The Encyclopaedia of

SCOTTISH FOOTBALL

The Encyclopaedia of SCOTTISH FOOTBALL

David Potter and Phil H. Jones

Published by Know the Score

Printed & Bound In Poland
www.polskabook.co.uk

ISBN: 978-1-84818-501-2

FOREWORD

It is a real pleasure to read this work on Scottish Football. Bringing together comprehensive accounts of the many different aspects and strands of Scottish football in a single volume is long overdue. Scottish football is steeped in history and sometimes important events are too soon forgotten. This book is a laudable attempt to make everything easily accessible to the reader. Football remains exceptionally important to most of the Scottish population, and it is said that more Scottish people per head of the population attend a football match every weekend that anywhere else in western Europe. Reading about the game remains one of its pleasures. This ambitious work aims to have something for everyone. I hope you enjoy it.

Gordon Brown

INTRODUCTION and ACKNOWLEDGEMENTS

The genesis of this book came some twenty or thirty years ago, when the two authors completed the pleasurable odyssey of watching a game at every one of Scotland's senior grounds. It was felt then that the game in Scotland needed a reference book to cover as many aspects of Scottish football as possible.

Work started in 2005 and the enormous amount of research required has been a labour of love for the past three years. The authors have travelled all over Scotland, visiting libraries, football grounds, and in particular the Scottish Football Museum at Hampden Park. Pitfalls and blind alleys have of course been encountered, but enthusiasm has never waned, nor has love of Scottish football ever been diminished.

There will, inevitably, be mistakes and omissions in a work of this complexity. For them we apologise and urge you to get in touch with us to tell us the error of our ways.

In the course of compiling this encyclopaedia, hundreds of books and websites have been consulted, and it is not possible to mention them all. There are some, however, that have been particularly useful, and without which this book would not be as informative as it is. The authors would particularly like to express their thanks to the compilers of the following well-thumbed volumes. We understand how much time and effort went into putting them together.

The Breedon Book of Football Records - Gordon Smailes
The First 100 Years:The Official Centenary History of the SFL - Bob Crampsey
The Juniors: 100 Years - David McGlone and Bill McLure
Rejected FC of Scotland (three volumes) - Dave Twydell
The Roar of the Crowd - David Ross
Sky Sports Football Yearbooks
The Ultimate Directory of English and Scottish Football League Grounds - Paul and Shirley Smith
Up for the Cup: British football clubs in Europe since 1955 - John Ladd
The Winners: Bernard Stocks

Websites may not be well thumbed, but the following sites have been accessed many times from the authors' list of favourites, and they have been invaluable sources of information.

www.scottishleague.net - Football histories website
www.nonleaguescotland.co.uk - Non-league Scotland
www.rsssf.com - Rec. Sport Soccer Statistics Foundation
www.geocities.com/br1anmccoll - Scottish Football History – an A to Z archive

Lastly, thank you to all the people who have gone out of their way to help the authors put this book together – in particular the staff at the Scottish Football Museum, who have provided the answers to many queries, John Grant of the Highland League and Ronnie Hutcheson at Girvan FC. Thank you also to friends and family who have provided encouragement, administrative help, and the opportunity to discuss the many issues that have arisen - in particular the authors' wives Rosemary and Margaret, and friends Ian Simpson, John Adamson and Tom Campbell.

Exhibits at the Scottish Football Museum at Hampden Park illustrate the way in which equipment has changed over the years: (b) An early laced football; (c) An 'orange segment' football; (d) A woollen shirt, as worn by the 'Auld Enemy'; (f) A Scotland shirt from the early 1960s; (g) & (h) Shirts from Hamilton Academical and Raith Rovers in the days when shirt sponsorship was still relatively new; (m) A shirt from the time when Scotland played in their 'Rosebery' colours; (n) An advertisement from an era when the 'T' football was an innovation; (o) The turnstile was once an innovation; (p) Early shinguards; (q) Early football boots.

The Museum also has many exhibits that recall the different ways in which success has been recognised: (a) A medal awarded to winners of a Victorian trophy in 1881/82; (e) A Scotland Cap awarded in 1922; (i) An English League medal awarded to John 'Sailor' Hunter when he was with Liverpool in 1900/01; (j) A Scotland shirt badge from 1878; (k) A Glasgow shirt badge from 1881; (l) A tie-pin worn by St. Bernard's players to commemorate their Scottish Cup success of 1894/95.

[h]

[i]

[j]

[k]

[l]

[m]

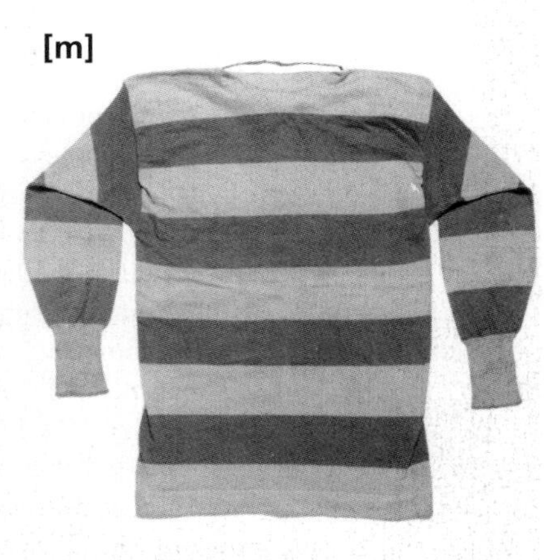

[n]

THE
IMPROVED 'T'
FOOTBALL

USED IN MORE INTERNATIONAL MATCHES THAN ANY OTHER BALL

SOLE MANUFACTURERS :

WM. THOMLINSON LTD.
450 DUMBARTON ROAD,
GLASGOW, W.I

[o]

RUSH-PREVENTIVE

TURNSTILES

(ELLISON'S PATENT).

Acknowledged to be the only Reliable

Registering Turnstile

For Football, Cricket, Athletic, Cycling, and Recreation Grounds; Baths, Exhibitions, Racecourses, Piers, Ferries, Public Gardens, Railway Companies, etc., etc.

They have been supplied to the following Football Clubs in Scotland:

QUEEN'S PARK, CELTIC, KILMARNOCK, etc., etc.

Also, Harbour Tunnel, Clyde Navigation Trustees, and Glasgow Subway.

Principal Association League Clubs in England supplied THIS YEAR with our Turnstiles:

Everton, Sunderland, Aston Villa, Bolton Wanderers, Sheffield United, Liverpool, Leicester, Blackburn Rovers, etc., etc., etc.

Also, The Liverpool Overhead Railway Co.

PRICE LIST ON APPLICATION.

W. T. ELLISON & CO., Engineers,
Irlams o' th' Height, near Manchester.

Telegraphic Address (two words): "ELLISON, IRLAMS O' TH' HEIGHT."

[See Testimonials on Back page.

[p]

[q]

ABANDONED GAMES

These are a comparative rarity but, such are the vagaries of the Scottish climate, they do occur, and sometimes games are abandoned for reasons other than the weather. Serious injury to Ross McCabe of Hamilton Academical, for example, caused the abandonment of the game against Clyde at New Douglas Park on 9 September 2006. Crowd encroachment was a common reason in the early days, when only a rope was used to separate the fans from the pitch. The Scottish Cup final of 12 March 1892 was abandoned (although played out as a friendly) for this reason as the authorities underestimated the size of the Celtic support.

On 8 May 1963, before a crowd of 95,000, an international friendly at Hampden Park was abandoned after seventy-nine minutes with Scotland leading Austria 4–1. It had all started when the Austrian centre half Nemec objected to Scotland's second goal, and after spitting at the referee, Mr Jim Finney of England, and threatening further violence, he was sent off. Later, with Scotland comfortably ahead, another Austrian, Hof, aimed a deliberate kick at Willie Henderson and was sent off. After a long debate involving the police, Hof eventually went, but not before an Austrian reserve had tried to attack Mr Finney. The violence continued (with some Scotland players not always totally innocent) and eventually, with eleven minutes to go, Mr Finney decided, after a foul by Linhart on Denis Law, that enough was enough and the game was abandoned.

Fog, snow and torrential downpours have all been responsible for the abandoning of games. The Scottish Cup final of 1889 between Third Lanark and Celtic, for example, was abandoned because of snow, yet, fearing trouble, the authorities decided to play a friendly instead and not to tell the fans! Hibs felt ill done-by on 19 October 1975 when they were winning 2–0 at Parkhead only to have the game abandoned because of fog, and there was a notorious game at Forfar on 21 January 1956 when referee Willie Brittle, apparently under pressure from the St Johnstone manager, abandoned a game after the snow had stopped. Forfar were winning 3–0 at the time. Abandonment of international games for weather reasons is rare, but Scotland's game against Spain on 3 September 2004 in Valencia was abandoned after sixty minutes because of a floodlight failure caused by torrential storms in the neighbourhood. The score was 1–1 at the time.

This game at Dens Park in 1936 should have been abandoned!

There have been seven occasions when a game has literally been abandoned with no attempt at a replay. The most famous was the Hampden riot of 17 April1909 when, in the second game of the Scottish Cup final between Celtic and Rangers, the crowd rioted and severely damaged Hampden Park because they were denied extra time. Crowd disturbances also meant that Dumbarton versus Clyde on 17 December 1892, Celtic versus Rangers on 25 March 1905, Clyde versus Rangers on 10 February 1912, and Celtic versus Dundee on 26 April 1920 were left unfinished. On these occasions the result was allowed to stand for fear of further trouble. The Dumbarton versus Vale of Leven game on 12 December 1891 was left unfinished at 8–0 for Dumbarton (it was reported that 'several Vale players left the field exhausted'), and the Dundee versus Hibs Scottish League Cup tie of 26 August 1950 was abandoned (because of weather conditions) at 0–2 and never replayed because Hibs had comfortably won the section in any case.

ABERCORN FC (former Scottish League club)

Home: **Paisley, Renfrewshire (grounds listed below)**
Highest League Position: **7th (1890/91)**
Best Scottish Cup Performances: **Last 4 (Semi-finals, 1887/88; 1889/90; 1890/91)**

Abercorn FC was one of the founder members of the Scottish Football League in 1890, along with Paisley rivals St Mirren. When they finished second bottom in its third season, 1892/93, they were relegated to the newly created second division, and therefore became founder members of Division Two as well. They won the Division Two title in 1895/96 and were elected to Division One, but after gaining just three points from eighteen games they were relegated again in 1897 and remained in Division Two until the end of the 1914/15 season.

Founded in 1877, shortly after St Mirren, the Abbies soon became one of Scotland's leading clubs. Like other top clubs of the time their fixtures included challenge matches against teams from south of the border and English champions Preston North End could only manage a 3–3 draw against them. By 1891 they had reached the Scottish Cup semi-finals for the third time, losing 3–1 to Dumbarton, and were attracting large crowds to their games.

Abercorn moved home several times and, after playing at East Park and Blackstoun Park, moved to Underwood Park in 1889. The following year the club was granted the honour of hosting the international match between Scotland and Wales, which Scotland won 5–0. Abercorn's prestige was now at its highest; membership of the new Scottish League was to bring disappointing results, lower crowds and increasing financial problems.

After ten years at Underwood Park the club was on the move again, first to Ralston Park and then New Ralston Park. The crowds briefly returned when they won the Scottish Qualifying Cup in 1912/13, beating Arbroath 4–1 in a final that was replayed twice, but then the onset of the first world war resulted in Division Two being abandoned in 1915.

The Abbies played in the Western League instead, but in 1920 the lease on their ground at New Ralston Park came to an end. The club found itself without a home, and Abercorn did not enter any league for 1920/21. Their last match was a first-round tie in that season's Scottish Qualifying Cup against Vale of Leven. The visit to Alexandria ended in an 8–2 defeat, and not long afterwards Abercorn FC went out of existence.

The table shows the grounds where Abercorn played in the Scottish League:

(East Park, Blackstoun Park, Underwood Park)		
Scottish League		
Underwood Park	1890	1899
Ralston Park	1899	1909
New Ralston Park	1909	1915

ABERDEEN FC

Ground: **Pittodrie**
Nickname: **The Dons**
Colours: **Red and white**
Record Attendance: **45,061 v Hearts (1954)**
Record Victory: **13-0 v Peterhead (1923)**
Record Defeat: **0-8 v Celtic (1965)**
Highest League Position: **1st (1954/55; 1979/80; 1983/84; 1984/85)**
Best Scottish Cup Performance: **Winners (1946/47; 1969/70; 1981/82; 1983/83; 1983/84; 1985/86; 1989/90)**
Best League Cup Performance: **Winners (1955/56; 1976/77; 1985/86; 1989/90; 1995/96)**

Aberdeen FC was formed in 1903 when three local clubs, Aberdeen, Orion and Victoria United, amalgamated. The 1903/04 season was spent in the Northern League, and in 1904 the club replaced Ayr Parkhouse in Division Two. Just one year later, despite finishing only seventh in the lower division, they were elected to Division One and have never been relegated since, although there have been two close calls. In 1995 they had to beat Dunfermline in a play-off and in 2000 they were only saved from another play-off by Falkirk's ineligibility, due to their ground failing to meet SPL requirements.

Jimmy Philip was manager of the Dons from their inception in 1903 until 1924, and just before he left, to be replaced by trainer Paddy Travers, he signed brothers Alec and Walter Jackson. Alec, who later scored a hat-trick for Scotland against England in the Wembley Wizards' victory of 1928, was one of the stars of the 1920s. He was transferred to Huddersfield Town after just one season, and it was said that his transfer fee helped to fund major improvements to Pittodrie stadium. By the outbreak of war in 1939 the Dons had finished in the top eight of the league for thirteen consecutive seasons, and in 1931 survived the departure of five of their regular players following allegations of corruption that were never proved or disproved. Forwards Willie Mills and Matt Armstrong were part of the new side, and as the 1930s progressed they became two of Pittodrie's legendary goal scorers.

Aberdeen in the 1930s with their black and gold vertical-striped jerseys.

In March 1939 the team adopted the red strip that is now so familiar to Scottish fans. Before this they played in black and gold stripes, and at one time this earned them the nickname of the Wasps, although this name appears to have been discarded in favour of the Dons a few years prior to the first world war.

Despite the consistent performances in the league, a major trophy didn't arrive at Pittodrie until 1947, when manager Dave Halliday led Aberdeen to a 2–1 victory over Hibernian in the Scottish Cup final. The team also reached the League Cup final that year, but lost 4–0 to Rangers. Some Dons fans claim that they actually won the Scottish League Cup in 1945/46, but technically this was a wartime tournament, known as the Southern League Cup, in what was still an unofficial season. As the 1950s unfolded, Aberdeen FC established itself as a powerful force in Scottish football. There were runners-up medals in the Scottish Cup finals of 1953 and 1954, and then the first league title was won in 1954/55, with the Dons winning twelve consecutive home games.

The following season brought a runners-up place in the league and a 2–1 victory over St Mirren in the final of the League Cup, but over the next decade the Dons were unable to scale these heights again. It wasn't until the appointment of Eddie Turnbull as manager in 1965 that they began to excite the fans once more. His new training methods, coupled with the signing of players like goalkeeper Bobby Clark and forward Jimmy Smith, kick-started a process that now brought European football to Pittodrie. The 1966/67 Scottish Cup final was lost to Celtic by two goals to nil, but it earned a first-round tie against KR Reykjavik in the European Cup-Winners' Cup. Aberdeen won the home-leg 10–0 and went through 14–1 on aggregate before losing to Standard Liege in the second round.

Joe Harper, signed from Morton in 1969, was scoring regularly and it wasn't long before another trophy arrived. A team that included the 17-year-old Arthur Graham and 21-year-old captain Martin Buchan beat Celtic 3–1 in the 1969/70 final. Eddie Turnbull left for Hibs in 1971 and was replaced by Jimmy Bonthrone, but it was only after Ally MacLeod became manager in 1975 that there was another trophy. Captain Willie Miller lifted the 1976/77 League Cup after Celtic were beaten 2–1 in the final. Ally MacLeod left to become manager of the national side, his successor Billy McNeill only stayed for a season before returning to Celtic, and then an appointment was made that changed the club's history forever.

Celtic v Aberdeen at Parkhead in 1955. Goalkeeper Fred Martin is forced to concede a corner.

Alex Ferguson arrived as manager in 1978 and in the years between 1978 and 1986 he presided over a period of spectacular success, with three more league titles, four Scottish Cups, and another League Cup win. As a result of the ensuing European campaigns, Aberdeen became a name that was recognised throughout the football world. There was European football in every year of his tenure, but the pinnacle came in 1982/83, when Real Madrid were beaten 2–1 in the final of the European Cup-Winners' Cup in Gothenburg. The following season the European Super Cup was added to the trophies, when Aberdeen beat the European Cup holders SV Hamburg, and the semi-finals of the Cup-Winners' Cup were reached for the second time, when Porto prevented another appearance in the final.

Aberdeen was the first British club to have an all-seated stadium and it has seen other European campaigns over the years, but after Alex Ferguson left to join Manchester United in 1986, his success has never been matched. Members of his winning side, such as Alex McLeish and Gordon Strachan, have gone on to establish themselves as successful managers in their own right.

There have been several other managers since Alex Ferguson, including Alex Smith and Jocky Scott, who acted as co-managers between 1988 and 1992. They led the Dons to a Scottish Cup and League Cup double in 1989/90, and a year later the title could have been won if defeat at Ibrox on the last day of the season had been avoided. There was another League Cup under Roy Aitken in 1995/96, when Dundee were beaten 2–0 in the final, but by the time Ebbe Skovdahl arrived from Brondby to take up the manager's post in 1999, Aberdeen appeared to be consistent under-achievers. His teams relied heavily on youth, and in 1999/2000 were losing finalists in both the Scottish Cup and League Cup, but it remained hard to avoid comparisons with Alex Ferguson's golden era.

Willie Miller, captain of the Dons during their glory years and club manager from 1992 until 1995, was appointed 'Director of Football' in 2004 and manager Steve Paterson was replaced with Jimmy Calderwood. His sides established themselves as consistent performers in the SPL, and a third-place finish in 2006/07 earned qualification for the UEFA Cup. The Dons got through the group stages, and then earned a deserved 2–2 home draw against Bayern Munich in the 'Round of 32', but the dream came to an end with a 5–1 defeat in Munich's Allianz Arena.

ADMINISTRATION

This refers to the legal process that enables a football club to keep operating when debts would otherwise mean the selling of assets in order to pay creditors. It begins with a club filing a notice of intention at the Court of Session in Edinburgh, and leads to the appointment of a named individual (the 'administrator'), who is usually an accountant, to take on the role of running the business. He or she will endeavour to obtain as much money as possible for the creditors, whilst enabling the club to still survive. The administrator is able to insist on changes to the way in which the club is run, such as introducing new practices that will cut costs, and a club in administration will not be able to sign new players. Dundee, Livingston, Morton and Motherwell have all gone down this route, but came out of administration when the administrators had done their job. When Gretna followed them in 2008 they felt the effect of an SPL rule, introduced in 2004, that requires the deduction of ten league points when an administrator is appointed.

ADVOCAAT Dick (1947 –)

Dick Advocaat was the Dutch-born manager of Rangers from 1998/99 until 2000/01, during which time Rangers won the treble of SPL championship, Scottish Cup and Scottish League Cup in 1998/99, and the double of SPL title and Scottish Cup in 1999/2000. When Alex McLeish arrived, he was moved to General Manager, but did not remain in that post for long, opting to become manager (for the second time) of his native Holland. Before arriving at Ibrox he had managed PSV Eindhoven, and after leaving Rangers he became manager of Borussia Munchengladbach, the United Arab Emirates, South Korea and Zenit St Petersburg.

AGE

The oldest player to have played in the Scottish Premier League is Andy Millen of St Mirren (born 10 June 1965). He was forty-two years, two hundred and seventy-nine days when he played for St Mirren against Hearts on 15 March 2008. Three days later he played for them against St Johnstone in the Scottish Cup. The second oldest is Jim Leighton, who was forty-one years, three hundred and two days when he played for Aberdeen against Dundee on 21 May 2000. He played in the Scottish Cup final six days later and was carried off injured with a broken jaw after two minutes. The youngest is Scott Robinson (born 11 March 1992), who was sixteen years, forty-five days when he played for Hearts against Inverness Caledonian Thistle on 26 April 2008.

In the Scottish Football League, Hamilton Academical brought on fifteen-year-old James McCarthy as a substitute in a game against Queen of the South at New Douglas Park on 30 September 2006. McCarthy was fifteen years, three hundred and twenty-three days. Jim Calder was aged over forty-six years and eight months when he played for Peterhead against Ayr United on 31 March 2007 at Balmoor Stadium. David Westwood of East Fife and Colin Cockle of Montrose might have beaten that record when they were nominated as substitute goalkeepers at the age of forty-eight in 2006 and 2007 respectively, but they were not called upon to play.

Jimmy Brownlie, then Dundee United's manager, was forced, because of injuries to his goalkeepers, to make a comeback as goalkeeper for a Scottish Cup replay against Hearts at Tynecastle in 1926 at the age of forty years and eight months.

Scotland's youngest internationalist remains John Lambie of Queen's Park, who was seventeen years ninety-three days when he appeared (as captain) for Scotland in their 7–2 defeat of Ireland in Belfast on 20 March 1886. Eight other players played their first game for Scotland at the age of eighteen – James Richmond of Clydesdale in 1877, Bob Christie of Queen's Park in 1884, Willie Sellar of Queen's Park in 1885, John Gow of Rangers in 1888, Dyke Berry of Queen's Park in 1894, Andy McLaren of St Johnstone in 1929, Denis Law of Huddersfield Town in 1958 and Willie Henderson of Rangers in 1962.

Ronnie Simpson's remarkable career is worthy of mention. He played in goal for Queen's Park on 2 June 1945 while still only fourteen years, two hundred and thirty-four days (possibly the youngest ever in Scottish football, albeit in an unofficial wartime game), and became Scotland's oldest-ever international debutant on 15 April 1967 in the 3–2 win over England at the age of thirty-six years one hundred and ninety-six days. He played his final game for Scotland on 6 November 1968. He was born on 11 October 1930, which means that he played for Scotland at the age of thirty-eight years and twenty-six days. His final game for Celtic on 13 October 1969 was almost a year after his last international appearance, and an injury to his shoulder in a League Cup semi-final against Ayr United compelled his substitution and brought an end to his career. This came only two days after he had been appointed captain for a game against Airdrieonians to celebrate his thirty-ninth birthday, and the crowd sang 'Happy Birthday' as he took the field.

John Fallon was Celtic's number 1 when they won the Scotish Cup in 1965, but he became deputy to Ronnie Simpson (right) who made a remarkable return to top-class soccer in 1967.

At least six other players have made their debut for Scotland while in their thirties – Tommy Pearson of Newcastle United in 1947, Jimmy Logie of Arsenal in 1953, Willie Summers of St Mirren in 1926, Peter Kerr of Hibernian in 1924, Donald Colman of Aberdeen in 1911 and Andrew Herd of Hearts in 1934. None of then, however, is Scotland's oldest international player. This honour belongs to Jim Leighton of Aberdeen, Manchester United and Hibernian, who was forty years, seventy-seven days when he played for Scotland against Estonia at Tynecastle on 10 October 1998. It was his ninety-first international appearance. Second oldest (and the record holder for an outfield player) is Jimmy McMenemy of Celtic, who was thirty-nine years, two hundred and three days when he played for Scotland against Ireland at Celtic Park on 13 March 1920. The following year Napoleon, as he was known, won a Scottish Cup medal with Partick Thistle at the age of forty.

An interesting combination of youth and age could be seen at Cowdenbeath on 9 December 2006 when, in a Scottish Cup tie against Edinburgh University, Cowdenbeath fielded Kyle Allison in goal at the age of sixteen and a half years. This was not in itself all that remarkable, but the substitute goalkeeper was goalkeeping coach John Martin at the age of forty-eight. Fortunately, Martin's services were not required, and Allison was nominated 'Man of the Match'.

AIRDRIEONIANS FC (former Scottish League club)

Home: **Airdrie, North Lanarkshire (grounds listed below)**
Highest League Position: **2nd (1922/23; 1923/24; 1924/25; 1925/26)**
Best Scottish Cup Performance: **Winners (1923/24)**
Best League Cup Performance: **Last 4 (Semi-finals, 1954/55; 1966/67; 1974/75; 1991/92; 1994/95; 1995/96; 1998/99)**

The club was founded in 1878, although it was known as 'Excelsior FC' until 1881. The Scottish League didn't begin until 1890, and Airdrieonians became members at the start of the 1894/95 season, when they were elected to Division Two. It was in 1886, whilst still participating in regional football, that they were responsible for Rangers' worst ever home defeat, when they won 10–2 at Ibrox.

Promotion to the top division came in 1903, and the most successful era of the club's history began. There were thirty-three continuous seasons in the top division, and from 1923 until 1926 there were four consecutive runners-up finishes. The Scottish Cup was won in 1924, when Hibs were beaten 2–0 in the final at Ibrox, and from 23 September 1922 until 5 December 1925 Airdrieonians were undefeated at home. Many famous players wore the diamond shirt during this period, including Hughie Gallacher, Bob McPhail and Jim Crapnell.

After relegation in 1936, these heights were never reached again. By 1955, eight out of thirteen seasons had been spent in the lower division, although after they won the Division B title in 1955, the club spent eighteen of the next twenty seasons in Division One. In 1971 they entered the record books when they beat Nottingham Forest in the Texaco Cup, by taking part in the UK's first penalty shoot-out. The following season they reached the final of the Texaco Cup, but lost 2–1 to Derby County.

At the time of league reconstruction in 1975, it was their misfortune to finish eleventh when only the top ten clubs formed the new Premier Division, and their disappointment was compounded by a 3–1 Scottish Cup Final defeat to Celtic. There were more runners-up medals in 1992, when Rangers won the Scottish Cup final 2–1, but this time there was the consolation of European football. Rangers played in the European Cup, and so Airdrieonians were given a place in the European Cup-Winners' Cup. Their one and only European tie ended with a 3–1 aggregate defeat to Sparta Prague in the first round.

The club never did reach the final of the League Cup, but they could hardly have come closer. There were four semi-final appearances in the 1990s, and the games against Dunfermline in 1991/92 and Raith Rovers in 1994/95 were only lost after penalty shoot-outs. There was, though, one more Scottish Cup final, which Celtic won 1–0 in 1995, and in both 2000 and 2001 Airdrieonians won the Scottish League Challenge Cup for clubs outwith the Premier Division.

After being placed there in 1975, the First Division (second tier) became Airdrie's home until their demise in 2002, apart from two two-season spells in the Premier Division. In the mid-1990s the club decided to sell Broomfield Park, its home since 1892, and ground-shared with Clyde at Cumbernauld for four years before moving to their new Excelsior stadium in 1998. However, severe financial problems had developed during this time and in 2002, after spending two years in administration, they became the first Scottish League club to go out of existence since Third Lanark in 1967.

These are the grounds where Airdrieonians played in the Scottish League:

(Old Mavisbank, Broomfield Park)		
Scottish League		
Broomfield Park	1894	1994
Broadwood Stadium	1994	1998
Excelsior Stadium	1998	2002

AIRDRIE UNITED FC

Ground: **Excelsior Stadium**
Nickname: **The Diamonds**
Colours: **White and red**
Record Attendance: **5,704 v Morton (2004)**
Record Victory: **7-0 v Dundee (2006)**
Record Defeat: **1-6 v Morton (2003)**
Highest League Position: **17th (5th in First Division, 2004/05)**
Best Scottish Cup Performance: **Last 16 (4th round, 2005/06)**
Best League Cup Performance: **Last 16 (3rd round, 2002/03)**

Airdrieonians went out of existence in May 2002. They had been in administration for two years and, when their financial problems finally became too great, their place in the Scottish League was given to Gretna. A group of Airdrie businessmen set about finding a way in which league football could continue in the town and they found the solution in Clydebank FC, another club in severe financial difficulties. The consortium bought up Clydebank and the Scottish League gave approval for the club's name to be changed to 'Airdrie United' and for its home to be at the Excelsior Stadium.

The new club took over Clydebank's place in the Second Division for the 2002/03 season and played in the familiar 'Diamond' strip of Airdrieonians. They finished that first season in a creditable third place, but in 2003/04 manager Sandy Stewart led them to even greater success. He built a team that contained experienced players such as Owen Coyle, and United not only reached the final of the Scottish League Challenge Cup, losing 2–0 to Inverness CT, they went on to win the Second Division title.

The Diamonds were therefore back in the First Division, which was where Airdrieonians had spent their final season, and for two seasons they could be found in mid-table. Former Airdrieonians player Kenny Black replaced Sandy Stewart in November 2006, but the team finished the 2006/07 season next to the bottom, and a 5–4 aggregate defeat to Stirling Albion in the final of the play-offs meant a return to the third tier. Twelve months later United again lost the play-off final, this time to Clyde, but were still promoted when the fall of Gretna FC created another place in the First Division.

AITKEN Andy (1877–1955)

Scotland Caps: 14

Andy Aitken was a player of the Edwardian era who earned fourteen caps for Scotland and was known as 'the Daddler'. He was an attack-minded central midfielder who played for Ayr Thistle, Ayr Parkhouse, Newcastle United, Middlesbrough, Leicester Fosse, Dundee, Kilmarnock, and then became manager of Gateshead Town. His greatest achievement was winning the English league championship with Newcastle in 1905. His international career included two victories over England in 1903 and 1906. In later years he became a scout for Arsenal and a journalist.

AITKEN George (1925 – 2003)

Scotland Caps: 8
Scottish League Cup medals: 2

George 'Dod' Aitken was a left half and centre half who played for East Fife, Third Lanark and Sunderland in the late 1940s and early 1950s. With East Fife's successful team of that era, he won two Scottish League Cup medals, and his eight Scottish caps saw some fine performances, notably a win over England in his international debut of 1949. When with East Fife he won five caps – a record for the club.

AITKEN Roy (1958 –)

Scotland Caps: 57
Scottish League Championship medals: 6
Scottish Cup medals: 5
Scottish League Cup medals: 1

Roy Aitken, sometimes called 'the Bear', was a strong, aggressive midfielder or defender. He was a player who was indelibly associated with the ups and downs of Celtic in the 1980s. He was, for example, ordered off in the 1984 Scottish Cup final defeat against Aberdeen, then in 1985 took the Scottish Cup final by the scruff of the neck to turn things round against Dundee United. He was the captain of Celtic's centenary-year league and cup double team of 1988, and played a massive 667 times for them.

Supporters argued about whether his best position was as a defender or a midfielder, but evidence would suggest that he was at his best in the centre of the park. He left Parkhead in January 1990 to go to Newcastle, where his career was less successful. He later returned to Scotland to play for St Mirren and Aberdeen as a player-coach. As manager of Aberdeen he won the Scottish League Cup in 1995/96. He subsequently joined David O'Leary at Leeds United and Aston Villa, and in January 2007 became assistant manager of Scotland before moving, along with Alex McLeish, to Birmingham City in November of that year.

ALBION ROVERS FC

Ground: **Cliftonhill Stadium, Coatbridge**
Nickname: **The Rovers; The Wee Rovers**
Colours: **Yellow and red**
Record Attendance: **27,381 v Rangers (1936)**
Record Victory: **12-0 v Airdriehill (1887)**
Record Defeat: **1-11 v Partick Thistle (1993)**
Highest League Position: **11th (11th in Division 1, 1921/22)**
Best Scottish Cup Performance: **Runners-up (1919/20)**
Best League Cup Performance: **Last 8 (Quarter-finals 1973/74; 1976/77)**

The Rovers played their first match at the new Cliftonhill Stadium on Christmas Day 1919, when St Mirren spoiled the party by winning 2–0. The club,

1920: Kilmarnock on the attack as Albion's Penman attempts a tackle in this first post-war Scottish Cup final.

which was formed in 1882 when Albion and Rovers merged together, had previously been based in Whifflet, an area of Coatbridge that was once an outlying village. In the years since then Cliftonhill has occasionally seen large crowds at cup-ties, but the stadium has steadily declined to the point where 'an urgent need for improvement' now represents an understatement, and the club may relocate to a new home.

In its formative years the club soon made its mark in local cup competitions, winning the Lanarkshire Cup for the first time in 1899/90. When the Scottish League was expanded for the 1903/04 season, the Rovers were elected to Division Two, and since then they have almost always been found in the lower reaches of the Scottish League. There have, however, been a total of nine seasons in the top flight.

The first four of these came soon after the end of the first world war. Division Two was suspended in 1915 and so the club played in the Western League, winning the title in 1917/18. Then, when the Scottish League decided to expand Division One in 1919, but not re-introduce Division Two for the time being, Albion Rovers and three other clubs became part of it. They never finished higher than eleventh, but this period also saw their greatest success, when they reached the final of the 1919/20 Scottish Cup after two replays against Rangers in the semi-finals. Whilst the record books show a 3–2 victory for Kilmarnock at Hampden Park, they also show that Rovers reached the final in the same season that they finished bottom of the Scottish League.

There was another semi-final against Rangers in 1920/21, but this time the Glasgow team won 4–1 at Celtic Park. A second-bottom finish in 1922/23 brought relegation to Division Two, and the club stayed in the lower division until 1934, when they won the Division Two championship. A second round Scottish cup-tie against Rangers in February 1936 brought Cliftonhill's record attendance, when Rovers lost 3–1. They were relegated in 1937, and promoted again in 1938, and in total the 1930s saw four more years in the top division.

After the second world war, the Rovers were placed in the new Division B, even though they had been in the top division when the league was suspended in 1939. It was at this time that Jock Stein was playing for the club, as well as working as a miner during the week, and after promotion in 1948 there was one more season in the top flight. It ended with just eight points from thirty matches. In 1961 Rovers abandoned their blue and white colours and adopted their now familiar yellow and red.

In the second half of the twentieth century there was another honour to celebrate, notwithstanding occasional triumphs in the Lanarkshire Cup. The Second Division (third tier) title was won in 1988/89 and in 2005 one of the stars of that side, Jim

The entrance to Cliftonhill in 1934, the year Rovers won the Championship of Division Two.

Chapman, accepted the challenge of becoming the club's head coach.

ALEXANDER Graham (1971 –)

Scotland Caps: 33

Graham Alexander, a reliable full back, played for Scotland from 2002 onwards, in spite of the fact that he was born in Coventry. By 2007 he had played for four English teams – Scunthorpe United, Luton Town, Preston North End and Burnley.

ALLOA ATHLETIC FC

Ground: **Recreation Park**
Nickname: **The Wasps**
Colours: **Gold and black**
Record Attendance: **15,467 v Celtic (1955)**
Record Victory: **9-0 v Selkirk (2005)**
Record Defeat: **0-10 v Dundee (1947); v Third Lanark (1953)**
Highest League Position: **16th (6th in First Div., 1982/83)**
Best Scottish Cup Performance: **Last 8 (4th round 1938/39; 1960/61)(5th round 1988/89)**
Best League Cup Performance: **Last 8 (Quarter-finals 1948/49; 1950/51; 1965/66)**

The club began as Clackmannan County in 1878, and was then known as Alloa AFC for a short time, until it became Alloa Athletic FC in 1883. Their home in those early years was West End Public Park, followed by Gaberston Park and then Bellevue Park, before they moved to Recreation Park in 1895. Between 1898 and 1974 the team played in black and gold hoops, which gave rise to their nickname of 'The Wasps', but since then the club colours have been gold shirts and black shorts. There have not been many memorable years in the history of the club since 1883, but 1921 was one. In the first round of the 1920/21 Scottish Cup non-league Alloa beat Falkirk 1–0 in a third replay and in the second round beat Clydebank 1–0 in a second replay. Then Alloa drew the mighty Rangers and earned a 0–0 draw in front of 54,000 spectators at Ibrox. They went back for yet another replay and lost 4–1, but they did score Alloa's first ever goal against Rangers.

In their early years Alloa played in the Central Combination, but by 1921 they were longstanding members of the Central League. 1921/22 was the season when the Scottish League re-introduced Division Two and sixteen of its twenty members, including Alloa, came from the Central League. Then the Wasps won the Division Two title at the first attempt, and earned promotion to Division One. 'Wee Willie Crilly' scored forty-nine goals that season, a figure that remains a club record.

Unfortunately, it was all downhill after that. Alloa finished bottom of Division One in their first season and found themselves back in Division Two. They were still there when the league was re-constructed in 1975, although there was a moment of irony along the way. Manager Jimmy McStay led them to a second-place finish in 1938/39 and the Wasps should have been promoted, but the Scottish League was suspended in 1939 at the start of the second world war. Jimmy McStay left to become manager of Celtic in 1940 and, when the league restarted in 1945, the club was placed back in the lower division.

After 1975, they hopped between the Second Division (third tier) and the First Division (second tier), with four promotions and four relegations, and then at the next league reconstruction in 1994 found themselves in the Third Division (fourth tier). There were more promotions and relegations, but they have never again reached the top flight. In 1999/2000 promotion to the First Division was accompanied by victory in the final of the Scottish League Challenge Cup, when Inverness Caledonian Thistle were beaten on penalties after a 4–4 draw, and so 2000 became another year to remember.

A series of ground improvements began at Recreation Park in the summer of 2007, the most notable being the installation of a synthetic playing surface, which enables members of the local community to use the facilities and also generates income for the club.

AMATEUR FOOTBALL

The Scottish Amateur Football Association, now based at Hampden Park, was founded in 1909 with three members, the Glasgow and District Fair Play League, Queen's Park and the Schools Association. Immediately they launched a Scottish Amateur Cup, which was won in the first year (1910) by John Neilson High School Former Pupils.

In the senior ranks, Queen's Park remains proudly and laudably amateur to this day, boasting the motto '*ludere causa ludendi*' – 'to play for the sake of playing'. They argued against professionalism throughout the 1880s and when professionalism was officially recognised in Scotland in 1893, they remained amateur and refused until 1900/01 to take part in the Scottish League. Sadly their decline as a major force in Scottish football is a result of their decision to stay amateur. For many years the 'Spiders', as they were nicknamed, would wear their jerseys outside their shorts to indicate their amateur status. As late as 1933, they provided players for Scotland – on 1 April 1933, the famous day of the birth of the Hampden roar, Bob Gillespie and James Crawford, both of Queen's Park, were in the Scotland team.

Amateur football is extremely popular in Scotland, as a visit to any public park on a Saturday or Sunday afternoon will testify. There are no fewer than ninety-five local leagues in Scotland, situated all over the country from Shetland to Bute, from Galashiels to Buckie, and the Association administers no fewer than nine cup competitions – the Scottish Amateur Cup, the Scottish Sunday Amateur Trophy, the North of Tay Amateur Cup, the Fife Amateur Cup, the Highland Amateur Cup and an Amateur Cup for each one of the four points of the compass i.e. north, south, east and west.

ANDERSON Andy (1909 – unknown)

Scotland Caps: 23

Andy Anderson was one of Hearts' greatest-ever players. He played for them throughout the 1930s and won twenty-three caps for Scotland. He was an aggressive right back and his tough tackling won him the nickname of 'Tiger'. His international debut was in 1933, in the famous game against England in which the "Hampden Roar" was born, and he was also on the winning side against the auld enemy in 1935, 1937 and 1938.

ANGLOS

An Anglo, or an Anglo-Scot (in contrast to a Home-Scot), is a player who plays for Scotland but is based in England, playing for an English club. Traditionally the awarding of caps to Anglos has been a bone of contention, and prior to 1896 no Anglo-Scot ever played for Scotland. On 4 April 1896, however, in the Scotland versus England game at Celtic Park, Ned Doig of Sunderland, Thomas Brandon of Blackburn Rovers, James Cowan of Aston Villa, Tommy Hyslop of Stoke City and Jack Bell of Everton became the first ever Anglo-Scots to play for Scotland in a game that Scotland won 2–1. Until 1905, Anglos played only in the game versus England, but on 3 March of that year Tommy Fitchie and Bobby Templeton of Woolwich Arsenal played in the game against Wales.

From time to time thereafter there have been disputes and arguments, but there has never been an official policy to exclude Anglos. However, in the Scottish team of 1925 that beat all three countries, Jimmy Nelson of Cardiff City was the only Anglo included, and the team that beat England 2–0 on 4 April 1925 consisted entirely of Home-Scots. Nevertheless, Anglos have been an integral part of Scottish teams. The Wembley Wizards team of 1928, which beat England 5–1, contained only three Home Scots.

There have often been problems getting Scottish players released from their English clubs – a problem that came to a head in December 1965, when Scottish players were in some cases made to play for their clubs on the Saturday before a vital World Cup qualifier in Italy. There was no legislation to compel managers to release their players and no effort was made to postpone fixtures in England (although they were postponed in Scotland). Yet in some cases the managers of the English clubs were themselves Scottish.

In addition it has often been (unfairly) suggested that Anglos are not sufficiently motivated to play for Scotland, in that they are earning enough in England. Yet the commitment of men like Billy Bremner and Denis Law, who never kicked a ball in Scottish domestic football, cannot be doubted. Some Anglos (notably Ian St John) have complained about unfair treatment and discrimination against Anglos, both in selection of teams and in the way that games were reported in the press. Such allegations remain unproved, and are in any case a matter of opinion. It is certainly true, however, that Anglos are not as well known in Scotland as Home-Scots, and it is therefore more difficult for them to catch the eye of the Scotland manager.

Jack Bell was one of the first-ever Anglo-Scot to play an international for Scotland.

ANGLO-SCOTTISH CUP

This knockout competition for clubs from Scotland and England was created in 1975 after the demise of the Texaco Cup. It lasted for six seasons before Scottish clubs ceased to enter due to lack of interest in Scotland. This was perhaps understandable when teams such as Chesterfield and Notts County were reaching the final, but Chesterfield did beat Rangers on the way. St Mirren was the only Scottish club to win the trophy. The results of the six finals are as follows:

Season	Home		Away	
1975/76	Middlesbrough	1	Fulham	0
	Fulham	0	Middlesbrough	0
	Middlesbrough won 1–0 on aggregate			
1976/77	Orient	1	Nottingham Forest	1
	Nottingham Forest	4	Orient	0
	Nottingham Forest won 5–1 on aggregate			
1977/78	St Mirren	1	Bristol City	2
	Bristol City	1	St Mirren	1
	Bristol City won 3–2 on aggregate			
1978/79	Oldham	0	Burnley	4
	Burnley	0	Oldham Athletic	1
	Burnley won 4–1 on aggregate			
1979/80	Bristol City	0	St. Mirren	2
	St. Mirren	3	Bristol City	1
	St. Mirren won 5–1 on aggregate			
1980/81	Chesterfield	1	Notts County	0
	Notts County	1	Chesterfield	1
	Chesterfield won 2–1 on aggregate (aet in second leg)			

APPEARANCES

Reference books often disagree about appearance records because some include European football; others include regional competitions and even friendlies. Some exclude wartime appearances; others include international matches and games played against English or foreign clubs in testimonial or benefit matches. In addition of course, some clubs play more games per season than anyone else. Billy McNeill, for example, played 790 times for Celtic between 1958 and 1975, but that is largely because Celtic did well in those years and therefore reached more semi-finals and finals than other teams. It is generally considered fairer to restrict the total to league appearances for one team in Scotland, and the players with the most appearances are:

Allan Ball	Queen of the South	1963-1982	731
Bobby Ferrier	Motherwell	1918-1937	626
David Narey	Dundee United	1973-1994	612
Willie Miller	Aberdeen	1973-1990	556
Alec McNair	Celtic	1904-1925	548
Ross Caven	Queen's Park	1982-2002	532
David Clarke	East Fife	1968-1986	517
Gary Mackay	Hearts	1980-1997	515
John Greig	Rangers	1962-1978	496
Billy McNeill	Celtic	1958-1975	486

The record number of appearances in one season is held by Carlos Cuellar, who turned out sixty-four times for Rangers in season 2007/08 in the SPL, Scottish Cup, Scottish League Cup, European Champions League and UEFA Cup.

ARBROATH FC

Ground: **Gayfield Park, Arbroath**
Nickname: **The Red Lichties; The Maroons**
Colours: **Maroon and white**
Record Attendance: **13,510 v Rangers (1952)**
Record Victory: **36-0 v Bon Accord (1885)**
Record Defeat: **1-9 v Celtic (1993)**
Highest League Position: **11th (1935/36; 1937/38)**
Best Scottish Cup Performance: **Last 4 (1946/47)**
Best League Cup Performance: **Last 4 (1959/60)**

The Scottish Cup has been an important part of the Lichties' history from the very beginning. Their first match was a 3–0 victory over Our Boys (from Dundee) in the first round of the 1878/79 competition, just a few weeks after their formation in July 1878. The game took place at Woodville, just outside Arbroath, and it would be another two years before the club moved to Gayfield. In September 1885 Arbroath beat Aberdeen Bon Accord 36–0 in the first round, and created a world record score that stands to this day. Centre forward Jocky Petrie scored a record thirteen goals. It was shortly after this that Ned Doig took over as goalkeeper. Capped for Scotland whilst still with Arbroath, he became one of the club's all-time great players and was eventually transferred to Sunderland. In 1891 Arbroath became founder members of the Northern League and in 1903 won the Scottish Qualifying Cup with a 4–2 victory over Albion Rovers at Dens Park. They moved to the newly created Central League in 1908, and in 1912/13 there was another appearance in the final of the Scottish Qualifying Cup, when Abercorn needed two replays before winning 4–1 at Cathkin Park.

After the first world war they played in the Scottish Alliance and then in 1921 became part of the new Division Two of the Scottish League. Gayfield Park was reconstructed in 1925, with the cost being met by a public fund-raising campaign, and the new ground hosted Division Two football until 1935, when a second-

place finish finally brought promotion. A successful four years followed, and it was during this period that Arbroath twice achieved their best ever league position. They were still in the top division when the league was closed down at the start of the second world war in September 1939.

When the league programme started again in 1945, the club was understandably surprised to find itself in Division B. It was to remain in the lower division for fourteen seasons and the highlights of this period were cup-ties against the bigger clubs. These included a memorable 2–1 home win over Hearts in 1946/47 that earned a semi-final tie against Aberdeen at Dens Park. The Dons won 2–0 and went on to lift the trophy. A second-place finish finally brought promotion to the top flight in 1959 and that year also saw a League Cup semi-final against Third Lanark at Ibrox, which was lost 3–0. The Lichties finished bottom of Division One after just one season in the top flight.

In 1962 Albert Henderson was appointed manager, a position he was to hold for over seventeen years, and he led Arbroath to promotion in both 1968 and 1972. There was a 3–2 victory over Rangers at Ibrox in 1974 and they were still in the top division when the Scottish League was reconstructed in 1975. Now they became part of the new First Division (second tier).

Albert Henderson was sacked at the beginning of 1980 and Arbroath were relegated to the Second Division (third tier) at the end of the season. They remained there for fourteen seasons and, when the league was reconstructed once again in 1994, became part of the new Third Division (fourth tier). It was not until 1998 that they were promoted, under manager Dave Baikie, and in 2001 his replacement John Brownlie took them back to the First Division for the first time since 1980. Unfortunately, this status was not to last; by 2005 they were back in the Third Division (fourth tier), but victory in the play-offs in May 2008 took them up to Division Two.

ARCHIBALD Sandy (1897–1946)

Scotland Caps: 8
Scottish League Championship medals: 13
Scottish Cup medals: 3

Sandy Archibald was arguably one of the best players in Rangers' very fine side of the 1920s and early 1930s. He was a right winger who was born in Aberdour, but lived in Crossgates, Fife. He joined Raith Rovers in 1915, and when Raith were compelled to go into abeyance because of the war in 1917, he went to Rangers, with whom he stayed until 1934. His thirteen Scottish League championship medals is a record.

He played eight times for Scotland, and many people felt that he deserved more caps. His best game for Scotland was the 1931 international against England at Hampden Park, when the forward line of Archibald, Stevenson, McGrory, McPhail and Morton was on everyone's lips for months afterwards for the way they ran England ragged. On leaving Rangers he returned to Raith Rovers to be manager, where he rallied the demoralised Kirkcaldy men and regained promotion to Division One in season 1937/38 with a magnificent side who still hold the record for goalscoring. In October 1939 he moved to Dunfermline Athletic, but the second world war denied him a real chance. He died in November 1946.

ARCHIBALD Steve (1956 –)

Scotland Caps: 27
Scottish League Championship medals: 1

Steve Archibald was a forward who played for Clyde, Aberdeen, Tottenham Hotspur, Barcelona, Blackburn Rovers, Hibs, St Mirren and East Fife, and who won twenty-seven caps for Scotland. He joined Alex Ferguson's Aberdeen in January 1978 and won a Scottish League championship medal with them in 1980 before joining Tottenham Hotspur for a then record fee between British clubs of £800,000.

Steve Archibald is congratulated by Danny McGrain after scoring for Scotland against New Zealand in the 1982 World Cup finals.

With Spurs he won the FA Cup in 1981 and 1982 and the UEFA Cup in 1984. He then went to Barcelona to win the Spanish League in 1985, and lose the 1986 European Cup final only on a penalty shoot-out. After his playing career finished, he turned his hand to management, notably with East Fife. At one point he was part of a consortium that tried to buy Airdrie. The tragedy about this undeniably talented player was that he was seldom able to turn his good form at club level to good use for Scotland, although he did play in the World Cup finals of both 1982 and 1986. Yet he 'never exactly became the darling of the Mount Florida terraces', as one television pundit put it.

ARGENTINA

The name that still sends a shiver down Scottish spines following the events of 1978. (See **ARGENTINA 1978**). Against Argentina themselves, however, Scotland's record is by no means a bad one – played three, won one, drawn one and lost one:

1977	18 June	Buenos Aires	1–1	Masson (pen)	Passarella (pen)
1979	2 June	Hampden Park	1–3	Graham	Luque (2) Maradona
1990	28 Mar	Hampden Park	1–0	McKimmie	

ARGENTINA 1978

This particular World Cup is worth an entry for the calamitous nature of the defeat, and the effect that it had on the Scottish psyche. Scotland had qualified in exhilarating circumstances with fine wins over Czechoslovakia and Wales in autumn 1977. As with four years previously, England had not. The media attention was therefore focussed firmly on Scotland, and the Scottish nation, under the influence of ebullient manager Ally MacLeod began to feel that the World Cup could actually be won. After all, the English League was the best in the world, the BBC told us, and the Scots, like Kenny Dalglish and Joe Jordan, were the stars of this competition.

Hype was the order of the day, even when the Home International Championship turned out to be a disaster containing a defeat from England at Hampden. In other circumstances this would have plunged the nation into the deepest melancholy, but such was the nationalist and jingoistic atmosphere, it was swept under the carpet as 'one of those things', however much wiser elements counselled caution.

The setting-off was reminiscent of the sailing to Darien in 1698 when William Paterson convinced the nation that a Scottish colony in Central America was to be the start of the Scottish Empire. No homework had been done by Paterson, and the whole enterprise was

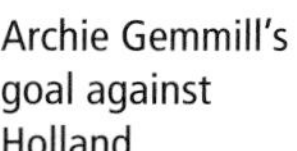

Archie Gemmill's goal against Holland.

built on nothing other than swagger and Scottish conceit. The results would be similar.

The Scottish nation has always had a tremendous penchant for self-destruction. No sooner had the squad reached Argentina than moans were heard about sub-standard accommodation and victimisation by the Argentine police, laced with a few complaints about not getting enough money, and scandalous stories about players enjoying themselves with drink and women. Even at that point reality did not kick in, and both in Argentina and Scotland itself, optimism was the order of the day.

It all exploded with a huge bang on 3 June 1978 when the team went down to Peru after taking a lead and missing a penalty. Worse was to come when Willie Johnston was sent home for taking illegal substances. A few days later, Scotland had a humiliating draw with Iran (needing an own goal from Iran to achieve even that), and the media and the fans turned on the hapless squad with a vengeance. Not for the first nor last time, Scotland became the laughing stock of the world, and crocodile tears were seen in great profusion south of Hadrian's Wall.

Then another facet of the Scottish character appeared when the team rallied and beat Holland to show what could have been done. Archie Gemmill's goal is arguably the most famous Scottish goal of all time, but there is something rather pathetic about the way that it continues, even now, to be celebrated. It has been 'praised not without cause, but without end'. The damage had been done by that time, and Scotland was a different place when the players came home thoroughly dejected.

ARMADALE FC (former Scottish League club)

Home: **Volunteer Park, Armadale, West Lothian**
Highest League Position: **25th (3rd in Div. Two, 1921/22)**
Best Scottish Cup Performance: **Last 8 (4th round 1919/20)**

It is believed that the club was first founded in 1879, but the 'Dale' appear to have gone out of existence and then re-emerged on more than one occasion during the 1880s and 1890s. By the end of the century the club had been officially wound up, but they re-formed in 1910 and played in the Scottish Union, before transferring to the Central League, which they won in 1914 and 1915, and then the Eastern League, which they won in 1916. After the end of the first world war, they returned to the Central League for the start of the 1919/20 season and then proceeded to earn themselves a reputation as Scottish Cup giant-killers, with two seasons of remarkable success. In 1919/20 they beat three Scottish League teams, Clyde, Hibernian and Ayr United, before a 2–1 home defeat to Kilmarnock prevented them from reaching the semi-finals.

The following season they beat St. Mirren and Bo'ness before coming up against Albion Rovers, the previous year's losing finalists, in the third round. Rovers needed three replays before they eventually triumphed 2–0 at Hampden Park.

The Scottish League re-introduced Division Two for the 1921/22 season after a six-year absence and its members were mostly clubs from the Central League, including Armadale. After a promising third-place finish in the first season, the Dale's performance soon fell away and they usually finished the season near the bottom of the table. By the early 1930s they were experiencing severe financial problems and were just managing to survive from year to year. At one point they even introduced whippet racing at their Volunteer Park ground in an attempt to boost their income.

There was one last moment of excitement in the Scottish Cup, when Rangers visited Armadale in the first round of the 1930/31 competition and won 7–1, but by 1932/33 the club's finances were in such bad shape that they couldn't even make the guaranteed payment to visiting clubs and were expelled from the Scottish League. Their fixtures were uncompleted, their records for that season were expunged, and it wasn't long before the club folded. However, football is still played at Volunteer Park, as three years later Armadale Thistle was formed as a junior club.

ARNOTT Wattie (1863 – 1931)

Scotland Caps: 14
Scottish Cup medals: 3

Wattie Arnott was one of the great players of the late Victorian era. He played mainly for Queen's Park, but was capped fourteen times for Scotland, leading them to victory against England in 1884 and 1887. He was a right back, a sturdy player, but not without speed, and was frequently described as the greatest player in the world. At club level he won Scottish Cup medals with Queen's Park in 1884, 1886 and 1890, and twice earned runners-up medals in the FA Cup when Queen's Park lost to Blackburn Rovers in the final in 1884 and 1885. He also told the story of how he (at the age of nine) and some friends saw the first-ever Scotland versus England international in 1872, hiring a taxi cab and standing on it to look over the fence at Hamilton Crescent to see the 0–0 draw.

ARTHURLIE FC (former Scottish League club)

Home: **Dunterlie Park, Barrhead, Renfrewshire**
Highest League Position: **Joint 19th (Joint 5th in Div. Two, 1904/05)**
Best Scottish Cup Performance: **Last 6 (6th round 1880/81)**

Founded in 1874, Arthurlie soon became a regular entrant in the Scottish Cup and reached the sixth round in 1880/81, beating Hearts 4–0 along the way before eventually losing 2–0 to Vale of Leven. There was an amalgamation with Barrhead Rangers in 1882, but the new club kept the Arthurlie name. Then in 1896/97 Arthurlie entered the record books by defeating Celtic, the reigning Scottish League champions, 4–2 in the first round of the Scottish Cup. However, they lost 5–1 to Morton in the second round and did not win again in the Scottish Cup (proper) until 1925.

In 1901 the club was admitted to Division Two and remained there until 1915, when the league was reduced to a single division. Although Division Two was re-introduced in 1921, Arthurlie wasn't part of it and it wasn't until the creation of Division Three in 1923 that the club once again participated in Scottish League football. The Division Three title, and promotion, was won at the first attempt.

In 1926/27 they reached the last eight of the Scottish Cup, when a crowd of 8000 saw them lose 3–0 at home to East Fife. Arthurlie remained in Division Two until 1929, but with four games to go in the 1928/29 season their mounting debts, coupled with low crowds, got so bad that they resigned from the Scottish League. There was a season of amateur football in 1929/30 before they reformed as a junior club and since then there have been many honours, including the Scottish Junior Cup in both 1937 and 1998. (see **JUNIOR FOOTBALL**)

ASSISTANT REFEREE (see REFEREE)

ATMOSPHERE

It is a matter of some regret that the arrival of all-seater stadia has led to a decline in what is called 'atmosphere' at Scottish football games. A football match is an act of drama with colours, rival groups, team spirit, 'us and them', all controlled by the man in the black that no one likes. For some reason, the fact that the audience is all seated has tended to calm them down. The good news about all this is that violence and aggression are less in evidence than they once were, but it is often felt that a little more enthusiasm from supporters would not go amiss.

In particular there has been a decline in the number of songs sung. Not all football songs are nice, and the lack of some of them is by no means to be deplored, but it used to be that the devotees of a particular team would sing a decent song that was in some way meant to represent their team. Rangers fans would sing *Follow, Follow* (a ditty pinched from the Salvation Army who used to sing 'Follow, Follow We Will Follow Jesus' and Celtic fans from 1961 onwards would have *Sure It's A Grand Old Team to Play For* while Aberdonians would sing about their *Northern Lights of Old Aberdeen* and Dundee fans sang the praises of Lord Graham of Claverhouse, Viscount Dundee ('Bonnie Dundee') who did so well at Killiecrankie in 1689. Hearts and Hibs also had their particular anthems, albeit with embarrassing lyrics, while the song of Dundee United *There's a grand stand, the finest in the land at Tannadice* was particularly awful for most non-Arabs.

An extract from: **The Match of the Vale Brigade!**
Hampden Park, December 30th, 1876

Have a kick, have a kick,
Have a kick onwards,
All into Queen's Park ground,
Rushed the Vale forwards.

"Forward the Leven team!
Charge for goal," they scream:
Down falls the fortress! – while
Cheered many a hundred.

"Forward the Vale Brigade!"
Was there a man dismayed?
Not that the players knew
That Queen's men ne'er blundered.

Theirs but to make a try,
Theirs not to reason why;
Theirs but to have a shy
Through the goal which had defied shots many a hundred.

Such community singing has virtually disappeared. There are still, sadly, obscene songs and sectarian songs, although Rangers are to be credited with making an effort in summer 2006 to improve the tone of Ibrox with the issuing of a booklet of politically correct and acceptable songs. Seldom, however, is there the singing (like a Welsh rugby match, for instance) that would make a Scottish football match more like a theatrical occasion. A Scotland versus England game at Hampden in the 1950s or 1960s was sometimes more memorable for the singing beforehand than it was for the game itself, as someone like Robert Wilson would lead the crowd in *Loch Lomond* or *Roamin' In The Gloamin'*.

Since the mid 1960s, there has also been a sad lack of the 'crawmill', the 'corncrake' or the 'rattle' with which to spur one's team to greater efforts. They were normally made of wood, and were twirled above one's head with the colours of the team draped from them.

'Put maroon on your rattles
For great Barney Battles
Is playing for Hearts today'

was a great chant of Hearts supporters in the 1930s.

Musical instruments were not uncommon either. Bells, drums and bugles used to be seen frequently at football grounds, and have now all but disappeared, although Rangers on occasion have had a band in the Broomloan Road end of Ibrox, and Stark's Park, Kirkcaldy was famous in the late 1990s for its lone trumpeter. Poignantly, on one occasion when the local side were doing badly, he played *The Last Post.*

ATTENDANCES

Attendances are often a matter for conjecture. There are vested interests in both exaggerating and minimising them, as exaggeration can be good for publicity purposes, whilst minimising can avoid taxes. The peak time for attendances was in the late 1940s and the early 1950s. Since then, there has been a general falling off and a polarisation towards the Old Firm, to the detriment of other teams in west central Scotland. Unimaginative stewardship of clubs has not helped. The selling of a star player can hardly be expected not to have an adverse effect on attendances, particularly when the buying club has been a rival, e.g. one or other of the Old Firm. Teams like Dundee, Hibernian and Motherwell have been particularly guilty in this respect. In addition, many clubs were slow to read the signs in the early 1960s that the public were beginning to demand better facilities in terms of all-seated stadia, catering, hygiene and general concern for spectators' welfare. Then, by the time that all-seated stadia were built, the prices were often too high for a family. It is a problem that many people feel must be addressed, for there are few more dispiriting sights on television than empty seats

The effect that live television has on attendances is often discussed. Many clubs now feel that they will earn at least as much from television revenues as they will from turnstile receipts, hence the willingness, indeed the imperative, to sign a lucrative television deal. In some ways this is to be welcomed because it means that the Scottish public's apparently insatiable desire for football is being addressed, albeit on television, whether in the home or the pub. On the other hand, the sight of half-empty all-seater stadia at provincial grounds, even when Rangers or Celtic are the visitors, must surely be deplored.

Scotland, and in particular Hampden Park, does however have an impressive number of record attendances, e.g. the European record for official attendance at any game is Scotland versus England on 17 April 1937 at Hampden Park, when 149,547 were there. A week later, 146,433 (some say 147,365) were at the same venue to see the Celtic versus Aberdeen Scottish cup final of that year. In 1948, on 27 March, 143,270 saw the Scottish Cup semi-final between Rangers and Hibernian, and then the final between Rangers and Morton, which went to two games, attracted a record aggregate of 265,199. The record for the European Cup was set on 15 April 1970 when 135,826 were at Hampden to see the Celtic versus Leeds semi-final, and the record for a European Cup final was Real Madrid versus Eintracht Frankfurt on 18 May 1960 with 127,621. The same Eintracht Frankfurt set the British record for a friendly when they played Rangers on 17 October 1961 in front of 104,679 people to inaugurate the Hampden Park floodlights. The record

Standing room only for the vast Hampden Park crowd, with over 110,000 attending this fixture against England in the 1920s.

Massed Scotland fans watch the World Cup qualifier against Ukraine at a sold out Hampden Park in October 2007.

attendance for a World Cup qualifier was Scotland versus Poland on 13 October 1965 (107,580), and ten days after that, on 23 October 1965 the record attendance for a League Cup final was recorded when 107,609 came to see the Old Firm clash. It must be stressed that these figures, although official, are approximate. On each occasion there will be many people who claim to have 'climbed over the wall' – a claim that will be substantiated by eyewitness accounts. In addition, it was always possible – indeed it was widespread – for impecunious youngsters to be given a 'lift-over' the turnstiles, so that all these attendances are probably an underestimate of reality.

Away from Hampden Park, the record for a Scottish League match is 118,567 for the clash between Rangers and Celtic on 2 January 1939, and the record for the Scottish League Premier Division was set on the first day of its existence at Ibrox Park on 30 August 1975, when 69,000 were at the Old Firm game. In the Scottish Premier League on several occasions, Celtic Park's capacity of 60,000 has been reached. Celtic Park's highest ever attendance is a matter of some doubt. Some sources say that 92,000 were there on New Year's Day 1938 to see the Old Firm game, but other more probable sources say 83,500. For junior football, the record is the Scottish Junior Cup final in 1951 when 77,650 were at Hampden to see Petershill versus Irvine Meadow.

Low attendances are similarly hard to prove, but Scotland's lowest home attendance in recent times is certainly the 7,843 who appeared to see Scotland versus Northern Ireland on Tuesday 6 May 1969 on a foul night when the game was televised live. Yet that is huge in comparison to the reported 600 who attended Scotland versus Wales in a snowstorm on 26 March 1892 at Tynecastle, 'sheltering behind the enclosure wall and begging the referee to let them go home'.

In domestic football, twenty-nine appeared on 31 July 1999 to see a Scottish League Cup game between Clydebank and East Stirlingshire, when Clydebank (who would go out of business in 2002) were sharing a ground with Morton at Cappielow. East Stirlingshire versus Leith Athletic on 15 April 1939 attracted thirty-two, on the same day that 149,269 (only a few hundred short of the record of two years previously) were at Hampden Park to see the Scotland versus England international. In the Scottish Premier League a record low was set on 5 April 2008 when only 431 were at Fir Park, Motherwell to see Gretna lose 2–1 to Inverness CT. This was perhaps an eloquent comment on the SPL's decision to compel Gretna to play their home games at Motherwell.

AUCHINLECK TALBOT FC (see JUNIOR FOOTBALL)

AULD Bertie (1938 –)

Scotland Caps: 3
Scottish League Championship medals: 5
Scottish Cup medals: 3
Scottish League Cup medals: 4
European Cup medal: 1

Bertie Auld was one of the Lisbon Lions, and one of Celtic's greatest-ever characters. He joined Celtic in 1955, and was one of the 'Kelly Kids' who showed promise. In Bertie's case, he had played three times for Scotland (being sent off in one of the games) before he fell out with Chairman Bob Kelly, who did not like his rebellious and flippant attitude. In 1961 he was transferred to Birmingham City, with whom he reached the Inter-Cities Fairs Cup final in that year, and won the English League Cup in 1963. Even before Jock Stein arrived as manager at Parkhead, he had indicated that

he wanted Bertie back, and Auld returned to Celtic in January 1965. After that, with Bertie as the midfield general, Celtic and Auld never looked back, as Celtic swept all before them.

Leaving Celtic in 1971, he joined Hibernian and soon became their coach. Afterwards he was manager of Partick Thistle (twice), Hamilton Accies, Hibs and Dumbarton. He will be remembered as the midfield general of the Lisbon Lions, but the downside of him was his aggression, which was not always channelled in the right direction. He was heavily involved in Celtic's South American fiasco in 1967, and on a trip to North America in 1970 he and Tommy Gemmell were sent home in disgrace. He remains, however, a great entertainer and Celtic supporter.

AUSTRALIA

Australia is not a country that has, until very recently, been associated with football, but Scotland have played them four times, winning twice, drawing once and losing once. The 1985 games were play-offs for the World Cup finals.

1985	20 Nov	Hampden Park	2–0	Cooper McAvennie	
1985	4 Dec	Melbourne	0–0		
1996	27 Mar	Hampden Park	1–0	McCoist	
2000	15 Nov	Hampden Park	0–2		Emerton Zdrilic

AUSTRIA

Austria is a country with which Scotland has a few similarities in that they are both under the shadow of a larger country which speaks the same language (England, Germany) and have both in the past been forced into Union or Anschluss with them (1707, 1938) through bribery, threats and general skulduggery. Scotland have played Austria eighteen times, but relations have not always been good, notably in the 1963 Hampden friendly when the game was abandoned by English referee Jim Finney in the face of Austria's dirty tactics after two Austrians had been sent off. In the game in 1951, Billy Steel was sent off, being the first man to receive this penalty in an international match for Scotland. The previous December, Austria had become the first foreign team to beat Scotland at Hampden. Of the twenty games, Scotland have won five, drawn six and lost eight with one abandoned.

Garry O'Connor (second from left) celebrates scoring against Austria in May 2007.

1931	16 May	Vienna	0–5		Zischek (2) Schall Vogel Sindelar
1933	29 Nov	Hampden Park	2–2	Meiklejohn McFadyen	Zischek Schall
1937	9 May	Vienna	1–1	O'Donnell	Jerusalem
1950	13 Dec	Hampden Park	0–1		Melchior
1951	27 May	Vienna	0–4		Hanappi (2) Wagner (2)
1954	16 June	Zurich	0–1		Probst
1955	19 May	Vienna	4–1	Robertson Smith Liddell Reilly	Ocwirk
1956	2 May	Hampden Park	1–1	Conn	Wagner
1960	29 May	Vienna	1–4	Mackay	Hanappi (2) Hof (2)
1963	8 May	Hampden Park	4–1	Wilson (2) Law (2)	Linhart
Match abandoned after 79 minutes					
1968	6 Nov	Hampden Park	2–1	Law Bremner	Starek
1969	5 Nov	Vienna	0–2		Redl (2)
1978	20 Sep	Vienna	2–3	McQueen Gray	Pezzey Schachner Kreuz
1979	17 Oct	Hampden Park	1–1	Gemmill	Krankl
1994	20 Apr	Vienna	2–1	McGinlay McKinlay	Hutter
1996	31 Aug	Vienna	0–0		
1997	2 Apr	Celtic Park	2–0	Gallacher (2)	
2003	30 Apr	Hampden Park	0–2		Kirchler Haas
2005	17 Aug	Graz	2–2	Miller O'Connor	Iberstberger Standfest
2007	30 May	Vienna	1–0	O'Connor	

AWAY GAMES

It is much more difficult to win away from home than at home. This is particularly true in European competitions, because of a hostile crowd, travelling, unfamiliarity with the quirks of the pitch, and many other associated problems. But a good team will overcome all these, which are in any case psychological to a certain extent. There is perhaps an argument in favour of awarding an extra point for an away win, in that it would encourage the away team to attack all the more, but on the other hand, football benefits from having a simple points structure. In any case, big teams like Celtic and Rangers have such a large away support that many away games are tantamount to home ones.

Teams who have done particularly well away from home include Rangers, who won all their away games in season 1888/89, and then again in season 1920/21 when they won thirty-seven out of forty-two possible points away from home by dint of winning sixteen games and drawing five. In the Scottish Premier League, Celtic in season 2003/04 went through the whole season without losing a game away from home. In fact they won them all apart from a draw at Dunfermline on the opening day, and then two draws at Hearts and Motherwell after the league had been comfortably secured.

AWAY GOALS RULE

This rule was introduced into European competitions in the late 1960s to avoid penalty shoot-outs, poorly attended play-offs in neutral countries, and the tossing of coins to decide winners. It has been the bane of many Scottish clubs. If the goals are equal on aggregate, the team who has scored the most goals away from home wins. Thus, for example, in season 1985/86 in the quarter-finals of the European Cup, Aberdeen drew 2–2 with FK Gothenburg at Pittodrie and 0–0 in Sweden. FK Gothenburg went through because they had scored two goals in Scotland, whereas Aberdeen had not scored in Sweden. This scenario has been replicated with Scottish teams in countless occasions eg Celtic versus Liverpool in 1997/78, Rangers versus Viktoria Zizkov in 2003/04.

Scotland's first encounter with the away goals rule was a bizarre one. It came on 3 November 1971 when Rangers were playing Sporting Lisbon in the second round of the European Cup-Winners' Cup. Rangers had won the first leg at Ibrox 3–2, and lost the second leg by a similar score in Lisbon. Extra time was ordered and, when both teams scored in the extra-time period, referee Van Ravens ordered a penalty shoot-out. Sporting Lisbon won the shoot-out and thought that they had won the tie. But a Scottish journalist approached Rangers' manager Willie Waddell with the rule book, then the UEFA representative was consulted, the penalty shoot-out was declared invalid, and Rangers were declared the winners on the grounds that they had scored three goals away from home, even though one of them was in extra time.

Scottish teams generally do badly on this rule. One possible reason for this is tactical naivety or lack of ability on the part of defenders, but another is perhaps more deeply embedded in the Scottish psyche, in that a Scottish team feels more obliged than those of other nations to attack unreservedly in front of their own fans, even at times when tactical considerations and common sense should dictate otherwise. Clichés like 'the back door was left open' are heard in the deathly silence that follows a foreign team scoring at a Scottish ground.

Despite Silvio Meissner being sent off by referee Runo Derrien in the UEFA Cup first round second leg match against Hearts at Tynecastle in September 2000. Ten-man VfB Stuttgart won on the away goals rule after the tie finished 3-3 on aggregate.

AYR FC (former Scottish League club)

Home: **Somerset Park, Ayr**
Highest League Position: **15th (3rd in Div. 2, 1902/03)**
Best Scottish Cup Performance: **Last 16 (5th round 1887/88; 2nd round 1895/96; 1900/01; 1902/03; 1906/07; 1909/10)**

Ayr FC, which went on to amalgamate with Ayr Parkhouse and form Ayr United, was itself the result of an amalgamation of two clubs, when Ayr Thistle and Ayr Academicals joined together in 1879. The new club spent its early years playing friendly matches and in cup competitions such as the Ayrshire Cup, and then in the 1890s went on to play in both the Scottish Alliance League and the Ayrshire Combination.

In 1897 they were elected to Division Two of the Scottish League, but success at national level proved elusive at first. They finished in the bottom half of the table in each of their first five seasons, but in 1903 their league form finally started to improve. By 1908 they had finished third on three occasions, but it was never quite enough to gain promotion to the top flight. Neighbours and rivals Ayr Parkhouse weren't doing well, and there was an increasing view that an amalgamated club would offer the best opportunity for first-division football. Thus it was that a new club was born, and at the start of the 1910/11 season Ayr United took the place of Ayr FC and Ayr Parkhouse.

AYR PARKHOUSE FC (former Scottish League club)

Home: **Beresford Park, Ayr**
Highest League Position: **24th (6th in Div. 2, 1907/08)**
Best Scottish Cup Performance: **Last 8 (3rd round 1894/95; 1897/98)**

Founded in 1886, the club took its name from Parkhouse Farm, where the first training sessions were held. Proud of their amateur status, Ayr Parkhouse played in both the Ayrshire League and the Ayrshire Combination in the 1890s. By the 1900s amateur clubs were dropping their resistance to national league football, and after finishing as runners-up in the Scottish Amateur League in 1903, Parkhouse successfully applied to join Division Two of the Scottish League. Unfortunately, they only won three of their twenty-two games and, after finishing in bottom place in 1904, failed to win re-election. Then it came to light that their fierce rivals Ayr FC had orchestrated a campaign to persuade other clubs not to vote for them.

Now playing in the Scottish Combination, the Parkhouse club finally embraced professionalism in 1905 and when the Scottish League was expanded in 1906 they were re-elected. However, this second chance did not bring league success and when the club finished in bottom place in 1910, the idea of amalgamating with Ayr FC began to gain ground. Their rival's form had also been poor and so a newly created Ayr United joined the Scottish League for the 1910/11 season, after which Ayr Parkhouse ceased to exist.

AYR UNITED FC

Ground: **Somerset Park**
Nickname: **The Honest Men**
Colours: **White and black**
Record Attendance: **25,225 v Rangers (1969)**
Record Victory: **11-1 v Dumbarton (1952)**
Record Defeat: **0-9 v Rangers (1929); v Hearts (1931); v Third Lanark (1954)**
Highest League Position: **4th (1915/16)**
Best Scottish Cup Performance: **Last 4 (1972/73; 1999/2000; 2001/02)**
Best League Cup Performance: **Runners-up (2001/02)**

Ayr United are known as 'The Honest Men' because of the poetry of Robert Burns, who wrote 'Auld Ayr, wham ne'er a toon surpasses, for honest men and bonnie lasses' in *Tam o' Shanter*. The only club in the Scottish League to have been formed by the amalgamation of two previous Scottish League clubs, their origins date back to 1910 when Ayr FC merged with Ayr Parkhouse. Neither of these clubs had ever been promoted out of Division Two of the Scottish League and that is where Ayr United started life at the beginning of the 1910/11 season.

The new club got off to a very good start. After finishing as runners-up in their first season, United topped Division Two in 1911/12, only to fail to win election to the top flight. They then topped Division Two again in 1912/13 and this time they were voted into Division One. As the years unfolded, this was where the club was usually to be found. In fact, by the time the league was suspended at the start of the Second World War, there had only been two brief spells outside Division One and on each occasion a Division Two championship was won in the course of the return. When this happened in the 1927/28 season, Jimmy Smith scored sixty-six league goals and created a British record that still stands.

It was therefore something of a surprise when the Scottish League resumed in 1945 and United found themselves in Division B – especially as three clubs that had finished below them in 1939 were in Division A. They did not escape from it until 1956 and now the club started to experience the opposite of what happened in the pre-war years – brief spells in the top division. It happened three times and it brought two more Division Two championships.

However, promotion in 1969 was different. Manager Ally MacLeod built a side that stayed in the top division until 1978 and United finished in the top eight clubs for five consecutive seasons. In 1969/70 they took Celtic to a replay in the semi-finals of the League Cup, before losing 2–1, and in 1972/73 they reached the semi-finals of the Scottish Cup, but lost 2–0 to Rangers.

After relegation in 1978, Ayr's usual home was the First Division (second tier), but now their form was characterised by brief spells in the Second Division. Two highlights of the early 1990s were appearances in the final of the Scottish League Challenge Cup, but they were lost 3–2 to Dundee and 1–0 to Hamilton. Then, in 2000, manager Gordon Dalziel led the Honest Men to another semi-final in the Scottish Cup. Once again the result was a defeat to Rangers, this time 7–0.

Two years later, however, Ayr United had a year to remember. Not only did they again reach the semi-finals of the Scottish Cup, this time losing 3–0 to Celtic, they

Ayr United 1960/61.

also went all the way to the final of the 2001/02 League Cup. A penalty from Eddie Annand was enough to overcome Hibernian in the semi-finals, but Rangers prevented Ayr from winning their first major trophy with a 4–0 victory in the final at Hampden Park.

Gordon Dalziel left in 2002 after seven years in charge, and in the years that followed United's form in the league diminished. A ninth-place finish in 2003/04 brought relegation to the Second Division, and after that they were regularly found in the middle of the third tier. In October 2007 former player Brian Reid became the club's fifth new manager since Dalziel's departure.

BANKS O'DEE FC (see JUNIOR FOOTBALL)

BATHGATE FC (former Scottish League club)

Home: **Mill Park, Bathgate, West Lothian**
Highest League Position: **23rd (3rd in Div. 2, 1923/24)**
Best Scottish Cup Performances: **Last 16 (2nd round 1904/05; 3rd round 1921/22, 1925/26)**

This Bathgate football club was founded in 1893, although there had been a previous Bathgate FC that had gone out of existence. The club is also not to be confused with Bathgate Rovers, a team that once achieved fame by holding Falkirk to a 5–5 draw in the third round of the 1891/92 Scottish Cup and then winning the replay 3–0.

In 1903 the club obtained the lease for some land near the town centre and this was developed into Mill Park, which became their home for nearly thirty years. They played in various leagues over the years, including the Central Combination League, the Midland League and the Scottish Union, which they won in 1907/08. In 1904/05 they almost knocked Aberdeen out of the Scottish Cup when they drew 1–1 away from home.

One of the club's early players was Bernard ('Barney') Battles, who went on to play for Hearts, Celtic, Liverpool, Dundee and Celtic again. He won three Scottish caps whilst with Celtic.

From 1908 until the first world war they played in the Central League and they joined it again after the war in 1919. The Scottish Qualifying Cup was won in 1919/20 and in 1921 Bathgate became members of the Scottish League when the Central League provided most of the members of the new Division Two. There were some successes in the early stages of the Scottish Cup during this period, including a 1–0 victory over first-division neighbours Falkirk in 1921/22.

Bathgate then remained in Division Two until 1928/29, when they resigned after playing only twenty-eight matches. They were in serious financial trouble by this time. The shale oil industry of West Lothian was in decline, there was high unemployment, and crowds were small.

After leaving Division Two they played in the East of Scotland League and won the Scottish Qualifying Cup again in both 1929/30 and 1930/31. They also won the East of Scotland League in three successive seasons, but the town council wanted to develop Mill Park and they played their last match in 1932. The Mill Park stand was sold to Stenhousemuir.

BATHGATE THISTLE FC (see JUNIOR FOOTBALL)

BAULD Willie (1928 – 1977)

Scotland Caps: 3
Scottish League Championship medals: 2
Scottish Cup medals: 1
Scottish League Cup medals: 2

Willie Bauld was the personality goal-scorer of Hearts in the 1950s. With only three Scottish caps, he could consider himself under-rewarded, but he did play in the 1950 game against England, when Scotland had said that they would go to the World Cup finals in Brazil only if they were the British champions. The game ended 0–1 and Bauld, late in the game, famously hit the bar with a

shot which would have drawn the game and given Scotland the Home International championship if it had gone in. But he was always considered to be the King Willie of Tynecastle, winning with Hearts the Scottish Cup of 1956, two league championship medals in 1958 and 1960, and two Scottish League Cup medals in 1954/55 and 1958/59. He is regarded as one of Hearts' greatest-ever players.

BAXTER Jim (1939 – 2001)

Scotland Caps: 34
Scottish League Championship medals: 3
Scottish Cup medals: 3
Scottish League Cup medals: 4

A naturally skilled player, Jim Baxter's charismatic personality and individual brilliance with a football earned him the status of one of Scotland's most entertaining footballers of all time. His first senior club

Jim Baxter after the defeat of England at Wembley in 1967.

was Raith Rovers, which he joined after working in the Fife coalfields. In 1960 he was transferred to Rangers, where he consistently demonstrated his ability to influence the outcome of a match, and he won at least one medal in each of his five seasons there. Moves to Sunderland (1965) and Nottingham Forest (1968) followed, and eventually he rejoined Rangers in 1969, but was not so successful this time.

His flamboyant character and total self-belief meant that he loved to rise to the big occasion, and he did so twice for Scotland at Wembley. On the winning side each time, he scored Scotland's two goals in 1963, and in 1967 dominated the game with an outstanding display of virtuosity against the World Cup holders. He won a total of thirty-four caps for Scotland. Jim Baxter's reputation was one of a man who loved to live life to the full, and later in life he suffered from poor health. A liver transplant prolonged his life by seven years, but he died in 2001, aged sixty-one.

BEATTIE Andy (1913 – 1983)

Scotland Caps: 7

Andy Beattie was a left back who played for Preston North End before the second world war, and he won the FA Cup with them in 1938. His international debut was the game against England in 1937 at Hampden Park, which established the world record attendance, and which Scotland won 3–1. After the war he became a manager with no fewer than seven English league clubs, and also earned a certain notoriety for being manager of Scotland in the 1954 World Cup in Switzerland – and resigning half-way through the competition before the 7–0 thrashing by Uruguay. No reason was given for this bizarre behaviour, but it was commonly believed to be interference by officialdom in the running of team affairs. Surprisingly after that, he was given a second spell as Scotland manager from 1959-1960.

BEITH FC (former Scottish League club)

Home: **Bellsdale Park, Beith, Ayrshire**
Highest League Position: **47th (7th in Div. 3, 1923/24)**
Best Scottish Cup Performance: **Last 8 (3rd round, 1904/05)**

Beith only belonged to the Scottish League for three seasons, from 1923 to 1926, but the history of the Ayrshire club dates back to 1875 and it enjoyed success in the years after it ceased to be part of the national league.

The first Beith FC was founded in 1875 and quickly made its mark in the Scottish Cup. They reached the fifth round in 1877/78, before losing to Third Lanark,

Andy Beattie, who was Scotland's manager for the 1954 World Cup.

and only the mighty Queens Park prevented them from reaching the fifth round again in 1880/81. However, this success attracted the attention of the bigger clubs and many of their best players left. The team suffered a severe loss of form and the situation got so bad that the club stopped playing altogether during 1882/83.

They re-formed for the 1891/92 season, but struggled to find success, and it wasn't long before they amalgamated with Beith Thistle. The situation now improved and the new club won the Scottish Combination in 1904/05. That same season they beat Kilmarnock, of Division One, in the Scottish Cup, winning 3–1 after a 2–2 draw at Rugby Park. One year later they reached the final of the Scottish Qualifying Cup, losing 2–0 to Leith Athletic.

The club moved on to play in both the Scottish Union and the Scottish Reserve League over the years and in 1919 Beith became part of the Western League. In 1923 most of its members were invited to become part of the new Division Three and so Beith's short membership of the Scottish League began. The introduction of the new division coincided with an economic downturn and crowds were low, particularly in small towns such as Beith. Even travelling costs became a problem for some clubs and Division Three folded in 1926.

Beith's league finishes of seventh, thirteenth and twelfth in Division Three had been unremarkable, but then they went on to show their ability by winning four Scottish Qualifying Cups. In 1927/28 they were victorious in one of its last years as a national competition and then they won the Scottish Qualifying Cup (South) in 1931/32, 1932/33 and 1934/35. However, it was a different story with league football. The club was now playing in the Scottish Alliance, which included the reserve teams of several Scottish League clubs, and success was hard to find. In 1937/38 they finished bottom and took the decision to adopt junior status.

BELARUS

Scotland have played Belarus four times with two wins, one draw and one defeat.

1997	8 June	Minsk	1–0	McAllister (pen)	
1997	7 Sep	Pittodrie	4–1	Gallacher (2) Hopkin (2)	Kachuro (pen)
2005	8 June	Minsk	0–0		
2005	8 Oct	Hampden Park	0–1		Kutuzov

BELGIUM

Scotland have played Belgium fourteen times with four wins, two draws and eight defeats.

1947	18 May	Brussels	1–2	Steel	Anoul (2)
1948	28 Apr	Hampden Park	2–0	Combe Duncan	
1951	20 May	Brussels	5–0	Hamilton (3) Mason Waddell	
1971	3 Feb	Liege	0–3		Van Himst (2) (1 pen) McKinnon o.g.
1971	10 Nov	Pittodrie	1–0	O'Hare	
1974	1 June	Bruges	1–2	Johnstone	Henrotay Lambert (pen)
1979	21 Nov	Brussels	0–2		Van der Elst Voordeckers
1979	19 Dec	Hampden Park	1–3	Robertson	Van der Elst (2) Vandenbergh
1982	15 Dec	Brussels	2–3	Dalglish (2)	Van der Elst (2) Vandenbergh
1983	12 Oct	Hampden Park	1–1	Nicholas	Vercauteren
1987	1 Apr	Brussels	1–4	McStay	Claesen (3) Vercauteren
1987	14 Oct	Hampden Park	2–0	McCoist McStay	
2001	24 Mar	Hampden Park	2–2	Dodds (2) (1 pen)	Wilmots Van Buyten
2001	5 Sep	Brussels	0–2		Van Kerckhoven Goor

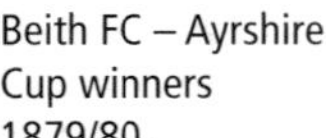
Beith FC – Ayrshire Cup winners 1879/80.

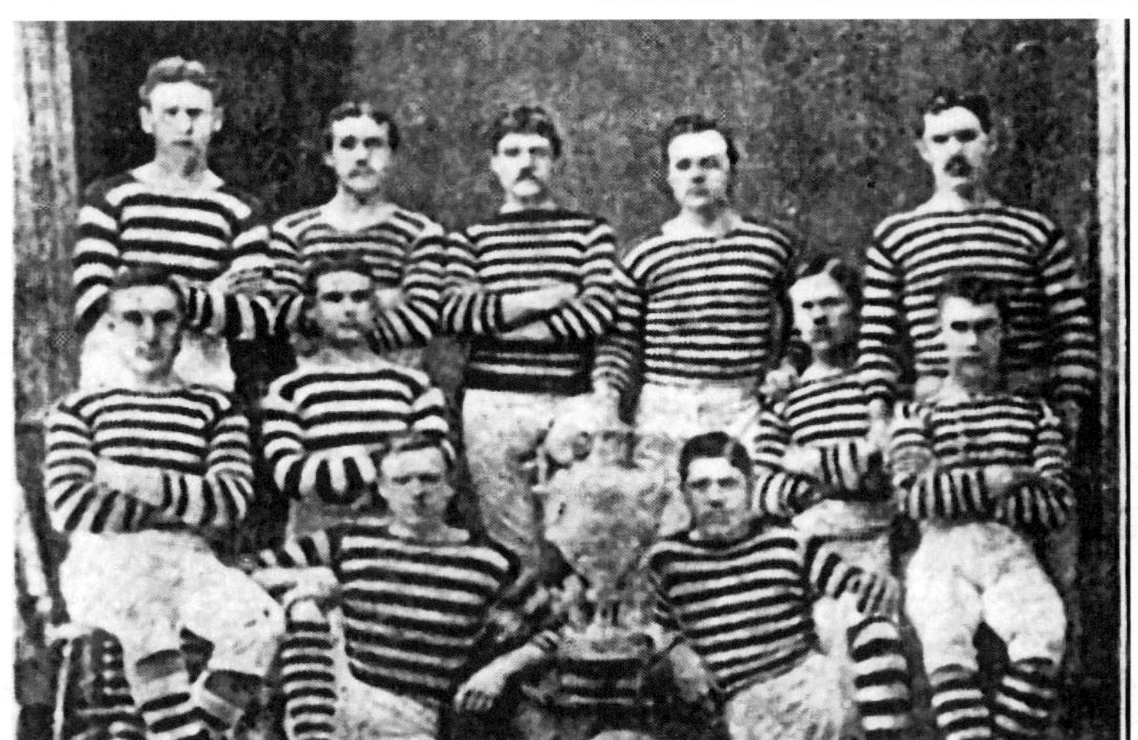

BENNETT Alec (1881 – 1940)

Scotland Caps: 11
Scottish League Championship medals: 7
Scottish Cup medals: 2

Alec Bennett was an outside right of the Edwardian era, who played equally successfully for both sides of the Old Firm, and earned eleven Scottish caps in the process. He joined Celtic in 1903 and almost immediately was a success, although it was not until season 1904/05 that he became established on the right wing, earning the nickname of 'the artful dodger'. He won four Scottish League championships with Celtic, and two Scottish Cup medals, before he moved to Rangers in 1908, to the great distress of those at Celtic Park who adored him. No reason was ever given, but suggestions were that it might have been for religious reasons or perhaps because of his inability to put up with the dictatorship of Willie Maley. With Rangers he won another three league championship medals. In later years he turned out for Dumbarton and Albion Rovers and was manager of Third Lanark and Clydebank. His Scottish caps included the epic win over England in 1910.

BERWICK RANGERS FC

Ground: **Shielfield Park**
Nickname: **The Borderers**
Colours: **Black and gold**
Record Attendance: **16,000 v Rangers (1960)**
Record Victory: **8-1 v Forfar Athletic (1965); v Vale of Leithen (1966)**
Record Defeat: **1-9 v Hamilton Academical (1980)**
Highest League Position: **22nd (12th in First Div., 1979/80)**
Best Scottish Cup Performance: **Last 8 (4th round 1953/54); (5th round 1979/80)**
Best League Cup Performance: **Last 4 (1963/64)**

Berwick Rangers are unique, because the club is the only one in first-class Scottish football that plays in England. The Northumberland club has a proud history of achievement in both the Scottish Cup and the Scottish League Cup, and the proudest achievement of all came on 28 January 1967. Led by player-manager Jock Wallace, they defeated Rangers 1–0 in the first round of the Scottish Cup and Sammy Reid's winning goal created one of the biggest shocks in the history of the competition.

The club was founded in late 1881 and has known many homes over the years. The Borderers first played at Bull Stob Close on land provided by Peter Cowe, a local fish trader, before moving to Pier Field, Meadow Field, Union Park and then Old Shielfield Park. Their current ground was opened in 1954 adjacent to the previous one. At first they switched between English and Scottish football, and won the North Northumberland League in 1899/1900 without losing a single match. After joining the Border League in 1902/03 they won the title at the first attempt, and then played in Northumberland again before finally settling in Scottish football in 1905/06. Berwick went on to win the championship of the East of Scotland League in its inaugural season of 1927/28 and won the title again in 1946/47.

Berwick Rangers.

Bobby Ancell was appointed player/manager in 1950, and in 1951 the Borderers were elected into Division C of the Scottish Football League. He moved on to Dunfermline Athletic, but the club he had left behind became part of an expanded Division B four years later when Division C was discontinued. Since then Berwick's league form has been unremarkable, the highlight being the championship of the Second Division (third tier) in 1979, which brought two seasons in the middle division. After league re-organisation in 1994 they divided their time between the Second and Third Divisions, and in 2006/07 manager John Coughlin led them into the third tier as Third Division champions.

The wee Rangers have played cup-ties against their Glasgow namesakes on several other occasions besides their famous win in 1967. They lost 4–0 at Ibrox whilst still a Division C club in 1954, after a 3–0 victory over Dundee had earned them a place in the last eight of the Scottish Cup. In January 1960 Rangers travelled to Northumberland for a first-round tie, and although the score was 1–1 at half time, the Glasgow giants won 3–1. In 1963/64 they met again in the semi-finals of the League Cup at Hampden Park, and this time Rangers won 3–1.

In 1979/80 the Borderers again reached the last eight of the Scottish Cup, when Hibs visited Shielfield Park, and a Hibernian side that included George Best could only draw 0–0. Berwick lost the replay 1–0, but their ability to cause a surprise in the Scottish Cup has continued into the twenty-first century. In 2000/01 they took Hearts to a replay at Tynecastle, after a 0–0 draw in the third round, which Hearts won 2–1. The following season there was yet another tie against Rangers, and a 0–0 draw at Shielfield Park in the third round. Rangers won the replay 3–0 at Ibrox and went on to win the trophy.

In 2007/08 the wee Rangers found life difficult in the Second Division of the league, and John Coughlin resigned in October 2007. He was replaced as manager by former Hibs defender Michael Renwick, but Berwick finished the season well adrift at the bottom of the division.

BETT Jim (1959 –)

Scotland Caps: 25
Scottish Cup medals: 3
Scottish League Cup medals: 2

Jim Bett was an industrious and creative midfield player, who played twenty-five times for Scotland between 1982 and 1990. His last game was the defeat to Costa Rica in the 1990 World Cup, for which he had to accept a disproportionate share of the blame. His career stared with Dundee and Airdrieonians, included two spells with Lokeren of Belgium, and time with Rangers and Aberdeen, as well as brief spells with Hearts and Dundee United at the end of his career. He won one Scottish League Cup and one Scottish Cup medal with Rangers, and one Scottish League Cup and two Scottish Cup medals with Aberdeen.

BETTING

Betting on the outcome of matches has always been a part of Scottish football, and the most common form of betting has been the football pools, which generated large amounts of money for the football authorities in return for the use of fixture lists. They began to appear shortly after the first world war; Littlewoods were the first to appear in 1923, followed by Vernon's in 1925, and their popularity increased rapidly through the 1930s, when people were desperate to win money to escape the crippling effects of the depression. The attraction was increased by the frisson of excitement brought about by the fact that football pools were technically illegal, although in practice very little was done to stop them, other than the occasional denunciation from a pulpit on a Sunday.

A further attraction was that the pools gave working people the chance to win vast sums of money when other forms of gambling, such as horse racing, did not. Their heyday was in the 1950s, when Littlewoods, Vernon's, Empire, Zetters and others offered the chance to win a fortune by forecasting eight draws on the 'treble chance'. If there had been any doubt about their morality and legality (and the pools companies themselves would argue that they were a game of skill, not chance, as players had to be able to use football knowledge to predict results), this was swept away in 1960, when the Betting and Gaming Act of that year officially sanctioned football pools and many other forms of gambling. They enjoyed great popularity until the early 1990s, when the National Lottery began to overshadow them as a means of getting rich quickly, although there was as much (or as little) likelihood of it happening.

The 'fixed odds' also became a popular form of betting, where scores in specific games are predicted. This was particularly popular in the 1950s, but it could lend itself to bribe taking and match fixing by unscrupulous players and managers. It would be naive to say that match fixing did not happen, but it would have been very difficult to arrange. It would have had to involve several players – usually including the goalkeeper, and perhaps the referee – and it would have to be done convincingly enough to fool the fans and the newspaper reporters. Yet there was an incentive for certain players, who believed that they were not earning enough money from the game itself, as the clubs were restricted by the maximum wage rule until 1961.

In the early 1960s clubs began to hit upon the idea of having their own football or development pools. Dundee United were one of the first, with 'Taypools', and very soon every team joined in. 'Rangers Pools' even had advertisements at other grounds, Dens Park, Dundee, for example, in the 1970s, but these pools gave way to the bigger concerns and the National Lottery.

At the beginning of the twenty-first century it was no uncommon sight to see a betting shop inside a ground, offering odds for '2–0 and a named player to score the first goal', for example.

As the climate of opinion in this country about gambling had changed over the twentieth century, from outright condemnation to indifference or benign tolerance, there appeared to be no objections. By then Scottish football had been totally free from the slightest whiff of any corruption of this sort for many years, probably because it was too difficult to arrange, too easy to be caught, and there was too much money in the game to make it worth anyone's while.

BLANTYRE VICTORIA FC (see JUNIOR FOOTBALL)

BO'NESS FC (former Scottish League club)

Home: **Newtown Park, Bo'ness, West Lothian**
Highest League Position: **19th (19th in Div. 1, 1927/28)**
Best Scottish Cup Performance: **Last 8 (4th round, 1922/23; 1926/27; 1930/31)**

Bo'ness belonged to the Scottish League from 1921 to 1933 and in 1927/28 spent one season in the top division. They finished second bottom and were only relegated by a narrow margin, but then declined so rapidly that five years later they were expelled from the Scottish League altogether, for failing to make guaranteed payments to visiting teams.

The club was founded in 1881 and soon amalgamated with nearby Vale of Kinnell FC. The new club was a regular entrant in the Scottish Cup from 1884 onwards and got as far as the fourth round in 1887/88. They played in several different leagues over the years and won the Eastern League in 1903/04, but then settled in the Central League from 1909 onwards. Bo'ness went on to win the title on three occasions, including 1921, which was the year when, along with most Central League clubs, they became part of the Scottish League.

They were one of four West Lothian clubs in the second division, along with Armadale, Bathgate and Broxburn United, but Bo'ness was the only one that went on to play in the first division, after winning the

Division Two championship in 1926/27. However, this was a time of economic hardship for the local community and as the team struggled against the top clubs the size of the crowds dropped dramatically. Several of their best players had to be sold to balance the books and consequently results and crowds suffered even more. After relegation in 1928 things went from bad to worse.

The 1930/31 Scottish Cup brought some relief when Kilmarnock were taken to a fourth-round replay, but by 1932/33 the financial situation had become so severe that the club was expelled. They played in various leagues throughout the 1930s, and even won the East of Scotland League in 1938/39, but after the second world war they amalgamated with Bo'ness Cadora and formed Bo'ness United Junior club. (see **JUNIOR FOOTBALL**)

BONNYRIGG ROSE ATHLETIC FC

(see JUNIOR FOOTBALL)

BOSMAN RULING

This is the name given to a legal ruling in 1995, which has had a far-reaching effect on European football, and has probably worked to the disadvantage of smaller Scottish clubs, who have to sell players to balance their financial books. In 1995 Jean-Marc Bosman won his legal case, which allowed him to move to whatever club he could arrange terms with, once his contract had expired with his current club. (Bosman wanted to move from Belgian club RFC Liege to French club Dunkerque.) Previously, the club for whom the player played was able to hold on to him until such time as a transfer could be arranged. Many people throughout Europe believed this to be wrong, and in Scotland fans could recall the events of 1964, when Dundee were able to block Alan Gilzean moving to any other club other than by a transfer which benefited Dundee.

Bosman used the 'restriction of trade' argument, and won the day before the European Court of Justice in Luxemburg. All this means that a Scottish team cannot be guaranteed a large transfer fee if a player decides to wait until the end of his contract. For this reason, Scottish clubs are sometimes pressurised to accept a lower transfer fee than they would have wanted, and at a time when the player still has some time of his contract to run. Since then, the phrase 'on a Bosman' has often come to replace 'on a free transfer', and players who have changed clubs on this basis include Gary McSwegan, who went from Dundee United to Hearts in 1998, and Chris Killen who joined Celtic from Hibs in 2007.

Gary McSwegan (pictured left) moved from Dundee United to Hearts in 1998 on a 'Bosman free'.

BOSNIA

Scotland have beaten Bosnia on both occasions that they have played them.

1999	4 Sep	Sarajevo	2–1	Hutchison Dodds	Bolic
1999	5 Oct	Ibrox	1–0	Collins (pen)	

BOYD Tom (1965 –)

Scotland Caps: 72
Scottish Premier League medals: 3
Scottish Cup medals: 3
Scottish League Cup medals: 3

Tom Boyd was a defender for Motherwell, Chelsea and Celtic, with the happy ability to play all over the defence. He earned seventy-two caps for Scotland, and it is a shame that he will be remembered for his own goal against Brazil in the opening match of the 1998 World Cup finals. He was not to blame for that unfortunate event, and in any case made up for it with many fine performances as player and captain. He joined Motherwell in 1983, and was their captain when they won the Scottish Cup in 1991. He went to Chelsea immediately afterwards, but returned to Scotland after a brief and unhappy spell to play for Celtic, for whom he became a legend throughout a turbulent time in their history. Not only did he lead Celtic to success on the field, he also became an excellent ambassador for the club, and for the game in Scotland. Tom Boyd was awarded the MBE for his services to Scottish football.

BRADSHAW Tom (Tiny) (1904 – 1986)

Scotland Caps: 1

Tom Bradshaw earned only one cap for Scotland, but it was the famous Wembley Wizards International of 1928, in which, according to legend, 'he did not give Dixie Dean (England's centre forward) a kick of the ball'. He was a man of huge build (hence his ironic nickname), and he is the only Bury player to have earned a Scottish cap whilst with the club. He might have won more caps if he had not been a contemporary of Davie Meiklejohn of Rangers. He joined Bury in 1922, was transferred to Liverpool in 1930, and returned to Scotland to play out the last years of his career with Third Lanark in 1938.

BRAZIL

Scotland have never beaten Brazil in the nine times that they have met (four times in World Cup finals) but they have never been outclassed, and have always enjoyed the respect of their opponents, with the atmosphere at such games being much commented on and praised for its colour and good nature. They have drawn twice, the 0–0 draw in the 1974 World Cup finals being the closest that Scotland have come to beating the nation that is acknowledged to be the best on earth.

1966	25 June	Hampden Park	1–1	Chalmers	Servilio
1972	5 July	Rio de Janeiro	0–1		Jairzinho
1973	30 June	Hampden Park	0–1		Johnstone o.g.
1974	18 June	Frankfurt	0–0		
1977	23 June	Rio de Janeiro	0–2		Zico Toninho Cerezo
1982	18 June	Seville	1–4	Narey	Zico Oscar Eder Falcao
1987	26 May	Hampden Park	0–2		Rai Valdo
1990	20 June	Turin	0–1		Muller
1998	10 June	Paris	1–2	Collins (pen)	Cesar Sampaio Boyd o.g.

BRECHIN CITY FC

Ground: **Glebe Park**
Nickname: **The City**
Colours: **Red and white**
Record Attendance: **8,122 v Aberdeen (1973)**
Record Victory: **12-1 v Thornhill (1926)**
Record Defeat: **0-10 v Cowdenbeath (1937); v Airdrie (1938); v Albion Rovers (1938)**
Highest League Position: **15th (5th in First Div., 1983/84)**
Best Scottish Cup Performance: **Last 16 (4th round 1984/85, 1986/87,1996/97)**
Best League Cup Performance: **Last 4 (1957/58)**

Brechin City FC was founded in 1906, when junior sides Brechin Hearts and Brechin Harp got together to form a senior side that would play in the Northern League, and the club went on to become its champions on two occasions (1907/08 and 1912/13). Not long after the end of the first world war they switched to the Eastern League and this is where they were playing when the short-lived Division Three was created in 1923. Brechin were members for all three seasons of its existence, but never finished out of the bottom seven.

Division Three folded in 1926 and City then played in the Scottish Alliance. In 1926/27 they reached the final of the Scottish Qualifying Cup, losing 4–1 to Mid-Annandale, and not long afterwards they were back in the Scottish League. In 1929 they filled one of the two vacancies in Division Two, following the resignations of Arthurlie and Bathgate, and they remained in the lower division until the abandonment of league football at the start of the second world war in 1939.

After the war they were placed in the new Division C and when they became champions of the northeast section in 1953/54 were promoted into Division B. They

Nearly a goal for Bremner against Brazil in the 1974 World Cup game that ended 0-0.

also won the Scottish Qualifying Cup (South) in 1950/51, beating Duns 12–2 on aggregate. However, this period of modest success was not to last. When the league was reconstructed in 1975, not only had Brechin never left the lower division, they had finished bottom of it on eight occasions.

They continued in the bottom division until 1983, when the Second Division championship was won under manager Ian Fleming, and Brechin became part of the second tier for four consecutive seasons. After relegation in 1987 their 'yo-yo' years commenced, and there was frequent movement between the bottom divisions, but City have never played in the top tier of Scottish football. There were further seasons in the First Division (second tier) in 1990/91, 1993/94, 2003/04 and 2005/06, but on each occasion they finished in bottom place.

The highlights of Brechin's history have been occasional cup-ties against some of the top clubs, including a 2–1 victory over Kilmarnock at Rugby Park in the first round of the 1936/37 Scottish Cup. In 1957/58 they played Rangers at Hampden Park in the semi-finals of the League Cup, losing 4–0. They had got there by topping their qualifying group on goal average and then beating Hamilton in the quarter-finals. There was a creditable 0–0 draw with Aberdeen at Pittodrie in the first round of the Scottish Cup in 1959/60, with the Dons winning the replay 6–3. In 1984/85 City took Hearts to a replay in the fourth round of the Scottish Cup, and only lost 1–0 at Tynecastle following a 1–1 draw at home.

Glebe Park has a hedge growing along part of its perimeter, and SPL side Kilmarnock were another top-flight club to play in front of this unusual back-drop when they visited for a second-round tie in the 2003/04 League Cup. A 1–0 victory for Brechin, thanks to a Steven Hampshire goal, resulted in City putting Killie out of a cup competition for the second time in their history.

BREMNER Billy (1942 – 1997)

Scotland Caps: 54

Billy Bremner was a red-haired terrier of a player who captained Scotland in the 1974 World Cup, but was banned from playing for Scotland for life following an irresponsible incident in Copenhagen in 1975. This had followed a warning after another incident the previous year. It was with Leeds United that he played most of his career. He was born in Stirling and joined Leeds in 1959. He became associated with manager Don Revie, who appreciated his tough style of play at right half. Leeds were in the Second Division at that point, but having reached the First Division, Bremner was in the side that was the most feared in all England, although they did tend to be runners-up rather than winners. Bremner won the English league with Leeds in 1969 and 1974, plus the FA Cup in 1972 and the League Cup in 1968, but also lost another three Wembley cup finals.

In 1970 the Football Writers' Association named Billy 'Player of the Year'. On the European scene, Leeds United won the Fairs Cup in 1968 and 1971, but lost the European Cup final of 1975 after seeming well on top at one point – and, most hurtful of all to Bremner, they also lost a European Cup semi-final to Celtic in 1970. Bremner's Scotland career included the famous 3–2 win over England in 1967 and the respectable but ultimately unhappy World Cup of 1974, in which Billy missed the chance that would have beaten Brazil. He joined Hull City in 1976 and, after his playing career was over, he became manager of Doncaster Rovers from 1978 to 1982. He then returned to Elland Road as manager, but had no great success, being perhaps too fiery and emotional for the demands of that job. Like many footballers, he died young. He had many critics in both Scotland and England, not least for his somewhat robust style of play – something that led him into trouble on many occasions, but no one could ever doubt his skill, enthusiasm or commitment for the cause.

BREWSTER Craig (1966 –)

Scottish Cup Medals: 1

Craig Brewster became the player/manager of Inverness Caledonian Thistle for the second time in 2007, and has had a remarkable career in Scottish football. He was born in Dundee, and first played for a junior football team called Dundee Stobswell before moving to Forfar Athletic, Raith Rovers and then his first love, Dundee United. With them, he reached one of the high-points of their history when he scored the only goal in the 1994 Scottish Cup final against Rangers. He then experienced both relegation and promotion in successive seasons with the Tannadice club, before moving under the Bosman ruling (see **BOSMAN RULING**) to the Greek club Ionikos between 1996 and 2001, for whom he appeared in the final of the Greek Cup in 2000 – a match that Ionikos lost to AEK Athens. His move to Greece probably put paid to his chances of international recognition, but he returned to Scotland in 2001 to play for a variety of Scottish clubs – Hibs, Dunfermline, Inverness Caledonian Thistle, Dundee United (both of these last two as player-manager) and Aberdeen. He was a fine centre forward with close to 200 goals to his credit for his various clubs.

BRITISH LEAGUE CUP

Otherwise known as the Glasgow Exhibition Trophy, or the Coronation Cup, the British League Cup was a one-off tournament held in 1902 for the Ibrox Disaster Fund. Rangers had won the Glasgow Exhibition Trophy in 1901 (a purely Scottish competition in which Rangers had beaten St. Mirren 8–1, Third Lanark 4–1 and Celtic 2–1), and put up this cup for the first-ever British tournament between themselves, Celtic, Sunderland and Everton, the champions and runners-up in each country. The Ibrox Disaster Fund would benefit, and the winners could claim to be the best in Britain. By coincidence, the tournament was played in the run-up to the coronation of King Edward VII, and is sometimes referred to as the Coronation Cup, but it should not be confused with that of 1953.

Semi-finals:

30 Apr 1902	Celtic	5	1	Sunderland	Celtic Park
	Own goal McDermott (2) McMahon Campbell			Ferguson	4,000

1 May 1902	Everton	1	1	Rangers	Goodison Park
	Young			Hamilton	8,000

Replay:

3 May 1902	Rangers	3	2	Everton	Celtic Park
	Speedie Hamilton Walker			Dilly Brierley	12,000

The game had to be played at Celtic Park as Ibrox was still out of action because of the disaster. Rangers did very well considering that this was the day that the international was being replayed at Villa Park, and they were without four players in Nick Smith, John Drummond, John Robertson and Alex Smith.

Final:

17 June 1902	Celtic	3	2	Rangers	Second Hampden Park
	Quinn (3)	a.e.t.		Hamilton Speedie	12,000

The late date of this game can be explained by the desire to have the game played as close as possible to the coronation of King Edward VII, which was scheduled for 26 June. In the event, King Edward VII took ill with appendicitis and the coronation had to be postponed until 9 August. The receipts from this final were a very healthy £314, and it took a late header from Jimmy Quinn, in the last minute of extra time, to decide the issue. Celtic had gone two goals ahead through Jimmy Quinn, but before half time Bob Hamilton had taken full advantage of a goalkeeping fumble to reduce the leeway, then Finlay Speedie equalized for Rangers. The second half saw no further scoring, and when full time came many of the public and the press had gone home, assuming that there would be a replay. But both teams agreed to extra time of ten minutes each way, and Jimmy Quinn scored at the very end.

Celtic: McPherson, Watson, Battles, Loney, Marshall, Orr, Crawford, Campbell, Quinn, McDermott, Hamilton.
Rangers: Dickie, N. Smith, Crawford, Gibson, Stark, Robertson, Lennie, Walker, Hamilton, Speedie, A. Smith.

BROADCASTING, RADIO AND TV

Broadcasting is now very much a part of the game, so much so that the finances of many clubs depend to a large extent on TV revenue. Yet, for many years, the policy of the authorities in Scotland towards television in particular was one of trying to keep it at arm's length. A primitive form of match commentating was first seen at games immediately after the first world war. So many men had been blinded in the conflict that some clubs, notably Dundee and East Fife, employed a man to give an account of what was going on to the blind in a special enclosure, normally in front of the main stand. To this day many hospitals provide commentary on a telephone line to local hospitals in a noble continuation of this tradition.

Radio broadcasting began in Scotland on 2 April 1927, when a running commentary was provided on the 'Glasgow' service from Hampden Park on the Scotland versus England international, which England won 2–1. Alan Morton of Rangers thus has the honour of scoring the first ever goal to be broadcast on the radio, but Dixie Dean of Everton then scored two for England. Then two weeks later on 16 April 1927 the Scottish Cup final between Celtic and East Fife was broadcast to the small proportion of the country that owned a radio. Enterprising ice cream parlours in Methil and Leven set up a

Setanta Sports won the right to televise SPL matches in a five year deal commencing from the 2004/05 season.

radio with a speaker, so that customers could hear the proceedings of the local team playing Celtic. No doubt they rose to applaud the headed goal by Jock Wood of East Fife, but Celtic eventually won 3–1.

By the mid 1930s, Scottish Cup finals, Scotland versus England internationals, and one-off events like the Empire Exhibition Trophy final of 1938 were broadcast to the nation. The second world war was the heyday of the radio, and wartime internationals were broadcast to overseas troops in places like Cairo, Alexandria and Tripoli, as well as to the domestic audience, with Rex Kingsley doing the commentary – on one famous occasion on New Year's Day 1940 he commentated on an Edinburgh derby that he could not see. This was because he was not allowed to say anything about fog, lest this might give some sort of advantage to listening Germans! He employed two boys as runners to stand behind each goal and come back to tell him what was going on.

By the 1950s, the Scottish Home Service offered the last half hour of an unspecified game every Saturday. The game was unspecified in case people might be deterred from going to a game if they knew that it was going to be on the wireless. Gradually this relaxed, until today we have blanket coverage of football as it happens. Yet the radio broadcasting of the 1950s and 1960s, with commentators like Peter Thomson, George Davidson and David Francey, did a great job within their limited compass. David Francey, in particular, became a cult figure with his "he tries a drive and – ooh! – over the bar" style of commentary being much impersonated, but perhaps proving that imitation is indeed the sincerest form of flattery.

In the early years of the twenty-first century, radio coverage has been excellent, and has been a tremendous boon to supporters who, for one reason or other, are unable to be at games. All SPL games are covered, and news and information about other games are rapidly relayed.

Television proved to be a bone of contention for many decades. BBC arrived in Scotland in 1952, but Queen's Park can claim to be the first Scottish team to appear on television – even before television arrived in Scotland! This was in March 1951 when, before a limited TV audience (all in the immediate area of London), they beat Walthamstow Avenue in a game at Walthamstow's ground, Derek Greirson scoring both goals in the 2–0 win.

It was rare in the 1950s, however, to watch a live football match. The first live Scottish game to be televised in Scotland was the second half of the Scotland versus Northern Ireland international match of 3 November 1954 at Hampden Park. Scotland were 2–1 down to the Irishmen when television joined the game, but viewers saw Bobby Johnstone of Hibs score the first televised Scottish goal when he equalised in the seventy-first minute. In those pre-floodlight days it was a Wednesday afternoon kick-off and, given the paucity of television owners in 1954, the viewing figures would have been minimal. The international match between Scotland and England at Hampden Park was televised live in 1956 and every Hampden game (apart from 1970) between the two countries was subsequently televised, with Wembley games from 1969 onwards. World Cup games were televised, although in the early days Scotland were at the mercy of whatever the foreign authorities decided to allow. Unfortunately, this meant that the 7–0 defeat at the hands of Uruguay on 19 June 1954 was shown in its entirety. World Cup qualifying matches tended not to be shown live until the early 1970s.

Yet, on the occasions in autumn 1973 and autumn 1977 when Scotland qualified for the West German and Argentinian World Cups, the relevant games were televised live from Hampden Park and Anfield (Liverpool), uniting the nation in the passion and triumph of it all. The converse of this came in 1978, when Scotland's shortcomings in Argentina were beamed back and made obvious, and the result was a collective national grief seldom seen since the Battle of Culloden in 1746.

The coverage of European football was patchy. The famous 1960 Real Madrid versus Eintracht Frankfurt game at Hampden Park, for example, was shown live, and from then on European Cup finals were live, including Celtic's glory night in Lisbon in 1967, but it was not until the 1990s that a fan could rely on seeing his team in Europe, although games like Rangers versus Real Madrid in 1963 were sometimes shown. There was one remarkable night on 19 April 1972 when both Celtic and Rangers were involved in European semi-finals in Glasgow on the same night (such was the strength of Scottish football then) and both games were televised live, including Dixie Deans' miss in the penalty shoot-out. The European Cup-Winners' Cup semi-final from Ibrox between Rangers and Bayern Munich was shown live in its entirety on STV, but the BBC did not show the Celtic versus Inter Milan semi-final from Parkhead until after the nine o'clock news had finished, effectively only the latter stages of a dull 0–0 draw, extra time and the penalty shoot-out.

Live domestic football was almost totally blacked out, usually on the grounds that it would deter people from going to other football matches. The Scottish Cup final of 1955 between Celtic and Clyde was televised live, with the BBC sending up Kenneth Wolstenholme from London to do the commentating, (such was the mistrust of 'regional accents' in BBC headquarters). Celtic thus have the distinction of having played in the first radio broadcast of a Scottish game and also the first televised broadcast of a Scottish game. Then the Scottish Cup final (first game) of Falkirk versus Kilmarnock was shown live in 1957, but there was not another Scottish domestic game televised live until the Scottish Cup final of 1977 (and this was apparently at the insistence of the sponsors). Scottish Cup finals have all been shown live since that date, and Scottish League Cup finals since 1984.

The reason for this paucity of live televised football was the attitude of the SFA. This sprang from a laudable desire to protect games that were taking place at the same time, but subsequent events have proved that although there always has been (and continues to be) a voracious appetite for live televised football, it does not necessarily affect attendances at other games. Rangers' supporters, for example, will not give up going to see their team just because Celtic versus Aberdeen is on the television. For many years the SFA objected to the screening of live English football matches in Scotland (even at times when there were no Scottish games being played), but after Channel 4 began showing games from Italy on Sunday afternoons in 1993, the SFA withdrew their objections.

From the 1950s onwards, both major channels provided a highlights programme, which was much looked forward to and enjoyed on a Saturday night or a Sunday afternoon. The first such programme was on the BBC on 3 September 1955 and featured the Scottish League Cup tie between Clyde and Aberdeen. The BBC had George Davidson, Peter Thomson and Archie McPherson, whereas STV's *Scotsport* began from Glasgow's Theatre Royal on Wednesday 18 September 1957, with a troika of Arthur Montford (with his eye-catching jackets), the erudite Bob Crampsey, and Alex 'Candid' Cameron, who was once famously and unceremonially moved out of the way by a police horse live on television outside Hampden Park. *Scotsport*, which made a laudable and ambitious attempt to broadcast a few junior matches with hand-held cameras in the early days, has now celebrated its fiftieth anniversary and is the longest lasting football programme in the world.
Both these programmes suffered from under-funding (in comparison with their English counterparts) and sometimes the camera techniques were so bad that goals were missed. In addition, the film reel had to be changed every ten minutes or so, and if, as luck would have it, a

A television gantry looms over Falkirk versus Hearts in October 2005.

goal was scored during the changing, then that goal was lost forever. There are several well-documented cases of a game being won 3–2, and the only goals shown being the two for the losing side, so the presenter had to apologise for the omissions! It was often suggested that *Scotsport* and *Sportscene* should be re-named 'Spot The Ball', and *Scotsport* was sometimes referred to disparagingly as 'Montford's Mad Movies', but they enjoyed high ratings.

Indeed the BBC programme managed to lose a whole Scottish League Cup final (the 7–1 Celtic versus Rangers game of 1957) because a technician went for his tea break and forgot to take the lens cap off the camera! In 1979, there was a thrilling finish to the Scottish League programme, as Celtic beat Rangers 4–1 on Monday 21 May, but both TV companies failed to produce even a highlights package because of a labour dispute, perhaps also coupled with a general lethargy.

Season 1985/86 was spoiled for television viewers by a dispute that kept Scottish domestic football totally off the screen, but when the dispute was settled live league football began to appear, beginning with a Hearts versus Aberdeen Sunday match on 20 April 1986. A few years later satellite television arrived and the attitude of the teams and the authorities changed. Far from 'keep football off the screen', there now was a scramble to get as much on as possible. Clubs may now be dangerously dependent on television money.

In January 1995, SKY television signed a three and a half year deal, worth about £10 million per season, and this contract was renewed in 1998 and lasted until 2002. As this agreement was coming to a close, the SPL dabbled with the idea of having its own TV channel, thus deterring SKY from a further renewal, and when these plans fell through they negotiated a deal with the BBC.

The money paid by the companies had a price, and this was the sometimes-crazy time of day when live games were shown. In the late 1990s for example, there was a Scottish Premier League game shown on SKY television at 6.05 pm on a Sunday, something that was hard to defend, and very unpopular with the clubs and the fans. Fortunately, when the contract passed first to the BBC in seasons 2002/03 and 2003/04, and then to the Irish channel Setanta from 2004 onwards, a more sensible time of Sunday afternoon was agreed. In season 2006/07 a Monday night slot was utilised occasionally for a televised Scottish domestic game. STV, the only terrestrial channel which showed SPL highlights in season 2006/07, broadcast at 11.00 pm on a Monday night, some forty-eight hours after the games were played. In season 2007/08 the BBC also showed a highlights programme – this time on a Wednesday night, more than four days after the full-time whistle.

The BBC deal referred to for seasons 2002/03 and 2003/04, however popular it was with the fans, nevertheless lost the SPL and its teams a lot of money, for the sum negotiated was a great deal less than what SKY television had paid. This precipitated a financial crisis, and was the trigger that resulted in three clubs, Motherwell, Livingston and Dundee, having to go into (temporary) administration.

In order to boost viewing figures, the game shown live on Setanta television tends to involve one or other of the Old Firm, usually whichever one of the two is playing away from home that weekend. Playing earlier or later can give an advantage to a team, but this point is usually submerged in the main agenda, which is mainly about money. Yet the Scottish public benefits too; the coverage is usually good and the commentators well informed. There can be little doubt that the arrival of large-scale television coverage has been a great help in allowing more people to see the game. The exciting last-day finishes to the SPL in 2003, 2005 and 2008 were all shown on television and thrilled the nation. The down side, of course, is that fewer people attend the games and the atmosphere suffers. This is not surprising, given what sometimes seem like exorbitant admission prices, but the sight of empty seats is dispiriting, and must have an effect on the players.

In 2007/08 the BBC showed live some Scottish League Cup games, Scottish Cup games (a commitment shared with SKY), some UEFA Cup games, and Scotland internationals away from home (SKY showed the home games), whereas STV's commitment tended to be for Champions League games. For seasons 2000/01 until 2005/6 there was also a programme on STV called *Football First*, which concentrated entirely on the First Division of the SFL. This was a laudable attempt to bring non-SPL football to the television audience, but the programme suffered from erratic scheduling and lack of sponsorship because of low ratings.

BROWN Bill (1931 – 2004)

Scotland Caps: 28
Scottish League Cup medals: 1

Bill Brown is considered by some to be Scotland's best-ever goalkeeper. Born in Arbroath, he won twenty-eight caps between 1958 and 1966 in his career with Dundee and Tottenham Hotspur, and never let Scotland down. He won a Scottish League Cup medal with Dundee in 1951/52, but it was when he was transferred to Spurs in 1959 for £16,500 that his career really took off. He was part of the famous Spurs team that won the double in 1961 (missing only one game in the whole season), then the FA Cup again the following year, before winning the European Cup-Winners' Cup in 1963 (the first British team to do so). Bill finished his career with Northampton Town, and then went to live in Canada.

BROWN Bobby (1923 –)

Scotland Caps: 3
Scottish League medals: 3
Scottish Cup medals: 3
Scottish League Cup medals: 2

Bobby Brown was a great goalkeeper for Rangers in the years of their 'Iron Curtain' defence, and was renowned for his immaculate appearance (he insisted on a new pair of white boot laces for every match!), and his gentlemanly and sporting approach to the game. He joined the Ibrox side from Queen's Park in 1946 and stayed with them, as a part-time player, until 1956 when he moved to Falkirk. He then became manager of St Johnstone, before accepting the Scotland job in February 1967. His first match was the famous 3–2 game against England at Wembley, but this success was not maintained, and Scotland qualified for neither the European Nations Cup in 1968 nor the World Cup in 1970. Brown gave up the job in 1971, and returned to his career as a teacher, which he had pursued when he was a player.

BROWN Craig (1940 –)

Following a relatively undistinguished footballing career, which included spells at Dundee and Falkirk, Craig Brown became a manager, doing so well at Clyde that he was appointed assistant to Andy Roxburgh as

Scotland manager. He took over from Roxburgh in 1993, and did well to take Scotland to Euro '96 in England and the World Cup in France in 1998, but his failure to reach Euro 2000 or the 2002 World Cup finals led to his resignation. He was then manager of Preston North End for a spell, and worked as a commentator on radio.

BROWN George (1907 – unknown)

Scotland Caps: 19
Scottish League Championship medals: 7
Scottish Cup medals: 4

George Brown was a talented and able left half for Rangers in the 1930s. With his fair hair and clean-cut image, he was regarded as an ideal role model for youngsters, and indeed he was a schoolteacher by profession. At Ibrox, in a period of almost unbroken success, George was regarded as one of the best players of that team, with the half back line of Meiklejohn, Simpson and Brown considered to be the best in the game at the time. For Scotland he played nineteen times, and was four times on the winning side against England. After the second world war he was a director with Rangers.

BROWNLIE Jimmy (1885 – 1973)

Scotland Caps: 16

Jimmy Brownlie was one of the most remarkable characters of Scottish football, and was well known for his association with two clubs, Third Lanark and Dundee United. A lithe and agile goalkeeper, he joined Third Lanark in 1906 and played more than 500 games for them, and also earned sixteen caps for Scotland between 1909 and the outbreak of the Great War in 1914. He had outstanding games in the victories over England at Hampden Park in 1910 and 1914. He became manager of Dundee Hibs (later Dundee United) in 1923, and raised their profile enough to take them to the first division and to establish them as a force in Scottish football. Suddenly dismissed in 1931 for reasons never adequately explained, he was brought back in 1934, sacked again in 1936, but became a director of the club in 1938 and, along with Sam Irving, took over the manager's role as well! The advent of the second world war ended his formal connection with the club, but he remained a supporter and a well-loved figure at Tannadice until his death in 1973 at the age of eighty-eight.

BROXBURN UNITED FC
(former Scottish League club)

Home: **Sports Park, Broxburn, West Lothian**
Highest League Position: **27th (7th in Div. 2, 1924/25)**
Best Scottish Cup Performance: **Last 8 (Quarter-finals, 1924/25)**

Broxburn United spent five seasons in the Scottish League and all were in Division Two. They finished bottom in 1926, which was the year when Division Three was scrapped, and they couldn't be relegated into a lower division. However, the club had been suffering financial difficulties for some time and crowds were small, so they decided to play in the Scottish Alliance instead.

They had been founded in 1912, as a result of the amalgamation of Broxburn FC and Broxburn Athletic, and both predecessors left their mark in the records of the Scottish Cup. Athletic reached the last sixteen in 1911/12, when they lost 6–1 away to Third Lanark, and Broxburn FC, who were previously known as Broxburn Thistle, reached the third round in 1890/91.

The town of Broxburn had been trying to support three clubs, as there was also Broxburn Shamrock, and in 1912 it made economic sense for two of them to join together. The new club took the place of Broxburn FC in the Central League, where they spent three unremarkable seasons, followed by two seasons in the wartime Eastern League. Then there were two years with no football at all, until United joined the re-formed Central League in 1919. There were occasional highlights in the Scottish Cup, such as a third-round tie at Ibrox in 1919/20, when Rangers won 3–0, and a second-round tie against Hearts in 1921/22, which went to two replays before Hearts won 3–1.

Division Two was re-introduced in 1921, with its members coming mainly from the Central League, and United commenced their five years in the Scottish League. They finished in the top ten of Division Two on three of the five occasions, but found themselves in the wrong place at the wrong time in 1926. By then the club's financial situation, like the West Lothian economy, was in a bad way and if it hadn't been for the cup run of 1924/25 it would have been even worse. Falkirk were beaten 2–1 in the third round and in the fourth round a single goal from Dundee prevented them from reaching the semi-finals. Then, little more than a year later, they were out of the Scottish League. By the 1927/28 season they couldn't even continue in the Scottish Alliance and United turned to junior football.

BUCHAN Martin (1949 –)

Scotland Caps: 34
Scottish Cup medals: 1

Martin Buchan was a polished centre half and captain for Aberdeen and Manchester United. He was Scotland's Player of the Year in 1971, then, astonishingly, Aberdeen, to the distress of their fans, sold him for £125,000 to Manchester United in 1972 in mid-season, when they still had a chance of winning the Scottish League. Some fans saw this as the equivalent of Winston Churchill selling the Spitfires in the middle of the Battle of Britain. Buchan won a Scottish Cup medal with Aberdeen in 1970, as well as an FA Cup medal with Manchester United in 1977, and has the distinction of being the only man to have captained a team that won the Scottish and the English Cup finals. He played his latter years with Oldham Athletic, and was manager of Burnley. For Scotland he played thirty-four times, taking part in the World Cup finals of 1974 and 1978. He must take at least part of the blame for the Argentina fiasco, but he did impress everyone with his quiet dignity in dreadful circumstances.

BULGARIA

Scotland have a good record against Bulgaria. They have never lost to them in their six games, have won three and drawn three. The most famous game was the one in 1987 when Gary MacKay's late strike prevented Bulgaria reaching the finals of the European Championship of 1988. Unfortunately it was Eire, not Scotland, who qualified as a result. One of Scotland's best performances in recent years has been the 5–1 victory over the Bulgarians in Japan in May 2006 in the Kirin Cup.

1978	22 Feb	Hampden Park	2–1	Gemmill Wallace	Mladenov
1986	10 Sep	Hampden Park	0–0		
1987	11 Nov	Sofia	1–0	MacKay	
1990	14 Nov	Sofia	1–1	McCoist	Todorov
1991	27 Mar	Hampden Park	1–1	Collins	Kostadinov
2006	11 May	Kobe	5–1	Boyd (2) Burke (2) McFadden	Todorov

BURLEY Craig (1971 –)

Scotland Caps: 46
Scottish Premier League medals: 1
Scottish League Cup medals: 1

The nephew of Scotland manager George Burley (q.v.), Craig Burley was a tenacious midfielder, who won forty-six caps for Scotland in a career that saw him play for Chelsea, Celtic, Derby County, Dundee, Preston North End and Walsall. He joined Chelsea in the early 1990s and won the FA Cup with them in 1997. In that same season he joined Celtic, and was outstanding in

the 1997/98 campaign, which saw Celtic win the Scottish League Premier Division and the Scottish League Cup. To the distress of Celtic fans, John Barnes sold him for £3million to Derby County in 1999, and from then on his career was dogged by ill luck. He sustained a serious injury when he was with Derby, and was also unlucky enough to be in the Dundee side that went into administration in 2003. His Scotland career is remembered for the goal that he scored against Norway in the 1998 World Cup finals, and for his consistently determined approach to all games. He went on to become a pundit with Setanta TV.

BURLEY George (1956 –)

Scotland Caps: 11

George Burley was a man with a long and varied career, with many clubs in both Scotland and England. He earned eleven Scottish caps when with Ipswich Town as a defender in the late 1970s and early 1980s, and also won the 1978 FA Cup with Ipswich. He subsequently

played for Sunderland and Gillingham, and became player-manager/coach at Motherwell, Ayr United and Colchester United. He was then manager of Ipswich Town and Derby County before he returned to Scotland in summer 2005 to take charge of Hearts. After a meteoric few months, Vladimir Romanov suddenly sacked him in October 2005 when Hearts were top of the SPL – a decision that baffled the world. George, however, soon resumed his managerial career, this time with Southampton, before accepting the Scotland manager's job in January 2008.

BURNS Kenny (1953 –)

Scotland Caps: 20

Kenny Burns was a tough, gritty central defender with a whole host of teams, including Rangers, Birmingham City, Nottingham Forest, Leeds United and Scotland, although he played better for his clubs than he did for

Scotland. It was his misfortune to be involved in the two 1978 disasters in Argentina against Peru and Iran. At club level, however, he won two European Cups with Nottingham Forest, and an English league medal and an English League Cup medal with the same team. He joined Forest from Birmingham City in 1977, and left to go to Leeds United in 1981.

BURNS Tommy (1956 – 2008)

Scotland Caps: 8
Scottish League Championship medals: 6
Scottish Cup medals: 4
Scottish League Cup medals: 1

Tommy Burns was a very talented, red-haired, midfield player, and he has made an outstanding contribution to Scottish football. He joined Celtic in 1975 and very soon made his way into the first team, winning eleven medals in the fourteen years that he played with them. He also won eight caps for Scotland. When his playing career finished, he turned to management, becoming in 1992 manager of Kilmarnock (for whom he had been playing since 1989). Two years later, the irresistible call to manage Celtic came, but Tommy lasted only three years, unable to break Rangers' stranglehold of the Premier League, although he did win the Scottish Cup in 1995. He continued to work at Parkhead in spite of ill health until his death in May 2008, and for a time combined his job with being assistant manager of Scotland.

BURNTISLAND SHIPYARD AMATEUR FC

Home: **Recreation Ground, Burntisland, Fife**
Best Scottish Cup Performance: **Last 32 (3rd round, 1994/95)**
(Participating club in Scottish Cup, but not member of East of Scotland League, Highland League or South of Scotland League)

Burntisland's shipyard may have closed in 1969, but it is not forgotten because of the amateur football club that still bears its name. Founded in 1925 as part of the shipyard's recreation club, the team played in the Lothian Amateur League, the Edinburgh and District Amateur League and then the Kirkcaldy and District Amateur League before joining the Kingdom Caledonian League in 1999.

The name regularly comes to national prominence through the Scottish Cup, which the club is eligible to enter because of its membership of the SFA. Over the years it has qualified for the Scottish Cup by virtue of the Scottish Qualifying Cup on several occasions. The first time was in 1929/30, but it was the Scottish Cup of 1938/39 when the club really hit the headlines. Celtic were drawn at home in the first round, and the 3–8 scoreline captured the country's imagination. In more recent times, victory over St Cuthbert's earned a third-round tie at Highland League Huntly in 1994/95, but it resulted in a 7–0 defeat.

When a new format was adopted for the Scottish Cup in 2007/08, and the Scottish Qualifying Cup was discontinued, the club reached the second round after a 5–3 away win at Wigtown & Bladnoch, but the run ended with an 8–0 defeat at Albion Rovers.

BUSBY Sir Matt (1909 – 1994)

Scotland Caps: 1

Sir Matt Busby was one of world football's outstanding managers, although his involvement with Scottish football was limited. He came from the Bellshill area of Lanarkshire, which has been the nursery for so many giants of the British game. He played as right half, mainly for Manchester City and Liverpool, and only had one full Scottish international cap – in a depressing defeat by Wales in October 1933. His best football years coincided with those of the second world war, during which time he 'guested' for Hibs, and captained Scotland's international side in unofficial internationals. It was after the war that he became famous as the manager of Manchester United, building up four great sides, including one that perished in the Munich air crash of 1958, and another that won the European Cup in 1968. He was briefly manager of Scotland, before and after Munich (in which he himself was badly injured), but found that two jobs were too much for him, and he concentrated on Manchester United. His retirement from the Manchester United job in 1971 saw the club plunge into more than a decade of chaos and under-achievement, a situation that was only resolved by the arrival of another Scotsman, Alex Ferguson.

Sir Matt (seated right) at the signing of Pat Crerand from Celtic in 1963

BUTCHER Terry (1958 –)

Scottish League Championship medals: 3
Scottish League Cup medals: 2

A central defender who was renowned for his strength and accuracy as a header of the ball, Terry Butcher joined the 'Souness revolution' at Ibrox in August 1986. Graeme Souness signed him for £750,000 from Ipswich Town, a club with whom he had won the UEFA Cup in 1981. He was made team captain, and in November 1986 became captain of England as well. During his time at Rangers he won the league championship in 1986/87, 1988/89 and 1989/90, achieving the last two titles after coming back from a broken leg. He also won two Scottish League Cup winners' medals. By the time he left Ibrox to become player/manager at Coventry City in 1990 Terry Butcher had made 176 appearances for Rangers.

He returned to Scotland in 2001 to become assistant manager to Eric Black at Motherwell, and a year later took over as manager. Although he was forced to rely on younger players, he took Motherwell to the final of the 2004/05 League Cup, losing 5–1 to Rangers. There were also top-six finishes in the league in both 2004 and 2005. After leaving Motherwell for Sydney FC in 2006, he briefly returned to Scotland once again in March 2007 to work as an assistant coach at Partick Thistle, but soon moved on to become manager of Brentford. In January 2008 newly appointed George Burley invited Terry to become part of his Scotland coaching team. Always a good ambassador for the Scottish game, he also worked as a match summariser on both radio and television. He also played cricket for Stirling County.

CAIRNS Tommy (1890 – 1967)

Scotland Caps: 8
Scottish League Championship medals: 7

Tommy Cairns was a talented inside left who, with Alan Morton, made up the most powerful left wing of all time, according to some Rangers historians. He had played for Bristol City and St Johnstone before he joined Rangers in November 1913. He stayed with them until he went to Bradford City in 1927. During his time with Rangers he won seven Scottish League medals but, as Rangers were going through their twenty-five year 'hoodoo' as far as the Scottish Cup was concerned, he never won that tournament. His eight Scottish caps included two victories over England, and in 1925 he played against all three British countries, with Scotland beating them all.

CALDERWOOD Colin (1965 –)

Scotland Caps: 36

Colin Calderwood was a tall, commanding centre half who played thirty-six times for Scotland between 1995 and 1999. The highlight of his international career was the World Cup finals of 1998. He played for Mansfield Town, Swindon Town, Tottenham Hotspur, Aston Villa and both the Nottingham teams. Having managed Northampton Town, he became manager of Nottingham Forest in 2006.

Colin Calderwood, now managing Nottingham Forest.

CALDOW Eric (1934 –)

Scottish Caps: 40
Scottish League Championship medals: 5
Scottish Cup medals: 2
Scottish League Cup medals: 3

Eric Caldow was a full back with both Rangers and Scotland who was renowned for his speed. He was capped forty times for Scotland, fourteen as captain. Originally from Cumnock in Ayrshire, he joined Rangers in 1952 and had played 407 games for them by the time he left in 1966. He won five Scottish League championship medals, two Scottish Cup medals and three Scottish League Cup medals. His play exuded class, he was never booked, and opponents respected him for his fair play. A member of the first Rangers side to play in Europe (against Nice in the 1956/57 European Cup), he was team captain in their first European final (against Fiorentina in the 1960/61 European Cup-Winners' Cup).

With Jim Baxter, Eric Caldow celebrates the League Cup victory over Celtic in 1964.

An automatic choice for Scotland from 1957 until he fractured his leg in three places at Wembley in 1963, a blow from which he only partially recovered, he became the first Rangers player to play in the World Cup finals, in Sweden in 1958. He is remembered for the penalty kick that he took at Hampden Park in 1962, to confirm Scotland's first home victory over England since 1937. After he left Rangers he went to Stirling Albion, and subsequently tried his hand at management with Corby Town and Stranraer, but was regarded by some people as a man who was too nice for football management, lacking the ruthlessness that is often required.

CALDWELL Gary (1982 –)

Scotland Caps: 27
Scottish Premier League medals: 2
Scottish Cup medals: 1

A versatile defender who has played twenty-seven times for Scotland in a career with Newcastle United, Hibernian and Celtic. He scored the goal that beat France at Hampden Park in October 2006 and, after a long lay-off with injury in season 2006/07, came back to win a league and cup double with Celtic, although it was with Hibs that he made his name. He won another SPL medal in 2008.

CAMBUSLANG FC (former Scottish League club)

Home: **Whitefield Park, Cambuslang, South Lanarkshire**
Highest League Position: **4th (1890/91)**
Best Scottish Cup Performance: **Runners-up (1887/88)**

As one of the founder members of the Scottish League, Cambuslang FC will always have an important place in the history of Scottish football. The club was founded in 1876, in what was then the small Lanarkshire town of Cambuslang, and soon made a name for itself in the Scottish Cup. The team regularly reached the later rounds throughout the 1880s and in 1887/88 went all the way to the final. After a 10–0 victory over Ayr in the fifth round, a 6–0 win against Our Boys in the sixth, and a 10–1 defeat of Abercorn in a replayed semi-final, Cambuslang eventually went down 6–1 to Renton in the final.

It therefore wasn't surprising that they were elected to the Scottish League when it was formed in 1890. However, after a promising start in their first season, the club finished second bottom in 1891/92, and their only victories came against the bottom club, Vale of Leven. They acknowledged that they were out of their depth by not even applying for re-election. The Scottish Alliance became their home for five seasons, but the debts were mounting and in 1897 the club went out of existence.

CAMBUSLANG RANGERS FC
(see JUNIOR FOOTBALL)

CAMELON JUNIORS FC (see JUNIOR FOOTBALL)

CAMERON Colin (1972 –)

Scotland Caps: 28
Scottish League Cup medals: 1

A creative midfielder, Colin Cameron (sometimes called Micky) has played twenty-eight times for Scotland. He played in Irish football for a spell with

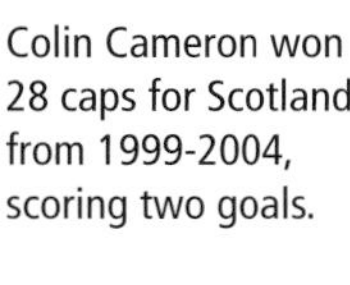

Colin Cameron won 28 caps for Scotland from 1999-2004, scoring two goals.

Sligo Rovers, but made his mark in the excellent Raith Rovers side of the early 1990s, winning promotion from the First Division in 1993 and a League Cup medal with them in 1994. He then joined Hearts in 1996, and later Wolves in 2001.

CAMPBELL Charles (c.1850 – 1927)

Scotland Caps: 13
Scottish Cup medals: 8
Charles Campbell was a midfield player for Queen's Park in the 1870s and 1880s. He won eight Scottish Cup medals, which would be a record, but some claim that the 1884 Scottish Cup Final, which was a walkover, should not put him above the seven medals of Bob McPhail, Billy McNeill and Jimmy McMenemy. He also played for Scotland on thirteen occasions, ten times against England. His record against the 'Auld Enemy' is seven wins, two draws and one defeat. After he retired he was president of the SFA in 1889/90. He also became a well-known referee, and officiated at the 1890 Scottish Cup final.

CAMPBELL Henry (1867 – 1915)

Scotland Caps: 1
Scottish Cup medals: 1
The first player to win both a Scottish Cup medal and an English FA Cup medal, Henry Campbell did so with Renton in 1888 and Blackburn Rovers in 1890. He was an excellent inside right, and won one cap for Scotland.

CAMPBELL Johnny (1871 – 1947)

Scotland Caps: 12
Scottish League medals: 4
Scottish Cup medals: 3
One of the greats of the 1890s and early 1900s, Johnny Campbell was normally a left winger (and it was here that he played his best games for Celtic), but could play all over the forward line, and indeed won his twelve Scottish caps in a variety of positions. He played for Celtic until 1895, then moved to Aston Villa for three seasons before returning to his beloved Celtic until 1903, when he moved to Third Lanark. He finished off his career with Thirds, winning the Scottish League in 1904. His array of medals is impressive – three Scottish league medals with Celtic and one with Third Lanark, three Scottish Cup medals with Celtic, and two English League medals and one FA Cup medal with Aston Villa. He was the key member of Aston Villa's team that won the Double in 1897. The 1901 Scotland versus Ireland international at Celtic Park is remarkable for two things. One was the 11–0 victory, and the other was the fact that John Campbell of Celtic was the right-winger, and his inside right partner was John Campbell of Rangers!

CAMPBELL Kenny (1892 – 1977)

Scotland Caps: 8
Scottish Cup medals: 1
Kenny Campbell was generally recognised as the best Scottish goalkeeper of the years immediately after the first world war. He won eight Scottish caps in the first

three official seasons after the armistice, distinguishing himself in the game at Villa Park in 1922, which Scotland won 1–0. The previous year he won a Scottish Cup winners' medal for Partick Thistle in their victory over Rangers in 1921. His first senior team was Liverpool, for whom he was unlucky not to win an FA Cup winners' medal in 1914, but he moved to Partick Thistle in 1920, before returning to England to play for Brighton, Stoke and Leicester City.

CANADA

Scotland have played Canada five times and beaten them every time. Canada is not one of the greatest football playing countries on earth, and most of the population are quite happy to admit that they are Scotland supporters! Canada used to be a favourite destination for Scottish teams on their close season tour.

1983	12 June	Vancouver	2–0	Strachan (pen) McGhee	
1983	16 June	Edmonton	3–0	Nicholas Gough Souness	
1983	20 June	Toronto	2–0	Gray (2)	
1992	21 May	Toronto	3–1	McAllister (2) McCoist	Catliff
2002	15 Oct	Easter Road	3–1	Crawford (2) Thompson	De Rosario (pen)

CAPS

The phrase 'earning a cap' or 'being capped for Scotland' is sometimes used loosely. From the very first international match in 1872 every player who played a game for Scotland was awarded a cap unofficially, and it was considered the pinnacle of a career to have a photograph taken with an international cap. In 1886 when the International Board of all British nations was formed, this practice of awarding a cap became official. When Scotland played the three home nations, a player would be given a cap per season with the details of the game(s) played embroidered upon it. But the Scots are not called mean for nothing, and no attempt was made to award a cap for any game played against foreign opposition, presumably on the grounds that foreign opposition was inferior. This changed in 1976, and from then onwards a cap was awarded for any Scotland game, but this welcome change of heart was not made retrospective for another 30 years until, after a certain amount of pressure from the press and the public, a cap was awarded to the survivors of any game that Scotland had played before 1976. The case highlighted was that of Eddie Turnbull, the talented inside forward of Hibs who had for example played three games in the 1958 World Cup in Sweden, but had never played against a home nation. In the course of this campaign, it was also pointed out that Turnbull had actually played nine games for Scotland, not eight as the record books tended to suggest. The SFA laudably decided to change their mind and Eddie was publicly given a cap (just one, though!) for services rendered. This was done at half time at Hampden during a Scotland versus Switzerland friendly on 1 March 2006. (See separate **APPENDIX** on Scotland Caps)

CARNOUSTIE PANMURE JUNIOR FC

(see JUNIOR FOOTBALL)

CASSIDY Joe (1896–1949)

Scotland Caps: 4
Scottish League medals: 2
Scottish Cup medals: 1

One of Celtic's greatest centre forwards, Joe Cassidy famously scored the goal that won the 1923 Scottish Cup final against Hibernian, thus scoring eleven goals in the 1923 Scottish Cup campaign. He was called 'Trooper Joe', following his service in the first world war, in which he won the Military Medal, and was much loved for his handsome appearance and superb forward play. He won four caps for Scotland, and as well as playing for Celtic, also appeared for Bolton Wanderers, Cardiff City, Dundee, Clyde, Ballymena, Morton and Dundalk in a much-travelled career.

CELTIC FC

Ground: **Celtic Park**
Nickname: **The Bhoys; The Hoops**
Colours: **Green and white**
Record Attendance: **83,500 v Rangers (1938)**
Record Victory: **11-0 v Dundee (1895)**
Record Defeat: **0-8 v Motherwell (1937)**
Highest League Position: **1st (1892/93; 1893/94; 1895/96; 1897/98; 1904/05; 1905/06; 1906/07; 1907/08; 1908/09; 1909/10; 1913/14; 1914/15; 1915/16; 1916/17; 1918/19; 1921/22; 1925/26; 1935/36; 1937/38; 1953/54; 1965/66; 1966/67; 1967/68; 1968/69; 1969/70; 1970/71; 1971/72; 1972/73; 1973/74; 1976/77; 1978/79; 1980/81; 1981/82; 1985/86; 1987/88; 1997/98; 2000/01; 2001/02; 2003/04; 2005/06; 2006/07; 2007/08)**
Best Scottish Cup Performance: **Winners (1891/92; 1898/99; 1899/1900; 1903/04; 1906/07; 1907/08; 1910/11; 1911/12; 1913/14; 1922/23; 1924/25; 1926/27; 1930/31; 1932/33; 1936/37; 1950/51; 1953/54; 1964/65; 1966/67; 1968/69; 1970/71; 1971/72; 1973/74; 1974/75; 1976/77; 1979/80; 1984/85; 1987/88; 1988/89; 1994/95; 2000/01; 2003/04; 2004/05; 2006/07)**
Best League Cup Performance: **Winners (1956/57; 1957/58; 1965/66; 1966/67; 1967/68; 1968/69; 1969/70; 1974/75; 1982/83; 1997/98; 1999/2000; 2000/01; 2005/06)**

The club played its first game in 1888, but it was in 1887 that Brother Walfrid and John Glass proposed the idea of a football team that would raise funds to help poor children in the east end of Glasgow. It would be called Glasgow Celtic, as this would enable people of both

Scottish and Irish descent to identify with it. A piece of land was leased and, thanks to volunteer labour, it was ready to host a match against Rangers on 28 May, which Celtic won 5–2. Willie Maley, who would go on to do so much for the club, and his brother Tom both played in that first match and Neil McCallum scored the club's first goal.

SFA membership was obtained for the 1888/89 season and the new club reached the final of the Scottish Cup at the first attempt, losing 2–1 to Third Lanark in a replay after the first match was declared a friendly because of the atrocious weather conditions. The Scottish League came into existence for the 1890/91 season and Celtic, who were founder members, finished that first season in third place. Two years later a team that had been built around Willie Maley and James Kelly won the first of Celtic's many league championships when they took the 1892/93 title.

Willie Maley was also an accountant and his administrative skills led to him being appointed club secretary. In 1892 he organised the club's move to a new ground about two hundred yards away and this site remains the club's home to this day. The year 1892 was underlined as one to remember for Celtic when they won the Scottish Cup for the first time, beating Queen's Park 5–1 at Ibrox in another replayed final, after crowd trouble at the first match.

By 1897 Willie Maley had become secretary/manager and when his team won their fourth title in 1897/98 they completed their league fixtures without being beaten. Then in 1900 he signed the powerful Jimmy Quinn and Celtic went on to win virtually everything from 1904 to 1910. There were six consecutive league titles and in 1906/07 they became the first team to win the double of league title and Scottish Cup.

When the title winning sequence came to an end in 1911 and Celtic entered a transition phase, Willie Maley made signings that included Patsy Gallacher from Clydebank Juniors and goalkeeper Charlie Shaw from Queens Park Rangers. By 1914 the championship had returned to Parkhead and it stayed there for four consecutive seasons. The years after the first world war saw the arrival of players such as the irrepressible Tommy McInally and Willie McStay, who was later joined by his brother Jimmy, but perhaps the greatest signing of this period was Jimmy McGrory, whose partnership with Patsy Gallacher was epitomised by their match-winning goals against Dundee in the 1924/25 Scottish Cup final. Gallacher's famous somersault goal is still talked about by Celtic fans.

Jimmy McGrory's goal scoring become legendary during the 1920s. In the 1926/27 season he scored five goals on three occasions and four goals on four occasions, and in January 1928 scored eight times against Dunfermline. However, another feature of this period was the way in which star players were allowed to leave, such as Tom 'Tully' Craig, who eventually ended up at Rangers, and Joe Cassidy, who was sold to Bolton Wanderers. Young talent was brought in and one such acquisition was John Thomson from Fife, who took over in goal during the 1926/27 season. He went on to play in that season's Scottish cup final, a 3–1 victory over East Fife, which was the first domestic match in Scotland to be broadcast on the radio.

On 5 September 1931 Celtic were playing a league match at Ibrox when John Thomson, by now a Scottish international, dived at the feet of Sam English, the Rangers centre forward. He suffered a depressed fracture of the skull, and tragically died in hospital later that night. There was a huge outpouring of grief amongst Celtic fans and it was said that some of them walked from Glasgow to Fife for the funeral.

Another important signing was made in 1933, when Jimmy Delaney joined the club. His crosses for Jimmy McGrory became a feature of Celtic's play and there were more league championships in 1935/36 and 1937/38. Glasgow hosted the Empire Exhibition in 1938 and Celtic celebrated their fiftieth anniversary by also winning the Empire Exhibition trophy, beating Everton in the final.

When Celtic and Willie Maley parted company on 1 February 1940, the club said goodbye to the only manager it had ever known. Jimmy McStay, a former club captain who had enjoyed some success as manager of Alloa Athletic, replaced him. He signed several teenagers who were to eventually make a big impact, including Bobby Evans, but in July 1945 he made way for Jimmy McGrory to return as manager. The Celtic legend remained in the job for twenty years, but these were lean times when compared with previous successes. There were, however, some notable exceptions.

The Scottish Cup was won in 1950/51 and in 1953 Celtic won the Coronation Cup in a tournament for four English and four Scottish teams. A Celtic team captained by Jock Stein won the double of league championship and Scottish Cup in 1953/54 and the eccentric Charlie Tully earned a reputation for scoring direct from corner kicks. The League Cup was won for the first time in 1956/57, when Partick Thistle were beaten 3–0, but it is the following year's League Cup victory that Celtic fans still sing about, when their side triumphed 7–1 over Rangers, and centre forward Billy McPhail headed a hat-trick.

This was to be the last major domestic trophy for seven years and several of the better players, such as Pat Crerand, left for other clubs. There was an appearance in the semi-finals of the 1963/64 European Cup-Winners' Cup, when a 3–0 home victory over MTK was overturned by a 4–0 defeat in Budapest, but the turning point came in March 1965, when Jock Stein returned as manager. He had been responsible for developing Celtic's younger players, such as Bobby Murdoch and Billy McNeill, in the 1950s before leaving to manage Dunfermline, and now he inherited a team in disarray.

He transformed this situation into the most successful period in the club's history. The Scottish Cup was won in April 1965, when Billy McNeill scored the winner in a 3–2 victory over Dunfermline, and six months later the League Cup was added with a 1–0 win over Rangers. The 1965/66 league title followed and this became the first of nine successive championships. It was the following season, however, when Celtic achieved their greatest-ever success, by becoming the first British club to win the European Cup. After going a goal behind to Inter-Milan, Tommy Gemmell and Steve Chalmers scored, to ensure that the 'Lisbon Lions' would go down in history. Celtic won every competition they entered in 1966/67 and followed this up with another domestic treble in 1968/69. In 1969/70 they once more reached the final of the European Cup, after beating Leeds United in the semi-finals. Tommy Gemmell scored again, but this time it ended with a 2–1 defeat to Feyenoord.

Celtic's Kenny Dalglish became one of the best-known names in British football in the 1970s and in 1977 he left to join Liverpool. Jock Stein, who suffered serious injuries in a car crash in 1975, had been unable to persuade him to stay and in 1978 he stepped down as manager. His replacement was Billy McNeill, by now a successful manager at Aberdeen, and between 1978 and 1983 he led the club to a major trophy in each of five consecutive seasons. Former player David Hay took over in 1983 and, although his period in charge brought another Scottish Cup victory and another league title, he made way for Billy McNeill to return after four years. The man who had been captain of the 'Lisbon Lions' went on to guide his team to the 1987/88 league and cup double in the club's centenary year.

The next few years saw more changes of manager. Billy McNeill left for the second time in 1991, Liam Brady was in charge for two years, and Lou Macari, another former player, was appointed in 1993. The club was required to make its ground all-seater by the start of the 1994/95 season and financial pressures were mounting. Scots-born Canadian businessman Fergus McCann took control of the club in 1994 and he organised a share flotation that enabled Celtic to rebuild Parkhead into one of the best grounds in Britain.

Lou Macari was replaced by Tommy Burns, the Scottish Cup was won in 1994/95, and then former Dutch international Wim Jansen became head coach for the 1997/98 season. His team not only won the League Cup, but also a league title that prevented Rangers from beating Celtic's own record of 'nine in a row'. Wim Jansen signed Henrik Larsson from Feyenoord, a player who went on to score 242 goals in 315 matches during his seven years with the club and become one of Celtic's greatest-ever players.

Further changes saw Slovakian Dr. Jozef Venglos become head coach for a season, and then former England international John Barnes followed him for seven months. His departure was hastened when Celtic suffered a 3–1 home defeat to Inverness Caledonian Thistle in the third round of the 1999/2000 Scottish Cup. Irishman Martin O'Neill was appointed manager in 2000 and by the end of the 2000/01 season Celtic had won the treble for the third time. Two seasons later they reached the final of the 2002/03 UEFA Cup, but lost 3–2 to F.C Porto after extra time. There was another league and cup double in 2003/04, but Martin O'Neill left after the 2004/05 Scottish Cup final, when Celtic beat Dundee United 1–0.

His replacement Gordon Strachan kept up the momentum and both the 2005/06 title and League Cup were won in his first season. In 2006/07 the championship was won with four games to spare when Shunsuke Nakamura scored from a last-minute free kick to give Celtic a 2–1 victory over Kilmarnock, and then a 1–0 win over Dunfermline in the Scottish Cup final secured the double. 2007/08 saw a much closer finish, but a seventh consecutive win on the last day of the season secured Celtic's third title in a row.

Henrik Larsson signed from Feyenoord in 1997.

CENTRAL LEAGUE

There have been other leagues with this name, but the one that existed between 1919 and 1921 played an important part in the history of Scottish football. The Scottish Football League decided not to re-introduce Division Two at the end of the first world war, and this meant that several clubs no longer had a place in the Scottish League. The league's lower division and the previous Central League had both been closed down in 1915 because of the hostilities, and when the Central League was re-formed for 1919/20 it provided a home for three clubs – Dunfermline Athletic, East Stirlingshire and St Bernard's – that had belonged to Division Two in 1914/15. Bo'ness won the title in 1919/20, just pipping Dunfermline Athletic, and the following season Cowdenbeath, Dundee Hibernian, Lochgelly United and St Johnstone, who had all spent 1919/20 in the Eastern League (q.v.), joined them in the Central League.

Sometimes referred to as the 'rebel' league, because it was not constrained by the rules of the Scottish League, member clubs were able to sign players without paying a transfer fee and several were lured away from the Scottish League by the prospect of higher wages. In 1921 the SFL finally agreed to bring back a lower division, which would be based almost entirely on the Central League. The agreement included the introduction of automatic promotion and relegation between the divisions for the first time, as well as the introduction of goal average to separate teams with equal points.

The case of Andrew Nesbit Wilson serves to illustrate how some players were affected by the creation of a new Division Two. He had signed for Middlesbrough in 1914, but then joined Dunfermline Athletic in the Central League after the end of the first world war. When Dunfermline became part of the Scottish League in 1921, the terms of the agreement required him to return to Middlesbrough, the team that he was first registered with.

The final Central League table at the end of the 1920/21 season looked like: -

	P	W	D	L	F	A	Pts.
Bo'ness	34	21	7	6	66	34	49
Hearts 'A'	34	22	4	8	84	36	48
Cowdenbeath	34	20	6	8	64	37	46
Dunfermline Athletic	34	16	7	11	65	52	39
East Fife	34	13	12	9	33	37	38
Bathgate	34	13	11	10	58	37	37
St. Bernard's	34	11	12	11	48	42	34
Stenhousemuir	34	15	4	15	51	56	34
Alloa Athletic	34	9	15	10	50	56	33
St. Johnstone	34	13	6	15	44	51	32
Falkirk 'A'	34	10	10	14	41	52	30
Broxburn United	34	12	5	17	44	58	29
Clackmannan	34	13	3	18	39	57	29
East Stirlingshire	34	10	8	16	44	60	28
Armadale	34	10	7	17	44	51	27
King's Park	34	9	9	16	39	51	27
Dundee Hibernian	34	10	7	17	39	52	27
Lochgelly United	34	11	5	18	39	73	27

Of these eighteen teams, all but Hearts 'A' and Falkirk 'A' joined Arbroath, Forfar Athletic, Johnstone and Vale of Leven to form a new Division Two of the Scottish League at the start of the 1921/22 season.

CHALMERS Steve (1936 –)

Scotland Caps: 5
Scottish League Championship medals: 4
Scottish Cup medals: 3
Scottish League Cup medals: 4
European Cup medals: 1

Steve Chalmers will always be remembered as the man who scored the winning goal in the European Cup final of 1967, as Celtic beat Inter Milan 2–1. He was a speedy centre forward, or right-winger, for Celtic in the 1960s and, although he won only five Scottish caps, he scored a famous goal in the first minute against Brazil in 1966. Surviving childhood illness, Steve became one of the Kelly Kids (the name given to the young Celtic players of the late 1950s and early 1960s). His early years at Celtic were not always happy ones as the supporters were particularly prone to turn on him if things were not going well. But he showed the strength of character to come through all that and, with the arrival of Jock Stein, things changed.

After leaving Celtic in 1971, having enjoyed almost unbroken success, Steve played for Morton and Partick Thistle before returning to Celtic in an administrative capacity, notably the Celtic Pools. Football management would not have been a success for Steve, for he is one of nature's gentlemen. It is said that of all the ex-professional golfers who play golf, Steve is one of the best.

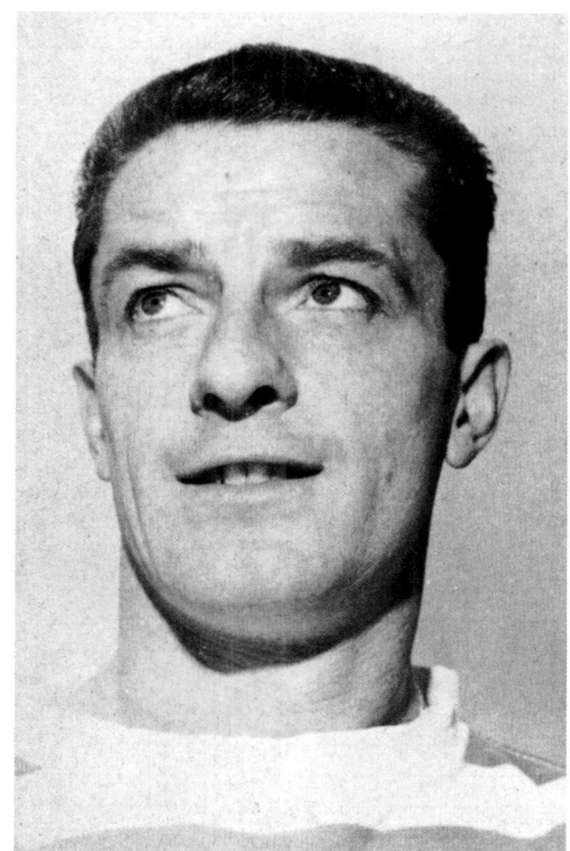

CHAMPIONSHIPS

(of the various divisions of the Scottish Football League and Scottish Premier League)

The numbers in the table below show the number of times that a club has won a particular title (up to the end of the 2007/08 season). A shaded area indicates that the club has never competed for that title. (In addition to these numbers: *Dumbarton and Rangers shared the Division One championship of 1890/91; **Leith Athletic and Raith Rovers shared the Division Two championship of 1909/10)

(Does not include Division C, which existed in various formats between 1946 and 1955, or Division 3, which existed from 1923 until 1926)

	Div. 1/ Div. A	Div. 2/ Div. B	Premier Div./ SPL (post 1975)	First Div. (post 1975)	Second Div. (post 1975)	Third Div. (post 1994)
Abercorn	0	2				
Aberdeen	1	0	3	0		
Airdrieonians	0	3	0	0		
Airdrie United				0	1	
Albion Rovers	0	1		0	1	0
Alloa Athletic	0	1		0	0	1
Arbroath	0	0		0	0	0
Ayr United	0	6	0	0	2	
Berwick Rgrs.		0		0	1	1
Bo'ness	0	1				
Brechin City		0		0	3	1
Celtic	29		13			
Clyde	0	5		0	4	
Clydebank	0	0	0	0	1	
Cowdenbeath	0	3		0	0	1
Dumbarton *	1	2	0	0	1	0
Dundee	1	1	0	3		
Dundee United	0	2	1	0		
Dunfermline Ath.	0	1	0	2	1	
East Fife	0	1		0	0	1
E. Stirlingshire	0	1		0	0	0
Elgin City						0
Falkirk	0	3	0	4	1	
Forfar Athletic		0		0	1	1
Greenock Morton	0	3	0	3	2	1
Gretna				1	1	1
Hamilton Ac.	0	1	0	3	0	1
Heart of Midl'n.	4		0	1		
Hibernian	4	3	0	2		
Inverness CT			0	1	0	1
Kilmarnock	1	2	0	0	0	
Leith Athletic **	0	2				
Livingston/M'bnk.		0	0	1	2	1
Montrose		0		0	1	0
Motherwell	1	2	0	2	0	
Partick Thistle	0	3	0	2	1	
Peterhead					0	0
Port Glasgow	0	1				
Queen Of The S.	0	1		0	1	
Queen's Park	0	2			1	1
Raith Rovers **	0	3	0	2	1	
Rangers *	34		16			
Ross County				0	1	1
St. Bernard's	0	2				
St. Johnstone	0	3	0	3	0	
St. Mirren	0	1	0	3	0	
Stenhousemuir		0		0	0	0
Stirling Albion	0	4		0	3	0
Stranraer		0		0	2	1
Third Lanark	1	2				

CHAMPIONS LEAGUE

In 1992/93 the European Cup, the top club competition in Europe, was re-branded as the UEFA Champions League and this formalised the mini-league system that had been used in 1991/92. The format has changed several times, with either one or two group stages providing varying numbers of clubs for a knockout competition. In recent times there have, on occasion, been two places offered to Scottish teams, although there is usually at least one qualifying round to negotiate first. In 2002 Hampden Park hosted the final for the second time and Real Madrid were the victors, just as they had been in 1960. This time they beat Bayer Leverkusen 2–1.

The record of Scottish teams is as follows:

Season	Scottish Club	Opposition	Agg	Round
1992/93	Rangers	Lyngby	3–0	First
		Leeds United	4–2	Second
		Marseille (H)	2–2	Group Stage
		CSKA Moscow (A)	1–0	
		FC Bruges (A)	1–1	
		FC Bruges (H)	2–1	
		Marseille (A)	1–1	
		CSKA Moscow (H)	0–0	
1993/94	Rangers	Levski Sofia	4–4	First
		Rangers lost on away goals		
1994/95	Rangers	AEK Athens	0–3	Qualifying
1995/96	Rangers	Anorthosis	1–0	Qualifying
		Steaua Bucharest (A)	0–1	Group Stage
		Borussia Dortmund (H)	2–2	
		Juventus (A)	1–4	
		Juventus (H)	0–4	
		Steaua Bucharest (H)	1–1	
		Borussia Dortmund (A)	2–2	
1996/97	Rangers	Vladikavkaz	10–3	Qualifying
		Grasshopper Zur. (A)	0–3	Group Stage
		Auxerre (H)	1–2	
		Ajax (A)	1–4	
		Ajax (H)	0–1	
		Grasshopper Zur. (H)	2–1	
		Auxerre (A)	1–2	
1997/98	Rangers	Gotu	11–0	1st Qualifying
		Gothenburg	1–4	2nd Qualifying
1998/99	Celtic	St Patrick's	2–0	1st Qualifying
		Croatia Zagreb	1–3	2nd Qualifying
1999/00	Rangers	FC Haka	7–1	2nd Qualifying
		Parma	2–1	3rd Qualifying
		Valencia (A)	0–2	1st Group Stage
		Bayern Munich (H)	1–1	

		PSV Eindhoven (A)	1–0	
		PSV Eindhoven (H)	4–1	
		Valencia (H)	1–2	
		Bayern Munich (A)	0–1	
2000/01	Rangers	Zalgiris Kaunas	4–1	2nd Qualifying
		Herfolge BK	6–0	3rd Qualifying
		Sturm Graz (H)	5–0	1st Group Stage
		Monaco (A)	1–0	
		Galatasary (A)	2–3	
		Galatasary (H)	0–0	
		Sturm Graz (A)	0–2	
		Monaco (H)	2–2	
2001/02	Celtic	Ajax	3–2	3rd Qualifying
		Juventus (A)	2–3	1st Group Stage
		Porto (H)	1–0	
		Rosenborg (H)	1–0	
		Porto (A)	0–3	
		Rosenborg (A)	0–2	
		Juventus (H)	4–3	
	Rangers	NK Maribor	6–1	2nd Qualifying
		Fenerbahce	1–2	3rd Qualifying
2002/03	Celtic	FC Basel	3–3	3rd Qualifying
		Celtic lost on away goals		
2003/04	Celtic	FBK Kaunas	5–0	2nd Qualifying
		MTK Hungaria	5–0	3rd Qualifying
		Bayern Munich (A)	1–2	Group Stage
		Lyon (H)	2–0	
		Anderlecht (A)	0–1	
		Anderlecht (H)	3–1	
		Bayern Munich (H)	0–0	
		Lyon (A)	2–3	
	Rangers	FC Copenhagen	3–2	3rd Qualifying
		VfB Stuttgart (H)	2–1	Group Stage
		Panathinaikos (A)	1–1	
		Manchester United (H)	0–1	
		Manchester United (A)	0–3	
		VfB Stuttgart (A)	0–1	
		Panathinaikos (H)	1–3	
2004/05	Celtic	Barcelona (H)	1–3	Group Stage
		AC Milan (A)	1–3	
		Shakhtar Donetsk (A)	0–3	
		Shakhtar Donetsk (H)	1–0	
		Barcelona (A)	1–1	
		AC Milan (H)	0–0	
	Rangers	CSKA Moscow	2–3	3rd Qualifying
2005/06	Celtic	Artmedia Bratislava	4–5	2nd Qualifying
	Rangers	Anorthosis Famagusta	4–1	3rd Qualifying
		Porto (H)	3–2	Group Stage
		Inter Milan (A)	0–1	
		Artmedia Bratislava (H)	0–0	
		Artmedia Bratislava (A)	2–2	
		Porto (A)	1–1	
		Inter Milan (H)	1–1	
		Villareal	3–3	1st Knockout
		Rangers lost on away goals		
2006/07	Celtic	Manchester United (A)	2–3	Group Stage
		FC Copenhagen (H)	1–0	
		Benfica (H)	3–0	
		Benfica (A)	0–3	
		Manchester United (H)	1–0	
		FC Copenhagen (A)	1–3	
		AC Milan	0–1aet	1st Knockout
	Hearts	Siroki Brijeg	3–0	2nd Qualifying
		AEK Athens	1–5	3rd Qualifying
2007/08	Celtic	Spartak Moscow	2–2	3rd Qualifying
		Celtic won on penalties		
		Shakhtar Donetsk (A)	0–2	Group Stage
		AC Milan (H)	2–1	
		Benfica (A)	0–1	
		Benfica (H)	1–0	
		Shakhtar Donetsk (H)	2–1	
		AC Milan (A)	0–1	
		Barcelona	2–4	1st Knockout
	Rangers	Zeta	3–0	2nd Qualifying
		Crvena Zvezda	1–0	3rd Qualifying
		VfB Stuttgart (H)	2–1	Group Stage
		Lyon (A)	3–0	
		Barcelona (H)	0–0	
		Barcelona (A)	0–2	
		VfB Stuttgart (A)	2–3	
		Lyon (H)	0–3	

The following table summarises the performance of Scottish clubs by showing which round/stage they reached each year. It also shows how the format of the competition has changed several times.

One group stage, followed by the final				
1992/93	Rangers	2nd in group		
One group stage, followed by semi-finals				
1993/94	Rangers	1st round		
One group stage, followed by quarter-finals				
1994/95	Rangers	QR		
1995/96	Rangers	4th in group		
1996/97	Rangers	4th in group		
1997/98	Rangers	2nd QR		
1998/99	Celtic	2nd QR		
Two group stages, followed by quarter-finals				
1999/2000	Rangers	3rd in 1st GS		
2000/01	Rangers	3rd in 1st GS		
2001/02	Rangers	3rd QR	Celtic	3rd in 1st GS
2002/03	Celtic	3rd QR		
One group stage, followed by first knockout round with sixteen clubs				
2003/04	Rangers	4th in group	Celtic	3rd in group
2004/05	Rangers	3rd QR	Celtic	4th in group
2005/06	Celtic	2nd QR	Rangers	1st KR
2006/07	Hearts	3rd QR	Celtic	1st KR
2007/08	Rangers	GS	Celtic	1st KR

QR-Qualifying round; GS-Group stage; 1st KR- First Knockout Round (sixteen clubs)

CHILE

Scotland did not manage to qualify for the 1962 World Cup held in Chile. They might have done well if they had done so, for Czechoslovakia, the team that beat Scotland narrowly in the qualifying section reached the final. Scotland have played Chile twice and won both times. The game in Santiago in 1977 provoked a certain amount of protest, because that was the stadium used in the repression, torture and murder of the supporters of Salvador Allende after the 'golpe' or coup of 11 September 1973.

1977	15 June	Santiago	4–2	Macari (2) Dalglish Hartford	Crisoto (2)
1989	30 May	Hampden Park	2–0	McInally MacLeod	

CLACKMANNAN FC (former Scottish League club)

Home: **Chapelhill Park, Clackmannan**
Highest League Position: **42nd (20th in Div. 2, 1921/22)**
Best Scottish Cup Performance: **Last 32 (2nd round, 1928/29)**

Clackmannan FC achieved remarkably little during its two lifetimes and this is born out by the circumstances surrounding the best performances. Their highest Scottish League position was achieved when they finished bottom of the entire league and their best Scottish Cup performance came after they had left the league and were only taking part in cup competitions. The club was founded in 1885 and first entered the Scottish Cup in 1890/91. In the early years they played in the Midland League, although this was punctuated by seasons with only friendlies and cup-ties. They won the Midland league in 1896/97 and this resulted in them losing their best players to bigger clubs. For example, Bolton Wanderers signed full back Bill Halley. This brief success was then followed by a rapid decline and after a spell in the Central Combination, and more years of only friendlies and cup-ties, the club folded in 1904.

Three years later, Clackmannan managed to reform, but the next few years were equally unremarkable, with time spent in both a new Midland League and the Eastern League. However, in 1914 a change took place that was to have a major impact on the club's future. They were accepted into the Central League and seven years later this got them into the new Division Two of the Scottish League, which was largely made up of the Central League clubs. Unfortunately, the team did not grasp the opportunity. They finished bottom in 1922 and had to leave the league after just one season.

Despite this setback, the club received a second chance when it was accepted into the newly formed Division Three in 1923. Three years of unremarkable league form followed and when Division Three came to an end in 1926 so did Clackmannan's time in the Scottish League. The club now decided to only play cup football and this resulted in very few matches being played. Eventually they couldn't continue any longer and went out of existence in 1931. Before that happened though, another club record was set. Their first round tie in 1928/29 gave them a walkover against Dunkeld & Birnam and the club made its only appearance in the second round. It resulted in an 8–1 defeat at Albion Rovers.

Scottish Cup final 1958. Johnny Coyle has just scored the only goal of the game for Clyde against Hibernian.

CLARK John (1941 –)

Scotland Caps: 4
Scottish League Championship medals: 3
Scottish Cup medals: 3
Scottish League Cup medals: 4
European Cup medal: 1

Often referred to as the 'quiet man', 'Luggy' or 'John the Brush', John Clark was the 'sweeper up' of Celtic's Lisbon Lions team, but although he was one of the less flamboyant characters of that squad, his contribution must not be under-estimated. He joined Celtic in 1958 and stayed with them until 1971, although by 1969 he had lost his place to Jim Brogan. He played his full part in that golden age for Celtic. He also played for Morton and, after he retired in 1973, was assistant manager to Billy McNeill at Aberdeen and Celtic. He later became manager at Cowdenbeath, Stranraer and Clyde, and then went on to take charge of the kit at Celtic Park.

CLYDE FC

Ground: **Broadwood Stadium, Cumbernauld**
Nickname: **The Bully Wee**
Colours: **White, with red and black**
Record Attendance: **48,000 (disputed by some) at Shawfield v Rangers (1912)**
8,200 at Broadwood v Celtic (2005)
Record Victory: **11-1 v Cowdenbeath (1951)**
Record Defeat: **0-11 v Dumbarton (1879); v Rangers (1880)**
Highest League Position: **3rd (1908/09; 1911/12; 1966/67)**
Best Scottish Cup Performance: **Winners (1938/39; 1954/55; 1957/58)**
Best League Cup Performance: **Last 4 (1956/57; 1957/58; 1968/69)**

Founded in 1877, Clyde FC played at Barrowfield Park in Rutherglen until 1897. They then moved to Shawfield Stadium, just south of the River Clyde, where they were to stay until 1986. Shawfield also hosted athletics and boxing, and in the 1930s the stadium became the venue for greyhound racing as well.

Clyde joined the Scottish League in 1891, which was only the second year of the league's existence. The early years were unremarkable, but things started to change

Action in the Queen's Park goalmouth as McLoughlin jumps to head a goal for Clyde.

when the club won promotion in 1906 after six seasons in Division Two. They soon became one of the best teams in Scotland and earned third-place finishes in both 1909 and 1912. By the start of the second world war in 1939 the club was still in the top flight and had only spent two seasons in the lower division since 1906. In 1938/39 Clyde won the Scottish Cup for the first time with a 4–0 victory over Motherwell in the final and, because of the war, they can claim to have held on to the trophy for a record eight years.

Most of the years between 1945 and league reconstruction in 1975 were spent in the top division, but during that period the club was relegated five times and on each occasion was promoted back to the top flight at the first attempt. There were two more Scottish Cup wins, in 1955 and 1958, and the 1955 final was the first Scottish domestic game to be televised live. It ended in a 1–1 draw against Celtic and in the replay, which wasn't televised, Clyde's Tommy Ring scored the only goal. By the time Hibernian were beaten 1–0 in the 1957/58 final, by virtue of a goal from John Coyle, there had been relegation in 1956, and then the championship of Division Two in 1956/57.

Another third-place finish was achieved in 1966/67, but the club was denied entry to the Inter-Cities Fairs Cup because Rangers had finished second and the rules only permitted one entrant per city. In 1975 they were placed in the new First Division (second tier) and have not been back in the top tier since. They had to leave Shawfield Stadium in 1986 and were forced to groundshare with other clubs. For five years they shared Firhill with Partick Thistle, and then Douglas Park in Hamilton became their home for a while, until in 1994 they finally moved to a permanent home at the newly built Broadwood stadium in Cumbernauld.

At the 1994 league reorganisation the Bully Wee were placed in the Second Division (third tier), but were promoted to the First Division in 2000 and this signalled the start of more successful times. In the opening years of the twenty-first century Clyde consistently finished in the top half of the First Division and in 2006, under manager Graham Roberts, they famously beat Celtic 2–1 in the third round of the Scottish Cup at Broadwood.

Graham Roberts was sacked in August 2006, and his assistant Joe Miller took over. Clyde reached the final of the 2006/07 League Challenge Cup, losing 5–4 on penalties to Ross County at McDiarmid Park, but at the end of the season Joe Miller decided to leave the club. Colin Hendry (q.v.) briefly replaced him, before former Rangers' youth coach John Brown became manager in January 2008, and at the end of his first season in charge the Bully Wee survived the play-offs to remain in the First Division.

CLYDEBANK FC (former Scottish League club)

Home: **Clydebank, Dunbartonshire (list of grounds below)**
Highest League Position: **5th (1919/20)**
Best Scottish Cup Performance: **Last 4 (Semi-finals, 1989/90)**
Best League Cup Performance: **Last 8 (Quarter-finals, 1971/72; 1975/76; 1976/77); (4th round, 1980/81)**

There has been a club called Clydebank in the Scottish League on three separate occasions, season 1914/15, then from 1917 to 1931, and finally from 1966 to 2002. However, the story of Clydebank FC goes back to 1888 and the years in the Scottish League tell only part of the story. The first Clydebank FC played between 1888 and 1894 and was a regular entrant in the Scottish Cup, reaching the fourth round in 1891/92. The Bankies also played in the Scottish Federation league, but plans for a new railway forced them to leave their Hamilton Park ground, and they soon went out of existence.

Junior football was played in Clydebank over the subsequent years, but another Clydebank FC was formed in 1914. The new club played at Clydeholm and was quickly accepted into the second division of the Scottish League. They competed for a single season until Division Two was suspended because of the first world war and then played in the Western League for two seasons, winning the championship in 1916/17. When Aberdeen, Dundee and Raith Rovers left the Scottish League because of the difficulties of wartime travel, Clydebank were re-admitted to it for 1917/18.

The club now spent five seasons in Division One, although it was a single-division set-up for four of them, and this period saw their highest-ever league finish, when they finished fifth in 1919/20. Then they finished bottom in 1921/22, which was the very year that automatic relegation to the new Division Two was introduced, and the club embarked upon a 'yo-yo' period of movement between the divisions. For five consecutive seasons they were either relegated or promoted, until they finally settled in Division Two in 1926. The Bankies' form in the league soon deteriorated and there was little of interest in the Scottish Cup. It was a time of economic depression and crowds were low. Finally, after finishing second bottom in 1930/31, the club resigned from the Scottish League.

Over thirty years later, moves were made to bring senior football back to Clydebank. The owners of East Stirlingshire FC decided to amalgamate with Clydebank Juniors and 'ES Clydebank' played Scottish League football at New Kilbowie Park, Clydebank, for the 1964/65 season. The amalgamation was controversial and the matter was eventually decided in court, when the new club was split back into its constituent parts. The Shire went back to Falkirk, and Clydebank spent the

1965/66 season in the Combined Reserve League. One year later they were admitted into Division Two of the Scottish League.

The new Bankies were part of the second tier for almost all their time in the Scottish League, but league reconstruction in 1975 placed them in Division Two (third tier). A team that included Davie Cooper won promotion in two consecutive seasons and the club spent the 1977/78 season in the Premier Division, making them the first club to play in all three divisions. A few years later they spent two more seasons in the top flight, from 1985 to 1987, and in 1989/90 they reached the semi-finals of the Scottish Cup, losing 2–0 to Celtic.

In 1996 the club had to leave its New Kilbowie Park home, which had been one of the first all-seater grounds in Britain, and shared grounds at Boghead Park, Dumbarton, and Cappielow Park, Greenock. Financial problems mounted and in 2002, when they were in administration, Airdrie United effectively bought them out. They offered more money than a bid that was backed by the Clydebank supporters and the club moved to Airdrie. Their fixtures were taken over by Airdrie United, but the club name and crest were transferred to a supporters trust. In 1993 a junior club, playing at Glenhead Park, took the name of Clydebank into the future.

These are the grounds where the Bankies played in the Scottish League:

(Hamilton Park)		
Scottish League		
Clydeholm	1914	1931
New Kilbowie Park	1966	1996
Boghead Park	1996	1999
Cappielow Park	1999	2002

COLLINS Bobby (1931 –)

Scotland Caps: 31
Scottish League Championship medals: 1
Scottish Cup medals: 1
Scottish League Cup medals: 2

A talented forward who played some marvellous football for Celtic, Everton and Leeds United in the 1950s and 1960s, Bobby Collins also won thirty-one caps for Scotland, taking part in the 1958 World Cup finals in Sweden. Celtic fans knew him as 'The Wee Barra', and the wonder is that he won only four Scottish medals in his years with Celtic. He is also remembered as one of the few players ever to score a hat-trick of penalties, a feat he achieved against Aberdeen at Parkhead in September 1953.

His best game for Celtic was probably the 7–1 victory against Rangers in the Scottish League Cup final of October 1957. A year later he was transferred to Everton for £23,500, where his career took a dip until he joined Leeds United in 1962. There he teamed up with Don Revie and captained Leeds, taking them into Division One and reaching the FA Cup Final. As late as 1965 he regained his place in the Scottish international team. A serious leg break seemed to have finished his career in

1965, but he came back to play for Bury and Morton, and then to coach and manage a variety of clubs.

COLLINS John (1968 –)

Scotland Caps: 58
Scottish Cup medals: 1

From the rugby-playing area of Galashiels, John Collins was an outstanding midfield player, who won fifty-eight caps for Scotland between 1988 and 2000 in a career that saw him play for Hibs, Celtic, Monaco, Everton and Fulham. He was renowned for his professional attitude and placid temperament. He played in the 1996 European Championships and the 1998 World Cup, but his Celtic career was unfortunate in that it coincided with a low point in the club's fortunes. He did nevertheless win a Scottish Cup medal with them, and then with Monaco he won a French League championship medal. In his later career, he played for Fulham but he must not be confused with another Fulham player called 'Collins John'! In autumn 2006, he returned to Scotland to

become manager of Hibs, achieving almost instant success with them when he won the Scottish League Cup in March 2007. However, to the surprise of Scottish football, he suddenly announced his resignation in December 2007.

COLOMBIA

Scotland have never beaten Colombia, nor have they ever played there. Colombia have once been to Hampden Park as part of a triangular tournament with Scotland and England called the Rous Cup, and the other games were played in the USA, when both teams were on tour before major tournaments.

1988	17 May	Hampden Park	0–0		
1996	29 May	Miami	0–1		Asprilla
1998	23 May	New York	2–2	Collins Burley	Valderrama Rincon

COMMONWEALTH OF INDEPENDENT STATES

Scotland have played this team once, and will almost certainly never do so again, for it was the name given to all the states of the former Soviet Union. They had started off playing as the Soviet Union, but as various states achieved independence during the qualification for the European Championships in Sweden in 1992, they refused to play under the Soviet banner and called themselves the CIS instead. Many people believe it was one of Scotland's best-ever performances.

1992	18 June	Norrkoping	3–0	McStay McClair McAllister	

CONN Alfie jr. (1952 –)

Scotland Caps: 2
Scottish League Championship medals: 2
Scottish Cup medals: 2
Scottish League Cup medals: 1
European Cup-Winners' Cup medals: 1

Alfie Conn had a remarkable career, which would have been far more illustrious if he had not suffered so much from injuries. He was the son of another Alfie Conn (see **TERRIBLE TRIO**), who had played for the great Hearts team of the 1950s. A versatile midfield player, Alfie joined Rangers in 1968, and in 1972 was part of the Rangers team that won the European Cup-Winners' Cup against Moscow Dynamo in Barcelona. Then, the following year, he scored a goal in the Scottish Cup final of 1973 against Celtic. In 1974 he moved on to Tottenham Hotspur, where his career suffered because of injury, but in March 1977, to the amazement of the football world, Jock Stein brought him back to Scotland to play for Celtic, where he immediately settled and played his part in the league and cup double of 1977. He thus has the unique record of having played in Old Firm Scottish Cup finals for both sides, and having won both games! He also won a Scottish League medal with Celtic in 1979, and finished his career with Hearts, Blackpool and Motherwell.

COOKE Charlie (1942 –)

Scotland Caps: 16

In the opinion of many people, Charlie Cooke was the most cultured player of his generation. He was a talented right-sided midfielder or inside right and was much

loved wherever he went. He started off at Aberdeen and joined Dundee in 1964, for whom he played a little over fifteen months. In that time the veterans compared him with Billy Steel and Alec Troup, and Dundee fans asked:

'I have for you a question
Its answer I do seek
How long before Prince Charlie Cooke
Will make a football speak?'

Sadly, Dundee succumbed to monetary temptations and Cooke went to Chelsea for £72,000 in 1966, and won an FA Cup medal with them in 1970, playing outstandingly in the final against Leeds United. He later played for Crystal Palace. He played consistently well for Scotland, and it is a shame that Scotland did not qualify for the 1966 or 1970 World Cup finals, so that the world could have seen Charlie Cooke at his best. He is now based in Cincinnati, Ohio, working for an organisation that is teaching football to youngsters all over America and the rest of the world.

COOPER Davie (1956 – 1995)

Scottish Caps: 22
Scottish League Championship medals: 3
Scottish Cup medals: 4
Scottish League Cup medals: 7

One of the best left-wingers of his generation and, according to some, of all time, Davie Cooper joined Rangers in 1977 from Clydebank (with whom he had won the Second Division Championship). He won a grand total of thirteen medals with them until 1989, when he went to Motherwell, with whom he won the Scottish Cup in 1991. He is remembered as 'The Moody Blue' (because he did not like to give interviews to journalists) and 'Super Cooper'. The twenty-two games that he played for Scotland included the 1986 World Cup finals in Mexico. It was he who scored the vital penalty at Cardiff that earned Scotland the play-off, and indirectly led to the tragic death of manager Jock Stein. Cooper himself died suddenly of a brain haemorrhage in March 1995.

CORNER KICK

A corner kick is awarded to the attacking side every time the ball goes out of play over the goal line, the ball having last touched a defender. A corner kick was first introduced in 1872. Law 17 describes how the ball must be placed inside the corner arc at the nearest flag post and the ball is kicked by a member of the attacking team. The flag post must not be removed to facilitate the taking of the kick, the opposition must remain ten yards from the corner arc, and the taker of the corner kick must not touch the ball a second time until it has touched another player. Some grounds now have a mark outside the playing area to mark ten yards from the corner flag on the touchline and the dead-ball line. It might be an idea to draw another arc to indicate the area into which the opposition must not encroach when a corner kick is being taken. At one point in the 1960s, Law 17 stated that a member of the attacking team should 'take a kick at the nearest flag post', until someone pointed out that the phrasing was ambiguous and unfortunate!

The award of a corner is significant, for it gives the attacking side a goal scoring opportunity and there remain fewer more spectacular sights that the heading home of a corner kick. At one point, particularly in regional competitions such as the Glasgow Cup and Glasgow Charity Cup, 'counting corners' was a recognised method of deciding a drawn cup-tie before anyone thought of the idea of a penalty shoot-out. During the second world war, Rangers won the Southern League Cup final in two successive years through corners. In 1943, they beat Falkirk 11–3 by this method, and in 1944 Hibs 6–5 when the amount of goals scored was equal. In some ways this was a fair method because the award of corners gives an indication of pressure applied to a defence.

A surprising number of football fans are unaware that a goal can be scored direct from a corner kick. This has been allowed since 1924, and the first player to achieve this feat was Billy Alston of St Bernard's who scored against Albion Rovers in the Scottish League second division on 21 August 1924. It is a rare phenomenon, but there are at least three famous occasions in Scottish football history when goals were scored direct from a corner kick. One was Alec Cheyne's late winner for Scotland against England at Hampden in 1929, and also at Hampden was Clyde's late equalizer against Celtic in the last minute of the 1955 Scottish Cup final, when Archie Robertson earned Clyde a replay, which they duly won.

But the most remarkable sequence of events would have to be those at Brockville in a Scottish Cup tie in 1953 when Charlie Tully of Celtic took a corner kick and scored direct. The crush barriers then collapsed in a corner of the dangerously overcrowded stadium as Celtic fans ran on to congratulate their hero. But the linesman had his flag up. The ball had been placed outside the arc. The kick had to be retaken. Tully waited patiently until the crowd were ushered back on to the terracing, then he politely asked the linesman to place the ball for him, lest he make another mistake. The official did so, and after a lapse of several minutes, Tully shaped up to take the corner kick again. Mayhem broke out when he scored for the second time!

Alec Cheyne, mentioned above, is the only player

It is the last minute of the 1955 Scottish Cup final and Clyde have just equalized direct from a corner kick against Celtic

known to have scored two goals direct from a corner kick in the one game. This was for Aberdeen in a Scottish Cup tie against Nithsdale Wanderers on 1 February 1930.

CORONATION CUP

This was a competition held in Glasgow to commemorate the coronation of Queen Elizabeth II in 1953. It should not be confused with the **BRITISH LEAGUE CUP** of 1902, sometimes called the Coronation Cup, because of its proximity to the coronation of Edward VII in 1902. In 1953 it was decided by both the English and the Scottish authorities that four teams from each country should he invited to take part. Newcastle United, Arsenal (English league champions), Manchester United and Tottenham Hotspur accepted the invitation, as did Hibernian, Rangers (Scottish league and cup winners), Celtic and Aberdeen. Blackpool, the winners of the FA Cup, did not take part, nor did Preston North End or Wolves, who finished second and third respectively in the English league. The Glasgow grounds of Hampden Park and Ibrox were chosen because it was felt that London would be too busy with the coronation itself.

The teams chosen were considered to be the best available crowd pullers and Celtic, who had had a poor season, finishing eighth in the Scottish League, were invited to take part only because of the size of their following and the fact that all games were to be played in Glasgow. Yet they ended up the winners in an epic final against Hibs, in which Johnnie Bonnar, the Celtic goalkeeper, aided by captain Jock Stein, famously defied Hibs 'Famous Five' forward line. The whole competition was a pleasant surprise for Scottish teams, particularly Hibs and Celtic, and was well attended throughout. The irony, however, of the Coronation Cup final being played on an occasion when 'all Hampden was covered in green, white and gold' rather than the red, white and blue which one might have expected, was not lost on supporters of Celtic and Hibernian.

Quarter Finals:

11 May 1953	Celtic	1	0	Arsenal	Hampden Park
	Collins				59,538
11 May 1953	Hibernian	1	1	Tottenham H.	Ibrox
	Smith			Walters	43,000
12 May 1953	Hibernian	2	1	Tottenham H.	Ibrox
	Reilly (2)			McClellan	13,000
13 May 1953	Manchester U.	2	1	Rangers	Hampden Park
	Pearson Rowley			McMillan	75,000
13 May 1953	Newcastle U.	4	0	Aberdeen	Ibrox
	Milburn White Hannah o.g.				10,000

Semi-finals:

16 May 1953	Hibernian	4	0	Newcastle U.	Ibrox
	Turnbull (2) Reilly Johnstone				35,000
16 May 1953	Celtic	2	1	Manchester U.	Hampden Park
	Peacock Mochan			Rowley	73,466

Final:

20 May 1953	Celtic	2	0	Hibernian	Hampden Park
	Mochan Walsh				117,060

Celtic: Bonnar, Haughney, Rollo, Evans, Stein, McPhail, Collins, Walsh, Mochan, Peacock, Fernie
Hibs: Younger, Govan, Paterson, Buchanan, Howie, Combe, Smith, Johnstone, Reilly, Turnbull, Ormond.
Referee – H. Phillips, Wishaw

The final was played on a very pleasant summer evening before a crowd given as 117,060, but with many more locked out of Hampden when the gates were closed, as the east terracing was dangerously over-crowded. Hibs, the form team, who had only narrowly lost the Scottish League on goal average, were expected to win. In addition Hibs had demolished Newcastle United in the semi-final with a breathtaking display of attacking football – but Celtic, strengthened by new signing Neil Mochan, who compensated for the absence of the injured Tully, scored first, then resisted the intense onslaught of the Hibs forward line throughout the second half until a breakaway led to another and decisive goal for Celtic.

COSTA RICA

It was against this third-world nation that Scotland achieved, in the 1990 World Cup finals, what was one of their worst ever results, plunging the country into gloom and earning worldwide ridicule. It was also a day on which Scotland lost international credibility.

1990	11 June	Genoa	0–1	Cayasso

COWAN Jimmy (1926 – 1968)

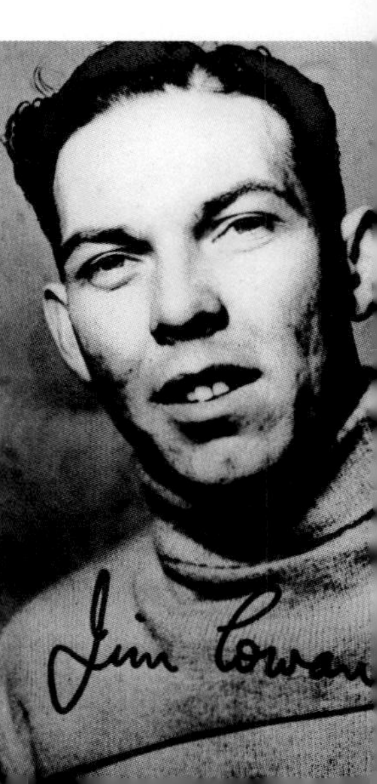

Scotland Caps: 25

Jimmy Cowan played twenty-five times in goal for Scotland (an unusual amount for a man from a provincial club), and was almost the automatic choice between the years of 1948 and 1952. He played mainly for Morton, but also for Sunderland and Third Lanark. With Morton he reached the final of the Scottish Cup in 1948, but he was immortalised for his displays in the 1949 and 1951 Scotland versus England internationals at Wembley. Scotland won both games, and the 1949 international in particular is known as 'Cowan's Wembley'. He died at the tragically young age of forty-two.

COWDENBEATH FC

Ground: **Central Park**
Nickname: **The Blue Brazil**
Colours: **Royal blue and white**
Record Attendance: **25,586 v Rangers (1949)**
Record Victory: **12-0 v Johnstone (1928)**
Record Defeat: **1-11 v Clyde (1951)**
Highest League Position: **5th (1924/25)**
Best Scottish Cup Performance: **Last 8 (4th round, 1930/31)**
Best League Cup Performance: **Last 4 (Semi-finals, 1959/60; 1970/71)**

Cowdenbeath FC came into existence when two Cowdenbeath clubs, Cowdenbeath Rangers (founded 1880) and Raith Rovers (founded 1881, and not the club from Kirkcaldy), amalgamated in 1882. Cowdenbeath Rangers had previously merged with Cowdenbeath Thistle and retained their name. Elected to Division Two of the Scottish Football League in 1905, they remained in the second tier until 1915. They won the championship of Division Two in 1913/14, but there was no automatic promotion and Cowdenbeath had to remain in the lower division. Then they won the title again in 1914/15, only to be denied promotion once more when the Scottish League was reduced to a single division during the first world war.

The club played at North End Park until 1917, when chairman Andrew Dick gifted Central Park to them. After the first world war they played in the Central League and, along with most of its members, became part of the new Division Two when it was formed in 1921. Promotion was achieved in 1923/24 and, when Cowdenbeath finished fifth in Division One in 1924/25, Willie Devlin was the first division's top scorer with thirty-three league goals. They remained in the top flight until 1934, and in 1930 goalkeeper Bob Middleton became the first Cowdenbeath player to be capped for Scotland. Jim Paterson (1931) and Alex Venters (1934) also represented Scotland during this period. Former player Scott Duncan was manager from 1925 to 1932, when he left to become manager of Manchester United.

The championship of Division Two was won again in 1938/39, when centre forward Rab Walls scored fifty-four league goals. Although automatic promotion and relegation had now been introduced, the advent of another world war meant that promotion was again denied. When the Scottish League resumed in 1945, the club was placed in Division 'B', which was now the name of the second tier. In 1949 Cowdenbeath became the first-ever team from the lower divisions to beat Rangers at Ibrox, a 3–2 victory in the first leg of the quarter-finals of the League Cup, and in 1959 they reached the semi-finals of the League Cup, when Hearts beat them 9–3 at Easter Road.

It was not until 1970 that the club was promoted back to Division One, when manager Andy Matthew's side spent a single season in the top division. The 1970/71 season also brought another appearance in the semi-finals of the League Cup, which resulted in a 2–0 defeat to Rangers. The club did not escape from the bottom division again until 1992, when they won promotion from the Second Division (third tier). They could only stay up in the First Division for one season and this period saw a run of thirty-eight home league matches without a win.

Craig Levein was manager between 1997 and 2000 and he made improvements that led to promotion from the Third Division (fourth tier) in 2001, but the club was relegated again in 2003. Two years later the Finnish international Mixu Paatelainen became manager and

led them to the 2005/06 Third Division championship, which was their first title since 1939. He left in October 2006 and Brian Welsh, the former Hibs and Dundee United defender, took over, but at the end of 2007/08 the Blue Brazil went down to the bottom tier once again after losing to Arbroath in the play-offs.

Central Park also doubles as a stock-car stadium and the rental is a source of income for the club. Crowds on race nights are frequently bigger than those on a Saturday afternoon.

COWIE Doug (1926 –)

Scotland Caps: 20
Scottish League Cup medals: 2

Doug Cowie was a very cultured centre half, who won twenty caps for Scotland during his career with Dundee, which lasted from 1945 to 1961. With Dundee he won the Scottish League Cup twice, and it is generally agreed that the half back line of Gallacher, Cowie and Boyd was the best in the history of the club. He subsequently played for Morton and managed Raith Rovers. His international career included appearances at the 1954 and 1958 World Cup finals.

COWLAIRS FC (former Scottish League club)

Home: **Springvale Park, Springburn, Glasgow**
Highest League Position: **10th (1890/91)**
Best Scottish Cup Performance: **Last 8 (7th round, 1891/92)**

Although Cowlairs spent only three seasons in the Scottish League, they made their mark in the record books. Firstly, they were one of the founder members of the Scottish League in 1890. They were also the first club to finish the season in bottom place, a situation that wasn't helped by having four points deducted for infringement of the rules regarding registration. Further, they were one of the small group of Scottish clubs that played in the English FA Cup before the SFA decided that they couldn't compete in both England and Scotland. In 1886/87 Cowlairs recorded FA Cup wins away to Darwen Old Wanderers and Rossendale before going out to Rangers.

Cowlairs had been a familiar name in the Scottish Cup since 1880 and over the years they recorded some high scoring wins, such as their 21–1 away victory against Victoria in 1889/90. In 1891/92 there was a remarkable tie against Royal Albert, with 6–6 and 4–4 draws before both teams were allowed to progress.

Professionalism was not officially recognised in Scotland until 1893, and the club's participation in that groundbreaking season of 1890/91 was overshadowed by allegations of illegal payments. At the end of the season their financial records failed an inspection and they had to leave the Scottish League. After a year without league football, they joined the Scottish Alliance league for 1892/93 and won the title. This was the year that the Scottish League introduced Division Two and Cowlairs became members for the 1893/94 and 1894/95 seasons. Although they took the runners-up spot at the first attempt, they finished bottom again the next year. Crowds were small, financial difficulties were mounting, and so they left the league once more. One year later they went out of existence.

COX Sammy (1924 –)

Scotland Caps: 24
Scottish League Championship medals: 4
Scottish Cup medals: 3
Scottish League Cup medals: 1

An excellent left-sided defender, who played for Rangers in the days of their famous 'Iron Curtain' defence, Sammy Cox was equally at home at left back and left half, and played for Scotland in both positions. His Ibrox career lasted from 1946 to 1955. He then played a few years for East Fife, and emigrated to Canada in 1959. A blot on his otherwise outstanding record was the violent foul that he committed on Charlie Tully in an Old Firm game at Ibrox on 27 August 1949.

CRAIG Jim (1943 –)

Scotland Caps: 1
Scottish League Championship medals: 7
Scottish Cup medals: 4
Scottish League Cup medals: 3
European Cup medals: 1

The right back of the Lisbon Lions, Jim Craig was a totally dependable and reliable full back. Surprisingly, he won only one Scottish cap. He also played in South Africa and for Sheffield Wednesday. In addition he is a dentist, journalist, and sporting historian and polymath.

CRAIGMYLE Peter (1893 – 1980)

Peter Craigmyle was a famous referee of the inter-war period, during which he officiated at many cup finals and international fixtures, taking over from Tom Dougray as Scotland's number one official. He came from Aberdeen, and was well respected for his fairness and fearlessness but also for his sense of the dramatic, in particular when a goal was scored and he would pause, have everyone look at him before he turned and pointed theatrically to the centre spot. Other stories about him include the time that, when assailed by players demanding a penalty, he ran away from them round the back of the goal and on to the field again! This happened in the 1931 Scottish Cup final when he denied Celtic a penalty, and on another occasion in 1925 he awarded a free kick outside the box in the last minute of the game when St Mirren thought it should have been a penalty.

After bending down to look at the exact spot where the offence occurred, he noticed that St Mirren were refusing to take the free kick, insisting that it was a penalty. Craigmyle took out his watch, counted down the seconds to full time, calmly picked the ball up and walked off the field!

CRAMPSEY Bob (1930 –)

Generally acknowledged to be an elder statesman of Scottish football, and a real expert, Bob came to prominence as part of a three-man team of himself, Arthur Montford and Alec Cameron who hosted STV's *Scotsport* when it started in the late 1950s. Bob has since worked for the BBC and Radio Clyde, and for many years was responsible for the *Now You Know* query column in the *Evening News*. He has also been 'Brain of Britain' in 1965 and was Headmaster at St Ambrose High School, Coatbridge. His deep throaty voice and knowledge and love of the game make him one of the best-loved characters of the Scottish media. He has written many books on football, and a few on cricket as well.

CRAWFORD Steve (1974 –)

Scotland Caps: 25
Scottish League Cup medals: 1

A man of many clubs, including Raith Rovers, Millwall, Hibs, Dunfermline, Plymouth Argyle, Dundee United, Aberdeen and Dunfermline Athletic again, Steve Crawford has played twenty-five times in the centre forward position for Scotland. In 1994 he attracted attention by his performance in the Scottish League Cup final, when he scored the first goal and won a medal with Raith Rovers.

Dunfermline's Stevie Crawford takes on Celtic's Steven Pressley in the 2007 Scottish FA Cup final.

CRERAND Pat (1939 –)

Scotland Caps: 16

One of the most accomplished passers of a ball ever seen in Scottish football, Pat Crerand played for Celtic between 1958 and 1963, and formed part of the magnificent Scotland half back line of Crerand, McNeill and Baxter that beat England 2–0 at Hampden Park in 1962. His problem was that he played for a poor team (as Celtic were then) and did not win anything with them. After he had an argument with assistant manager Sean Fallon in the dressing room at Ibrox at half time on New Year's Day 1963, Celtic went on to lose 4–0 and Crerand never played for them again. He moved to Manchester United for £65,000 in February of that year, and went on to win an FA Cup medal, two English league medals and a European Cup medal in 1968. He won sixteen caps for Scotland, and was manager of Northampton Town for a spell.

CRICKETERS

It is now comparatively rare for Scottish footballers to be cricketers as well, because the seasons overlap. But Scotland can boast of two players who have represented their country at both sports – Scott Symon and Andy Goram. Scott Symon played for Dundee, Portsmouth and Rangers before the second world war, after which he became manager of East Fife, Preston North End and Rangers. In cricket he was a bowler for Perthshire and Scotland. Andy Goram was a goalkeeper for Oldham Athletic, Hibs and Rangers, and kept wicket for Penicuik, Kelso and Scotland. In addition there was Donald Ford, who played for West Lothian and Hearts in the 1960s, and Celtic's mighty full backs of the turn of the nineteenth/twentieth centuries, James Welford and Davie Storrier, were both cricketers. Welford even played first class cricket for Warwickshire, and Storrier for Arbroath and Forfarshire.

The two Scottish caps who came from Montrose in the 1890s, George Bowman and Sandy Keillor, were also famous cricketers. Gil Herron was a Jamaican who played for Celtic and Third Lanark in the early 1950s during the winter, and for Poloc and Ferguslie in the summer. Queen of the South had an England international playing for them in the mid 1970s in the form of Leicestershire's Chris Balderstone, and Terry Butcher played a few games for Stirling County in the late 1980s and early 1990s.

There are many other examples, for the football season used to end fairly predictably at the end of April and not resume until the middle of August, allowing a reasonable chance for a footballer to be a cricketer as well. Wise football clubs would have encouraged their players to do just that, for it was a good way of keeping fit – although Willie Maley of Celtic even frowned on golf sometimes. (This was surprising for he himself had played many other sports.) As the football season now goes on until well into May, and pre-season training can resume as early as midsummer's day in June, there is little scope for a double career.

CROATIA

All Scotland's games against Croatia have been drawn.

2000	11 Oct	Zagreb	1–1	Gallacher	Boksic
2001	1 Sep	Hampden Park	0–0		
2008	26 Mar	Hampden Park	1–1	Miller	Kranjcar

CROSSBAR

A necessary part of the furniture of the football field, crossbars were introduced to the game in 1875. Prior to that there was no height restriction at all, as long as the ball passed between imaginary continuations of the posts. There is a story about a game in 1871 when the famous Queen's Park went to Airdrie to play a team called the Airdrie Hammer Drivers. The Hammer Drivers had stretched a tape over the top of their goalposts. Queen's Park objected to this innovation and at first refused to play, but eventually a compromise was reached whereby the tape would be used in the second half only. After their inevitable victory, Queen's Park began to see the advantages of using a tape or, perhaps a rope, to restrict the height of the goal. As Queen's Park were the leading lights of Scottish football in the 1870s, their influence on other teams was considerable.

By the time that the first international was played in 1872, however, there were references in the report of the game to the ball passing over the tape, and indeed in 1874, when Scotland beat England 2–1 at Hamilton Crescent, England opened the scoring when Kingsford fired 'under the tape'. This was clearly unsatisfactory, so it is no surprise to find that a bar was introduced in 1875, and that by 1882 the international conference in Manchester decreed that crossbars should be compulsory. Not every single Scottish game from 1882 onwards would have been played with a crossbar, for such changes would have taken time to reach the lower reaches of the game. It is, for example, possible (although there is no photographic or other hard evidence) that the record score of 36–0 for Arbroath versus Aberdeen Bon Accord on 12 September 1885 may have happened with a rope or a tape rather than a wooden or solid crossbar. The crossbar now should be white (like the rest of the goal) and should be eight feet off the ground. It must be no wider than the maximum width of the touch line (five inches), but it may be square, cylindrical, round or any other reasonable shape. Very often what determines whether a ball enters the net is the shape of the crossbar. The referees are instructed that in the event of a crossbar being broken, or in some way constituting a danger to the players, the game should be delayed until such time as a suitable replacement can be found, and if that is not possible, the game should be abandoned. A rope or tape is not acceptable. Fortunately such cases are extremely rare. Perhaps the most famous instance of someone hitting the bar was Willie Bauld for Scotland, versus England at Hampden in 1950. A draw would have allowed Scotland to go to the 1950 World Cup in Brazil as joint British Champions (the SFA refused to go otherwise) and with six minutes remaining and England 1–0 up, Willie Bauld of Hearts was through the defence and crashed the ball off the underside of the bar. The ball decided to bounce back into play rather than into the net, and Scotland were denied their first-ever trip to a World Cup finals tournament.

CRUM Johnny (1912 – 1969)

Scotland Caps: 2
Scottish League Championship medals: 2
Scottish Cup medals: 1

A forward for Celtic in the late 1930s, Johnny Crum is immortalised for the goal that he scored which won the **EMPIRE EXHIBITION TROPHY** (q.v.), and the highland fling that he did afterwards to celebrate. He played as an inside forward until Jimmy McGrory retired, and he was called upon to take over that mantle. He played for Morton during the second world war.

CUMNOCK JUNIORS FC (see JUNIOR FOOTBALL)

CUNNINGHAM Andy (1891 – 1973)

Scotland Caps: 12
Scottish League Championship medals: 7
Scottish Cup medals: 1

A tall, golden-haired inside forward, Andy Cunningham is generally acknowledged to have been one of Rangers' best ever players. His first senior team was Kilmarnock, but he joined Rangers in 1915 and stayed with them until 1929 when he went to Newcastle United. At Newcastle he became, at thirty-eight, the oldest-ever debutant in the English league and, after he became their manager in 1930, he took them to victory in the FA Cup Final of 1932. Decline soon followed, however, and he resigned in 1935 before becoming the manager of Dundee from 1937 to 1940. After the second world war, he was a journalist with the *Scottish Daily Express*. He won twelve caps for Scotland, and was only once on the losing side – against England in 1927. He had been on the winning side against them in 1921 and 1926.

CUNNINGHAM Willie (1930 – 2007)

Scottish Cup medals: 1

Born in Mallusk, County Antrim, Willie Cunningham was an Ulsterman who made Scotland his home. He won a total of thirty caps for Northern Ireland, but the highlight of his international career was the World Cup finals of 1958, when his country reached the quarter-finals. In 1964, when Jock Stein resigned from his post as Dunfermline manager, it was team coach and former club captain Willie Cunningham who replaced him, and he went on to manage the Pars during one of the most successful periods in their history.

Signed by St Mirren from junior side Ardrossan Winton Rovers, Willie Cunningham made his professional debut in October 1950. After developing into an outstanding full back, he was transferred to Leicester City in 1954 for £4750. He helped them win the English Division Two title in 1956/57, and then returned to Scotland in the autumn of 1960, signing for Dunfermline Athletic for a fee of £1850. Success soon followed, with the Pars winning the 1960/61 Scottish Cup at the end of his first season. The following season Dunfermline reached the quarter-finals of the European Cup-Winners' Cup, with captain Willie Cunningham playing a commanding role in defence.

His first season as Dunfermline manager saw continued success, with the Pars being runners-up in the 1964/65 Scottish Cup and finishing third in the league. The following season they reached the quarter-finals of the Inter-Cities Fairs Cup. He resigned as manager in June 1967, but later went on to manage both Falkirk and St Mirren. After leaving St Mirren in 1974, he became manager of a sports shop in Dunfermline until he retired.

CUPS

The table opposite shows the number of times that each club in the Scottish Premier League and Scottish Football League has won the Scottish Cup, Scottish League Cup, Scottish League Challenge Cup or Scottish Qualifying Cup (up to the end of the 2007/08 season). It also shows the record of former league clubs that have won one of these trophies.

The Scottish Qualifying Cup was played as a single competition from 1895/96 to 1930/31, and from then until 2006/07 there were both 'North' and 'South' competitions. A 'Midlands' one also existed in 1946/47 and 1947/48.

A shaded area indicates that a club has never competed for a particular trophy.

	Scottish Cup	League Cup	Scottish League Challenge Cup	Scottish Qualifying Cup
Abercorn	0			1 (single)
Aberdeen	7	5		1 (single)
Airdrieonians	1	0	3	0
Airdrie United	0	0	0	
Albion Rovers	0	0	0	1 (single)
Alloa Athletic	0	0	1	0
Arbroath	0	0	0	1 (single)
Ayr United	0	0	0	0
Bathgate	0			3 (single)
Beith	0			1 (single); 3 (south)
Berwick Rangers	0	0	0	1 (south)
Brechin City	0	0	0	1 (south)
Celtic	34	13		
Clyde	3	0	0	0
Cowdenbeath	0	0	0	0
Dumbarton	1	0	0	0
Dundee	1	3	1	
Dundee Utd / Hibernian	1	2	0	0
Dunfermline	2	0	0	1 (single)
East Fife	1	3	0	1 (single)
East Stirlingshire	0	0	0	2 (single)
Elgin City	0	0	0	8 (north)
Falkirk	2	0	3	0
Forfar Athletic	0	0	0	1 (midlands)
Galston	0			1(single); 1 (south)
Greenock Morton	1	0	0	0
Gretna	0	0	0	
Hamilton Academical	0	0	2	0
Hearts	7	4		
Hibernian	2	3	0	
Inverness CT	0	0	1	
Kilmarnock	3	0	0	1 (single)
Leith Athletic	0	0		3 (single); 2 (south)
Liv'ston / M'bank / Ferranti	0	1	0	1 (south)
Mid-Annandale	0			1 (single)
Montrose	0	0	0	1 (single); 1 (midlands)
Motherwell	2	1		1 (single)
Partick Thistle	1	1	0	0
Peebles Rovers	0			1 (south)
Peterhead	0	0	0	6 (north)
Port Glasgow	0			1 (single)
Queen of the South	0	0	1	1 (single)
Queen's Park	10	0	0	0
Raith Rovers	0	1	0	1 (single)
Rangers	32	25		
Renton	2			0
Ross County	0	0	1	1 (north)
Royal Albert	0			2 (single)
St. Bernard's	1			2 (single)
St. Johnstone	0	0	1	0
St. Mirren	3	0	1	
Stenhousemuir	0	0	1	2 (single)
Stirling Albion	0	0	0	0
Stranraer	0	0	1	1 (south)
Third Lanark	2	0		
Vale of Leven	3			1 (single)

The Scottish Cup was withheld in 1908/09 following 2–2 and 1–1 draws between Celtic and Rangers in the final.

CYPRUS

Scotland has a 100% record against Cyprus, having won all four games played against them. The game in February 1989 was a close-run thing however, for Scotland needed six minutes of extra time before they scored the winner.

1968	11 Dec	Nicosia	5–0	Gilzean (2) Stein (2) Murdoch	
1969	17 May	Hampden Park	8–0	Stein (4) Gray McNeill Henderson Gemmell	
1989	8 Feb	Limassol	3–2	Gough (2) Johnston	Koliandris Ioannou
1989	26 Apr	Hampden Park	2–1	Johnston McCoist	Nicolaou

CZECHOSLOVAKIA

This country no longer exists, being now divided into the Czech Republic and Slovakia. Scotland beat them twice to qualify for the World Cup finals in 1973 and 1977, but the Czechs won on a play-off in 1961. (Czechoslovakia went on to reach the World Cup final in Chile the following year.) All in all, Scotland played them 10 times, winning five, drawing one and losing four.

1937	15 May	Prague	3–1	Simpson McPhail Gillick	Puc
1937	8 Dec	Hampden Park	5–0	McCulloch (2) Black Buchanan Kinnear	
1961	14 May	Bratislava	0–4		Pospichal (2) Kvasnak Kadraba
1961	26 Sep	Hampden Park	3–2	Law (2) St. John	Kvasnak Scherer
1961	29 Nov	Brussels	2–4 aet	St. John (2)	Hledik Scherer Pospichal Kvasnak
1972	2 July	Porto Alegre	0–0		
1973	26 Sep	Hampden Park	2–1	Holton Jordan	Nehoda
1973	17 Oct	Bratislava	0–1		Nehoda (pen)
1976	13 Oct	Prague	0–2		Panenka Petras
1977	21 Sep	Hampden Park	3–1	Jordan Hartford Dalglish	Gajdusek (pen)

CZECH REPUBLIC

All outings against this talented team have been defeats.

1999	31 Mar	Celtic Park	1–2	Jess	Elliott o.g. Smicer
1999	9 June	Prague	2–3	Ritchie Johnston	Repka Kuka Koller
2008	30 May	Prague	1–3	Clarkson	Sionko (2) Kadlec

Ian St John, seen here on under-23 duty with Matt Busby, twice was on the score sheet against Czechoslovakia.

DAILLY Christian (1973 –)

Scotland Caps: 67
Scottish Cup medals: 1
Scottish League Cup medals: 1

Christian Dailly is a defensive midfielder who was an established internationalist for Scotland between 1997 and 2008. He was born in Dundee, and first made a name for himself in Jim McLean's Dundee United side of the early 1990s. The highlight of his career with Dundee United was his winning of the Scottish Cup in 1994. He moved to Derby County in 1996, Blackburn Rovers in 1998, and West Ham United in 2000. His international appearances included three games in the World Cup finals of 1998 in France, but he earned a certain notoriety when his somewhat forthright opinions of the German team were overheard on television, while Berti Vogts was being interviewed after a European Championship qualifier in Dortmund on 10 September 2003. In January 2008 he moved to Rangers.

DALGLISH Kenny (1950 –)

Scotland Caps: 102
Scottish League Championship medals: 4
Scottish Cup medals: 4
Scottish League Cup medals: 1

Kenny Dalglish, in the opinion of many people, is the most famous Scottish player of the last fifty years. He gained 102 Scottish Caps between 1971 and 1987, and appeared in the World Cup finals of 1974, 1978 and 1982. He was always the consummate professional on and off the field, and failed to live up to his expectations only because the expectations were too high. He was a disappointment in particular in Argentina in 1978, although his name was conspicuously absent from the list of those dubbed troublemakers. He was a centre forward with a great eye for goal, but also with the ability to lead the line. He joined Celtic in 1967, and really made his mark at the start of the 1971/72 season. From then until 1977 he was seldom absent from the Celtic side, being one of those players who tended to be lucky enough to avoid injury. He had the misfortune to play in a Celtic team which was in decline, but he did a great deal to arrest and slow down that decline.

His transfer to Liverpool in 1977 at £440,000 was a record between British clubs, a source of tremendous distress to Celtic supporters, and the cause of a loss of credibility for Jock Stein. For Liverpool, the success (agonising for some Scottish supporters) continued – three European Cup-Winners' medals, six English League championship medals, four English League Cup medals and one FA Cup medal. In particular, the famous picture of Kenny jumping over the advertising hoardings in the 1978 European Cup Final at Wembley haunts Scottish supporters, for here was Scotland's most talented player winning a European trophy for an English club when he could not win the World Cup for Scotland. On several occasions he was also voted the Player of the Year in England. His playing days over, he became Liverpool's player-manager, and subsequently managed Blackburn Rovers, Newcastle United and, briefly on a temporary basis, Celtic in 2000 after the sacking of John Barnes. Like all great players, he has his detractors. In particular, the Celtic fans often felt short-changed by him, but no one can deny his superb ability and always-positive attitude to the game. He was in every way a credit to the game and to his country, and continues to be so.

DALLAS Hugh (1957 –)

Hugh Dallas, who comes from Bonkle near Motherwell, is one of Scotland's best-known and most respected referees. His first European match was in 1988, when he was a linesman in the European Cup-Winners' Cup-tie between Sampdoria and Carl Zeiss Jena. This was the start of a journey that saw him refereeing at the World Cup finals of 1998 and 2002, as well as the Euro 2000 competition. In 2002 he was the fourth official at the World Cup final. In 2001 he was invited to referee a World Cup qualifying fixture between Uruguay and Brazil in Montevideo, which demonstrates the respect in which he is held throughout the world. The match was a magnificent game, and free of controversy. He retired 'at the top' in 2005, but still speaks affectionately of his first match in charge, when Motherwell Bridgeworks played Victoria.

DEANS John (Dixie) (1946 –)

Scotland Caps: 2
Scottish League Championship medals: 3
Scottish Cup medals: 2
Scottish League Cup medals: 1

A remarkable scorer of goals for Celtic, in particular in the early 1970s, John Deans' tally was 124 in 184 appearances. He joined Celtic from Motherwell in October 1971 with a bad disciplinary record, and when he was in the middle of a suspension, but he immediately became hugely popular with the Celtic fans. The nadir of his Celtic career, however, came in the semi-final of the European Cup, against Inter Milan on 19 April 1972, when he was the only player of ten to miss in the penalty shoot-out. Seventeen days later, however, he became an immortal when he scored a hat-trick in the 1972 Scottish Cup final against Hibs, thereby equalling the achievement of Jimmy Quinn in 1904. He also scored a hat-trick against the same opponents on 26 October 1974 in the Scottish League Cup final. On 17 November, against Partick Thistle, he scored six goals, a post-war record for Celtic. He was twice capped for Scotland in 1974, and subsequently played for Luton Town, Carlisle and Partick Thistle.

DEBACLES

There are probably four outstanding debacles, plus many minor ones, in Scottish football history. One was the Scotland versus England game on 17 March 1888 when Scotland, who had beaten England the previous year, appalled the country by going down 0–5 at the First Hampden Park in a performance that was described as listless and complacent.

Complacency was also a contributory cause to the World Cup fiasco of 1954 when Scotland, with only 13 players in the squad and a manager who resigned half way through, lost respectably 0–1 to Austria, but then held themselves up to scorn and ridicule with a 0–7 defeat to Uruguay. 1961 brought a Scotland team that looked good on paper to Wembley for a 9–3 thrashing which might well have been double figures, and then there was the World Cup of 1978 in Argentina. The Scotland team were talented and confident with an exuberant manager, but complained about the accommodation once they got there, wanted more money, and failed to do some elementary research on their opponents Peru and Iran. The results were catastrophic, and if that was not bad enough, one of the players was sent home for taking illegal substances. (See **ARGENTINA 1978**)

Other debacles worth a mention, although perhaps not as traumatic as the four previously mentioned, were three other defeats to England – the 2–7 defeat at Wembley in 1955, the 1–5 defeat at the same venue in 1975, and the 0–5 defeat at Hampden in 1973 in a game that was meant to mark the centenary of the SFA. There was also the 0–1 defeat by the 'banana republic' of Costa Rica in 1990, and Celtic's two disastrous foreign expeditions – one to South America in quest of the World Club Championship in 1967, and the European

Dixie Deans is congratulated by Evan Williams, with trainer Neilly Mochan in attendance, after the 6-0 victory over Hibernian in the Scottish Cup final, 1972.

Cup final of 1970. Yet Scottish football has always shown its ability to bounce back.

DEBUTS

A debut (a word borrowed from French society language) refers to the first appearance of a player. See **AGE** for the ages of debutants. Many players have marked their debut by scoring goals or even hat-tricks. The most remarkable debut in Scottish football must be that of James Dyet who made his first appearance for King's Park, a now defunct Stirling team, against Forfar Athletic in the Scottish League Division Two on 2 January 1930. King's Park won 12–2 and Dyet scored eight of the goals

Joe Craig of Celtic enjoyed a most unusual international debut for Scotland against Sweden on 27 April 1977 in that he scored a goal before he kicked a ball. He was brought on as a substitute in the seventy-sixth minute in his one and only international cap, and headed a goal three minutes later!

DEFEATS

No team has ever played a whole season without at least one defeat. Even the Rangers team of 1898/99 that managed a 100% record in the Scottish League lost to Celtic in the Scottish Cup final of that year. The previous year, Celtic had been undefeated in the league, but had drawn three times, and lost to Third Lanark in the Scottish Cup. In season 1967/68 both Celtic and Rangers went through the whole season with only one defeat, Celtic winning the title on the basis of having drawn three times, as distinct from the five draws that Rangers recorded. Even more remarkably, Rangers' one defeat came in their last game of the season, at home to Aberdeen. The teams with the best records of avoiding defeat in a league season are as follows:

Scottish Premier League	Celtic	2001/02	1 defeat
Scottish League Premier Division	Celtic	1987/88	3 defeats
	Rangers	1995/96	3 defeats
Scottish League Division One	Celtic	1897/98	0 defeats
	Rangers	1898/99	0 defeats
	In both these seasons only 18 games were played		
	Rangers	1920/21	1 defeat
	Celtic	1967/68	1 defeat
	Rangers	1967/68	1 defeat
Scottish League Division Two	Clyde	1956/57	1 defeat
	Morton	1966/67	1 defeat
	St Mirren	1967/68	1 defeat
Scottish League First Division	St Mirren	1976/77	2 defeats
Scottish League Second Division	Raith Rovers	1975/76	1 defeat
Scottish League Third Division	Gretna	2004/05	2 defeats

In the Scottish Cup, the record for consecutive lack of defeats belongs to Celtic, who lost to Hearts on 24 February 1906 and not again until the semi-finals of 12 March 1910, when they went down to Clyde. In the meantime they won the Scottish Cup in both 1906/07 and 1907/08, and the cup was withheld in 1908/09, making a total of twenty-four games without defeat.

At the other end of the spectrum, the following teams hold the record for the most defeats in a season:

Scottish Premier League	St Johnstone	2001/02	27 defeats
Scottish League Premier Division	Morton	1984/85	29 defeats
Scottish League Division One	St Mirren	1920/21	31 defeats
	Lochgelly United	1923/24	30 defeats
	Brechin City	1962/63	30 defeats
	Forfar Athletic	1974/75	30 defeats
Scottish League First Division	Cowdenbeath	1992/93	34 defeats
Scottish League Second Division	Stranraer	1997/98	27 defeats
Scottish League Third Division	East Stirlingshire	2003/04	32 defeats

Scottish fans taste defeat in Euro 96 against the Auld Enemy at Wembley.

DEFENSIVE RECORDS

It is often said that the prevention of another team from scoring is not a particularly outstanding trait in the Scottish game, with its traditional emphasis on 'blood and thunder' attacking. Nevertheless, teams who have been able to restrict the goals against have usually done very well. Rangers' 'Iron Curtain' defence of the cold war era, in which Young, Woodburn, Cox and others conceded very few goals, and the twin centre-half pairing of Miller and McLeish at Aberdeen in the 1980s, are good examples. At the same time, there was the Dundee United defence of Malpas, Hegarty and Narey, which ensured that the club had consistent success in European competitions. The best defensive records (i.e. conceding the fewest goals) in Scottish domestic competitions are as follows:

Scottish Premier League	Celtic	2001/02	18
Scottish League Premier Division	Rangers	1989/90	19
Scottish League First Division	Dundee	1902/03	12
This is the record, but only 22 games were played in season 1902/03. Credit should perhaps also be given to Celtic in 1913/14, who conceded only 14 goals in 38 games			
Scottish League Second Division	Morton	1966/67	20
Scottish League Third Division	Brechin City	1995/96	21

Two teams (Queen's Park in 1874 and Celtic in 1911) have won the Scottish Cup without conceding a goal.

Three teams (Aberdeen in 1985/86, Celtic in 1997/98, and Celtic in 1999/2000) have won the Scottish League Cup without conceding a goal.

Queen's Park can claim to have gone seven and a half years without losing a goal. They were founded in July 1867 and did not lose a goal until 16 January 1875, when Vale of Leven breached their defence. However, they did not play many games in this period.

DELANEY Jimmy (1914 – 1989)

Scotland Caps: 13
Scottish League Championship medals: 2
Scottish Cup medals: 1

Jimmy Delaney was one of the real romantic figures of British football history, in that he won a Scottish Cup medal with Celtic in 1937, an English FA Cup medal with Manchester United in 1948, and an Irish Cup medal with Derry City in 1954 – three medals in three countries in three decades. He almost made it four with Cork Athletic in 1956, but they lost in the final of the FAI Cup. He was a speedy right winger, and had four very successful seasons with Celtic in the late 1930s until he broke his arm very badly in April 1939, thereby losing a couple of seasons to injury. He was transferred to Manchester United in 1946, and then subsequently played for Aberdeen, Falkirk, Derry City, Cork Athletic and Elgin City, before finally retiring in 1957. He played thirteen times for Scotland, at least twice with distinction. One occasion was the game at Ibrox in 1936,

when he scored the two goals that 'put Hitler off his tea' as Scotland beat Germany 2–0, and the other was the goal he scored in the (unofficial) Victory International of 1946, to bring joy to a football-starved nation. His son Pat played for Motherwell and Dunfermline Athletic in the 1960s, and his grandson is John Kennedy of Celtic.

DENMARK

Scotland have played Denmark on fourteen occasions, having won eight and lost six. There has never been a draw. Scotland beat them the first four times they played, but after two Scotland victories in 1975 the Danes have emerged on top.

1951	12 May	Hampden Park	3–1	Steel Reilly Mitchell	Hansen
1952	25 May	Copenhagen	2–1	Thornton Reilly	Rasmussen
1968	16 Oct	Copenhagen	1–0	Lennox	
1970	11 Nov	Hampden Park	1–0	O'Hare	
1971	9 June	Copenhagen	0–1		Laudrup
1972	18 Oct	Copenhagen	4–1	Macari Bone Harper Morgan	Laudrup
1972	15 Nov	Hampden Park	2–0	Dalglish Lorimer	
1975	3 Sep	Copenhagen	1–0	Harper	
1975	29 Oct	Hampden Park	3–1	Dalglish Rioch MacDougall	Bastrup
1986	4 June	Nezahualcoyotl	0–1		Elkjaer-Larsen
1996	24 Apr	Copenhagen	0–2		M. Laudrup B. Laudrup
1998	25 Mar	Ibrox	0–1		B. Laudrup
2002	21 Aug	Hampden Park	0–1		Sand
2004	28 Apr	Copenhagen	0–1		Sand

DERBIES

Derby fixtures add spice to the season. The origin of this use of the word is uncertain, but it is defined in the Chambers Dictionary as "a sporting fixture of strong local interest" and it is used when two local teams clash. New Year's Day in Scotland was the traditional day for Rangers versus Celtic, Hearts versus Hibs, Dundee versus Aberdeen (not Dundee United, who would play St. Johnstone on that day, then Dundee on 2 January), and hosts of other local games, such as Arbroath versus Forfar, East Fife versus Raith Rovers, Partick Thistle versus Clyde, and Ayr United versus Kilmarnock. Such games were keenly contested and the phrase 'bragging rights' has come to be applied to the supporters of those who won the fixture. In recent years, the New Year fixture is not necessarily a 'derby'. There are several reasons for this. One is the fear of disorder at a time when local constabularies are undermanned, and another is that it can no longer be guaranteed that the teams will be in the same division.

It is also worth remembering the derby matches of days gone by, when fans eagerly anticipated fixtures involving clubs that are no longer part of the Scottish League. (see **FORMER LEAGUE CLUBS**). Some local clashes in the Scottish League used to be:

Ayrshire	Ayr FC v Ayr Parkhouse or Kilmarnock Ayr Parkhouse v Ayr FC
Dunbartonshire (& Nearby Area)	Clydebank v Dumbarton or Partick Thistle Renton v Dumbarton or Vale of Leven Vale of Leven v Dumbarton or Renton
Edinburgh	Leith Athletic v Hearts, Hibernian, or St. Bernard's St. Bernard's v Hearts, Hibernian or Leith Athletic
Fife	Lochgelly United v Cowdenbeath, Dunfermline Athletic or East Fife
Glasgow	Third Lanark v Celtic, Clyde, Partick Thistle, Queen's Park or Rangers
Renfrewshire	Abercorn v Arthurlie, Johnstone or St. Mirren Arthurlie v Abercorn or Johnstone Johnstone v Abercorn or Arthurlie Port Glasgow Athletic v Morton
West Lothian	Armadale v Bathgate, Bo'ness or Broxburn Utd Bathgate v Armadale, Bo'ness or Broxburn Utd Bo'ness v Armadale, Bathgate, Broxburn Utd or Falkirk Broxburn Utd v Armadale, Bathgate or Bo'ness

John Greig celebrates after Celtic's Young put through his own goal in the 1965 League Cup final at Hampden. It was Celtic, though, who lifted the trophy with a 2-1 win.

DISASTERS

There have been two really sad days in Scotland's football history – by sheer coincidence, both of them at Ibrox Stadium. Yet as far as crowd disasters are concerned, it was only by the 'Grace of God' that more such things have not happened. Hampden Park when housing an over 100,000 crowd was by no means a safe place to be, and apparently at half time in the European Cup semi-final of 1970 between Celtic and Leeds United, Jock Stein confided to his opposite number Don Revie that he was worried about the amount of swaying on the dangerously overcrowded East Terracing. Fortunately no fatalities or serious injuries occurred on that particular night.

The first Ibrox Disaster happened on 5 April 1902 at the Scotland versus England game. Behind what is now the Broomloan Road end of the ground was a wooden stand, and by 'stand' it meant what it said in that people stood to watch the game, having climbed a wooden staircase to do so. The 'stand' was about 20 feet above the ground. The floor of the stand was made of wood, and the timbers had been rotted by Glasgow's extensive rainfall. The creaking of the timbers was not looked upon to be particularly significant – in fact if anything it added to the atmosphere of the occasion. Some time in the first half a cross ball was sent to Bobby Templeton on Scotland's left wing. The crowd followed the ball and the weight shifted from one part of the stand to the other. The floorboards gave way and 25 people either fell to their deaths or were crushed in the ensuing panic. Another 25 were seriously injured and over 400 were slightly injured. The game continued, the authorities thinking that abandonment would cause more panic (for there was in 1902 a justified fear of anarchist terrorism) but the game was declared unofficial and a replay was held at Villa Park a month later.

This disaster shocked Edwardian Glasgow to its core and although Rangers won the Scottish Cup in the following year 1903, they did not do so again until twenty-five years later in 1928. Many people thought that the reason for this was a 'haunting' by some of the spirits of the dead of the disaster in 1902!

The second Ibrox disaster took place on 2 January 1971 at the end of the Rangers versus Celtic game. For a long time, it was believed that because Celtic scored late in the game, the Rangers fans started to go home but when Rangers immediately equalized some tried to come back and met other fans coming down the stairway, but this is not the case. It was simply that the barriers on Stairway 13 had been suffering from metal fatigue for some time and quite simply gave way. Sixty-six fans were either crushed or trampled to death. Yet this disaster now looks as if it had been coming for some time. Ten years previously on 16 September 1961 (again after an Old Firm game) two fans had met their death in similar circumstances, and there had been another warning with a few injuries on New Year's Day 1969. To their credit, Rangers, in the wake of this disaster, were one of the first teams in Great Britain to build an all-seater stadium ten years later.

DISCIPLINE

This is the province of the SFA, which deals with disciplinary matters in every competition. The key number of penalty points is eighteen. A sending off carries an automatic suspension for the next game, and also twelve, eight, or five points according to the severity of the offence. 'Serious foul play' for example carries twelve points, 'offensive, abusive or insulting language' is eight, whereas the so-called 'professional foul' of attempting to deny an opponent a goalscoring opportunity is five. A caution or a yellow card is normally three, so a sending off for two yellow cards would be six. Once the eighteen points have been reached, a trip to the Disciplinary Committee is necessary, and they may award fines or suspensions as they consider appropriate. The procedure varies slightly in the Scottish Cup, the Scottish League Cup, the SPL and the SFL, and normally suspensions incurred in international matches and European competitions have no bearing on domestic competitions.

DOCHERTY Tommy (1928 –)

Scotland Caps: 25

Tommy Docherty was one of the really charismatic figures of Scottish football. A wing half, he began his senior career for Celtic in 1948, but very soon moved to Preston North End and then Arsenal. He won twenty-five Scottish international caps between 1952 and 1959, and participated in both the 1954 and 1958 World Cup campaigns (although not in the finals in 1958). His greatest achievement lay in his playing for, and captaining, the side that beat Switzerland and Spain to qualify for the World Cup in Sweden in 1958. He captained Scotland on many occasions, but was never in a Scottish team that beat England. Throughout his subsequent colourful managerial career, in which it was

Skippers Tommy Docherty of Scotland and Billy Wright of England lead out their teams for an international at Hampden in April 1958.

said that he 'had more clubs than golfer Jack Nicklaus', his patriotism and love of Scotland were never in any doubt, although he was one of the Scottish managers of English clubs who were much criticised for refusing to release Scotland players before important games. In September 1971 he became the Scotland team manager to general delight, and certainly played his part in setting Scotland on the road for qualification to the 1974 World Cup, before, to the distress of his many admirers, finding the attraction of Manchester United too strong for him in December 1972. Five years later, a liaison with a physiotherapist's wife at Old Trafford led to his departure.

DODDS Billy (1969 –)

Scotland Caps: 26
Scottish Premier League medals: 2
Scottish Cup medals: 1
Scottish League Cup medals: 2

A man of many clubs and twenty-six caps for Scotland, Billy Dodds is one of the few players to have played for the three Tayside clubs of Dundee United (twice), Dundee and St Johnstone. Always a dangerous striker and predatory attacker, he also had spells at Rangers, Aberdeen, Partick Thistle (twice) and Chelsea, and was well regarded by all the clubs he played for. He had a degree of success everywhere that he went, winning for example a League Cup medal with both Aberdeen and Rangers. He now works as a commentator on radio and television, and owns a racehorse.

DOIG Ned (1866 – 1919)

Scotland Caps: 5

Ned Doig was one of the great personality goalkeepers of the late nineteenth and early twentieth century. He shares with four others the distinction of being one the first Anglo-Scots included in a Scotland team (4 April 1896). He started his career by playing for Arbroath, but moved to Sunderland in 1890. He played fourteen years for the Wearsiders, in their great side that won four

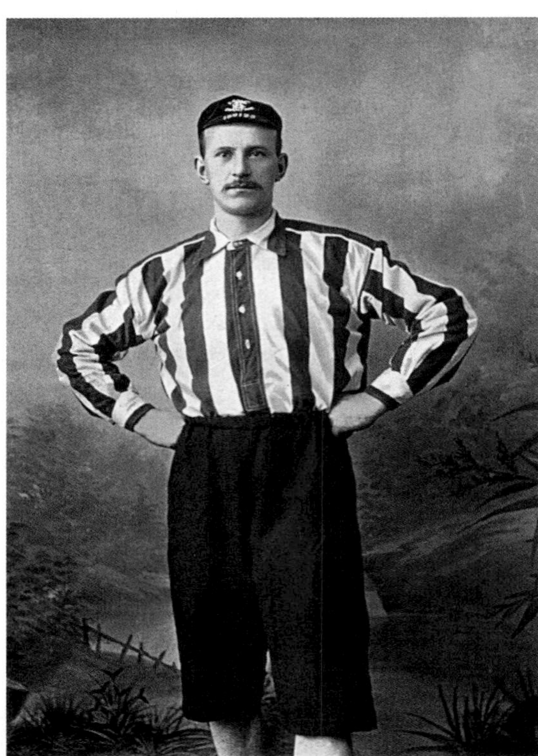

English League championships, and then in 1904 he moved to Liverpool, with whom he won the second division championship. He played for Scotland five times, and this might have been more if it had not been for the attitude of the Sunderland management, who often refused to release him. His most famous international was the England versus Scotland game at Bramall Lane, Sheffield in 1903 when, almost single-handedly, he defied a strong England team and allowed the hard-working Scottish side to win 2–1.

DONACHIE Willie (1951 –)

Scotland Caps: 35

A left back who played thirty-five times for Scotland in the mid-1970s, including the games against Iran and Holland in the Argentina World Cup of 1978, Willie Donachie was a respected player, but will always be remembered for an own goal that he scored in the game against Wales prior to the departure for Argentina. The bulk of his career was with Manchester City, with whom he won the English League Cup in 1976, but he also played in the USA, and had spells with Norwich City, Burnley and Oldham Athletic.

Willie Woodburn heads clear from a Clyde attack in the 1949 Scottish Cup final which Rangers won 4-1. Rangers became the first club to win the League championship, the Scottish Cup and the League Cup in the same season.

DOUBLES

A double of winning the Scottish League (i.e. being champions of Scotland, whether it be the old Division One, the Premier Division or the Scottish Premier League) and Scottish Cup in the same season is not such a rare phenomenon in Scotland as it is in England.. Celtic first achieved it in 1907, after it was commonly believed that such a feat was impossible. Rangers however have achieved a double on a record sixteen occasions – 1928, 1930, 1934, 1935, 1949, 1953, 1963, 1964, 1976, 1978, 1992, 1993, 1996, 1999, 2000 and 2003, whereas Celtic have done it on fourteen occasions - 1907, 1908, 1914, 1954, 1967, 1969, 1971, 1972, 1974, 1977, 1988, 2001, 2004 and 2007. The only other team to win such a double is Aberdeen, who did it in 1984.

The advent of the Scottish League Cup after world war two has made it possible to win a treble (See **TREBLES**), but teams who have won a double of the Scottish League and the Scottish League Cup (but not the Scottish Cup) in the same season include Rangers who have done it eight times in 1947, 1961, 1987, 1989, 1991, 1994, 1997 and 2005. Celtic have won this particular double five times in 1966,1968,1970 1998 and 2006. Hearts achieved this feat in 1960. East Fife managed a remarkable and unique double in season 1947/48 when they managed to win the Scottish League Cup and the Scottish League Division Two.

Rangers in 1962, Celtic in 1975, Rangers in 1979, Aberdeen in 1986 and 1990, and Rangers in 2002 and 2008 achieved the double of winning both the Scottish Cup and the Scottish League Cup, but not the league.

DRAWS

A draw is often considered to be a disappointing result, particularly for the home side, and the introduction of three points for a win in the mid 1990s was an effort to deter teams from settling for a draw, which still offered one point. The record for drawn games in Scotland for a season is shared between Aberdeen and East Fife, who have both managed twenty-one draws out of forty-four games. Aberdeen did this in the Scottish League Premier Division in 1993/94, and East Fife in the Scottish League First Division in 1986/87.

The highest draw is a Scottish Cup tie on 8 September 1883 when Queen on the South Wanderers and South Kirkcubrightshire Rifle Volunteers drew 7–7 at Hunholm in Dumfries, and on two occasions in the Scottish League there has been a 6–6 draw. These were Queen of the South versus Falkirk in Division A on 20 September 1947, and Motherwell versus Dumbarton in Division B on 10 April 1954.

DRUMMOND Jock (1870 – 1935)

Scotland Caps: 14
Scottish League Championship medals: 3
Scottish Cup medals: 4

Jock Drummond was a left back for Falkirk and Rangers who won fourteen caps for Scotland. He joined Falkirk as a teenager in 1886, and joined Rangers in 1892. With them he won many honours, and was part of the

Rangers team that won four league championships in a row from 1899-1902. He was half of the potent full back partnership with Nick Smith, before he returned to Falkirk in 1904. His international career included wins over England in 1896 and 1900. In later years he was a director with Falkirk.

DRYBURGH CUP

This was a pre-season tournament that was little lamented when it disappeared. The problem was that although the weather was good, and the attendances tolerable, clubs resented having to start as early as July. In addition, people felt that the clubs were already playing each other too often. This was especially so in the second spell of the Dryburgh Cup's existence in the late 1970s when, with the advent of the Premier Division, clubs were already playing each other at least four times. For many clubs a friendly match against an English team appeared a more sensible option. The winners were:

1971	Aberdeen	1972	Hibernian	1973	Hibernian
1974	Celtic	1975	No competition	1976	No competition
1977	No competition	1978	Rangers	1979	Rangers
1980	Aberdeen				

DUMBARTON FC

Ground: **Strathclyde Homes Stadium**
Nickname: **The Sons**
Colours: **White, black and gold**
Record Attendance: **18,000 at Boghead Park v Raith Rovers (1957)**
2,011 at Strathclyde Homes Stadium v Morton (2004)
Record Victory: **13-1 v Kirkintilloch (1888)**
Record Defeat: **1-11 v Albion Rovers (1926); v Ayr United (1952)**
Highest League Position: **Joint 1st (1890/91) 1st (1891/92)**
Best Scottish Cup Performance: **Winners (1882/83)**
Best League Cup Performance: **Last 4 (Semi-finals, 1970/71)**

Dumbarton's Strathclyde Homes Stadium is overlooked by the famous Dumbarton Rock and is a regular venue for Scotland's national squad training sessions.

In the early days of Scottish football, Dumbarton was one of the country's major clubs. Founded in 1872, they had appeared in six Scottish Cup finals by 1897, although their only victory was a 2–1 defeat of Vale of Leven in 1883. Following this match they played Blackburn Olympic for the so-called 'Championship of Britain' and won 6–1.

The club was one of the founder members of the Scottish League in 1890/91 and finished joint top with Rangers. In the days before goal average was taken into account there was a play-off to decide the title and, after it finished in a 2–2 draw, the two clubs were declared joint champions. The following season Dumbarton won the championship outright.

Only five years later the picture looked very different. In 1895/96 the club finished bottom of Division One for the second consecutive season and was voted into Division Two. Then they finished bottom of Division Two in 1896/97 and, despite reaching the final of the Scottish Cup, failed to gain re-election to the Scottish League at all.

They were not re-admitted until 1906, but then enjoyed a successful spell that culminated in promotion in 1913. Strangely, they finished sixth that year and were elected to Division One, whereas when they finished top in 1911 they failed to gain promotion. This second period in the top flight came to an end with relegation in 1922, and then the Sons began fifty years in the second tier that were only interrupted by a season in Division C after finishing bottom in 1954.

Things finally changed for the better in the early 1970s, under manager Jackie Stewart. In 1970/71 they drew 0–0 with Celtic in the semi-finals of the League Cup and only lost the replay 4–3 after extra time. The following season they finally returned to Division One after finishing top of Division Two, with Kenny Wilson scoring a record thirty-eight goals in the league. There then followed three relatively successful seasons and their time in the top division only came to an end when the league was reconstructed in 1975. By finishing in fourteenth place the Sons became members of the First Division (second tier).

They escaped for a single season in the Premier Division in 1984/85, but by 1988 there had been two relegations and the club was in the Second Division (third tier). The Second Division championship was won in 1991/92, but then league re-construction intervened once again and in 1994 the club found itself back in the Second Division (third tier). Player-coach Murdo MacLeod led the club to promotion in 1995 and this brought one more season in the First Division, but since 1996 the club has played its football in either the Second Division or the Third Division (fourth tier).

The year 2000 brought a milestone in the club's history when the Sons moved to the purpose-built Strathclyde Homes Stadium. Situated beneath Dumbarton Rock, their new home brings them closer to the place that gives them the name 'Sons of the Rock'. In 2001/02 a second-place finish in the Third Division brought promotion, but after four seasons in the third tier the Sons slipped back down again.

DUMBARTON HARP FC
(former Scottish League club)

Home: **Meadow Park, Dumbarton**
Highest League Position: **50th (10th in Div. 3, 1923/24)**
Best Scottish Cup Performance: **Last 64 (1st round 1921/22; 1923/24)**

The club was a member of the Scottish League for less than two seasons. In the 1920s there was a Division Three from 1923 until 1926 and Harp was a founder member. At the end of the 1923/24 season the club finished in mid-table, but the following year they weren't even able to complete their fixtures and went out of existence.

Dumbarton Harp FC is thought to have been founded by Irish immigrants in 1894, although the date is uncertain. The early years were spent playing friendly matches and cup-ties, and at one point the club participated in the Glasgow Junior League. In 1908 they became members of the Scottish Union, a league that included the reserve teams of some first division clubs, and in 1909/10 they won the championship. Harp remained in the Scottish Union until it was disbanded in 1915, when they joined the newly formed Western League, and in 1918/19 they won the championship of this league too.

Along with other members of the Western League, Harp became members of Division Three in 1923, but results were poor and crowds were low. By early 1925 financial problems were so severe that the club was having difficulty in meeting the guaranteed payments for visiting teams, and they resigned from the Scottish League after just seventeen matches. Their record was expunged, and Dumbarton Harp joined the ranks of Scotland's defunct clubs.

DUNBAR UNITED FC (see JUNIOR FOOTBALL)

DUNBARTONSHIRE CUP

The Dunbartonshire Cup competition was created upon the formation of the Dunbartonshire Football Association in 1884, and survived until the beginning of the second world war. (Note the different spelling for the town of Dumbarton and the county of Dunbartonshire).

1884/85	Dumbarton	1903/04	No competition	1922/23	Dumbarton
1885/86	Vale of Leven	1904/05	Vale of Leven	1923/24	Clydebank
1886/87	Renton	1905/06	Vale of Leven	1924/25	Helensburgh
1887/88	Vale of Leven	1906/07	Vale of Leven	1925/26	Dumbarton
1888/89	Dumbarton	1907/08	Renton	1926/27	Helensburgh
1889/90	Dumbarton	1908/09	Dumbarton	1927/28	Clydebank
1890/91	Dumbarton	1909/10	Dumbarton Harp	1928/29	Clydebank
1891/92	Dumbarton	1910/11	Vale of Leven	1929/30	Dumbarton
1892/93	Dumbarton	1911/12	Dumbarton Harp	1930/31	Dumbarton
1893/94	Dumbarton	1912/13	Dumbarton Harp	1931/32	Dumbarton
1894/95	Dumbarton	1913/14	Renton	1932/33	Dumbarton
1895/96	Renton	1914/15	Dumbarton	1933/34	Vale Ocoba *
1896/97	Vale of Leven	1915/16	Clydebank	1934/35	Vale Ocoba *
1897/98	Dumbarton	1916/17	Clydebank	1935/36	Dumbarton
1898/99	Dumbarton	1917/18	Clydebank	1936/37	Dumbarton
1899/00	Vale of Leven	1918/19	Clydebank	1937/38	No competition
1900/01	Vale of Leven	1919/20	Clydebank	1938/39	No competition
1901/02	Vale of Leven	1920/21	Dumbarton	1939/40	Dumbarton
1902/03	No competition	1921/22	Dumbarton		

* Vale of Leven Old Church Old Boys Association

DUNCAN Douglas (Dally) (1909 – 1990)

Scotland Caps: 14

Douglas Duncan was an outstanding outside left who played fourteen times for Scotland in the late 1930s, and scored seven goals for them. His most famous game was the one against England in 1935, when he scored twice

from Charlie Napier corner kicks. He was born in Aberdeen, and then joined Hull City in 1928 before being transferred to Derby County in 1932 for £2,000. He was still with Derby County in the first season after the second world war, when they won the FA Cup.

DUNDEE FC

Ground: **Dens Park**
Nickname: **The Dark Blues**
Colours: **Dark blue, with red and white**
Record Attendance: **43,024 v Rangers (1953)**
Record Victory: **10-0 v Alloa (1947); v Dunfermline (1947)**
Record Defeat: **0-11 v Celtic (1895)**
Highest League Position: **1st (1961/62)**
Best Scottish Cup Performance: **Winners (1909/10)**
Best League Cup Performance: **Winners (1951/52; 1952/53; 1973/74)**

Dundee FC was founded in 1893, when Our Boys and East End amalgamated to form a new club. Although this was the year that the first Division Two was incorporated into the Scottish League, they were elected straight into Division One, along with St. Bernard's, to replace the relegated Abercorn and Clyde. They played briefly at West Craigie Park before moving to Carolina Port, where they stayed until the opening of Dens Park in August 1899, and Dundee soon established themselves as one of Scotland's leading clubs. The Scottish Cup was won in 1910, when Clyde were beaten 2–1 at Ibrox after a 0–0 draw, and by 1914 they had only once finished the season outside the top ten clubs.

In 1917, with Scotland facing wartime transport difficulties, Dundee was deemed 'remote' and, along with Aberdeen and Raith Rovers, the club left the Scottish League for two seasons. Whilst they were away they won the Eastern League in 1917/18, and then they celebrated their return to the national league with three consecutive top-four finishes. There was also another cup final appearance in 1925, but this ended with a 2–1 defeat to Celtic. Performance then tailed off in the 1930s, and in 1938 the club was relegated for the first time. There was one season in the lower division before the second world war and two seasons following it but, after promotion in 1947, Dundee was a member of Division One all the way through to league reconstruction in 1975.

In 1950 manager George Anderson signed Billy Steel from Derby County. The fee was a Scottish record at the time, but Dundee acquired a man who was a national celebrity. It is said that crowds increased by thousands wherever he played and he helped Dundee win the League Cup in two consecutive seasons. There was a 3–2 victory over Rangers in the 1951/52 final and twelve months later Kilmarnock were beaten 2–0. Dundee almost always finished in the top ten of the league during the 1950s, but the club's finest hour came when they won the 1961/62 league championship under manager Bob Shankly.

This brought qualification for the European Cup and a campaign that became a showcase for the goal scoring talents of Alan Gilzean. There was a hat-trick against Cologne, another against Sporting Lisbon, two goals against Anderlecht in the quarter-final, and he headed the only goal of the game in the second leg of the semi-final against AC Milan. The Italians won on aggregate and went on to win the trophy. Gilzean was scoring just as freely in the league and netted seven against Queen of the South in December 1962. He was transferred to Tottenham Hotspur in 1964.

Dundee were given a place in the 1967/68 Inter-Cities Fairs Cup, despite finishing sixth in the league, when Clyde were not allowed to take part because only one representative could come from each city. Bobby Ancell's team reached the semi-finals and this time the result was a 2–1 aggregate defeat to Leeds United after a 1–1draw at Dens Park. They reached the final of the 1967/68 League Cup, losing 5–3 to Celtic, but went one better in 1973/74, beating Celtic 1–0 with a goal from Gordon Wallace.

When the league was reconstructed in 1975 Dundee were placed in the new Premier Division, but a ninth-place finish no longer ensured survival, and the club was relegated for the second time in its history after just one season. This was unfortunately a sign of things to come, and by the time of the next reconstruction in 1994 Dundee had spent a total of six seasons in the second tier, although they had also won two First Division championships.

After 1994 there were four more seasons in the First Division before promotion to the newly created Scottish Premier League in 1998 under manager Jocky Scott. This brought seven consecutive seasons in the SPL until relegation in 2005, and they proved to be an eventful chapter in the history of Dundee FC. Italian Ivano Bonetti was appointed as manager and he, together with his brother Dario, introduced a more continental approach, with an emphasis on structured training and diet. They signed high-profile foreign players such as Claudio Caniggia, who had won the World Cup with

1963: A fine view of Alan Gilzean heading a goal against Third Lanark at Cathkin Park.

Argentina, and Fan Zhiyi, the captain of the Chinese national team. The fans enjoyed some entertaining football, but the debts were mounting, and in 2003 the club went into administration for a time.

However, Dundee showed that it could bounce back. The debts were reduced and money raised by the "Dee4Life" Supporters' Trust enabled fans to have a bigger say in the running of the club. The Dark Blues reached the semi-finals of the 2005/06 Scottish Cup under manager Alan Kernaghan, but a 3–0 defeat by Gretna prevented them from reaching the final, and a few weeks later Alex Rae was unveiled as their new manager.

DUNDEE UNITED FC
(Formerly Dundee Hibernian FC)

Ground: **Tannadice Park**
Nickname: **The Terrors; The Arabs**
Colours: **Tangerine and black**
Record Attendance: **28,000 v Barcelona (1966)**
Record Victory: **14-0 v Nithsdale (1931)**
Record Defeat: **1-12 v Motherwell (1954)**
Highest League Position: **1st (1982/83)**
Best Scottish Cup Performance: **Winners (1993/94)**
Best League Cup Performance: **Winners (1979/80, 1980/81)**

In 1909 members of Dundee's Irish community formed a new football club, known as Dundee Hibernian. The new club took over Clepington Park, which was where Dundee Wanderers had been playing, and renamed it Tannadice Park. The Hibs spent the 1909/10 season in the Northern League, and were then elected into Division Two of the Scottish League in 1910. They remained there until 1915, when Division Two was abandoned because of the first world war, and reached the final of the Qualifying Cup in 1914, when they lost to Albion Rovers after two replays.

In 1915 the club switched to the Eastern League, and won the title in 1919/20. They moved again for the 1920/21 season, this time to the Central League, which included six other former members of Division Two who were no longer part of the Scottish League. In 1921 the Central League was taken under the umbrella of the Scottish League to form the basis of a new Division Two, but Dundee Hibs finished second bottom in its first season and had to leave. They replaced Celtic 'A' in the Scottish Alliance for 1922/23, and also played five fixtures in the Eastern League that season – one of them being a 1–1 away draw against Dundee 'A' on 21 April 1923.

But major changes were on the way – there was a debate about replacing the name 'Hibernian', the club colours were changed from green and white to black and white, and later that year the club was re-elected to Division Two for the 1923/24 season. Some favoured 'Dundee City' as a new name, but on 17 October 1923 the SFA approved a proposal to change to 'Dundee United'. However, older fans could still be heard shouting "C'mon the Hibs" as late as 1955.

Over the next few years, United became a 'yo-yo' club, and by 1932 they had been both promoted and relegated three times. This was then followed by many years in the lower division and it wasn't until 1960, under manager Jerry Kerr, that they achieved promotion. This, however, was the beginning of another new era. In the 1960s, not only did United change their colours to tangerine and black, they also went on to become one of Scotland's leading clubs over a period of many years and remained in the top division until 1995.

United made great progress under Jerry Kerr and in 1971 Jim McLean replaced him as manager. A long period of success followed, and from 1976 to 1993 United never finished the season outside the top five. The League Cup was won in both 1979/80 and 1980/81, with both finals taking place at nearby Dens Park. The score was 3–0 on both occasions, with Aberdeen being beaten in 1980 and Dundee the following year. Dens Park was again the venue when United won the league championship of 1982/83. The date of 14 May 1983 has gone down in United history as the day when a 2–1 victory over Dundee made Paul Hegarty one of the few captains outwith the Old Firm to hold the championship trophy aloft.

The consistently high finishes in the league brought regular qualification for Europe. When United entered the European Cup for the first time in 1983/84, they reached the semi-finals and went out 3–2 to AS Roma after a 2–0 victory at Tannadice Park. In 1986/87 they became the first Scottish club to reach the final of the UEFA Cup, only to lose 2–1 on aggregate to IFK Gothenburg. United's ties with Barcelona merit special mention. In 1966/67, on their first European adventure, they played them twice in the Inter-Cities Fairs Cup and won on both occasions. In the 1986/87 UEFA Cup, on their way to the final, they again won both home and away.

By the time Jim McLean stepped down as manager in 1993, United had appeared in six Scottish Cup finals and

Dundee United with the Premier League trophy in 1982/83.

two more League Cup finals, but none of these matches was won. All eight of these finals took place at Hampden Park and the headline writers began referring to United's 'Hampden Hoodoo', but it was a phase in United's history that would soon be at an end.

Ivan Golac became manager after Jim McLean and the Scottish Cup was finally won in 1994, when a Craig Brewster goal was enough to beat Rangers 1–0 in the final. In 1994/95 United were relegated for the first time since 1932 and Ivan Golac departed during the season. However, life in the First Division (second tier) only lasted for one season and United bounced back thanks to a play-off victory against Partick Thistle.

The years that followed were a period of mixed fortunes. The League Cup final of 1997/98 and the Scottish Cup final of 2004/05 were both reached and lost, but United found it hard to repeat the outstanding league form of previous years. Eddie Thompson acquired a controlling interest in the club in September 2002 and by October 2006 Craig Levein had become the sixth manager in just over four years. He took over a team that was facing the prospect of relegation, and turned it into one that comfortably survived the drop after taking points from fixtures against the leading clubs. In January 2008 he took on the additional role of Director of Football.

DUNDEE WANDERERS FC
(former Scottish League club)

Home: **Clepington Park, Dundee**
Highest League Position: **19th (9th in Div. 2, 1894/1895)**
Best Scottish Cup Performance: **Last 8 (6th round, 1887/1888)**

In 1885 a group broke away from the 'Our Boys' club in Dundee and formed a new club called 'Wanderers'. They entered the Scottish Cup from 1886 onwards and in 1887/88 went all the way to the sixth round, where they lost 5–1 to eventual winners Renton.

In the early 1890s the club became known as Johnstone Wanderers, and in 1892 they joined the Northern League. Two years later they combined with local rivals Strathmore and, after briefly using the name 'Dundonians', became known as 'Dundee Wanderers'. In 1894 they were elected to Division Two of the Scottish League and it was not long before they adopted amateur status (like Port Glasgow).

However, 1894/95 was to be the club's only season in the Scottish League, as they finished next to the bottom, and were not re-elected. They then rejoined the Northern League, winning the championship in 1899/1900.

The club's ground was Clepington Park, and in 1909 the lease was bought out by the newly formed Dundee Hibernian. Dundee Hibs later become Dundee United and Clepington Park became Tannadice Park. This left the Wanderers without a permanent home and they started to lose their supporters as well. They played in Lochee for a while, but the club eventually went out of existence in 1913.

DUNFERMLINE ATHLETIC FC

Ground: East End Park
Nickname: **The Pars**
Colours: **Black and white**
Record Attendance: **27,816 v Celtic (1968)**
Record Victory: **11-2 v Stenhousemuir (1930)**
Record Defeat: **1-11 v Hibs (1889); 0-10 v Dundee (1947)**
Highest League Position: **3rd (1964/65; 1968/69)**
Best Scottish Cup Performance: **Winners (1960/61; 1967/68)**
Best League Cup Performance: Runners-up: **(1949/50; 1991/92; 2005/06)**

The club's origins go back to a time when members of Dunfermline Cricket Club played football during the winter months. In 1885 the footballers broke away from the cricket club to form Dunfermline Athletic FC, and rented land from the North British Railway that became East End Park. However, some twenty-five years were to pass before the team enjoyed a series of successes that would serve as a springboard into the Scottish League. In 1910/11 they won both the championship of the Scottish Central League and the Fife Cup, and the following season they not only won the title again, they added the Scottish Qualifying Cup to the trophy cabinet. Then, when the Scottish League was expanded in 1912, the club was elected to Division Two.

There were three seasons in the Scottish League before Division Two came to an end because of the first world war, and then Dunfermline played in the Eastern League (q.v.) before becoming part of the re-formed Central League from 1919 to 1921 (see **CENTRAL LEAGUE** for 1920/21 table). They became part of the re-born Division Two in 1921, and the Pars were to spend a large part of the next forty years in the lower division. By 1957 there had been three promotions, including the Division Two title in 1926, but each one had been followed by relegation two or three years later. It was the promotion at the end of the 1957/58 season, under manager Andy Dickson, that proved to be the turning point, although it wasn't apparent on the last day of the 1958/59 season. The Pars needed a big win against Partick Thistle to avoid relegation, but they beat Thistle 10–1, with six goals from Harry Melrose, and went on to stay in the top flight until 1972.

The 1960s was a golden decade for Dunfermline Athletic, and a major factor in their success was the appointment of Jock Stein as manager in 1960. By the time he left in 1964, Celtic had been beaten 2–0 in the 1960/61 Scottish Cup final and there had been two European campaigns, including an appearance in the quarter-finals of the 1961/62 European Cup-Winners' Cup. His successors Willie Cunningham and George Farm maintained the momentum, and in the 1960s the Pars finished in the top ten of the league on nine occasions, took part in seven European campaigns, and won the Scottish Cup again in 1967/68, when Hearts were beaten 3–1. In 1968/69 they reached the semi-finals of the European Cup-Winners' Cup, before losing 2–1 on aggregate to Slovan Bratislava.

When the league was reconstructed in 1975 Dunfermline found themselves in the First Division (second tier) and, by the time it was next reconstructed in 1994, they had spent only four more seasons in the Premier Division, and there had been six seasons in the Second Division (third tier). One of the highlights of this era was when manager Jim Leishman led them to consecutive promotions from the Second Division to the Premier Division in 1986 and 1987.

Bert Paton enjoyed some success as manager in the 1990s and when the First Division championship was won in 1995/96, it was followed by three seasons in the top division. Jimmy Calderwood led them back into the Scottish Premier League in 2000, and then in 2004 a milestone was reached, when an appearance in the 2003/04 Scottish Cup final took them back into Europe for the first time since 1969/70, despite losing 3-1 to Celtic. It was something of an anticlimax when they fell at the first hurdle of the UEFA Cup to FH Hafnarfjordur of Iceland. The home leg had to be played at McDiarmid Park, Perth when UEFA ruled that the Pars' synthetic pitch was not suitable for European football.

The charismatic Jim Leishman was re-appointed as manager with just three matches of the 2004/05 season remaining. He guided the Pars to SPL survival, and also to the 2005/06 League Cup final, although Celtic beat them 3–0. In October 2006 he became Director of Football and soon afterwards Stephen Kenny arrived from Derry City to be the new manager. The Pars reached the 2006/07 Scottish Cup final and qualified for the UEFA Cup, even though they lost 1–0 to Celtic. The new manager was unable to keep them in the SPL, however, and Dunfermline finished bottom despite a late run of good results.

When they played BK Hacken of Sweden in the second qualifying round of the UEFA Cup on 16 August 2007, it was the first European tie at East End Park since the 3–2 win over Anderlecht in the Inter-Cities Fairs Cup on 14 January 1970. This time they drew 1–1 on the night, but lost 2–1 on aggregate. By the end of 2007 Stephen Kenny had returned to Derry City, and striker Jim McIntyre made the move up to player/manager, but the Pars were unable to challenge for an immediate return to the SPL.

DUNN Jimmy (1900 – 1963)

Scotland Caps: 9

The red-haired inside right of the Wembley Wizards of 1928, Jimmy Dunn joined Hibs in 1920 and won his first Scottish cap in 1925. Shortly after the Wembley Wizards game of 31 March 1928 he was transferred to Everton, with whom he won the English league Championship in 1932 and the FA Cup in 1933.

DURIE Gordon (1965 –)

Scotland Caps: 43
Scottish Premier League medals: 4
Scottish Cup medals: 1
Scottish League Cup medals: 1

Gordon Durie was a hard-running centre forward who earned forty-three caps for Scotland in a lengthy and varied career that lasted almost twenty years from 1983. His first club was East Fife. From there he moved to

Hibernian, Chelsea, and then Tottenham Hotspur, before returning to Scotland for a transfer fee of £1.2 million to play for Rangers in 1993. With Rangers he won many domestic honours, scoring a hat-trick in the 1996 Scottish Cup final (a feat which puts him in the same bracket as Jimmy Quinn and Dixie Deans) against Hearts, the team he subsequently moved to. His Scotland career included participation in the 1998 World Cup finals.

DURRANT Ian (1966 –)

Scotland Caps: 20
Scottish League Championship medals: 6
Scottish Cup medals: 3
Scottish League Cup medals: 4

A speedy forward, Ian Durrant played for Rangers and Kilmarnock (and briefly for Everton on loan) from 1985 until 2002, in spite of losing three years to a horrendous tackle by Neil Simpson of Aberdeen in 1988. He was a fast runner, with the ability to take a goal, and became one of the stars of the Rangers side of the 1990s. He joined Kilmarnock in 1998 and played a good four years with them, earning nine of his twenty Scotland caps with the Ayrshire side.

DYKEHEAD FC (former Scottish League club)

Home: **Parkside, Dykehead, near Shotts, North Lanarkshire**
Highest League Position: **44th (4th in Div. 3, 1925/26)**
Best Scottish Cup Performance: **Last 16 (3rd round, 1924/25)**

Dykehead's life in the Scottish League was restricted to the three seasons of Division Three football that existed from 1923 to 1926. Many teams in the third division were struggling to keep afloat in 1926 and, even though Dykehead was just managing to survive financially, the Scottish League took the decision to abandon Division Three.

The club's origins date back to around 1880. They first entered the Scottish Cup in 1884/85, but it was a competition in which they were low achievers. The club only progressed beyond the first round on three occasions and only once got as far as the third round. They did, however, enter the record books in 1914/15 when they reached the final of the Scottish Qualifying Cup and only lost to St. Bernard's after two replays.

Dykehead played in various leagues over the years, including the Scottish Alliance, the Eastern League, the Football Combination and the Scottish Union and there were periods in between when they just played in friendly and cup matches. After the first world war they were playing in the Western League and in 1923 most of the members, including Dykehead, became members of the new Division Three. The three seasons of Scottish League football were modestly successful and at one point in 1924/25 the club was amongst those vying for promotion. In the end it didn't matter and they went into the Scottish Alliance, followed by the Provincial League.

Dykehead was situated in a mining area. Crowds were small and by early 1928 the club's finances were feeling the effect of industrial disputes. Things were so bad that they were unable to fulfil a Scottish Cup tie against Hibernian. The SFA was so concerned that it refused to give approval for a move to yet another league (the Scottish Intermediate League) and Dykehead FC soon went out of existence.

EASTERN LEAGUE

There had been previous short-lived leagues with this name, but the Eastern League with the greatest historical significance was the regional league formed in 1915 when Division Two was discontinued because of the first world war (also see **WESTERN LEAGUE**). A mix of former league clubs and non-league clubs, it eventually served as a route to the Scottish League for some of them. Its membership fluctuated considerably over the years, and in 1917/18 it provided a temporary home for Dundee and Raith Rovers, who (along with Aberdeen) had been asked to leave the Scottish League because of transport problems during the war. Dundee won the championship that season.

In season 1918/19 there were no fixtures at all, but the Eastern League re-started in 1919/20, and this time Dundee Hibernian won the title, with the table at the end of the season looking as follows:

	P	W	D	L	Pts
Dundee Hibernian	18	13	2	3	28
Dundee A	18	10	5	3	25
Cowdenbeath	18	10	4	4	24
St Johnstone	18	8	4	6	20
Arbroath	18	9	2	7	20
Forfar Athletic	18	8	2	8	18
Lochgelly United	18	6	4	8	16
Raith Rovers A	18	7	0	11	14
Montrose	18	4	2	12	10
Brechin City	18	1	3	14	5

When the league came to an end in 1923, it had practically fizzled out. Dundee Hibs, for example, played only five fixtures in 1922/23, and also competed in the Scottish Alliance throughout that season (see **SCOTTISH ALLIANCE**). However, four member clubs were elected into the Scottish League for the 1923/24 season. Brechin City, Clackmannan and Montrose joined the newly created Division Three, and Dundee Hibernian went straight into Division Two under their new name of Dundee United.

Some years later, Brechin City, Dundee 'A', East Stirlingshire, Edinburgh City, Forfar Athletic, Montrose and Stirling Albion played in another Eastern League for the 1945/46 season before joining the new Division 'C' for 1946/47.

EAST FIFE FC

Ground: **Bayview Stadium, Methil**
Nickname: **The Fifers**
Colours: **Black and gold**
Record Attendance: **22,515 at Bayview Park v Raith Rovers (1950)**
1,996 at Bayview Stadium v Queen's Park (2003)
Record Victory: **13-2 v Edinburgh City (1937)**
Record Defeat: **0-9 v Hearts (1957)**
Highest League Position: **3rd (1951/52; 1952/53)**
Best Scottish Cup Performance: **Winners (1937/38)**
Best League Cup Performance: **Winners (1947/48; 1949/50; 1953/54)**

The Levenmouth area of Fife was once home to a team that scaled the heights of Scottish football. It started when the Fifers won the Scottish Cup in 1938, and continued after the second world war when they won more trophies, set new records, and finished higher in the league than many of the big names in Scottish football. By 1958 it had come to an end and the fans' expectations have never again been so high.

Founded in 1903, East Fife spent their first two years in the Fife League and the Eastern League, before playing in the Northern League from 1905 to 1909. They then joined the Central League and remained there until 1921, apart from a brief period in the reformed Eastern League during the first world war (see **CENTRAL LEAGUE** for 1920/21 table). The Fifers won the Scottish Qualifying Cup in 1920/21, when Bo'ness were beaten 3–1 in the final at Central Park, Cowdenbeath, and at the end of that season, along with most of the Central League, East Fife became part of the Scottish League's new Division Two.

1972: Dave Gorman of East Fife at Bayview.

They reached the final of the Scottish Cup in 1926/27, losing 3–1 to Celtic in a match that was the first domestic match to be broadcast live on the radio (or 'wireless' as it was then called) by the BBC, and in 1929/30 achieved promotion to Division One. Although they were back in Division Two after just one year, these achievements were surpassed in 1937/38, when they became the first club from Division Two to win the Scottish Cup. Manager Dave McLean's strong and skilful side beat Kilmarnock 4–2 after extra time, in a replayed final that followed a 1–1 draw, and goalscorers Dan McKerrell (2), Eddie McLeod and Davie Millar entered the history books.

Former Rangers and Scotland player Scot Symon was appointed manager in 1947 and by the end of that year they had also become the first club from a lower division to win the League Cup, with a 4–1 victory over Falkirk in the final. Winger Davie Duncan scored a hat-trick after captain Tommy Adams had opened the scoring. At the end of the 1947/48 season the club finished top of Division B and the League Cup was complemented with promotion to the top division.

East Fife's golden age was now under way. Not only did the Fifers stay in the top flight for ten seasons, they won the League Cup on two more occasions, with victories against Dunfermline Athletic (3–0) in 1949/50 and Partick Thistle (3–0) in 1953/54. They also reached the Scottish Cup final for a third time in 1949/50, when they lost 3–0 to Rangers. Centre forward Henry Morris became a Methil legend, and Charlie Fleming, Allan Brown and Jimmy Bonthrone were all prolific goal scorers.

There was another record on Wednesday 8 February 1956, when first-class competitive football was played under floodlights for the first time in Scotland. There had previously been floodlit friendly football, but the SFA gave permission for the Fifer's re-arranged fifth-round Scottish cup-tie against Stenhousemuir to be played under their Bayview Park lights. They lost 3–1, but entered the history books, along with Hibernian, who hosted another re-arranged tie that night.

When East Fife were relegated back to Division Two at the end of the 1957/58 season they had won the League Cup on more occasions than any other club, including Rangers and Celtic. There were three more seasons in the top division, from 1971 to 1974, but over the years since then East Fife have fluctuated between the lower divisions. Manager Steve Archibald led them to the First Division in 1996, but he parted company with the club later that year and there was only one season in the second tier.

In 1998 they moved to New Bayview Stadium at Methil Docks, but soon afterwards, in 1999, they slipped down to the Third Division (fourth tier) for the first time. They did manage to return to the Second Division (third tier) in 2003, but a year later they were back in the Third Division. Much has changed since the days when East Fife was one of Scotland's leading clubs, but the history was brought to mind in March 2008 when manager Dave Baikie led them to the Third Division title - their first championship since 1948.

EAST KILBRIDE THISTLE FC

(see JUNIOR FOOTBALL)

EAST OF SCOTLAND LEAGUE

This is usually referred to as 'non-league' football because its status is below that of the Scottish Football League, but it is nevertheless a 'senior' league in that it is not part of Scottish junior football (the Highland League and the South of Scotland League also fall into this category). The league was founded in 1927 and Berwick Rangers won the first championship at the end of the 1927/28 season. In 1987 it was re-organised into a Premier Division and a First Division, with two teams being promoted and relegated at the end of each season. Two members, Annan Athletic and Dalbeattie Star, also have a team that competes in the South of Scotland League. Threave Rovers used to compete in both leagues, but they resigned in 2004 to concentrate on the South of Scotland League, and in 2007 Berwick Rangers Reserves replaced them.

Several clubs regularly raise their profile at a national level when they take part in the Scottish Cup. Before 2007/08 they qualified by virtue of reaching the last four of the Scottish Qualifying Cup (South), but on 1 June 2007 the SFA decided that, in future, EOSL clubs that met their criteria would automatically be entered into a revamped Scottish Cup.

In 2005/06 Spartans reached the fourth round of the Scottish Cup for the second time in three seasons. They drew 0–0 at home to St. Mirren before losing the replay 3–0. When Edinburgh University beat Keith in the first round of the 2006/07 competition, not only were their players unpaid, they had to pay an annual fee to be members of the club.

Member Club	Premier Division Champions (1987/88 onwards)	First Division Champions (1987/88 onwards)	Best Post-War Scottish Cup Performance (1946/47 onwards)
Annan Athletic Galabank, Annan	1989/90 1999/00 2000/01 2006/07	1987/88	Last 32 (third round 1997/98)
Civil Service Strollers Civil Service Sports Ground, Muirhouse, Edinburgh		1992/93	Last 40 (second round 1973/74; 1975/76; 1977/78; 1987/88; 1991/92)
Coldstream Home Park, Coldstream		1989/90	Last 32 (second round 1953/54; 1958/59)
Craigroyston St. Mark's Park, Edinburgh		2005/06	Non-participant
Dalbeattie Star Islecroft Stadium, Dalbeattie		2006/07	Last 44 (second round 1998/99; 1999/2000)
Easthouses Lily MW Newbattle Complex, Easthouses, Midlothian	1991/92	1990/91 1998/99 2004/05	Non-participant
Edinburgh Athletic, (formerly Manor Thistle) Civil Service Sports Ground, Muirhouse, Edinburgh			Non-participant
Edinburgh City (formally Postal United) Meadowbank Stadium, Edinburgh	2005/06	1995/96	Last 32 (third round 1997/98)
Edinburgh University East Peffermill, Edinburgh		2002/03	Last 40 (second preliminary round 1964/65)
Eyemouth United Warner Park, Eyemouth			Last 8 (fourth round 1959/60)
Gala Fairydean Netherdale, Galashiels	1988/89 1990/91		Last 16 (third round 1962/63)
Hawick Royal Albert Albert Park, Hawick			Last 32 (first round 1967/68)
Heriot Watt University Riccarton, Edinburgh		2007/08	Non-participant
Kelso United Woodside Park, Kelso		2003/04	Non-participant
Lothian Thistle Saughton Enclosure, Edinburgh		1996/97	Non-participant
Ormiston (formerly Pencaitland & Ormiston) Recreation Park, Ormiston, East Lothian		2000/01	Non-participant
Peebles (formed from Peebles Rovers and others) Whitestone Park, Peebles		(As Peebles Rovers) 1988/89 1997/98	(As Peebles Rovers) Last 32 (second round 1953/54; 1958/59; 1959/60; 1960/61)
Preston Athletic The Pennypit, Prestonpans		2001/02	Last 42 (second round 2006/07)
Selkirk Yarrow Park, Selkirk			Last 40 (second round 1976/77; 1993/94)
Spartans City Park, Ferry Road, Edinburgh	1996/97 2001/02 2003/04 2004/05		Last 16 (fourth round 2003/04; 2005/06)
Tynecastle (formerly Tollcross Utd) Fernieside Recreation Ground, Edinburgh			Non-participant
Vale of Leithen Victoria Park, Innerleithen			Last 32 (second round 1961/62; third round 1977/78)
Whitehill Welfare Fergusson Park, Rosewell	1987/88 1992/93 1993/94 1994/95 1995/96 1997/98 1998/99 2002/03 2007/08		Last 32 (third round 1986/87; 1995/96)

EAST OF SCOTLAND SHIELD

This tournament, once vigorously contested, has now virtually disappeared. Until 1891 it was called the Edinburgh Challenge Cup. The problem was that it tended to become a Hearts versus Hibs clash and, with the advent of the Premier League in 1975, these teams (providing they were in the same division) would play each other four times per season anyway. Thus interest from both the clubs and the fans tended to drain away.

The winners were:

1885	Hibernian	1886	Hibernian	1887	Hearts
1888	Mossend Swifts	1889	Hearts	1890	Hearts
1891	Hearts	1892	Hearts	1893	Hearts
1894	Hearts	1895	Bo'ness	1896	Mossend Swifts
1897	St Bernard's	1898	Hearts	1899	Hearts
1900	Hibernian	1901	Raith Rovers	1902	Hearts
1903	Hibernian	1904	Hearts	1905	Hibernian
1906	Hibernian	1907	Hearts	1908	Hibernian
1909	Hibernian	1910	Hearts	1911	Hibernian
1912	Hibernian	1913	Hibernian	1914	Hearts
1915	Hearts	1916	No Competition	1917	No Competition
1918	Hibernian	1919	Hearts	1920	Hearts
1921	Hibernian	1922	Hearts	1923	Hibernian
1924	Hibernian	1925	Hibernian	1926	Hibernian
1927	Hearts	1928	Hibernian	1929	Hibernian
1930	Hearts	1931	Hearts	1932	Hearts
1933	Hearts	1934	Hearts	1935	Hibernian
1936	Hearts	1937	Hearts	1938	Hibernian
1939	Hibernian	1940	Hearts	1941	No Competition
1942	Hearts	1943	Hibernian	1944	Hearts
1945	Hibernian	1946	Hearts	1947	Hibernian
1948	Hibernian	1949	Hearts	1950	Hearts
1951	Hibernian	1952	Hibernian	1953	Hibernian
1954	Hearts	1955	Hearts	1956	Hearts
1957	Hibernian	1958	Hearts	1959	Hibernian
1960	Hibernian	1961	Hibernian	1962	Hearts
1963	Hibernian	1964	Hearts	1965	Hearts
1966	Hearts	1967	Hearts	1968	Hibernian
1969	Hearts	1970	Hearts	1971	Hibernian
1972	No Competition	1973	No Competition	1974	Hearts
1975	Hearts	1976	Hearts	1977	Hibernian
1978	Hibernian	1979	No Competition	1980	Hibernian
1981	Berwick Rangers	1982	Hearts	1983	Hibernian
1984	Berwick Rangers	1985	No Competition	1986	Hearts
1987	Hibernian	1988	Hearts	1989	Hearts
1990	Hibernian	1991	Hibernian	1992	Hibernian
1993	Hearts	1994	Hibernian	1995	Hearts
1996	Hibernian	1997	No Competition	1998	Hearts
1999	Hearts				

Edinburgh clubs also played for two other trophies, both now long defunct. One was the Rosebery Charity Cup, played for by all Edinburgh clubs between 1883 and 1945, and won by Hearts on thirty-three occasions, Hibs on twenty-two, St.Bernard's four, Leith Athletic three and Mossend Swifts one. The other was the Wilson Cup, specifically for the fixture between Hearts and Hibs on New Year's Day (which was of course traditionally the date for the Scottish League fixture as well). It was presented by a Hearts Director called Robert Wilson and, between 1906 and 1946 (since when it appears to have been discontinued), Hearts won the trophy twenty-four times and Hibs sixteen.

EAST STIRLINGSHIRE FC

Ground: **Firs Park, Falkirk**
Nickname: **The Shire**
Colours: **Black and white**
Record Attendance: **12,000 v Partick Thistle (1921)**
Record Victory: **11-2 v Vale of Bannock (1888)**
Record Defeat: **1-12 v Dundee United (1936)**
Highest League Position: **18th (1963/64)**
Best Scottish Cup Performance: **Last 8 (6th round 1888/89; 5th round 1980/81)**
Best League Cup Performance: **Last 18 (Play-offs for 2nd round 1973/74)**

In 1880 the iron industry was thriving in the area to the north of Falkirk, and the village of Bainsford, on the road to Stenhousemuir, was no exception. That year the local cricket club, Bainsford Bluebonnets, formed a football club called Bainsford Britannia, and in 1881 the name was changed to East Stirlingshire. The Shire played at Burnhouse and Randyford Park, before settling down at Merchiston Park, where they would remain until they moved to Firs Park in neighbouring Falkirk in 1921.

The new club was a regular entrant in the Scottish Cup, and in 1888/89 went all the way to the last eight, before losing 2–1 away to Celtic. Welsh international Humphrey Jones won five of his fourteen caps whilst with the Shire during this period, and this remains a club record for international appearances. When the Scottish Qualifying Cup was introduced in 1895/96, the men from Bainsford reached the final four times in its first six years - bringing home the trophy in 1898/99 and losing on the other three occasions.

In 1900/01 East Stirlingshire replaced Linthouse in Division Two of the Scottish League and the lower division became their home. They escaped for a single season in 1931/32 when they topped Division Two on goal average, but they finished bottom of Division One the next season and were relegated back down. Following the end of the second world war, the Shire were placed in the new Division C (third tier) and won the title in 1947/48. They were promoted to Division B, but only for one season, as they finished bottom and were replaced by Forfar Athletic. Their exile from Division Two lasted for six years, until the Scottish League was expanded in 1955 and East Stirlingshire became one of five new members.

When the Shire finished the 1962/63 season as runners-up in Division Two, promotion brought a further single year in the top flight, and once again it ended with a bottom-place finish. Jack and Charles Steedman, who were Glasgow businessmen, had bought control of the club in 1957 and the subsequent period of decline after relegation resulted in them taking the club to Kilbowie Park, Clydebank for the 1964/65 season. It was amalgamated with Clydebank Juniors and renamed 'ES Clydebank'. Legal action ensued and, after a ruling from the Court of Session, the Shire's fans were able to celebrate the club's return to Falkirk in 1965.

1963: Steve Chalmers has just scored for Celtic against East Stirlingshire at Firs Park. The players are McQueen and Collumbine.

Lawrence Binnie became the first manager in 1966, but it was the man who took the job in 1974 who went on to become famous throughout the world of football. Firs Park was the starting point for Sir Alex Ferguson's career in football management, although he left after less than four months to become the manager of St Mirren. In 1980 the club again finished the season as runners-up, but by this time they were in the third tier, although it was called the Second Division. Two years in the First Division ensued, although it was actually the second tier. This brief period of success also brought another appearance in the last eight of the Scottish Cup and once again it ended with a defeat by Celtic, this time 2–0.

When the league was again restructured in 1994, the Shire's position in the bottom eight clubs of the Second Division resulted in them becoming founder members of a new fourth tier, known as the Third Division. Over the ensuing years they established themselves as one of the Scottish League's worst performing clubs and in 2003/04 gained just eight points from thirty-six games. This unfortunate reputation attracted the attention of the press, and Littlewoods football pools decided to sponsor the club. The Shire increased their profile, and off-field improvements included a slick new website.

By 2007 East Stirlingshire had finished bottom of Division Three for five consecutive seasons, and by finishing bottom in both 2005/06 and 2006/07 they had broken the SFL's rule 21.5, which meant that their status could have been reduced to 'Associate Member'. They were given another chance to improve, and the club pressed ahead with plans to sell Firs Park for a housing development, which would mean ground sharing at Stenhousemuir's Ochilview. In March 2008 Jim McInally replaced Gordon Wylde as manager, and he faced the challenge of lifting Shire off the bottom of the league. In the end it came down to the last day of the season, and interest in their fate was so great that even *The Times* featured a full-page preview of the match against Montrose. East Stirlingshire won 3–1, and when they finished second bottom it seemed like a triumph.

ECLIPSE OF THE SUN

This rare phenomenon affected Scottish football on the afternoon of 24 January 1925. The partial eclipse reached Scotland at 3.00 pm during the Scottish Cup games being played that afternoon, which would normally have kicked off at 2.30 p.m. Some games were started earlier, and referees were given the authority to suspend play if necessary. It turned out to be a beautiful crisp afternoon and little disruption occurred, but the *Fife Free Press* reports that the play between Raith Rovers and Clackmannan (3-0 for the home side) was so boring that most of the time it was "heads upwards for the crowd". Third Lanark, ever anxious for good relations with the press, laid on candles for their use if necessary.

ECUADOR

Scotland have played Ecuador once, in the Kirin Cup in Japan, and won 2–1.

1995	24 May	Toyama	2–1	Robertson Crawford	Hurtado (pen)

EDINBURGH CITY FC
(former Scottish League club)

Home: **Edinburgh (list of grounds below)**
Highest League Position: **35th (15th in Div. 2, 1935/36)**
Best Scottish Cup Performance: **Last 24 (2nd round, 1931/32)**

Founded in 1928 as an amateur club, Edinburgh City was admitted to Division Two of the Scottish League in 1931, following the resignation of Clydebank. They then became Edinburgh's fifth league club, along with Heart of Midlothian, Hibernian, St Bernard's and Leith Athletic.

They completed eight seasons in Division Two before the advent of the second world war, and finished bottom on six occasions. In their first season they conceded a record-breaking 146 goals. City never progressed beyond the second round of the Scottish Cup, but in 1937/38 they pulled off a famous victory when they beat Hibs 3–2 at Easter Road in the first round.

City played at three different venues over the years. They commenced their time in the league at New Powderhall Stadium, but the pitch was very narrow and they left after three seasons. After a season of ground sharing with Leith Athletic at Marine Gardens, Portobello, they moved to City Park. The following table lists the grounds where Edinburgh City played in the Scottish League:

(Marine Gardens)		
Scottish League		
New Powderhall	1931	1934
Marine Gardens	1934	1935
City Park	1935	1949

After the war, City spent the 1945/46 season in the Eastern League, and then became part of the newly created Division C of the Scottish League in 1946. They competed in it for three seasons and their dismal league form continued, as they finished bottom twice and next to the bottom on the other occasion. They did, however, enjoy some success when they won the Scottish Qualifying Cup (South) in 1946/47. In 1949 they became a junior club, and six years later, in 1955, they went out of existence.

In 1986 a new Edinburgh City emerged in the East of Scotland League, and in 1997/98 they reached the third round of the Scottish Cup before losing 7–2 away to Dunfermline Athletic.

EGYPT

Scotland have played Egypt once, and it was a humiliating defeat.

1990	16 May	Pittodrie	1–3	McCoist	Abdelhamid Hassan Youssef

EIRE

See **IRELAND, REPUBLIC**. The republic's governing body is the Football Association of Ireland (FAI), which is not to be confused with Northern Ireland's Irish Football association (IFA). The southern part of Ireland broke away from the IFA in 1921, and Scotland's fixture in February of that year was the last occasion on which Scotland played a team that represented the whole of Ireland. Scotland did not play the Republic until 1961.

ELGIN CITY FC

Ground: **Borough Briggs**
Nickname: **The City; Black and whites**
Colours: **Black and white**
Record Attendance: **12,608 v Arbroath (1968)**
Record Victory: **18-1 v Brora Rangers (1960)**
Record Defeat: **1-14 v Hearts (1939)**
Highest League Position: **37th (5th in Third Division, 2005/06)**
Best Scottish Cup Performance: **Last 8 (3rd round 1967/68)**
Best League Cup Performance: **Last 28 (2nd round 2006/07)**

The club was formed in 1893, when Elgin Rovers amalgamated with Vale of Lossie, and became a member of the Highland League at the start of the 1895/96 season. With the exception of three seasons (1896/97, 1900/01 and 1901/02) they remained there until 2000, when they were admitted to the Scottish Football League. Their first Highland League title eluded them for thirty-seven years, until Bert Maclachlan led them to the championship in 1931/32, but before then some of their players moved on to greater things – such as Bob Hamilton, who was capped eleven times for Scotland whilst with Rangers and Dundee.

City won the Highland League championship fifteen times in total and in the 1960s they came to dominate Highland football. The title was won eight out of eleven times in the years from 1960 to 1970 and the championship of 1969/70 marked a famous 'three in a row'. The strength of the side in this era was further demonstrated by the 1967/68 Scottish Cup campaign, when Albion Rovers, Forfar Athletic and Arbroath were all beaten as the Highland League club reached the quarter-finals. A 2–1 defeat away to Morton prevented them from reaching the semi-finals.

However, this was not the only occasion when the Scottish Cup enabled City to raise their profile at a national level. When they reached the last sixteen in 1976/77, losing 3–0 at Ibrox, it was the fourth time they had gone out at this stage and the third time it had been against the Old Firm. Celtic won 2–1 at Elgin in 1959/60, and in 1966/67 City lost 7–0 at Parkhead, whilst in 1971/72 Kilmarnock travelled north and won 4–1.

The Scottish Qualifying Cup (North) was won for the seventh time in 1989/90 and then in 1992/93 they became known as the 'Six Day Champions' when they were stripped of the Highland League title for allegedly bringing forward a crucial fixture so that they could play before two players began a suspension. City's disappointment turned to joy in 2000 when the Scottish League was expanded and they were awarded one of two new places, but league success at a national level proved elusive, and the lower reaches of the Third Division was where they were usually to be found.

EMPIRE EXHIBITION TROPHY

This was a one-off tournament, played between four leading sides of Scotland and four leading sides of England, in late May and early June 1938, to commemorate the Empire Exhibition being held at Bellahouston Park, Glasgow. The Exhibition was to be 'an exposition of the work, life, culture and progress' of the British Empire, and was a much needed propaganda counterblast to what was coming from Nazi Germany. As Glasgow, the 'Second City of the Empire', was frequently described as the football capital of the world, it was felt that a football tournament between eight invited sides would be a fitting part of the 'work, culture, life and progress' of Glasgow. A trophy was commissioned in the image of the Tait Tower, the symbol of the Empire Exhibition. All the games were played at Ibrox, because of its proximity to Bellahouston Park. Sadly, neither Arsenal (the English league winners) nor

Celtic's team of 1938 which won the Scottish League and the Empire Exhibition Trophy. Back row, left to right: Geatons, Hogg, Kennaway, Morrison, Crum, Paterson. Front row: Delaney, MacDonald, Lyon, Divers, Murphy.

Preston North End (the FA Cup winners) took part, but the tournament was still hotly contested, and the winners could claim to be the champions of Britain.

Quarter-final:

25 May 1938	Celtic	0	0	Sunderland	53,976
26 May 1938	Celtic	3	1	Sunderland	20,000
	Crum Divers (2)			Burbank	
27 May 1938	Aberdeen	4	0	Chelsea	30,000
	Strauss Thomson Armstrong Hamilton				
30 May 1938	Hearts	1	0	Brentford	45,403
	Briscoe				
1 June 1938	Everton	2	0	Rangers	47,682
	Lawton Cunliffe				

Semi-final:

3 June 1938	Celtic	1	0	Hearts	50,000
	Crum				
6 June 1938	Everton	3	2	Aberdeen	20,000
	Gillick Boyes Lawton			Armstrong Strauss	

Final:

10 June 1938	Celtic	1	0	Everton	82,000
	Crum	a.e.t.			

Celtic: Kennaway, Hogg, Morrison, Geatons, Lyon, Paterson, Delaney, MacDonald, Crum, Divers, Murphy
Everton: Sagar, Cook, Greenhalgh, Mercer, Jones, Thomson, Geldard, Cunliffe, Lawton, Stevenson, Boyes
Referee: T.Thomson, Northumberland.

This was an epic final between two great teams. "Fetch a polis man, Everton's getting murdered" was the cry of the Celtic fans before the game, but the reality was quite different, for the game was tight and hard-fought, with a winner possible at either end. Celtic had Jimmy Delaney back from injury and his presence was probably crucial, although it was Johnny Crum who broke the deadlock when he scored the only goal of the game after seven minutes of extra time. Famously, he then ran behind the goal and did a 'Highland fling' for the benefit of the fans. The second half of the game and the extra time was broadcast on radio on the BBC Regional Service, beginning at 7.50 pm, and the commentator was the Sunday Mail journalist Rex Kingsley. Johnny Crum, the hero of the hour, was married the following Wednesday.

ENGLAND

England was referred to as Scotland's 'auld enemy', and for many years it was 'the' game of the calendar. The annual game was often referred to as 'the international'. The first international between the two of them on 30 November 1872 was the world's first international match. Yet it might not have been so described had Queen's Park, who supplied all of Scotland's eleven players, not decided to call themselves Scotland rather than Queen's Park. They did this presumably for reasons of attracting a large crowd to Hamilton Crescent, and thereby started the whole concept of international football.

There had been five previous England versus Scotland games, all played at the Oval in London, but Scotland's players were all based in the London area and chosen by the English authorities! In fact they were supplemented by a few Englishmen, including some men who later went on to play for England. These five games played between 1870 and 1872 are therefore rightly deemed unofficial. Of these five games, two were 1–1 draws and the other three were victories for England with the scores of 0–1, 1–2 and 0–1.

It is a matter of some regret that the annual match has now disappeared, a victim of hooliganism and a crowded fixture calendar, for it used to be the most eagerly awaited game of the season. 1928 and 1967 are still etched into the memory of every Scotsman, but perhaps credit should also be given to the mighty men of the early 1880s who won five in a row, or the Scotland teams between the wars who never lost to England at Hampden apart from 1927 (when the whole country was plunged into mourning as a result) and in 1939 when everyone was more concerned about Hitler. Most of these games until the mid 1980s were in the Home International Championship, but the games in 1950 and 1954 were World Cup qualifying games as well, whereas those in 1967 and 1968 doubled as European Nations Cup Qualifying games. The game in 1996 was in the European Championships and those in 1999 were play-offs for the European Championships. 110 games have been played, forty-one won, forty-five lost and twenty-four drawn.

1872	30 Nov	Hamilton Crescent	0–0		
1873	8 Mar	Kennington Oval	2–4	Renny-Tailyour Gibb	Kenyon-Stanley (2) Bonsor Chenery
1874	7 Mar	Hamilton Crescent	2–1	Anderson MacKinnon	Kingsford
1875	6 Mar	Kennington Oval	2–2	McNeil Andrews	Wollaston Alcock
1876	4 Mar	Hamilton Crescent	3–0	MacKinnon McNeil Highet	
1877	3 Mar	Kennington Oval	3–1	Ferguson (2) Richmond	Lyttleton
1878	2 Mar	1st Hampden Park	7–2	McDougall (3) McGregor McNeil (2) MacKinnon	Wyllie Cursham
1879	5 Apr	Kennington Oval	4–5	MacKinnon (2) McDougall Smith	Mosforth Bambridge (2) Goodyer Bailey
1880	13 Mar	1st Hampden Park	5–4	Ker (3) Baird Kay	Bambridge (2) Mosforth Sparks
1881	12 Mar	Kennington Oval	6–1	Smith (3) Ker (2) Hill	Bambridge
1882	11 Mar	1st Hampden Park	5–1	Ker (2) Harrower McPherson Kay	Vaughton
1883	10 Mar	Bramall Lane	3–2	Smith (2) Fraser	Mitchell Cobbold
1884	15 Mar	Cathkin Park	1–0	Smith	

1885	21 Mar	Kennington Oval	1–1	Lindsay	Bambridge
1886	27 Mar	1st Hampden Park	1–1	Somerville	Lindley
1887	19 Mar	Blackburn	3–2	McCall Keir Allan	Lindley Dewhurst
1888	17 Mar	1st Hampden Park	0–5		Dewhurst (2) Lindley Hodgetts Goodall
1889	13 April	Kennington Oval	3–2	Munro Oswald McPherson	Bassett Weir
1890	5 April	2nd Hampden	1–1	McPherson	Wood
1891	4 April	Blackburn	1–2	Watt	Goodall Chadwick
1892	2 April	Ibrox	1–4	Bell	Goodall (2) Chadwick Southworth
1893	1 April	Richmond	2–5	Sellar (2)	Spiksley (2) Gosling Coterill Reynolds
1894	7 April	Celtic Park	2–2	Lambie McMahon	Goodall Reynolds
1895	6 April	Goodison Park	0–3		Bloomer Gibson o.g. Smith
1896	4 April	Celtic Park	2–1	Lambie Bell	Bassett
1897	3 April	Crystal Palace	2–1	Hyslop Millar	Bloomer
1898	2 April	Celtic Park	1–3	Millar	Bloomer (2) Wheldon
1899	8 April	Villa Park	1–2	Hamilton	Smith Settle
1900	7 April	Celtic Park	4–1	McColl (3) Bell	Bloomer
1901	30 Mar	Crystal Palace	2–2	Campbell Hamilton	Blackburn Bloomer
1902	3 May	Villa Park	2–2	Templeton Orr	Settle Wilkes
	Original match played at Ibrox on 5 April, but declared unofficial after collapse of west stand, which led to twenty-six people being killed in what became known as the first Ibrox disaster. The first game was a 1–1 draw.				
1903	4 April	Bramall Lane	2–1	Speedie Walker	Woodward
1904	9 April	Celtic Park	0–1		Bloomer
1905	1 April	Crystal Palace	0–1		Bache
1906	7 April	3rd Hampden Park	2–1	Howie (2)	Shepherd
1907	6 April	Newcastle	1–1	Crompton o.g.	Bloomer
1908	4 April	Hampden Park	1–1	Wilson	Windridge
1909	3 April	Crystal Palace	0–2		Wall (2)
1910	2 April	Hampden Park	2–0	McMenemy Quinn	
1911	1 April	Goodison	1–1	Higgins	Stewart
1912	23 Mar	Hampden Park	1–1	Wilson	Holley
1913	5 April	Stamford Bridge	0–1		Hampton
1914	4 April	Hampden Park	3–1	Thomson McMenemy Reid	Fleming
1920	10 April	Hillsborough	4–5	Miller 2 Wilson Donaldson	Kelly (2) Quantrill Cock Morris
1921	9 April	Hampden Park	3–0	Wilson Morton Cunningham	
1922	8 April	Villa Park	1–0	Wilson	
1923	14 April	Hampden Park	2–2	Cunningham Wilson	Kelly Watson
1924	12 April	Wembley	1–1	Cowan	Walker
1925	4 April	Hampden Park	2–0	Gallacher (2)	
1926	17 April	Old Trafford	1–0	Jackson	
1927	2 April	Hampden Park	1–2	Morton	Dean (2)
1928	31 Mar	Wembley	5–1	Jackson (3) James (2)	Kelly
1929	13 April	Hampden Park	1–0	Cheyne	
1930	5 April	Wembley	2–5	Fleming (2)	Watson (2) Rimmer (2) Jack
1931	28 Mar	Hampden Park	2–0	Stevenson McGrory	
1932	9 April	Wembley	0–3		Waring Barclay Crooks
1933	1 April	Hampden Park	2–1	McGrory (2)	Hunt
1934	14 April	Wembley	0–3		Bastin Brook Bowers
1935	6 April	Hampden Park	2–0	Duncan (2)	
1936	4 April	Wembley	1–1	Walker (pen)	Camsell
1937	17 April	Hampden Park	3–1	McPhail (2) O'Donnell	Steele
1938	9 April	Wembley	1–0	Walker	
1939	15 April	Hampden Park	1–2	Dougall	Beasley Lawton
1947	12 April	Wembley	1–1	McLaren	Carter
1948	10 April	Hampden Park	0–2		Finney Mortensen
1949	9 April	Wembley	3–1	Mason Steel Reilly	Milburn
1950	15 April	Hampden Park	0–1		Bentley
1951	14 April	Wembley	3–2	Johnstone Reilly Liddell	Hassall Finney
1952	5 April	Hampden Park	1–2	Reilly	Pearson (2)
1953	18 April	Wembley	2–2	Reilly (2)	Broadis (2)
1954	3 April	Hampden Park	2–4	Brown Ormond	Broadis Nicholls Allen Mullen
1955	2 April	Wembley	2–7	Reilly Docherty	Wilshaw (4) Lofthouse (2) Revie
1956	14 April	Hampden Park	1–1	Leggat	Haynes
1957	6 April	Wembley	1–2	Ring	Kevan Edwards
1958	19 April	Hampden Park	0–4		Kevan (2) Douglas Charlton
1959	11 April	Wembley	0–1		Charlton
1960	9 April	Hampden Park	1–1	Leggat	Charlton (pen)
1961	15 April	Wembley	3–9	Mackay Wilson Quinn	Greaves (3) Smith (2) Haynes (2) Robson Douglas
1962	14 April	Hampden Park	2–0	Wilson Caldow (pen)	
1963	6 April	Wembley	2–1	Baxter (2) (1 pen)	Douglas
1964	11 April	Hampden Park	1–0	Gilzean	
1965	10 April	Wembley	2–2	Law St. John	Charlton Greaves
1966	2 April	Hampden Park	3–4	Johnstone (2) Law	Hunt (2) Hurst Charlton
1967	15 April	Wembley	3–2	Law Lennox McCalliog	Charlton Hurst
1968	24 Feb	Hampden Park	1–1	Hughes	Peters
1969	10 May	Wembley	1–4	Stein	Peters (2) Hurst (2)
1970	25 April	Hampden Park	0–0		
1971	22 May	Wembley	1–3	Curran	Chivers (2) Peters
1972	27 May	Hampden Park	0–1		Ball
1973	14 Feb	Hampden Park	0–5		Clarke (2) Lorimer o.g. Channon Chivers
	A special game to mark the centenary of the SFA				

Scotland versus England 3 May 1902 before the game which has held at Villa Park following the Ibrox Disaster of the previous month.

1973	19 May	Wembley	0–1		Peters
1974	18 May	Hampden Park	2–0	Jordan Todd o.g.	
1975	24 May	Wembley	1–5	Rioch (pen)	Francis (2) Beattie Bell Johnson
1976	15 May	Hampden Park	2–1	Masson Dalglish	Channon
1977	4 June	Wembley	2–1	McQueen Dalglish	Channon (pen)
1978	20 May	Hampden Park	0–1		Coppell
1979	26 May	Wembley	1–3	Wark	Barnes Coppell Keegan
1980	24 May	Hampden Park	0–2		Brooking Coppell
1981	23 May	Wembley	1–0	Robertson (pen)	
1982	29 May	Hampden Park	0–1		Mariner
1983	1 June	Wembley	0–2		Robson Cowans
1984	26 May	Hampden Park	1–1	McGhee	Woodcock
1985	25 May	Hampden Park	1–0	Gough	
1986	23 April	Wembley	1–2	Souness (pen)	Butcher Hoddle
1987	23 May	Hampden Park	0–0		
1988	21 May	Wembley	0–1		Beardsley
1989	27 May	Hampden Park	0–2		Waddle Bull
1996	15 June	Wembley	0–2		Shearer Gascoigne
1999	13 Nov	Hampden Park	0–2		Scholes (2)
1999	17 Nov	Wembley	1–0	Hutchison	

ESTONIA

Scotland have played Estonia seven times and drawn twice. They have never lost to them. There were bizarre events on 9 October 1996 in the World Cup when Scotland, having complained about the floodlights, managed to get the game changed from 6.45 pm to an afternoon kick-off at 3.00 pm – or so they thought. The Estonians did not turn up, and thus Scotland, and the referee and linesmen, appeared – but no opposition! Scotland lined up in front of the TV cameras, the referee Miroslav Radoman blew his whistle, Billy Dodds took the kick-off, passed to John Collins who kicked the ball upfield, and the referee blew his whistle again to finish the game. Everyone then shook hands and went away home! Scotland then claimed three points. FIFA, not for the first time in their history, showed their ability to be taken for a ride, and rearranged the game in the neutral venue of Monaco the following February. It was a breathtaking piece of fence sitting, and may well have imperilled Scotland's chances of qualification, but fortunately Scotland, although only drawing in Monaco, managed to qualify for France.

1993	19 May	Tallinn	3–0	Gallacher Collins Booth	
1993	2 June	Pittodrie	3–1	Nevin (2) (1 pen) McClair	Bragin
1997	11 Feb	Monaco	0–0		
1997	29 Mar	Rugby Park	2–0	Boyd Meet o.g.	
1998	10 Oct	Tynecastle	3–2	Dodds (2) Hohlov-Simson o.g.	Hohlov-Simson Smirnov
1999	8 Sep	Tallinn	0–0		
2004	27 May	Tallinn	1–0	McFadden	

EUROPEAN COEFFICIENT

This complicated system determines how many clubs from each country are able to participate in the Champions League and UEFA Cup. For the European Champions League, the places are allocated to the previous year's winners, then three countries are given four places each, three are given three, nine are given two and the remaining countries have one each. Scotland has never had more than two places. For the UEFA Cup, the places are given to the previous year's winners, then two countries are given four places each, twelve countries are given three places each, three countries are given one each and the remaining countries (Scotland are normally in this group) two each. This is in addition to extra entries through the Intertoto Cup and the Fair Play assessment.

How countries are placed depends on the coefficient of how all their teams have played in European ties over the past five seasons, and an announcement is made at the end of each season. Two points are given for a win, and one for a draw (one for a win in qualifying round matches and a half for a draw), and a game that is resolved as a penalty shoot-out is deemed a draw. Then an extra point is awarded for reaching the first knockout round, quarter-final, semi-final and final of the Champions League, and three points for actual participation in the Champions League. In the UEFA Cup an extra point is awarded for reaching the quarter-final, the semi-final and the final. Then the total of points for each country is counted, and divided by the number of clubs who have participated in European competition from that country. That becomes the national coefficient.

It is clear therefore that it is in the interests of all Scottish clubs that the other Scottish clubs do well. Parochial rejoicing at the demise of one's city rivals is indeed just that – parochial and contrary to the best interests of all Scottish football.

The national association (SFA) then nominates which clubs will take part in which competitions the following year on the basis of the number of places allocated. Normally the SPL champions are given a place in the Champions League and the Scottish Cup winners a place in the UEFA Cup. Other allocations depend on league positions and the number of places. For example, if Scotland were allowed two entries to the Champions League, and the team which won the Scottish Cup was also second in the SPL, they would then be allocated a place in the Champions League. This happened in 2006 with Hearts.

There is also the club coefficient to determine seedings. This is calculated on the number of points obtained by a particular club over the past five seasons, plus 33% of the national coefficient. Celtic's good run in the UEFA Cup of 2003, therefore, helped to ensure that in season 2006/07 they were allocated a place in the Champions League itself rather than having to qualify, for they had a better coefficient than Arsenal. Yet had Arsenal won the 2006 Champions League final, their coefficient would have been much improved and Celtic would have had to play in a qualifying round.

EUROPEAN CUP

The brainchild of French journalist Gabriel Hanot in the 1950s, this was a knockout competition between the league champions of each European country. It was played on a home and away basis, with the final being a single game at a neutral venue. It first saw Scottish participation in 1955/6, when Hibs were invited to take part (even though they had only finished fifth in the Scottish League). To Hibs thus belongs the honour of kicking the first ball for Scotland in the European Cup on 14 September 1955 away to Rot-Weiss Essen, and to Eddie Turnbull belongs the honour of scoring the first goal. Jock Buchanan scored the first home goal at Easter Road.

After that it was always the league champions of the previous season who played in this tournament, and Scotland's record was good considering that it is a small nation – one win, one runner-up and six semi-final appearances. Hampden Park hosted the final in 1960, when Real Madrid beat Eintracht Frankfurt 7–3 in a classic match. In 1992/93 it was re-branded as the Champions League, formalising the mini-league system that had been used in 1991/92.

The record of Scottish teams is as follows:

Season	Scottish Club	Opposition	Agg.	Round
1955/56	Hibernian	Rot-Weiss Essen	5–1	First
		Djugaarden	4–1	Quarter-final
		Reims	0–3	Semi-final
1956/57	Rangers	Nice	3–3	First
			1–3	Play-off
1957/58	Rangers	St Etienne	4–3	Preliminary
		AC Milan	1–6	First
1958/59	Hearts	Standard Liege	3–6	Preliminary
1959/60	Rangers	Anderlecht	7–2	Preliminary
		Red Star Bratislava	5–4	First
		Sparta Rotterdam	3–3	Quarter-Final
			3–2	Play-off
		Eintracht Frankfurt	4–12	Semi-final
1960/61	Hearts	Benfica	1–5	Preliminary
1961/62	Rangers	Monaco	6–4	Preliminary
		Vorwaerts	6–2	First
		Standard Liege	3–4	Quarter-final
1962/63	Dundee	FC Cologne	8–5	Preliminary
		Sporting Lisbon	4–2	First
		Anderlecht	6–2	Quarter-final
		AC Milan	2–5	Semi-final
1963/64	Rangers	Real Madrid	0–7	Preliminary
1964/65	Rangers	Red Star Belgrade	5–5	Preliminary
			3–1	Play-off
		Rapid Vienna	3–0	First
		Inter Milan	2–3	Quarter-final
1965/66	Kilmarnock	Nendori Tirana	1–0	Preliminary
		Real Madrid	3–8	First
1966/67	Celtic	Zurich	5–0	First
		Nantes	6–2	Second
		Vojvodina	2–1	Quarter-final
		Dukla Prague	3–1	Semi-final
		Inter Milan	2–1	Final
Played in Lisbon on 25 May 1967. Celtic's team was: Simpson; Craig; Gemmell; Murdoch; McNeill; Clark; Johnstone; Wallace; Chalmers; Auld; Lennox. Scorers: Gemmell and Chalmers				
1967/68	Celtic	Dinamo Kiev	2–3	First
1968/69	Celtic	St Etienne	4–2	First
		Red Star Belgrade	6–2	Second
		AC Milan	0–1	Quarter-final
1969/70	Celtic	Basle	2–0	First
		Benfica	3–3	Second
		Celtic won on the toss of a coin		
		Fiorentina	3–1	Quarter-final

		Leeds United	3–1	Semi-final
		Feyenoord	1–2	Final
1970/71	Celtic	KPV Kokkola	14–0	First
		Waterford	10–2	Second
		Ajax	1–3	Quarter-final
1971/72	Celtic	BK 1903 Copenhagen	4–2	First
		Sliema Wanderers	7–1	Second
		Ujpest Dozsa	3–2	Quarter-final
		Inter Milan	0–0	Semi-final
		Celtic lost on penalties		
1972/73	Celtic	Rosenborg	5–2	First
		Ujpest Dozsa	2–4	Second
1973/74	Celtic	Turku	9–1	First
		Vejle	1–0	Second
		Basle	6–5	Quarter-final
		Atletico Madrid	0–2	Semi-final
1974/75	Celtic	Olympiakos	1–3	First
1975/76	Rangers	Bohemians	5–2	First
		St Etienne	1–4	Second
1976/77	Rangers	Zurich	1–2	First
1977/78	Celtic	Jeunesse D'Esch	11–1	First
		SW Innsbruck	2–4	Second
1978/79	Rangers	Juventus	2–1	First
		PSV Eindhoven	3–2	Second
		FC Cologne	1–2	Quarter-final
1979/80	Celtic	Partizan Tirana	4–2	First
		Dundalk	3–2	Second
		Real Madrid	2–3	Quarter-final
1980/81	Aberdeen	Austria Vienna	1–0	First
		Liverpool	0–5	Second
1981/82	Celtic	Juventus	1–2	First
1982/83	Celtic	Ajax	4–3	First
		Real Sociedad	2–3	Second
1983/84	Dundee United	Hamrun Spartans	6–0	First
		Standard Liege	4–0	Second
		Rapid Vienna	2–2	Quarter-final
		Dundee United won on away goals		
		AS Roma	2–3	Semi-final
1984/85	Aberdeen	Dinamo Berlin	3–3	First
		Aberdeen lost on penalties		
1985/86	Aberdeen	Akranes	7–2	First
		Servette	1–0	Second
		IKF Gothenburg	2–2	Quarter-final
		Aberdeen lost on away goals		
1986/87	Celtic	Shamrock Rovers	3–0	First
		Dinamo Kiev	2–5	Second
1987/88	Rangers	Dinamo Kiev	2–1	First
		Gornik Zabrze	4–2	Second
		Steaua Bucharest	2–3	Quarter-final
1988/89	Celtic	Honved	4–1	First
		Werder Bremen	0–2	Second
1989/90	Rangers	Bayern Munich	1–3	First
1990/91	Rangers	Valletta	10–0	First
		Red Star Belgrade	1–4	Second
1991/92	Rangers	Sparta Prague	2–2	First
		Rangers lost on away goals		

(see **CHAMPIONS LEAGUE** for seasons 1992/93 onwards)

Rangers defenders clear as Red Star put on the pressure in Bratislava.

Milan centre-forward Beane hands the ball to Rangers galkepper Ritchie after a goal was scored in this European Cup-tie at Ibrox in 1960.

The following table summarises the performance of Scottish clubs by showing which round they reached each year:

1955/56	Hibernian	semi-final
1956/57	Rangers	1st
1957/58	Rangers	1st
1958/59	Hearts	1st
1959/60	Rangers	semi-final
1960/61	Hearts	1st
1961/62	Rangers	quarter-final
1962/63	Dundee	semi-final
1963/64	Rangers	preliminary round
1964/65	Rangers	quarter-final
1965/66	Kilmarnock	1st
1966/67	Celtic	winners
1967/68	Celtic	1st
1968/69	Celtic	quarter-final
1969/70	Celtic	runners-up
1970/71	Celtic	quarter-final
1971/72	Celtic	semi-final
1972/73	Celtic	2nd
1973/74	Celtic	semi-final
1974/75	Celtic	1st
1975/76	Rangers	2nd
1976/77	Rangers	1st
1977/78	Celtic	2nd
1978/79	Rangers	quarter-final
1979/80	Celtic	quarter-final
1980/81	Aberdeen	2nd
1981/82	Celtic	1st
1982/83	Celtic	2nd
1983/84	Dundee United	semi-final
1984/85	Aberdeen	1st
1985/86	Aberdeen	quarter-final
1986/87	Celtic	2nd
1987/88	Rangers	quarter-final
1988/89	Celtic	2nd
1989/90	Rangers	1st
1990/91	Rangers	2nd
1991/92	Rangers	1st

EUROPEAN CUP-WINNERS' CUP 1961 – 1999

This tournament is now defunct, but was once held in great esteem. As the name suggests, the winners of each domestic cup competition competed for it. On occasion, when the same team won the league and the cup, the defeated finalist would enter the competition. It would thus be possible to win the European Cup-Winners' Cup without winning the domestic cup. Scotland did well, winning the trophy on two occasions, reaching the final on another two and on many other occasions having a team in the semi-final. The trophy began to lose its value when it became apparent that other nations did not always hold their cup competition in as much value as British nations did. Cup winners now qualify for the UEFA Cup. The results of Scottish clubs were as follows:

Season	Scottish Club	Opposition	Agg.	Round
1960/61	Rangers	Ferencvaros	5–4	Preliminary
		Borussia M'gladbach	11–0	Quarter-final
		Wolves	3–1	Semi-final
		Fiorentina	1–4	Final
1961/62	Dunfermline	St Patrick's Athletic	8–1	First
		Vardar Skopje	5–2	Second
		Ujpest Dozsa	3–5	Quarter-final
1962/63	Rangers	Seville	4–2	First
		Tottenham Hotspur	4–8	Second
1963/64	Celtic	Basle	10–1	First
		Dinamo Zagreb	4–2	Second
		Slovan Bratislava	2–0	Quarter-final
		MTK	3–4	Semi-final
1964/65	Dundee	Real Zaragoza	3–4	Second
1965/66	Celtic	Go Ahead Deventer	7–0	First

Stevie Chalmers' goal hits the back of the Inter Milan net and Celtic are now 2-1 up in Lisbon and the club's greatest triumph, the 1967 European Cup final.

		Aarhus	3–0	Second
		Dinamo Kiev	4–1	Quarter-final
		Liverpool	1–2	Semi-final
1966/67	Rangers	Glentoran	5–1	First
		Borussia Dortmund	2–1	Second
		Real Zaragoza	2–2	Quarter-final
		Rangers won on toss of a coin		
		Slavia Sofia	2–0	Semi-final
		Bayern Munich	0–1 aet	Final
1967/68	Aberdeen	KR Reykjavik	14–2	First
		Standard Liege	2–3	Second
1968/69	Dunfermline	Apoel Nicosia	12–1	First
		Olympiakos Piraeos	4–3	Second
		West Bromwich Alb.	1–0	Quarter-final
		Slovan Bratislava	1–2	Semi-final
1969/70	Rangers	Steaua Bucharest	2–0	First
		Gornik Zabrze	2–6	Second
1970/71	Aberdeen	Honved	4–4	First
		Aberdeen lost on penalties		
1971/72	Rangers	Rennes	2–1	First
		Sporting Lisbon	6–6	Second
		Rangers won on away goals		
		Torino	2–1	Quarter-final
		Bayern Munich	3–1	Semi-final
		Moscow Dynamo	3–2	Final
Played in Barcelona on 24 May 1972. Rangers' team was: McCloy; Jardine; Mathieson; Greig; D. Johnstone; Smith; McLean; Conn; Stein; MacDonald; W. Johnston. Scorers: Stein; W. Johnston (2)				

1972/73	Hibernian	Sporting Lisbon	7–3	First
		Besa	8–2	Second
		Hadjuk Split	4–5	Quarter-final
1973/74	Rangers	Ankaragucu	6–0	First
		Borussia M'gladbach	3–5	Second
1974/75	Dundee United	Jiul Petrosani	3–2	First
		Bursaspor	0–1	Second
1975/76	Celtic	Valur	9–0	First
		Boavista	3–1	Second
		Zwickau	1–2	Quarter-final
1976/77	Hearts	Lokomotiv Leipzig	5–3	First
		SV Hamburg	3–8	Second
1977/78	Rangers	Young Boys	3–2	Preliminary
		Twente Enschede	0–3	First
1978/79	Aberdeen	Marek Stanke	5–3	First
		Fortuna Dusseldorf	2–3	Second
1979/80	Rangers	Lillestrom	3–0	First
		Fortuna Dusseldorf	2–1	Second
		Valencia	2–4	Quarter-final
1980/81	Celtic	Diosgyor	7–2	First
		Poli Timosarara	2–2	Second
		Celtic lost on away goals		
1981/82	Rangers	Dukla Prague	2–4	First
1982/83	Aberdeen	Sion	11–1	Preliminary
		Dinamo Tirana	1–0	First
		Lech Posnan	3–0	Second
		Bayern Munich	3–2	Quarter-final
		Waterschei	5–2	Semi-final

Bayern Munich's Roth scores the winning goal against Rangers in the 1967 European Cup-Winners' Cup final in Nuremburg.

		Real Madrid	2–1	Final
Played in Gothenburg on 11 May 1983. Aberdeen's team was: Leighton; Rougvie; McMaster; Cooper; McLeish; Miller; Strachan; Simpson; McGhee; Black (Hewitt); Weir. Scorers: Black; Hewitt				
1983/84	Aberdeen	Akranes	3–2	First
		Beveren	4–1	Second
		Ujpest Dozsa	3–2	Quarter-final
		Porto	0–2	Semi-final
	Rangers	Valletta	18–0	First
		Porto	2–2	Second
		Rangers lost on away goals		
1984/85	Celtic	Gent	3–1	First
		Rapid Vienna	4–3	Second
		Home leg ordered to be replayed at Old Trafford, and Celtic lost 0–1 (Instead of 3–0 win).		
1985/86	Celtic	Atletico Madrid	2–3	First
1986/87	Aberdeen	Sion	2–4	First
1987/88	St Mirren	Tromso	1–0	First
		Mechelen	0–2	Second
1988/89	Dundee United	Floriana	1–0	First
		Dinamo Bucharest	1–2	Second
1989/90	Celtic	Partizan Belgrade	6–6	First
		Celtic lost on away goals		
1990/91	Aberdeen	Salamis	5–0	First
		Legia Warsaw	0–1	Second
1991/92	Motherwell	Katowice	3–3	First
		Motherwell lost on away goals		
1992/93	Airdrieonians	Sparta Prague	1–3	First
1993/94	Aberdeen	Valur	7–0	First
		Torino	3–6	Second
1994/95	Dundee United	Tatran Presov	4–5	First
1995/96	Celtic	Dinamo Batumi	7–2	First
		Paris St Germain	0–4	Second
1996/97	Hearts	Red Star Belgrade	1–1	First
		Hearts lost on away goals		
1997/98	Kilmarnock	Shelbourne	3–2	Qualifying
		Nice	2–4	First
1998/99	Hearts	Lantana	6–0	Qualifying
		Real Mallorca	1–2	First

The following table summarises the performance of Scottish clubs by showing how far they progressed each year:

1960/61	Rangers	runners-up		
1961/62	Dunfermline	quarter-final		
1962/63	Rangers	2nd		
1963/64	Celtic	semi-final		
1964/65	Dundee	2nd		
1965/66	Celtic	semi-final		
1966/67	Rangers	runners-up		
1967/68	Aberdeen	2nd		
1968/69	Dunfermline	semi-final		
1969/70	Rangers	2nd		
1970/71	Aberdeen	1st		
1971/72	Rangers	winners		
1972/73	Hibernian	quarter-final		
1973/74	Rangers	2nd		
1974/75	Dundee United	2nd		
1975/76	Celtic	quarter-final		
1976/77	Hearts	2nd		
1977/78	Rangers	1st		
1978/79	Aberdeen	2nd		
1979/80	Rangers	2nd		
1980/81	Celtic	1st		
1981/82	Rangers	1st		
1982/83	Aberdeen	winners		
1983/84	Rangers	2nd	Aberdeen	semi-final
1984/85	Celtic	2nd		
1985/86	Celtic	1st		
1986/87	Aberdeen	1st		
1987/88	St. Mirren	2nd		
1988/89	Dundee United	2nd		
1989/90	Celtic	1st		
1990/91	Aberdeen	2nd		
1991/92	Motherwell	1st		
1992/93	Airdrieonians	1st		
1993/94	Aberdeen	2nd		
1994/95	Dundee United	1st		
1995/96	Celtic	2nd		
1996/97	Hearts	qual. round		
1997/98	Kilmarnock	1st		
1998/99	Hearts	1st		

Colin Stein celebrates his goal in Rangers' 3–2 win over Moscow Dynamo in the 1972 European Cup-winners' Cup final in Barcelona.

EUROPEAN FINALS PLAYED IN SCOTLAND

There have been a total of eight European cup-finals played in Scotland:

European Cup/Champions League

18 May 1960	Real Madrid	7	3	Eintracht Frankfurt	Hampden Park
					135,000
12 May 1976	Bayern Munich	1	0	St Etienne	Hampden Park
					54,864
15 May 2002	Real Madrid	2	1	Bayer Leverkusen	Hampden Park
					52,000

European Cup-Winners' Cup

17 May 1961	Rangers	0	2	Fiorentina	Ibrox
					80,000
(First leg: - Rangers lost 1–2 in the second leg on 27 May, and lost 1–4 on aggregate)					
10 May 1962	Atletico Madrid	1	1	Fiorentina	Hampden Park
					27,389
(Atletico Madrid won the replay 3–0 at Stuttgart on 10 September 1962)					
5 May 1966	Borussia Dortmund	2	1	Liverpool	Hampden Park
a.e.t.					41,657

UEFA Cup

20 May 1987	Dundee United	1	1	IFK Gothenburg	Tannadice
					20,911
(Second leg: - Dundee United lost 0–1 in the first leg on 6 May, and lost 1–2 on aggregate)					
16 May 2007	Sevilla	2	2	Espanol	Hampden Park
(a.e.t: - Sevilla won 3–1 on penalties)					50,670

Fiorentina's assistant coach comes on to the field to argue with referee Steiner after he had awarded Rangers a dubious penalty in the first leg of the European Cup-Winners' Cup final at Ibrox in May 1961.

EUROPEAN FOOTBALL CHAMPIONSHIP

Once known as the European Nations' Cup, this tournament is held every four years, at two-year intervals from the World Cup. Scotland showed no interest in the first two tournaments of 1960 or 1964 (a shame, perhaps, because the Scottish team of 1964 was a strong one) but have entered every competition since. The British international championships of 1966/67 and 1967/68 were used as a qualifying section. Since then there has been a draw for the qualifying sections. However, Scotland's record is a poor one, for only in 1992 and 1996 have they qualified.

1968 Qualifying Section

16 Oct 1966	Northern Ireland	Hampden Park	2–1
22 Oct 1966	Wales	Cardiff	1–1
15 Apr 1967	England	Wembley	3–2
21 Oct 1967	Northern Ireland	Belfast	0–1
22 Nov 1967	Wales	Hampden Park	3–2
24 Feb 1968	England	Hampden Park	1–1
Scotland failed to qualify for Italy			

1972 Qualifying Section

11 Nov 1970	Denmark	Hampden Park	1–0
3 Feb 1971	Belgium	Liege	0–3
21 Apr 1971	Portugal	Lisbon	0–2
9 June 1971	Denmark	Copenhagen	0–1
13 Oct 1971	Portugal	Hampden Park	2–1
10 Nov 1971	Belgium	Pittodrie	1–0
Scotland failed to qualify for Belgium			

1976 Qualifying Section

20 Nov 1974	Spain	Hampden Park	1–2
5 Feb 1975	Spain	Valencia	1–1
1 June 1975	Romania	Bucharest	1–1
3 Sep 1975	Denmark	Copenhagen	1–0
29 Oct 1975	Denmark	Hampden Park	3–1
17 Dec 1975	Romania	Hampden Park	1–1
Scotland failed to qualify for Yugoslavia			

1980 Qualifying Section

20 Sep 1978	Austria	Vienna	2–3
25 Oct 1978	Norway	Hampden Park	3–2
29 Nov 1978	Portugal	Lisbon	0–1
7 June 1979	Norway	Oslo	4–0
17 Oct 1979	Austria	Hampden Park	1–1
21 Nov 1979	Belgium	Brussels	0–2
19 Dec 1979	Belgium	Hampden Park	1–3
26 Mar 1980	Portugal	Hampden Park	4–1
Scotland failed to qualify for Italy			

1984 Qualifying Section

13 Oct 1982	East Germany	Hampden Park	2–0
17 Nov 1982	Switzerland	Berne	0–2
15 Dec 1982	Belgium	Brussels	2–3
30 Mar 1983	Switzerland	Hampden Park	2–2
12 Oct 1983	Belgium	Hampden Park	1–1
16 Nov 1983	East Germany	Halle	1–2
Scotland failed to qualify for France			

Archie Gemmill nets from the penalty spot as Scotland defeat Norway 3-2 in a European Football Championship qualifier at Hampden Park in October 1978.

1988 Qualifying Section

10 Sep1986	Bulgaria	Hampden Park	0–0
15 Oct 1986	Republic of Ireland	Dublin	0–0
12 Nov 1986	Luxemburg	Hampden Park	3–0
18 Feb 1987	Republic of Ireland	Hampden Park	0–1
1 Apr 1987	Belgium	Brussels	1–4
14 Oct 1987	Belgium	Hampden Park	2–0
11 Nov 1987	Bulgaria	Sofia	1–0
2 Dec 1987	Luxemburg	Esch	0–0
Scotland failed to qualify for Germany			

1992 Qualifying Section

12 Sep 1990	Romania	Hampden Park	2–1
17 Oct 1990	Switzerland	Hampden Park	2–1
14 Nov 1990	Bulgaria	Sofia	1–1
27 Mar 1991	Bulgaria	Hampden Park	1–1
1 May 1991	San Marino	Serravalle	2–0
11 Sep 1991	Switzerland	Berne	2–2
16 Oct 1991	Romania	Bucharest	0–1
13 Nov 1991	San Marino	Hampden Park	4–0

Finals in Sweden

12 June 1992	Holland	Gothenburg	0–1
15 June 1992	Germany	Norrkoping	0–2
18 June 1992	CIS	Norrkoping	3–0

It was felt by many observers that Andy Roxburgh's side did not enjoy the best of fortunes in the 1992 championships. The first game saw Scotland against the strong Dutch side, and after Scotland had weathered an early storm, they held their own until a late Dennis Bergkamp goal. Against Germany, Scotland lost a goal in the first half, then early in the second half a wicked deflection from Stefan Effenberg deceived Andy Goram and put Germany two up. Hard though Scotland tried, they could not get back into the game. In the final game, with only pride at stake, Scotland turned on some of the best football seen by any team at the tournament, against the Commonwealth of Independent States, who had previously been known as the USSR. Paul McStay was outstanding in midfield, and he scored one of the goals, the other two coming from Brian McClair and Gary McAllister.

1996 Qualifying Section

7 Sep 1994	Finland	Helsinki	2–0
12 Oct 1994	Faeroe Islands	Hampden Park	5–1
16 Nov 1994	Russia	Hampden Park	1–1
18 Dec 1994	Greece	Athens	0–1
29 Mar 1995	Russia	Moscow	0–0
26 Apr 1995	San Marino	Serravalle	2–0
7 June 1995	Faeroe Islands	Toftir	2–0
16 Aug 1995	Greece	Hampden Park	1–0
6 Sep 1995	Finland	Hampden Park	1–0
15 Nov 1995	San Marino	Hampden Park	5–0

Finals in England

10 June 1996	Holland	Villa Park	0–0
15 June 1996	England	Wembley	0–2
18 June 1996	Switzerland	Villa Park	1–0

Scotland, under Craig Brown, were very unfortunate not to qualify from this section. The first game was a creditable 0–0 draw with Holland at Villa Park, and then it was on to Wembley for the key match against England. Scotland held their own until Alan Shearer scored early in the second half, then Gary McAllister missed the penalty that has haunted him ever since before Paul Gascoigne, minutes later, scored a wonder goal to defeat Scotland 2–0.

Even then Scotland might just have qualified if they had scored one more goal more against Switzerland, or Holland one goal fewer against England. Although Ally McCoist scored for Scotland, the game finished 1–0, and Holland scored a late consolation goal against England, which was enough to put them into the next round.

2000 Qualifying Section

5 Sep 1998	Lithuania	Vilnius	0–0
10 Oct 1998	Estonia	Tynecastle	3–2
14 Oct 1998	Faeroe Islands	Pittodrie	2–1
31 Mar 1999	Czech Republic	Celtic Park	1–2
5 June 1999	Faeroe Islands	Toftir	1–1
9 June 1999	Czech Republic	Prague	2–3
4 Sep 1999	Bosnia	Sarajevo	2–1
8 Sep 1999	Estonia	Tallinn	0–0
5 Oct 1999	Bosnia	Ibrox	1–0
9 Oct 1999	Lithuania	Hampden Park	3–0

Play Offs

13 Nov 1999	England	Hampden Park	0–2
17 Nov 1999	England	Wembley	1–0
Scotland failed to qualify for Holland / Belgium			

2004 Qualifying Section

7 Sep 2002	Faeroe Islands	Toftir	2–2
12 Oct 2002	Iceland	Reykjavik	2–0
29 Mar 2003	Iceland	Hampden Park	2–1
2 Apr 2003	Lithuania	Kaunas	0–1
7 June 2003	Germany	Hampden Park	1–1
6 Sep 2003	Faeroe Islands	Hampden Park	3–1
10 Sep 2003	Germany	Dortmund	1–2
11 Oct 2003	Lithuania	Hampden Park	1–0

Play Offs

15 Nov 2003	Holland	Hampden Park	1–0
19 Nov 2003	Holland	Amsterdam	0–6
Scotland failed to qualify for Portugal			

2008 Qualifying Section

2 Sep 2006	Faeroe Islands	Celtic Park	6–0
6 Sep 2006	Lithuania	Kaunas	2–1
7 Oct 2006	France	Hampden Park	1–0
11 Oct 2006	Ukraine	Kiev	0–2
24 Mar 2007	Georgia	Hampden Park	2–1
28 Mar 2007	Italy	Bari	0–2
6 June 2007	Faeroe Islands	Toftir	2–0
8 Sep 2007	Lithuania	Hampden Park	3–1
12 Sep 2007	France	Paris	1–0
13 Oct 2007	Ukraine	Hampden Park	3–1
17 Oct 2007	Georgia	Tbilisi	0–2
17 Nov 2007	Italy	Hampden Park	1–2
Scotland failed to qualify for Austria / Switzerland			

EUROPEAN SUPER CUP

This tournament used to match the winners of the previous season's European Cup and European Cup-Winners' Cup. Scottish teams have twice competed. The first was Rangers, who lost 3–6 on aggregate to Ajax in January 1973 (1–3 at Ibrox on 16 January and 2–3 in Amsterdam on 24 January). This was the first time that the Super Cup (the idea of Dutch journalist Anton Witkamp) had been held, and doubt persists about whether or not it was an official tournament that year, not least because Rangers were banned from European competition following the rioting of their fans in Barcelona the previous May.

There is no doubt, however, about Aberdeen's triumph in December 1983, when they became the first British team to lift the trophy by drawing in Hamburg and then winning 2–0 at Pittodrie.

1983	22 Nov	SV Hamburg	0	0	Aberdeen	Hamburg
Aberdeen: Leighton, Cooper, Rougvie, Simpson, McLeish, Miller, Strachan, Hewitt, McGhee, Bell, Weir						
						15,000

1983	20 Dec	Aberdeen	2	0	SV Hamburg	Pittodrie
		Simpson McGhee				
Aberdeen: Leighton, McKimmie, McMaster, Simpson, McLeish, Miller, Strachan, Hewitt (Black), McGhee, Bell, Weir						
						22,500

Since 1999/2000, following the demise of the European Cup-Winners' Cup, the tournament has matched the European champions against the winners of the UEFA Cup.

EVANS Bobby (1927 – 2001)

Scotland Caps: 48
Scottish League Championship medals: 1
Scottish Cup medals: 2
Scottish League Cup medals: 2

Bobby Evans was right half and centre half for many clubs, Celtic in particular, in a lengthy career that ran from 1944-1967. He won forty-eight caps for Scotland, and his red hair and habit of keeping his jersey outside his shorts made him instantly recognisable. He played in the 1958 World Cup finals in Sweden but missed those of 1954, although many people thought that

Scotland missed him a lot more. He joined Celtic in 1944 as an inside forward, and it took some time before it was realised that his best position was further back. There can be little doubt that he would have won far more medals with Celtic if he had been in a better-managed side. He was captain of Celtic briefly, but it became a cliché for the newspapers to say 'Evans, as usual, was superb'.

His bad days, notably the 1956 Scottish Cup final and the 1957 Scottish Cup semi-final, were significant, in that it usually meant that Celtic would lose. He was a player around whom circulated (perhaps unfairly) rumours of match-fixing, but it was probably because his bad games were so infrequent that fans found it hard to believe that he could play so poorly. In 1960, to the surprise of the fans, he moved on to Chelsea, then in 1961 to Newport County, before returning to Scotland in 1962 to play for Morton, Third Lanark (whom he managed as well), and finally Raith Rovers until he retired in 1967, but not before guiding them to promotion to the top flight. Many thought that Bobby might have been invited to join Jock Stein's Celtic set-up, but no invitation came.

FACILITIES

The facilities at Scottish football grounds improved dramatically towards the end of the twentieth century, but this is not to say that they are ideal. All-seater stadia became compulsory in the SPL and, generally speaking, they are places where families can be taken, – except, perhaps, for the prices. Yet good facilities are not always apparent at the grounds of the smaller clubs, where there are too often complaints about unhygienic toilets, inadequate catering facilities, and having to stand on a terracing, although there is now some sort of shelter available from the elements.

It is sometimes said that if humans are treated like animals they will behave appropriately, and one of the reasons why some men used to urinate on the terracing at big games was because such toilets as existed were overused and filthy. It was always said that 'Scottish football was no place for softies', and that the facilities at football grounds mirrored the conditions that once prevailed in the urban slums. However, many clubs paid the price for not treating their fans well enough when attendances dropped in the early 1960s, because by then fans tended to live in houses with modern conveniences and did not see any great corresponding improvement at football grounds.

As far as facilities for female spectators are concerned, there has been a slow, but by no means spectacular, or indeed universal, improvement. Even at clubs like St Johnstone and Aberdeen, which always had a large female support, toilet facilities were once scant, but as women formed an increased percentage of the average crowd for most clubs, the facilities began to reflect this. Some teams, notably the now defunct Clydebank, supplied crèche facilities to encourage families to attend.

Food is normally now available at grounds, although the length of the queue can be a deterrent at half time. There is the traditional Bovril, tea and coffee, as well as a wide selection of multi-national junk foods, but Kilmarnock reputedly have the best pies, and at Forfar there is the local speciality called the bridie.

FA CUP

Eight Scottish clubs entered the FA Cup in the nineteenth century before the practice was brought to an end in 1887. This remained the total number of participants until 2002, when the number increased to nine because Gretna, a club that had previously entered the FA Cup, joined the Scottish League.

Queen's Park took part in the very first FA Cup competition in 1871/72 and were given byes because of the long distance they had to travel. They reached the semi-final without playing a match and at this time hadn't conceded a goal since their formation in 1867. After a 0–0 draw against Wanderers at Kennington Oval they had to withdraw because they couldn't afford the cost of travelling south for a replay. There were more withdrawals in subsequent years, but then they reached the final in both 1883/84 and 1884/85. The venue for their semi-final replay against Nottingham Forest in 1884/85 was Merchiston Castle School, Edinburgh and this is the only FA Cup semi-final to be played in Scotland.

In those far-off days of amateur football Rangers scratched against Rawtenstall in the 1885/86 competition, rather than play against professionals, and were fined ten shillings by the English FA. The following season they reached the semi-finals, losing 3–1 to Aston Villa in March 1887. Later that year the Scottish FA told its members that they could no longer be involved in the FA Cup.

This might have been the end of the story, but for the involvement of Gretna over a hundred years later, when

The original FA Cup, so nearly won by Queen's Park, who twice reached the final in 1884 and 1885.

they were part of the Northern League First Division. Their first round tie in 1993/94 was switched to Burnden Park and they were beating Bolton Wanderers 2–1 with about ten minutes to go, but then two goals from Owen Coyle brought their cup run to an end.

Clydesdale

1875/76	scratched against South Norwood

Cowlairs

1886/87	1st Rnd	Darwen Old Wdrs.	1	Cowlairs	4
1886/87	2nd Rnd	Rossendale	2	Cowlairs	10
1886/87	3rd Rnd	Rangers	3	Cowlairs	2

Gretna

1991/92	1st Rnd	Gretna	0	Rochdale	0
1991/92	Replay	Rochdale	3	Gretna	1
1993/94	1st Rnd	Gretna	2	Bolton Wdrs.	3

Heart of Midlothian

1885/86	1st Rnd	scratched against Padiham			
1886/87	1st Rnd	Darwen	7	Hearts	1

Partick Thistle

1885/86	1st Rnd	Queen's Park	5	Partick Thistle	1
1886/87	1st Rnd	Blackburn Olympic	1	Partick Thistle	3
1886/87	2nd Rnd	Partick Thistle	7	Fleetwood	0
1886/87	3rd Rnd	Cliftonville	1	Partick Thistle	11
1886/87	4th Rnd	bye			
/87	5th Rnd	Old Westminsters	1	Partick Thistle	0

Renton, Scottish Cup-winners in 1888, which included many of the team that played in the 1886/87 FA Cup matches, and below their 1885 Scottish Cup winning team.

Queen's Park

1871/72	1st Rnd	bye				
1871/72	2nd Rnd	Walkover against Donington School, Spalding				
1871/72	3rd Rnd	bye				
1871/72	S-Final	Wanderers	0	Queen's Park	0	Kennington Oval
1871/72	Replay	scratched against Wanderers				
1872/73	1st Rnd	bye				
1872/73	2nd Rnd	bye				
1872/73	3rd Rnd	bye				
1872/73	4th Rnd	bye				
1872/73	S-Final	scratched against Oxford University				
1876/77	1st Rnd	bye				
1876/77	2nd Rnd	bye				
1876/77	3rd Rnd	scratched against Oxford University				
1879/80	1st Rnd	scratched against Sheffield				
1880/81	1st Rnd	scratched against Sheffield Wednesday				
1881/82	1st Rnd	scratched against Accrington Stanley				
1882/83	1stRnd	scratched against Grimsby				
1883/84	1st Rnd	Crewe	0	Queen's Park	10	
1883/84	2nd Rnd	Queen's Park	15	Manchester	0	
1883/84	3rd Rnd	Oswestry	1	Queen's Park	7	
1883/84	4th Rnd	Queen's Park	6	Aston Villa	1	
1883/84	5th Rnd	Old Westminsters	0	Queen's Park	1	
1883/84	S-Final	Blackburn Olympic	0	Queen's Park	4	Nottingham
1883/84	Final	Blackburn Rovers	2	Queen's Park	1	Kennington Oval
1884/85	1st Rnd	walkover against Stoke				
1884/85	2nd Rnd	Queen's Park	2	Crewe	1	
1884/85	3rd Rnd	Leek	2	Queen's Park	3	
1884/85	4th Rnd	Queen's Park	7	Old Wykehamists	0	
1884/85	5th Rnd	bye				
1884/85	6th Rnd	Notts County	2	Queen's Park	2	
1884/85	Replay	Queen's Park	2	Notts County	1	
1884/85	S-Final	Nottingham For	1	Queen's Park	1	Derby
1884/85	Replay	Nottingham For	0	Queen's Park	3	Edinburgh (*)
1884/85	Final	Blackburn Rovers	2	Queen's Park	0	Kennington Oval
1885/86	1st Rnd	Queen's Park	5	Partick Thistle	1	
1885/86	2nd Rnd	scratched against South Shore				
1886/87	1st Rnd	Queen's Park	0	Preston	3	
(*) Merchiston Castle School, Edinburgh						

Rangers

1880/81	1st Rnd	walkover against Wanderers				
1880/81	2nd Rnd	Bye				
1880/81	3rd Rnd	Royal Engineers	6	Rangers	0	
1881/82	1st Rnd	scratched against Romford				
1885/86	1st Rnd	scratched against Rawtenstall				
1886/87	1st Rnd	walkover against Everton				
1886/87	2nd Rnd	Rangers	2	Church	1	
1886/87	3rd Rnd	Rangers	3	Cowlairs	2	
1886/87	4th Rnd	Bye				
1886/87	5th Rnd	Rangers	3	Lincoln City	0	
1886/87	6th Rnd	Rangers	5	Old Westminsters	1	
1886/87	S-Final	Aston Villa	3	Rangers	1	Crewe

Renton

1886/87	1st Rnd	Renton	1	Accrington	0
1886/87	2nd Rnd	Renton	2	Blackburn Rovers	2
1886/87	Replay	Blackburn Rovers	0	Renton	2
1886/87	3rd Rnd	Renton	0	Preston	2

Third Lanark

1885/86	1st Rnd	Third Lanark	4	Blackburn Park Rd.	2
1885/86	2nd Rnd	scratched against Church			
1886/87	1st Rnd	Third Lanark	5	Higher Walton	0
1886/87	2nd Rnd	Third Lanark	2	Bolton Wdrs.	3

FAEROE ISLANDS

These small islands have twice held Scotland to a draw, and even Scottish fans conceded that they were unlucky not to win on both occasions. For many followers of the national team it seems that Scotland reserve their worst performances for such fixtures, but they remain undefeated.

Eight games have been played, with six victories and two draws:

1994	12 Oct	Hampden Park	5–1	Collins (2) McGinlay McKinlay Booth	Muller
1995	7 June	Toftir	2–0	McGinlay McKinlay	
1998	14 Oct	Pittodrie	2–1	Burley Dodds	Petersen (pen)
1999	5 June	Toftir	1–1	Johnston	Hansen
2002	7 Sep	Toftir	2–2	Lambert Ferguson	Petersen (2)
2003	6 Sep	Hampden Park	3–1	McCann Dickov McFadden	Johnsson
2006	2 Sep	Celtic Park	6–0	Boyd (2) (1 pen) Miller (pen) Fletcher McFadden O'Connor	
2007	6 June	Toftir	2–0	Maloney O'Connor	

FAIR PLAY COMPETITION

UEFA introduced fair play rankings in 1995, and four years later offered the opportunity of an extra place in the UEFA Cup to three countries that achieve a high position. The country that tops the list automatically receives an entry for the club that heads its domestic fair play table and the other two places are decided by a draw amongst the remaining countries that meet a qualifying standard. Scotland topped the rankings in 1999 and Kilmarnock was awarded the extra place.

FALKIRK FC

Ground: **The Falkirk Stadium**
Nickname: **The Bairns**
Colours: **Navy blue and white**
Record Attendance: **23,100 at Brockville Park v Celtic (1953)**
7,245 at Falkirk Stadium v Rangers (2006)
Record Victory: **12-1 v Laurieston (1893)**
Record Defeat: **1-11 v Airdrie (1951)**
Highest League Position: **2nd (1907/08; 1909/10)**
Best Scottish Cup Performance: **Winners (1912/13; 1956/57)**
Best League Cup Performance: **Runners-Up (1947/48)**

It is generally believed that the club was founded in 1876, although there is some doubt about the exact year. Falkirk didn't join the Scottish League until 1902 and by then they were well established as a strong side whose successes included the championship of the Central Football Combination in 1899/1900. In 1901/02 they had reached the last eight of the Scottish Cup and, when the Scottish League was expanded that year, Falkirk were one of the two clubs elected into Division Two.

Three years later they were elected into Division One for the 1905/06 season, even though they had only finished second and the club above them, Clyde, was not promoted. Nevertheless the Bairns soon made their mark and, by the time they beat Raith Rovers 2–0 in the 1912/13 Scottish Cup final, they were on a run that

Bert Slater, of Falkirk saves at Ibrox. Later he was transferred to Dundee.

eventually brought nine consecutive top ten finishes in the league. Then in 1922 they hit the headlines by paying the record sum of £5,000 to sign Syd Puddefoot from West Ham.

Over the following years their form in the league was unexceptional, but they were consistent performers. By the time of league reconstruction in 1975 they had spent only six seasons outside the top division since 1905 and had collected three Division Two titles in the course of 'bouncing back'. One of their most memorable years was 1957, when Englishman Reggie Smith was manager. Season 1956/57 had been disappointing in the league, with relegation only avoided by four points, but then they reached the final of the Scottish Cup. Their opponents Kilmarnock were firm favourites, but Falkirk took them to a replay after a 1–1 draw. Once again it was 1–1 after ninety minutes, but a goal in extra time from Dougie Moran was enough to take the cup back to Brockville.

Alex Ferguson joined from Rangers in 1969 and the Division Two title was won in 1970. The following season the Bairns finished seventh in the league, but by 1974 they were back in Division Two, and in 1975 the Division Two title only earned them a place in the new First Division (second tier). Then the team's form slipped even more, and between 1977 and 1980 there were three seasons in the Second Division (third tier). Defender Gary Gillespie attracted attention from the bigger clubs when he captained the side at the age of seventeen, and in 1978 he was transferred to Coventry City.

Falkirk-born Kevin McAllister joined the club in 1983, and his attacking play made him a favourite with the supporters. He would eventually have four different spells with the Bairns, and many years later the fans voted him their 'player of the millennium'. In the 1990s, with Jim Jefferies in charge, Falkirk enjoyed success and First Division titles in 1990/91 and 1993/94 were each followed by two seasons in the Premier Division. In 1993/94 they also won the Scottish League Challenge Cup, for clubs outwith the Premier Division, and they won it again in 1997/98, by which time Alex Totten had become manager.

At the end of the 1990s the club faced financial problems, but survived a period in provisional liquidation. Then it was Brockville Stadium, their home since 1885, that made the news. It failed to meet the requirements of the Scottish Premier League, and this denied Falkirk an opportunity for promotion on two occasions. At the end of the 1999/2000 season they weren't allowed to take part in the intended play-offs for a place in the SPL, despite finishing as runners-up in the First Division, and then they were denied promotion when they won the First Division title in 2002/03, saving Motherwell from relegation.

The result was the sale of Brockville in 2003 and the construction of the purpose-built Falkirk Stadium. After one season of sharing Ochilview with Stenhousemuir, the club moved into its new home in August 2004 and embarked on a season that brought the First Division championship, not to mention a third Scottish League Challenge Cup. This time promotion followed, and the Bairns moved up to the SPL, where their first two seasons both ended in the middle of the table.

FAMILIES

Families are a vital part of Scottish football, and Scottish football will in the long run lose out by not encouraging families enough. True, there were 'family enclosures' at grounds, a phenomenon of the 1990s and still there at some grounds, but there can be little doubt that the price rises of those days have done a great deal to deter

Falkirk in the early 1960s on a rainy day at Tynecastle.

a father from bringing his children to a game. There is a danger that a whole generation will lose interest in the game, particularly at some of the less well supported SPL grounds where empty stands hardly project the best image of Scottish football. It would surely be far better to admit school children for a nominal charge.

A particularly dreadful journalistic cliché is sometimes employed to describe a Scottish Cup final in which neither Rangers nor Celtic are involved. It is sometimes called 'the family final', a clear and insulting implication that Old Firm fans do not have families. Similarly, one often hears the atmosphere at some clubs described as a 'family atmosphere'. Those who say that have clearly little inkling of what goes on in many families!

Such is the tribal nature of football that families do tend to follow the same team. This is certainly true in the West of Scotland, although possibly less true in the East. There is also a great deal of evidence of football ability running in families. The best example of this must surely be the McStays. In the 1920s Willie and Jimmy McStay played for Celtic with Willie earning a thirteen caps for Scotland. In the 1980s Paul and Willie, their grand nephews also played for Celtic, and Paul of course seventy–six times with distinction for Scotland. In 1923, 1925, 1927 and 1985 Celtic won the Scottish Cup with two McStays in the team! The Callaghan brothers also won the Scottish Cup for Dunfermline in 1968. The same two also played in a losing cause in the final of 1965, as did Derek and Darren Young (also of Dunfermline) in 2004.

Rangers hold the record of having four brothers playing together in the same side. On several occasions in 1874 (the second year of their formation) Rangers fielded four brothers – William, Harold, Moses and Peter McNeil. A remarkable example of brothers who played together where the O'Donnells, Hugh and Frank. Hugh was a left winger and Frank a centre forward. They started playing together for St Agatha's School, Leven then moved together to Denbeath Violet, Wellesley Juniors, Celtic, Preston North End, Blackpool, Hearts and Liverpool! But their careers were not entirely parallel. Frank earned six caps for Scotland, while Hugh won the Scottish Cup with Celtic in 1933 and the English Cup with Preston in 1938.

There was the case of the Shaw brothers, both left backs with a similar 'no-nonsense', but totally sporting approach to the game. They were even rivals in the years immediately after the second world war for a place in the Scotland team. Jock 'Tiger' Shaw played for Rangers while his younger brother Davie played for Hibs. They never played together in the Scottish team in a full international, although they did so twice in 1946 in 'Victory' unofficial internationals.

At least nineteen pairs of brothers have played for Scotland, not necessarily in the same game, but a good recent example is Gary and Steven Caldwell against Switzerland in 2006. In one case, a trio of brothers have worn the Scotland colours. They are Alexander, Gladstone and James Hamilton who played for Scotland a total of eight times between 1885 and 1906. Brothers playing against each other are hardly unusual, but several times in the 1980s there were brothers on opposite sides of the Old Firm. This was the McAdam family, Tom playing for Celtic and Colin for Rangers. On three occasions, Scottish Cup finals have been contested by managers who are brothers. In 1912, Celtic v. Clyde saw Willie Maley in opposition to his brother Alec and the same thing happened in 1923, except by this time Alec was manager of Hibs. Then in 1991, the Scottish Cup final between Dundee United and Motherwell brought Jim and Tommy McLean together. What made this one more poignant was that their father had died days before the final. Returning to the Maley family, Willie was the manager of Celtic as they won the Scottish Cup in 1904, then the following week his brother Tom won the English Cup as manager of Manchester City.

Craig Burley is George Burley's nephew.

Twin brothers Ian and Dick Campbell have had a long association with Scottish football. In February 2005 both won the manager of the month award, Dick with Partick Thistle in the First Division and Ian with Brechin City in the Second Division.

The Shankly brothers, Bob and Bill, seldom crossed paths on the football field, but both led their respective clubs to league championships – Bob with Dundee in 1962 and Bill on three occasions in 1964, 1966 and 1973 with Liverpool. Even more remarkable was that when Bob became manager of Stirling Albion in 1970, both their clubs played at Anfield (albeit with slightly different spelling).

Fathers and sons have also been known to play a part in Scottish football. There have been Barney Battles senior and junior, Kenny and Paul Dalglish, Jackie McNamara senior and junior, John Divers senior and junior, Alfie Conn senior and junior, Joe McBride senior and junior and a few others, but the most remarkable father and son are surely the Simpsons – Jimmy and Ronnie. Both were capped for Scotland and both played with distinction, but Jimmy played for Rangers, whereas Ronnie played in goal for (among others in a long and

Neil Gibson was Jimmy Gibson's father, and both played for Partick Thistle.

remarkable career) Celtic. Other fathers and sons who have played for Scotland are the Battles and the Conns (supra), James Blair senior and junior, Neil Gibson and Jimmy Gibson and Alex Higgins senior and junior.

One grandfather and grandson have played for Scotland in William McColl of Renton in 1895 and Ian McColl of Rangers in the 1950s. There have been father and son referees in Willie and Davie Syme.

FAMOUS FIVE

This was the name given to the Hibs forward line of the early 1950's - Gordon Smith, Bobby Johnstone, Lawrie Reilly, Willie Ormond and Eddie Turnbull. The name was first bestowed upon them by Rex Kingsley in the Sunday Mail, and was taken from the series of children's novels written by Enid Blyton. Hibs did well in the Scottish League in those days, winning it in 1948, 1951, 1952 and losing only on goal average in 1953 although they remained 'trophy shy' as far as the cup competitions went. The forward play was devastatingly successful, often getting the better even of Rangers 'Iron Curtain' defence.

Gordon Smith went on to win league championship medals with Hearts and Dundee, thus creating a record of winning three league medals with separate clubs (and none of them were with the Old Firm!), Bobby Johnstone went on to Manchester City, Lawrie Reilly became famous for his last minute goals, notably for Scotland versus England at Wembley in 1953, and Willie Ormond and Eddie Turnbull went on to have distinguished careers in football management, Ormond with St.Johnstone, Scotland, Hearts and Hibs and Turnbull with Queen's Park, Aberdeen and Hibs.

FANZINES

Most league clubs have one or more fanzines associated with them. The word 'fanzine' makes the point that they are magazines produced by fans, as opposed to official club publications. Usually written on poor quality paper, they can be scurrilous and contain obscene language, but are written by people whose love for their club is both transparent and real. The titles are often amusing – *the Loonatic* of Forfar Athletic (Forfar's nickname is the Loons), *Stark's Bark* of Raith Rovers (who play at Stark's Park), and *Wendy* of St Johnstone ('Oh, wen dee saints go marching in').

First coming to the fore in the 1980s, they soon proliferated and, as use of the internet increased, some fanzines, e.g. Rangers' *Follow, Follow* and Celtic's *Not The View* (Celtic's official magazine is the *Celtic View*), also became available on-line. There are also more serious publications such as *The Celt* and *The Rangers Historian,* which have a historical slant, but in general fanzines are popular for their irreverence and humour.

FARMER Sir Tom (1940 –)

Sir Tom Farmer is a businessman and philanthropist who describes himself as a Leither. He came to the rescue of Hibernian FC in 1991, when the club was in receivership and was being threatened with extinction. At that time proposals were being made for a merger with Heart of Midlothian FC, but Sir Tom said he felt that the continued existence of Hibs was important to the community of Leith.

His company paid almost three million pounds to buy the club and its related properties from the receiver, and in later years he also guaranteed loans for the improvement of the club's facilities. With an emphasis on the reduction of debt, he transformed the club from a position of vulnerability to one of stability.

FAULDHOUSE UNITED FC
(see JUNIOR FOOTBALL)

FERGUSON Sir Alex (1941 –)

The legendary Manager of Manchester United also made a significant contribution to Scottish football, particularly in the management of Aberdeen in the early 1980s, when he took them to four Scottish Cups, three Scottish League championships, one Scottish League Cup, and the European Cup-Winners' Cup in 1983. He had previously been the manager of East Stirlingshire and St Mirren. He was the assistant manager of the Scotland national team in 1985 and was called upon to take them to the World Cup finals of 1986 in Mexico following the sudden death of Jock Stein. In his playing career he turned out for Queen's Park, St Johnstone, Dunfermline, Rangers, Falkirk and Ayr United as a forward, but he never won any major honour and, like many great managers, was a good but not a great player. He never played again for Rangers following the Scottish Cup final of 1969, in which he failed to mark Billy McNeill for Celtic's first goal early in the game. His main contribution to Scottish football has been as a manager.

Sir Alex Ferguson (left) and Barry Ferguson of Rangers (right).

FERGUSON Barry (1978 –)

Scotland Caps: 43
Scottish Premier League medals: 4
Scottish Cup medals: 4
Scottish League Cup medals: 5

A talented midfielder with Rangers, for whom he first played in 1996, Barry Ferguson took time out with Blackburn Rovers from 2003 to 2005, after he had been the youngest-ever captain of Rangers in season 2001/02. He was transferred to Blackburn for over £6.2 million and went back to Ibrox for £4.5 million. In 2003 he won both the Football Writers' and the Professional Football Players' Player of the Year award for the part he played in winning a domestic treble for Rangers, even though he had been in pain with pelvic trouble. He is no stranger to controversy, but has been a regular member of the Scotland team since 1999, having won forty-three caps.

FERGUSON Hughie (1896 – 1930)

Hughie Ferguson was a famous and tragic figure, who scored 364 goals in a career that saw him play for Motherwell, Cardiff City and Dundee. At one point he held the British record for goalscoring, and he is famous for two things. He was 'the Scotsman who scored the goal which took the English Cup to Wales', when Cardiff City won the FA Cup in 1927, and then, tragically, in 1930 he took his own life at Dens Park, Dundee, being found one morning in a gas-filled room. He had been suffering from illness and injury for some time. Amazingly for a man who scored so many goals, he was never capped for Scotland.

FERNIE Willie (1928 –)

Scotland Caps: 12
Scottish League Championship medals: 1
Scottish Cup medals: 1
Scottish League Cup medals: 2

Willie Fernie was a great dribbler of the ball in the 1950s, when he starred for Celtic and Scotland, with whom he won twelve caps. A famously sporting and gentlemanly player, he came from Kinglassie in Fife. He could play inside forward or right half, and with Celtic he won several honours, one of them being the 7–1 beating of Rangers, in which he starred at right half and scored a last-minute penalty. He also played on the left wing in the Coronation Cup final of 1953. In the late 1950s he had a couple of successful seasons with Middlesbrough before returning to Celtic for a year, and then finishing his career with St Mirren and Alloa. He was a coach with Celtic for a spell, and manager of Kilmarnock for four years in the mid 1970s. He did not play as often as expected for Scotland, but he did take part in the World Cup finals of 1954 and 1958.

FIFE CUP

This tournament has proved to be more robust than most other regional tournaments. Indeed in the heydays of East Fife and Raith Rovers, it was much prized. Since its inception in 1883 it has only missed 1899, 1900, 1919, 1938-46 and (mysteriously) 1948. Like a few regional trophies, it managed to keep going during the Great War, but the Spanish flu epidemic of 1919 was too much for it. The term 'Fife' is sometimes used loosely, for Alloa and Clackmannan were regular competitors in the early days. Since the turn of the century, however, it has struggled, and such games as have been played have seen small crowds and little interest.

1883	Dunfermline	1884	Dunfermline	1885	Cowdenbeath
1886	Alloa Athletic	1887	Dunfermline Ath.	1888	Lassodie
1889	Cowdenbeath	1890	Cowdenbeath	1891	Cowdenbeath
1892	Raith Rovers	1893	Cowdenbeath	1894	Raith Rovers
1895	Clackmannan	1896	Clackmannan	1897	Dunfermline Ath.
1898	Raith Rovers	1899	No competition	1900	No competition
1901	Hearts of Beath	1902	Cowdenbeath	1903	Hearts of Beath
1904	Cowdenbeath	1905	Cowdenbeath	1906	Raith Rovers
1907	Kirkcaldy United	1908	East Fife	1909	Raith Rovers
1910	Cowdenbeath	1911	Dunfermline Ath.	1912	Dunfermline Ath.
1913	Kirkcaldy United	1914	Dunfermline Ath.	1915	Raith Rovers
1916	Cowdenbeath	1917	Cowdenbeath	1918	Dunfermline Ath.
1919	No competition	1920	Dunfermline Ath.	1921	Raith Rovers
1922	Raith Rovers	1923	Raith Rovers	1924	Cowdenbeath
1925	Raith Rovers	1926	Cowdenbeath	1927	Dunfermline Ath.
1928	Cowdenbeath	1929	Cowdenbeath	1930	Raith Rovers
1931	East Fife	1932	East Fife	1933	East Fife
1934	Dunfermline Ath.	1935	Cowdenbeath	1936	East Fife
1937	East Fife	1938	No competition	1939	No competition
1940	No competition	1941	No competition	1942	No competition
1943	No competition	1944	No competition	1945	No competition
1946	No competition	1947	Dunfermline Ath.	1948	No competition
1949	Raith Rovers	1950	East Fife	1951	Raith Rovers
1952	Dunfermline Ath.	1953	East Fife/Raith R.	1954	East Fife
1955	East Fife/Raith R.	1956	Raith Rovers	1957	Dunfermline/ Raith R.
1958	Dunfermline Ath.	1959	Dunfermline Ath..	1960	East Fife
1961	Dunfermline Ath.	1962	Raith Rovers	1963	Dunfermline Ath..
1964	Dunfermline Ath.	1965	Dunfermline Ath..	1966	Dunfermline/ Raith R.
1967	Raith Rovers	1968	Raith Rovers	1969	Raith Rovers
1970	Dunfermline Ath.	1971	Cowdenbeath	1972	Raith Rovers
1973	Dunfermline Ath.	1974	East Fife	1975	Dunfermline Ath.
1976	Raith Rovers	1977	Dunfermline Ath.	1978	East Fife
1979	East Fife	1980	Dunfermline Ath.	1981	Raith Rovers
1982	Dunfermline Ath.	1983	Dunfermline Ath.	1984	Cowdenbeath
1985	East Fife	1986	East Fife	1987	Raith Rovers
1988	Cowdenbeath	1989	Raith Rovers	1990	Raith Rovers
1991	Raith Rovers	1992	Dunfermline Ath.	1993	Raith Rovers
1994	Raith Rovers	1995	Raith Rovers	1996	Cowdenbeath
1997	Dunfermline Ath.	1998	Raith Rovers	1999	Raith Rovers
2000	Raith Rovers	2001	Dunfermline Ath.	2002	Raith Rovers
2003	Dunfermline Ath.	2004	Raith Rovers	2005	East Fife
2006	East Fife	2007	Dunfermline Ath.		

FINLAND

Scotland's record against the Finns is a good one. Eight games have been played, six won and two drawn.

1954	25 May	Helsinki	2–1	Ormond Johnstone	Lahtinen
1964	21 Oct	Hampden Park	3–1	Law Chalmers Gibson	Peltonen
1965	27 May	Helsinki	2–1	Wilson Greig	Hyvarinen
1976	8 Sep	Hampden Park	6–0	A. Gray (2) E. Gray Rioch Masson Dalglish	
1992	25 Mar	Hampden Park	1–1	McStay	Litmanen
1994	7 Sep	Helsinki	2–0	Shearer Collins	
1995	6 Sep	Hampden Park	1–0	Booth	
1998	22 Apr	Easter Road	1–1	Jackson	Johansson

FIXTURES

These are usually produced around the middle of June, after the computers of the SPL and SFL have done their work trying to avoid clashes such as Dundee and Dundee United being at home on the same day, and allowing for the preferences of clubs about whether they would like to play on 2 January, Boxing Day etc. No one is ever totally satisfied with the outcome, but an attempt is made to alleviate obvious problems. Then television companies make their choice of the fixtures they want under the terms of their contract (with understandable but dismal frequency they usually go for whichever of the Old Firm is playing away from home). There sometimes appears to be a strange desire NOT to publish fixtures in some newspapers, even though it is a vital part of what can be a dull summer season for football fans.

In the SFL, postponed games are played off in the month of March as far as possible. Any fixture that has been lost to the weather may be played off whenever the teams agree, although there is no compulsion to do so in the months of January or February. By March, however, a date is assigned by the SFL.

There is another issue in the SPL, and it concerns the 'split'. After thirty-three games, (i.e. after each team has played everyone else three times) the SPL splits into two sections, so that the top six play each other and the bottom six do likewise. The top six then compete for the championship and European places, whilst the bottom six play to avoid relegation. This is not unique in world football, but is certainly unusual. No matter how well a team does in the bottom half of the split, it cannot overtake the team at the bottom of the top half of the split. Every effort is made to ensure that each team has nineteen home fixtures over the season. This means that in some cases teams will have played each other four times, three times at one ground, and only once at the other. This appears both wrong and unfair to many people, but it the SPL are to have this 'split' it is inevitable. It is not, however, the most embarrassing question about the 'split' that is asked by English and foreign journalists. The question that floors everyone is 'How is it possible for the team that ends up seventh to have more points than the team that ends up sixth?'

FLEETING Julie (1980 –)

One of the country's most successful woman footballers, Julie Fleeting is a striker with an outstanding goal scoring record. Born in Kilwinning, Ayrshire, she began her career with Ayr Ladies, and then moved to San Diego Spirit in 2002. When the United States league disbanded she joined Ross County Ladies on loan and then signed for Arsenal Ladies in January 2004. Her record with Arsenal did much to raise the profile of Scottish women's football in England, particularly her winning hat-trick in the 2004 Women's FA Cup final against Charlton Athletic.

After making her debut for Scotland against Wales in November 1996, she became captain of the national team in 2002, and for much of her international career her goal scoring average was higher than one goal per game. A goal against Slovakia on 27 October 2007 took her total to one hundred goals in ninety-nine matches, and then four days later she became only the second woman to play one hundred times for Scotland (along with Pauline Hamill) when she took part in the 1–0 defeat against Denmark at McDiarmid Park. In June 2008 she was awarded the MBE for services to women's football.

FLETCHER, Darren (1984 –)

Scotland Caps: 36

A midfielder, Darren Fletcher was not always a regular with Manchester United, but nevertheless won all three of the major English honours with them. He has also played thirty-six times for Scotland and, when he captained the national side at the age of twenty in a 1–0 victory over Estonia in Tallinn on 26 May 2004, he was the youngest Scotland captain since John Lambie in 1886.

FLOODLIGHTS

Nowadays floodlights are the *sine qua non* of any football ground. Indeed it is hard to imagine football without them, for they allow the playing of football in the evening. Even on Saturday afternoons in the winter floodlights allow games to kick off at 3pm instead of the 2pm that used to be necessary in the months of November to January. European football would simply not be possible without floodlights. Indeed both phenomena arrived on the scene at the same time in the mid 1950s.

It is reported that an attempt was made to use floodlights on a football field as early as the night of 25 October 1878. Third Lanark invited Vale of Leven to play a game under lights. Electricity was in its infancy then, and disappointment ensued until a single beam was deployed from a platform some fifty feet above the pitch, presumably operated by a man in a very precarious position. While everyone applauded his courage, they were less impressed by his technique, for he found it difficult to keep up with play and much of the game had to be played in darkness while the intrepid technician struggled to bring his lamp into position. A long punt up field would have caused tremendous problems. Third Lanark beat Vale of Leven 2–1.

A few weeks after that the idea spread to Edinburgh – to Powderhall where Hibs were to take on a motley crew referred to as an 'Association Team', or the 'Rest of Edinburgh', on 11 November 1878. Mr E. Patterson of London was to supply three electric lights for this fixture. The idea failed, however, because of a snowstorm which restricted the crowd, and also because two of the lights failed to function – one from the outset

Floodlight football in the 1950s in this unofficial international match between Scotland and South Africa at Ibrox. Scotland's Tommy Younger saves from Johnny Hubbard of Rangers and South Africa.

September 1959: Rangers v Anderlecht in the European Cup at Ibrox. Observe the floodlights and the half-time scoreboard.

and one at half time. But the show (and the snow) went on, with Hibs winning 3–0, but little more was heard of this idea.

Ten years later in 1888 at the Glasgow International Exhibition, a floodlit match took place between Vale of Leven and Rangers under the illuminating rays of the 'Well's Light', on Tuesday 6 November with a 7.00 p.m kick-off. Vale of Leven won 8–0, and the Scottish Sport's report on the game jokes that Rangers were "in the dark", whereas the Vale players "were fairly on the dot, and rattled away as if artificial light was their native element". But, for one reason or another, 'Well's Light' soon disappears into the mists of oblivion.

Various teams experimented with floodlights in the 1890s, notably Celtic, Morton and Clyde, but the experiments were not deemed a success because electric cables and bulbs were a danger to the players, suspended as they were, in some cases, a mere twelve feet above the ground. In March 1890 Morton played St Mirren in a game floodlit by oil lamps. Celtic tried an experiment with lights in a game against Clyde on Christmas Night 1893 – wires were attached to a dozen huge wooden posts fifty feet high, and lamps were attached to wires stretched over the park. There were also a hundred gas jets stretched along the top of the covered enclosure. The problem was that the wires sagged and the ball hit them. Yet Celtic might have persevered with 'Madden's Shipyard', (as the fans called the floodlit arena after their famous forward Johnny Madden), if St Bernard's had not threatened to object when the ball kept hitting the wires in a Scottish Cup game (played in daylight) in January 1894.

After Celtic lost interest, few other teams thought about floodlights and the idea died a death for over fifty years. Midweek games in winter until the second world war had to be played before miniscule crowds in the afternoon, although there was a tendency for games to kick off as late as possible in autumn and spring to take advantage of what daylight there was, and to allow as many people as possible to get to the match. In particular, press reports would frequently carry stories about the mass influx of schoolboys in time to see the second half.

The earliest floodlit Scottish football game in modern times took place on 7 November 1951 at Ochilview Park, Stenhousemuir when the local team took on Hibs. The Edinburgh side won 5–3 in this friendly, and the spectators thought it was a good idea, but the establishment, conservative as always, took some time to be won round. Nevertheless friendlies continued to be played, often against English or European opposition, and sometimes, crucially, in front of television cameras. By 1956 floodlit games were allowed in official competitions.

There had been some considerable debate about the wisdom of playing under lights, with people worrying about the effect that they would have on the eyesight of players and spectators, whether a ball would swing 'like a cricket ball' in the artificial light, and what would happen in the event of a power cut. But on Monday 6 February 1956 the SFA gave permission for two Scottish Cup ties to be played under floodlights on Wednesday 8 February. These games were East Fife versus Stenhousemuir and Hibs versus Raith Rovers, both games having been postponed the previous Saturday because of bad weather. Stenhousemuir are therefore the first Scottish team to win a competitive floodlight game, for they beat East Fife 3–1 while Hibs and Raith Rovers drew 1–1.

The first Scottish League game to be played under floodlights was Rangers' 8–0 beating of Queen of the South at Ibrox on 7 March 1956, (Don Kitchenbrand scored five goals) and Ibrox was also the venue for the floodlit replay of the Scottish League Cup semi-final of 9 October 1956, when Partick Thistle beat Dundee 3–2. Scotland's first floodlit international was the game against Wales at Hampden Park on 8 November 1961, when Ian St John scored twice in Scotland's 2–0 victory. Some grounds (notably Hampden Park, whose floodlights were not 'hanselled' until October 1961 in a friendly between Rangers and Eintracht Frankfurt) were late to get their pylons. Nevertheless such pylons soon became a landmark in most Scottish towns and cities, often giving an indication to travelling supporters of how to reach a ground. Queen of the South claim that theirs are the highest in the country, at eighty-four feet.

In time pylons came to be replaced, in some grounds at least, by strong lights from the top of the stands, and very seldom nowadays are there complaints of floodlights not being strong enough. (See **ESTONIA** for an example of how football can make an international fool of itself).

Celtic and Hibs once tried to get a League Cup semi-final at Ibrox moved to Hampden Park because of inadequate floodlighting. This was in October 1965, and when the first game went to a replay, the protests became even stronger. The Scottish League refused, perhaps reckoning that this was nothing more than a piece of political propaganda brought by Celtic to unsettle Rangers.

If the lights fail, the game must be abandoned or postponed. This happened, for example, at a League Cup game between Livingston and Celtic on 28 November 2001, to the intense disappointment of the players and the STV crew, whose commentator had to tell the frustrated Celtic and Livingston fans that they would be watching the royal variety performance instead!

FOREIGN PLAYERS

As a rule, until about the mid 1980s, foreign players were a rarity in Scottish football. There were several reasons for this.

In the first place, Scotland suffered from a surfeit of arrogance, believing that Scottish players were good enough in any company, and that foreigners could not tell them very much. To be fair to this seemingly blinkered view of things, it would have to be admitted that, given Scotland's mastery of the Home International Championship, a good case could be made out for Scotland being the best in the world.

Secondly, foreign players were reluctant to come to Scotland, where (according to reputation) the climate was harsh, the tackles were hard, and only the really tough survived. In addition, the remuneration was not as attractive as it is now. There were very few exceptions to this trend, and the first known Danish professional footballer in Scotland, for example, is Carl 'Shoemaker' Hansen, who joined Rangers in 1921. Normally, the furthest anyone was likely to come would be from England or Ireland, although Celtic employed a Canadian goalkeeper called Joe Kennaway in the mid 1930s. Dundee's Albert Juliussen of the late 1940s was in fact from County Durham, although his parents were Norwegian.

In the early 1960s, however, first Morton and then Dundee United engaged players from Scandinavia, where the game was still amateur and whose players were thus open to offers from Scotland. The best was perhaps Orjan Persson, who played for Dundee United and then Rangers while still playing international football for Sweden. Hamilton Accies became the first Scottish club to bring in players from eastern Europe, when Polish international players Witold Szygula and Roman Strzalkowski were recruited in 1971.

Shunsuke Nakamura of Celtic

Dundee FC's Claudio Caniggia in action at Dens before he was transferred to Rangers.

14 April 2000: Rangers' Jorg Albertz, centre left, celebrates with teammate Tugay Kerimoglu, after scoring for Rangers against Dundee United.

This trend did not last long however, and from the early 1970s until 1986 very few non-Scots took part in the Scottish game, although there was, for example, the Icelander Johannes Edvaldsson who played for Celtic. But in 1986, Rangers appointed Graeme Souness to Ibrox and gave him as much money as he wanted to buy players. First came Englishmen like Terry Butcher and Ray Wilkins, and then players of all nationalities including the black Mark Walters, whose arrival was sadly greeted by banana throwing and monkey noises.

By the mid 1990s, foreign players were here in sufficient numbers for their presence not to be an issue, but it cannot be said that in every case they were a success. There was Brian Laudrup who starred for Rangers, and Henrik Larsson who did equally well for Celtic, but many clubs were let down by their foreign mercenaries, who in many cases seemed to lack the commitment or attitude of mind to do well in Scotland, however talented they may have been. Celtic in particular suffered a great deal from the personality problems of many of their expensive foreigners. Yet clubs, particularly the Old Firm, remained willing to pay out attractive money. Jonas Thern, for example, one-time captain of Sweden, is on record as saying that he came to Rangers in 1997 because they were willing to pay more than anyone else.

Nor did this trend work well for the national side, for many young Scottish players were being denied the chance to play for a Scottish team. It is no coincidence that the fortunes of the national side have taken a severe dip since the arrival of foreign players in such large numbers to Scotland (and England), and some teams seem to be taking positive steps to redress the balance. Yet in these post-Bosman days, where any player can go where he wishes at the end of his contract, it is even more difficult to hang on to talented young Scots, and sometimes it is easier to replace them by mediocre foreigners, particularly from Eastern Europe.

Yet in the early years of the twenty-first century, with the freedom of movement allowed in the European Union as well as by the Bosman ruling, it is hard to imagine Scottish football without names like Paatelainen, Boruc, Darcheville, Invincibile, Beuzelin, and the myriad of Lithuanian names from Tynecastle. Scottish football is surely all the richer for such diversity.

FORFAR ATHLETIC FC

Ground: **Station Park**
Nickname: **The Loons**
Colours: **Navy blue and sky blue**
Record Attendance: **10,780 v Rangers (1970)**
Record Victory: **14-1 v Lindertis, Kirriemuir (1888)**
Record Defeat: **2-12 v Kings Park (1930)**
Highest League Position: **14th (4th in First Div., 1985/86)**
Best Scottish Cup Performance: **Last 4 (1981/82)**
Best League Cup Performance: **Last 4 (1977/78)**

The club can trace its origins back to May 1885 and the founding members are believed to be a group of reserve team players from Angus Athletic, who broke away to form a new club. After playing friendly matches and entering local cup competitions, they began playing league football in 1891/92, when they joined the Northern League. Although they won the title in 1895/96, re-election had to be sought on more than one occasion.

James Black, a man who led the club for decades, dominates the early history of Forfar Athletic. He initially introduced a policy of using local players whenever possible and under his guidance a long tradition of cup success began. It started with the Forfarshire Cup, which was won for the first time in 1906, and in 1910/11 there was a famous 2–0 victory against high-flying Falkirk in the second round of the Scottish Cup. In 1914 he signed Alec Troup, who went on to play alongside Dixie Dean at Everton, and was arguably Forfar's best-ever player.

When the new Division Two was formed for the 1921/22 season, Forfar became one of the founder members, but in 1925 they finished bottom and were relegated to Division Three for the 1925/26 season. This turned out to be the last season for this first attempt at a third-tier division, and the fixtures were uncompleted. Forfar finished third in the table and it might have been the end of their time in the Scottish League, but when Broxburn United resigned, Forfar were given their place in Division Two.

There were occasional cup successes, such as winning the Forfarshire Cup in 1931, and an impressive 2–2 away draw against Hibernian in the 1932/33 Scottish Cup, but the club was an ever-present in the lower division until the Scottish League was suspended at the start of the second world war in 1939. At the end of the hostilities, the club found itself in Division C for the 1946/47 season, but managed to escape by topping the table and winning promotion to Division B in 1948/49.

Since then the club's successes have mainly come by way of cup competitions. Manager Archie Knox led them to the semi-finals of the League Cup in 1977/78, when they lost 5–2 to Rangers after being 2–1 ahead with less than ten minutes to play, and then they reached the last four of the 1981/82 Scottish Cup under Alex Rae. Once again it was Rangers who beat them at Hampden Park, this time 3–1 after a 0–0 first game. Then, in 1986/87, Dundee United needed a late equaliser and a replay before preventing them from reaching the semi-finals of the Scottish Cup for a second time.

Forfar's team that won the Second Division Championship in 1984.

Forfar's league form has been relatively poor. They finished bottom of the Scottish League on three occasions in the 1960s and 1970s, but their best years came in the 1980s, under manager Doug Houston. They won the Second Division title by sixteen points in 1983/84 and in 1985/86 they finished fourth in the First Division (second tier), only one point behind promoted Falkirk, but the club has never made that final leap into the top flight. After relegation from the First Division in 1992, the Loons have spent their time in the third and fourth tiers of Scottish football. Their former goalkeeper Jim Moffat was appointed manager in March 2007, just a few weeks before they ended the season twenty points adrift at the bottom of the Second Division, but he left in April 2008, after a dismal season that saw Forfar finish at the foot of the Scottish Football League.

FORFARSHIRE CUP

This was a competition played for by the teams of Angus (or Forfarshire as it was once known) and Dundee, and latterly including others, for instance St Johnstone. Enthusiasm was never high for this trophy. Dundee would frequently enter their reserve side, and the games tended to be played at the end of the season or the beginning of the next season. As interest diminished, the trophy almost fizzled out at the turn of the century, although for teams like Forfar Athletic, a victory in this competition was a great event. The list of winners contains a team called Dundee Hibernian. That was before they changed their name to Dundee United. There was also a Forfarshire Charity Cup, which did not even last until the turn of the nineteenth to the twentieth century, but was won five times by Forfar, twice by Montrose and once by Arbroath.

The winners of the Forfarshire Cup (in the years that it was competed for) were:

1883/84	Arbroath	1884/85	Dundee Harp	1885/86	Dundee Harp
1886/87	Dundee Harp	1887/88	Arbroath	1888/89	Arbroath
1889/90	Our Boys	1890/91	Our Boys	1891/92	Montrose
1892/93	Arbroath	1893/94	Dundee	1894/95	Dundee
1895/96	Arbroath	1896/97	Arbroath	1897/98	Dundee Wdrs.
1898/99	Arbroath	1899/00	Arbroath	1900/01	Dundee
1901/02	Dundee Wdrs.	1902/03	Dundee	1903/04	Dundee Wdrs.
1904/05	Dundee	1905/06	Forfar Athletic	1906/07	Arbroath
1907/08	Forfar Athletic	1908/09	Dundee	1909/10	Brechin City
1910/11	Dundee Hibs.	1911/12	Dundee	1912/13	Dundee
1913/14	Arbroath	1914/15	Dundee Hibs.	1915/16	Montrose
1916/17	No competition	1917/18	No competition	1918/19	No competition
1919/20	Dundee Hibs.	1920/21	Arbroath	1921/22	Montrose
1922/23	Dundee	1923/24	Arbroath	1924/25	Dundee
1925/26	No competition	1926/27	No competition	1927/28	No competition
1928/29	Dundee United	1929/30	Dundee United	1930/31	Forfar Athletic
1931/32	Montrose	1932/33	Montrose	1933/34	Arbroath
1934/35	Dundee	1935/36	Arbroath	1936/37	Arbroath
1937/38	Dundee	1938/39	Arbroath	1939/40	Arbroath
1940/41	No competition	1941/42	No competition	1942/43	No competition
1943/44	No competition	1944/45	Dundee	1945/46	Dundee
1946/47	Dundee	1947/48	Dundee United	1948/49	Dundee
1949/50	Dundee	1950/51	Dundee United	1951/52	Montrose
1952/53	Brechin City	1953/54	Dundee United	1954/55	Dundee
1955/56	Dundee	1956/57	Not completed	1957/58	Arbroath
1958/59	Brechin City	1959/60	Dundee	1960/61	Dundee United
1961/62	Montrose	1962/63	Dundee United	1963/64	Not completed
1964/65	Dundee United	1965/66	Dundee	1966/67	Dundee
1967/68	Dundee United	1968/69	Dundee United	1969/70	Not completed
1970/71	Dundee	1971/72	Not completed	1972/73	Montrose
1973/74	Not completed	1974/75	Dundee United	1975/76	Dundee United
1976/77	Dundee United	1977/78	Not completed	1978/79	Forfar Athletic
1979/80	Dundee United	1980/81	Not completed	1981/82	Not completed
1982/83	Not completed	1983/84	Forfar Athletic	1984/85	Dundee United
1985/86	Dundee	1986/87	Dundee United	1987/88	Dundee United
1988/89	Dundee	1989/90	Dundee	1990/91	Forfar Athletic
1991/92	Montrose	1992/93	St Johnstone	1993/94	Not completed
1994/95	Forfar Athletic	1995/96	Forfar Athletic	1996/97	Brechin City
1997/98	Not completed	1998/99	St Johnstone	1999/00	Dundee
2000/01	Not completed	2001/02	Montrose	2002/03	Not completed
2003/04	St Johnstone	2004/05	Dundee United	2005/06	Dundee United
2006/07	St Johnstone				

FORMER SCOTTISH LEAGUE CLUBS

Thirty-eight clubs have seen their membership of the Scottish Football League come to an end, and an individual account of each one is provided elsewhere. Not all of their names have disappeared, as some junior teams still carry the name of a senior predecessor, for example Arthurlie, Beith, Clydebank, Royal Albert and Vale of Leven. Some names have been used again in senior non-league football, such as Edinburgh City in the East of Scotland League and Nithsdale Wanderers in the South of Scotland League.

The bleakest year was 1926, when Division Three folded, and thirteen clubs ended their association with the Scottish League. There would have been seventeen, but Leith Athletic, Forfar Athletic, Montrose and Brechin City were later given another opportunity. Leith Athletic left once more in 1953 and Forfar, Montrose and Brechin are the only clubs to remain from that doomed division.

The ending of a club's membership has usually been because of severe financial problems, dismal league form, or a combination of both. Sometimes, however, it has been when a club has lost its home and never recovered from the blow. Examples of this are the unfortunate King's Park, whose ground in Stirling was bombed during the second world war, and Abercorn, when the lease for their ground in Paisley came to an end. Ayr and Ayr Parkhouse combined to form Ayr United, a club that provides the only example of a Scottish League club being formed by the amalgamation of two previous Scottish League clubs.

The table below shows the years when the thirty-eight clubs played in the Scottish Football League.

Leith Athletic FC 1931.

Dykehead FC 1896/97.

King's Park FC 1932/33.

Edinburgh City FC 1931.

Club	From	Until	
Abercorn FC	1890	1915	
Airdrieonians FC	1894	2002	
Armadale FC	1921	1932	(g)
Arthurlie FC	1901	1915	
	1923	1929	(e)
Ayr FC	1897	1910	
Ayr Parkhouse FC	1903	1904	
	1906	1910	
Bathgate FC	1921	1929	(f)
Beith FC	1923	1926	(d)
Bo'ness FC	1921	1932	(g)
Broxburn Utd. FC	1921	1926	
Cambuslang FC	1890	1892	
Clackmannan FC	1921	1922	
	1923	1926	(d)
Clydebank FC	1914	1915	
	1917	1931	
	1966	2002	(i)
Cowlairs FC	1890	1891	
	1893	1895	
Dumbarton Harp FC	1923	1925	(c)
Dundee Wanderers FC	1894	1895	
Dykehead FC	1923	1926	(d)
Edinburgh City FC	1931	1949	
Galston FC	1923	1926	(d)
Gretna FC	2002	2008	
Helensburgh FC	1923	1926	
Johnstone FC	1912	1915	
	1921	1926	(d)
King's Park FC	1921	1939	(h)
Leith Athletic FC	1891	1915	
	1924	1926	(d)
	1927	1953	
Linthouse FC	1895	1900	
Lochgelly United FC	1914	1915	
	1921	1926	(d)
Mid-Annandale FC	1923	1926	(d)
Nithsdale Wanderers FC	1923	1927	
Northern FC	1893	1894	
Peebles Rovers FC	1923	1926	(d)
Port Glasgow Athletic FC	1893	1911	
Renton FC	1890	1890	(a)
	1891	1897	(b)
Royal Albert FC	1923	1926	(d)
St. Bernard's FC	1900	1915	
	1921	1939	
Solway Star FC	1923	1926	(d)
Third Lanark FC	1890	1967	
Thistle FC	1893	1894	
Vale of Leven FC	1890	1892	
	1905	1915	
	1921	1926	(d)

a) Expelled after five matches
b) Resigned after four matches of the 1897/98 season, after which Hamilton Ac. took over their fixtures
c) Did not complete their fixtures in 1924/25 and their record for that season was expunged
d) Did not complete their fixtures in 1925/26, when Division Three came to an end
e) Did not complete their fixtures in1928/29, but their record for that season was allowed to stand
f) Did not complete their fixtures in 1928/29 and their record for that season was expunged
g) Did not complete their fixtures in 1932/33 and their record for that season was expunged
h) Played four matches of the 1939/40 season before the league was abandoned because of the second world war
i) In addition, an amalgamated team called East Stirlingshire Clydebank competed in Division Two in 1964/65

Lochgelly United FC 1902/03.

Solway Star FC 1921/22.

FORSYTH Tam (1949 –)

Scotland Caps: 22
Scottish League Championship medals: 3
Scottish Cup medals: 4
Scottish League Cup medals: 2

Tam Forsyth was nicknamed 'Jaws', after the famous film of the 1970s, but there was a great deal more to his play than mere hard tackling. He was very versatile, playing at times in midfield and at other times as a defender. He was enthusiastic, committed, and well deserved his twenty-two caps for Scotland. Like many another international career, Forsyth's did not survive the return from the Argentina World Cup. He joined Motherwell in 1967, and then moved to Rangers in 1972, playing for the Ibrox side until injury compelled his retirement in 1982. He scored very few goals, but his most famous one was in the 1973 Scottish Cup final, when he squeezed the ball over the line with his studs. His best season was probably 1975/76, during which his solid defensive work helped Rangers to a treble of domestic honours. After he retired, he was manager at Dunfermline and assistant manager at Motherwell, but without any great success at either club.

FOURTH OFFICIAL (see REFEREE)

FRANCE

Scotland have played France fifteen times, winning eight and losing seven – not a bad performance in the light of the relative populations of the countries – although most of Scotland's successes were in the early years. The victories in 2006 and 2007, in the qualifying section for the 2008 European Football Championships, were tremendous triumphs for the nation, considering that the star-studded French were the beaten World Cup finalists of 2006.

1930	18 May	Paris	2–0	Gallacher (2)	
1932	8 May	Paris	3–1	Dewar (3)	Langilier (pen)
1948	23 May	Paris	0–3		Bongiorni Flamion Baratte
1949	27 Apr	Hampden Park	2–0	Steel (2)	
1950	27 May	Paris	1–0	Brown	
1951	16 May	Hampden Park	1–0	Reilly	
1958	15 June	Orebro	1–2	Baird	Kopa Fontaine
1984	1 June	Marseilles	0–2		Giresse Lacombe
1989	8 Mar	Hampden Park	2–0	Johnston (2)	
1989	11 Oct	Paris	0–3		Deschamps Cantona Nicol o.g.
1997	12 Nov	St Etienne	1–2	Durie	Laigle Djorkaeff
2000	29 Mar	Hampden Park	0–2		Wiltord Henry
2002	27 Mar	Paris	0–5		Trezeguet (2) Zidane Henry Marlet
2006	7 Oct	Hampden Park	1–0	Caldwell	
2007	12 Sep	Paris	1–0	McFadden	

FRIENDLIES

In today's overcrowded calendar, friendlies are a rarity and often give the impression of getting in the way. There are basically two types of friendlies played in the early twenty-first century – one is the pre-season friendly which counts for very little as it merely gives a manager a chance to assess his new squad before the serious stuff begins. Substitutions are frequent, and the result is not all that important and quickly forgotten about. There is also a testimonial game, which counts for even less, for it is a way to say thank you to a player for long service.

International friendlies do at least give the national manager a rare opportunity to glimpse some of his players playing for Scotland, but they are held in low esteem by the Scottish public and are particularly ill attended by supporters suspicious of the amount of call-offs though 'injuries'. The downside of these games is well illustrated by the tragic case of John Kennedy who lasted about 15 minutes in a friendly against Romania before being horrifically injured in a way that threatened his career.

Yet historically friendlies, whether for the national team or at club level, were highly regarded. Games played by Scotland against foreign opposition at Hampden attracted huge crowds and engendered great enthusiasm. 123,751 people, for example, were attracted to Hampden on Wednesday 26 April 1950 to see Scotland beat Switzerland 3–1, and on Wednesday 30 April 1952 107,765 saw Scotland defeat the USA 6–0. On the day that Scotland lost her proud record of never being beaten at Hampden by foreign opposition, Wednesday 13 December 1950 with a 2pm. kick-off in those pre-floodlight days, 68,468 people 'departed in funereal silence into the December gloom' according to a newspaper report – and that game was a friendly!

Club friendlies have always been played against English and Irish teams, and have been taken very seriously. On 6 August 1966, for example, the week after England won the World Cup, Celtic beat Manchester United 4–1 and Rangers beat Arsenal 2–0, before large crowds in each case. But it was not only pre-season that friendlies were played. Often a way of supplementing cash reserves after an early exit from the Scottish Cup would be to arrange a friendly against an attractive English team in a similar position.

GALLACHER Hughie (1903 – 1957)

Scotland Caps: 20
Scottish Cup medals: 1

Hughie Gallacher is perhaps the archetypal example of Scottish brilliance on the one hand, and self-destruction on the other. Arguably the greatest player of his day, but unable to abstain from alcohol, Hughie remains one of the real tragic figures of Scottish football. As a centre forward he had few equals, and scored 387 goals in 543 league matches. His first senior team was Airdrieonians, with whom he won a Scottish Cup medal in 1924, but the poverty of Airdrie compelled his transfer to Newcastle United, where he spearheaded the winning of the English league championship in 1927. He then moved to Chelsea in 1930, and subsequently played for Derby County, Notts County, Grimsby Town and Gateshead before his retiral at the start of the second world war.

For Scotland he won twenty caps, including the famous Wembley Wizards game of 1928. He scored five goals for Scotland against Northern Ireland at Windsor Park, Belfast on 23 February 1929, a Scotland record, and he also scored a hat-trick on another two occasions. But perhaps his best Scotland appearance was in 1925, when he scored the two goals at Hampden that beat England and confirmed the treble over the other British countries. Gallacher had scored in every game!

On Tyneside, where he lived after his football career, his fame remained. As late as the 1950s, children would sing the rhyme:

Dae ye mind o' Hughie Gallacher
The wee Scots lad?
The best centre forward
The Geordies ever had!
Dae ye mind o' Hughie Gallacher
The hero o' the toon
And he fairly scored the goals
For the Geordies!

But in spite of such hero status, alcoholism, the death of his wife, and depression marred Gallacher's later life. His end was very sad. On 11 June 1957, while facing a charge of child neglect, he threw himself in front of the York to Edinburgh express as it passed through Newcastle, at a place called, ironically enough, Dead Man's Railway Crossing, Low Fell, Gateshead. 'Wee Hughie's' death was as spectacular as his life had been.

GALLACHER Kevin (1966 –   )

Scotland Caps: 53

Kevin Gallacher was the grandson of Patsy Gallacher (see below), and his first breakthrough was with Jim McLean's Dundee United in the mid 1980s. He moved to Coventry City in 1989, Blackburn Rovers in 1993, and Newcastle United in 1999, before finishing his career with Preston North End, Sheffield Wednesday and Grimsby Town.

He was a strong attacking midfielder who earned fifty-three caps for Scotland, and played in the 1992 European Championship finals and the 1998 World Cup

finals. His best moment for Scotland was the excellent goal that he scored against Austria in a World Cup qualifying game in 1997 at Parkhead. In recent years he has involved himself in the media and writing about the game.

GALLACHER Patsy (1891 – 1953)

Scottish League Championship medals: 6
Scottish Cup medals: 4

Although an Irishman, Patsy Gallacher lived most of his life in Scotland and was, in the opinion of most who were alive at the time, the greatest player of them all. He made his debut for Celtic in December 1911 and played for them until 1926, when he joined Falkirk, for whom he played until 1932. He was best remembered for the phenomenal goal that he scored (he somersaulted into the net with the ball wedged between his legs) in the Scottish Cup final against Dundee in 1925, and during the first world war he was generally recognised as the 'most talked about man in the trenches'. He played eleven times for Ireland.

GALSTON FC (former Scottish League club)

Home: **Portland Park, Galston, East Ayrshire**
Highest League Position: **51st (11th in Div. 3, 1924/25)**
Best Scottish Cup Performance: **Last 16 (2nd round, 1906/07; 1907/08; 1910/11)**

The small town of Galston once had a football team in the Scottish League, but only because it was part of the short-lived Division Three that existed between 1923 and 1926. This was a time of depression in the Ayrshire mining industry and the consequence was low crowds and financial problems. The situation eventually got so bad that Galston had little choice but to resign from the Scottish League in February 1926 and their fixtures were uncompleted.

Believed to have been founded in 1886, the club's first appearance in the records of the Scottish Cup is a 2–1 first round defeat at Dumbarton in 1894/95. A few years later, in 1899/1900, they went on to win the Scottish Qualifying Cup with a 5–2 victory over Arbroath. There were three consecutive titles in the Scottish Football Combination between 1906 and 1909, and the championship of the Scottish Football Union in 1911/12, but most memorable of all were Scottish Cup ties against the old firm. A 2–1 home win over Motherwell in the first round of the 1906/07 competition earned a visit from Rangers, who progressed with a 4–0 victory, and then Galston restricted Celtic to a 1–0 second-round win at Celtic Park in 1910/11.

When league football resumed after the first world war, Galston became part of the Western League and occasionally made their presence felt in the Scottish Cup with results such as a 0–0 draw against Hibernian in 1919/20 and a 1–0 win against Stenhousemuir in 1922/23. Then came the ill-fated three years in Division Three.

When their time in the Scottish League was over, they played amateur football for a time and then, after reverting to semi-professional status in 1932, went on to enjoy the Scottish Cup once more. In 1934/35 neighbours Kilmarnock made the four-mile journey to Galston in order to record a 1–0 first-round win, and the following year, after winning the 1935/36 Scottish Qualifying Cup (South), Galston beat Stranraer 5–3 before losing 5–2 at Dunfermline in the second round. The onset of the second world war meant the suspension of organised football in 1939 and sadly Galston didn't reappear in 1945.

GATE RECEIPTS AND OTHER REVENUE

It used to be that gate receipts were always published along with the attendance after any big game such as a cup final or an international match. Such has been inflation in recent decades, particularly the 1970s, that the figures given then mean very little now to the historian. Gate receipts now, though significant, are only a fraction of the way that clubs and the game in general are financed, as other income comes from sponsorship or television money.

It is the practice now in the SPL for the home club to 'keep the gate'. This practice clearly works to the benefit of the better-off clubs. All operating expenses of running the SPL are covered by central broadcasting and commercial revenues. In contrast to other leagues and competitions, SPL broadcasting revenues are not split on a match-by-match basis that depends on which clubs are featured. All monies received from deals (Setanta Sports, BBC, STV, Bank of Scotland etc.) are put into a central 'pot'. From this are subtracted running costs, payments to the SFL, 'parachute' payments to recently relegated clubs, and staff/referee costs. Everything else that is left is distributed to the clubs, with 48% split equally and 52% split according to where a club finishes in the league. The end result is that the champion club will receive 17% of what is left in the pot, whilst the twelfth-placed club will receive 4.5%. In season 2006/07 the pot for the clubs totalled approximately £16 million, after approximately £3-3.5 million had been deducted from total revenues of £19-19.5 million.

In the SFL the home club also 'keeps the gate'. Clubs also receive money from any surplus of the league's trading account, on the basis of 75% to be divided equally among all member clubs, and 25% on an incentive-based system (55% going to First Division clubs, 33% to Second Division clubs, and 12% to Third Division clubs). The absence of a television deal clearly amounts to a major blow for SFL clubs.

In the Scottish League Cup (and the League Challenge Cup), after 15% has gone to the home club, the remainder of the gate money is shared between the participating clubs. The semi-final gates are pooled between the four teams after 5% has been retained by the SFL and 20% has gone to the host clubs. The 'gate' in the final is similarly divided. There is of course a TV deal for the Scottish League Cup, and this makes a great difference for both the clubs and the SFL. A similar system obtains in the Scottish Cup, which is, of course, organized by the SFA.

GEMMELL Tommy (1943 –)

Scotland Caps: 18
Scottish League Championship medals: 6
Scottish Cup medals: 3
Scottish League Cup medals: 4
European Cup medal: 1

One of the great characters of the Celtic team of the late 1960s, Tommy Gemmell was a real personality in Scottish football. He joined Celtic in 1961, but at first struggled to break into the first team. Even when he did come through, the nature of Celtic in those days counted against the development of this attacking left

back. It was only with the arrival of Jock Stein in 1965 that his career took off, for he was a vital factor in the great Celtic team of that era. He scored the equalizing goal in the final against Inter Milan, and Celtic's only goal in the European Cup final of 1970 against Feyenoord. He left for Nottingham Forest in 1971, then moved to Dundee in 1973, leading them to a Scottish League Cup win in December 1973 against his old team Celtic. He later became the manager of Dundee, and then Albion Rovers, before working on radio.

He played eighteen times for Scotland, his most famous outing being the 3–2 game against England at Wembley in 1967. He was famous for his attacking play, and in particular his goals from free kicks and long distance. He had his moments of notoriety too. He scored an own goal for the USSR against Scotland in May 1967, was sent off while playing for Scotland against West Germany in 1969, was sent home in disgrace from a Celtic tour of America in 1970, and in the infamous games against Racing Club in the World Championship, the whole world saw him take his revenge on an aggressive Argentinian. In spite of all this, he made a tremendous contribution to Celtic and to Scottish football in general.

GEMMILL Archie (1947 –)

Scotland Caps: 43

Archie Gemmill was a remarkable little midfielder, famous in Scottish history for two things. One was that he was the first-ever substitute in Scottish football history, in a game against Clyde in the Scottish League Cup on 13 August 1966, and the other was the great goal that he scored against Holland in Argentina in 1978, to give Scotland their only moment of glory in a disastrous tournament. Archie joined St Mirren in 1964, and played three years with them before moving to Preston North End, Derby County, Nottingham Forest and Birmingham City. In 1979 he tried football in the United States, before returning to play for Wigan Athletic and eventually Notts Forest for the second time.

He played forty-three times for Scotland, and never did the Tartan Army feel short changed by Gemmill's contribution. He won three English league championship medals, twice with Derby County (1972 and 1975) and once with Notts Forest (1978). He also won a League Cup medal with Forest the following year, but was unlucky to be left on the substitutes' bench for the European Cup final of that year. In 2006 he and Tommy Wilson earned plaudits for coaching the Scotland Under 19 team to the final of the European Championship.

GEMMILL Scott (1971 –)

Scotland Caps: 26

The son of Archie, Scott Gemmill was often compared unfavourably with his father, but he still managed to win

Father and son, Archie Gemmill (left) and Scott Gemmill (right).

twenty-six Scottish caps in his career with Nottingham Forest, Everton, Preston North End, Leicester City and Oxford United. He was an energetic midfield player, but his international career possibly suffered in that he played in poor Scottish teams.

GEORGIA

Scotland played Georgia twice in the qualifying campaign for the 2008 European Championship, winning at home and losing away.

2007	24 Mar	Hampden Park	2–1	Boyd Beattie	Arveladze
2007	17 Oct	Tbilisi	0–2		Mchedlidze Siradze

GERMANY

Although it was divided between the years of 1945 and 1990, Scotland have played a united Germany seven times, winning twice, drawing twice and losing three times.

Allegedly, Scotland's 1936 victory at Ibrox greatly displeased the Fuhrer. Jimmy Delaney scored twice for Scotland, thereby 'putting Hitler aff his tea'.

1929	1 June	Berlin	1–1	Imrie	Ruch
1936	14 Oct	Ibrox	2–0	Delaney (2)	
1992	15 June	Norrkoping	0–2		Riedle Effenberg
1993	24 Mar	Ibrox	0–1		Riedle
1999	28 Apr	Bremen	1–0	Hutchison	
2003	7 June	Hampden Park	1–1	Miller	Bobic
2003	10 Sep	Dortmund	1–2	McCann	Bobic Ballack (pen)

GERMANY (EAST)

Played six, won two, drawn one, lost three

1974	30 Oct	Hampden Park	3–0	Hutchison Burns Dalglish	
1977	7 Sep	East Berlin	0–1		Schade
1982	13 Oct	Hampden Park	2–0	Wark Sturrock	
1983	16 Nov	Halle	1–2	Bannon	Kreer Streich
1985	16 Oct	Hampden Park	0–0		
1990	25 Apr	Hampden Park	0–1		Doll (pen)

GERMANY (WEST)

Played eight, won two, drawn three, lost three

1957	22 May	Stuttgart	3–1	Collins (2) Mudie	Siedl
1959	6 May	Hampden Park	3–2	White Weir Leggat	Seeler Juskowiac
1964	12 May	Hanover	2–2	Gilzean (2)	Seeler (2)
1969	16 Apr	Hampden Park	1–1	Murdoch	Muller
1969	22 Oct	Hamburg	2–3	Johnstone Gilzean	Fichtel Muller Libuda
1973	14 Nov	Hampden Park	1–1	Holton	Hoeness
1974	27 Mar	Frankfurt	1–2	Dalglish	Breitner Grabowski
1986	8 June	Queretaro	1-2	Strachan	Voller Allofs

GIANT KILLING

This is a comparatively rare phenomenon in Scottish football, certainly in comparison with England. It means

Giant killing in the Scottish League Cup as Partick Thistle beat Celtic in 1971

the defeat of a rich, wealthy and powerful team by a team in a lower division. Only once has this happened in the Scottish Cup final and that was in 1938 when second division East Fife defeated Kilmarnock after a replay. Celtic have been giant-killed in the Scottish Cup on six occasions - by Arthurlie in 1897, by Dundee in 1947, Dundee United in 1949, Inverness Caledonian Thistle in 2000 and 2003 and by Clyde in 2006. The defeats by Arthurlie in 1897 and Inverness Caledonian Thistle in 2000 led to regime change on both occasions. Rangers have fallen less often but certainly their 1967 defeat by the other Rangers, those from Berwick, was a spectacular one, considering that they reached the final of the European Cup-Winners' Cup that same season! Aberdeen's highest-profile giant-killing defeat was to Queen of the South in the semi-final of 2008, but they also lost in an earlier round to Stenhousemuir in 1995, while Hearts went out to Forfar Athletic in 1982. Dundee fell to Fraserburgh in 1959. East Fife were unlucky to receive few headlines in 1967 when they Motherwell 1–0 on 28 January – a result that would surely have hit the headlines, had it not been for the fact that it was the same day that Berwick Rangers beat Glasgow Rangers! A few days later on 1 February (the original tie having been postponed) Elgin City beat Ayr United 2–0. Yet, unlike in England where most years can be guaranteed to produce a shock, such events are rare.

The Scottish League Cup has also produced some giant-killing moments, two in particular in season 2006/07, when Aberdeen went out to Queen's Park, then Rangers to St Johnstone. There have been two in the final. Raith Rovers beat Celtic in the final of 1994/95 (although they needed a penalty shoot-out to do so), and East Fife beat Falkirk 4–1 in season 1947/48. The 1971/72 final when Partick Thistle beat Celtic, unexpected and a shock though it was, cannot really be considered a giant killing, for both teams were in the old first division.

GIBSON Jimmy (1901 – 1978)

Scotland Caps: 8

Jimmy Gibson was a right half, whose main claim to fame is that he was the right half of the Wembley Wizards of 1928.

His father Neil played for both Partick Thistle and Rangers, and Jimmy joined Thistle in 1921, winning the first of his eight Scottish caps in 1926 when Scotland beat England 1–0 at Old Trafford. In 1927 he was transferred to Aston Villa for a record fee of £7,500, and played out his career with Villa until he retired in 1936

GILLICK Torry (1915 – 1971)

Scotland Caps: 5
Scottish League Championship medals: 1
Scottish Cup medals: 2
Scottish League Cup medals: 2

Torry Gillick was a talented inside forward for Rangers in the years after the second world war. He had joined Rangers in 1933, and been good enough to win a Scottish Cup medal with them in 1935, before he was surprisingly sold to Everton later that year. He then played in the very fine Everton side of the late 1930s, and won five Scottish caps before war was declared. In 1945 manager Struth broke one of his own rules by signing a player twice and brought him back to Ibrox, where he starred for Rangers, winning medals in each of Scotland's domestic tournaments. He finished his career with Partick Thistle.

GILZEAN Alan (1938 –)

Scottish Caps: 22
Scottish League Championship medals: 1

A prolific goal scorer with Dundee and Tottenham Hotspur, Alan Gilzean was capped twenty-two times for Scotland. He was born in Coupar Angus and joined Dundee in 1956, scoring many goals in their winning of

Alan Gilzean with Dundee FC, April 1962, when they won the Championship. Back row: (left to right) P. Liney, R. Wishart, A. Gilzean, R. Waddle, R. Seith, G. Smith. Front row: A. Penman, I. Ure, R. Cox, A. Hamilton, A. Cousin, H. Robertson.

the Scottish league championship in 1962, and their European Cup run the following year. His greatest achievement with Dundee was the seven goals he scored against Queen of the South on 1 December 1962. All this time, he remained an unpretentious man who played cricket in the summer for his native Coupar Angus team. Sadly for Scottish football, he was transferred to Tottenham Hotspur for £72,500 in December 1964. With Spurs, and utilising the service of Jimmy Greaves and others, Alan won an Inter-Cities Fairs Cup medal, an FA Cup medal, and two English League Cup medals. Scotland fans will always remember him for his glorious header which gave Scotland three victories in a row over England in the rain at Hampden Park in April 1964, and indeed it is his heading ability for which he was most renowned.

GIRVAN FC

Home: **Hamilton Park, Girvan, South Ayrshire**
Best Scottish Cup Performance: **Last 40 (2nd round, 1976/77)**

(Participating club in Scottish Cup, but not member of East of Scotland League, Highland League or South of Scotland League)

Founded in 1944, Girvan FC became a junior club in June 2004 after previously playing in the South of Scotland League, but the club retained its membership of the SFA as well as becoming a member of the SJFA. The Seasiders are therefore eligible to enter the Scottish Cup without having to win one of the junior competitions.

2006/07 was a disappointing season for the club, as it finished bottom of the West Region Superleague First Division but, in spite of being relegated, Girvan participated in the first round of the 2007/08 Scottish Cup, following the discontinuation of the Scottish Qualifying Cup that year. They scored a 2–0 home victory over Highland League Forres Mechanics, and in the second round they only went out at home to Third Division Stranraer after conceding a late penalty. By the end of the season they had been promoted back to the First Division.

Back in 1976/77, the Seasiders qualified for the Scottish Cup as a senior club. After receiving a bye in the first round, they were beaten 3–0 by Queen's Park at Hamilton Park.

GLASGOW CHARITY CUP

This tournament is no longer played for, a fact that many Scottish football fans regard as a shame. It is the second-oldest trophy in Scottish football, having been launched in 1876/77 by Glasgow merchants for the laudable purpose of raising money for charities, and it served that purpose for many decades. Until 1961 it was competed for at the end of every season (including war years) by Glasgow clubs, although on special occasions like the aftermath of the Ibrox disaster of 1902, teams from outwith the city were invited to compete. Hibernian won the trophy that year.

Even with the arrival of professionalism in the 1890s, it was expected that the players would provide their services free, although some observers suspected that they did not always do so. The tournament was taken seriously but, being played at the end of the season, it

lacked the status of the Scottish Cup or even the Glasgow Cup. By 1961 the month of May, when the Charity Cup was usually held, was becoming crowded with overseas tours, international fixtures and a later finish to the season, and clubs were withdrawing from the competition. The device of 'counting corners' was used to decide a winner so that a replay would not be necessary, and the trophy was shared on two occasions in latter years. After 1960/61 the tournament was abandoned in its existing format, but for the next five years there was a pre-season game between a Glasgow Select and a top English team, until in 1966 the tournament was finally abandoned after a draw between Leeds United and a Glasgow Select. The magnificent trophy now resides in the museum at Hampden Park. The results of the finals were:

1876/77	Queen's Park	4	0	Rangers
1877/78	Queen's Park	1	0	Vale of Leven
1878/79	Rangers	2	1	Vale of Leven
1879/80	Queen's Park	2	1	Rangers
1880/81	Queen's Park	3	1	Rangers
1881/82	Vale of Leven	1	0	Dumbarton
1882/83	Queen's Park	4	1	Rangers
1883/84	Queen's Park	8	0	Third Lanark
1884/85	Queen's Park	1	0	Dumbarton
1885/86	Renton	3	1	Vale of Leven
1886/87	Renton	1	0	Vale of Leven
1887/88	Renton	4	0	Cambuslang
1888/89	Renton	3	1	Queen's Park
1889/90	Third Lanark	2	1	Queen's Park
1890/91	Queen's Park	9	1	Northern
1891/92	Celtic	2	0	Rangers
1892/93	Celtic	5	0	Rangers
1893/94	Celtic	2	1	Queen's Park
1894/95	Celtic	4	0	Rangers
1895/96	Celtic	2	1	Queen's Park
1896/97	Rangers	6	1	Third Lanark
1897/98	Third Lanark	1	0	Rangers
1898/99	Celtic	2	0	Rangers
1899/00	Rangers	5	1	Celtic
1900/01	Third Lanark	3	0	Celtic
1901/02	Hibernian	6	2	Celtic
1902/03	Celtic	5	2	St Mirren
1903/04	Rangers	5	2	Celtic
1904/05	Celtic	2	0	Partick Thistle
1905/06	Rangers	3	2	Queen's Park
1906/07	Rangers	1	0	Celtic
1907/08	Celtic	3	0	Queen's Park
1908/09	Rangers	4	2	Celtic
1909/10	Clyde	1	1	Third Lanark
	Clyde won 8–3 on corners			
1910/11	Rangers	2	1	Celtic
1911/12	Celtic	0	0	Clyde
	Celtic won 7–0 on corners			
1912/13	Celtic	3	2	Rangers
1913/14	Celtic	6	0	Third Lanark
1914/15	Celtic	3	2	Rangers
1915/16	Celtic	2	0	Partick Thistle
1916/17	Celtic	1	0	Queen's Park
1917/18	Celtic	2	0	Partick Thistle
1918/19	Rangers	2	1	Queen's Park
1919/20	Celtic	1	0	Queen's Park
1920/21	Celtic	2	0	Rangers
1921/22	Rangers	3	1	Queen's Park
1922/23	Rangers	4	0	Queen's Park
1923/24	Celtic	2	1	Rangers
1924/25	Rangers	1	0	Clyde
1925/26	Celtic	2	1	Queen's Park
1926/27	Partick Thistle	6	3	Rangers
	After Extra Time			
1927/28	Rangers	3	1	Queen's Park
1928/29	Rangers	4	2	Celtic
1929/30	Rangers	2	2	Celtic
	Rangers won by the toss of a coin after extra time, with the score at two goals and four corners each			
1930/31	Rangers	2	1	Queen's Park
	After Extra Time			
1931/32	Rangers	6	1	Third Lanark
1932/33	Rangers	1	0	Queen's Park
1933/34	Rangers	1	0	Celtic
1934/35	Partick Thistle	2	1	Queen's Park
1935/36	Celtic	4	2	Rangers
1936/37	Celtic	4	3	Queen's Park
1937/38	Celtic	2	0	Rangers
1938/39	Rangers	0	0	Third Lanark
	Rangers won 7–3 on corners			
1939/40	Rangers	1	1	
	Rangers won 7–2 on corners			
1940/41	Rangers	3	0	Partick Thistle
1941/42	Rangers	3	1	Clyde
1942/43	Celtic	3	0	Third Lanark
1943/44	Rangers	2	1	Clyde
1944/45	Rangers	2	1	Celtic
1945/46	Rangers	2	0	Third Lanark
1946/47	Rangers	1	0	Celtic
1947/48	Rangers	2	0	Celtic
1948/49	Partick Thistle	2	1	Celtic
1949/50	Celtic	3	2	Rangers
1950/51	Rangers	2	0	Partick Thistle
1951/52	Clyde	2	2	Third Lanark
	Trophy Shared			
1952/53	Celtic	3	1	Queen's Park
1953/54	Third Lanark	1	0	Rangers
1954/55	Rangers	3	1	Queen's Park
1955/56	Third Lanark	4	2	Partick Thistle
1956/57	Rangers	2	1	Queen's Park
1957/58	Clyde	4	0	Rangers
1958/59	Celtic	5	0	Clyde
1959/60	Rangers	2	0	Partick Thistle
1960/61	Celtic	1	1	Clyde
	Trophy shared			
1962	Glasgow Select	2	4	Manchester United
1963	Glasgow Select	2	1	Manchester United
1964	Glasgow Select	4	2	Tottenham Hotspur
1965	Glasgow Select	0	3	Chelsea
1966	Glasgow Select	1	1	Leeds United

GLASGOW CUP

This competition, with its magnificent Victorian trophy, is no longer competed for by senior clubs, but in its heyday it was much prized and valued, next to the Scottish Cup. It came into being when the SFA ruled in 1887 that teams like Queen's Park and Rangers could no longer take part in the English FA Cup as well as the Scottish Cup. The loss of English Cup revenue was a serious one, and to offset this, and to prevent the whole season being nothing other than the Scottish Cup and meaningless friendlies, a new trophy was provided for Glasgow clubs. Because of seniority (it is three years older than the Scottish League) it was able to claim precedence about fixtures, and the final tended to be played in October, usually the autumn Glasgow holiday weekend. The competition was played for during both wars (unlike the Scottish Cup), mainly because it involved few transport problems. After the second world war, the appearance of the Scottish League Cup removed the Glasgow Cup from its autumn slot, and eventually the tournament disappeared altogether under pressure from increasing European and international fixtures. Yet as late as 1967 in Celtic's *annus mirabilis*, the club were proud to claim the Glasgow Cup as one of the five trophies that they entered and won. In the following year, Rangers withdrew from the tournament, claiming fixture congestion, which allowed Celtic fans to describe their decision as 'cowardice'. Rangers won the trophy forty-four times and Celtic twenty-nine, with the others some distance behind. The formula was normally 'two ties and two byes' for the six Glasgow teams of Celtic, Rangers, Partick Thistle, Third Lanark, Clyde and Queen's Park, then semi-finals, and then a final at Hampden Park. The results of the finals were:

1887/88	Cambuslang	3	1	Rangers
1888/89	Queen's Park	8	0	Partick Thistle
1889/90	Queen's Park	3	2	Celtic
1890/91	Celtic	4	0	Third Lanark
1891/92	Celtic	7	1	Clyde
1892/93	Rangers	3	1	Celtic
1893/94	Rangers	1	0	Cowlairs
1894/95	Celtic	2	0	Rangers
1895/96	Celtic	6	3	Queen's Park
1896/97	Rangers	2	1	Celtic
	After a 1–1 draw			
1897/98	Rangers	4	0	Queen's Park
1898/99	Queen's Park	1	0	Rangers
1899/1900	Rangers	1	0	Celtic
	After a 1–1 draw			
1900/01	Rangers	3	1	Partick Thistle
1901/02	Rangers walkover after Celtic scratched, following a 2–2 draw at Ibrox. Celtic claimed the replay should have been played at Celtic Park.			
1902/03	Third Lanark	3	0	Celtic
1903/04	Third Lanark	1	0	Celtic
	After a 1–1 draw			
1904/05	Celtic	2	1	Rangers
1905/06	Celtic	3	0	Third Lanark
1906/07	Celtic	3	2	Third Lanark
1907/08	Celtic	2	1	Rangers
	After 2–2 and 0–0 draws			
1908/09	Third Lanark	4	0	Celtic
	After 1–1 and 2–2 draws			
1909/10	Celtic	1	0	Rangers
1910/11	Rangers	3	1	Celtic
1911/12	Rangers	1	0	Partick Thistle
1912/13	Rangers	3	1	Celtic
1913/14	Rangers	3	0	Third Lanark
1914/15	Clyde	1	0	Partick Thistle
	After a 1–1 draw			
1915/16	Celtic	2	1	Rangers
1916/17	Celtic	3	1	Clyde
1917/18	Rangers	4	1	Partick Thistle
1918/19	Rangers	2	0	Celtic
1919/20	Celtic	1	0	Partick Thistle
1920/21	Celtic	1	0	Clyde
1921/22	Rangers	1	0	Celtic
1922/23	Rangers	1	0	Clyde
	After a 0–0 draw			
1923/24	Rangers	3	1	Third Lanark
1924/25	Rangers	4	1	Celtic
1925/26	Clyde	2	1	Celtic
1926/27	Celtic	1	0	Rangers
1927/28	Celtic	2	1	Rangers
1928/29	Celtic	2	0	
1929/30	Rangers	4	0	Celtic
	After a 0–0 draw			
1930/31	Celtic	2	1	Rangers
1931/32	Rangers	3	0	Queen's Park
1932/33	Rangers	1	0	Partick Thistle
1933/34	Rangers	2	0	Clyde
1934/35	Partick Thistle	1	0	Rangers
1935/36	Rangers	2	0	Celtic
1936/37	Rangers	6	1	Partick Thistle
	After a 2–2 draw			

Rangers 1925/26 with the Scottish League championship trophy, the Glasgow Cup and the Glasgow Merchants' Charity Cup Back row (left to right): Hamilton, Archibald, Gray, Osborne, Ireland, Purdon, McGregor, Hodge, Muirhead. Middle row: W.Struth (manager), Henderson, Meiklejohn, A.Kirkwood, D.Kirkwood, Cunningham, Dick, Henderson, Marshall, Robb. Front row: Craig, McCandless, McKay, Cairns, Dixon, Morton, Jamieson, G.Livingstone (trainer).

1937/38	Rangers	2	1	Third Lanark
1938/39	Celtic	3	0	Clyde
1939/40	Rangers	3	1	Queen's Park
1940/41	Celtic	1	0	Rangers
1941/42	Rangers	6	0	Clyde
1942/43	Rangers	5	2	Third Lanark
1943/44	Rangers	2	0	Clyde
1944/45	Rangers	3	2	Celtic
1945/46	Queen's Park	2	0	Clyde
1946/47	Clyde	2	1	Third Lanark
1947/48	Rangers	4	1	Third Lanark
1948/49	Celtic	3	1	Third Lanark
1949/50	Rangers	2	1	Clyde
1950/51	Partick Thistle	3	2	Celtic
	After a 1–1 draw			
1951/52	Clyde	2	1	Celtic
1952/53	Partick Thistle	3	1	Rangers
1953/54	Rangers	3	0	Third Lanark
1954/55	Partick Thistle	2	0	Rangers
1955/56	Celtic	5	3	Rangers
	After a 1–1 draw			
1956/57	Rangers	2	0	Clyde
1957/58	Rangers	4	2	Third Lanark
	After a 1–1 draw			
1958/59	Clyde	1	0	Rangers
	After a 0–0 draw			
1959/60	Rangers	2	1	Partick Thistle
1960/61	Partick Thistle	2	0	Celtic
1961/62	Celtic	3	2	Third Lanark
	After a 1–1 draw			
1962/63	Third Lanark	2	1	Celtic
1963/64	Celtic	2	0	Clyde
1964/65	Celtic	5	0	Queen's Park
1965/66	No competition			
1966/67	Celtic	4	0	Partick Thistle
1967/68	Celtic	8	0	Queen's Park
1968/69	Rangers	3	2	Partick Thistle
1969/70	Celtic	3	1	Rangers
1970/71	Rangers	2	1	Clyde
1971/72	No competition			
1972/73	No competition			
1973/74	No competition			
1974/75	Rangers	2	2	Celtic
	Teams declared joint winners			
1975/76	Rangers	3	1	Celtic
1976/77	No competition			
1977/78	No competition			
1978/79	Rangers	3	1	Celtic
1979/80	Final between Celtic and Rangers not played after a riot at the Scottish Cup final			
1980/81	Partick Thistle	1	0	Celtic
1981/82	Celtic	2	1	Rangers
1982/83	Rangers	1	0	Celtic
1983/84	No competition			
1984/85	Rangers	5	0	Queen's Park
1985/86	Rangers	3	2	Celtic
1986/87	Rangers	1	0	Celtic
The competition as such was then abandoned, and re-launched as a youth tournament				

GLASGOW UNIVERSITY FC

Home: **Garscube Sports Complex, West of Scotland Science Park, Glasgow**
Best Scottish Cup Performance: **Last 32 (1st round, 1968/69)**

(Participating club in Scottish Cup, but not member of East of Scotland League, Highland League or South of Scotland League)

Glasgow became the first Scottish University to form a football club in 1877, and by 1884/85 they were participating in the first round of the Scottish Cup, losing 6–4 away to Northern. After the introduction of the Scottish Qualifying Cup in 1895 they occasionally qualified for the competition proper, for example in 1928/29 when they lost 8–1 away to Kilmarnock in the first round. To this day their membership of the SFA makes them eligible to enter the Scottish Cup and when the Scottish Qualifying Cup was discontinued for season 2007/08, they went straight into the first round, losing 2–1 at home to Highland League Buckie Thistle.

Glasgow University won the Scottish Qualifying Cup (South) in both 1968/69 and 1970/71, and on the former occasion they once again drew Kilmarnock at Rugby Park in the first round of the competition proper. They lost 6–0 in a season when the use of preliminary rounds meant that the first round contained the last thirty-two clubs.

GLENAFTON ATHLETIC FC

(see JUNIOR FOOTBALL)

GLENROTHES JUNIOR FC

(see JUNIOR FOOTBALL)

GOAL AVERAGE/DIFFERENCE

Goal AVERAGE was the device used in the Scottish League from 1921/22 until 1970/71 to differentiate teams when they were equal on points. After 1971 goal DIFFERENCE was used. Prior to the introduction of goal average in season 1921/22, there could be joint champions of the Scottish League, as for example in 1891 when Dumbarton and Rangers both finished with twenty-nine points from their eighteen games. A play-off was held at Hampden Park, but when this finished 2–2, the teams were declared joint champions. In 1905, when Celtic and Rangers both finished with forty-one points from their twenty-six games, a play-off was held at Hampden Park, and Celtic emerged victorious 2–1. In the second division, Raith Rovers and Leith Athletic were declared joint champions in season 1909/10 after they had declined to play off, while in 1915 there was an even more complicated situation involving three teams, Cowdenbeath, Leith Athletic and St Bernard's, from which Cowdenbeath emerged victorious, having defeated the other two in play-offs.

Goal average involved dividing the goals scored by the goals conceded. Thus, for example in 1953, when the championship was decided on goal average, Rangers had scored eighty goals but lost thirty-nine, whereas Hibs had scored ninety-three but lost fifty-one. Thus, although Hibs would have won the title on goal DIFFERENCE, they in fact lost it on goal AVERAGE, for Rangers' goal average was 2.05 as against Hibs' 1.82. An even closer finish involving goal average came in 1965. On the morning of 24 April, the last day of the season, Hearts had fifty points with a goal average of 1.91 and

Kilmarnock had forty-eight points with a goal average of 1.81. Hearts appeared to have the advantage, but Kilmarnock were due at Tynecastle that day and it was calculated that a 2–0 win would be sufficient for them to win the title (3–1 or 4–2 for Killie would have done the job equally well). Amidst incredible excitement, Willie Waddell's Kilmarnock proceeded to achieve just that.

The disadvantage of goal average was that it tended to encourage defensive football, with the emphasis being on not losing a goal, and the change to goal difference from season 1971/72 onwards also made calculations simpler. In 1986 Hearts once again missed out on the last day, when Celtic had to beat St Mirren by at least 4–0 (it was 5–0 in the event) if Hearts lost at Dundee. Once again Hearts 'blew up' on the last day of the season, and lost out on goal difference. Ironically, had goal DIFFERENCE been in vogue in 1965 and AVERAGE in 1986, they would have won the championship on both occasions. Celtic were the unlucky ones in 2003 when, on the last day of the season, Rangers scored more goals against Dunfermline than Celtic did at Kilmarnock.

On several occasions goal average/difference has been called into play to decide the championship winners, or promotion and relegation issues, in the minor divisions; notably in 1930, 1932, 1949, 1951 and 1972 in the old Division Two, when Leith Athletic, East Stirlingshire, Raith Rovers, Queen of the South and Dumbarton were the beneficiaries. In 1978 Morton won the Scottish League First Division on goal difference from Hearts, but the Tynecastle men were nevertheless promoted.

Eric Sorensen of Morton (top), and (left) Dr James Marshall of Rangers heads the ball out of the reach of Hearts goalkeeper Jack Harkness at Ibrox in the 1930s.

GOALKEEPERS

It is often claimed that goalkeepers are mad to do the job that they do, in that they get all the blame when a goal is lost, but seldom get due praise for good saves and shutouts. It is certainly true that Scottish football has always had its fair share of real goalkeeping characters, for example Ned Doig, Dan McArthur, Harry Rennie, Jimmy Brownlie, Charlie Shaw, Jack Harkness, John Thomson, Jerry Dawson, Bill Brown, Ronnie Simpson, Alan Rough, and Andy Goram.

Yet if we look at a picture of a pre-first world war football team, it often seems that there is no goalkeeper! This is because it was not necessary in those days for the goalkeeper to be dressed differently, and he was expected to play forward at times when he was not required for defensive duties. We are surprised to discover that until 1912 he could handle the ball in any part of his own half of the field (a privilege rarely claimed, one presumes), and it was only in that year that his handling activities were restricted to the penalty area. On 15 August 1910, in a game at Cathkin Park, both goalkeepers, Jimmy Brownlie of Third Lanark and Clem Hampton of Motherwell scored in Motherwell's 4–2 victory, and this phenomenon was one of the reasons why the goalkeeper's handling activities were to be restricted. It was about this time as well that goalkeepers began to dress differently, and the normal equipment of a 'custodian' was a thick yellow pullover and a bunnet!

An aspect of British and in particular Scottish football that often attracted criticism was 'charging'. A goalkeeper could be 'charged' i.e. bundled into the net with the ball in his hands by a burly centre forward like Jimmy Quinn of Celtic, as long as the charging was done with the shoulder (not the elbow) and the goalkeeper's feet were on the ground. This practice gradually died out in both Scotland and England following two dreadful charges on goalkeepers in the 1957 and 1958 English Cup finals, and under pressure from the increasing European influence.

Yet, although goalkeepers were (and are) frequently injured, fatalities were almost unknown at any level of football until one of Scottish football's most tragic days on 5 September 1931. This was the day at Ibrox when Celtic and Scotland's goalkeeper John Thomson was killed when his skull came into contact with the knee of

Rangers' Sam English. It was a total accident but Thomson died of a fractured skull later that night.

Scotland's most capped goalkeeper is Jim Leighton who won 91 caps between 1983 and 1999 in a lengthy career that saw him play for Aberdeen, Manchester United, Hibs and Aberdeen again. Jim wore contact lenses and on one occasion in 1985 had to be replaced by Alan Rough at half time because he had lost a contact lens! Jimmy Cowan of Morton in 1949 had such a tremendous game at Wembley that the victory is often called 'Cowan's Wembley'. On the other hand, Fred Martin of Aberdeen in 1955, Frank Haffey of Celtic in 1961 and Stewart Kennedy of Rangers in 1975 were held disproportionately responsible for Wembley disasters and never forgiven by the Scottish media and public.

For a long time, Scottish goalkeepers were much ridiculed in England. This was because of the way that Scottish games were highlighted on English television. A goalkeeping error is, naturally enough, good television and played again and again. It just happened that some Scottish goalkeepers made some high profile errors in the 1970s and 1980s, and the media generalised from a few unfortunate instances.

For a long time Bobby Clark of Aberdeen held the Scottish and British record of having gone 1,156 minutes without conceding a goal. This was achieved in season 1970/71. The man who beat this record was an Englishman playing for a Scottish club in Scottish football. It was Chris Woods of Rangers who managed 1,196 minutes on 31 January 1987. He must have wished that he could have held on to his record a little longer, for the goal that eventually beat him put Rangers out of the Scottish Cup. It was a shock defeat too, for the goal was scored by Adrian Sprott of Hamilton Academical, then bottom of the Premier Division of the Scottish League!

GOAL NETS

Nets are not really compulsory. The appropriate part of Law One states *Nets may be attached to the goals and the ground behind the goal, provided that they are properly supported and do not interfere with the goalkeeper*. The operative word is 'may', and hundreds of games are played every weekend in Scotland without this luxury, although they have been standard practice in senior football in Scotland since the beginning of the twentieth century.

A few English teams employed them in the 1880s but they first appeared in Scotland at a friendly match on New Year's Day 1892 between Celtic and Dumbarton, and their use spread quickly throughout 1892 and 1893. But Queen's Park, conservative as always, opposed their use. Queen's Park felt that the goalkeeper would feel 'cabined, cribbed and confined', that the forwards would be so unfamiliar with them that this 'in the act of shooting, would cause their vision to be engrossed with the unusual arrangement outside the post' – a reference, one assumes to the poles used to support the nets – and that in any case the players were in the habit of practising without them.

Matters came to a head however in the 1893 Scottish Cup final when Celtic protested that one of the goals scored by Queen's Park had gone past the post and that the referee Mr Harrison of Kilmarnock had only allowed the goal because some of the Queen's Park players had said 'It's a goal, Mr. Harrison!' Compulsory use of goal nets would solve the problem, and at the SFA AGM in May 1893, it was proposed and carried by 41 votes to 35 that goal nets should be mandatory at Scottish Cup finals and semi-finals. As they cost £3 a pair, however, it was felt unfair that smaller clubs should be compelled to buy them. Their use however was recommended, and indeed following a dispute, Raith Rovers were ordered to replay their 1894/95 Scottish Cup first round game against the Fifth Kings Rifle Volunteers for 'failing to provide goal nets'.

GOALSCORING RECORDS (INDIVIDUAL)

Before the advent of modern technology, and evidence such as video replays, the identification of goal scorers relied on newspaper reports and there were occasional inaccuracies. Nevertheless, it is apparent that Celtic's Jimmy McGrory was head and shoulders above all others in the goalscoring stakes. He scored 550 goals

Ally McCoist with Derek Ferguson and Ian Durrant. McCoist was to net 355 goals for Rangers.

overall, including 408 in the Scottish League between 1923 and 1937 (395 for Celtic and thirteen for Clydebank). David McLean who played for Forfar Athletic, Celtic, Preston, Sheffield Wednesday, Third Lanark, Rangers, Bradford Park Avenue, Dundee and Forfar Athletic again, between the years of 1906 and 1932, actually scored 412 league goals, (four more than McGrory), but many of them were in war-time and in second division football with Forfar Athletic. Hughie Gallagher, between the years of 1921 and 1939, scored 387, although very few of his were for a Scottish team (Airdrieonians). Hugh Ferguson of Motherwell and Cardiff City in the 1920s scored 352, and in more recent years, Ally McCoist with Rangers and Kilmarnock scored 355 (281 in the Scottish League).

In a season, Henrik Larsson hit fifty-three overall in season 2000/01, including thirty-five league goals. For the old Division One, Willie McFadyen of Motherwell, who scored fifty-three in season 1931/32, holds the record, closely followed by Jimmy McGrory, who scored fifty in season 1935/36. The British record for a season, however, is held by Jimmy Smith of Ayr United, who found the net sixty-six times in season 1927/28. For the Scotland international team the record is thirty goals, shared by Denis Law and Kenny Dalglish. Law scored his in fifty-five appearances, whereas Dalglish played 102 times for Scotland.

Since the end of the second world war the best goal scorers in league matches in the top tier (be it Division One, Premier Division of the SFL, or the SPL) have been as follows:

1946/47	Bobby Mitchell	Third Lanark	22
1947/48	Archie Aikman	Falkirk	20
1948/49	Alec Stott	Dundee	30
1949/50	Willie Bauld	Hearts	30
1950/51	Lawrie Reilly	Hibernian	22
1951/52	Lawrie Reilly	Hibernian	27
1952/53	Lawrie Reilly	Hibernian	30
	Charlie Fleming	East Fife	30
1953/54	Jimmy Wardhaugh	Hearts	27
1954/55	Willie Bauld	Hearts	21
1955/56	Jimmy Wardhaugh	Hearts	28
1956/57	Hugh Baird	Airdrieonians	33
1957/58	Jimmy Wardhaugh	Hearts	28
	Jimmy Murray	Hearts	28
1958/59	Joe Baker	Hibernian	25
1959/60	Joe Baker	Hibernian	42
1960/61	Alex Harley	Third Lanark	42
1961/62	Alan Gilzean	Dundee	24
1962/63	Jimmy Millar	Rangers	27
1963/64	Alan Gilzean	Dundee	32
1964/65	Jim Forrest	Rangers	30
1965/66	Joe McBride	Celtic	31
	Alex Ferguson	Dunfermline Athletic	31
1966/67	Stevie Chalmers	Celtic	23
1967/68	Bobby Lennox	Celtic	32
1968/69	Kenny Cameron	Dundee United	26
1969/70	Colin Stein	Rangers	24
1970/71	Harry Hood	Celtic	22
1971/72	Joe Harper	Aberdeen	33
1972/73	Alan Gordon	Hibernian	27
1973/74	Dixie Deans	Celtic	26
1974/75	Andy Gray	Dundee United	20
	Willie Pettigrew	Motherwell	20
1975/76	Kenny Dalglish	Celtic	24
1976/77	Willie Pettigrew	Motherwell	21
1977/78	Derek Johnstone	Rangers	25
1978/79	Andy Ritchie	Morton	22
1979/80	Doug Somner	St Mirren	25
1980/81	Frank McGarvey	Celtic	23
1981/82	George McCluskey	Celtic	21
1982/83	Charlie Nicholas	Celtic	29
1983/84	Brian McClair	Celtic	23
1984/85	Frank McDougall	Aberdeen	22
1985/86	Ally McCoist	Rangers	24
1986/87	Brian McClair	Celtic	35
1987/88	Tommy Coyne	Dundee	33
1988/89	Mark McGhee	Celtic	16
	Charlie Nicholas	Aberdeen	16
1989/90	John Robertson	Hearts	17
1990/91	Tommy Coyne	Celtic	18
1991/92	Ally McCoist	Rangers	34
1992/93	Ally McCoist	Rangers	34
1993/94	Mark Hateley	Rangers	22
1994/95	Tommy Coyne	Motherwell	16
1995/96	Pierre van Hooijdonk	Celtic	26
1996/97	Jorge Cadete	Celtic	25
1997/98	Marco Negri	Rangers	32
1998/99	Henrik Larsson	Celtic	29
1999/00	Mark Viduka	Celtic	25
2000/01	Henrik Larsson	Celtic	35
2001/02	Henrik Larsson	Celtic	29
2002/03	Henrik Larsson	Celtic	28
2003/04	Henrik Larsson	Celtic	30
2004/05	John Hartson	Celtic	25
2005/06	Kris Boyd	Kilmarnock and Rangers	32
2006/07	Kris Boyd	Rangers	20
2007/08	Scott MacDonald	Celtic	25

Henrik Larsson of Celtic scored 53 goals in 2000/01, including 35 league goals.

Joe Baker, who scored nine for Hibernian against Peebles Rovers.

In a single match, it is unlikely that anyone will beat the thirteen scored by John Petrie of Arbroath on 12 September 1885 when Arbroath beat Aberdeen Bon Accord 36–0. Both the 36–0 scoreline and Petrie's thirteen goals, well documented in contemporary accounts, should be accepted as genuine, but the actual validity of the fixture should be called into question, for there is a certain amount of evidence to suggest that 'Aberdeen Bon Accord' were in fact Orion Cricket Club, to whom the notification of the game had been sent by mistake. In addition, the referee, Mr Stormont, clearly a humane man, admitted afterwards to disallowing several other goals 'in order to keep the score down'.

Nevertheless, this was officially a Scottish Cup tie, and also in the Scottish Cup, the Baker brothers did well. Gerry scored ten for St Mirren in a 15–0 win over Glasgow University on 30 January 1960, and the following year on 11 February 1961, his brother Joe scored nine for Hibernian against Peebles Rovers in a 15–1 win – and missed a penalty as well. The feat of scoring nine goals in a Scottish Cup tie has been achieved on another two occasions, by Johnny Simpson of Partick Thistle against Royal Albert on 17 January 1931, and by Jim Fleming of Rangers against Blairgowrie on 20 January 1934.

In the Scottish League, five players have scored eight goals in a game. In the old Division One, Jimmy McGrory scored eight against Dunfermline on 14 January 1928, and in Division Two, the feat of scoring eight goals in a game was achieved by Owen McNally for Arthurlie against Armadale on 1 October 1927, Jim Dyet of King's Park versus Forfar Athletic on 2 January 1930, John Calder of Morton versus Raith Rovers on 18 April 1936 and Norman Haywood on 20 August 1937 for Raith Rovers against Brechin City. Dyet's performance for King's Park was all the more remarkable as he was making his debut that day.

In the Scottish Premier League and Scottish Premier Division, four players have scored five goals in a game. Paul Sturrock for Dundee United versus Morton on 17 November 1984, Marco Negri for Rangers versus Dundee United on 23 August 1997, Kenny Miller for Rangers versus St Mirren on 4 November 2000 and Kris Boyd for Kilmarnock versus Dundee United on 25 September 2004.

The Scottish League Cup record is five, shared by Jim Fraser of Ayr United versus Dumbarton on 13 August 1952 and Jim Forrest of Rangers versus Stirling Albion on 17 August 1966. Forrest also holds the record for a League Cup final by scoring four against Morton on 26 October 1963.

The record for a Scotland international match was set by Hughie Gallacher, who scored five against Ireland in a 7–3 victory in Belfast on 23 February 1929. Some sources say that Charlie Heggie also scored five for Scotland against Ireland on 20 March 1886, but most sources say four.

Men who have scored four for Scotland in a game are Denis Law (twice), Charlie Heggie, Willie Dickson, Willie Paul, Johnny Madden, Sandy McMahon, Bob Hamilton, Jimmy Quinn, Billy Steel and Colin Stein. No one has scored four against England, but there have been five hat-tricks against the Auld Enemy – John McDougall (1878), George Ker (1880), John Smith (1881), Robert McColl (1900) and Alec Jackson (1928).

There are four curious cases of international hat-trick scorers who scored their hat-tricks on their international debuts and were never chosen to play for Scotland again. There were Charlie Heggie and Willie Dickson, mentioned above, plus James Gillespie of Third Lanark, who scored three against Wales on 19 March 1898. In more recent times there was also the luckless Henry Morris of East Fife, who scored a hat-trick against Northern Ireland on 1 October 1949 in his only Scotland appearance.

(Left) Marco Negri scored five goals against Dundee United in 1997. Here, Rangers' Gordon Durie and Marco Negri celebrate after Negri had scored the second goal against Hearts at Tynecastle, 20 December 1997. Rangers won the match 5-2.

(Bottom) Billy Steel, scorer of four goals in a game for Scotland is second right, next to Stanley Matthews, with Wilf Mannion to his right, Raich Carter behind him, and George Young at the very back.

GOALSCORING RECORDS (TEAMS)

The most goals scored by a team in a Scottish League season is the 142 scored by Raith Rovers in Division Two in season 1937/38, closely followed by Morton's 135 in the same division in 1963/64, and Falkirk's 132 in 1935/36. In the Third Division, Gretna hit 130 in season 2004/05. In the top flight, the record is the 132 of Hearts in their successful quest for the league championship of season 1957/58. In the Scottish Premier League, Celtic, who scored 105 in season 2003/04, hold the record.

Those who have the less enviable records of the most goals scored against them include Morton, who twice managed to concede 100 goals in the Scottish League Premier Division, in 1984/85 and 1987/88. The Division One record is 137 and the Division Two record is 146, held respectively in the same year of 1931/32 by teams that are now defunct – Leith Athletic and Edinburgh City. In the Third Division, East Stirlingshire conceded 118 in 2003/04.

In individual competitions, records and other notable scores are as follows:

S. Premier League	Dunfermline	1	8	Celtic	19 Feb 2006
S. Lge. Premier Div.	Aberdeen	8	0	Motherwell	26 Mar 1979
	Hamilton	0	8	Celtic	05 Nov 1988
	Kilmarnock	1	8	Rangers	06 Sep 1980
S. Lge. Div. One	Celtic	11	0	Dundee	26 Oct 1895
	Airdrieonians	1	11	Hibernian	24 Oct 1959
S. Lge. Div. Two	Airdrieonians	15	1	Dundee Wndrs.	01 Dec 1894
The highest aggregate score in the top flight of the Scottish League is Hearts 10 Queen's Park 3 on 24 Aug 1912. The highest in recent years is Brechin City 5 Cowdenbeath 7 on 18 Jan 2003. In the Premier Division, Celtic beat Hamilton Academical 8–3 on 03 Jan 1987.					
Scottish Cup	Arbroath	36	0	Aberdeen B.Ac.	12 Sep 1885
	Dundee Harp	35	0	Aberdeen Rov.	12 Sep 1885
	Stirling Albion	20	0	Selkirk	08 Dec 1984
Scottish League Cup	Alloa	0	10	Third Lanark	08 Aug 1953
	Clyde	10	0	Stranraer	14 Aug 1957
	Dumbarton	10	3	Stranraer	24 Aug 1957
Internationals	Scotland	11	0	Ireland	23 Feb 1901
	Scotland	9	0	Wales	23 Mar 1878
	England	9	3	Scotland	15 Apr 1961
Scotland's biggest win over England is 7–2 at the first Hampden Park on 02 Mar 1878					

GOLDEN GOAL

This method of deciding a game has been used in recent years by UEFA and FIFA. It means that the first goal scored in extra time, when the teams are level after ninety minutes, finishes the game. Fewer people are aware that, under the name of 'sudden death', it has been used in the Scottish Cup on two occasions on the one day. It was on 29 March 1947, the first post-war season. Austerity measures prohibited the playing of midweek football, for in those pre-floodlight days, the games would have been played on a Wednesday afternoon and would have encouraged absenteeism, particularly from the coal mines. Coal production was vital in 1947 in the wake of the very bad winter, which had also, of course, postponed many football matches. The result was that the SFA were compelled to insist that the quarter-finals and semi-finals of the 1947 Scottish Cup had to be played to a finish, even though replays had been allowed in previous rounds of the tournament, in order for the Scottish Cup final to be played, as arranged, on 19 April.

On 29 March 1947, Hibs were playing Motherwell at Hampden Park in the semi-final, while Dundee and Aberdeen were a round behind, playing in the quarter-final at Dens Park. The arrangement was that the teams would play ninety minutes, then if still level, would play twenty minutes extra time (or less if a team scored), then change ends and play another ten (or less if a team scored), then change ends and another ten minutes, and so on, until such time as one team actually did score. It took until the 142nd minute before Hibs scored the winner after the exhausted Motherwell goalkeeper Johnston cleared the ball down the field to Hibs midfielder Howie, who saw Johnston sauntering back to his goal line and kicked the ball over Johnston's head from about forty yards. The game at Dens Park did not last quite so long, for Stan Williams scored in the 130th minute for Aberdeen "with the defence too exhausted to tackle" according to one report.

The press was united in their condemnation of this method of settling a tie, using words like "farce" and "freak", and it must have been a relief for Aberdeen to beat Arbroath 2–0 in ninety minutes when their semi-final was played. This method was never used again.

GOLSPIE SUTHERLAND FC

Home: **King George V Park, Golspie, Sutherland**
Best Scottish Cup Performance: **Last 64 (2nd round, 2007/08)**

(Participating club in Scottish Cup, but not member of East of Scotland League, Highland League or South of Scotland League)

Golspie Sutherland is an amateur club that plays in the North Caledonian League. The Blues, who can trace their history all the way back to 1877, enjoyed a particularly good year in 2007. Not only did they finish the 2006/07 season as league champions, they came to national prominence through their participation in the Scottish Cup, which they are eligible to enter as members of the SFA.

Prior to 2007 they took part in the Scottish Qualifying Cup (North), but when this was discontinued for season 2007/08 they went straight into the first round of the competition proper. The campaign got off to a good start, with a 3–1 home victory over Preston Athletic of the East of Scotland League, but it came to an end at Rosewell in the second round, when Whitehill Welfare beat them 6–1.

GORAM, Andy (1964 –)

Scotland Caps: 43
Scottish Premier League medals: 6
Scottish Cup medals: 3
Scottish League Cup medals: 2

An occasionally controversial character, Andy Goram is one of the few Englishmen who have played for Scotland (he qualified through parentage), and he has also played for Scotland at cricket. He was an excellent goalkeeper and never let Scotland down in any of the forty-three

games that he played for the country, being particularly good in the 1992 European Championships in Sweden. Born in Oldham, it was for Oldham Athletic that he first played. It was also with them that he finished his career. He subsequently moved to Hibernian, and then Rangers in 1991, where he had an outstanding few years for the Ibrox side. He was voted the greatest Rangers goalkeeper of all time, and subsequently played for a number of other clubs – Motherwell, Notts County, Sheffield United, Manchester United, Coventry City, Queen of the South and Elgin City. However, many people believe that his associations with various sectarian groups in Northern Ireland are a blot on his record.

GORDON, Craig (1982 –)

Scotland Caps: 31
Scottish Cup medals: 1

An outstanding goalkeeper for Hearts and Sunderland, Craig Gordon won a Scottish Cup medal with Hearts in 2006, and has been capped thirty-one times for Scotland. In August 2007 he was transferred to Sunderland for nine million pounds, a British record for a goalkeeper.

GORDON Jimmy (1888 – 1954)

Scotland Caps: 10
Scottish League Championship medals: 5

Jimmy Gordon is regarded as one of Rangers' greatest-ever players, and it was often said that he was the architect of their three successive Scottish League championship wins from 1911 to 1913. He arrived at Ibrox in 1907, and was versatile enough to play in almost any position before settling down at right half. The first world war affected his career badly, but he became a sergeant in the H.L.I., guesting for various teams, and helping Rangers win the championship in 1918. The highlight of his international career was when he captained Scotland to an epic 3-1 victory over England at Hampden Park in 1914. After leaving Ibrox in 1920, he played briefly for Dunfermline Athletic, and owned a chain of billiard halls in Glasgow.

GOUGH Richard (1962 –)

Scotland Caps: 61
Scottish League Championship medals: 9
Scottish Cup medals: 3
Scottish League Cup medals: 6

A tough and sometimes controversial character, Richard Gough won sixty-one caps for Scotland, in a career which saw him play for Dundee United, Tottenham Hotspur, Rangers, Nottingham Forest and Everton between 1980 and 2002. He also played in the USA, and in later years was manager of Livingston. He learned his craft in the stern school of Jim McLean at Dundee United, but it was with Rangers that he won the honours – playing 427 times for them, and winning many domestic trophies as captain and commanding centre half. In 1989 the Scottish Football Writers' Association nominated him as Player of the Year, an honour that his fellow professionals had bestowed upon him in 1986. His international career had its moments, notably the goal that he scored to give Scotland victory over England in 1985 at a rainy Hampden Park, but there was also controversy in his ill-disguised inability to get on with manager Andy Roxburgh, and his being sent off in a World Cup qualifier against Switzerland in 1992. He was held mainly responsible for the 0–5 defeat by Portugal in 1993, and never played for Scotland again.

Mark Walters and Richard Gough in a crowded goalmouth during the goalless draw between Rangers and St Johnstone in the 1989 Scottish Cup semi-final tie at Celtic Park.

GRAY Andy (1955 –)

Scotland Caps: 20

Now an enthusiastic commentator and pundit with Sky Sport, Andy Gray is a well-known character. He was a courageous, hard-running, and predatory goal scorer

Andy Gray and Graeme Sharp when they both played for Everton; (right) Eddie Gray starred on the left wing for Leeds United and Scotland.

who won twenty caps for Scotland. He began his career with Dundee United, but was transferred to Aston Villa in 1975, then Wolves in 1979 for a British record £1.46 million, before moving to Everton in 1983, and back to Aston Villa again in 1985. He also saw service with Notts County and West Bromwich Albion before returning to Scotland to play a few games for Rangers in season 1988/89. It was with Everton that his greatest moments came, for he won an English league medal, an FA Cup medal, and a European-Cup Winners' Cup medal to add to the English League Cup medals he had won with Wolves in 1980 and with Aston Villa in 1977. For Scotland, his career was disappointing, but he did well to avoid the Argentina disgrace of 1978.

GRAY Dougie (1905 – 1972)

Scotland Caps: 10
Scottish League Championship medals: 10
Scottish Cup medals: 6

Dougie Gray was one of the stars of the Rangers team of the inter-war period. He was born in Alford, Aberdeenshire, but joined Rangers in 1925. He played a record 879 times for them between the years of 1925 and 1945, and won ten Scottish caps, although only once against England, and that was the time when England won 5–2 in 1930. His determined defending entitles him to be considered an Ibrox all-time great.

GRAY Eddy (1948 –)

Scotland Caps: 12

Eddie Gray, a left-winger for Leeds United, played twelve times for Scotland, the highlight being the victory over

England in 1976 at Hampden Park. For Leeds he won the Inter-Cities Fairs Cup in 1968, the English league in 1969, and the FA Cup in 1972. He was seen as an integral part of Don Revie's great side of that time. He was also manager of Leeds for a spell between 1982 and 1985, and was awarded the MBE for his services to football.

GRAY Frank (1954 –)

Scotland Caps: 32

The younger brother of Eddy, Frank Gray was an attack-minded left back who played for Leeds United, Nottingham Forest, Leeds United again, Sunderland and Darlington between 1971 and 1992. He played alongside his brother Eddy for a spell with Leeds United, but it was with Nottingham Forest that he won a European Cup medal in 1980. He won thirty-two Scottish caps, and was widely regarded as one of the best defenders in the 1982 World Cup finals in Spain.

GREAT DAYS

There have been few enough of these! A 'great day' is defined as a day in which the rest of the footballing world has been compelled to sit up and take notice of Scotland. Six such days have been identified.

15 March 1884 Scotland 1 England 0 Cathkin Park

Scotland beat England to register their fifth win in a row against the Auld Enemy. 1880 and 1883 had seen narrow victories, 1881 and 1882 had been 'Bannockburn thrashings' as a newspaper put it, but 1884 was significant in that it really did convince the Scottish public, particularly the Scottish working class, that here was an activity in which Scotland could regularly beat England. Now newspapers began to highlight football matches to an extent that they had never before, and the football clubs began to proliferate throughout the land. In England, the effects were no less dramatic, for the movement to allow professionalism in the game became irresistible. It was legalised in 1886 in England, although Scotland stayed amateur (at least officially) until 1893.

The game itself attracted a huge crowd of well over 10,000 to Cathkin in spite of incessant rain throughout the morning. As many of Scotland's players played for Dunbartonshire teams, there was a steady stream of trains into Glasgow's stations that day from that direction, and even a few supporters from Edinburgh and Dundee. Scotland's goal was scored by Dr John Smith, previously of Mauchline but now of Queen's Park, towards the end of the first half with a shot which grazed the underside of the crossbar before going in. Had it been a few years earlier before crossbars were in vogue, his shot probably would have gone over the top of the goal. England rallied in the second half but goalkeeper Jim McAuley of Dumbarton 'the prince of goalkeepers' had some fine saves. Charlie Campbell of Queen's Park was excellent throughout as Scotland adapted better than England to the energy-sapping conditions. Indeed Scotland almost scored in the last minute through Bob Christie of Queen's Park.

Scotland: McAulay (Dumbarton), Arnott (Queen's Park), Forbes (Vale of Leven), Campbell (Queen's Park), McPherson (Vale of Leven), Anderson (Queen's Park), Shaw (Pollokshields), Smith (Queen's Park), Lindsay (Dumbarton), Christie (Queen's Park), McKinnon (Dumbarton)

England: Rose (Swifts), Dobson (Notts County), Beverley (Blackburn Rovers), Bailey (Clapham Rovers), Macrae (Notts County), Wilson (Hendon), Bromley–Davenport (Oxford University), Gunn (Notts County), Bambridge (Swifts), Vaughton (Aston Villa), Holden (Wednesbury Old Athletic)

Referee Mr Sinclair, Ireland Crowd 10,000

31 March 1928 England 1 Scotland 5 Wembley

This is the game and the team who became known as the 'Wembley Wizards'. Alex Jackson scored a hat trick and Alex James the other two, England's solitary counter coming through Bob Kelly in the last minute. Everton's legendary 'Dixie' Dean was subdued throughout. A great deal of the mystique about this game lies in the fact that it was at Wembley, which was considered to be the greatest football stadium in the world. 1928 was the first Scottish team to win at the new Empire Stadium at Wembley, the only previous visit having ended up in a draw in 1924. There was not a Celtic player in the team and only one Ranger, Alan Morton. Indeed he and Jack Harkness the goalkeeper of Queen's Park (he would later move to Hearts) and red-haired Jimmy Dunn, the inside right of Hibs, were the only three 'Home Scots' in the side, the rest being 'Anglos' i.e. they played for English clubs. There is a cartoon of the three Home Scots on the train looking for someone else to join them for a game of whist!

The match day preparations included a trip to the River Thames to see the Oxford versus Cambridge Boat Race! On a dreary wet afternoon Alex Jackson opened the scoring with a fine header in three minutes and it looked as if Scotland would go in at half time only one goal up (a scant reward for their superiority) until Alex James, after a mazy dribble, scored on the stroke of half time. In the second half Scotland attacked throughout and scored again through Jackson, James and Jackson again. The English defence deserve credit for keeping the score down. The Duke of York (the future King George VI) and his guest King Amanullah of Afghanistan must have been impressed, and the Duke's Scottish wife (Lady Elizabeth Bowes-Lyon of Glamis Castle who became the Queen and the Queen Mother) would have been interested to hear how well her compatriots had done. Until Lisbon in 1967, this was the most famous Scottish game of them all, even though England have on several occasions reversed and even bettered this scoreline. Five players of Huddersfield Town played in this game.

Hughie Gallacher in action against England.

Ivan Sharpe, the greatest of 1920s journalists, and as an Englishman not someone one would have thought prone to hyperbole about this game, nevertheless writes in the *Athletic News*:

'Real football at last! Clockwork passing. The triangle – prettiest of all tunes that football can provide – tinkling for an hour or so on both sides of the field. Gibson (at his best) behind Jackson and the little Dunn; McMullen (generally great in attack) inspiring Morton and James. James! He needs no inspiration. But he got it and taking the game through, was the mastermind of this clockwork Scottish forward line…

To say the whole crowd was delighted with the Scottish cleverness was beyond question as Cockney voices resounded with 'Go it Scotland, you devils!"

England: Hufton (West Ham), Goodall (Huddersfield Town), Jones (Blackburn Rovers), Edwards (Leeds United), Wilson (Huddersfield Town), Healless (Blackburn Rovers), Hulme (Arsenal), Kelly (Huddersfield Town), Dean (Everton), Bradford (Birmingham), Smith (Huddersfield Town).

Scotland: Harkness (Queen's Park), Nelson (Cardiff City, Law (Chelsea), Gibson (Aston Villa), Bradshaw (Bury), McMullan (Manchester City) captain, Jackson (Huddersfield Town), Dunn (Hibs), Gallacher (Newcastle United), James (Preston North End), Morton (Rangers)

Referee W Bell, Scotland Crowd 80,968

15 April 1967 Scotland 3 England 2 Wembley

On this day Scotland became the first team to beat England after they had won the World Cup of 1966. Scotland had had a bitter experience during that World Cup for they always felt that they were a better team than England, and that had it not been for the obstructionist tactics of the English League teams who refused to postpone games and release Scottish players, Scotland would have qualified. In fact, this is only half true, for there were many other factors in the equation, and in any case, any belief that Scotland were better than England in 1966 was shattered when England beat them 4–3 at Hampden in the April of that year.

Nevertheless this was Scotland's first attempt to play England after the World Cup, and it was an opportunity they grabbed with both hands. Scotland's storm petrels Denis Law and Jim Baxter both played at their best and they had four members of the Celtic team that was soon to win the European Cup. With the backing of a massive Scottish support, the team played to their potential under the guidance of manager Bobby Brown to win 3–2. Denis Law scored first, and Scotland were leading 1–0 until the last ten minutes when both teams scored two goals each, Scotland's two coming from Bobby Lennox and Jim McCalliog.

There were many memorable things about this game – Jim Baxter's 'keepie uppie', Ronnie Simpson's International debut at the age of 36, Bobby Lennox becoming the first Celtic player ever to score at Wembley and the invasion of Scottish fans at the end of the game.

England: Banks (Leicester City), Cohen (Fulham), Wilson (Everton), Stiles (Manchester United), J. Charlton (Leeds United), Moore (West Ham United), Ball (Everton), Greaves (Tottenham Hotspur), R. Charlton (Manchester United), Hurst (West Ham United), Peters (West Ham United)

Scotland: Simpson (Celtic), Gemmell (Celtic), McCreadie (Chelsea), Greig (Rangers), McKinnon (Rangers), Baxter (Sunderland), Wallace (Celtic), Bremner (Leeds United), McCalliog (Sheffield Wednesday), Law (Manchester United), Lennox (Celtic)

Referee G Schulenburg, West Germany Crowd 99,063

25 May 1967 Celtic 2 Inter Milan 1 Lisbon

This was undeniably Scottish football's greatest ever day to date as Celtic became the first British and northern European team to win the European Cup. They did this with a magnificent display of attacking football following the loss of an early goal. This game completed an *annus mirabilis* for Jock Stein's Celtic who won every competition that they entered for – an achievement that can clearly only be equalled, never beaten.

The game with a 5.30 pm kick-off was televised live throughout Europe and it was a night on which Scotland almost came to a standstill until the final whistle. It was also a triumph that was shared by nearly

Jim McCalliog is congratulated by fellow debut-maker Ronnie Simpson at the end of the game, having just beaten World Cup winners England at Wembley in Aprtil 1967.

Training in Lisbon on the eve of the European Cup Final.

all the nation, for everything about the team was undeniably Scottish. Indeed all the team, including the manager, had been born within a thirty-mile radius of Glasgow. Some Labour MPs in the House of Commons were moved to table a message of congratulations, and any hint of religious bigotry was swept aside when the Church of Scotland, then in its General Assembly in Edinburgh, sent a telegram to the victorious team!

Celtic had gone behind to a debatable penalty conceded by Jim Craig as early as the seventh minute, but this clearly delineated the tactics that the team had to employ. Attack had to be the order of the day, and for the remaining eighty-three minutes of the game the Inter Milan goal was besieged. The wonder was that Celtic scored only two goals, but they eventually came when Tommy Gemmell hammered home in the sixty-third minute, and just as we were expecting extra time or a replay, Steve Chalmers touched in a Murdoch shot. Bill Shankly of Liverpool told Jock Stein that he was immortal. So he and this game will prove to be!

Celtic: Simpson, Craig, Gemmell, Murdoch, McNeill, Clark, Johnstone, Wallace, Chalmers, Auld, Lennox
Inter Milan: Sarti, Burgnich, Facchetti, Bedin, Guarneri, Picchi, Domenghini, Cappellini, Mazzola, Bicicli, Corso
Referee – K. Tschescher, West Germany Crowd 55,000

24 May 1972 Rangers 3 Moscow Dynamo 2 Barcelona
This was Rangers' first victory in the now defunct European Cup-Winners' Cup, although they had twice previously, in 1961 and 1967, lost in the final. Yet it was a bittersweet occasion for the Ibrox side, for the whole thing was tarnished by the behaviour of their fans, which was so bad in the immediate aftermath of the game that no public presentation of the trophy to captain John Greig was possible. Rangers would be banned from European competition for the following year. Yet this must not in any way detract from the performance of the team, who had played second fiddle to Celtic in Scotland all season. The goals scored by Colin Stein and Willie Johnston (2) were excellent, and although Moscow Dynamo staged a late rally and came close to earning extra time, Rangers held out to record their victory.

The causes of the trouble were complex, but cheap wine was probably the main one. General Franco's *guardia civil,* the prickly Spanish police force, were certainly quick off the mark and behaved with considerably less restraint than the Glasgow Con-

Colin Stein in action against Moscow Dynamo.

stabulary would have, but they might have felt threatened by the manifestly anti-Catholic tone of some of the chants, songs and banners of the Rangers supporters. In addition, an invasion of the field was simply something that was not tolerated in the Spanish dictatorship of 1972.

Rangers: McCloy, Jardine, Mathieson, Greig, Johnstone, Smith, McLean, Conn, Stein, MacDonald, Johnston
Moscow Dynamo: Pilgui, Basalev, Dolmatov, Zykov, Dobbonosov (Gerschkovitch), Zhukov, Baidatchni, Jakubik (Estrekov), Sabo, Makovihov, Evryuzhikin
Referee – J. M. Ortiz de Mendibil, Spain Crowd 35,000

11 May 1983 Aberdeen 2 Real Madrid 1 Gothenburg
This was a great triumph for Alex Ferguson's Aberdeen side who deservedly earned the plaudits of the whole of Europe for their capture of the European Cup-Winners' Cup, particularly as they beat Bayern Munich en route. Aberdeen would also win the Scottish Cup that year although the Scottish League Premier Division went to Dundee United and the Scottish League Cup to Celtic. The geography and the weather were both kind to Aberdeen, in that the game was played in Sweden rather than a hot Mediterranean country and the pitch was almost waterlogged. Thus the conditions were more like Aberdeen than Madrid, and it was no surprise when Eric Black put Aberdeen ahead. Madrid however fought back and earned a penalty to equalize, and for a long time in the second half were well on top. But the Dons kept plugging away and John Hewitt eventually notched the winner.

As is the way with Aberdeen supporters, there was no great exuberant celebration, and the whole affair was very dignified and a credit to Scotland. As with the triumphs of Celtic in 1967 and Rangers in 1972, everyone connected with Aberdeen was Scottish.

Aberdeen: Leighton, Rougvie, Miller, McLeish, McMaster, Cooper, Strachan, Simpson, Weir, McGhee, Black (Hewitt)
Real Madrid: Augustin, Metgod, Bonet, Camacho (San Jose), Juan Jose, Angel, Gallego, Steilike, Juanito, Santillana, Isidro (Salguero)
Referee – G Menegali, Italy Crowd 17,804

GREECE

Scotland have played Greece twice, with the score being 1–0 for the home side on each occasion. Many people have asked, "If Greece can become European champions (as they did in Portugal 2004), why can't Scotland?"

1994	18 Dec	Athens	0–1		Apostolakis (pen)
1995	16 Aug	Hampden Park	1–0	McCoist	

GREENOCK MORTON FC

Ground: **Cappielow Park**
Nickname: **The Ton**
Colours: **Blue and white**
Record Attendance: **23,500 v Celtic (1922)**
Record Victory: **11-0 v Carfin Shamrock (1886)**
Record Defeat: **1-10 v Port Glasgow Athletic (1894); v St. Bernard's (1933)**
Highest League Position: **2nd (2nd in Div. 1, 1916/17)**
Best Scottish Cup Performance: **Winners (1922)**
Best League Cup Performance: **Runners-up (1963/64)**

Founded in 1873, the club originally played on land near Morton Terrace, Greenock. This could explain the origin of the name 'Morton', but no one is absolutely sure. In

Morton, First Division champions 1977/78. Back row, left to right: Neil Orr, George Anderson, Barry Evans, Denis Connaghan, Andy Ritchie, John Goldthorpe, Tommy Veitch. Front row: Jim Holmes, Charlie Brown, Davie Hayes, Bobby Russell, Jimmy Miller, Billy Thomas.

Morton celebrate their victory over Dumbarton and winning the Second Division Championship in 1995.

1893 they went professional and became a founder member of the original Division Two. Promotion to Division One was achieved in 1900 and top-flight status was then maintained until 1927. This was a very successful period for the club, although it got off to a difficult start when Morton finished bottom in both 1902 and 1903, but survived when Division One was expanded on both occasions. They went on to enjoy a respectable position in the league table for nearly three decades and in 1922 won the Scottish Cup with a 1–0 victory over Rangers.

After relegation in 1927 they went on to be promoted and then relegated again on two occasions before 1939. When the Scottish League closed down at the start of the second world war Morton were in the lower half of Division B, but when the league programme resumed in 1945 they were put in Division A. In 1948 they reached another Scottish Cup final, which went to a replay before Rangers won 1–0.

The 1950s was not a successful period for the club and most of the decade was spent in the lower division. However, things changed dramatically when the charismatic Hal Stewart became manager in 1961. In 1963/64 his team secured promotion to Division One with a leap-year victory over Forfar on 29 February. They went on to gain sixty-seven points out of seventy-two and Allan McGraw scored fifty-eight league goals that season. There was also an appearance in the 1963/64 League Cup final against Rangers, which ended in a 5–0 defeat. In 1968 their sixth-place finish in Division One brought qualification for the Inter-Cities Fairs Cup, but their only European campaign didn't progress beyond an aggregate 9–3 defeat to Chelsea in the first round.

When the league was reconstructed in 1975, Morton found themselves in the First Division (second tier) and, by the time it was reconstructed again in 1994, they had been promoted to the Premier Division and then relegated again three times.

Their position at the end of the 1993/94 season meant that they were placed in the new Second Division (third tier), and it was at this time that the club began to emphasise the name of 'Greenock Morton', as opposed to simply being known as 'Morton'. Greenock Morton achieved promotion at the first attempt, and they maintained their First Division status until 2001. Then the new millennium brought one of the darkest periods in the club's history. Not only did they go into administration, they dropped into the Third Division (fourth tier) in 2002 after relegation in two consecutive seasons.

Fortunately Greenock Morton came through this difficult time; a buyer stepped in to save them, and the Third Division championship was won at the first attempt in 2003. After four seasons in the Second Division they finished the 2006/07 season as divisional champions, but in February 2008 manager Jim McInally resigned after a run of bad results. He was replaced by David Irons, with former Morton captain Derek Collins as his assistant.

GREIG John (1942 –)

Scotland Caps: 44
Scottish League Championship medals: 5
Scottish Cup medals: 6
Scottish League Cup medals: 4
European Cup-Winners' Cup medal: 1

John Greig will always be associated with Rangers, for whom he has been player, captain, manager, administrator and director. He joined the club in 1960 from Whitburn Juniors, and first came to prominence on a close-season tour of Russia in 1961. Between 1961 and 1978 he played 857 times for Rangers, winning many honours with the club as well as being voted 'Player of the Year' in both 1966 and 1976. He is also the only player in Scottish football to have won three domestic trebles. He did this in 1963/64, 1975/76 and 1977/78.

In 1977 he was awarded the MBE for his services to football. Unfortunately, most of John's career coincided with Jock Stein's Celtic at their best, and there were times

John Greig with Willie Johnston (left) and Colin Stein (right).

when he carried the Rangers team virtually on his own. When his career finished in 1978, John was appointed manager, a job in which he was markedly less successful than he was as a player, and he was dismissed in 1983. He was then an excellent commentator for BBC Radio Scotland before returning to his beloved Ibrox in an administrative capacity in 1990. He played forty-four times for Scotland, scoring a famous goal against Italy at Hampden Park in 1965, and captaining the side in the epic 3–2 win at Wembley in 1967, but he was unfortunate in that Scotland did not make the finals of the World Cup in 1966 and 1970 when he was in his prime. In 2008 he and his contemporary Billy McNeill of Celtic were awarded honorary degrees from the University of Glasgow.

GRETNA FC (former Scottish League club)

Ground: **Raydale Park**
Nickname: **Black and whites**
Colours: **Black and white**
Record Attendance: **3000 (disputed by some) at Raydale Park v Dundee United (2005)**
6137 at Fir Park v Rangers (2008)
Record Victory: **8-0 v Cowdenbeath (2004); (also 20-0 v Silloth)**
Record Defeat: **0-5 v Greenock Morton (2003); (also 0-6 v Worksop Town; v Bradford Park Avenue)**
Highest League Position: **12th (2007/08)**
Best Scottish Cup Performance: **Runners-up (2005/06)**
Best League Cup Performance: **Last 16 (3rd Round, 2006/07; 2007/08)**

Gretna achieved promotion to the Scottish Premier League in 2007, just five years after finishing seventh in the Unibond League First Division, the second tier of England's Northern Premier League. In the intervening five years they had been promoted through the ranks of Scottish football in three successive seasons, and played in both the Scottish Cup final and European football.

Founded in 1946, Gretna played in the Dumfriesshire Junior League for just one season before joining the Carlisle and District League and earning the distinction of being a Scottish team that played in England. Apart from 1951/52, when they were part of the short-lived Cumberland League, they stayed there until 1982. After winning the Carlisle and District title for six consecutive seasons they moved on to the Northern League Second Division. Promoted to the First Division at the first attempt, they went on to win the Northern League championship in both 1990/91 and 1991/92, which brought promotion to the Northern Premier League (Unibond League). Ten years later they were admitted to the Third Division of the Scottish League when Airdrieonians went out of existence in 2002.

Rowan Alexander had become manager at the end of 2000, and then Brooks Mileson, a successful businessman, bought control of the club when it was in the Third Division. Shrewd transfer dealing brought experienced players such as Alan Main, Steve Tosh and James Grady to the club and they joined Derek Townsley, a player who had played for Gretna in the English FA Cup when they were part of the Unibond League. Promotion to the Second Division was achieved at the third attempt in 2004/05 and a year later the Second Division title was won with an eighteen-point margin. In May 2006 the Scottish Cup final against Hearts was only lost on penalties, following a 1–1 draw. Hearts had already qualified for the Champions League, and so Gretna took part in the 2006/07 UEFA Cup. Their first European campaign got off to a bad start with a 5–1 home defeat to Derry City, but a 2–2 draw away from home restored some pride.

Promotion to the Second Division was achieved at the third attempt in 2004/05 and a year later the Second Division title was won with an eighteen-point margin. In May 2006 the Scottish Cup final against Hearts was only lost on penalties, following a 1–1 draw. Hearts had already qualified for the Champions League, and so Gretna took part in the 2006/07 UEFA Cup. Their first European campaign got off to a bad start with a 5–1 home defeat to Derry City, but a 2–2 draw away from home restored some pride.

Assistant manager David Irons took over on a caretaker basis in March 2007 when Rowan Alexander suffered ill health, and he was still in charge on 28 April 2007 when the final step up to the SPL was achieved. Gretna had seen their lead over St Johnstone gradually reduced over the preceding weeks and a draw against Ross County at Dingwall would not have been enough, but a last-minute goal from James Grady in the final game of the season secured a 3–2 victory. The club announced that their SPL home games would be played at Motherwell's Fir Park, and for a time there was talk of a new all-seater stadium being constructed.

It was David Irons, now Head Coach, and Director of Football Mick Wadsworth who took on the challenge of keeping the Black and Whites in the top flight, and Rowan Alexander was dismissed in November 2007. By February 2008 there was much speculation about Gretna's financial situation, and David Irons left for

Greenock Morton. Mick Wadsworth and a young squad of players were left to carry on the fight to get off the bottom of the SPL, but in March, with Brooks Mileson suffering severe health problems, the club went into administration and the deduction of ten points by the SPL meant that relegation was inevitable.

On 29 May 2008, after the administrator said he could not guarantee that Gretna would be able to fulfil the next season's fixtures, the SFL announced that, if the club was going to survive at all, it would spend 2008/09 in the Third Division. It soon became apparent that there would be no financial rescue package, and Gretna's short, but dramatic, time in Scottish league football came to an end.

A ticket for Gretna's last League game at Raydale Park, when they drew 0-0 with Clyde.

GROUNDS

Scottish football has a wide diversity of types of ground, and many people find it a pleasurable odyssey to visit as many as possible. In the last two decades of the twentieth century many grounds disappeared (usually to be built upon by supermarkets or housing) and were replaced by newer, all-seated enclosures. Even the grounds which remain on the same site have undergone radical changes, usually with more seating accommodation as this is now a requirement by the SPL. Yet some grounds still retain their individuality and charm. There is for example the long, obtuse-angled main stand at Dens Park, Dundee, or the L-shaped main stand at Stark's Park, Kirkcaldy. Both of these structures have been in place since the early 1920s.

Examples of grounds that have gone are Muirton Park in Perth, Brockville in Falkirk, Broomfield (with its quaint, Victorian cricket-type pavilion on the corner) in Airdrie, Annfield in Stirling and Boghead in Dumbarton. In the case of Kilbowie Park, Clydebank or Cathkin Park, Glasgow, where Third Lanark used to play, the team has disappeared as well, yet they were once the 'theatre of dreams' of many who contributed to Scottish football. There still remain the pitch and parts of the terracing at Cathkin Park, and it can be very evocative for the visitor, particularly when it is remembered that Scotland versus England internationals were played there before the present Hampden Park was built.

Ross County's Victoria Park.

Many Scottish grounds have quaint names. Fir Park, for example, is where Motherwell play, whereas Firs Park is the home of East Stirlingshire, and both of them are distinct from Firhill. Trivia quizzes sometimes ask 'Which Scottish grounds have the same name as a British Prime Minister, an English County Cricket team and a different sport?' Palmerston, Somerset and Rugby Parks are the homes of Queen of the South, Ayr United and Kilmarnock. Pittodrie in Aberdeen is said to have originally meant 'dung heap'! The names of some grounds are mundane eg Central Park, Cowdenbeath and The Falkirk Stadium. Others tell us about the history of the ground eg Glebe Park, Brechin used to belong to the Church of Scotland, for the glebe was land owned by the minister. Some tell us a little geography, eg Bayview of East Fife tells us that the old ground had a good view of Methil docks, whereas the most ironically named is Station Park, Forfar. Forfar Station used to be 100 yards away from the ground, but the station closed in 1967 and Forfar Athletic are now further away from a railway line than any other club in Scotland except Peterhead!

The first all-seated stadium in the United Kingdom was that at Pittodrie, which was built in 1980. All-seated stadia were a result of the Taylor Report, which was set up in the wake of the Hillsborough disaster of 1989, and there can be little doubt that comfort, hygiene and particularly safety have been greatly enhanced. The SPL now insists on all-seated stadia for its clubs. Yet there is a down side as well, for on a winter's day it is colder to sit than to stand and in an all-seated stadium it is more difficult to move away from an unpleasant individual. There is also more than an element of truth in the statement that all-seated stadia destroy the atmosphere.

In addition, an all-seated stadium with more than half the seats empty can be a depressing experience, and many people believe there is little point in paying for such developments if the seats are seldom going to be used, but there is little doubt that attendance at a Scottish football match in the early years of the twenty-first century is a far more civilised experience than in the 1960s or 1970s. Hooliganism has been all but eradicated, overcrowding hardly exists, and grounds

Queen of the South's Palmerston Park.

have toilets where hands can be washed. Some fans yearn for a return to the atmosphere of yesteryear, but the clock will not be turned back.

It is impossible to make a list of ground capacities that will remain accurate for long, as they are constantly changing. Some clubs make use of additional temporary seating from time to time, seats are sometimes removed to make room for television cameras, and sometimes changes are dictated by safety considerations. Every season brings news of ground developments, and new grounds are usually designed so that they can be expanded at a later date. All these factors affect capacities, and so the following table has categorised grounds into different bands, which serve to illustrate how Scotland's football clubs operate on very different scales.

Motherwell's Fir Park.

Rangers' Ibrox Stadium.

Rothes' Mackessack Park.

(a) Greater than 50,000

Capacity	Club	Ground
	Celtic	Celtic Park
	Queen's Park	Hampden Park
	Rangers	Ibrox Stadium

(b) Between 5,000 and 25,000

Capacity	Club	Ground
20,000 – 25,000	Aberdeen	Pittodrie Stadium
15,000-20,000	Heart of Midlothian	Tynecastle Park
	Hibernian	Easter Road
	Kilmarnock	Rugby Park
10,000-15,000	Airdrie United	Excelsior Stadium
	Ayr United	Somerset Park
	Dundee	Dens Park
	Dundee United	Tannadice Park
	Dunfermline	East End Park
	Greenock Morton	Cappielow Park
	Livingston	Almondvale Stadium
	Motherwell	Fir Park
	Partick Thistle	Firhill Stadium
	Raith Rovers	Stark's Park
	St Johnstone	McDiarmid Park
	St Mirren	St Mirren Park
5,000-10,000	Clyde	Broadwood Stadium
	Falkirk	The Falkirk Stadium
	Forfar Athletic	Station Park
	Hamilton Academical	New Douglas Park
	Inverness CT	Caledonian Stadium
	Queen of the South	Palmerston Park
	Ross County	Victoria Park
	Stranraer	Stair Park

(c) Less than 5000

Capacity	Club	Ground
2,500-5,000	Alloa Athletic	Recreation Park
	Arbroath	Gayfield Park
	Berwick Rangers	Shielfield Park
	Brechin City	Glebe Park
	Cowdenbeath	Central Park
	Elgin City	Borough Briggs
	Montrose	Links Park
	Peterhead	Balmoor Stadium
	Stenhousemuir	Ochilview Park
	Stirling Albion	Forthbank Stadium
less than 2,500	Albion Rovers	Cliftonhill Stadium
	Dumbarton	Strathclyde Homes Stadium
	East Fife	First2Finance Bayview Stadium
	East Stirlingshire	Firs Park

GROUND SHARING

This has taken place on several occasions when a club has had to leave its home before it was able to move into a new stadium. In the case of Dumbarton, Falkirk and Stirling Albion this was only for a single season, but Airdrieonians, Clyde, Clydebank and Hamilton Academical were 'on the road' for several years. The unfortunate Clydebank never did find a new permanent new home whilst they were part of the Scottish Football League, as Airdrie United effectively bought them out when they were in administration.

The grounds of Inverness Caledonian Thistle and Gretna did not meet SPL requirements when they were promoted to the top flight and they both had to share with another SPL club for a time. Inverness shared Pittodrie with Aberdeen for six months when they were promoted in 2004 and Gretna were given permission to share Fir Park with Motherwell when they went up in 2007 (They had already played a UEFA Cup tie against Derry City at Fir Park in August 2006). However, a combination of increased use and wet weather meant that the Fir Park pitch deteriorated into a poor condition, and some matches had to be postponed.

There have been additional instances of a club playing just a handful of matches at another's ground, and these are not included in the list below. In the case of Tynecastle Park it should be noted that four other clubs have used the ground as well as Hearts. These are Hibernian and St. Bernard's in 1924, Berwick Rangers in 1989 and Meadowbank Thistle in 1992.

Guest Club	Shared Stadium	Host Club	From	To
Airdrieonians	Broadwood Stadium	Clyde	1994	1998
Clyde	Firhill	Partick Thistle	1986	1991
	Douglas Park	Hamilton Ac.	1991	1994
Clydebank	Boghead	Dumbarton	1996	1999
	Cappielow	Greenock Morton	1999	2002
Dumbarton	Cliftonhill	Albion Rovers	1999	2000
Edinburgh City	Marine Gardens	Leith Athletic	1928	1931
			1934	1935
Falkirk	Ochilview	Stenhousemuir	2003	2004
Greenock Morton	St Mirren Park	St Mirren	1949	1949
Gretna	Fir Park	Motherwell	2007	2008
Hamilton Ac.	Firhill	Partick Thistle	1994	1996
	Cliftonhill	Albion Rovers	1996	1998
	Firhill	Partick Thistle	1998	2001
Inverness CT	Pittodrie	Aberdeen	2004	2005
Leith Athletic	New Logie Green	St Bernard's	1899	1899
St Bernard's	Tynecastle	Hearts	1924	1924
Stirling Albion	Ochilview	Stenhousemuir	1992	1993
Third Lanark	Hampden Park	Queen's Park	1903	1904

HAFFEY Frank (1938 –)

Scotland Caps: 2

Frank Haffey was the goalkeeper held responsible for the 9–3 defeat by England at Wembley on 15 April 1961. It was not all his fault by any manner of means, but sympathy tended to evaporate when he appeared to milk the situation by having his photograph taken under a station platform sign which said '9', for example. On the other hand, he saved a penalty the previous year at Hampden Park against England, and had many fine performances for Celtic, notably in the first game of the 1963 Scottish Cup final. He played in only these two internationals for Scotland.

HALL OF FAME

This is part of the Scottish Football Museum at Hampden Park, and contains inductees who are considered to have made an outstanding contribution to Scottish football, either as a player, manager or both. Originally the idea was that everyone with fifty caps would be a member, but this was considered to be unfair as so few international matches were played before the second world war, many outstanding players would have been omitted.

Those inducted in 2004 (the originals) were:
Willie Woodburn, Jim Baxter, Sir Alex Ferguson, Graeme Souness, John Greig, Jock Stein, Bill Shankly, Billy McNeill, Jimmy McGrory, Danny McGrain, Bobby Murdoch, Jimmy Johnstone, Sir Matt Busby, Billy Bremner, Dave Mackay, Denis Law, Gordon Smith, Willie Miller, Hughie Gallacher, Kenny Dalglish.

Another eleven were added in 2005:
Alan Morton, Alex McLeish, Bobby Lennox, Charles

Added to the Hall of Fame in 2006 was Billy Steel.

In 2007 Eddie Turnbull was added to the Hall of Fame. Turnbull holds aloft the Dryburgh Cup with Pat Stanton (left) and Alan Gordon (right).

Campbell, George Young, Jim McLean, Joe Jordan, John White, Lawrie Reilly, Willie Waddell, Alex James;

And 2006's eleven inductees were:

Brain Laudrup, Henrik Larsson, Sandy Jardine, Billy Steel, Willie Ormond, John Neilson Robertson (Notts Forest), Tommy Walker, Willie Henderson, Davie Cooper, Tommy Gemmell, Richard Gough.

They were followed in 2007 by another nine:

Willie Bauld, Eric Caldow, Alan Hansen, Walter Smith, Gordon Strachan, Ally McCoist, Eddie Turnbull, Jimmy Cowan, and the first-ever female inductee, Rose Reilly.

It would be difficult to argue against any of these fifty-one, for their contribution to the game has been immense, but many Scots have been surprised to see that there is as yet no R S McColl, Wattie Arnott, Jimmy Quinn, Andrew Nesbit Wilson, John Thomson, Jimmy Delaney or Bobby Walker - for all of whom a strong case could be made.

HAMILL Pauline (1971 –)

Pauline Hamill entered the record books in August 2007, when she became Scotland's first woman footballer to play one hundred times for her country. When she took the field for Scotland's 3–2 victory over Belgium in a friendly at McDiarmid Park, she joined Kenny Dalglish as the only Scottish footballers with a hundred caps. Her international debut was against England in 1992.

An outstanding striker with the Hibernian Ladies team, Pauline spent two seasons in England with Doncaster Belles before returning to Hibernian in 2007. She combined her playing career with Hibs with the post of Football Development Officer for Falkirk FC, working to attract more women into Scottish football.

HAMILTON Alex (1939 – 1993)

Scotland Caps: 24
Scottish League Championship medals: 1

Alex Hamilton was a flamboyant, but effective, right back for Dundee in the early 1960s. His twenty-four caps for Scotland make him Dundee's most capped player. The highlights of his international career were the hat-trick of victories over England between 1962 and 1964, and he was a regular until he was made the scapegoat for Scotland's defeat by Poland on 13 October 1965 at Hampden Park. He won the Scottish League championship with Dundee in 1962, and featured in their run to the European Cup semi-final the following year.

HAMILTON Bob (1877 – 1948)

Scotland Caps: 11
Scottish League Championship medals: 4
Scottish Cup medals: 2

Centre forward for Rangers and Scotland at the turn of the nineteenth and twentieth centuries, Bob Hamilton won eleven caps for Scotland, but is most famous for the goal-scoring role he played in Rangers' four league championships in a row, from 1899-1902. He left Rangers in 1906, to play for a variety of clubs (including a brief return to Ibrox) and was surprisingly given a Scottish cap as late as 1911 when with Dundee, seven years after his previous one. He came from Elgin and was their Lord Provost for a spell in the 1930s.

HAMILTON ACADEMICAL FC

Ground: **New Douglas Park**
Nickname: **The Accies**
Colours: **Red and white**
Record Attendance: **28,690 at Douglas Park v Hearts (1937)**
5,078 at New Douglas Park v Dundee (2008)
Record Victory: **11-1 v Chryston (1885)**
Record Defeat: **1-11 v Hibernian (1965)**
Highest League Position: **4th (1934/35)**
Best Scottish Cup Performance: **Runners-up (1910/11; 1934/35)**
Best League Cup Performance: **Last 4 (Semi-final 1948/49; 1960/61; 1979/80)**

The club's first recorded fixture took place in 1874, not long after it was founded by James Blacklock, the rector of Hamilton Academy. At first there was no letter 's' at the end of 'Academical', but one was later adopted, and in recent times the 's' has been dropped again. The Acas, as they were known in the early years, first entered the Scottish Cup in 1876, losing their first-round tie away to Barrhead, and in 1888 they moved from South Haugh to Douglas Park, which would be their home until 1994. The opportunity to join the Scottish League came in 1897, when Renton resigned after just four matches. Hamilton took over their four results and their remaining fixtures for that season. They stayed in Division Two until 1906 and, because of the re-election system, were not promoted when they won the title in 1904 and were promoted when they finished fourth in 1906. The Accies then remained in the top division until after the second world war, and enjoyed some very successful times. Their successes included reaching two Scottish Cup finals. Celtic beat them 2–0 in the replayed 1910/11 final after a 0–0 draw, and in the 1934/35 final Bertie Harrison scored as they lost 2–1 to Rangers. 1934/35 also saw Hamilton end the season with a fourth-place finish in the league.

When league football resumed after the war, the club's fortunes soon took a turn for the worse. In 1947 they finished bottom of Division A with just eleven points from thirty games and were relegated to the lower division. With the exception of the 1953/54 and 1965/66 seasons, when they briefly enjoyed top-flight status, they stayed there until league reconstruction in 1975. It was during this period that the Accies became the first Scottish club to bring in players from eastern Europe, when Polish international players Witold Szygula and Roman Strzalkowski were recruited in 1971.

In 1975 they were placed in the First Division, the second of three tiers, and history repeated itself. With the exception of the 1986/87 and 1988/89 seasons, when they briefly experienced Premier Division football, they remained there until the next league reconstruction in 1994. The Accies did manage to enter the record books during this period, though, when their charismatic manager John Lambie led them to a famous 1–0 win at Ibrox in the third round of the 1986/87 Scottish Cup. Adrian Sprott scored the goal. They also won the Scottish League Challenge Cup in 1991/92, beating Ayr United 1–0 in the final, and then won it again in 1992/93 with a 3–2 victory over Morton.

The last Scottish League match to be played at Douglas Park took place in May 1994 and there now followed several years of ground sharing, first with Partick Thistle, and then with Albion Rovers. The nomadic period didn't come to an end until 2001, when Accies played their first match at New Douglas Park, just down the road from the supermarket that stands where they played for over a hundred years.

Since 1994 the club has, at various times, played in every division. The lowest point came in 1999/2000, when the players didn't turn up for a Second Division fixture at Stenhousemuir, because the club was having difficulty in paying their wages, and fifteen points were deducted. They were relegated to the Third Division at the end of the season, but it didn't take the Accies long to bounce back, and promotions in both 2001 and 2004 took them up to the First Division (second tier).

After former player Billy Reid was appointed manager in 2005, Hamilton reached the final of the 2005/06 Scottish League Challenge Cup, losing 2–1 to St Mirren. A strong team, which included players from a successful youth development programme, began to regularly challenge for promotion and in 2007/08 a remarkable recovery was completed when they won the First Division championship after remaining undefeated at home in the league throughout the season. The Accies had arrived in the SPL.

HAMPDEN PARK

'On Hampden's battle field
The results shall be revealed
England's fate shall be sealed
And the Saxon foe shall yield'

This ground, sometimes known nowadays as 'The National Stadium' is the very epicentre of Scottish football, and there is now an excellent museum there to impress the visitor. The ground is owned by Queen's Park, although it has been leased out to the SFA on a ten-year deal. Their lower division fixtures are played there in a sometimes melancholy, but still impressive, silence. Hampden is the normal home for Scotland internationals, Scottish Cup finals and semi-finals, and Scottish League Cup finals. It has an impressive list of attendance records to its name, simply because for a long time, there was no other ground in the world anything like as big. Apart from football, the ground has been in the past used for other events like boxing, rugby, American football and even rock concerts.

The current ground is actually the third Hampden Park. Ironically, the name Hampden has connections with a great English Parliamentarian hero, John Hampden, of the seventeenth century, who refused to pay taxes to Charles I. The first Hampden Park was opposite a street called Hampden Terrace, which was named after this great man! Queen's Park had leased this ground from Glasgow Corporation, but had to yield when the rent rose and the Cathcart Circle Railway line was planned to go through their ground. In 1883, they bought their second ground and opened it in 1884.

For a while, second Hampden Park was the best ground in Scotland and attracted the biennial international fixture between Scotland and England, holding crowds up to 20,000. But then in 1892, the ambitious Celtic club built their fine new ground, which was bigger than second Hampden, and Celtic Park 'won' the Internationals for 1894, 1896, 1898 and 1900. Queen's Park now decided to build the biggest stadium in the world on their present site, and it was duly opened in a game against Celtic on 31 October 1903. Celtic Park still staged the Scotland versus England international of 1904, but the Scottish Cup final of 1904 (the famous one of Jimmy Quinn's hat-trick) was staged at the new Hampden before 64,472 fans. Second Hampden now became the home of Third Lanark and was known as New Cathkin Park.

Now, Celtic Park's day having passed, and Ibrox being ruled out following the disaster in 1902 in which twenty-five people were killed, Hampden Park was staging the England internationals, and in 1906 astonished the world by housing a six-figure crowd of 102,741. By this time they had acknowledged the importance of the press by building the first ever Press Box 'with telegraphic facilities'. In 1908 there were 121,452 people (a world record), 1910 was down a little to 106,205, 1912 housed 127,307 (a world record in spite of a rail strike!) and 1914 saw over 115,000 with another 40,000, it was reckoned, locked outside. This was astonishing stuff, as Hampden was not yet as big as it would become, for the east terracing (with its extra layer) was not totally completed until after the first world war.

In between times, Hampden Park had survived the riot of 1909 when, in the Scottish Cup final, the supporters of Celtic and Rangers united in their demands to have extra time, which they felt they were being cheated out of, and set fire to the stand, goalposts, pay boxes etc. This allowed Queen's Park to rebuild, and to modify and improve the design, but it is curious that although Hampden Park was given the Scotland versus England internationals in 1910, 1912 and 1914, the Scottish Cup finals were given to either Ibrox and Celtic Park until the first world war, when Hampden Park became the almost-automatic choice.

The period from the 1920s onwards was the heyday of Hampden Park, with two magnificent stands – the south or main stand holding 10,000 and with a magnificent clock hanging from its front, and the north stand holding 4,000. The large clock, which stayed suspended from the south stand until 1945, was often significant in the results of games, for the players could instantly know how long was left. The west terracing (the Mount Florida or the Rangers End) held 41,000 and the east terracing (the King's Park or Celtic End) held 62,000. When full for cup finals and internationals, Hampden was a sight to behold, often astounding English and foreign journalists with its size and its pioneering use of facilities now taken for granted, such as turnstiles (rather than the primitive pay boxes) and a loudspeaker system.

At least two occasions claim to be the birth of the 'Hampden Roar' – the international against England of 1929 when Alec Cheyne scored direct from a corner kick, and (more likely) the great goal of Jimmy McGrory when he picked up a through pass from Bob McPhail to win the 1933 international against the same opponents. 1931 and 1933 both beat previous world records and, following serious overcrowding at the 1935 international, the 1937 match was made all-ticket. But, with forgeries and people climbing over the wall, it was reckoned that far more than the official world record of 149,547 (although Queen's Park insist it was only 149,415) were there on 17 April 1937. A week later, to see the Scottish Cup final between Celtic and Aberdeen, 147,365 (the figure is also disputed) were there, with at

Hampden Park for Scotland v England 1908.

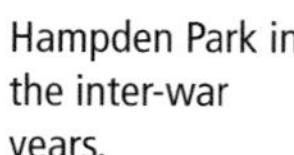

Hampden Park in the inter-war years.

least 20,000 denied admission and forced to follow the game by the roar of the crowd.

After the second world war, Hampden Park (its limit now set at 134,000) continued unchallenged in British and European football, hosting games like Great Britain versus Rest of Europe on 10 May 1947 and, famously, the European Cup final of 1960 between Real Madrid and Eintracht Frankfurt, when it was said that the applause for Real Madrid's magnificent victory was heard all over the city of Glasgow. This was in addition to the usual complement of cup finals and internationals, with six-figure crowds a commonplace and accommodated without any serious problems. Floodlights came in 1961, and the west terracing was covered in 1968.

By the late 1960s, however, criticism was being heard about how decrepit and out of date the stadium was. Certainly, toilets were a disgrace and often at big games, the SFA, in a misguided attempt to save money, would not employ enough gate checkers – so that the crowd could not get in on time! Exiting from the ground, in particular going down the stairways, was more than a little dangerous (although it took the tragic events at Ibrox in 1971 to highlight that problem in the eyes of the authorities). The cinders on the terracing meant that after Scotland scored and the crowd jumped around to acclaim it, a cloud of dust would hang around for some time afterwards! Another Hampden riot at the Scottish Cup final of 1980 may have raised questions about religious bigotry in Scotland and the failure of the Scottish educational system, but it also highlighted the lack of facilities at Hampden Park. In particular it was felt that an all-seater stadium might have made the riot a lot less likely, and a lot less serious.

But little action was taken until the 1990s, when eventually the authorities were shamed into doing something about it. Hampden was closed for a while, but re-opened in 1999 as an all-seated stadium with a much-reduced capacity of 52,000. Although it does have its critics, particularly about the lack of car park facilities and consequent traffic jams, it is indeed a stadium fit for a football-mad country, as Scotland undeniably is. In 2002, Hampden Park hosted the Champions League final, and did the job brilliantly as Real Madrid beat Bayer Leverkusen.

HANSEN Alan (1955 –)

Scotland Caps: 26

An established and respected BBC television pundit, Alan Hansen was one of the most successful Scottish players in England of them all. He won twenty-six caps for Scotland, and many people believe he should have won more, but much of his career clashed with the Aberdeen pairing of Willie Miller and Alex McLeish. His first senior team was Partick Thistle, whom he joined in 1973, and he won the Scottish First Division title with them in 1976. He was soon recognised as an accomplished defender, a tremendous reader of the game, and a man who possessed the ability to be in the right position at the right time.

Alan Hansen, standing centre, is joined by two other Scotland greats, Kenny Dalglish and Graeme Sounness

He was transferred to Liverpool for £100,000 in 1977, and with them he won three European Cup medals, eight league championship medals, two FA Cup medals and three League Cup medals, in a career that lasted until 1991. He had been their captain since 1985. As is the case with many other players, his achievements with his club overshadow those with his country. His international career was not without its good moments, but he will be remembered for the game against USSR in the World Cup finals of 1982, when his accidental collision with Willie Miller effectively allowed Shengalia to score and put Scotland out of the tournament. In June 2007 he received the award of Doctor of the University from the University of Stirling, in recognition of his outstanding contribution to sport.

HARKNESS Jack (1907 – 1985)

Scotland Caps: 11

Jack Harkness was an outstanding goalkeeper for Queen's Park and Hearts in the years between the two world wars. He won eleven caps between 1927 and 1934, notably the Wembley Wizards game of March 1928, when he was still an amateur with Queen's Park, although he turned professional and joined Hearts later that summer. He was renowned for his sporting and gentlemanly approach to the game (see **JACK HARKNESS TROPHY**), on one occasion diving to push Jimmy McGrory of Celtic away from a post on which he might have done himself serious harm. After the second world war, he was a journalist with the *Dundee Courier* and the *Sunday Post*, becoming almost as popular a Scottish character as Oor Wullie and Pa Broon, and referred to simply as 'Jack'. He told many stories about himself, notably about the time when he saw Jimmy McGrory on the other side of Sauchiehall Street. McGrory nodded, and Harkness dived into the gutter, so conditioned was he to diving whenever Jimmy inclined his head!

HARTFORD Asa (1950 –)

Scotland Caps: 50

A midfielder, Asa Hartford played for a variety of English clubs and won fifty Scottish caps in an international career that included appearances in the 1978 and 1982 World Cup Finals. His first club was West Bromwich Albion in 1966, but in November 1971 he was due to be transferred to Leeds United only to find that he failed their medical because of a 'hole in the heart' condition. This condition did not stop him going on to play over the next fifteen years for Manchester City (twice), Nottingham Forest, Everton, Norwich City, Bolton Wanderers, Stockport County, Oldham Athletic and Shrewsbury Town. He won two English League Cup medals with Manchester City and Norwich City, and was always rated highly with any club that he played, but he never entirely won the affection of the Scotland crowd, who felt that they never saw the best of him. After the 'fiasco' of the 1978 World Cup finals, it was generally believed that he had to accept his share of the blame.

HAT-TRICK

This is the term used for a player scoring three goals in a game. The origin of this is in Victorian cricket, where an amateur player (not allowed to accept money in those days, of course) would often be presented with a new hat, if he took three wickets – hence the term, presumably, 'bowler' hat. It very soon became common parlance in football, and the honour of scoring the earliest international hat-trick belongs to John McDougal of Vale of Leven who performed this feat on 2 March 1878 as Scotland beat England 7–2.

Alex Haddow of King's Park scored five consecutive hat-tricks in 1932 against Armadale (23 January), Stenhousemuir (6 February), Edinburgh City (13 February), Montrose (20 February) and Brechin City (27 February). In fact he scored four against Armadale and five against Stenhousemuir, so it was a total of eighteen goals. Having been knocked out of the Scottish Cup, King's Park had no game on 30 January. Two Hearts players have also scored a hat-trick of hat-tricks – Jack White on 1 February 1926 against Dundee United, on 6 February against Alloa and on 10 February against Hamilton Accies (all within ten days) and Barney Battles junior did the same in 1930 against Motherwell, Dundee and St. Mirren on 15, 22 and 29 November.

There are two claimants for the fastest hat-trick in Scottish football. One is Jimmy McGrory who on 14 March 1936 scored a hat-trick inside three minutes against Motherwell in a 5–0 victory at Parkhead, and the

St Mirren goalkeeper Tom Morrison (second left) punches clear from Celtic's Jimmy McGrory with teammates Bill Summers (left) and Finlay (right) in attendance. This was the 1926 Scottish Cup final and Celtic (unusually) were wearing white shirts.

other is Ian St John who on 15 August 1959 in a League Cup match against Hibs at Easter Road performed the same feat. Jimmy McGrory scored a phenomenal fifty-four hat-tricks for Celtic if we count Glasgow Cup and Glasgow Charity Cup games, a feat which makes Henrik Larsson's record of twelve in the Scottish Premier League appear somewhat modest! Little wonder that one of the Celtic fans' favourite songs in the 1930s was:

'Tell me the old, old story
A hat-trick for McGrory!'

But Jimmy McGrory never scored a hat-trick in a Scottish Cup final. Only three players have done this – Jimmy Quinn for Celtic versus Rangers in 1904, Dixie Deans for Celtic versus Hibs in 1972, and Gordon Durie for Rangers versus Hearts in 1996. Some sources claim that Sandy McMahon scored three or even four for Celtic versus Queen's Park in 1892, but the balance of evidence is that Sandy only scored two. A similar claim has been made about an earlier Cup final, namely that of 1881 where some newspapers seem to say that Dr John Smith scored three for Queen's Park, but more reliable sources say that Geordie Ker scored one of the goals in the 3–1 defeat of Dumbarton. It is now generally agreed that in the 1888 Scottish Cup final when Renton beat Cambuslang 6–1, no player scored more than two goals.

Nine hat-tricks have been scored in the Scottish League Cup final – Davie Duncan of East Fife in 1947/48, Willie Bauld of Hearts in 1954/55, Billy McPhail of Celtic in 1957/58, Jim Forrest of Rangers in 1963/64, Bobby Lennox of Celtic in 1968/69, Dixie Deans of Celtic in 1974/75, Joe Harper of Hibs in 1974/75, Ally McCoist of Rangers in 1983/84 and Henrik Larsson in 2000/01. Jim Forrest actually scored four in the League Cup final of 1963/64 against Morton, and he therefore holds the record, but spare a thought for Joe Harper of Hibs who actually scored a hat-trick in the League Cup Final of 1974/75 against Celtic – but still ended up on the losing side, for Dixie Deans of Celtic also scored a hat-trick and three other Celts also scored in the 6–3 victory.

HAY David (1948 –)

Scotland Caps: 27
Scottish League Championship medals: 5
Scottish Cup medals: 2
Scottish League Cup medals: 1

One of the best players in Scottish football in the early 1970s, David Hay earned twenty-seven caps for Scotland. Later he had a career in management, which had its highs as well as its lows. He joined Celtic in 1965 and was very soon one of the 'quality street kids', as Celtic reserves were known, before he broke into the first team in about 1969, reaching the final of the European Cup in his first year. He was an attacking full back, but later on became a midfield player with the nickname 'the quiet assassin' and many people thought that he was Scotland's best player in the 1974 World Cup. But he had

fallen out with Jock Stein the previous season over the issue of injured players not being paid enough, and Stein was looking for an opportunity to get rid of him. On his return from Germany he was transferred for £225,000 to Chelsea, where his career was much less successful, with injuries and the necessity to have an eye operation. When his playing career finished in 1979, Hay turned to management with Motherwell, Celtic, Lillestrom (Norway), St Mirren, Dunfermline, Livingston and elsewhere. He was not without success here, for he won the Scottish Cup and the Scottish League with Celtic, and the Scottish League Cup with Livingston.

HAY James (1880 – 1940)

Scotland Caps: 11
Scottish League Championship medals: 6
Scottish Cup medals: 4

Nicknamed 'Dun', James Hay was one of the great figures of Edwardian football, the captain of the outstanding Celtic side that won six championships in a row, and part of the immortal half back line of Young, Loney and Hay before his departure to Newcastle United in 1911. He was capped eleven times for Scotland, being involved in the wins over England at Hampden Park in 1910 and 1914. After the first world war, he turned to management with Clydebank and Ayr United. A man of the utmost integrity, he resigned from Ayr United in 1926, after accusing a director of being involved in a bribery scandal.

HEART OF MIDLOTHIAN FC

Ground: **Tynecastle Park, Edinburgh**
Nickname: **Hearts; The Jam Tarts; The Jambos**
Colours: **Maroon and white**
Record Attendance: **53,396 at Tynecastle v Rangers (1932)**
32,459 at Murrayfield v AEK Athens (2006)
Record Victory: **21-0 v Anchor (1880)**
Record Defeat: **1-8 v Vale of Leven (1888)**
Highest League Position: **1st (1894/95; 1896/97; 1957/58; 1959/60)**
Best Scottish Cup Performance: **Winners (1890/91; 1895/96; 1900/1901; 1905/06; 1955/56; 1997/98; 2005/06)**
Best League Cup Performance: **Winners: 1954/55; 1958/59; 1959/60; 1962/63**

The club's year of formation is documented as 1874, and there was a centenary match against Tottenham Hotspur in 1974, but Tom Purdie, Hearts' first captain, always insisted that it was founded in 1873. The early Hearts teams played in red, white and blue, but soon after formation they amalgamated with St. Andrew Boys' Club and the new club played in maroon. There are several explanations of how the club got its name, and a favoured one is that the founders were patrons of 'The Heart of Midlothian', a dance hall just off the Royal Mile. Others believe that the young footballers played in the streets around the site of the old jail near St. Giles' cathedral that was known as the Heart of Midlothian.

In those early years the club played at the Meadows, then Powburn, and then Powderhall, before moving to 'Old' Tynecastle in 1881. Five years later they crossed Gorgie Road, and took up residence in their current home. It was around this time that Hearts entered the English FA Cup. In 1885/86 they were drawn away to Padiham, in Lancashire, but 'scratched' because the English side contained professionals and there was a risk of the Scottish amateurs being punished. By the following season this was no longer an issue and Hearts played a first-round tie at Darwen, also in Lancashire, losing 7–1. Not long afterwards the SFA put a stop to their members taking part in the English competition.

Hearts were regular entrants in the Scottish Cup from 1875/76 onwards, and by the end of the century they had twice won the competition, beating Dumbarton 1–0 in the 1890/91 final and triumphing 3–1 over Hibernian in 1895/96. This latter fixture took place at Logie Green, Edinburgh, which was the home of St. Bernard's. The cup was won again in 1900/01, when Celtic were beaten 4–3 in what became known as the 'Walker final' because of the immense contribution of captain Bobby Walker. He also played a major role in Hearts' 1–0 victory over Third Lanark in the 1905/06 final.

Hearts were founder members of the Scottish League in 1890/91 and they also won the league title on two occasions before the end of the century, in 1894/95 and 1896/97. There was to be a long wait before the club next won the league championship, but they consistently finished in a high position. The memory lives on of one particular Hearts team that consistently finished near the top of the league, and might well have gone on to greater things. It was lost when all the players volunteered for service at the outbreak of the first world war; seven players were killed, and others wounded or gassed.

Heart of Midlothian FC 1960/61 with the Scottish League Cup and the Scottish League Championship trophy.

The wait for another trophy did not come to an end until October 1954, when manager Tommy Walker led Hearts to the 1954/55 League Cup. The young Hearts team, containing players such as Alfie Conn, Willie Bauld, Jimmy Wardhaugh and Dave Mackay, then brought the 1955/56 Scottish Cup back to Tynecastle after a 3–1 victory over Celtic. Dave Mackay took over the captaincy for the 1957/58 season and the team went from strength to strength, winning the 1957/58 championship and beating Partick Thistle 5–1 in the 1958/59 League Cup final. Dave Mackay left for Tottenham Hotspur in 1959, but the team went on to win the title again in 1959/60, and there were two more League Cup victories when Third Lanark were beaten 2–1 in 1959/60, and Kilmarnock defeated 1–0 in 1962/63.

Hearts' forays into the European Cup were disappointing, and they twice fell at the first hurdle, losing to Standard Liege in 1958/59 and Benfica in 1960/61. They qualified for the Inter-Cities Fairs Cup on three occasions in the 1960s, but never got beyond the third round, although they only lost to Real Zaragoza in a replay.

After league reconstruction in 1975, ninth and tenth-place finishes no longer provided safety from relegation, and Hearts dropped down to the First Division in 1977, 1979 and 1981. They quickly bounced back each time and almost won the league championship in 1986, when the final day's results meant that they lost the title to Celtic on goal difference. For many Hearts fans this brought back memories of previous last days of the season. In 1965 a 2–0 defeat to Kilmarnock gave the title to the Ayrshire side on goal average, whilst in 1959 their failure to beat Celtic meant that Rangers were champions instead of Hearts. They finished second again in both 1987/88 and 1991/92, and the 1988/89 UEFA Cup campaign saw them reach the quarter-finals of a European competition for the first time, only losing 2–1 on aggregate to Bayern Munich.

Jim Jefferies, a former club captain, was appointed manager in 1995, and he led the team to victory in the 1997/98 Scottish Cup final, when Rangers were defeated 2–1 at Celtic Park. In December 2000 Craig Levein, another former captain, replaced him, and Hearts achieved consecutive third-place league finishes in 2002/03 and 2003/04. This was achieved despite mounting financial problems, and Hearts went on to reach the new group stage of the 2004/05 UEFA Cup by beating Portuguese side S.C. Braga 5–3 on aggregate. Craig Levein left for Leicester in October 2004, and, although his replacement John Robertson led the side to an away victory in Basel, they failed to progress to the last sixteen.

Vladimir Romanov acquired a controlling interest in the club in February 2005, and it wasn't long before many changes were taking place at Tynecastle. John Robertson left in April and by the start of the 2005/06 season George Burley had been appointed. He left in October and by the end of March 2006 his replacement Graham Rix had also departed. Lithuanian Valdas Ivanauskas became head coach and Hearts not only finished second in the SPL, they also won the 2005/06 Scottish Cup, beating Gretna on penalties.

The ensuing European campaign ended in disappointment, with failure to qualify for the group stages of either the Champions League or the UEFA Cup, but the pace of change did not diminish. International players Steven Pressley and Paul Hartley both left to join Celtic and, after Valdas Ivanauskas also departed, Director of Sport Anatoly Korobochka, a 'Master of Sport' in the former USSR, became interim head coach. Hearts went on to finish fourth in the 2006/07 SPL, which was not quite enough to secure a place in the UEFA Cup.

Erik Sorensen is congratulated by his Morton teammates after saving a penalty in a cup-tie against Hearts.

In August 2007 the club announced plans for a redevelopment of Tynecastle stadium that would increase its capacity by nearly 6,000 to 23,000, and that same month Scotland goalkeeper Craig Gordon was transferred to Sunderland. The frequent changes were becoming associated with a degree of uncertainty amongst fans and journalists, and this now extended to the management structure. Former player Stephen Frail and Bulgarian coach Angel Chervenkov were both working with Anatoly Korobochka, and then in January 2008 Stephen Frail was appointed caretaker manager, but despite all these changes the Jam Tarts finished the season in a disappointing eighth place.

HEIGHT

No reliable evidence exists about who has been the tallest or smallest footballer in Scottish football history, but Kevin James of Falkirk and St Johnstone (six feet seven inches) in the 1990s and early twenty-first century, and Ian McWilliam of Queen's Park and Celtic (six feet five inches) in the 1970s would be strong contenders for the tallest. As men are now generally taller than they were in the days before the welfare state, the smallest footballer would almost certainly be someone in the Victorian era or the early years of the twentieth century, but in modern times Jimmy Johnstone of Celtic (five feet four inches) was one of the smallest.

HELENSBURGH FC (former Scottish League club)

Home: **Ardencaple Park, Helensburgh, Dunbartonshire**
Highest League Position: **41st (1st in Div. 3, 1925/26)**
Best Scottish Cup Performance: **Last 3 (Semi-final, 1878/79)**

A glance at the record books gives the impression that Helensburgh were unlucky. They were part of the short-lived Division Three that existed from 1923 until 1926 and finished top of the table for the 1925/26 season. Unfortunately, this was the season when the Scottish League decided not to continue with Division Three and because some of the clubs (not Helensburgh) had failed to complete their fixtures, there was no automatic promotion to Division Two. Forfar Athletic, who had finished third, were voted into Division Two instead. Closer inspection of the table shows that if some of the teams below them had been able to complete their fixtures, Helensburgh might well have been overtaken.

Prior to involvement with Division Three, the club's history went all the way back to 1874. In those days, when the Scottish Cup was in its infancy, Helensburgh soon made their mark in the early rounds, but it was a shock when they reached the semi-finals in 1878/79. Hibs were beaten 2–1 in Edinburgh along the way, but they were helped by receiving a bye in the sixth round and the cup run finally came to an end with a 3–0 defeat to Vale of Leven.

Not long after this success, the club went through the process of reforming itself, but both the 'new' and the 'old' Helensburgh existed on a diet of cup-ties and friendly matches. The first league football didn't come until 1920, when the club spent two seasons in the Scottish Amateur League. In 1922 they stepped up to the Western League and this provided the launch pad for their membership of the Scottish League a year later.

After it all came to an end in 1926, they spent the 1926/27 season in the Scottish Alliance, followed by the Intermediate League (Western Division) for 1927/28. However, their financial problems had now become too great and in 1928 the club reverted to amateur status.

HENDERSON Willie (1944 –)

Scottish Caps: 29
Scottish League Championship medals: 2
Scottish Cup medals: 4
Scottish League Cup medals: 1

An outside right for Rangers from 1960 until 1972, Willie Henderson won twenty-nine Scottish caps in the process. He was a 'child prodigy' when he joined Ibrox, being good enough at the age of seventeen to unseat Alec Scott on the right wing, and to be the second-youngest player to play for Scotland (also see **AGE**). He won the Scottish League championship twice, the Scottish Cup four times, and the Scottish League Cup

once. He was frequently compared to his friend Jimmy Johnstone of Celtic. He was perhaps less of an entertainer, but more direct. Frequently in the late 1960s he was made the scapegoat for poor performances by both Rangers and Scotland, but his Scotland career included wins over England in 1963 and 1964.

HENDRY Colin (1965 –)

Scotland Caps: 51
Scottish Premier League medals: 1
Scottish Cup medals: 1
Scottish League Cup medals: 1

A rugged, determined, fair-haired centre half, Colin Hendry won fifty-one caps for Scotland in a career that lasted from 1983 until 2004. He was born in Keith, but his first senior team was Dundee before he moved to Blackburn Rovers, with whom he won the Premiership

in 1995. This was his second spell with a Lancashire club, for he also played with Manchester City from 1989 to 1991. In 1998 he moved to Rangers and won a domestic treble with them, but personality clashes with manager Dick Advocaat meant a return to English football – to Coventry City, Bolton Wanderers, Preston North End and Blackpool. His international career ended in unfortunate circumstances when he was banned for six games following the use of an elbow on a San Marino player, but he was always much loved by the Tartan Army, not least for his fine performances in the European Championships in 1996 and the World Cup Finals of 1998. He was manager of Clyde from June 2007 until January 2008.

HEWIE John (1928 –   )

Scotland Caps: 19

John Hewie was a tall full back, who played nineteen times for Scotland in the late 1950s, including the World Cup finals of 1958. He was born in South Africa of Scottish parents and played his football in England for Charlton Athletic, on four occasions being picked as their goalkeeper during an injury crisis!

HIBERNIAN FC

Ground: **Easter Road, Leith, Edinburgh**
Nickname: **The Hibees**
Colours: **Green and white**
Record Attendance: **65,860 v Hearts (1950)**
Record Victory: **22-1 v 42nd Highlanders (1881)**
Record Defeat: **0-10 v Rangers (1898)**
Highest League Position: **1st (1902/03; 1947/48; 1950/51; 1951/52)**
Best Scottish Cup Performance: **Winners (1886/87; 1901/02)**
Best League Cup Performance: **Winners (1972/73; 1991/92; 2006/07)**

Founded in 1875, Hibernian began as a team for the Young Men's Society of St. Patrick's Catholic church in Edinburgh's Cowgate, where there was a strong Irish community. The club played its first Scottish Cup tie in 1877/78, beating Hearts in the first round after a replay, and reached the fifth round before losing to South Western. The early games were played at the Meadows, then Powderhall and then Mayfield, before the club moved to Easter Road in 1880. The Scottish Cup was won in 1886/87, when Dumbarton were beaten 2–1 at Hampden Park, and Hibs became the first club to take the cup out of the west of Scotland. They went on to play Preston North End in a match that was advertised as being for the championship of the world and won 2–1.

The first Easter Road ground was eventually lost to developers and the club ceased to exist for a while until it was reformed in 1892 as a non-sectarian organisation. A new ground was created to the north of the previous one and the club was elected to the Scottish League in 1893, becoming a founder member of Division Two. Hibs won the Division Two championship at the first attempt, but because of the election system had to remain in the lower division. When they won it again in the 1894/95 season, they were promoted and then remained in Division One for thirty-six years.

Hibs won the Scottish Cup again in 1901/02, when Celtic were beaten 1–0, and after they had won the 1902/03 league championship they were established as one of Scotland's leading clubs. This has been the case ever since, although there have been occasional dips in performance. One such dip occurred between 1931 and 1933, when two years were spent in Division Two, but the arrival of Willie McCartney as manager in 1936 was the catalyst that would result in a period of spectacular success in the years following the second world war. It was Willie McCartney who signed Gordon Smith, Bobby Johnstone, Lawrie Reilly, Eddie Turnbull and Willie Ormond, a forward line that was so successful they became known as 'The Famous Five', but his death in January 1948 meant that he did not witness their triumphs.

It was his successor Hugh Shaw who was manager when the league championship was won in 1947/48, 1950/51 and 1951/52, but the foundations had been laid by Willie McCartney. In 1955/56 Hibs went on to become the first British team to play in a European competition, when they reached the semi-finals of the European Cup in its first year, only to lose 3–0 on aggregate to Reims. They also reached the semi-finals of their second European campaign, the 1960/61 Inter-Cities Fairs Cup, when they played AS Roma after beating Barcelona 3–2 in a quarter-final tie at Easter Road, following a memorable 4–4 draw in Spain. Hibs eventually took Roma to a replay, after 2–2 and 3–3 draws, but then lost 6–0. Their prolific goal scorer Joe Baker, who played for England although he had been raised in Motherwell, scored three times against each of Barcelona and Roma and during his career he scored sixteen hat-tricks for Hibs.

On Wednesday 8 February 1956 first-class competitive football was played under floodlights for the first time in Scotland, although Hibs had already taken part in the first floodlit match, a friendly at Stenhousemuir in 1951. Their fifth-round Scottish cup-tie at home

Hibernian in 1964.

Action in the 1972/73 Scottish League Cup final between Celtic and Hibs.

to Raith Rovers had been postponed four days earlier, and the re-arranged fixture was played under the lights of Easter Road. Hibs drew 1–1 and then lost the replay 3–1, but nevertheless entered the record books along with East Fife, who also hosted a re-arranged tie under floodlights that evening.

Under the management of former player Eddie Turnbull, the team known as 'Turnbull's Tornadoes' won the 1972/73 League Cup, beating Celtic 2–1 at Hampden Park. From 1972 until 1979 they always finished in the top six clubs in the league and a highlight for their fans was the 7–0 victory away to Hearts in the New Year's game in 1973.

There was another memorable European night in the first round of the 1972/73 European Cup- Winners' Cup when Sporting Lisbon were beaten 6–1 at Easter Road, but the campaign eventually ended with a 5–4 aggregate defeat to Hadjuk Split in the quarter-finals.

Eddie Turnbull left in 1980, after taking them to a second replay in the 1978/79 Scottish Cup final against Rangers, which they lost 3–2. There now followed not only a season in the First Division (second tier) in 1980/81, but also a long spell without European competition, which eventually ended with entry to the 1989/90 UEFA Cup. Videoton of Hungary were beaten in the first round, but Hibs went out in the second round with a 1–0 aggregate defeat to Liege of Belgium after extra time.

By 1991 the club was experiencing severe financial problems and there was much speculation about a merger between Hibernian and Heart of Midlothian. Many Hibs fans saw this as an attempted takeover rather than a merger, and they joined a 'Hands Off Hibs' campaign in their thousands. Hibs eventually went into receivership, but then Sir Tom Farmer bought the club, and stability was restored. Manger Alex Miller brought Murdo MacLeod back to Scotland from Borussia Dortmund, Leith-born Keith Wright was signed from Dundee and the experienced John Burridge took over in goal when Andy Goram left for Rangers. Less than a year after being a club in crisis, Hibs now had a winning team and the 1991/92 League Cup was added to the trophy cabinet. Keith Wright's headed goal had been enough to beat Rangers in the semi-final and then Dunfermline were beaten 2–0 in the final. There was also a League Cup final appearance in 1993/94, but this ended with a 2–1 defeat to Rangers.

The 1998/99 season was spent in the First Division (second tier), but with Alex McLeish as manager they returned to the top flight at the first attempt. In 2001 he led them to their first Scottish Cup final appearance since 1979, although it ended with a 3–0 defeat to Celtic. Alex McLeish left for Ibrox at the end of 2001 and then both Frank Sauzee and Bobby Williamson had spells as manager. Bobby Williamson's team reached the 2003/04 League Cup final, beating both Celtic and Rangers, but ultimately lost 2–0 to Livingston.

Tony Mowbray became the new manager in May 2004 and led Hibs to third place in the league in 2004/05. Qualification for the 2005/06 UEFA Cup marked the fiftieth anniversary of the first European campaign, but this one ended with a 5–1 aggregate defeat to Ukrainians Dnipro Dnipropetrovsk in the first round. Despite this disappointment Hibs maintained their good league form, but when the 2006/07 season was just a few weeks old, Tony Mowbray accepted an offer to join West Bromwich Albion.

His replacement was former Hibs star John Collins, who returned to Easter Road to take up his first managerial post. By March 2007 his team had won a trophy, with a 5–1 victory over Kilmarnock in the League Cup final, but 2006/07 was also a season when the club lost some of its top players, such as Kevin Thomson, who left for Rangers, and Scott Brown, who signed for Celtic. In December 2007, just after Hibs had unveiled their superb new training centre in East Lothian, John Collins announced his resignation and not long afterwards Mixu Paatelainen, another former player, took his place. Young players such as Steven Fletcher began to fill the gap left by the high-profile departures, and he finished the 2007/08 season as leading scorer.

HIGHLAND LEAGUE

Founded in 1893, this is a competition played for by teams in the north of Scotland, although the word 'highland' can be misleading, for most teams are in the Moray/Nairn/Buchan/Banff area. Just seven teams competed in that first 1893/94 season – Camerons, Caledonian, Clachnacuddin, Forres Mechanics, Inverness Citadel, Inverness Thistle and Union. The league was weakened by the loss of Caledonian, Inverness Thistle, Ross County, Elgin City and Peterhead to the Scottish League, but Wick Academy and Inverurie Loco Works replaced them, taking the number of member clubs to fifteen.

Highland League clubs have traditionally done well in the Scottish Cup and both newcomers soon qualified for the competition proper. They had to do so by virtue of reaching the last four of the Scottish Qualifying Cup (North), but on 1 June 2007 the SFA decided that in future HL clubs that met their criteria would automatically be entered into a revamped Scottish Cup. There is also a Highland League Cup.

Winners of the Highland League are:

1894	Inverness Thistle	1895	Clachnacuddin	1896	Caledonian
1897	Clachnacuddin	1898	Clachnacuddin	1899	Caledonian
1900	Caledonian	1901	Clachnacuddin	1902	Caledonian
1903	Clachnacuddin	1904	Clachnacuddin	1905	Clachnacuddin
1906	Clachnacuddin	1907	Inverness Thistle	1908	Clachnacuddin
1909	Inverness Citadel	1910	Inverness Thistle	1911	Caledonian
1912	Clachnacuddin	1913	Aberdeen 'A'	1914	Caledonian
1915	Not completed	1916	No competition	1917	No competition
1918	No competition	1919	No competition	1920	Buckie Thistle
1921	Clachnacuddin	1922	Clachnacuddin	1923	Clachnacuddin
1924	Clachnacuddin	1925	Aberdeen 'A'	1926	Caledonian
1927	Buckie Thistle	1928	Buckie Thistle	1929	Inverness Thistle
1930	Huntly	1931	Caledonian	1932	Elgin City
1933	Fraserburgh	1934	Buckie Thistle	1935	Elgin City
1936	Inverness Thistle	1937	Buckie Thistle	1938	Fraserburgh
1939	Clachnacuddin	1940	No competition	1941	No competition
1942	No competition	1943	No competition	1944	No competition
1945	No competition	1946	No competition	1947	Peterhead
1948	Clachnacuddin	1949	Peterhead	1950	Peterhead
1951	Caledonian	1952	Caledonian	1953	Elgin City
1954	Buckie Thistle	1955	Undecided #	1956	Elgin City
1957	Buckie Thistle	1958	Buckie Thistle	1959	Rothes
1960	Elgin City	1961	Elgin City	1962	Keith
1963	Elgin City	1964	Caledonian	1965	Elgin City
1966	Elgin City	1967	Ross County	1968	Elgin City
1969	Elgin City	1970	Elgin City	1971	Caledonian
1972	Inverness Thistle	1973	Inverness Thistle	1974	Elgin City
1975	Clachnacuddin	1976	Nairn County	1977	Caledonian
1978	Caledonian	1979	Keith	1980	Keith
1981	Keith	1982	Caledonian	1983	Caledonian
1984	Caledonian	1985	Keith	1986	Forres Mechanics
1987	Inverness Thistle	1988	Caledonian	1989	Peterhead
1990	Elgin City	1991	Ross County	1992	Ross County
1993	Elgin City*	1994	Huntly	1995	Huntly
1996	Huntly	1997	Huntly	1998	Huntly
1999	Peterhead	2000	Keith	2001	Cove Rangers
2002	Fraserburgh	2003	Deveronvale	2004	Clachnacuddin
2005	Huntly	2006	Deveronvale	2007	Keith
2008	Cove Rangers				

* Championship subsequently withheld
# Season abandoned, following abnormal weather conditions

Member Club	Highland League Champions	Best Post-War Scottish Cup Performance (1946/47 onwards)
Brora Rangers Dudgeon Park, Brora		Last 32 (third round 1982/83)
Buckie Thistle Victoria Park, Buckie	1919/20; 1926/27; 1927/28; 1933/34; 1936/37; 1953/54; 1956/57; 1957/58	Last 16 (third round 1953/54; sixth round 1954/55; third round 1957/58)
Clachnacuddin Grant Street Park, Inverness	1894/95; 1896/97; 1897/98; 1900/01; 1902/03; 1903/04; 1904/05; 1905/06; 1907/08; 1911/12; 1920/21; 1921/22; 1922/23; 1923/24; 1938/39; 1947/48; 1974/75; 2003/04;	Last 32 (third round 1970/71; 1974/75)
Cove Rangers Allan Park, Cove, Aberdeen	2000/01, 2007/08	Last 32 (third round 1990/91; 1992/93; 1994/95)
Deveronvale Princess Royal Park, Banff	2002/03; 2005/06	Last 16 (fourth round 2006/07)
Forres Mechanics Mosset Park, Forres	1985/86	Last 32 (fifth round 1954/55; 1956/57; third round 2001/02)
Fort William Claggan Park, Fort William		Last 40 (second round 1985/86)
Fraserburgh Bellslea Park, Fraserburgh	1932/33; 1937/38; 2001/02	Last 32 (second round 1957/58; 1963/64)
Huntly Christie Park, Huntly	1929/30; 1993/94; 1994/95; 1995/96; 1996/97; 1997/98; 2004/05	Last 16 (fourth round 1991/92; 1994/95)
Inverurie Loco Works Harlaw Park, Inverurie		Last 42 (second round 2003/04; 2005/06)
Keith Kynoch Park, Keith	1961/62; 1978/79; 1979/80; 1980/81; 1984/85; 1999/00; 2006/07	Last 16 (fourth round 1979/80)
Lossiemouth Grant Park, Lossiemouth		Last 32 (second round 1957/58)
Nairn County Station Park, Nairn	1975/76	Last 32 (second round 1962/63; third round 1985/86)
Rothes Mackessack Park, Rothes	1958/59	Last 40 (second round 1980/81; 1986/87)
Wick Academy Harmsworth Park, Wick		Last 50 (first round 2001/02)

HILL Frank (1906 – 1993)

Scotland Caps: 3

Frank Hill contributed hugely to the game in both Scotland and England, but there was a certain whiff of scandal around him that was never completely dispelled. Frank joined Aberdeen in 1928 from his native Forfar, and became part of their legendary half back line of Black, McLaren and Hill. Yet Aberdeen were never a great team in those days, failing to win anything, and this half back line would come to grief in spectacular fashion. Before this happened Hill was capped three times for Scotland, making his debut for Scotland in Paris in May 1930 in a comfortable 2–0 victory, and then playing against Ireland and Wales the following season. He earned the nickname of 'tiger' for his tenacious style of play.

But in November 1931 Hill, along with three others,

was suddenly dropped from the Aberdeen team. This followed a series of strange results in the autumn of that year when they had gone down to St Mirren, Third Lanark and Hamilton in circumstances that manager Paddy Travers had found puzzling. No charge of match fixing was ever brought, and no evidence exists to incriminate Hill, but the mud associated with the scandal stuck. A line was drawn under the affair when he was transferred for £3,000 to Herbert Chapman's Arsenal in spring 1932. With Arsenal he won two English league championships, and then went on to Blackpool, Southampton and Preston North End before the second world war broke out. After the war he was player/manager for Crewe Alexandra, and then managed Burnley, Preston North End (managing men like Tom Finney, Tommy Docherty and Willie Cunningham), Notts County and Charlton Athletic, before finishing his long and varied career in 1965, after which he emigrated to the USA.

HILL OF BEATH HAWTHORN JUNIOR FC

(see JUNIOR FOOTBALL)

HOLLAND (sometimes called THE NETHERLANDS)

Scotland have played Holland sixteen times, the most famous being the game in Mendoza in Argentina in 1978 when Archie Gemmill scored his wonder goal, praised as 'not without cause, but without end' by a defeated and disgraced nation. On the other hand there was the disgraceful 0–6 defeat in 2003 which knocked Scotland out of the play-off for the 2004 European Championship, a defeat which came all the worse for Scotland as they had won the first leg. Played sixteen, won six, drawn four, lost six

1929	4 June	Amsterdam	2–0	Fleming Rankin (pen)	
1938	21 May	Amsterdam	3–1	Black Murphy Walker	Vente
1959	27 May	Amsterdam	2–1	Collins Leggat	Van der Gijp
1966	11 May	Hampden Park	0–3		Van der Kuijlen (2) Nuninga
1968	30 May	Amsterdam	0–0		
1971	1 Dec	Amsterdam	1–2	Graham	Cruijff Hulshott
1978	11 June	Mendoza	3–2	Gemmill (2) (1 pen) Dalglish	Rensenbrink Rep
1982	23 Mar	Hampden Park	2–1	Gray (pen) Dalglish	Kieft
1986	29 Apr	Eindhoven`	0–0		
1992	12 June	Gothenburg	0–1		Bergkamp
1994	23 Mar	Hampden Park	0–1		Roy
1994	27 May	Utrecht	1–3	Shearer	Roy Van Vossen Irvine o.g.
1996	10 June	Villa Park	0–0		
2000	26 Apr	Arnhem	0–0		
2003	15 Nov	Hampden Park	1–0	McFadden	
2003	19 Nov	Amsterdam	0–6		Van Nistelrooy (3) Sneider Ooijer de Boer

April 1966: Denis Law has just scored for Scotland in the Home International game against England. Jim Baxter rushes to congratulate him.

HOME INTERNATIONAL CHAMPIONSHIP

This was the name given to the British International Championship between the years of 1884 and 1984. It was at one point considered to be the most important tournament in football, being the only international football played. But the arrival of the World Cup and European competitions, both for clubs and countries, from the 1950s onwards meant that this competition lost prestige and ended up being played at the end of the season. Players were often not available, and it was no longer an economic success for Scotland and England to play against Northern Ireland and Wales.

Scotland won the tournament outright twenty-four times (out of eighty-nine), and shared it on another seventeen occasions. Goal average or goal difference was never used to determine the winner in this competition, in which each country played only three games, and in 1956 there was the unique occurrence of every nation winning one game, losing one, and drawing the other, so that the tournament was shared by all four nations! Originally, all the games were played in the spring, towards the end of the season, but from the mid 1920s onwards some games were played in the autumn, although the showpiece of the season, the Scotland versus England clash, was always reserved for April. Scotland's performances were as follows:

1884	Winners	1934	Fourth
1885	Winners	1935	Winners (shared with England)
1886	Winners (shared with England)	1936	Winners
1887	Winners	1937	Second
1888	Second	1938	Second Equal
1889	Winners	1939	Winners (shared with E & W)
1890	Winners (shared with England)	1947	Third Equal
1891	Second	1948	Fourth
1892	Second	1949	Winners
1893	Second	1950	Second
1894	Winners	1951	Winners
1895	Second Equal	1952	Third
1896	Winners	1953	Winners (shared with England)
1897	Winners	1954	Second
1898	Second	1955	Second
1899	Second	1956	Winners (shared with E, NI, W)
1900	Winners	1957	Second
1901	Second	1958	Third Equal
1902	Winners	1959	Third
1903	Winners (shared with E & Ire)	1960	Winners (shared with E & W)
1904	Third Equal	1961	Third
1905	Third Equal	1962	Winners
1906	Winners (shared with England)	1963	Winners
1907	Third	1964	Winners (shared with E & NI)
1908	Winners (shared with England)	1965	Third
1909	Third	1966	Third
1910	Winners	1967	Winners
1911	Second	1968	Second
1912	Winners (shared with England)	1969	Second
1913	Second Equal	1970	Winners (shared with E & W)
1914	Second	1971	Fourth
1920	Second Equal	1972	Winners (shared with England)
1921	Winners	1973	Third
1922	Winners	1974	Winners (shared with England)
1923	Winners	1975	Second
1924	Second	1976	Winners
1925	Winners	1977	Winners
1926	Winners	1978	Third
1927	Winners (shared with England)	1979	Third
1928	Third	1980	Fourth
1929	Winners	1981	Abandoned - civil unrest in N Ire
1930	Second	1982	Second
1931	Winners (shared with England)	1983	Second
1932	Second	1984	Fourth
1933	Second		

HONG KONG

Scotland have played in Hong Kong several times, the most recent being on 23 May 2002 when they beat the home side 4–0. Unfortunately these matches were not recognised by FIFA as official international matches.

2002	23 May	Hong Kong	4–0	Kyle Thompson Dailly Gemmill	

HONOURS

The following table lists the winners of the major trophies since 1873/74, which was the inaugural year of the Scottish Cup. (See **SCOTTISH FOOTBALL LEAGUE** for a chart that shows how the names of the different tiers of the Scottish League have changed over the years).

Year	Scottish Cup winners	Scottish League champions	Scottish League Cup winners	Scottish League second tier	Scottish League third tier	Scottish League fourth tier
1873/74	Queen's Park					
1874/75	Queen's Park					
1875/76	Queen's Park					
1876/77	Vale of Leven					
1877/78	Vale of Leven					
1878/79	Vale of Leven					
1879/80	Queen's Park					
1880/81	Queen's Park					
1881/82	Queen's Park					
1882/83	Dumbarton					
1883/84	Queen's Park					
1884/85	Renton					
1885/86	Queen's Park					
1886/87	Hibernian					
1887/88	Renton					
1888/89	Third Lanark					
1889/90	Queen's Park					
1890/91	Hearts	Dumbarton & Rangers				
1891/92	Celtic	Dumbarton				
1892/93	Queen's Park	Celtic				
1893/94	Rangers	Celtic		Hibernian		
1894/95	St. Bernard's	Hearts		Hibernian		
1895/96	Hearts	Celtic		Abercorn		
1896/97	Rangers	Hearts		Partick Thistl.		
1897/98	Rangers	Celtic		Kilmarnock		
1898/99	Celtic	Rangers		Kilmarnock		
1899/00	Celtic	Rangers		Partick Thistl.		
1900/01	Hearts	Rangers		St.Bernard's		
1901/02	Hibernian	Rangers		Port Glasgow		
1902/03	Rangers	Hibernian		Airdrieonians		
1903/04	Celtic	Third Lanark		Hamilton Ac.		
1904/05	Third Lanark	Celtic		Clyde		
1905/06	Hearts	Celtic		Leith Athletic		
1906/07	Celtic	Celtic		St. Bernard's		
1907/08	Celtic	Celtic		Raith Rovers		
1908/09	Withheld	Celtic		Abercorn		
1909/10	Dundee	Celtic		Leith Athletic & Raith Rvrs.		
1910/11	Celtic	Rangers		Dumbarton		
1911/12	Celtic	Rangers		Ayr United		
1912/13	Falkirk	Rangers		Ayr United		
1913/14	Celtic	Celtic		Cowdenbeath		
1914/15	No Comptn.	Celtic		Cowdenbeath		
1915/16	No Comptn.	Celtic		No Comptn.		
1916/17	No Comptn.	Celtic		No Comptn.		
1917/18	No Comptn.	Rangers		No Comptn.		
1918/19	No Comptn.	Celtic		No Comptn.		
1919/20	Kilmarnock	Rangers		No Comptn.		
1920/21	Partick Thistl.	Rangers		No Comptn.		
1921/22	G. Morton	Celtic		Alloa Athletic		
1922/23	Celtic	Rangers		Queen's Park		
1923/24	Airdrieonians	Rangers		St. Johnstone	Arthurlie	
1924/25	Celtic	Rangers		Dundee Utd.	Nithsdale Ws.	
1925/26	St. Mirren	Celtic		Dunfmln. Ath	Helensburgh	
1926/27	Celtic	Rangers		Bo'ness		
1927/28	Rangers	Rangers		Ayr United		
1928/29	Kilmarnock	Rangers		Dundee Utd.		
1929/30	Rangers	Rangers		Leith Athletic		
1930/31	Celtic	Rangers		Third Lanark		
1931/32	Rangers	Motherwell		E Stirlingshire		

Celebrations after Rangers' 3-1 win over Hearts in the 1976 Scottish Cup Final.

League Champions 1962: Dundee FC players and officials before the celebratory dinner in the City Chambers.

Morton - Winners of the 1967 Division Two championship.

1932/33	Celtic	Rangers		Hibernian		
1933/34	Rangers	Rangers		Albion Rvrs.		
1934/35	Rangers	Rangers		Third Lanark		
1935/36	Rangers	Celtic		Falkirk		
1936/37	Celtic	Rangers		Ayr United		
1937/38	East Fife	Celtic		Raith Rovers		
1938/39	Clyde	Rangers		Cowdenbeath		
1946/47	Aberdeen	Rangers	Rangers	Dundee	Stirling Alb'n.	
1947/48	Rangers	Hibernian	East Fife	East Fife	E Stirlingshire	
1948/49	Rangers	Rangers	Rangers	Raith Rovers	Forfar Ath.	
1949/50	Rangers	Rangers	East Fife	G. Morton	Hibs II + Clyde II #	
1950/51	Celtic	Hibernian	Motherwell	Queen of Sth.	Hearts II * Clyde II #	
1951/52	Motherwell	Hibernian	Dundee	Clyde	Dundee II * Rangers II #	
1952/53	Rangers	Rangers	Dundee	Stirling Alb'n.	Aberdeen II * Rangers II #	
1953/54	Celtic	Celtic	East Fife	Motherwell	Brechin City* Rangers II #	
1954/55	Clyde	Aberdeen	Hearts	Airdrieonians	Aberdeen II * Partick T II #	
1955/56	Hearts	Rangers	Aberdeen	Queen's Park		
1956/57	Falkirk	Rangers	Celtic	Clyde		
1957/58	Clyde	Hearts	Celtic	Stirling Alb'n.		
1958/59	St. Mirren	Rangers	Hearts	Ayr Utd.		
1959/60	Rangers	Hearts	Hearts	St. Johnstone		
1960/61	Dunfmln. Ath	Rangers	Rangers	Stirling Alb'n.		
1961/62	Rangers	Dundee	Rangers	Clyde		
1962/63	Rangers	Rangers	Hearts	St. Johnstone		
1963/64	Rangers	Rangers	Rangers	G. Morton		
1964/65	Celtic	Kilmarnock	Rangers	Stirling Alb'n.		
1965/66	Rangers	Celtic	Celtic	Ayr United		
1966/67	Celtic	Celtic	Celtic	G. Morton		
1967/68	Dunfmln. Ath	Celtic	Celtic	St. Mirren		
1968/69	Celtic	Celtic	Celtic	Motherwell		
1969/70	Aberdeen	Celtic	Celtic	Falkirk		
1970/71	Celtic	Celtic	Rangers	Partick Thistl.		
1971/72	Celtic	Celtic	Partick Thistl.	Dumbarton		
1972/73	Rangers	Celtic	Hibernian	Clyde		
1973/74	Celtic	Celtic	Dundee	Airdrieonians		
1974/75	Celtic	Rangers	Celtic	Falkirk		
1975/76	Rangers	Rangers	Rangers	Partick Thistl.	Clydebank	
1976/77	Celtic	Celtic	Aberdeen	St. Mirren	Stirling Alb'n.	
1977/78	Rangers	Rangers	Rangers	G. Morton	Clyde	
1978/79	Rangers	Celtic	Rangers	Dundee	Berwick Rgrs.	
1979/80	Celtic	Aberdeen	Dundee Utd	Hearts	Falkirk	
1980/81	Rangers	Celtic	Dundee Utd	Hibernian	Queen's Park	
1981/82	Aberdeen	Celtic	Rangers	Motherwell	Clyde	
1982/83	Aberdeen	Dundee Utd.	Celtic	St. Johnstone	Brechin City	
1983/84	Aberdeen	Aberdeen	Rangers	G. Morton	Forfar Ath.	
1984/85	Celtic	Aberdeen	Rangers	Motherwell	Montrose	
1985/86	Aberdeen	Celtic	Aberdeen	Hamilton Ac.	Dunfmln. Ath	
1986/87	St. Mirren	Rangers	Rangers	G. Morton	Meadowb'k T	
1987/88	Celtic	Celtic	Rangers	Hamilton Ac.	Ayr United	
1988/89	Celtic	Rangers	Rangers	Dunfmln. Ath	Albion Rvrs.	
1989/90	Aberdeen	Rangers	Aberdeen	St. Johnstone	Brechin City	
1990/91	Motherwell	Rangers	Rangers	Falkirk	Stirling Alb'n.	
1991/92	Rangers	Rangers	Hibernian	Dundee	Dumbarton	
1992/93	Rangers	Rangers	Rangers	Raith Rovers	Clyde	
1993/94	Dundee Utd.	Rangers	Rangers	Falkirk	Stranraer	

1994/95	Celtic	Rangers	Raith Rovers	Raith Rovers	G. Morton	Forfar Ath.
1995/96	Rangers	Rangers	Aberdeen	Dunfmln. Ath	Stirling Alb'n.	Livingston
1996/97	Kilmarnock	Rangers	Rangers	St. Johnstone	Ayr United	Inverness C T
1997/98	Hearts	Celtic	Celtic	Dundee	Stranraer	Alloa Athletic
1998/99	Rangers	Rangers	Rangers	Hibernian	Livingston	Ross County
1999/00	Rangers	Rangers	Celtic	St. Mirren	Clyde	Queen's Park
2000/01	Celtic	Celtic	Celtic	Livingston	Partick Thistl.	Hamilton Ac.
2001/02	Rangers	Celtic	Rangers	Partick Thistl.	Queen of Sth.	Brechin City
2002/03	Rangers	Rangers	Rangers	Falkirk	Raith Rovers	G. Morton
2003/04	Celtic	Celtic	Livingston	Inverness C T	Airdrie Utd.	Stranraer
2004/05	Celtic	Rangers	Rangers	Falkirk	Brechin City	Gretna
2005/06	Hearts	Celtic	Celtic	St. Mirren	Gretna	Cowdenbeath
2006/07	Celtic	Celtic	Hibernian	Gretna	G. Morton	Berwick Rgrs.
2007/08	Rangers	Celtic	Rangers	Hamilton Ac.	Ross County	East Fife

+ south-east section; # south-west section; * north-east section

HUGHES John (1943 –   )

Scotland Caps: 8
Scottish League Championship medals: 6
Scottish Cup medals: 1
Scottish League Cup medals: 4

Commonly known as 'Big Bad John' or 'Yogi Bear', John Hughes played for Celtic all through the 1960s, before moving to Crystal Palace and then Sunderland in the early 1970s. He did not play in the European Cup final in 1967, but won a losers' medal in 1970. He was famous for his individual runs and great goals, but his problem was inconsistency. On occasion he was a world-beater, other times he looked lethargic and uninterested. It was this unpredictable behaviour that caused his frequent personality clashes with Jock Stein, but he still won many honours with Celtic, as well as eight caps for Scotland. He is not to be confused with the other John Hughes, who played for Falkirk, Celtic and Hibs in the 1990s before becoming the manager of Falkirk. There was also a Johnny Hughes in the 1960s, who was the secretary of the Players Union.

Hughes smashes the ball into the roof of Airdrie's net. This goal was disallowed for offside, but Hughes became one of the highest goalscorers in Celtic history, with a grand total of 189 goals.

HUNGARY

Scotland have played Hungary eight times, winning two games, drawing twice, and losing four times. The game in December 1954 is often said to be one of the best ever played at Hampden Park, as Scotland did well to hold the World Cup finalists to a 4–2 defeat.

1938	7 Dec	Ibrox	3–1	Walker Black Gillick	Sarosi
1954	8 Dec	Hampden Park	2–4	Ring Johnstone	Bozsik Hidegkuti Sandor Kocsis
1955	29 May	Budapest	1–3	Smith	Hidegkuti Kocsis Fenyvesi
1958	7 May	Hampden Park	1–1	Mudie	Fenyvesi
1960	5 June	Budapest	3–3	Hunter Herd Young	Sandor Gorocs Tichy
1980	31 May	Budapest	1–3	Archibald	Torocsik (2) Kereki
1987	9 Sep	Hampden Park	2–0	McCoist (2)	
2004	18 Aug	Hampden Park	0–3		Huszti (2) (1 pen) Marshall o.g.

HUNTER John (Sailor) (1879 – 1966)

Scottish Cup medals: 1

John Hunter was the legendary manager of Motherwell who painstakingly built up the great Motherwell team that won the Scottish League in 1932, and also reached the Scottish Cup final in 1931, 1933 and 1939. After a career in England, in which he won a league championship medal with Liverpool in 1900/01, he scored the winning goal for Dundee in the 1910 Scottish Cup final. Immediately after that he became manager of Motherwell for the astonishingly long time of 1911-1946, and even after he resigned as manager, he remained their secretary until 1959, when he was eighty years old.

HUSBAND Jackie (1918 – 1992)

Scotland Caps: 1

A Partick Thistle legend (arguably their most famous-ever player), Jackie Husband earned only one Scottish cap. Sadly for him, the second world war got in the way of his career, but he did play for Scotland in the unofficial Victory International of 1946. He was a left half who was famous for his accurate free kicks and long throw-ins, and has the honour of having a stand named after him at Firhill.

HUTTON Alexander (1853 – 1936)

Known in Argentina as 'el padre del futbol argentino' ('the father of Argentinian football'), Alexander Hutton was a Scot whose enthusiasm and organisational skills were a major influence on the development of the game in that country. He was born in the Gorbals in 1853, became a teacher, and emigrated to Argentina in 1882. He and his wife formed the English (sic) High School in Buenos Aires and introduced football to the pupils. In 1898 some former pupils founded a team called Alumni FC, which played successfully in the Argentine Football League that Hutton had instigated in 1893. He later became president of the Argentinian Football Association, and a plaque in a Buenos Aires cemetery states 'escoces ilustre – introductor y organizador del futbol en la Republica Argentina' ('a famous Scotsman – pioneer and organiser of football in the Argentine Republic').

HUTTON Jock (1898 – unknown)

Scotland Caps: 10

A legend of the 1920s, with his burly girth and sense of humour, Jock Hutton joined Aberdeen immediately after the first world war, and played for them until 1926 when he joined Blackburn Rovers for £4,000. He won the FA Cup with them in 1928, and won ten caps for Scotland, including the success against England of 1926.

HUTCHISON Don (1971 –)

Scotland Caps: 26

An attacking midfielder, Don Hutchison played twenty-six times for Scotland. Unusual in certain respects, not least because he played for both Liverpool and Everton, and twice joined West Ham United for record fees, he was born in Gateshead and qualified for Scotland on the parentage rule. Hartlepool United, Sheffield United, Sunderland, Millwall and Coventry City are clubs that

Don Hutchison won 26 caps, scoring six goals for Scotland, despite being born in England and never having played for a Scottish club. His finest moment was scoring the winning goal in a 1-0 victory at Wembley in 1999.

he played for as well. He never really let Scotland down, but was unfortunate in that his time of playing for Scotland coincided with a low point in the country's football history. However, it was Don Hutchison who scored the winning goal for Scotland against England at Wembley in November 1999.

ICELAND

Scotland have a perfect record against the Icelanders. They have won all four games that they have played against them.

1984	17 Oct	Hampden Park	3–0	McStay (2) Nicholas	
1985	28 May	Reykjavik	1–0	Bett	
2002	12 Oct	Reykjavik	2–0	Dailly Naysmith	
2003	29 Mar	Hampden Park	2–1	Miller Wilkie	Gudjohnsen

INJURIES

Injuries have always been a sad fact of the game. In a contact sport like football, it is hard to see how they can be avoided. Sometimes the injuries are slight and can be 'run off' following a little attention from the physiotherapist (with his suitcase and pharmacopoeia) who has now replaced the trainer with his sponge and smelling salts. On the other hand, there can be very serious injuries such as leg breaks, cartilage problems, or the one that is a real threat to anyone's career – the cruciate ligaments.

Some players have managed to come back from broken legs – including Eric Caldow, Jim Baxter, Willie Ormond, Dave Mackay and many others who have defied medical wisdom and played again. In recent years, surely one of the most horrific was that sustained by Henrik Larsson of Celtic in a European game in Lyon on 21 October 1999. The game was televised, and all of Europe saw how badly broken his leg was in one of the more disturbing images ever shown in a football transmission. Yet Larsson was back in action by the start of the following season in which he scored fifty goals!

A disturbing trend in recent years (and not confined to Scottish football) has been the faking of injuries to 'con' the referee into sending an opponent off. It can be argued that this has been part and parcel of the game for many decades, or that it only started when European football began to be broadcast on television in the 1960s, but it really is something that clubs have a responsibility to stamp out. An experienced referee knows what is a real injury and what is not. An injury to the head normally would require the referee to stop the game instantly rather than wait for a convenient moment when the ball goes out of play, for instance. Sporting etiquette would expect an opponent to put the ball out of play for attention to be administered, and equally, it is expected that the ball would be returned when play starts again.

There is another kind of faking of injuries that causes distress. This is the spurious claim by an unscrupulous manager that a player is injured and unavailable for an international fixture with the player himself being given every encouragement to keep quiet about it. He will then recover and be available for his club's next game. But against that, there is the case of John Kennedy of Celtic, who was given his international debut in a pointless

5 September 1931: Celtic's John Thomson is stretchered off suffering from a depressed fracture of the skull.

John Kennedy of Celtic.

friendly game against Romania at Hampden Park on 31 March 2004. After fifteen minutes, he was carried off injured and was out of the game for more than two years.

When one considers the amount of football played in Scotland on any given day, it is remarkable how few fatal injuries are sustained. There was the John Thomson tragedy of 5 September 1931 (see **THOMSON John**), but other cases are mercifully seldom – William Walker of Leith Athletic on 12 January 1909 in a game versus Vale of Leven, John Main of Hibs was injured in a game versus Partick Thistle on Christmas Day 1909 and died a few days later, and Joshua Williamson, the goalkeeper of Dumbarton in a game versus Rangers on 12 November 1921.

INTER-CITIES FAIRS CUP

The 'International. Inter-City Industrial Fairs Cup', which was usually shortened to the 'Inter-Cities Fairs Cup', was the original name of the tournament that became the UEFA Cup in 1971. It was created for cities that hosted trade fairs and was designed so that each participating city would be represented by a single team. At first there was no qualification system based on league performance, which explains why a London representative side was invited to take part in the first tournament, which lasted from 1955 to 1958. By the mid 1960s, however, only clubs were invited, after taking account of their performance the previous season.

The first Scottish side to take part was Hibernian, who participated in the 1960/61 competition, by which time it had become an annual event. Entry was denied to Clyde in 1967/68, even though they had finished the 1966/67 season in third place, because Rangers had finished second and only one club per city was allowed to enter. Hibernian took their place. The results of Scottish clubs are as follows:

Season	Scottish Club	Opposition	Agg.	Round
1960/61	Hibernian	Barcelona	7–6	Quarter-final
		AS Roma	5–5	Semi-final
			0–6	Play-off
1961/62	Hearts	Union St Gilloise	5–1	First
		Inter Milan	0–5	Second
	Hibernian	Belenenses	6–4	First
		Red Star Belgrade	0–5	Second
1962/63	Celtic	Valencia	4–6	First
	Dunfermline	Everton	2–1	First
		Valencia	6–6	Second
			0–1	Play-off
	Hibernian	Stavenet	7–2	First
		DOS Utrecht	3–1	Second
		Valencia	2–6	Quarter-final
1963/64	Hearts	Lausanne	4–4	First
			2–3	Play-off
	Partick Thistle	Glentoran	7–1	First
		Spartak Brno	3–6	Second
1964/65	Celtic	Leixoes	4–1	First
		Barcelona	1–3	Second
	Dunfermline	Oergryte	4–2	First
		Stuttgart	1–0	Second
		Atletico Bilbao	1–1	Quarter-final
			1–2	Play-off
	Kilmarnock	Eintracht Frankfurt	5–4	First
		Everton	1–6	Second
1965/66	Dunfermline	KB Copenhagen	9–2	Second
		Spartak Brno	2–0	Third
		Real Zaragoza	3–4	Quarter-final
	Hearts	Valerengen	4–1	Second
		Real Zaragoza	5–5	Third
			0–1	Play-off
	Hibernian	Valencia	2–2	First
			0–3	Play-off
1966/67	Dundee United	Barcelona	4–1	Second
		Juventus	1–3	Third
	Dunfermline	Frigg Oslo	6–2	First
		Dinamo Zagreb	4–4	Second
		Dinamo Zagreb won on toss of a coin		
	Kilmarnock	Antwerp	8–2	Second
		La Gantoise	3–1	Third
		Lokomotiv Leipzig	2–1	Quarter-final
		Leeds United	2–4	Semi-final
1967/68	Dundee	DWS Amsterdam	4–2	First
		FC Liege	7–2	Second
		Zurich	2–0	Quarter-final
		Leeds United	1–3	Semi-final
	Hibernian	Porto	4–3	First
		Napoli	6–4	Second
		Leeds United	1–2	Third
	Rangers	Dinamo Dresden	3–2	First
		FC Cologne	4–3	Second
		Leeds United	0–2	Quarter-final
1968/69	Aberdeen	Slavia Sofia	2–0	First
		Real Zaragoza	2–4	Second
	Hibernian	Ljubljana	5–1	First
		Lokomotiv Leipzig	4–1	Second
		SV Hamburg	2–2	Third
		SV Hamburg won on away goals		
	Morton	Chelsea	3–9	First
	Rangers	Vojvodina	2–1	First

		Dundalk	9–1	Second
		DWS Amsterdam	4–1	Third
		Atletico Bilbao	4–3	Quarter-final
		Newcastle United	0–2	Semi-final
1969/70	Dundee United	Newcastle United	1–3	First
	Dunfermline	Bordeaux	4–2	First
		Gwardia Warsaw	3–1	Second
		Anderlecht	3–3	Third
		Anderlecht won on away goals		
	Kilmarnock	Zurich	5–4	First
		Slavia Sofia	4–3	Second
		Dinamo Bacau	1–3	Third
1970/71	Dundee United	Grasshoppers	3–2	First
		Sparta Prague	2–3	Second
	Hibernian	Malmo	9–2	First
		Vitoria Guimares	3–2	Second
		Liverpool	0–3	Quarter-final
	Kilmarnock	Coleraine	3–4	First
	Rangers	Bayern Munich	1–2	First

(see **UEFA CUP** for seasons 1971/72 onwards)

The following table summarises the performance of Scottish clubs by showing which round they reached each year:

1960/61	Hibernian	SF						
1961/62	Hearts	2nd	Hibernian	2nd				
1962/63	Celtic	1st	Dunfermline	2nd	Hibernian	QF		
1963/64	Hearts	1st	Partick Thstl.	2nd				
1964/65	Celtic	2nd	Kilmarnock	2nd	Dunf'mline	3rd		
1965/66	Hibernian	1st	Hearts	3rd	Dunf'mline	QF		
1966/67	Dunf'mline	2nd	Dundee Utd.	3rd	Kilmarnock	SF		
1967/68	Hibernian	3rd	Rangers	QF	Dundee	SF		
1968/69	Morton	1st	Aberdeen	2nd	Hibernian	3rd	Rangers	SF
1969/70	Dundee Utd.	1st	Dunf'mline	3rd	Kilmarnock	3rd		
1970/71	Kilmarnock	1st	Rangers	1st	Dundee Utd.	2nd	Hibernian	3rd

QF- Quarter-final; SF- Semi-final

INTER-LEAGUE

Inter-league games have now gone out of existence, a victim of the crowded fixture list that has been with us since the arrival of European football from the 1950s onwards. The game between the Scottish League and the Football League (as the English League used to call itself) used to be a highlight of the season, often being used as a trial for youngsters aspiring to a full Scotland cap. The Scottish League team consisted only of players currently playing domestic football in Scotland. Seventy-five games were played between 1892 and 1976, with the Scottish League winning nineteen games as against forty-two wins for the Football League and fourteen draws. Deprived of 'Anglos' (Scotsmen playing in England or elsewhere), it is not surprising that Scotland did so badly.

On the other hand, between 1893 and 1980, out of sixty-two games the Scottish League beat the Irish League (the league of Northern Ireland) fifty-six times as against five, with surprisingly only one draw (in the penultimate game), and between 1939 and 1980 beat the League of Ireland (the league of the Irish Republic) eighteen times as against two, with two draws, out of twenty-two games. In the five years from 1910 to 1914, the Scottish League played five games against the Southern League of England, winning two, drawing one and losing two. A total of three games were arranged between the Scottish League and the Italian League, with two draws (1961 and 1978) and one defeat (1962); one game was played against the Danish Football Combination (4–0 in 1955) and, after a humiliating 0–3 reverse to the Welsh League in 1952, no further fixtures were sought in the principality!

League international matches should not be relegated to a footnote in football history. They were extremely highly rated in their time, and caps were awarded to the participants. The Inter-League international between the Scottish League and the Football League on 1 March 1913 attracted over 96,000 to Hampden Park to see a rampant Scottish side demolish their England counterparts 4–1, and 66,996 were enticed to Hampden on the dreadful night of 1 November 1961 to see the Scottish League draw 1–1 with the Italian League, who contained in their ranks one Denis Law! Also in the 1960s, the Scottish League had two great victories over the English League – a 4–3 win in 1962 at Villa Park, Birmingham (in a game televised live) and a 3–1 win in 1966 at St James' Park, Newcastle, when John Hughes ran riot through the English defence.

Some players, who were perhaps a little short of the word 'great', were blooded in league internationals. A notable example of this was Jock Stein (he described himself with deliberate ambiguity as 'a passable centre half'), who never won a full Scottish cap, but played once for the Scottish League at Stamford Bridge in 1954. A few Englishmen and foreigners, who would have been

English League v Scottish League, 5th November 1930, White Hart Lane, which ended 7-3 to the English League.

November 1929: Scotland's Inter-League team that beat the English League at Ibrox 2-1.

debarred from playing for Scotland, found themselves representing their adopted homeland in the Scottish League. In this category we find Willie Lyon of Celtic, Bobby Ferrier of Motherwell and Joe Baker of Hibs. Joe Kennaway, the Canadian born Celtic goalkeeper, was eventually allowed to play for the full Scotland team but cut his teeth with the Scottish League side.

Attendances peaked in the years between 1910 and 1960, and by the early 1970s it was becoming obvious that the fixture was often an embarrassment, with players becoming 'injured' or otherwise unavailable. In 1976 (the last Inter-League game against the Football League) the attendance was a pitiful 8,874 at Hampden Park, ironically not all that far short of the first such game at Pike Lane, Bolton in 1892 when 9,500 Lancastrians attended.

Three players share the record of scoring five goals for the Scottish League in an Inter-League game, all against the Irish League – Barney Battles junior of Hearts at Firhill on 31 October 1928, Hughie Gallacher of Airdrie at Windsor Park, Belfast on 11 November 1925, and Bobby Flavell of Airdrie at Windsor Park, Belfast on 30 April 1947.

The results were as follows:

Football (English) League

1891/92	Bolton	2–2	1892/93	Celtic Park	3–4
1893/94	Goodison Park	1–1	1894/95	Celtic Park	1–4
1895/96	Goodison Park	1–5	1896/97	Ibrox	3–0
1897/98	Villa Park	2–1	1898/99	Celtic Park	1–4
1899/00	Crystal Palace	2–2	1900/01	Ibrox	6–2
1901/02	Newcastle	3–6	1902/03	Celtic Park	0–3
1903/04	Manchester	1–2	1904/05	Hampden Park	2–3
1905/06	Chelsea	2–6	1906/07	Ibrox	0–0
1907/08	Villa Park	0–2	1908/09	Celtic Park	3–1
1909/10	Blackburn	3–2	1910/11	Ibrox	1–1
1911/12	Middlesbrough	0–2	1912/13	Hampden Park	4–1
1913/14	Burnley	3–2	1914/15	Celtic Park	1–4
1918/19	Birmingham	1–3	1918/19	Ibrox	3–2
(Victory Internationals)					
1919/20	Celtic Park	0–4	1920/21	Highbury	0–1
1921/22	Ibrox	0–3	1922/23	Newcastle	1–2
1923/24	Ibrox	1–1	1924/25	Goodison Park	3–4
1925/26	Celtic Park	0–2	1926/27	Leicester	2–2
1927/28	Ibrox	2–6	1928/29	Villa Park	1–2
1929/30	Ibrox	2–1	1930/31	Tottenham	3–7
1931/32	Celtic Park	4–3	1932/33	Manchester	3–0
1933/34	Ibrox	2–2	1934/35	Chelsea	1–2
1935/36	Ibrox	2–2	1936/37	Liverpool	0–2
1937/38	Ibrox	1–0	1938/39	Wolverhampton	1–3
1941/42	Blackpool	2–3			
(Wartime International)					
1946/47	Hampden Park	1–3	1947/48	Newcastle	1–1
1948/49	Ibrox	0–3	1949/50	Middlesbrough	1–3
1950/51	Ibrox	1–0	1951/52	Sheffield	1–2
1952/53	Ibrox	1–0	1953/54	Chelsea	0–4
1954/55	Hampden Park	3–2	1955/56	Sheffield	2–4
1956/57	Ibrox	3–2	1957/58	Newcastle	1–4
1958/59	Ibrox	1–1	1959/60	Highbury	0–1
1960/61	Ibrox	3–2	1961/62	Villa Park	4–3
1963/64	Sunderland	2–2	1964/65	Hampden Park	2–2
1965/66	Newcastle	3–1	1966/67	Hampden Park	0–3
1967/68	Middlesbrough	0–2	1968/69	Hampden Park	1–3
1969/70	Coventry	2–3	1970/71	Hampden Park	0–1
1971/72	Middlesbrough	2–3	1972/73	Hampden Park	2–2
1973/74	Maine Road	0–5	1975/76	Hampden Park	0–1

Irish League

1892/93	Belfast	2–3	1893/94	Celtic Park	6–0
1894/95	Belfast	4–1	1895/96	Celtic Park	3–2
1896/97	Belfast	2–0	1897/98	Carolina Port	5–0
1898/99	Belfast	1–3	1899/00	Easter Road	6–0
1900/01	Belfast	2–1	1901/02	Dens Park	3–0
1902/03	Belfast	0–1	1903/04	Love Street	3–1
1908/09	Belfast	2–1	1909/10	Firhill	2–0
1910/11	Belfast	3–1	1911/12	Firhill	3–0
1912/13	Belfast	3–1	1913/14	Belfast	2–1
1914/15	Belfast	2–1	1919/20	Belfast	2–0
1920/21	Ibrox	3–0	1921/22	Shawfield	3–0
1922/23	Celtic Park	3–0	1923/24	Belfast	1–0
1924/25	Edinburgh	3–0	1925/26	Belfast	7–3
1926/27	Tynecastle	5–2	1927/28	Belfast	2–1
1928/29	Firhill	8–2	1929/30	Belfast	4–1
1930/31	Firhill	5–0	1931/32	Belfast	2–3
1932/33	Ibrox	4–1	1933/34	Belfast	0–3
1934/35	Firhill	3–2	1935/36	Belfast	3–2
1936/37	Ibrox	5–3	1937/38	Belfast	3–2
1938/39	Ibrox	6–1	1939/40	Belfast	3–2
1946/47	Belfast	7–4	1947/48	Celtic Park	3–0
1948/49	Belfast	1–0	1949/50	Ibrox	8–1
1950/51	Belfast	4–0	1951/52	Ibrox	3–0
1952/53	Belfast	5–1	1953/54	Ibrox	4–0
1954/55	Belfast	5–1	1955/56	Ibrox	3–0
1956/57	Belfast	7–1	1957/58	Ibrox	7–0
1958/59	Belfast	5–0	1959/60	Ibrox	7–1
1960/61	Belfast	2–1	1961/62	Ibrox	7–0
1963/64	Belfast	4–1	1965/66	Ibrox	6–2
1967/68	Belfast	2–0	1969/70	Ibrox	5–2
1978/79	Fir Park	1–1	1979/80	Belfast	4–2

League of Ireland

1938/39	Dublin	1–2	1947/48	Dublin	2–0
1948/49	Ibrox	5–1	1949/50	Dublin	1–0
1950/51	Celtic Park	7–0	1951/52	Dublin	2–0
1952/53	Celtic Park	5–1	1953/54	Dublin	3–1
1954/55	Shawfield	5–0	1955/56	Dublin	4–2
1956/57	Shawfield	3–1	1957/58	Dublin	5–1
1958/59	Ibrox	1–0	1959/60	Dublin	4–1
1960/61	Celtic Park	5–1	1961/62	Dublin	1–1
1962/63	Celtic Park	11–0	1963/64	Dublin	2–2
1965/66	Celtic Park	6–0	1967/68	Dublin	0–0
1969/70	Celtic Park	1–0	1979/80	Dublin	1–2

Welsh League

1952/53	Cardiff	0–3

Italian League

1961/62	Hampden Park	1–1	1962/63	Rome	3–4
1977/78	Verona	1–1			

Danish Football Combination

1954/55	Copenhagen	4–0

Southern League

1910/11	Millwall	0–1	1911/12	Shawfield	3–2
1912/13	Millwall	0–1	1913/14	Cathkin Park	5–0
1914/15	Millwall	1–1			

INTERTOTO CUP

Originally conceived by Ernst Thommen of Switzerland and Karl Rappen of Austria as a summer tournament that would generate income for pools companies, the

Intertoto Cup has become an established way of gaining qualification for the UEFA Cup. The first tournament was held in 1961, but British clubs generally ignored it, and it was only in 1995 that UEFA awarded places in the UEFA Cup for two 'winners'. A third place was added in 1996, and there was an expansion in 2006/07 when the eleven successful clubs in the third round were given places in the second qualifying round of the UEFA Cup. There is now no Intertoto Cup final as such, for the 'winners' are decided by who progresses furthest in the UEFA Cup.

It would be fair to say that the tournament is not held in high esteem by fans, and the fact that it is played in midsummer has counted against it, but Hibernian, Dundee and Partick Thistle have all participated, although without much success. A place in the second round is available to the SPL club that finishes highest at the end of the season without qualifying for the Champions League or UEFA Cup, as long as the club submits an application. If the highest such club does not apply, then the place goes to the next highest club that has applied, as long as it finished in one of the four positions immediately below those that qualified for the UEFA Cup.

INVERNESS CALEDONIAN THISTLE FC

Ground: **Tulloch Caledonian Stadium**
Nickname: **Caley Thistle; Caley Jags**
Colours: **Royal blue, red and white**
Record Attendance: **9,530 at Pittodrie v Aberdeen (2004)**
7,753 at Tulloch Caledonian Stadium v Rangers (2008)
Record Victory: **8-1 v Annan Athletic (1998)**
Record Defeat: **0-6 v Airdrieonians (2001)**
Highest League Position: **7th (2005/06)**
Best Scottish Cup Performance: **Last 4 (Semi-finals, 2002/03; 2003/04)**
Best League Cup Performance: **Last 8 (Quarter-finals, 2001/02; 2005/06; 2007/08)**

The story of Caley Thistle is the story of how enormous changes can be brought about in just ten years. A new club, membership of the Scottish Football League, a new stadium, a change of name, a team whose giant-killing grabbed the attention of the world's press, and then membership of the Scottish Premier League. The change was so successful that SPL football in the Highlands became part of the norm.

When the Scottish League was expanded and restructured in 1994, one of the two extra places was awarded to Caledonian Thistle, a new club from Inverness that had been formed by the merger of Caledonian FC and Inverness Thistle FC. These were two clubs that had been founder members of the Highland League, Caledonian having won the Highland League title eighteen times, and Thistle five times. Both had a reputation for knocking league clubs out of the Scottish Cup.

Sergei Baltacha, a former USSR international, was manager for the first season of 1994/95 and he helped to lay the foundations for what was to come. At first Caley Thistle played at Telford Street Park, the former home of Caledonian FC, but work started on a new stadium in October 1995. By now it had become clear that the majority of fans wanted the word 'Inverness' included in the club's name, and it also became clear that those providing funding for the new ground shared this view. Steve Paterson replaced Sergei Baltacha at the end of the first season, and the club finished its second season in the Third Division in third place.

The name was changed to Inverness Caledonian Thistle for the start of the 1996/97 season and, after a few more games at Telford Street, the new stadium was opened in November 1996. By the end of the season the Third Division title had been won, and 1997 saw the start of full-time football. Former Scotland international Duncan Shearer signed in September of that year, and 1997/98 was a season of consolidation in the Second Division.

Bobby Mann, who would later become club captain, arrived from Forfar in February 1999, and a few months

Inverness Caledonian Thistle's Tulloch Caledonian Stadium.

later a second-place finish earned promotion to the First Division and a season that will always be remembered in ICT history. In February 2000 the team came away from Celtic Park with a 3–1 victory in the third round of the Scottish Cup and shockwaves reverberated around Scottish football. There was a 1–1 draw with Aberdeen in the next round, but the Dons won the replay 1–0.

Duncan Shearer was now assistant manager, and Caley Thistle's attacking side included Charlie Christie, who would go on to make 314 appearances for the club. In January 2002 the team caused another major shock in the Scottish Cup when they beat Hearts 3–1 at Tynecastle in the fourth round. Partick Thistle then provided the opposition in the quarter-final, and once again Caley Thistle took the tie to a replay, which they lost 1–0.

Steve Paterson and Duncan Shearer left for Aberdeen in December 2002 and it wasn't long before replacements John Robertson and Donald Park were leading the club to another cup victory over Celtic. This time it was a 1–0 victory at home in the quarter-finals, with Dennis Wyness scoring the winner, but the ensuing semi-final at Hampden Park resulted in a 1–0 defeat to Dundee.

It was the following season, 2003/04 that became the most memorable of all. The League Challenge Cup was won in October, when Airdrie United were beaten 2–0 at McDiarmid Park, and there was another Scottish Cup semi-final, which was lost 3–2 to Dunfermline in a replay at Pittodrie. The biggest prize, however, was won on the last day of the season, when a 3–1 home victory over St Johnstone brought the championship of the First Division.

At first the Caledonian stadium did not meet the criteria for the SPL, but after two votes the SPL agreed that Caley Thistle could play their home fixtures at Pittodrie, over 100 miles away in Aberdeen, for the time being. In November 2004 manager John Robertson left to re-join Hearts and two months later the improvements to the stadium were deemed to be sufficient. New player-manager Craig Brewster scored one of the goals

A consequence of Caley Thistle's rapid rise was that Ross Tokely became the first player to play in all four divisions whilst remaining at the same club. Canadian international Richard Hastings also played in all four divisions with Caley Thistle, but he left in 2001 and returned three years later. Craig Brewster left in January 2006 and was replaced by Charlie Christie, who helped the club consolidate its position in the SPL. When he resigned in August 2007 Craig Brewster returned for a second spell as manager, and a period of transition saw the emergence of players such as Inverness-born Don Cowie.

IRAN

Scotland have played Iran only once, but it was quite a 'once'. Their second game of the 1978 World Cup in Argentina, the match ended in a draw. It is widely regarded as a disastrous game, and possibly their worst-ever, although there is strong competition for that title.

1978	7 June	Cordoba	1–1	Eskandarian o.g.	Danaifar

IRELAND

Scotland have played Ireland since 1884 in the Home International Championship with some fixtures doubling as World Cup or European Championship Qualifying games. Ireland has had many troubles since 1884, and this means that games against Ireland until 1922 were against the whole of Ireland, whereas since that date it has been Northern Ireland. For games against southern Ireland see **IRELAND, REPUBLIC**. In addition, the troubles of the 1970s meant that all fixtures in that decade had to be played at Hampden Park. Ninety-two fixtures have been played, Scotland have won sixty-one, lost fifteen and drawn sixteen. Ireland were always considered to be the weakest of the British international countries, and for this reason, particularly in the early days, the side that Scotland fielded was anything but the strongest available eleven.

Danny McGrain (right) shakes hands with Northern Ireland captain Martin O'Neill before the teams meet in 1981.

1884	26 Jan	Belfast	5–0	Harrower (2) Gosland (2) Goudie	
1885	14 Mar	2nd Hampden Park	8–2	Higgins (3) Lamont Turner Calderwood Marshall Barbour	Gibb (2)
1886	20 Mar	Belfast	7–2	Heggie (4) Lambie Dunbar Gourlay	Condy Johnston
1887	19 Feb	2nd Hampden Park	4–1	Watt Jenkinson Johnstone Lowe	Browne
1888	24 Mar	Belfast	10–2	Dickson (4) Dewar Breckenridge Aitken McCallum A. Stewart Wilson o.g.	Dalton (2)
1889	9 Mar	Ibrox	7–0	Groves (3) Watt (2) Black McInnes	
1890	29 Mar	Belfast	4–1	Rankin (2) Wylie McPherson	Peden
1891	28 Mar	(Old) Celtic Park	2–1	Low Waddell	Stanfield
1892	19 Mar	Belfast	3–2	Keillor Lambie Ellis	Williamson Gaffikin
1893	25 Mar	(New) Celtic Park	6–1	Sellar (2) McMahon Kelly Hamilton S. Torrans o.g.	Gaffikin
1894	31 Mar	Belfast	2–1	Taylor Torrans o.g.	Stanfield
1895	30 Mar	Celtic Park	3–1	Walker (2) Lambie	Sherrard
1896	28 Mar	Belfast	3–3	McColl (2) Murray	Barron (2) Milne (pen)
1897	27 Mar	Ibrox	5–1	McPherson (2) Gibson McColl King	Pyper
1898	26 Mar	Belfast	3–0	Robertson McColl Stewart	
1899	25 Mar	Celtic Park	9–1	McColl (3) Hamilton (2) Campbell (2) Christie Bell	Goodall
1900	3 Mar	Belfast	3–0	Campbell (2) A. Smith	
1901	23 Feb	Celtic Park	11–0	McMahon (4) Hamilton (4) J W Campbell (2) Russell	
1902	1 Mar	Belfast	5–1	Hamilton (3) Walker Buick	Milne
1903	21 Mar	Celtic Park	0–2		Connor Kirwan
1904	26 Mar	Dublin	1–1	Hamilton	Sheridan
1905	18 Mar	Celtic Park	4–0	Thomson (2) Walker Quinn	
1906	17 Mar	Dublin	1–0	Fitchie	
1907	16 Mar	Celtic Park	3–0	O'Rourke Walker Thomson	
1908	14 Mar	Dublin	5–0	Quinn (4) Galt	
1909	15 Mar	Ibrox	5–0	McMenemy (2) MacFarlane Thomson Paul	
1910	19 Mar	Belfast	0–1		Thompson
1911	18 Mar	Celtic Park	2–0	Reid McMenemy	
1912	16 Mar	Belfast	4–1	Aitkenhead (2) Reid Walker	McKnight (pen)
1913	15 Mar	Dublin	2–1	Reid Bennett	McKnight
1914	14 Mar	Belfast	1–1	Donnachie	Young
1920	13 Mar	Celtic Park	3–0	Wilson Morton Cunningham	
1921	26 Feb	Belfast	2–0	Wilson (pen) Cassidy	
1922	4 Mar	Celtic Park	2–1	Wilson (2)	Gillespie
1923	3 Mar	Belfast	1–0	Wilson	
1924	1 Mar	Celtic Park	2–0	Cunningham Morris	
1925	28 Feb	Belfast	3–0	Meiklejohn Gallacher Dunn	
1926	27 Feb	Ibrox	4–0	Gallacher (3) Cunningham	
1927	26 Feb	Belfast	2–0	Morton (2)	
1928	25 Feb	Firhill	0–1		Chambers
1929	23 Feb	Belfast	7–3	Gallacher (5) Jackson (2)	Rowley (2) Bambrick
1930	22 Feb	Celtic Park	3–1	Gallacher (2) Stevenson	McCaw
1931	21 Feb	Belfast	0–0		
1931	19 Sept	Ibrox	3–1	Stevenson McGrory McPhail	Dunne
1932	17 Sept	Belfast	4–0	McPhail (2) McGrory King	
1933	16 Sept	Celtic Park	1–2	McPhail	Martin (2)
1934	20 Oct	Belfast	1–2	Gallacher	Martin Coulter
1935	13 Nov	Tynecastle	2–1	Walker Duncan	Kelly
1936	31 Oct	Belfast	3–1	Napier Munro McCulloch	Kernaghan
1937	10 Nov	Pittodrie	1–1	Smith	Doherty
1938	8 Oct	Belfast	2–0	Delaney Walker	
1946	27 Nov	Hampden Park	0–0		
1947	4 Oct	Belfast	0–2		Smyth (2)
1948	17 Nov	Hampden Park	3–2	Houliston (2) Mason	Walsh (2)
1949	1 Oct	Belfast	8–2	Morris (3) Waddell (2) Steel Reilly Mason	Smyth (2)
1950	1 Nov	Hampden Park	6–1	Steel (4) McPhail (2)	McGarry
1951	6 Oct	Belfast	3–0	Johnstone (2) Orr	
1952	5 Nov	Hampden Park	1–1	Reilly	D'Arcy
1953	3 Oct	Belfast	3–1	Fleming (2) Henderson	Lockhart (pen)
1954	3 Nov	Hampden Park	2–2	Davidson Johnstone	Bingham McAdams
1955	8 Oct	Belfast	1–2	Reilly	J.Blanchflower Bingham
1956	7 Nov	Hampden Park	1–0	Scott	
1957	5 Oct	Belfast	1–1	Leggat	Simpson
1958	5 Nov	Hampden Park	2–2	Herd Collins	McIlroy Caldow o.g.
1959	3 Oct	Belfast	4–0	Leggat Hewie White Mulhall	
1960	9 Nov	Hampden Park	5–2	Brand (2) Law Caldow Young	D.Blanchflower (pen) McParland
1961	7 Oct	Belfast	6–1	Scott (3) Brand (2) Wilson	McLaughlin
1962	7 Nov	Hampden Park	5–1	Law (4) Henderson	Bingham
1963	12 Oct	Belfast	1–2	St. John	Bingham Wilson
1964	25 Nov	Hampden Park	3–2	Wilson (2) Gilzean	Best Irvine
1965	2 Oct	Belfast	2–3	Gilzean (2)	Dougan Crossan Irvine

September 1931: Scotland v Ireland.

1966	16 Nov	Hampden Park	2–1	Murdoch Lennox	Nicholson
1967	21 Oct	Belfast	0–1		Clements
1969	6 May	Hampden Park	1–1	Stein	McMordie
1970	18 Apr	Belfast	1–0	O'Hare	
1971	18 May	Hampden Park	0–1		Greig o.g.
1972	20 May	Hampden Park	2–0	Law Lorimer	
1973	16 May	Hampden Park	1–2	Dalglish	O'Neill Anderson
1974	11 May	Hampden Park	0–1		Cassidy
1975	20 May	Hampden Park	3–0	MacDougall Dalglish Parlane	
1976	8 May	Hampden Park	3–0	Gemmill Masson Dalglish	
1977	1 June	Hampden Park	3–0	Dalglish (2) McQueen	
1978	13 May	Hampden Park	1–1	Johnstone	O'Neill
1979	22 May	Hampden Park	1–0	Graham	
1980	16 May	Belfast	0–1		Hamilton
1981	25 Mar	Hampden Park	1–1	Wark	Hamilton
1981	19 May	Hampden Park	2–0	Stewart Archibald	
1981	14 Oct	Belfast	0–0		
1982	28 Apr	Belfast	1–1	Wark	McIlroy
1983	24 May	Hampden Park	0–0		
1983	13 Dec	Belfast	0–2		Whiteside McIlroy
1992	19 Feb	Hampden Park	1–0	McCoist	

Goals from Denis Law and Peter Lorimer settled this game at Hampden in 1972 against Northern Ireland.

IRELAND, REPUBLIC of (otherwise known as EIRE)

Scotland have played eight times against the Republic of Ireland and won three, drawn two, and lost three.

1961	3 May	Hampden Park	4–1	Brand (2) Herd (2)	Haverty
1961	7 May	Dublin	3–0	Young (2) Brand	
1963	9 June	Dublin	0–1		Cantwell
1969	21 Sep	Dublin	1–1	Stein	
1986	15 Oct	Dublin	0–0		
1987	18 Feb	Hampden Park	0–1		Lawrenson
2000	30 May	Dublin	2–1	Hutchison Ferguson	Burley o.g.
2003	12 Feb	Hampden Park	0–2		Kilbane Morrison

IRON CURTAIN

This was the name given to the Rangers defence of the late 1940s and early 1950s. Containing men of the calibre of George Young, Jock Shaw, Sammy Cox and Willie Woodburn, the Rangers defence of that era was notoriously mean in conceding goals, and to actually score a goal against them was said to be like crossing the 'iron curtain'. The 'iron curtain' in the broader political context of that era referred to the dividing line in Europe between the West, which was under British/American control, and the East, which was held by the Soviet Union. It was Winston Churchill who coined the term, when he said in a speech in Fulton, Missouri in March 1946 "From Stettin in the Baltic to Trieste in the Adriatic, an iron curtain has descended across the continent". Radio commentators took up this impressive phrase and would say things like "after Rangers went ahead, an iron curtain descended over Ibrox".

IRVINE MEADOW XI FC (see JUNIOR FOOTBALL)

ISRAEL

Scotland have played Israel three times and always beaten them, although never too convincingly.

1981	25 Feb	Tel Aviv	1–0	Dalglish	
1981	28 Apr	Hampden Park	3–1	Robertson (2) pens Provan	Sinai
1986	28 Jan	Tel Aviv	1–0	McStay	

ITALY

Scotland have only beaten Italy once, and drawn twice out of ten starts, but then again Italy are one of the best teams in the world, and World Cup winners in 1934, 1938, 1982 and 2006. The time that Scotland beat them was a World Cup qualifier at Hampden when a late John Greig goal gave Scotland a chance of reaching the World Cup finals in England, a chance that sadly evaporated a month later when Scotland went to Naples. Sadly, Scotland have never even drawn in Italy.

1931	20 May	Rome	0–3		Constantino Meazza Orsi
1965	9 Nov	Hampden Park	1–0	Greig	
1965	7 Dec	Naples	0–3		Pascutti Facchetti Mora
1988	22 Dec	Perugia	0–2		Giannini Berti
1992	18 Nov	Ibrox	0–0		
1993	13 Oct	Rome	1–3	Gallacher	Donadoni Casiraghi Eranio
2005	26 Mar	Milan	0–2		Pirlo (2)
2005	3 Sep	Hampden Park	1–1	Miller	Grosso
2007	28 Mar	Bari	0–2		Toni (2)
2007	17 Nov	Hampden Park	1–2	Ferguson	Toni Panucci

JACK HARKNESS TROPHY

This is a trophy awarded by the *Sunday Post* every year to the team with the best 'Crime Count' in the SPL i.e. with the fewest fouls conceded or yellow and red cards awarded. It is named after Jack Harkness (see **HARKNESS Jack**), who was legendary for his sportsmanship in his playing career and also was a respected journalist for many years in the *Sunday Post*. It is remarkable how often the team that wins this trophy also does well in the SPL itself. There is of course a lesson here, sadly not always heeded by managers and players.

JACKSON ALEX (1905 – 1946)

Scotland Caps: 17

Alex Jackson was the man who scored a hat-trick in the Wembley Wizards international of 1928, and is reckoned to be one of the greatest wingers of all time, being called

'The Flying Scotsman', 'The Laughing Cavalier', or even 'The Gay Cavalier', for his flamboyant style of play. He played seventeen times for Scotland. He started his career with Dumbarton in 1922, then had a year in the USA before playing for Aberdeen for a season, during which time he impressed so much that Huddersfield paid £5,000 for him in May 1925. With the strong-going Huddersfield team of that era, he won the English league championship of 1926 and twice reached the final of the FA Cup before moving on to Chelsea in 1930.

After two years with Chelsea he picked a foolish argument with them on the subject of the maximum wage, and disappeared from top class professional football when he was still young enough to go on. In his Scotland appearances, apart from his Wembley hat-trick, he also scored the only goal of the game in 1926 which beat England at Old Trafford. In 1929, after having been carried off injured and taken to hospital with a dislocated elbow, he was the man who knew that Scotland had won the game when he heard the roar of the crowd from his hospital bed. In the seventeen times that he played for Scotland, Scotland lost only once and drew once. After service in the RAF during the second world war, he met his death in a tragic motor accident in Cairo.

JACKSON Darren (1966 –)

Scotland Caps: 28
Scottish Premier League medals: 1

A player of many clubs, Darren Jackson won twenty-eight caps with Scotland. He played for Meadowbank Thistle, Newcastle United, Dundee United, Hibs, Celtic, Hearts, Coventry City, Livingston and others in a long and interesting career. He could score fine goals (one for Scotland against Latvia in Riga in 1996 is generally considered to be particularly good), and was an expert at winding up opponents and rival crowds. He was signed for Celtic in 1997, and won the Premier League with them, but during his time there he suffered from a life-threatening brain tumour. Happily, he made a full recovery, and it did not prevent him from taking part in the 1998 World Cup finals. He is one of the few players to have taken part in all three city derbies in Dundee, Edinburgh and Glasgow.

Alex James (left), with Arsenal teammate Cliff Bastin.

JAMES Alex (1901 – 1953)

Scotland Caps: 8

Alex James was one of the real characters of Scottish football, whose trademark was his baggy shorts. Small of stature, and looking on occasion more in need of a good feed than anything else, Alex, a dribbling inside forward, was one of the best players that the game has ever seen. He earned nicknames like the 'Wee Wizard'. The baggy shorts were apparently to cover another pair of shorts underneath, made necessary by his being prone to rheumatism. He joined Raith Rovers in 1922, and fairly soon made a name for himself in the excellent Kirkcaldy side of that era.

He was transferred to Preston North End for £3,000 in 1925, but it was with the great Arsenal side of the early 1930s that he became famous under their legendary manager Herbert Chapman. He won four league championships and two FA Cup medals with that Arsenal side, which he helped to transform from a rich, but under-performing, outfit into the best in the world. He played eight times for Scotland, the most famous occasion being the 'Wembley Wizards' international of 31 March 1928, in which he scored twice as Scotland beat England 5–1. He also played in the team that beat England at Hampden Park in 1929. He did some coaching in Poland immediately before the second world war, and died of cancer in London on 1 June 1953, the very eve of the coronation of Queen Elizabeth II.

JAPAN

Scotland have only twice played against Japan, and no one has as yet scored a goal.

1995	21 May	Hiroshima	0–0		
2006	13 May	Saitama	0–0		

JARDINE Sandy (1948 –)

Scotland Caps: 38
Scottish League Championship medals: 3
Scottish Cup medals: 5
Scottish League Cup medals: 5
European Cup-Winners' Cup medals: 1

His real name is William Jardine, but he prefers to be called Sandy. He was right back for Rangers and Hearts, at one time being the co-manager of the Edinburgh club. In 1986, at the age of thirty-seven he was named Scotland's Player of the Year. He played thirty-eight games for Scotland and took part in the World Cup finals of 1974 and 1978. He joined Rangers in 1965, and won a European Cup-Winners' Cup medal with them in 1972. Sandy was also a vital part of their treble-winning teams of 1975/76 and 1977/78. He left Rangers to go to Hearts in 1982 and, as player and co-manager in 1986, came within a whisker of winning the league and cup double for the Tynecastle side. He is one of the few players in Scottish football history to have played more than 1,000 games, and is also one of the very few to have been named Player of the Year twice, in 1975 and 1986.

JOHNSTON Maurice (1963 –)

Scotland Caps: 38
Scottish League Championship medals: 3
Scottish Cup medals: 1

A marvellous player, with sharp reflexes and the ability to score many goals, Maurice Johnston will always be remembered for the amazing events of summer 1989. His senior career began with Partick Thistle, but then he was transferred to Elton John's Watford in 1983. He reached the FA Cup final with them, before returning to Glasgow in November 1984, to Celtic ('the only team he ever wanted to play for'), where he earned the nickname 'Supermo'. He became a regular in the Scotland squad, although Alex Ferguson, when caretaker manager, was less than enthusiastic about playing him.

In 1987 he left Celtic for Nantes, then on the day before the Scottish Cup final of 1989, returned to Celtic Park, was duly paraded with a green and white scarf, and gave the impression that he had 'returned home', saying once again that Celtic were 'the only team he ever wanted to play for'. But there was a snag with the deal, involving income tax payments, and he never signed. Two months later, in July, he signed for Graeme Souness's Rangers! He was thus the first Roman Catholic to play for Rangers in modern times, but he was never totally accepted by the Ibrox support, although he won Scottish League medals with them in 1990 and 1991. Nor is he ever likely to be forgiven by Celtic fans. He subsequently played for Everton, Hearts and Falkirk. He won thirty-eight Scottish caps, and featured in the 1990 World Cup finals. It is sad that such a talented player will probably always be tainted by controversy.

JOHNSTON Willie (1946 –)

Scotland Caps: 22
Scottish Cup medals: 1
Scottish League Cup medals: 2
European Cup Winners Cup medals: 1

Willie Johnston will always be remembered as the man who was sent home from the Argentina World Cup in 1978 for taking an illegal substance, but he was an excellent player who won several honours in his lengthy career. He also holds the record for being sent off twenty-one times (seven with Rangers, six with West Bromwich Albion, four with Vancouver Whitecaps, three with Hearts and one with Scotland), yet he was never really a violent player, and became a pleasant and affable host in the Port Brae Inn, Kirkcaldy. 'Bud' joined Rangers in 1962, and played for them for the next ten years. Unfortunately his best years at Ibrox coincided with the zenith of Jock Stein's Celtic, and he did not win as many medals as he would have liked, although he did win a Scottish Cup medal in 1966, two Scottish League Cup medals in 1964 and 1970, and the European Cup-Winners' Cup in 1972. In December of that year he moved to West Bromwich Albion, for whom he starred until 1979. Then, after a spell in Canada with Vancouver Whitecaps, Johnston returned to Ibrox in 1980, before moving to Hearts, where he teamed up with old Ibrox teammates Alex MacDonald and Sandy Jardine. His career was bedevilled by clashes with authority, referees and managers, but this must not deflect attention from the undeniable fact that he was a fine winger. He was a close friend of his near namesake Jimmy Johnstone of Celtic, but was a different type of winger, with lots of

Rangers' Willie Johnston.

speed, and the ability to send over devastatingly accurate crosses. He played twenty-two times for Scotland, his international career coming to a shuddering halt after the distressing events of Argentina in 1978.

JOHNSTONE FC (former Scottish League club)

Home: **Newfield Park, Johnstone, Renfrewshire**
Highest League Position: **26th (8th in Div. 2, 1912/13)**
Best Scottish Cup Performance: **Last 16 (2nd round, 1906/07; 1910/11)**

In 1912 Division Two of the Scottish League was expanded from twelve to fourteen clubs and Johnstone FC, along with Dunfermline Athletic, was chosen to be elevated. Their misfortune was to finish second bottom in 1925, when a Division Three briefly existed. They were relegated and spent one season in the third tier before it was abandoned, which meant that Johnstone's time in the Scottish League came to an end.

The club had been founded in 1877 and initially played in friendly matches and cup-ties, sometimes reaching the early rounds of the Scottish Cup. Their first encounters with league football were a season in the Scottish Alliance and then two separate spells in the Scottish Combination. In 1908 they joined the Scottish Union and became one of its more successful clubs. They also reached the final of the 1910/11 Scottish Qualifying Cup, which was only lost to East Stirlingshire after a replay, and by 1912 their performances had been good enough to merit an opportunity in the Scottish League.

Johnstone's league form was unremarkable and, when Division Two was suspended in 1915, they joined the reformed Western League. They won the 1920/21 Western League title and when Division Two was revived that year they were given a place. Once again their Scottish League form was disappointing and it culminated in relegation in 1925. When they found themselves out of the Scottish League one year later they played a further season in the Scottish Alliance, but results were poor, financial problems were mounting, and they didn't even complete their fixtures.

The final irony came at the start of the 1927/28 season. The club somehow reached the first round of the Scottish Cup proper, by virtue of a walkover and a bye. There was difficulty raising a team and a makeshift eleven lost 12–0 at Cowdenbeath. Soon after that Johnstone FC went out of existence.

JOHNSTONE BURGH FC (see JUNIOR FOOTBALL)

JOHNSTONE Bobby (1929 – 2001)

Scotland Caps: 17
Scottish League Championship medals: 2

A superb inside forward, Bobby Johnstone played for Hibernian, Manchester City, Hibs (again) and Oldham

Athletic. Born in the rugby-playing town of Selkirk, Bobby is well known as one of the 'famous five' forward line of Hibs, and he won the Scottish League championship with them in both 1951 and 1952. Following his transfer to Manchester City in March 1955, he created history by becoming the first player to score in two successive FA Cup finals, once in a losing cause in 1955 and once for the winning team in 1956. He played seventeen times for Scotland between 1951 and 1956, and once for Great Britain against the Rest of Europe in Belfast in 1955. He is possibly the least known of Hibs' immortal forward line, but was as good a player as any of the others.

JOHNSTONE Derek (1953 –)

Scotland Caps: 14
Scottish League Championship medals: 3
Scottish Cup medals: 5
Scottish League Cup medals: 5
European Cup-Winners' Cup medal: 1

Derek Johnstone was both a centre forward and centre half for Rangers. Very strong, determined and versatile, he was born and brought up in Dundee, but joined Rangers and came to prominence in 1970 when, as a

sixteen-year-old, he scored the only goal in the Scottish League Cup final with a header. With Rangers he won many domestic honours throughout the 1970s as well as the European Cup-Winners' Cup in 1972. He won fourteen caps for Scotland, but one of the big mysteries of the Argentina disaster of 1978 was why Ally McLeod didn't use him, when both the Football Writers and the Professional Footballers had named him Player of the Year for 1978. In later days he became a radio and TV pundit.

JOHNSTONE Jimmy (1944 – 2006)

Scotland Caps: 23
Scottish League Championship medals: 9
Scottish Cup medals: 4
Scottish League Cup medals: 5
European Cup medals: 1

Jimmy Johnstone was arguably one of Scotland's greatest ever players, and certainly the trickiest winger and ball player in living memory. Most of his career is associated with Jock Stein's Celtic, but he also played for Sheffield United, Dundee and Elgin City, as well as having spells in both the USA and Ireland. He made his debut for Celtic in 1963, and virtually his first game was the Scottish Cup final of 1963, in which he played well to help Celtic draw with Rangers. From then on he was the darling of the Celtic fans, but when Celtic unaccountably dropped him for the replay in 1963, the team lost 3–0. A fiery redhead, Jimmy was seldom away from trouble. When he was sent off in the New Year's Day game at Ibrox in 1965, it was felt that his career might not survive the arrival of the strict disciplinarian Jock Stein. Johnstone was not Stein's first choice for the right wing spot, but eventually he won his way into Stein's squad, and his appearances for Celtic in Europe were always great 'tourist attractions'. Jimmy was shamefully hacked down by defenders, but was always courageous enough to come back for more, never letting anyone know that they had got the better of him.

On at least two occasions Stein suspended Johnstone – once for an attack on an opponent and on another occasion for publicly disputing Stein's decision to substitute him, but he was often suspended by the SFA as well, for violent retaliations on the occasions that the 'red mist' descended. Yet it was Johnstone to whom Celtic gave the ball in the first few minutes of the 1967 European Cup final, so that he could have a few mazy dribbles and win over the Portuguese and neutral fans, and it was Johnstone who was the architect of Celtic's victory over Leeds United in 1970. Stories of Johnstone are plentiful, for example the time that he would be allowed to miss the trip to Red Star Belgrade (Johnstone was afraid of flying) if Celtic were four goals up at Parkhead, and he inspired Celtic to a 5–1 victory. There was also the time with the Scotland squad in 1974 that he started to row out to sea when he had been on a night out with the boys, and had to be rescued by the coastguard. What can never be disputed is that Jimmy Johnstone on his day was one of the greatest players on earth, and it is to the eternal credit of Jock Stein that he managed to keep him in the game when, with weaker management, he might well have drifted away. There remained with Johnstone the typically Scottish qualities of self-destruction, but also those of sociability, courtesy, and essentially being one of the fans who so adored him. He eventually retired in 1980. In a poll of Celtic supporters, he was voted the greatest ever, although his inconsistency and temperament caused a few to dispute that verdict. In latter years he suffered from Motor Neurone disease, to which he succumbed in March 2006.

JORDAN Joe (1951 –)

Scottish Caps: 52

A great centre forward, who represented Scotland fifty-two times, Joe Jordan is the only Scotsman to have scored in the final stages of three World Cup tournaments - 1974, 1978 and 1982. He was a powerful header of the ball, and was never afraid to go in hard, occasionally losing a few teeth in the process. He is famous for the part he played in Scotland's qualification for the World Cup finals in Argentina, when the referee awarded a penalty for Scotland, thinking that a Welsh defender had punched the ball, whereas in fact it was Joe's arm! He was born in Cleland, and his boyhood hero was the great Jimmy Delaney. He started his career with Blantyre Victoria, and then moved to Morton in 1968.

He moved to Leeds United in 1970 for £15,000, winning with them the English League in 1974, but being on the wrong end of defeats in the FA Cup final of 1973 and the European Cup final of 1975. He was transferred to Manchester United in 1978 for £350,000, but again failed to win anything for them. He subsequently moved to Italy to play for AC Milan and Verona, before returning to the UK to play the rest of his career with Southampton and then Bristol City. He

then managed Hearts, and for a very short time he was the assistant to Liam Brady at Celtic, before doing managerial stints at Bristol City, Huddersfield Town, Stoke City and Portsmouth.

JUNIOR FOOTBALL

The Scottish Junior Football Association, as opposed to the SFA, governs the junior game. Whilst the SJFA is affiliated to the SFA, it is an independent organisation with its own constitution and rules. It was formed on 2 October 1886, at a time when junior clubs around Scotland were organising themselves into local associations and inaugurating local cup competitions. The creation of a national association brought uniformity to junior football and ensured that clubs throughout the country conformed to the same set of rules.

The word 'junior' sometimes misleads those who are not familiar with the traditions of the Scottish game. It does not necessarily mean younger and is in fact used to make a distinction from the SFA's 'senior' game, which operates at a higher grade. A key element of junior football is that it enables small communities to play against each other. When the SJFA was formed the SFA had already been in existence for over thirteen years, and after 1886 small clubs that did not aspire to compete at the highest level also had a structured organisation of their own.

Players sometimes take part after they have previously played in senior football, although the rules of junior football require a player to be formally 'reinstated' if he has been participating in the senior game. It is often amateur, although professionalism does exist as well. The game's roots in Scottish culture may be partly explained by the belief that a strong community base for the game of football is more important than financial rewards, and spectators can enjoy a match that is often as exciting as one in the senior game for a modest admission charge.

Junior football is quite distinct from the senior version, with no promotion or relegation between them, and until 2007 there was no competition between the two. However, on 1 June 2007 the SFA took the historic decision to admit the winners of junior football's four main competitions into the Scottish Cup. Thus in 2007/08 Culter (North Region Premier League), Linlithgow Rose (Scottish Junior Cup and East Region Superleague) and Pollok (West Region Superleague Premier Division) became the first three junior clubs to take part.

Although junior football may be described as a form of non-league football, it should be remembered that senior non-league football also exists – in the Highland League, East of Scotland League and South of Scotland League. The junior system is unique to Scotland, but there are occasional junior international matches, when Scotland will compete against teams from an equivalent level in another country's system.

When the SJFA was first formed only local associations (JFAs), and not clubs, were allowed to be members. One of its first tasks was to organise a cup competition for the 1886/87 season, and if a club wished to take part it had to be a member of a local JFA. That first tournament attracted thirty-nine entries and Fairfield, a team from Glasgow, emerged as winners after beating Edinburgh side Woodburn 3–1 in a final that was replayed after a protest. The number of associations and clubs quickly multiplied, and in 1922/23 a record 412 clubs entered the Scottish Junior Cup.

In the late 1920s the junior game was split by a dispute about transfer fees, as a junior club at that time received little or no compensation when a player moved to a senior club. This was a source of much resentment, particularly when a promising young player was starting a journey that would lead to a career at the top level. In 1926 fifty-five clubs broke away and formed a new grade of football, the 'intermediate' grade, which was not subject to the restriction. This situation lasted until 1931, when arrangements for reasonable compensation were finally agreed and the breakaway clubs returned to the SJFA.

Many of Scotland's most famous players started their career at a junior club, for example Dave Mackay (Hearts and Tottenham Hotspur) and Alex Young (Hearts and Everton) both played for Newtongrange Star before stepping up. Many more examples are to be found in the section on individual clubs, and actor Sir Sean Connery played for Bonnyrigg Rose in the early 1950s before he became known through his film character of James Bond.

Junior clubs often possess unique and lovely names, such as Irvine Meadow, Kilbirnie Ladeside, Kirkintilloch Rob Roy and Dundee Violet, and these reinforce the sense of community spirit. However, the local communities that supported many junior clubs before the second world war changed considerably in the second half of the twentieth century. Many former mining communities disappeared, and Scotland's inner-city populations broke up. Coupled with the rise of

alternative leisure pursuits, particularly television, it meant that quite a few junior football teams became defunct.

A major re-structure of the junior game took place in 1968, with the replacement of the country's many associations by just six district committees, which were under the jurisdiction of the SJFA, and which were given responsibility for organising competitions within their area. In 2002 there was further change with the division of the country into just three regions, West, East and North. These regions decided upon different ways of organising their leagues, and the different structures are shown in the table below.

West Region			East Region			North Region
Superleague Premier Division			Superleague			Premier League (also known as the North Superleague)
Superleague First Division			Premier League (from season 2006/07)			Division One
Ayrshire District	Central District First Div.	Central District Second Div.	South Div. (from 2006/07)	Central Div. (from 2006/07)	North Div. (from 2006/07)	Division Two

The Scottish Junior Cup has been competed for every year since its inception (including war years). At first the final was held at different venues, but from 1943 until 1981 it was always Hampden Park, and was considered to be the official end of the season. In the late 1940s and early 1950s the crowds regularly exceeded 50,000, and when Petershill defeated Irvine Meadow 1–0 in 1951 the attendance was 77,650. These numbers fell away, however, and from 1977 onwards the finals were televised live. After 1981 they were not always held at Hampden Park and venues such as Ibrox and Firhill were frequently chosen. The trophy was 'retired' in 2006, and in 2007 Linlithgow Rose became the first club to lift its replacement when they beat Kelty Hearts at East End Park, Dunfermline.

The results of the Scottish Junior Cup finals are as follows:

1886/87	Fairfield Govan	3	Edinburgh Woodburn	1
1887/88	Wishaw Thistle	3	Maryhill	1
1888/89	Burnbank Swifts	3	West Benhar Violet	1
1889/90	Burnbank Swifts	3	Benburb	1
1890/91	Vale of Clyde	2	Chryston Athletic	0
1891/92	Minerva	5	West Benhar Violet	2
1892/93	Vale of Clyde	3	Dumbarton Fern	2
1893/94	Ashfield	3	Renfrew Victoria	0
1894/95	Ashfield	2	West Calder Wanderers	1
1895/96	Cambuslang Hibs	3	Parkhead	1
1896/97	Strathclyde	2	Dunfermline Juniors	0
1897/98	Dalziel Rovers	2	Parkhead	1
1898/99	Parkhead	4	Westmarch	1
1899/1900	Maryhill	3	Rugby	2
1900/01	Burnbank Athletic	2	Maryhill	0
1901/02	Glencairn	1	Maryhill	0
1902/03	Parkhead	3	Larkhall Thistle	0
1903/04	Vale of Clyde	3	Parkhead	0
1904/05	Ashfield	2	Renfrew Victoria	1
1905/06	Dunipace Juniors	1	Kirkintilloch Rob Roy	0
1906/07	Strathclyde	1	Maryhill	0
1907/08	Larkhall Thistle	1	Queen's Park Hampden XI	0
1908/09	Kilwinning Rangers	1	Strathclyde	0
1909/10	Ashfield	3	Kilwinning Rangers	0
1910/11	Burnbank Athletic	1	Petershill	0
1911/12	Petershill	5	Denny Hibs	0
1912/13	Inverkeithing United	1	Dunipace Juniors	0
1913/14	Larkhall Thistle	1	Ashfield	0
1914/15	Parkhead	2	Port Glasgow Athletic	0
1915/16	Petershill	2	Parkhead	0
1916/17	St Mirren Juniors	1	Renfrew Juniors	0
1917/18	Petershill awarded cup after no final took place because Parkhead and Renfrew failed to agree a date for the semi-final			
1918/19	Glencairn	1	St Anthony's	0
1919/20	Parkhead	2	Cambuslang Rangers	0
1920/21	Kirkintilloch Rob Roy	1	Ashfield	0
1921/22	St Roch's	2	Kilwinning Rangers	1
1922/23	Musselburgh Bruntonians	2	Arniston Rangers	0
1923/24	Parkhead	3	Baillieston	1
1924/25	Saltcoats Victoria	2	St Anthony's	1
1925/26	Strathclyde	2	Bridgeton Waverley	0
1926/27	Glencairn	2	Cambuslang Rangers	1
1927/28	Maryhill Hibs	6	Burnbank Athletic	2
1928/29	Dundee Violet	4	Denny Hibs	0
1929/30	Newtongrange Star	3	Hall Russell's	0
1930/31	Denny Hibs	1	Burnbank Athletic	0
	Prolonged protests followed. Denny eventually allowed to keep cup.			
1931/32	Perthshire	2	Kirkintilloch Rob Roy	1
1932/33	Yoker Athletic	4	Tranent Juniors	2
1933/34	Benburb	3	Bridgeton Waverley	1
1934/35	Tranent Juniors	6	Petershill	1
1935/36	Benburb	1	Yoker Athletic	0
1936/37	Arthurlie	5	Kirkintilloch Rob Roy	1
1937/38	Cambuslang Rangers	3	Benburb	2
1938/39	Glencairn	2	Shawfield	1
1939/40	Maryhill	1	Morton Juniors	0
1940/41	Perthshire	3	Armadale Thistle	1
1941/42	Clydebank	4	Vale of Clyde	2
1942/43	Kirkintilloch Rob Roy	3	Benburb	1
1943/44	Perthshire	1	Blantyre Victoria	0
1944/45	Burnbank Athletic	3	Cambuslang Rangers	1
1945/46	Fauldhouse United	2	Arthurlie	0
1946/47	Shawfield	2	Bo'ness United	1
1947/48	Bo'ness United	2	Irvine Meadow	1
1948/49	Auchinleck Talbot	3	Petershill	2
1949/50	Blantyre Victoria	3	Cumnock	0
1950/51	Petershill	1	Irvine Meadow	0
1951/52	Kilbirnie Ladeside	1	Camelon	0
1952/53	Vale of Leven	1	Annbank United	0
1953/54	Sunnybank	2	Lochee Harp	1
1954/55	Kilsyth Rangers	4	Duntocher Hibs	1
1955/56	Petershill	4	Lugar Boswell Thistle	1

1956/57	Aberdeen Banks O' Dee	1	Kilsyth Rangers	0
1957/58	Shotts Bon Accord	2	Pumpherston	0
1958/59	Irvine Meadow	2	Shettleston	1
1959/60	St Andrews	3	Greenock	1
1960/61	Dunbar United	2	Cambuslang Rangers	0
1961/62	Kirkintilloch Rob Roy	1	Renfrew	0
1962/63	Irvine Meadow	2	Glenafton Athletic	1
1963/64	Johnstone Burgh	3	Cambuslang Rangers	0
1964/65	Linlithgow Rose	4	Baillieston	1
1965/66	Bonnyrigg Rose	6	Whitburn	1
1966/67	Kilsyth Rangers	3	Glencairn	1
1967/68	Johnstone Burgh	4	Glenrothes	3
1968/69	Cambuslang Rangers	1	Kirkintilloch Rob Roy	0
1969/70	Blantyre Victoria	1	Penicuik Athletic	0
1970/71	Cambuslang Rangers	2	Newtongrange Star	1
1971/72	Cambuslang Rangers	3	Bonnyrigg Rose	2
1972/73	Irvine Meadow	1	Cambuslang Rangers	0
1973/74	Cambuslang Rangers	3	Linlithgow Rose	1
1974/75	Glenrothes	1	Glencairn	0
1975/76	Bo'ness United	3	Darvel	0
1976/77	Kilbirnie Ladeside	3	Kirkintilloch Rob Roy	1
1977/78	Bonnyrigg Rose	1	Stonehouse Violet	0
1978/79	Cumnock	1	Bo'ness United	0
1979/80	Baillieston	2	Benburb	0
1980/81	Pollok	1	Arthurlie	0
1981/82	Blantyre Victoria	1	Baillieston	0
1982/83	East Kilbride Thistle	2	Bo'ness United	0
1983/84	Bo'ness United	2	Baillieston	0
1984/85	Pollok	3	Petershill	1
1985/86	Auchinleck Talbot	3	Pollok	2
1986/87	Auchinleck Talbot	1	Kilbirnie Ladeside	0
1987/88	Auchinleck Talbot	1	Petershill	0
1988/89	Cumnock	1	Ormiston Primrose	0
1989/90	Hill O' Beath	1	Lesmahagow	0
1990/91	Auchinleck Talbot	1	Newtongrange Star	0
1991/92	Auchinleck Talbot	4	Glenafton	0
1992/93	Glenafton	1	Tayport	0
1993/94	Largs Thistle	1	Glenafton	0
1994/95	Camelon	2	Whitburn	0
1995/96	Tayport	2	Camelon	0
1996/97	Pollok	3	Tayport	1
1997/98	Arthurlie	4	Pollok	0
1998/99	Kilwinning Rangers	1	Kelty Hearts	0
1999/2000	Whitburn	2	Johnstone Burgh	2
	(Whitburn won on penalties)			
2000/01	Renfrew	0	Carnoustie Panmure	0
	(Renfrew won on penalties)			
2001/02	Linlithgow Rose	1	Auchinleck Talbot	0
2002/03	Tayport	1	Linlithgow Rose	0
2003/04	Carnoustie Panmure	0	Tayport	0
	(Carnoustie Panmure won on penalties)			
2004/05	Tayport	2	Lochee United	0
2005/06	Auchinleck Talbot	2	Bathgate Thistle	1
2006/07	Linlithgow Rose	2	Kelty Hearts	1
2007/08	Bathgate Thistle	2	Cumnock	1

The following clubs have all won the Scottish Junior Cup since the second world war, and their best performances in the first years of the new league set-up are also shown.

Arthurlie

Home: Dunterlie Park, Barrhead, East Renfrewshire
Colours: Sky blue and white
Scottish Junior Cup winners: 1936/37; 1997/98
West Region Superleague Premier Division: Runners-up 2003/04; 2004/05

Arthurlie reformed as a junior club in 1931 but, as a senior club, the 'Lie once knocked Celtic out of the Scottish Cup and also won the championship of Division Three in 1923/24. The Scottish Junior Cup was won with a 5–1 victory over Kirkintilloch Rob Roy at Celtic Park in 1937, but over sixty years elapsed before

the feat was repeated. A 4–0 victory over Pollok at Fir Park was revenge for a 1–0 defeat to the same team in the 1980/81 final.

Among the Arthurlie players who stepped up to senior football is James Grady, who went on to become part of the Gretna team that rapidly achieved success after joining the Scottish Football League.

Auchinleck Talbot

Home: Beechwood Park, Auchinleck, Ayrshire
Colours: Black and gold
Scottish Junior Cup winners: 1948/49; 1985/86; 1986/87; 1987/88; 1990/91; 1991/92; 2005/06
West Region Superleague Premier Division: Champions 2005/06

The 'Bot were formed in 1909, and take their name from Lord Talbot de Maldahide, who gave them their ground. It now has a stand that used to grace Douglas Park, Hamilton until the Accies vacated their Douglas Park ground. Auchinleck first won the Junior Cup in 1949, with a 3–2 defeat of Petershill at Hampden Park, in front of 68,837 fans. When they beat Bathgate Thistle 2–1 at Rugby Park, Kilmarnock in 2006, the crowd of 7,479 was somewhat lower, but it amounted to a record breaking seventh victory. This was not the first time that Auchinleck had gone into the record books, as they had already become the first club to win the Scottish Junior Cup three times in a row.

The club has played its league football in the West Region Premier Division since 2002/03, and when they won the title in 2005/06 it gave them a league and cup 'double'.

Banks O' Dee

Home: Spain Park, Aberdeen
Colours: Sky and navy blue
Scottish Junior Cup winners: 1956/57
North Region Premier League: Champions 2007/08

Formed in 1902, the Dee won the Scottish Junior Cup in 1957 when they beat Kilsyth Rangers 1–0. Their former players include Martin Buchan (q.v.) (Aberdeen and Manchester United) and Graham Leggat (q.v.) (Aberdeen and Fulham), who both played for Scotland. Their Spain Park ground has been refurbished, and in 2008 this was complemented by the championship of the North Region Premier League, which brought qualification for the 2008/09 Scottish Cup.

Bathgate Thistle
Home: Creamery Park, Bathgate, West Lothian
Colours: Blue and white
Scottish Junior Cup winners: 2007/08
East Region Superleague: 2nd 2005/06
Thistle reached their first Junior Cup final in 2006,when they lost 2–1 to Auchinleck Talbot at Rugby Park, but two years later they were back in Kilmarnock for the 2007/08 final. This time Paul McGrillen's winning goal earned them a 2–1 victory over Cumnock, and Willie Hill's side took the trophy back to West Lothian. Founded in 1937, Thistle is the club where goalkeeper Billy Ritchie began his career before moving to Rangers in 1955. Billy played once for Scotland (see **SUBSTITUTES**).

Blantyre Victoria
Home: Castle Park, Blantyre, South Lanarkshire
Colours: Blue and white
Scottish Junior Cup winners: 1949/50; 1969/70; 1981/82
West Region Central District League-First Division: 9th 2006/07
The Vics were formed in 1889 and first won the Junior Cup in 1950, when a crowd of 44,402 watched them defeat Cumnock 3–0 at Hampden Park. Their victory hit the headlines for the wrong reasons though, when the cup was stolen and later discovered buried in a bing.

They returned to Hampden twenty years later to beat Penicuik 1–0, and their third Junior Cup victory was at Ibrox Park in 1982, when they overcame Baillieston 1–0. Several famous players began their careers with the Vics, including Jock Stein (q.v.), Billy McNeill (q.v.), and Joe Jordan (q.v.).

Bo'ness United
Home: Newton Park, Bo'ness, West Lothian
Colours: Royal blue and white
Scottish Junior Cup winners: 1947/48; 1975/76; 1983/84
East Region Superleague: 6th 2003/04; 2004/05; 2005/06
Bo'ness FC was a senior club that once played in Division One of the Scottish League, but in 1945 they amalgamated with junior club Bo'ness Cadora to form Bo'ness United.

The new club went to Hampden Park in 1948 and won the Scottish Junior Cup in front of a crowd of over 55,000, beating Irvine Meadow 2–1. By the time they won the trophy for a second time, a 3–0 victory over Darvel in 1976, the final was attracting much smaller crowds and only just over 20,000 people made the journey to Hampden. The third victory, a 2–0 defeat of Baillieston in 1984, was witnessed by only 15,000 fans at Ibrox Stadium.

John Blackley (Hibernian) and Donald Ford (Hearts) are Scotland international players who began their careers with United and former Northern Ireland international George O'Boyle played for the club in the early years of the twenty-first century. The BUs were promoted to the Superleague in 2003, and after slipping down to the Premier League for a season in 2007/08, bounced straight back as champions of the second tier.

Bonnyrigg Rose Athletic
Home: New Dundas Park, Bonnyrigg, Midlothian
Colours: Red and white
Scottish Junior Cup winners: 1965/66; 1977/78
East Region Superleague: 2rd 2006/07
A club with a history that goes all the way back to 1890, the Rose have twice won the Scottish Junior Cup at Hampden Park, with a 6–1 victory over Whitburn in 1966 and a 1–0 defeat of Stonehouse Violet twelve years later. They were also runners-up in 1972, losing 3–2 to Cambuslang Rangers.

The legendary John White (q.v.) once wore the red and white hoops, before leaving for Alloa, Falkirk and Tottenham Hotspur. He was part of Spurs' double-winning team in 1960/61 and helped them win the European Cup-Winners' Cup in 1963, before being tragically killed by lightning the following year. Another famous former player is Pat Stanton (q.v.), who played for Hibernian and Celtic and eventually returned to Hibs as Manager.

Cambuslang Rangers
Home: Somervell Park, Cambuslang
Colours: Royal blue
Scottish Junior Cup winners: 1937/38; 1968/69; 1970/71; 1971/72; 1973/74
West Region Superleague First Division: 10th 2004/05
The Lang can trace their roots back to a juvenile team named Leeside that became a junior club called Clyde Rovers in 1892. The name was changed to Cambuslang Rangers in 1899.

Cambuslang first won the Scottish Junior Cup in 1938, when they defeated Benburb 3–2 at Parkhead, but it was in the 1970s that they became one of junior football's greatest ever teams. They reached the final five times in six years, and became the first club to retain the trophy when they defeated Bonnyrigg Rose 3–2 in 1972. If they had not lost to Irvine Meadow in the following year's final, they would have won the cup four times in a row.

Many Cambuslang players have gone on to achieve fame with senior clubs, with Bobby Murdoch (q.v.) of Celtic and Arthur Graham of Aberdeen and Leeds United being two of the most well known. Successive relegations took them down to the Central District Second Division in 2007.

Camelon
Home: Carmuirs Park, Camelon, near Falkirk
Colours: Red and white
Scottish Junior Cup winners: 1994/95
East Region Superleague: 3rd 2007/08
The Mariners were founded in 1920 and reached their first Scottish Junior Cup final in 1952, when a crowd of 69,959 at Hampden Park saw them lose 1–0 to Kilbirnie Ladeside. They didn't reach the final again until the 1990s, and then they did it in two consecutive years, beating Whitburn 2–0 in 1995 and losing 2–0 to Tayport a year later.

Scotland international goalkeeper Jerry Dawson was with Camelon before joining Rangers in 1931, and several of the club's players, including Kevin McAllister, have joined neighbours Falkirk FC over the years. In 2006 they were promoted to the East Region Superleague.

Carnoustie Panmure
Home: Laing Park, Carnoustie
Colours: Red and white
Scottish Junior Cup winners: 2003/04
East Region Superleague: 4th 2006/07
Formed in 1936, the 'Gowfers' left their Westfield Park ground in 2004 and moved to a brand new home at Laing Park. This was also the year when they won the first ever Scottish Junior Cup final between two Tayside teams, beating Tayport on penalties after a 0–0 draw at Firhill. Three years earlier they had they lost the final at the same venue when Renfrew beat them on penalties after a 0–0 draw. The club's most famous former player is Scotland goalkeeper Bill Brown (q.v.), who played for Dundee and then went on to become part of Tottenham Hotspur's double-winning side in 1961.

Cumnock
Home: Townhead Park, Cumnock, Ayrshire
Colours: Black and white
Scottish Junior Cup winners: 1978/79; 1988/89
West Region Superleague Premier Division: 4th 2003/04
The 'Nock' reached their first Scottish Junior Cup final in 1950, thirty-eight years after the club was founded. On that occasion they lost 3–0 to Blantyre Vics at Hampden Park, but their second Hampden final in 1979 resulted in a 1–0 victory over Bo'ness United. Ten years later they reached the final again, and this time beat Ormiston Primrose 1–0 at Rugby Park.

Eric Caldow (q.v.), the former Rangers and Scotland full back, managed the team for a short time in the 1970s, and in 2006 former St Mirren goalkeeper Campbell Money became manager.

Dunbar United
Home: New Countess Park, Dunbar, East Lothian
Colours: Black and white
Scottish Junior Cup winners: 1960/61
East Region South Division: 9th 2006/07
Formed in 1925, The Seasiders' finest hour came in 1961 when they won the Scottish Junior Cup, with a 2–0 win over Cambuslang Rangers in a replayed final after a 2–2 draw, and the victorious team paraded along Edinburgh's Princes Street in an open-top bus. In 2001 they moved from Countess Park to a purpose-built new stadium, but when the East Region's leagues were re-structured in 2006, they became part of the third tier.

Alex Smith played for Dunbar in the 1950s before moving to Dunfermline Athletic, where he later became part of the Jock Stein side that won the 1960/61 Scottish Cup. He also took part in some of the Pars' memorable European campaigns before moving to Rangers in 1966.

East Kilbride Thistle
Home: The Showpark, East Kilbride, South Lanarkshire
Colours: Black and white
Scottish Junior Cup winners: 1982/83
West Region Superleague First Division: 6th 2007/08
The Jags won the Scottish Junior Cup when they beat Bo'ness United 2–0 at Ibrox in 1983, just fifteen years after their formation in 1968. One of their most famous former players is Scotland international Willie Pettigrew, who went on to score two goals for Dundee United in the replayed 1980 League Cup final against Aberdeen.

In 2006 they achieved promotion to the First Division of the West Region Superleague when manager John Brogan led them to second place in the Central District First Division.

Fauldhouse United
Home: Park View, Fauldhouse, West Lothian
Colours: Red and white
Scottish Junior Cup winners: 1945/46
East Region South Division: Champions 2007/08
When the East Region reconstructed its leagues in 2006, United became part of the third tier for two seasons. This modest status contrasted with the high profile that they had achieved sixty years earlier, when Fauldhouse

Action from the 1969 Scottish Junior Cup final between Cambuslang Rangers and Kirkintilloch Rob Roy.

won the Scottish Junior Cup at Hampden Park. More than 44,000 fans celebrated the return of peacetime finals by watching Fauldhouse defeat Arthurlie 2–0. This remains the only appearance in the final for the club, which was founded in 1919.

Celtic's John Fallon, who was 'farmed out' to the West Lothian club not long after he had signed for the Hoops, provides another contrast. These modest beginnings were the start of a career that included keeping goal in the 1967 World Club Cup final in Argentina.

Glenafton Athletic
Home: Loch Park, New Cumnock, Ayrshire
Colours: Red and white
Scottish Junior Cup winners: 1992/93
West Region Superleague Premier Division: 3rd 2002/03
The Glens, who were formed in 1930, reached their first Scottish Junior Cup final in 1963 when they lost 2–1 to Irvine Meadow, but it was in the 1990s that they made a name for themselves. They reached the final in three consecutive years, but only won the trophy once, beating Tayport 1–0 at Firhill in 1993. In 1992 they lost 4–0 to Auchinleck Talbot and in 1994 it was a 1–0 defeat by Largs Thistle that stopped them becoming consecutive winners.

Former Scotland goalkeeper Alan Rough (q.v.) joined the club as player-manager in 1990 and was manager of the cup-winning team. Before that Ted McMinn played for the Glens in the 1980s before moving on to Queen of the South and Rangers.

Glenrothes
Home: Warout Stadium, Glenrothes, Fife
Colours: Red and white
Scottish Junior Cup winners: 1974/75
East Region Superleague: 4th 2004/05
The club from Fife's new town was formed in 1964 and reached the final of the Scottish Junior Cup only four years later. A crowd of 28,000 at Hampden Park in 1968 watched them draw 2–2 with Johnstone Burgh, but Johnstone went on to win the replay 4–3. Seven years later there was some consolation when the Glens returned to Hampden and defeated Rutherglen Glencairn 1–0 to take the trophy. In 2006/07 they became the first champions of the East Region's newly created Premier League (second tier), after a one-year absence from the Superleague.

Former players include Derek Stark, who won trophies with Dundee United in the 1980s, and Joe Watson, who went on to play international football for Australia.

Hill of Beath Hawthorn
Home: Keirs Park, Hill of Beath, Fife
Colours: Red and white
Scottish Junior Cup winners: 1989/90
East Region Superleague: 2nd 2002/03
The Haws won the Scottish Junior Cup in 1990, only fifteen years after they were formed, with a 1–0 victory over Lesmahagow at Rugby Park. After a second place finish in the Superleague in 2002/03 they were relegated the following season, but bounced back at the first attempt and then finished third in 2005/06.
One of their former players, David Westwood, went on to be goalkeeping coach at both Cowdenbeath and East Fife, and in 2006 he featured in newspaper articles after appearing on the bench for East Fife at the age of forty-eight.

Captains Shaw of Petershill and McLean of Irvine Meadow shake hands before the Scottish Junior Cup final of 1951.

Irvine Meadow
Home: Meadow Park, Irvine, North Ayrshire
Colours: Royal blue and white
Scottish Junior Cup winners: 1958/59; 1962/63; 1972/73
West Region Superleague Premier Division: 2nd 2007/08
The Medda (also sometimes known as the 'Dow), who were founded in 1897, appeared in three Scottish Junior Cup finals that attracted more than 55,000 fans to Hampden Park. Runners-up in both 1947/48 and 1950/51, they won at the third attempt with a 2–1 victory over Shettleston in 1958/59. Crowds were smaller by the time of their second victory in 1962/63, when they beat Glenafton Athletic 2–1, and when they won the trophy for a third time in 1972/73 they required two replays before overcoming Cambuslang Rangers 1–0.

Thirty years later they had become a yo-yo club in the league. Relegated from the Superleague Premier Division in 2002/03, they were demoted to the third tier two years later and, after bouncing straight back with consecutive promotions in 2005/06 and 2006/07, they finished second in the Superleague in 2007/08.

Scotland fans who watch replays of the famous goal scored by Archie Gemmill (q.v.) in Argentina in 1978 may care to reflect that he started his football career at Meadow Park before leaving for St Mirren in 1964.

Johnstone Burgh
Home: Keanie Park, Johnstone, Renfrewshire
Colours: Red and white
Scottish Junior Cup winners: 1963/64; 1967/68
West Region Superleague Premier Division: 5th 2002/03
Within twelve years of their foundation in 1956, the Burgh had twice won the Scottish Junior Cup final at Hampden Park. At the end of their first fifty years they had yet to win it again, although they only lost the 2000 final on penalties after a 2–2 draw with Whitburn. That

Kilwinning Rangers celebrate their 1998/99 Junior Cup triumph.

year they attracted a crowd of more than two thousand fans to their home tie against Glenafton.

Frank McAvennie wore the red and white of the Burgh before moving to St. Mirren, and a career that would later see him score on his international debut for Scotland. In the league, Johnstone started well after the creation of the Superleague, but by 2008 they had been relegated to the third tier.

Kilbirnie Ladeside
Home: Valefield, Kilbirnie, Ayrshire
Colours: Amber and black
Scottish Junior Cup winners: 1951/52; 1976/77
West Region Superleague Premier Division: 6th 2002/03
The Blasties have twice won the Scottish Junior Cup at Hampden Park. In 1952 just under 70,000 fans saw them beat Camelon 1–0, but their 3–1 victory over Kirkintilloch Rob Roy twenty-five years later was the first final to be televised live, and the crowd was a mere 11,476. Successive relegations saw them fall to the third tier of the league in 2005, but two years later they were back in the First Division.

The club was formed in 1901 and takes its name from a 'lade' or small burn. Ernie McGarr, who twice kept goal for Scotland, once played for the club, as did fellow international George Stevenson, who helped Motherwell win the Scottish League title in 1931/32 and later became their manager.

Kilsyth Rangers
Home: Duncansfield Park, Kilsyth, North Lanarkshire
Colours: Royal blue and white
Scottish Junior Cup winners: 1954/55; 1966/67
West Region Superleague Premier Division: 7th 2005/06
When the Gers won the 1954/55 Scottish Junior Cup in a replayed final at Hampden Park, Alex Querrie scored all four of their goals with his head. The first match, which had finished in a 0–0 draw, had been played in front of a crowd of just under 65,000. Their next visit to Hampden, two years later, ended in a 1–0 defeat, but then they went back in 1967 and claimed the trophy once again after another replay.

The club, which was originally formed in 1913 and re-formed in 1945, has produced several players who have gone on to win Scotland caps, including George Mulhall, Drew Jarvie, Frank McGarvey, David Stewart and 'Lisbon Lion' Willie Wallace (q.v.). The Gers' league form steadily improved after the introduction of the Superleague, with two promotions in two years taking them into the Premier Division, but in 2008 they were relegated back to the First Division.

Kilwinning Rangers
Home: Abbey Park, Kilwinning, Ayrshire
Colours: Blue and white
Scottish Junior Cup winners: 1908/09; 1998/99
West Region Superleague Premier Division: Champions 2003/04
Formed in 1899, the Buffs were the first Ayrshire team to win the Scottish Junior Cup when they beat Strathclyde 1–0 at Rugby Park in 1909, following a 0–0 draw at Shawfield. Ninety years later they celebrated their centenary by also becoming the last Ayrshire team to win it in the twentieth century, beating Kelty Hearts 1–0 at Firhill. Twelve months after winning the 2003/04 championship they were relegated to the First Division. This is the club where Scotland international Lou Macari (q.v.) began a playing career that was to take him to Celtic and Manchester United.

Kirkintilloch Rob Roy
Home: Adamslie Park, Kirkintilloch, East Dunbartonshire
Colours: Red and black
Scottish Junior Cup winners: 1920/21; 1942/43; 1961/62
West Region Superleague First Division: Champions 2007/08
The Rabs, who were founded in 1878, are one of the oldest football clubs in Scotland. As well as winning three Scottish Junior Cup finals at Hampden Park, they have been runners-up on five occasions, and their 1977 defeat to Kilbirnie Ladeside was the first final to be televised live. They won promotion to the First Division of the Superleague in 2004, were relegated back into the Central District First Division two years later, and then went straight up to the Premier Division in two successive seasons.

Many of their former players have gone on to become well known in the senior game. They include George Young (q.v.), who won fifty-three caps for Scotland and was a member of Ranger's famous 'iron curtain' defence, and Steve Chalmers (q.v.), who scored the winning goal for Celtic in the 1967 European Cup final.

Largs Thistle
Home: Barrfields Stadium, Largs, Ayrshire
Colours: Black and yellow
Scottish Junior Cup winners: 1993/94
West Region Superleague First Division: 3rd 2005/06
When Thistle took the Scottish Junior Cup back to Largs in 1994, after beating Glenafton 1–0 at Ibrox stadium, over a hundred years had elapsed since their formation in 1890. A decade later they won the 2004/05 championship of the Ayrshire District league and followed this up with a third place finish in the Superleague First Division in 2005/06.

Gordon McQueen (q.v.) began his career with Thistle, before joining St Mirren in 1970 and embarking on a journey that would see him win an English league championship medal with Leeds United and an FA Cup winner's medal with Manchester United.

Linlithgow Rose

Home: Prestonfield, Linlithgow, West Lothian
Colours; Maroon and white
Scottish Junior Cup winners: 1964/65; 2001/02; 2006/07
East Region Superleague: Champions 2003/04; 2006/07
The Rose can trace their history back to 1889, but their most famous signing was made in the 1930s. Tommy Walker, who gained twenty caps for Scotland, joined the club in 1931 and stayed for a year before joining Hearts.

The Linlithgow club has enjoyed three exceptional seasons. In 1964/65 they beat Baillieston 4–1 at Hampden Park to take the Scottish Junior Cup, and also won their league and three other cups that year. When they won the Scottish Junior Cup in 2002, with a 1–0 victory over Auchinleck Talbot at Firhill, they completed their season by winning four other cups as well as the league title.

They won the Scottish Junior Cup again in 2006/07, beating Kelty Hearts 2–1 after extra time at East End Park, and also topped the East Region Superleague. Each of these achievements was enough to earn entry to the 2007/08 Scottish Cup competition, and the Rose embarked on a cup run that took them all the way to the last thirty-two, when they lost 4–0 away to Queen of the South.

Petershill

Home: Petershill Park, Southloch Street, Glasgow
Colours: Maroon and white
Scottish Junior Cup winners: 1911/12; 1915/16; 1917/18; 1950/51; 1955/56
West Region Superleague Premier Division: 3rd 2007/08
Petershill Football and Athletic Club occupies an important place in the history of Scottish Junior football. Founded in 1897, the Peasy have won the Scottish Junior Cup on five occasions and been runners-up four times. Their Hampden victories in 1951 and 1956 were achieved in front of crowds of 77,650 and 64,702 respectively, and in 1950/51 they attracted 19,800 people to a quarter-final tie against Bo'ness United at Petershill Park. Built by volunteer labour in 1935, this large ground entered a period of reconstruction in 2005, with the club sharing the stadium of fellow juniors Ashfield (along with Glasgow Tigers speedway).

Many Petershill men have gone on to play senior football, including two famous Scotland internationalists of the 1930s – Torry Gillick (q.v.), of Rangers and Everton, and Alec Massie (q.v.) of Hearts and Aston Villa.

Pollok

Home: Newlandsfield Park, Shawlands, Glasgow
Colours: Black and white
Scottish Junior Cup winners: 1980/81; 1984/85; 1996/97
West Region Superleague Premier Division: Champions 2002/03; 2004/05; 2006/07; 2007/08
Formed in 1908, Pollok FC is a well-supported club that regularly attracts bigger crowds than some of the lesser teams in the Scottish Football League. Bobby Collins (q.v.) (Celtic) and Bob McPhail (q.v.) (Airdrieonians and Rangers) both wore the black and white stripes before they moved up to senior football.

After topping the West Region Superleague in both 2003 and 2005, they twice went on to beat the best teams from the other regions by winning the SJFA Supercup. Prior to the formation of the Superleague, they won the Central League Premier Division six times. They won the Scottish Junior Cup at Hampden Park in 1981 by beating local rivals Arthurlie 1–0, and four years later they went back to record a 3–1 victory over Petershill. In 1997 they took the trophy for a third time with a 3–1 win over Tayport at Fir Park, Motherwell.

When they won the West Region Superleague once again in 2006/07, a change in the rules for the Scottish Cup meant that Pollok earned a place in the first round, along with Linlithgow Rose and Culter. After beating St Cuthbert Wanderers, they held SFL side Montrose to a 2–2 draw in the second round before going out 1–0 in the replay.

Petershill (dark shirts) and Cummnock do battle.

Renfrew

Home: Western Park, Renfrew
Colours: Blue and white
Scottish Junior Cup winners: 2000/01
West Region Superleague Premier Division: Runners-up 2005/06
The Frew reached their first Scottish Junior Cup final in 1917, five years after they were founded in 1912. After a 0–0 draw with St. Mirren Juniors at Firhill, they lost the replay 1–0. Forty-five years later they lost their second final after a replay too. A crowd of 49,000 saw them draw 1–1 with Kirkintilloch Rob Roy at Hampden Park in 1962, and they again lost the second match 1–0.

Then, after another long wait, it was a case of third time lucky. In 2001 they went back to Firhill and this match would have gone to a replay if it hadn't been for the introduction of the penalty-shoot-out. Renfrew beat Carnoustie Panmure 6–5 on penalties after the match finished 0–0. In the league, they were relegated to the second tier just twelve months after finishing as runners-up.

Several Renfrew players have gone on to play for Scotland after joining a senior club, including Harry Haddock (Clyde), Charlie Cooke (q.v.) (Dundee and Chelsea) and John Divers, both senior and junior, (Celtic).

St Andrews United
Home: Recreation Park, St. Andrews, Fife
Colours: White and black
Scottish Junior Cup winners: 1959/60
East Region Premier League: 10th 2006/07
Saints qualified for the East Region's new Premier League in 2006, by finishing second in the Fife League; twelve months later they had been relegated to the third tier.

However, the club's biggest day came nearly fifty years earlier when they won the Scottish Junior Cup by beating Greenock 3–1 at Hampden Park. The club from the university town was formed in 1920, and one of its most famous former players is full back Willie Mathieson, who went on to become part of the Rangers side that beat Dynamo Moscow in the 1971/72 European Cup-Winners' Cup final in Barcelona.

Shotts Bon Accord
Home: Hannah Park, Shotts, North Lanarkshire
Colours: Maroon
Scottish Junior Cup winners: 1957/58
West Region Superleague Premier Division: 4th 2005/06
The Bon Accord won the Scottish Junior Cup just eight years after the club was founded, when Pumpherston were beaten 2–0 at Hampden Park in 1958. Their own Hannah Park ground boasts an exceptionally large pitch, and in the late 1990s it was the scene of three successive championships, when the club bounced back from demotion by winning the Central League's Division Two, Division One and Premier Division in consecutive seasons.

John 'Yogi' Hughes (q.v.), who won eight Scotland caps and played for Celtic in the 1970 European Cup final, wore the maroon strip for a short time in 1959.

Sunnybank
Home: Heathryfold Park, Aberdeen
Colours: Black and white
Scottish Junior Cup winners: 1953/54
North Region Premier League: Champions 2002/03
Sunnybank, who were formed in 1946, won the North Region Premier League in its inaugural season of 2002/03, but it was almost fifty years earlier that the club had taken the Scottish Junior Cup back to Heathryfold Park. Fans from both Aberdeen and Dundee made the journey to Glasgow in 1954 to see Sunnybank beat Lochee Harp 2–1 at Hampden Park.

Several Sunnybank players have stepped up to play for neighbours Aberdeen FC over the years, including Teddy Scott, who also became part of the Dons' backroom team. Colin Jackson of Rangers and George Mitchell of Dundee United are also former players.

Vale of Leven in their senior existence with the Scottish Cup which they won three years in a row from 1877-1879.

Tayport
Home: The Canniepairt, Tayport, Fife
Colours: Red and white
Scottish Junior Cup winners: 1995/96; 2002/03; 2004/05
East Region Superleague: Champions 2002/03; 2005/06
Although they were founded in 1947, Tayport only became a junior club in 1990. They first won the Scottish Junior Cup in 1996, beating Camelon 2–0, but when they won it again in 2003 their 1–0 victory over Linlithgow Rose gave them a special 'double'. As well as winning the cup, they became champions of the East Region Superleague in its inaugural season. Prior to this they had topped the Tayside Premier Division for four consecutive seasons.

In 2005 a crowd of 6668 at Tannadice Park, Dundee saw them take the Scottish Junior Cup for the third time with a 1-0 win over Lochee United. The previous year Tayport's fans had travelled to Firhill in Glasgow to watch them lose the final to another Tayside team, Carnoustie Panmure.

Vale of Leven
Home: Millburn Park, Alexandria, West Dunbartonshire
Colours: Dark blue, white and red
Scottish Junior Cup winners: 1952/53
West Region Central District League – First Division: 4th 2002/03; 2003/04
The name 'Vale of Leven' once belonged to a club that won the Scottish Cup on three occasions and played in the Scottish League until 1925/26. The present club was formed in 1939, and even plays at the same ground, but it entered the record books for winning a different cup. In 1953 the Vale beat Annbank United at Hampden Park in front of over 55,000 people.

Numerous former players have gone on to make a career in senior football, and one even went on to become manager of Scotland's national team. Ian McColl (q.v.), who won fourteen caps for Scotland, became part of Rangers' famous 'Iron Curtain' defence, and then managed Scotland in the 1960s.

Whitburn
Home: Central Park, Whitburn, West Lothian
Colours: Claret and amber
Scottish Junior Cup winners: (1999/2000)
East Region Superleague: 2nd 2007/08
One of Whitburn's claims to fame is that John Greig (q.v.) used to play for them before he went on to become captain of Rangers and Scotland. The club was formed in 1934 and they had to wait until 1966 for their first

appearance in a Scottish Junior Cup final, which ended in a 6–1 defeat to Bonnyrigg Rose.

In 1995 they once again lost to a fellow East Region club, Camelon, but in 2000 it was a case of third time lucky. This time they were playing a club from the west of Scotland and they defeated Johnstone Burgh on penalties after a 2–2 draw. They were promoted to the Superleague in 2005, after winning the Division One title in the Lothian League, and quickly established themselves as one of the leading clubs.

KELLY James (1865 – 1932)

Scotland Caps: 8
Scottish League Championship medals: 3
Scottish Cup medals: 3

James Kelly was one of those who played in Celtic's first team of 1888, having joined them from Renton. He was an attacking centre half, and probably the most famous player in Victorian Scotland. He won eight caps with Scotland and captained them on several occasions. He was also the first Scottish captain to be introduced to royalty when, at Richmond in 1893, he was presented to Princess Mary of Teck, who would be the future Queen Mary. He became director and chairman of Celtic, and it is to him that much is owed for Celtic's early success. Less happily, his family ran the club in an autocratic and not always beneficial way, culminating in the collapse of the Board in 1994.

KELLY Sir Robert (1900 – 1971)

Sir Robert Kelly was the son of James Kelly (above) and the controversial chairman of Celtic in the years from 1947 until his death in 1971. Bob was a stockbroker's clerk to trade, and became a director of Celtic on the death of his father in 1932. He had a withered arm and could not play the game, but he involved himself in the running of Celtic and the SFA (he was chairman at one point) with enthusiasm and determination. As chairman of Celtic, he won the battle to be allowed the fly the Irish flag over Celtic Park on match days, but his control of the club was sometimes stifling and unhealthy. In 1965, after a prolonged period of lack of success and fan unrest, it was Kelly who made the significant decision to appoint Jock Stein, (a Protestant) to be manager of the club. Following the capture of the European Cup in 1967, Kelly was knighted in the New Year's Honours list of 1 January 1969.

KENNEDY Stewart (1949 –)

Scotland Caps: 5
Scottish League Championship medals: 2
Scottish League Cup medals: 2

An excellent goalkeeper, who played five times for Scotland, Stewart Kennedy is forever identified with the 1-5 Wembley disaster of 1975, for which he was not entirely to blame. He started his senior career with Dunfermline Athletic, but then returned to the juniors before reappearing in the senior ranks for Stenhousemuir, where he attracted the attention of Rangers. After he left Rangers in 1980 he joined Forfar Athletic, for whom he soon became a local hero, as they won the Scottish League Second Division in 1984 and frequently came close to embarrassing Rangers, whom they met several times in cup competitions.

KILBIRNIE LADESIDE FC (see JUNIOR FOOTBALL)

KILMARNOCK FC

Ground: **Rugby Park**
Nickname: **Killie**
Colours: **Blue and white**
Record Attendance: **35,995 v Rangers (1962)**
Record Victory: **11-1 v Paisley Academical (1930)**
Record Defeat: **1-9 v Celtic (1938)**
Highest League Position: **1st (1964/65)**
Best Scottish Cup Performance: **Winners (1919/20, 1928/29, 1996/97)**
Best League Cup Performance: **Runners-up (1952/53; 1960/61; 1962/63; 2000/01; 2006/07)**

Founded in 1869, Killie's roots can be traced back to former pupils of Kilmarnock Academy. The club has competed in the Scottish Cup since the inaugural competition in 1873/74, but did not gain entry to Division Two of the Scottish League until 1895.

The Division Two championship was won in both 1898 and 1899, but promotion was not automatic and it was not until 1899 that the club was voted into the top division. In 1888/89 they remained undefeated throughout the season.

The Scottish Cup was won in 1920, when 95,000 people saw a 3–2 victory over Albion Rovers in the first final after the war, and in 1929 the trophy returned to Rugby Park when Rangers were defeated 2–0. Membership of Division One was maintained until the second world war, when the Rugby Park ground was requisitioned by the military. It was returned as a virtual wreck in 1945 and relegation to Division B followed in 1947. The runners-up place in 1953/54 finally took them back to the top division and this was soon followed by a period of unprecedented success.

Full-time football was introduced in 1959 and the club competed in the Inter-Cities Fairs Cup of 1964/65 after finishing second in the league for the fourth time in five years. Although they went out to Everton in the second round, the first round brought a memorable victory, when a 3–0 away defeat to Eintracht Frankfurt was overturned by a 5–1 win at home.

Then in 1965, under manager Willie Waddell, the Division One championship was won on the last day of the season. In second place, two points behind Hearts on the morning of the match, Kilmarnock needed a two-goal victory at Tynecastle in order to win the title, and a 2–0 win brought the club's only league

Willie Waddell, manager of Kilmarnock leads the celebrations after his team have won the League by beating Hearts 2-0 at Tynecastle in 1965

championship. The ensuing European Cup campaign ended with a first round defeat by Real Madrid, despite a 2–2 draw at home.

Kilmarnock again competed in the Inter-Cities Fairs Cup in 1966/67,1969/70 and 1970/71, and in 1967 only a semi-final defeat by Leeds United stopped them from reaching the final. However, the 1970s and 1980s brought a period of decline and the club was relegated from the top flight in 1973, 1977 and 1981. In 1989 the club sank into the Second Division (third tier), and this brought about a series of changes that turned things around. Financial investment in the club enabled it to go full-time once again and manager Jim Fleeting signed Tommy Burns from Celtic, who went on to become player-manager in 1992. In 1993 he took Kilmarnock back into the Premier Division, but left to return to Celtic a year later.

Rugby Park was rebuilt and transformed into an all-seater stadium in 1994 and the Scottish Cup was won for a third time in 1997, with a 1–0 victory over Falkirk in the final. European football returned with the European Cup-Winners' Cup, but after beating Shelbourne the campaign ended with a defeat to Nice. There was more European football in 1998/99, 1999/2000 and 2001/02, when fourth-place finishes brought qualification for brief UEFA Cup campaigns, and in 2001 the club reached its fourth League Cup final, only to lose for a fourth time with a 3–0 defeat to Celtic.

Jim Jefferies replaced Bobby Williamson as manager in February 2002 and under his leadership Killie became established as a team that could consistently challenge the SPL's wealthier clubs, but in 2006/07 another League Cup final was lost - this time a 5–1 defeat to Hibernian.

KILSYTH RANGERS FC (see JUNIOR FOOTBALL)

KILWINNING RANGERS FC
(see JUNIOR FOOTBALL)

KING'S PARK FC (former Scottish League club)

Home: **Forthbank Park, Stirling**
Highest League Position: **23rd (3rd in Div. 2, 1927/28)**
Best Scottish Cup Performance: **Last 8 (3rd round, 1894/95)**

When King's Park FC was founded in 1875 the club took its name from the area in Stirling where the ground was situated. They did not stay there long and eventually settled at Forthbank Park, a name that was later adopted by Stirling Albion when they moved to a new ground in 1993. They first entered the Scottish Cup in 1879/80, but only once progressed as far as the quarter-finals, which resulted in a 4–2 away defeat to Hearts in 1894/95.

King's Park became founder members of the Scottish Alliance when it was formed in 1891 and subsequently played in the Midland League, Central Combination and Scottish Union, before joining the Central League in 1909. Apart from a period of inactivity during the first world war, they were still part of this league in 1921, when the Scottish League invited most of the members, including King's Park, to join its re-introduced Division Two.

This was where they spent the next eighteen years and the highest they ever finished was third, in 1927/28. In the Scottish Cup, they reached the third round on three occasions during this period, 1927/28, 1929/30 and 1934/35. Their record crowd of 8911 was achieved for a first-round tie in 1924/25, when they lost 4–0 to an Airdrieonians side that contained stars such as Hughie Gallacher and Bob McPhail.

In 1939 the second world war forced the abandonment of the Scottish League after just four games and the following year the stadium was badly damaged by a German bomb. There was an attempt to re-form King's Park FC, but the club never did recover from the loss of its ground and went out of existence not long afterwards. By 1947 Stirling's league club was the newly formed Stirling Albion and King's Park became a memory.

KINNAIRD Lord (1847 – 1923)

Scotland Caps: 1

The Honourable Arthur Fitzgerald Kinnaird, son of Baron Kinnaird of Rossie Priory in Perthshire, was one of the pioneers of the game in England, winning five FA Cup medals with the Old Etonians and the Wanderers. He played for Scotland in the second international in 1873 at the Oval. After he retired, at the age of forty-six in 1893, he became an administrator of the game in England, being president of the Football Association for thirty-three years. He was an all-round sportsman, playing fives, tennis, swimming, cricket and canoeing, and in his later life served as Lord High Commissioner of the Church of Scotland.

KIRIN CUP

This is a competition played in Japan to which Scotland have been invited twice. In 1995 they drew with Japan but lost to Ecuador, but in 2006 they won the tournament with a fine 5-1 win over Bulgaria followed by a goalless draw with Japan.

KIRKINTILLOCH ROB ROY FC
(see JUNIOR FOOTBALL)

LAMBERT Paul (1969 –)

Scotland Caps: 40
Scottish Premier League medals: 4
Scottish Cup medals: 2
Scottish League Cup medals: 2

Paul Lambert was one of the best players in Scotland in the latter years of the twentieth century. His forty Scottish caps include creditable performances in the 1998 World Cup finals. A defensive-minded midfielder, he began his career with St Mirren in 1986, and with the Buddies he won the Scottish Cup in 1987. He then moved to Motherwell in 1993, before joining Borussia Dortmund in 1996 and winning a European Cup medal with them. He is the only Scotsman to have won a European Cup medal with an overseas team. Home-

sickness brought him back to Scotland, and he joined Celtic in late 1997, where he became a very influential and popular captain, working well with Martin O'Neill. In 2002 he was voted Player of the Year by the Football Writers. On his retirement from the playing side of the game in 2005, he was briefly manager of Livingston, before moving to Wycombe Wanderers.

LARGS THISTLE FC (see JUNIOR FOOTBALL)

LARSSON Henrik (1971 –)

Scottish Premier League medals: 4
Scottish Cup medals: 2
Scottish League Cup medals: 2

Henrik Larsson is Swedish, but well worthy of inclusion in any book of Scottish football because of his outstanding contribution to Scottish football, and to Celtic in particular in the years from 1997-2004, during which time he scored 242 goals in 315 matches. He joined Celtic from Feyenoord in 1997, already an established Swedish internationalist. He was fast, lithe, agile, totally professional and committed to his cause.

He survived a horrendous leg break against Lyon in November 1999, to return the following summer, and it was when Martin O'Neill took over in 2000 that he reached his peak, scoring thirty-five league goals, and fifty-three in all competitions in season 2000/01 to win the European Golden Boot. He was twice the Scottish Players' Player of the Year (1999 and 2001) and twice the Scottish Writers' Player of the Year (the same years). He scored Celtic's two goals in Seville in their losing UEFA Cup final against Porto in 2003, and left on a free transfer to Barcelona in 2004. In 2006, he and Brian Laudrup became the first foreign players to be inducted into the Hall of Fame.

LATVIA

Scotland enjoy a good record against Latvia. They have won all the four games that they have played against them.

1996	5 Oct	Riga	2–0	Collins Jackson	
1997	11 Oct	Celtic Park	2–0	Gallacher Durie	
2000	2 Sep	Riga	1–0	McCann	
2001	6 Oct	Hampden Park	2–1	Freedman Weir	Rubins

LAUDRUP Brian (1969 –)

Scottish Premier League medals: 3
Scottish Cup medals: 1
Scottish League Cup medals: 1

Brian Laudrup was a tremendous midfield player for Rangers between the years of 1994 and 1998. He was already an established Danish internationalist when he arrived at Ibrox, and won many honours with Rangers,

soon becoming the darling of the Ibrox fans. He was Player of the Year in both 1995 and 1997 and, along with Henrik Larsson, in 2006 became the first non-Scot to be inducted into the Hall of Fame. He also enjoyed the reputation of being one of the most sporting players of the game.

LAW Denis (1940 –)

Scotland Caps: 55

Born in Aberdeen, and considered to be one of Scotland's most famous football players, Denis Law never played in Scotland other than at Hampden Park for the national side, in some of the fifty-five appearances in which he scored thirty goals. When he made his international debut in 1959, he was the youngest player to do so in modern times at eighteen years and 236 days. It was indeed sad that Law's career coincided with a time when Scotland never made it to the World Cup finals, other than in 1974 when Law, well past his prime, played his final international game against Zaire. Indeed, this turned out to be his final game in professional football.

He joined Huddersfield Town in 1955, then Manchester City in 1960, before moving in a high profile transfer to Torino the following year. When with Manchester City, he scored six goals in an English Cup tie against Luton Town on 28 January 1961. The only problem was that the game was rained off with Manchester City 6–2 in the lead, and then Luton won the rearranged game 3–1. Law scored City's consolation goal! He returned to the United Kingdom in July 1962 to play for the team that he is best known for – Manchester United. With Matt Busby's Manchester United, and in the company of other Scotsmen such as Pat Crerand and David Herd, he won two English league championship medals and one FA Cup medal, unluckily missing,

Nobby Stiles (no.4) heads off the line at Hampden in April 1966. Denis Law is to his left.

through injury, the European Cup final of 1968. In 1964 he was voted the European Footballer of the Year. In 1973, he moved back to Manchester City and, with supreme irony, with virtually his last kick of the ball for Manchester City, Denis scored the goal that relegated Manchester United. After his career was over, he became a radio and TV pundit, and in recent years has survived a cancer scare, showing the same bravery that he used to show on the field.

LAW Tommy (1908 – 1976)

Scotland Caps: 2

When the Wembley Wizards team of 1928 was chosen with Law of Chelsea at left back, many Scottish fans would not have known who he was. He played well in that famous game, but earned only one other Scottish cap. He joined Chelsea in 1925 from Bridgeton Waverley, and finished his career with them in 1939.

LAWS OF THE GAME

One of the great things about football is that the laws are relatively easy to understand, unlike those of rugby or cricket for example, and they change very seldom. In recent years there have been few significant changes – although one, the pass-back rule, was introduced in 1992 and states that a goalkeeper may not pick up a ball that has been passed to him by another member of his team. The goalkeeper may of course kick the ball in these circumstances, and he may also handle a ball that has been headed by one of his teammates, but if he picks up a ball that has been kicked by one of them, an indirect free kick is awarded at the place where the ball was picked up. An example of this occurred in the Scottish League Cup semi-final of 2006 between Celtic and Motherwell, and a mistake by the Motherwell goalkeeper cost his team the tie, for a goal was scored from the resulting indirect free kick.

Offside is now even more of a grey area than it was before, because a player should not be flagged offside, even if he is in an offside position, until he becomes 'active', i.e. plays the ball or 'interferes with play'. Offside has always caused problems, and it was the SFA who were partly responsible for a major change in 1925, reducing the number of players who had to be between a player and the opponents' goal from three to two for a player to be onside. This was because there was a genuine concern that not enough goals were being scored for the public's liking.

An aspect of the laws that has often seemed very draconian is the automatic red card awarded to a goalkeeper who handles the ball outside the penalty area, even in circumstances where it is obvious that there was nothing deliberate involved, and that the goal-keeper's impetus in catching a ball carried him over the line, or he was simply trying to avoid a collision with an opponent. An example of such a punishment involved Scott Thomson of Raith Rovers, who received a red card for overstepping the line in the League Cup semi-final of 1994/95 against Airdrie at McDiarmid Park. Previously the punishment had been simply an indirect free kick, which many people believed to be fairer.

For a long time an important part of British, and particularly Scottish, football was 'charging' i.e. a forward could 'charge' the goalkeeper, and try to barge him over the line as long as the goalkeeper had the ball in his hands, his feet were on the ground, and the shoulder (not the elbow) was used. Jimmy Quinn, Celtic's legendary centre forward in the Edwardian era, excelled in this art, as did many others, but the arrival of European football in the 1950s, added to two bad fouls on goalkeepers in the 1957 and 1958 English FA Cup finals, led to justified criticism of this aspect of the game and its eventual disappearance.

The first codification of the laws of football came in 1848 at Cambridge University. When the Scottish Football Association was formed in 1873, it naturally adopted the Code of Laws in operation at the time (those of the English Football Association of 1862), but such was the strength of the game in Scotland (as evidenced by the strong Scottish performances against England), that Scotland had a large say in the development of the laws.

The early years of the game allowed things such as 'handling', 'collaring' (presumably grabbing an opponent's shirt), 'hacking', and even 'shinning'. Originally there were two umpires, one for each half of the field, each with a flag and one appointed by each team. As in cricket, a player had to appeal to an umpire for a decision. By 1881, however, a referee was appointed, presumably to adjudicate if the umpires disagreed. Ten years later in 1891, the umpires were relegated to the touchline and called linesmen, and in 1894 it was confirmed that the referee should have total control of the game, and that it was no longer necessary to appeal to him.

Other landmarks in the evolution of the laws were:

1865 A tape to be stretched five feet from the ground at the top of the goal

1871 A goalkeeper (and only a goalkeeper) was allowed to handle the ball

1872 A corner kick was allowed for the attacking team

1875 A crossbar was allowed instead of a tape, and in 1882 this was recommended for international matches

1890 A penalty kick was introduced, but two years later it was decreed that the penalty taker could only kick the ball once

1895 Goalposts and crossbars must not exceed five inches in width

1902 The penalty box was set at eighteen yards from the goal line, and eighteen yards from each goal post. Previously it had been a line running the entire breadth of the field, twelve yards from goal.

1912 A goalkeeper was not allowed to handle the ball outside his own penalty area.

1913 Players were not allowed to stand within ten yards of a free kick. (Previously it had been just six yards).

1924 A goal could be scored direct from a corner kick. (In the 1929 international between Scotland and England, Alec Cheyne scored direct from a corner kick. Half the crowd at Hampden Park went mad with delight, whilst the other half looked on in stunned silence for a spell, not sure whether such a goal was legal or not).

1928 The goalkeeper had to stand still on his line when a penalty kick was being taken.

1931 The goalkeeper was allowed to carry the ball four steps as long as he bounced it.

1992 A pass-back to the goalkeeper was not allowed.

The laws of the game are now decided by FIFA, but Scotland does occasionally have its own experimental laws, e.g. in season 1973/74, in the Dryburgh Cup and the Scottish League Cup, a player could only be offside inside his opponent's penalty area and its lateral extension. The idea behind this was to encourage more attacking football and more goals, but it was quickly abandoned.

Scottish FA Chief Executive David Taylor attends the 120th International FA Board summit which regulates the Laws of the Game in 2006.

LEGGAT Graham (1934 –)

Scotland Caps: 18
Scottish League Championship medals: 1
Scottish League Cup medals: 1

A fast right-winger and a good goal scorer, Graham Leggat made his name with his hometown side, Aberdeen, playing for them with distinction in the mid 1950s. Having recovered from a broken leg, he moved to Fulham in 1958 for £16,000, and played with the Craven Cottage men for almost a decade before moving to Birmingham City, and later Rotherham United. He played eighteen games for Scotland, including two games in the 1958 World Cup finals in Sweden, but he is best remembered for the two goals he scored for Scotland against England at Hampden Park in 1956 and 1960.

LEIGHTON James (1958 –)

Scotland Caps: 91
Scottish League Championship medals: 2
Scottish Cup medals: 4
Scottish League Cup medals: 1
European Cup-Winners' Cup medals: 1

Jim Leighton was probably the greatest Scottish-born goalkeeper of recent years. He played ninety-one times for Scotland (by far the most capped goalkeeper) between the years of 1983 and 1998, in a lengthy career that saw him play for Aberdeen, Manchester United, Reading, Dundee, Hibernian and Aberdeen again. He was Aberdeen's goalkeeper in their European Cup-

Winners' Cup side of 1983, performing miracles in the archetypal Scottish conditions of mud and glaur at Gothenburg. When he joined Manchester United, his manager Alex Ferguson (with whom he had worked at Aberdeen) once famously dropped him for an FA Cup final replay in 1990, and relationships between the two men were never quite the same again. He was lithe, agile, and overcame the handicap of shortsightedness by wearing contact lenses. It was a problem with these contact lenses that compelled Jock Stein to substitute him at half time, and replace him with Alan Rough, in the World Cup game against Wales at Cardiff in 1985. He played for Scotland in three World Cup finals, in 1986, 1990 and 1998, and his total of ninety-one caps is bettered only by Kenny Dalglish. In 1997 he rejoined Aberdeen and played for them until receiving an injury in the Scottish Cup final of 2000. He also holds the record for being Scotland's oldest international player (see **AGE**)

LEISHMAN Jim (1953 –)

One of the real characters of Scottish football, Jim Leishman is always associated with Dunfermline Athletic but has also managed Montrose, Inverness Thistle and Livingston. He played for the Pars in the early 1970s, but when injury curtailed his playing career he turned to coaching. Between 1985 and 1987 he led Dunfermline to successive promotions from the Second Division and First Division, but left the club in 1990. He went to Livingston, with whom he won the Third Division and then both the Second Division and First Division. In the SPL of 2001/02, Livingston finished third and earned a place in Europe. He returned to Dunfermline Athletic in 2003 as director of football, and then became manager once again with just three games remaining of the 2004/05 season. The Pars had been facing relegation, but he inspired them to SPL survival. He stepped down from the manager's post in October 2006 and returned to being director of football. He is also a poet, takes part in musicals and pantomimes, and is an excellent after-dinner speaker. In June 2007 he was awarded an MBE for services to sport.

LEITCH Archibald (1865 – 1939)

Archie Leitch was a Glasgow-born architect who designed the main stand in many stadia throughout the United Kingdom. A Rangers supporter, Leitch won the contract for the 'New Ibrox' in 1899, and his design feature of criss-cross balustrades on the section that separated the upper tier from the lower tier was subsequently copied at grounds such as Sunderland's Roker Park and Everton's Goodison Park. Another design feature was a triangular pediment on the middle of the roof of the stand, with the name of the team inscribed. He lost a little credibility after the Ibrox disaster of 1902, but learned lessons and continued to be much in demand, contributing, at least in part, to the design of more than twenty grounds in England and Scotland.

LEITH ATHLETIC FC (former Scottish League club)

Home: **Edinburgh (list of grounds below)**
Highest League Position: **4th (Div. 1, 1891/92)**
Best Scottish Cup Performance: **Last 8 (6th round, 1889/90; 1890/91; 3rd round, 1903/04)**
Best League Cup Performance: **Last 8 (Quarter-finals, 1947/48)**

Most people who travel along Seafield Road, on the edge of Portobello, do not know that they are passing the site of the Marine Gardens, a former entertainment complex that once occupied twenty-seven acres. They are even less likely to realise that this was the home of Leith Athletic from 1928 to 1936, and when Athletic spent the 1930/31 and 1931/32 seasons in Division One, Scotland's top teams used to change in its elaborate Empress Ballroom.

Founded in 1887, the club had played at several other grounds before moving to Marine Gardens, including Old Logie Green and New Powderhall, which were also home to St Bernard's at various times. Although the Portobello site boasted many other attractions during its lifetime, including a scenic railway and even an African village, it had a reputation for being a cold and windy place during the winter months, and Athletic moved to Meadowbank in 1936.

Leith Athletic first joined the Scottish League for the 1891/92 season, which was only the second season of its existence, and played in Division One until 1895, when they finished second bottom. Because of the election system they were relegated to Division Two even though the bottom club, Dumbarton, stayed up. They won the Division Two championship in 1906, but Clyde and Hamilton were promoted instead. This was also the year when 'Athletic' was dropped from their name, and it was not re-adopted until 1919. Leith FC topped Division Two in 1909/10, and this time Raith Rovers were elected to Division One instead.

Leith stayed in Division Two until 1915, when it was abandoned during the first world war, but when it was reformed in 1921 there was no longer a place for them. When Division Three was created in 1923 they weren't part of that either. However, the club did get into Division Three in 1924 and actually came second in 1925/26. Their bad luck continued though, when Division Three ceased to exist at the end of that season and there was no automatic promotion. Forfar Athletic, who had finished third, were voted into Division Two instead. Then Nithsdale Wanderers left the league in 1927 and Leith were given their place.

Sometimes referred to as 'The Zebras' because of their black and white striped shirts, they won the Division Two championship on goal average in 1929/30, but the resulting promotion brought only two seasons in Division One and then they stayed in Division Two until the second world war. When the war was over they were placed in Division C for the 1946/47 season. They did escape into Division B for one season in 1947/48, but most of the teams in Division C were reserve sides and by 1953 Leith decided they had had enough. After refusing to play their fixtures for 1953/54, they were expelled from the league. There was one last Scottish Cup-tie in January 1954, when they lost 5–4 at Fraserburgh in the first round, but the club was eventually wound-up in May 1955. There was still an ironic twist to come though, because later that year the clubs whose first teams played in Division C were all given membership of Division B.

The following table lists the various grounds in the Edinburgh area where Leith played in the Scottish League:

(Hawkhill, Bank Park)	
Scottish League	
Bank Park (renamed Beechwood Park in 1895)	1891 - 1899
New Logie Green	1899 - 1899
Hawkhill	1899 - 1900
Chancelot Park	1900 - 1904
Old Logie Green	1904 - 1915
(Old Logie Green, Chancelot Park, Wardie Park)	
Scottish League	
Old Logie Green	1924 - 1926
(New Powderhall)	
Scottish League	
New Powderhall	1927 - 1928
Marine Gardens	1928 - 1936
Meadowbank	1936 - 1939
New Meadowbank	1946 - 1947
Old Meadowbank (reconstructed Meadowbank)	1947 - 1953

Bobby Lennox looks back as Jock Stein is chaired off the pitch by Bertie Auld, Bobby Murdoch and Billy McNeill.

LENNOX Bobby (1943 –)

Scotland Caps: 10
Scottish League Championship medals: 11
Scottish Cup medals: 8
Scottish League Cup medals: 4
European Cup medals: 1

No one typified the Jock Stein era of Celtic history more than the 'buzzbomb' Bobby Lennox. Coming from Saltcoats in Ayrshire, he was fast, intelligent, and had a tremendous zest for the game, which lasted throughout his career of almost twenty years from 1961 to 1980. He scored 273 goals for Celtic, which makes him second only to the great Jimmy McGrory. Yet until Jock Stein arrived in 1965, it looked as if Lennox was going nowhere, playing sporadically and badly on the left wing. But Jock Stein gave him more of an inside role and teamed him up with Bertie Auld. The results were electrifying and immediate, as Bobby became one of the greatest Celtic players of all time.

His eight Scottish Cup medals is a record, although he did not start in all these finals. His goals were usually well taken, and he could have had more if linesmen could have believed his acceleration, for he was frequently flagged by officials who believed that he must have been in an offside position. It is now generally agreed that the goal he scored for Celtic against Liverpool in the semi-final of the European Cup-Winners' Cup at Anfield in April 1966 was a legitimate one, but chalked off by an over-enthusiastic linesman. He played ten times for Scotland, including the famous 3–2 game at Wembley in April 1967, during which he became the first Celtic player to score at Wembley. He is also the first Celtic player to score a hat-trick at Ibrox, a feat he achieved in the Glasgow Cup in August 1966. In 1978 he tried American football for a spell with the Houston Hurricanes, but returned to Celtic Park to play, and then to take up a coaching post from 1980 to 1993. Modest and gentlemanly, but enthusiastic and energetic, he remains an excellent role model for youngsters and well worthy of the MBE that he received for his efforts.

LIDDELL Billy (1922 – 2001)

Scotland Caps: 28

Born in Dunfermline, Billy Liddell became a very talented left winger, and played twenty-eight times for Scotland during his career with Liverpool. He is still believed to be one of the best players ever to play for them (so much so that the supporters often talked about 'Liddellpool'), but he never played domestic football in Scotland other than a few wartime appearances. He joined Liverpool just at the outbreak of the second world war, during which time he served in the RAF. He was in the Liverpool side that won the English league in 1947, by which time he had earned his first Scottish cap. It was unfortunate that he did not feature in the World Cup of 1954, for it is hard to believe that he would not have made some kind of a difference to the lacklustre Scottish side. He twice played for Great Britain, against

Billy Liddell (left) watches team-mate Lawrie Reilly challenge the Austrian goalkeeper, Schmeit, in Vienna, May 1955.

the Rest of Europe and the Rest of the World in 1947 and 1955, an honour he shared with Stanley Matthews. He was a practising Christian, and was renowned for his gentlemanly demeanour on the field of play as well as for his footballing talent.

LINLITHGOW ROSE FC (see JUNIOR FOOTBALL)

LINTHOUSE FC (former Scottish League club)

Home: **Langlands Park, Govan, Glasgow**
Highest League Position: **15th (5th in Div. 2, 1897/98)**
Best Scottish Cup Performance: **Last 24 (4th round, 1889/90)**

Linthouse spent five seasons in the Scottish League, from 1895 to 1900, but coming from Govan, they were always overshadowed by Rangers. Clyde and Third Lanark were not far away, not to mention Celtic, and eventually it proved impossible to survive with so many successful teams in the vicinity.

The club was founded in 1881 and most of the early years were spent playing friendlies and cup-ties. The only league football played before 1895 was three seasons in the Scottish Alliance from 1891 to 1894, and the Alliance championship was won in 1891/92. The Linties had competed in the Scottish Cup since 1885, but achieved little of significance. Their main impact on the record books was an 8–0 victory at Hamilton in the first round of 1890/91.

Then in 1895, along with Kilmarnock, Linthouse was elected to Division Two of the Scottish League to replace Dundee Wanderers and Cowlairs. The Linties never finished higher than mid-table and it was always a struggle. After finishing bottom in 1900, they didn't even apply for re-election and soon went out of existence.

LITHUANIA

Scotland have played Lithuania six times. They have won all the home games, and in Lithuania have won one, drawn one and lost one.

1998	5 Sep	Vilnius	0–0		
1999	9 Oct	Hampden Park	3–0	Hutchison McSwegan Cameron	
2003	2 April	Kaunas	0–1		Razanauskas (pen)
2003	11 Oct	Hampden Park	1–0	Fletcher	
2006	6 Sep	Kaunas	2–1	Dailly Miller	Miceika
2007	8 Sep	Hampden Park	3–1	Boyd McManus McFadden	Danilevicius (pen)

LIVINGSTON FC (Formerly Meadowbank Thistle FC)

Ground: **Almondvale Stadium**
Nickname: **Livi Lions**
Colours: **Black and gold**
Record Attendance: **10,024 v Celtic (2001)**
Record Victory: **7-0 v Queen of the South (2000)**
Record Defeat: **0-8 v Hamilton Academical (1974)**
Highest League Position: **3rd (2001/02)**
Best Scottish Cup Performance: **Last 4 (2003/04)**
Best League Cup Performance: **Winners (2003/04)**

The Livingston story starts in the 1940s, when the works team of Ferranti Ltd. in Edinburgh played in the Lothian Welfare League as Ferranti Thistle. In 1953 they stepped up to the East of Scotland League and in 1972 became full members of the SFA, which meant that they could take part in the Scottish Cup. Good performances in the Scottish Qualifying Cup (South), which they won in 1973/74, got them into the tournament proper and they enjoyed a high profile for a non-league club. When the Scottish Football League was being increased to

Livingston's Almondvale Stadium.

thirty-eight clubs in 1974, Thistle applied for membership and won the ballot. However, attitudes to sponsorship at that time meant that the word 'Ferranti' had to be removed from their name and there were concerns about standards at their City Park ground. Edinburgh City Council offered the use of Meadowbank Stadium and part of the agreement was a change of name to 'Meadowbank Thistle'.

A runners-up place in the Second Division (third tier) in 1982/83 brought two seasons in the First Division and then the Second Division championship was won in 1986/87. The following season Meadowbank finished as runners-up in the First Division and only missed promotion to the Premier Division because it was being decreased from twelve clubs to ten.

In 1991 the ambitious Bill Hunter joined the board and soon afterwards moves began which ultimately brought about big changes to the way in which the club was run. At first the club was relegated back to the Second Division and the team was playing in front of very small crowds in a stadium that had been designed for athletics. There were complaints about the lack of atmosphere, and the cancellation of games because of competing events made matters worse.

There was much discussion about moving the club to an area where there would be more paying customers and the idea of moving to Livingston, a town with a growing population, gained popularity. There were protests from some of the fans, but Livingston Development Corporation supported the idea and eventually funding was put in place that would enable the club to move to a new stadium. The SFA gave permission to change the name to Livingston FC.

At the end of the 1994/95 season Meadowbank Thistle was relegated to the Third Division (fourth tier) in the club's last season under that name. The arrival of Jim Leishman as manager towards the end of the season couldn't save them, but the following year an impressive rise up the table began.

The Third Division title was won at the first attempt, despite having to play a few games at Meadowbank before making the move to West Lothian, and three years later the 1998/99 Second Division championship was achieved.

This success led to a substantial growth in home support and experienced players were now being signed. After only two seasons in the First Division, Livingston won the 2000/01 championship and arrived in the Scottish Premier League.

An impressive third place in that first 2001/02 season earned them a place in the UEFA Cup and later in 2002 Sturm Graz were beaten 4–3 in a first round tie at Almondvale, although the Austrians went through on aggregate. The following year Livi became the first British club to have a Brazilian head coach, when Marcio Maximo Barcellos arrived. He left for personal reasons after just four months and then his replacement David Hay led them to their first major trophy when Hibs were beaten 2–0 in the final of the 2003/04 League Cup. This was all less than nine years after relegation to the Third Division.

This success was unfortunately accompanied by financial difficulties and the club entered administration for a time, but then the 'Lionheart Consortium', led by Irish businessman Pearse Flynn, took control in May 2005 and this heralded a new beginning. However, the club's position in the SPL became ever more precarious, and culminated in relegation to the First Division at the end of the 2005/06 season. Manager Paul Lambert resigned in February 2006 and it was then John Robertson who was charged with taking them back to the top tier. He was sacked in April 2007 after results did not match expectations, but in 2007/08, with Mark Proctor now in charge, Livi were not amongst the challengers for promotion.

LOAN DEALS

These are allowed at certain points of the season, although some clubs may insist that the loaned player does not play against them. Celtic for example refused permission for on-loan David Fernandez to play against them in the Scottish Cup semi final of 2004. It may be a case of a young player being 'farmed out' from a larger club to a smaller club for experience or it may be that a club has a problem in a specialist position, notably goalkeeper and has to borrow a goalkeeper from another club. The most remarkable example of this was Tom Sinclair of Rangers in 1906. Celtic's goalkeeper Davie Adams had injured himself playing in a benefit match for a Rangers player, so with a guilty conscience bothering them, Rangers offered reserve goalkeeper Tom Sinclair. Sinclair then had eight shut-outs for Celtic (six in the league and two in the Glasgow Cup). When he eventually did concede a couple of goals in the Glasgow Cup final of 6 October 1906, Celtic won the game anyway, so that Sinclair returned to Ibrox with a medal, more than he had ever done for Rangers! It is hard to imagine this happening a century later!

LOCHGELLY UNITED FC
(former Scottish League club)

Home: **Recreation Park, Lochgelly, Fife**
Highest League Position: **30th (10th in Div. 2, 1914/15; 1922/23)**
Best Scottish Cup Performance: **Last 16 (3rd round, 1919/20)**

Lochgelly United FC was founded in 1890, when Lochgelly Athletic merged with Fifeshire Hibernians. Originally based at School's Park, they moved to Reid's Park in 1901, and then found a new home at Recreation Park in 1910. Known locally as 'The Reccy', the ground was on land where houses now stand, not far from the 'Lochgelly Centre' building. In the early years the club played friendly matches and entered cup competitions such as the Fife Cup and the East of Scotland Cup. In 1891 they entered the Scottish Cup for the first time.

United played some fixtures in the short-lived Central League that existed from 1896 to 1898, and then in 1902 they tried league football once again when they joined the Northern League. Although they never won the championship, the club enjoyed some good seasons, with the result that their best players were frequently lost to bigger clubs. In 1905 the Scottish Cup brought the excitement of a second-round tie away to Celtic, which was lost 3–0.

In 1909 United were one of the clubs that formed a new Central League, but after three seasons they were in severe financial difficulties, which were exacerbated by a miners' strike. The club reformed, without limited company status, and played a season in each of the Northern League and Central League, until in 1914 their dreams came true. The Scottish League was expanding and they were elected to one of the two new places. United played in Division Two for the 1914/15 season, after which the first world war brought Division Two to a temporary halt.

It wasn't reformed until 1921 and from 1919 to 1921 United played in the new Eastern League and then the new Central League. After the re-birth of Division Two, their league form was indifferent, but once again there were Scottish Cup ties against the top teams. In 1922/23 Celtic won a first round tie at Lochgelly by three goals to two and in both 1923/24 and 1925/26 there were defeats at Ibrox.

United's third post-war season in Division Two was disastrous. They finished bottom in 1924, with only 12 points from 38 games, and were relegated to Division Three, which had just completed its first season. When Division Three went out of existence in 1926, they had not managed to gain promotion back to Division Two and their short time in the Scottish League came to an end.

Although they then played in the Scottish Alliance for a season, as well as in cup matches, their financial problems finally became too great and in 1928 they went out of existence. The final match was a 3–1 away defeat to Brechin City in the first round of the Scottish Cup on 21 January 1928.

LOGAN James (1890 –)

James Logan was the manager of Raith Rovers in their glory years immediately after the first world war. In 1922 Raith Rovers were third in the Scottish League, and in 1924 they were fourth, as Logan built up a strong team with men like Dave Morris, Will Collier, John 'Tokey' Duncan and Alec James. Logan played in the Raith Rovers team that reached the final of the Scottish Cup in 1913, and in the first world war he joined up at the outbreak and reached the rank of Captain by 1918.

LONG SERVICE

Long service is not a phrase that comes readily to one's lips in the context of twenty-first century Scottish football, for neither players, managers nor anyone else last very long in any one particular post. But Willie Maley was manager of Celtic from 1897 until 1940. He was match secretary before that, after he retired from playing for the club in 1896. He had played in their first match in 1888, so his involvement with Celtic lasted an astonishing 52 years. On the playing side there are two players who have played 22 seasons for their club – Dougie Gray of Rangers from 1925 until 1947, and Alec McNair of Celtic from 1903 until 1925, but Gray has the edge over McNair in that he played more games (879 as against 740), and in any case McNair was farmed out to Stenhousemuir for his first season.

Dougie Gray of Rangers.

The short service record is a difficult one to check up on for there are several claims that a man had been appointed five minutes before a phone call came to offer him another and better job, but one that can certainly be substantiated is that of Steve Murray who was appointed manager of Forfar Athletic on 19 August 1980 and resigned on 22 August 1980 without ever having seen them play a competitive game! The one training session that he saw must have been pretty dreadful!

LONGEST GAMES

A game should, of course, last ninety minutes, but a welcome innovation in recent years has been the appearance of a man holding up a board (the fourth official), indicating the number of extra minutes to be added on. Famously on 8 February 1989, in a World Cup qualifier in Cyprus, Scotland scored a winner in the ninety-sixth minute, six minutes having been added on because of Cypriot time wasting.

In the Scottish Cup, since the introduction of a penalty shoot-out after extra time in a replay in season 1989/90, ties have had to be decided after two games, i.e. after a game at each of the venues of the two clubs. Some people feel this is unfair, but it is generally considered the best way of resolving issues, because a penalty shoot-out is a footballing skill. The 1990 and 2006 Scottish Cup finals were resolved this way, without even the recourse to a replay. Many fans felt that one replay was not too much to ask for, but it was not hard to see the interest of worldwide television in this issue, for they naturally enough wanted to see the issue settled in one day. As it happened, excitement in 1990 was intense as Aberdeen beat Celtic 9–8 on penalties after neither side had found the net in ninety minutes plus the added thirty for extra time, and 2006 was similarly exciting, exhilarating, or heartbreaking, depending on one's standpoint, with something like two-thirds of Scotland's population watching the penalty shoot-out, although they hadn't all necessarily watched the game!

Prior to the introduction of penalty shoot-outs, five games were necessary to find a winner on one occasion in Scottish Cup history (i.e. the original game and four replays). This was Broxburn versus Beith on Saturday 23 January, Saturday 30 January, Wednesday 3 February, Thursday 4 February and Friday 5 February 1909, before Beith eventually won 4–2 at Love Street. They did not have long to celebrate, however, because they lost in the next round to St Mirren on Saturday February 6, on the same ground where they had eventually won through in the previous round! Four games have been necessary on eleven occasions. These were:

1888/89	Third Lanark	v	Abercorn
1900/01	St Mirren	v	Third Lanark
1905/06	Port Glasgow Athletic	v	Kilmarnock
1919/20	Raith Rovers	v	East Stirlingshire
1920/21	Falkirk	v	Alloa
1920/21	Armadale	v	Albion Rovers
1923/24	Airdrie	v	Ayr United
1929/30	Falkirk	v	Leith Athletic
1934/35	Ayr United	v	King's Park
1955/56	Brechin City	v	Peebles Rovers
1982/83	Partick Thistle	v	Kilmarnock

The Scottish Cup final has never needed four games, but three games have been necessary on four occasions, namely:

1877	Vale of Leven	3	2	Rangers
	(After 0–0 and 1–1)			
1903	Rangers	2	0	Hearts
	(After 0–0 and 1–1)			
1910	Dundee	2	1	Clyde
	(After 2–2 and 0–0)			
1979	Rangers	3	2	Hibernian
	(After 0–0 and 0–0)			

The 1979 Scottish Cup final was eventually finished on 28 May, the latest day up to that point for an official Scottish domestic game in peace time, for 1979 had been a bad winter, and international fixtures had caused further delays. In 1909 a third game should have been played to decide the issue between Celtic and Rangers, but the crowd rioted after the second game, believing (not entirely without justification) that they had been cheated out of extra time, and that the third game was scheduled simply for more money.

The 1938 Scottish Cup was remarkable because it was won by second division East Fife, the only team to have done so from a lower division, but also because it took them eleven games and seventeen and a half hours (including replays and extra time) to do so. They beat Airdrie and Dundee United at the first time of asking, but then took two games each to beat Aberdeen and Raith Rovers, three to beat St Bernard's in the semi-final and two games plus extra time to get the better of Kilmarnock in the final. In 1947, the first official season after the second world war, 142 minutes were played in the semi-final between Motherwell and Hibs on 29 March at Hampden Park. Rather than have a replay, both teams had agreed to play on after extra time until a goal was scored. After extra time, the score was still 1–1, but they played on until Hibs scored a decisive goal. It was a primitive example of the 'golden goal' rule!

Another 'longest game' record is held by Airdrie versus Stranraer, whose Scottish Cup first round tie was scheduled for 12 January 1963, and was eventually played on 11 March 1963, having been postponed thirty-three times in the intervening two months of the infamous 1963 freeze-up. A close second is the Inverness Thistle versus Falkirk game of 1979, which was postponed twenty-nine times, and which caused referee Brian McGinlay of Balfron to name his house 'Kingsmills' after the name of the Inverness Thistle ground! He had been there so often just to say 'Match off'!

LORIMER Peter (1946 –)

Scotland Caps: 21

Born in Dundee, Peter Lorimer spent more or less his entire career with Leeds United from 1963 until 1986, although he did have an interlude with York City, Toronto Blizzard and Vancouver Whitecaps between 1979 and 1983. After he left Elland Road for the second time he also briefly played in Israel.

Youngsters (and Billy Bremner) mob Peter Lorimer after he scores a goal for Scotland.

He played twenty-one times for Scotland, and was a fine centre forward with a cannonball shot. He was only fifteen when he played his first game for Leeds United. Under Don Revie, he won the Inter Cities Fairs Cup in 1968, the English league (twice), the FA Cup and the English League Cup. For Scotland, he played in the 1974 World Cup finals, scoring the first goal against Zaire.

LUXEMBOURG

Scotland have registered two victories over tiny Luxembourg, but in 1987 a side captained by Alex McLeish only managed a disappointing 0–0 draw.

1947	24 May	Luxembourg-Ville	6–0	Flavell (2) Steel (2) McLaren Forbes	
1986	12 Nov	Hampden Park	3–0	Cooper (2) Johnston	
1987	2 Dec	Esch-sur-Alzette	0–0		

McALLISTER Gary (1964 –)

Scotland Caps: 57

Gary McAllister was a midfielder who won fifty-seven caps for Scotland in the 1990s, playing in the European Championships of 1992 and 1996, and being awarded the MBE for 'Services to Football' in 2001. Unfortunately, he will always be remembered as the man who missed a penalty for Scotland against England at Wembley in 1996. Cruelly, many Scottish fans never forgave him, and when he was substituted in a game against the Czech Republic at Celtic Park in 1999, the crowd booed him in a way that was uncharacteristic of the Tartan Army. He played for Motherwell, Leicester City, Leeds United, Coventry City, Liverpool and then Coventry City as player/manager. With Leeds United he won the English league championship in 1992, but it was with Liverpool, in the Indian summer of his career, that he won most honours. He won five cup medals with the Anfield club in 2001/02 – the English League Cup, the FA Cup, the UEFA Cup, the Charity Shield, and the European Super Cup, often making a decisive contribution, and (annoyingly for Scottish fans) converting penalties! In January 2008 Gary was appointed manager of Leeds United.

MACARI Lou (1949 –)

Scotland Caps: 24
Scottish League Championship medals: 2
Scottish Cup medals: 2

Lou Macari (left), seen here with George Graham.

A talented but controversial character, Lou Macari won twenty-four caps for Scotland. He joined Celtic in 1966, and was at once recognised as having talent, becoming known as one of the 'quality street kids' who included Danny McGrain, Kenny Dalglish and Davie Hay. He broke through into the Celtic team about 1970, and won two Scottish League championship medals and two Scottish Cup medals before he shook the Celtic fans by asking for a transfer. They adored his cheekiness, style of play, and ability to take a goal, and the famous American cowboy song was adapted to 'Lou, Lou, skip to my lou, skip to my Lou Macari.' He then joined Manchester United in early 1973 for £200,000 (a record at the time for a Scottish player) and, although Manchester United were relegated in 1974, Macari was with them as they bounced back to win the Second Division championship in 1975 and the FA Cup in 1977. He was seldom far from controversy – on one occasion in a Manchester derby being sent off and refusing to go. All in all, he won twenty-four international caps for Scotland. His international debut was in 1972 but he dropped out of the scene for a few years before coming back to take part in the Argentina World Cup of 1978. He had a poor World Cup, and then stated that he never wanted to play for Scotland again, a request that was granted. Once his playing career was over he became a manager with Swindon Town (where he was sacked and then re-instated seven days later), West Ham United, Birmingham City, Stoke City, Celtic, Stoke City (again) and Huddersfield Town. He was never far from the headlines in an eventful career. His time as manager of Celtic was at the nadir of the club's history in 1993/94, and it is unfair to blame him for all that went wrong there, for this was the time when the Kelly board collapsed and Fergus McCann took over. He did not long survive the arrival of McCann.

McCALL Stuart (1964 –)

Scotland Caps: 40
Scottish League Championship medals: 6
Scottish Cup medals: 3
Scottish League Cup medals: 2
An intelligent midfielder, who won forty caps for Scotland in the 1990s, Stuart McCall took part in the 1990 World Cup finals in Italy and the 1992 European Championships in Sweden. The highlight of his international career was the goal he scored against Sweden in the 1990 World Cup. He was born in Leeds of Scottish parentage, and his first senior team was Bradford City. He moved to Everton in 1988 for £875,000, and then to Rangers for £1.2 million in 1991, before returning to Bradford City in 1998 and helping them reach the English Premiership. In 2002 he moved to Sheffield United and later became their assistant manager. He again returned to Bradford City in June 2007, this time as manager.

McCANN Fergus (1942 –)

The Canadian tycoon who bought Celtic from the Kelly regime in 1994, Fergus McCann was responsible for the building of the massive new stadium, and the saving of the club from bankruptcy and mediocrity, particularly through the share issue to fans. He was born in Scotland and travelled on the Croy Celtic supporters' bus to games before he went to Canada and made his fortune.

McCANN Neil (1974 –)

Scotland Caps: 26
Scottish Premier League medals: 3
Scottish Cup medals: 5
Scottish League Cup medals: 1
Neil McCann is an attack-minded forward from Greenock, who has won twenty-six caps for Scotland and has played for Dundee (1992-1996), Hearts (1996-1999), Rangers (1999-2003), Southampton (2003-2006), and Hearts again from January 2006.

McCLAIR Brian (1963 –)

Scotland Caps: 30
Scottish League Championship medals: 1
Scottish Cup medals: 1
Brian McClair was a talented goal scorer for Motherwell, Celtic and Manchester United. He was known as 'Choccy', because his name rhymes with '(chocolate) éclair'! His first team was Aston Villa, for whom he made little impact, but then, after a couple of successful seasons with Motherwell, he joined Celtic in 1983. With

them he won the Scottish Cup and the Scottish League, scoring 121 goals, and becoming the Scottish Player of the Year in 1987 in the opinion of both the Football Writers and the Professional Footballers. He then went to Manchester United for £850,000 (as a transfer tribunal judged), and with United won the English league four times, the FA Cup twice, and the English League Cup and the European Cup-Winners' Cup once each. He won thirty caps for Scotland, and took part in the European Championships in Sweden in 1992. He then returned to Motherwell, but after his career was over he involved himself in coaching.

McCOIST Ally (1962 –)

Scotland Caps: 61
Scottish League Championship medals: 9
Scottish Cup medals: 1
Scottish League Cup medals: 9
A striker for St Johnstone, Sunderland, Rangers and Kilmarnock, Ally McCoist won sixty-one caps for Scotland between 1986 and 1999. He also developed a

successful media career, particularly in the BBC programme *Question of Sport,* where he typified the gallus Scottish attitude with his 'cheeky chappie' image. He played for St Johnstone until 1981, when he was transferred to Sunderland for the least successful part of his career. It was with Rangers (to whom he came in 1983) that he played his best football, scoring 355 goals and winning nine Scottish League championship medals, one Scottish Cup medal, and nine Scottish League Cup medals. He is the highest Scottish goal scorer since the second world war.

He was a predatory striker, teaming up well with Mark Hateley in the successful Rangers team of the 1990s, and earning the nickname 'Super Ally'. He was awarded the MBE for his efforts, as well as Player of the Year by both the Football Writers and Professional Footballers in 1992. He finished his career with Kilmarnock and was still being picked for Scotland as late as 1999, although, controversially, he was not in the squad for the 1998 World Cup. He had been working with Scotland as a coach on a match-to-match basis before returning to Ibrox in January 2007 as assistant manager to Walter Smith.

McCOLL Ian (1927 –)

Scotland Caps: 14
Scottish League Championship medals: 6
Scottish Cup medals: 5
Scottish League Cup medals: 2
Grandson of William McColl, who once played for Scotland in 1895, Ian McColl was a wing half who won fourteen caps for Scotland in the 1950s. He was born in Alexandria, that cradle of Scottish football, and made his name with Queen's Park in the latter years of the second world war. He then went to Rangers, having turned professional in 1945 while studying at Glasgow University for a B.Sc. in Engineering. Playing for

Rangers between 1945 and 1960, his play was characterised by rugged aggression (he was a member of Rangers Iron Curtain defence), as well as cultured and visionary passing. He became Scotland team manager from 1960 until 1965. His big failures included the 3–9 defeat at Wembley in April 1961 and the disappointment of not qualifying (after a heart–breaking play-off against Czechoslovakia in Brussels) for the Chile World Cup of 1962, in which Scotland might have done well. On the other hand he deserves a great deal of credit for the three consecutive victories against England in 1962, 1963 and 1964 – a feat not achieved since the 1880s. He left in 1965 to become manager of Sunderland, where he remained for three years before taking up a job outside football.

McCOLL Robert (1876 – 1959)

Scotland Caps: 13
Nicknamed 'Toffee Bob' because of his confectionery shops, Robert McColl is well known today as the famous R S McColl of modern day high streets. A centre forward, he was originally an amateur with Queen's Park from 1894 onwards, before turning professional by joining Newcastle in 1901. He then returned to Rangers in 1904, before in 1907 (most unusually) reinstating himself as an amateur with Queen's Park. On 26 April 1910 he scored all six goals as Queen's Park beat Port Glasgow Athletic 6-1. In spite of his great skills, he never won any domestic honour in either Scotland or England, although he was on the losing side in two cup finals.

His international career of thirteen caps is remarkable in that he three times scored hat-tricks, including his immortal three goals against England in what became known as the Rosebery International at Celtic Park in 1900. He was famous for his sporting attitude to the game, and he built his business on the strength of his success at football.

McCREADIE Eddie (1940 –)

Scotland Caps: 23

A steady, reliable left back for Scotland during the late 1960s, McCreadie was famous for his hard unflinching tackles, although he was never a dirty player. He won twenty-three Scottish caps, and although he never appeared in any major finals for Scotland, he did play in the famous 1967 game against England. He joined Chelsea in 1962 from East Stirlingshire, and from then on was a one-club man until the mid 1970s, when he became Chelsea's manager for a spell. He won the FA Cup with Chelsea in 1970, and the English League Cup in 1965, playing in the latter game as centre forward and scoring a goal.

McFADDEN Jamie (1983 –)

Scotland Caps: 37

A forward for Motherwell and Everton, Jamie McFadden is an established Scotland internationalist. He earned worldwide admiration for the goal that he scored for Scotland against France in Paris in September 2007, and has scored other great goals for his country. He first played for Motherwell in 2000, and was transferred to Everton in September 2003. In January 2008 he left Merseyside to join former Scotland manager Alex McLeish at Birmingham City.

McGHEE Mark (1957 –)

Scotland Caps: 4
Scottish League Championship medals: 3
Scottish Cup medals: 5
European Cup Winners Cup medals: 1

A player with a good record of goalscoring, Mark McGhee played for Greenock Morton, Newcastle United (twice), Aberdeen, Hamburg, Celtic and Reading. He was named Player of the Year in 1981, and won a European Cup-Winners' Cup medal with Aberdeen in 1983. Turning to management, he was in charge of Leicester City, Reading, Wolves, Millwall and Brighton. The highlight of his managerial career was reaching the semi-finals of the FA Cup with Wolves in 1998, when many people thought they were unlucky to go down 1–0 to Arsenal. In 2007, after a short spell out of the game, he became the manager of Motherwell, whom he took to third place in the SPL in 2007/08.

Mark McGhee won the Cup-Winners' Cup with Aberdeen as a player, and as manager took Motherwell to their first European qualification for 13 years by finishing 3rd in the SPL in 2007/08.

McGRAIN Danny (1950 –)

Scotland Caps: 62
Scottish League champions medals: 7
Scottish Cup medals: 5
Scottish League Cup medals: 2

Danny McGrain, acknowledged throughout the game as one of Celtic's and Scotland's best-ever right backs, joined Celtic in 1967 and thus began a career that

Danny McGrain with Kenny Dalglish and the Home International Championship trophy, won in 1976.

Jimmy McGrory and Aberdeen's Willie Cooper chase the ball during the 1937 Scottish Cup final.

spanned almost twenty years. His sixty-two caps for Scotland included some fine performances with his hard tackling, strength of character, and visionary passing. His career was plagued with many minor injuries and three major problems that would have ended the career of lesser men. In 1972, in a game against Falkirk at Brockville, he fractured his skull; in 1974, immediately after the World Cup finals in West Germany, he was diagnosed with diabetes; and in 1978 he was kept out of the Argentina World Cup with a mysterious foot injury which deprived him of about eighteen months football. In later years he was manager of Arbroath for a while, and is one of the few players in Scottish football to have sported a beard. Jock Stein, according to legend, disapproved but could do nothing about it because Danny was such a great and loyal player. He was awarded the MBE in 1983.

McGRORY James (1904 – 1982)

Scotland Caps: 7
Scottish League Championship medals: 2
Scottish Cup medals: 4

One of Scotland's most famous players of all time, James McGrory played centre forward for Celtic between 1922 and 1937. He then became manager of Kilmarnock, before returning to Parkhead in 1945 to serve as manager until 1965. When Jock Stein took over that year McGrory remained as public relations officer. He scored 522 goals for Celtic (including seventy-four in the Scottish Cup), plus another sixteen in season 1923/24 when he was 'farmed out' to Clydebank. His six goals for Scotland and six for the Scottish League brought his career total to 550. However, this does not tell the whole story. He scored fifty goals in season 1935/36, a hat-trick in three minutes against Motherwell in March 1936, and eight in one game against Dunfermline in January 1928. He is remembered for his brilliant diving headers, notably in the 1925 Scottish Cup final. On the internat-ional scene, he scored for Scotland against England in 1931 and 1933; the 1933 game being the famous one in which he picked up a ball from Bob McPhail and scored the goal which, according to legend, caused the birth of the Hampden Roar. He was never picked for Scotland against England at Wembley, and no one has been able to explain satisfactorily why he only played a total of seven times for Scotland. As a manager with Celtic he was less successful, lacking the necessary ruthlessness, but even so deserves credit for the Coronation Cup win in 1953, the league and cup double of 1954 and the 7–1 defeat of Rangers in the Scottish League Cup final of 1957/58. He was renowned throughout Scotland as a gentleman, both as a player and a manager, and was much mourned when he died in October 1982.

McINALLY Tommy (1900 – 1955)

Scotland Caps: 2
Scottish League Championship medals: 2
Scottish Cup medals: 1

Tommy McInally was a charismatic but ultimately disappointing player. He made his debut for Celtic in 1919 as a free-scoring forward, and was adored by the Celtic faithful, who loved his ability to entertain and show off. He fell out with manager Maley and was transferred to Third Lanark in 1922, but returned in 1925 to the great delight of the Celtic crowd. He led Celtic to the league championship in 1926 and the Scottish Cup in 1927. But he could never quite handle the strict discipline required to be a professional footballer, and his career must be considered to be one of under-achievement, even though he was possibly one of the most talented players that Scotland ever produced. He moved to Sunderland in 1928, but is another classic example of the Scottish penchant for self-destruction.

MACKAY Dave (1934 –)

Scotland Caps: 22
Scottish League Championships medals: 1
Scottish League Cup medals: 2

Dave Mackay was a right half who won twenty-two caps for Scotland in a lengthy career that spanned the 1950s and 1960s. He joined Hearts from Newtongrange Star in 1952, and was part of the excellent Hearts team of the 1950s. To the intense disappointment of the Tynecastle fans, he was transferred to Tottenham Hotspur in 1959 for £32,000, and with Spurs he won both the English League championship and the FA Cup in 1960/61 (the first team to win the English double in the twentieth century). He won the FA Cup again with Spurs in 1961/62 and 1966/67. He then moved to Derby County and played a great part in taking them back to Division One of the English league. He was later manager of Swindon Town, Nottingham Forest, Derby County (with whom he won the English league championship in 1975) and Walsall. He was renowned as a hard man and a great fighter, as was proved by the way that he twice came back from a broken leg.

Tosh McKinlay.

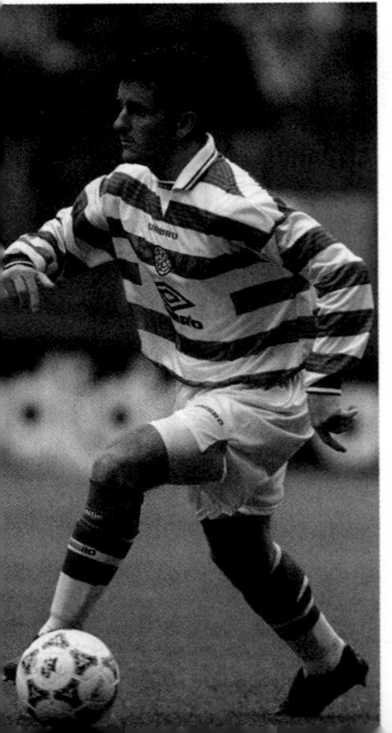

McKIMMIE Stewart (1962 –)

Scotland Caps: 40
Scottish League Championship medals 2
Scottish Cup medals: 3
Scottish League Cup medals: 3

A right back, Stewart McKimmie won forty caps for Scotland, and featured in the 1990 World Cup finals as well as the European Championships of 1992 and 1996. He was born in Aberdeen, but his first senior team was Dundee, to whom Alex Ferguson paid £90,000 for him in 1983. He arrived at Pittodrie just too late to play in the European Cup-Winners' Cup triumph of 1983, although he did take part in the European Super Cup. He then played for the Dons for most of his footballing life before finishing his career with Dundee United.

McKINLAY Billy (1969 –)

Scotland Caps: 29

Billy McKinlay was an energetic midfielder with twenty-nine caps for Scotland, including an appearance against Brazil in the 1990 World Cup finals. He joined Dundee United in 1986 and soon made an impact, but sadly missed Dundee United's Scottish Cup win in 1994 because of suspension. He then joined Blackburn Rovers for £1.75 million in 1995 and subsequently played for Leicester City (twice), Bradford City, Preston North End, Clydebank and Fulham.

McKINLAY Tosh (1964 –)

Scotland Caps: 22
Scottish Cup medals: 1

Tosh McKinlay was a useful left sided defender and midfield player, who won twenty-two caps for Scotland, taking part in the 1996 European Championships in England and the 1998 World Cup finals in France. He joined Dundee in 1983, moved to Hearts in 1988, and then in November 1994 to Celtic, with whom he won a Scottish Cup medal in 1995. He is one of the very few players to have played in all three city derbies in Dundee, Edinburgh and Glasgow. He later played for Stoke City and Kilmarnock, but then became an agent.

McKINNON Ron (1940 –)

Scotland Caps: 28
Scottish League Championship medals: 2
Scottish Cup medals: 4
Scottish League Cup medals: 3

A centre half for Rangers in the 1960s, Ron McKinnon won twenty-eight caps for Scotland (including the famous 3–2 win over England at Wembley in 1967) and, as a player for both club and country, radiated calm and assurance. For Rangers, the half back line of Greig, McKinnon and Baxter of the early sixties was rated one of their best ever, but a broken leg prevented him appearing in the European Cup-Winners' Cup final of 1972, and brought his career to a premature close.

McLAREN Alan (1971 –)

Scotland Caps: 24
Scottish League Championship medals: 3
Scottish Cup medals: 1

A full back who played for Hearts and Rangers in the late 1980s and 1990s, Alan McLaren won twenty-four caps for Scotland. With Rangers, whom he joined in 1994 for £2.1 million in a part-exchange deal with Dave McPherson, he won many honours, but his career was bedevilled by serious injury to the extent that he had to retire early from the game.

McLEAN Archie (1886 – 1971)

A textile engineer from Paisley, Archie McLean is remembered in Brazil as a man who was influential in the development of Brazilian football. In 1912, having already played for Johnstone and Ayr United, he went to work in the Sao Paulo factory of his employers, J & P Coats. He soon formed the 'Scottish Wanderers' football team, and discovered that local players based their game on long-ball tactics. Under Archie McLean's guidance, the Brazilians started to improve their skill and technique, and the short passing game became a feature of their play. His outstanding form on the wing for teams in Sao Paulo resulted in him representing Sao Paulo state, but many people believe that his legacy lies in the skilful football that has become associated with teams from Brazil.

McLEAN James (1937 –)

One of the real characters of Scottish football, James McLean is the man responsible for taking Dundee United from virtually nothing to being a successful team in Europe, reaching a UEFA Cup Final in 1987 (beating Barcelona en route) and a European Cup semi final in 1984, although sadly, he never quite won a trophy. He was born in Lanarkshire of a footballing family (his brothers Tommy and Willie both took part in professional football), and played for Clyde, Dundee and Kilmarnock but he was a good, rather than a great, player.

Dundee United manager Jim McLean (left) with Gundar Bengtson, coach-manager of IFK Gothenburg.

He became coach with Dundee in 1970, but then amazed the city by moving across the road to the manager's job at Tannadice Park in December 1971. Slowly, and determinedly, he built up Dundee United, concentrating on good defence but also bringing on flair players like Andy Gray and Paul Sturrock. He took them to ten Scottish Cup and League Cup finals but never won a final at Hampden, losing repeatedly to Celtic, Rangers, St Mirren and, poignantly, in 1991 to a Motherwell side managed by his brother Tommy on the same week that their father had died. He won the Scottish League Cup twice, beating Aberdeen in 1979 and Dundee in 1980, and curiously both games were played at Dens Park. It was fitting too that his greatest domestic triumph – the lifting of the Scottish Premier League trophy – should also occur at Dens Park. This was in 1983 when United beat Dundee on the last day of the season.

In the late 1980s he was a director as well as a manager, but finally relinquished the managerial chair in 1993. For a while, his brother Tommy managed the club that he directed, so that Dundee United earned the nickname 'the Brothers Grimm'. Jim's formal involvement with Dundee United ended sadly in October 2000 when he was involved in a violent altercation with a BBC reporter. Reputed to be dour and unsociable, Jim is nevertheless one of the best loved characters in the Scottish game, and no one can deny what he has achieved with his beloved Dundee United.

McLEISH Alex (1959 –)

Scotland Caps: 77
Scottish League Championship medals: 3
Scottish Cup medals: 5
Scottish League Cup medals: 2
European Cup-Winners' Cup medals: 1

Alex McLeish was a dignified and resolute defender for Aberdeen and Scotland, and continues to retain the

Alex McLeish, statistically one of Scotland's most successful managers, with a win percentage of 70%.

quality of dignity in his managerial career. He won the first of his seventy-seven Scotland caps in 1980, and retained an almost automatic place in the team, along with his Aberdeen partner Willie Miller, until 1993, playing in the World Cup finals of 1982, 1986 and 1990. His club career as a player was entirely with Aberdeen after he joined them in 1976. In a period of unparalleled success for the Dons, McLeish won a European Cup-Winners' Cup medal in 1983, three Scottish League championship medals, five Scottish Cup medals and two Scottish League Cup medals.

When he retired from playing he moved into management, managing Motherwell, Hibernian and Rangers. 'Eck' took Hibs to the Scottish Cup final in 2001, and with Rangers he won seven domestic honours – the SPL in 2003 and 2005, the Scottish Cup in 2002 and 2003, and the Scottish League Cup in 2002, 2003 and 2005, but a season without trophies in 2005/06 ensured his departure. He was not idle for long, because in January 2007 he was appointed manager of Scotland. After a certain amount of success, which took Scotland to the brink of qualification for the European Championships, he departed to Birmingham City, to the distress of the nation, in November 2007.

MacLEOD Ally (1931 – 2004)

Ally MacLeod is the man who will forever be remembered for taking Scotland to the Argentina World Cup of 1978, for which he deserves credit, and the subsequent disaster once we got there, for which he must accept his portion of the blame. He was no bad player himself as left half for Third Lanark, St Mirren, Blackburn Rovers, Hibs and Ayr United, but he won neither an international cap nor a winner's medal. The highlight of his playing career was the 1960 English FA Cup final, in which he played brilliantly for Blackburn Rovers, but the team lost to Wolves. On retiring from the playing side of the game, he became the outspoken manager of Ayr United until 1975, when he moved to Aberdeen, immediately transforming the douce city into a football-mad centre, where Union Street resounded to the peeping of car horns in November 1976 when the Dons won the Scottish League Cup and briefly challenged for the league championship.

However, in spring 1977 Ally MacLeod could not resist the challenge of becoming the manager of Scotland. He beat England at Wembley in June 1977, then took the team on a successful tour of South America before winning the two crucial World Cup qualifiers against Czechoslovakia and Wales to take Scotland to the Argentina World Cup of 1978.With the nation swept away by euphoria (encouraged to no small extent by MacLeod himself) he made the fatal mistake of not heeding the warnings of a defeat by England on the eve of departure and of neglecting to go and watch the opponents. Disaster followed disaster in Argentina (not all of it MacLeod's fault e.g. the superior attitude of some of the players and Willie Johnston's being sent home for taking illegal substances) and even though Scotland beat Holland at the end, MacLeod's sacking was inevitable.

This was by no means the end of his managerial career, for he managed Motherwell, Airdrie, Ayr United (again) and Queen of the South, before finally bowing out of the game in the mid 1990s. In his latter years, he was unable to remember much of his playing and managerial career.

MacLEOD Murdo (1958 –)

Scotland Caps: 20
Scottish League Championship medals: 4
Scottish Cup medals: 2
Scottish League Cup medals 1

An intelligent and creative midfielder, Murdo MacLeod won twenty caps for Scotland, and many people felt that he should have won more. His first team was Dum-

Midfielder Murdo Macleod won 22 Scotland caps and played for Celtic, Dumbarton, Hibernian, Partick Thistle and Borussia Dortmund.

barton, but he moved to join Billy McNeill's Celtic in late 1978, and very quickly became a favourite of the Parkhead support. He left Parkhead in 1987 to try his luck in German football with Borussia Dortmund. In later years he had spells in management with Hibs and Dumbarton, and was assistant manager to Wim Jansen in season 1997/98 at Celtic, when they won the Scottish League and the Scottish League Cup. On leaving Parkhead, he became a radio and TV pundit. He was known as 'Rhino', and his international career included the 1990 World Cup finals in Italy.

McMENEMY Jimmy (1880 – 1965)

Scotland Caps: 12
Scottish League Championship medals: 11
Scottish Cup medals: 7

One of the greatest inside forwards that Scottish football has ever seen, Jimmy McMenemy was nicknamed 'Napoleon', and played for Celtic between 1902 and 1920, followed by Partick Thistle until 1922, and then, briefly, Stenhousemuir. He also won twelve caps for Scotland and holds the record for being Scotland's oldest outfield player (see **AGE**). He was part of the great Celtic side of the Edwardian era, and the other great Celtic side during the first world war. His record of eleven Scottish League medals and seven Scottish Cup medals (one with Partick Thistle in 1921) speaks for itself. His international career is distinguished by the part he played in Scotland's victories against England in 1910 and 1914. Having been out of the game for several years, Napoleon was brought back to be the trainer for Celtic in the late 1930s. Given the advancing years and infirmity of manager Willie Maley, this in fact meant that he ran the team, and he therefore deserves great credit for the fine Celtic side of that era, which distinguished itself by winning the Empire Exhibition Trophy of 1938. His son John McMenemy played for Celtic and Motherwell, and the legendary Southampton manager Lawrie McMenemy is his great-nephew.

McMILLAN Ian (1931 –)

Scotland Caps: 6
Scottish League Championship medals: 3
Scottish Cup medals: 2
Scottish League Cup medals: 2

Ian McMillan is generally believed to be one of the best ball players that Airdrie and Rangers ever had, and it was his misfortune to play at a time when ball skills such as dribbling were beginning to go out of the game. He began his career with Airdrieonians and, by the time that Rangers came for him in 1958, he had already won five of his six Scottish caps. For Rangers he was a superb player, disdaining physical contact and concentrating on actually playing the game, so that he was given the nickname 'the Wee Prime Minister', for the Prime Minister of Great Britain at the time was Harold McMillan. In 1964 he returned to his native town of Airdrie and served as player, coach, manager, and director of Airdrieonians.

McMULLAN Jimmy (1895 – 1964)

Scotland Caps: 16

The captain of Scotland in the famous Wembley Wizards international of 1928, Jimmy McMullan is generally regarded as the man who inspired the side and kept the wilder elements in check. He was also captain of the Scotland side that beat England 1–0 at Hampden Park in 1929. In total he won sixteen caps for Scotland, and was only once on the losing side. His career started at Third Lanark, then he went to Partick Thistle, where he played both sides of the first world war, before being transferred to Manchester City in 1926 for £4,700. When he retired from playing in 1933 he became manager of a variety of English clubs, namely Oldham Athletic, Aston Villa, Notts County and Sheffield Wednesday.

McNAIR Alec (1883 – 1951)

Scotland Caps: 15
Scottish League Championship medals: 12
Scottish Cup medals: 6

From Stenhousemuir, Alec McNair was the mainstay of the great Celtic side that won six league championships in a row between 1905 and 1910, then another four between 1914 and 1917, and yet another two in 1919 and 1922. His 584 League appearances for the Parkhead side actually tops those of Billy McNeill, but Billy McNeill played more games if all competitions are counted. He won the Scottish Cup six times between 1907 and 1923, as well as fifteen caps for Scotland, a number that would have been greatly increased if it had not been for the first world war. His best game for Scotland was in April 1914, when the team beat England 3–1 and 'McNair never gave Smith or Mosscrop a kick of the ball'. 'Eck' was the right back of the two famous

Celtic teams that began 'Adams, McNair and Orr' and 'Shaw, McNair and Dodds'. Intelligent, thoughtful and gentlemanly, he was so cool under pressure that he was called 'the Icicle', and it is a matter of some surprise that he was never made captain of Celtic until after the first world war, when he was captain of Scotland for a short while as well. When his lengthy career came to a halt in 1925, he became manager of Dundee for a while, but met with little success. In his later years he was also a referee supervisor, but his career outside football was in stockbroking.

McNAMARA Jackie (1973 –)

Scotland Caps: 33
Scottish Premier League medals: 4
Scottish Cup medals: 3
Scottish League Cup medals: 2

The son of another Jackie McNamara, who played for Hibs and Celtic in the 1970s, Jackie McNamara was one of Celtic's best and most consistent defenders in the Martin O'Neill years from 2000 until 2005, winning thirty-three caps for Scotland in the process. He joined Celtic from Dunfermline Athletic for £650,000 in September 1995, and suffered a little from the constant changes of management until the arrival of O'Neill. He could play on both sides of the defence, and at full back as well as midfield. With Celtic, McNamara won four Scottish Premier League championships, three Scottish Cups, and two Scottish League Cups before his departure to Wolves at virtually the same time as Martin O'Neill left Celtic in 2005. In season 2007/08 he played for Aberdeen.

McNIEL (sometimes McNEIL) Moses (1855–1938)

Scotland Caps: 2

A legendary figure in the history of Rangers, Moses McNeil came from Rhu in Dumbartonshire, and his brother Henry played for Queen's Park. He was one of the founding members of the Fleshers' Haugh side in 1873, playing on the left wing. He is given the credit for calling this team 'Rangers', because it is claimed that he read the name in an English rugby union almanac. He played for Scotland against Wales in 1876, and against England in 1880.

McNEILL Billy (1940 –)

Scotland Caps: 29
Scottish League Championship medals: 9
Scottish Cup medals: 7
Scottish League Cup medals: 6
European Cup medals: 1

Billy McNeill joined Celtic in 1957 from Blantyre Vics, and became one of the greatest-ever figures in Scottish

Billy McNeill with Willie Wallace and Jim Craig after winning the Scottish Cup in 1967

football, centre half and captain of the great Celtic team between 1965 and 1975. With Celtic he won a grand total of twenty-three medals. He also won twenty-nine caps for Scotland, and was named Player of the Year in 1965, soon after his header won the Scottish Cup for Celtic against Dunfermline that year. His debut for Celtic was in 1958, and his international debut was the appalling 3–9 defeat by England at Wembley in 1961. Yet the selectors persevered with him, and the following year he was in the team that beat England 2–0 at Hampden Park, although in later years he would have competition from Ian Ure and Ron McKinnon.

For Celtic he was a commanding figure at centre half, particularly good in the air, and he could score a few goals with his head as well, often at pivotal points of Celtic history, e.g. versus Dunfermline in the Scottish Cup final of 1965, and versus Vojvodina in the quarter final of the 1967 European Cup. As a manager he was less successful, although he was not without his moments as well, always winning one honour per season in his first spell as Celtic manager, and in his second spell winning the league and cup double with Celtic in 1988. He had started off managing Clyde in 1976 and then, after a year at Aberdeen, joined Celtic in 1978. He left after a dispute in 1983 to go to Manchester City, and then joined Aston Villa for a spell, before returning to Celtic in 1987. He stayed there until summer 1991, doing well to avoid the problems thrown up by the dysfunctional directorate in the next few years.

In later years he remained high profile, doing some television commentary and punditry. He was an excellent ambassador for the game, as was proved when he and his old adversary John Greig were awarded honorary degrees from the University of Glasgow in 2008.

McPHAIL Bob (1905 – 2000)

Scotland Caps: 17
Scottish League Championship medals: 9
Scottish Cup medals: 7

Bob McPhail was one of the real legends of Scottish football, and one of the mainstays of Rangers' sustained success in the 1920s and 1930s. He was a broad and bustling inside left, but he could also score goals, netting 281 for Rangers. Although he was known as 'Greetin' Boab', because of his perceived perpetual mouthing on the field, he was nevertheless a true gentleman off the field, and his longevity was in no small measure due to his fitness and healthy lifestyle. He first came to prominence in the Airdrie team that won the Scottish Cup in 1924, but Rangers bought him in 1927, and with them he won nine Scottish league championships and six Scottish Cup medals. His Scotland career of seventeen caps was particularly impressive, for he was on the winning side against England in 1931, 1933, 1935 and 1937 (when his two late goals won the day), but was never chosen to play at Wembley.

MacPHERSON Archie (1937 –)

Archie MacPherson is one of the best-known broadcasters of the Scottish game. He was born in Glasgow and, after being a teacher and headmaster, joined the BBC in 1969 and hosted the television programme *Sportscene* for many years. He left the BBC in 1990 to work for a variety of broadcasting organizations – Radio Clyde, Eurosport, STV and Setanta. He has commentated at six World Cup finals and four Olympic Games, and has written several books on Scottish football.

McPHERSON Dave (1964 –)

Scotland Caps: 27
Scottish League Championship medals: 2
Scottish Cup medals: 2
Scottish League Cup medals: 4

Dave McPherson was a commanding centre half for Hearts, Rangers and Scotland, for whom he won twenty-seven caps between 1987 and 1993, featuring in the 1992 European Championships in Sweden. It is small wonder that he entitled his book *A Tale of Two Cities,* for he was forever moving back and forward along the M8. He began with Rangers in 1980; moved to Hearts in 1987 for £325,000, back to Rangers for £1,300,000 in 1992, then back to Hearts in a player exchange deal in 1994 before he finished off his career with Morton.

McQUEEN Gordon (1952 –)

Scotland Caps: 30

Gordon McQueen was a great central defender for Leeds United and Manchester United in the 1970s, with thirty Scottish caps to his name. In 1977 he scored for Scotland against England in the 2–1 win at Wembley. He was part of the squad for Argentina in 1978, but unfortunately injury prevented him from playing in any of the games. Arguably he should not have gone, for he was seen to hobble out to the aeroplane. (He was not, however, carried out on a stretcher, as some malicious rumours stated after the return from the Argentina cataclysm!) He began his playing career with St Mirren, and then moved to Leeds United for £40,000 in 1972, followed by Manchester United for a British record of £450,000 in 1978. With Leeds United, he won the English league

Defender Dave McPherson (left) played well over 250 SPL games for both Hearts and Rangers.

championship in 1974, and then the FA Cup with Manchester United in 1983.

McSTAY Paul (1964 –)

Scotland Caps: 76
Scottish League Championship medals: 3
Scottish Cup medals: 4
Scottish League Cup medals: 1

One of the best midfield players of his generation, it was Paul McStay's misfortune that his career coincided with a time of mediocrity for both Celtic and Scotland. He was born of a Celtic family (both his great-uncles played for the club in the 1920s and 1930s, and his brother Willie also played for Celtic at the same time as he did) and he made his debut in 1982. He had already impressed the nation in a schoolboys' international at Wembley in 1980 before he joined Celtic. He made an immediate good impression with Celtic in 1982, helping them to the league championship that year, and by the following year he won the first of his seventy-six Scottish caps. With Celtic, he played until 1997, winning the respect of opposition supporters by his mature and sensible approach to the game. Yet his career was often dogged by misfortune in the shape of injuries, and his unfortunate miss in a penalty shoot-out at the Scottish League Cup final of 1994/95 against Raith Rovers. He more or less carried that mediocre Celtic team through innumerable managerial changes, yet managed to retain his dignity throughout it all. His Scotland career saw McStay at his best in the European Championships of 1992, and he also performed creditably in the World Cup finals of 1986 and 1990.

MALEY Willie (1868 – 1958)

Scotland Caps: 2
Scottish League Championship medals: 3
Scottish Cup medals: 1

Known as "the man who made Celtic", Willie Maley was involved in that club from their first game in 1888 until his retirement or dismissal in early 1940. His playing career was respectable, but not brilliant, and he played twice for Scotland, even though he was born in Ireland. But it was his managerial abilities that made Celtic the great team that they are, his greatest years being the Edwardian era when his strong side won six Scottish League championships in a row between 1905 and 1910. He was manager from 1897 until 1940, something that is surely a world record. He may have been the man who made Celtic, but there were many who questioned in the 1930s whether he had been with the club too long, for his brooding despotism was not always something that worked in the club's favour.

The players in particular had little love for him. His departure from the club in 1940 was messy and undignified and, for years after that, Maley never went near the club, preferring indeed on occasion to go to Ibrox, until he and the club were happily reconciled in the early 1950s.

MALPAS Maurice (1962 –)

Scotland Caps: 55
Scottish League Championship medals: 1
Scottish Cup medals: 1

Maurice Malpas was an outstanding full back and captain for Dundee United, for whom he holds the record number of appearances with 646 league and cup games. He also played fifty-five times for Scotland, and he performed creditably at the World Cup finals of 1986 and 1990, as well as at the European Championships of 1992. He made his debut for Dundee United in 1981 and retired in 2000, and seldom had a really bad game for the club. He was part of Dundee United's very proficient defence that gained them much respect in Scotland and Europe. He won the Scottish Premier League in 1983 and the Scottish Cup in 1994, and runners-up medals on numerous occasions, not least the UEFA Cup in 1987. In 1991 the Scottish Football Writers elected him Player of the Year. His detractors called him 'Maurice Backpass', because of an apparent defensive obsession, but he had very few detractors in the Dundee United faithful. He became a coach, and then manager, at Motherwell, but left after one season in charge. In January 2008 he became manager of Swindon Town.

MALTA

Played five, won four, drawn one

1988	22 Mar	Valletta	1–1	Sharp	Busuttil
1990	28 May	Valletta	2–1	McInally (2)	Degiorgio
1993	17 Feb	Ibrox	3–0	McCoist (2) Nevin	
1993	17 Nov	Valletta	2–0	McKinlay Hendry	
1997	1 June	Valletta	3–2	Jackson (2) Dailly	Suda Sultana

MANAGER OF THE YEAR

This is an award given annually by the Scottish Football Writers' Association to the manager who has done the most in the past season, given his resources and other factors. The winners have been:

1987	Jim McLean	Dundee United
1988	Billy McNeill	Celtic
1989	Graeme Souness	Rangers
1990	Andy Roxburgh	Scotland
1991	Alex Totten	St Johnstone
1992	Walter Smith	Rangers
1993	Walter Smith	Rangers
1994	Walter Smith	Rangers
1995	Jimmy Nicholl	Raith Rovers
1996	Walter Smith	Rangers
1997	Walter Smith	Rangers
1998	Jim Jefferies	Hearts
1999	Dick Advocaat	Rangers
2000	Dick Advocaat	Rangers
2001	Martin O'Neill	Celtic
2002	John Lambie	Partick Thistle
2003	Alex McLeish	Rangers
2004	Martin O'Neill	Celtic
2005	Tony Mowbray	Hibernian
2006	Gordon Strachan	Celtic
2007	Gordon Strachan	Celtic
2008	Walter Smith	Rangers

MANAGERS

When Scottish football clubs were being formed at the end of the nineteenth century the position of manager did not exist, and the first managers of Rangers and Celtic, William Wilton and Willie Maley, were both initially appointed as match secretary. The title might have been unfamiliar, but these men possessed many of the qualities that are required by a successful manager in the twenty-first century. Not only could they spot talented players and then get the best out of them, they also had a vision of what was required to take their club forward, and possessed the ability to communicate that vision.

It was not long before English football clubs were also benefiting from the skills of a Scottish manager. In 1903 Maley's brother Tom led Manchester City to the championship of the English Division Two, and the following year they won the FA Cup. However, when he went on to manage Bradford Park Avenue, he exported more than his managerial skills. Bradford swapped their traditional red, amber and black for green and white hoops.

William Struth, manager at Rangers for 34 years.

John 'Sailor' Hunter was a manager who, like Willie Maley and William Wilton, earned his reputation in Scottish club football. Hunter managed Motherwell from 1911 to 1946, and was responsible for an important milestone in Scottish football history when his free-scoring team broke the Old Firm's twenty-seven year monopoly on the title in 1932. To do this he had to break down the power of Bill Struth's Rangers. Struth took over at Ibrox in 1920, following the death of William Wilton, and lasted until 1954. With an iron will and an emphasis on discipline and hard work, he built teams that won a total of twenty-five championships out of thirty-four, if the war years are counted.

In the mid-1930s in Edinburgh, a change took place that would make another impact on Scottish football. Willie McCartney crossed the city from Tynecastle to Easter Road, and became manager of Hibernian. McCartney had been manager of Hearts from 1919 to 1935 but, although his sides contained talented players, they won neither the league title nor the Scottish Cup. At Hibernian he put his faith in youth, signed the 'famous five' forward line, and built a team that went on to achieve spectacular success for Hibs in the 1940s and 1950s. The tragedy was that he died in 1948 and it was

Dick Advocaat.

his successor Hugh Shaw (who managed Hibs from 1948 to 1962) who witnessed their triumphs.

As professional football gathered momentum once again after the second world war, two of Scottish football's 'gentlemen' began their careers in club management, with a 'tracksuit' style that was seen as innovative at the time. In Manchester, Matt Busby became manager of United, and his sides won five English championships, two FA Cups and ultimately the 1968 European Cup. In Edinburgh, Tommy Walker returned from Chelsea to become assistant manager, and then manager, of Hearts. Thus began one of the most successful periods in Hearts' history. The 1954 League Cup was their first major trophy in nearly fifty years, and it was followed by the Scottish Cup, the 1957/58 league title and another League Cup. Both men had a special talent for blending players into teams that won trophies.

One manager who did not have a 'tracksuit' style was Scot Symon. He was known as a quiet man, but he had an exceptional ability to build winning teams and did so in both the east and west of Scotland. His first job as a manager took him to East Fife in 1947, where the Fifers won both the 1947/48 League Cup and the Division B title in his first season. In 1949/50 they won the League Cup again and also reached the Scottish Cup final. He then took Preston North End to the 1953/54 English FA Cup final before joining Rangers, and embarking on a period of outstanding success. He took Rangers into Europe for the first time (the 1956/57 European Cup), and his teams not only won six championships, they also reached the final of the European Cup-Winners' Cup in both 1960/61 and 1966/67.

The entries on individual clubs refer to further managers who have left their mark on Scottish football. Jock Wallace of Rangers (above) and Ivano Bonetti of Dundee (below right, with Claudio Caniggia) have both done so, but their styles were very different.

Bill Shankly did not manage a Scottish club, and yet he acquired a legendary status in both England and Scotland. He signed a fifteen-year-old Denis Law for Huddersfield Town, but it is his passion for the game of football that he is most remembered for. A man of immense enthusiasm and commitment, he transformed the fortunes of Liverpool, whom he managed from 1959 to 1974. His sides won three English titles and two FA Cups, as well as the 1973 UEFA Cup, but the canny Shankly was also building a formidable backroom team that would be the foundation for even more success in the future.

In Scotland Jock Stein (manager of Celtic from 1965 to 1978) was an equally shrewd operator. A wily tactician, he epitomised the increasing emphasis on tactics being adopted by managers in Scotland. Always remembered as the man who built the first British team to win the European Cup in 1967, his teams won many other trophies, including nine consecutive league titles between 1965/66 and 1973/74. As manager of Scotland from 1978 to 1985 he took his country to the 1982 World Cup finals in Spain.

Many Scottish managers have been described as 'charismatic', but a man whose charisma extended into flamboyance, and even controversy, was Tommy Docherty. Not only was he a good judge of a player's potential, his exceptional motivational skills were aided by a ready wit. His managerial career began with Chelsea in 1961, and he subsequently became manager of the Scottish national team between 1971 and 1972. He left to become manager of Manchester United, and never did manage a Scottish club side, although he managed clubs in Portugal and Australia as well as England.

Another Scot with charisma in abundance was Ally MacLeod. A successful manager with both Ayr United and Aberdeen between 1966 and 1977, he then became manager of the Scottish national team. His enthusiasm was so great that expectations were running high when Scotland competed in the 1978 World Cup finals in Argentina, and the subsequent lack of success resulted in intense disappointment throughout the country. He managed Motherwell, Airdrieonians and other clubs after Argentina, and as the years have gone by he is remembered as a larger than life character who also had his successes.

In Perth in 1967 a former member of the Hibs' 'famous five', Willie Ormond, began a distinguished managerial career that also led to the World Cup finals. Another manager with a talent for building winning teams, he took St Johnstone into Europe for the first time, and then managed the Scotland side that qualified for the 1974 World Cup finals in Germany. His team was the only undefeated one in the tournament. He later became manager of Hearts, and then followed in Willie McCartney's footsteps by also managing Hibs.

Sir Alex Ferguson.

Whilst managers such as Tommy Docherty moved between several different clubs, one man who stayed at the same club was Jim McLean at Dundee United, who was their manager from 1971 to 1993. He had a reputation for being dour and a strict disciplinarian, but he instituted a youth policy that eventually took his club to unprecedented heights. He led United to two League Cups and the 1982/83 league title, as well as an appearance in the 1986/87 UEFA Cup final, and their name became respected throughout Europe.

One of the most successful Scottish managers of all time took his first steps in management at Firs Park, Falkirk in 1974. Alex Ferguson only stayed with East Stirlingshire for four months, but his no-nonsense disciplined approach was already starting to pay dividends when he left for St Mirren in 1975. The Paisley club eventually sacked him in 1978, and this proved to be a turning point that led to a wealth of honours with Aberdeen and Manchester United. Under his leadership Aberdeen became the third Scottish club to win a European trophy when they won the 1982/83 European Cup-Winners' Cup in Gothenburg. They followed this by winning the European Super Cup the following season. The man who would become Sir Alex Ferguson left for Manchester United in 1986, where his astute tactical skills won him more trophies than any other manger in English football.

Graeme Souness made history during his time as manager of Rangers (1986-1991). He had already brought a succession of top English players, such as England captain Terry Butcher, to Ibrox when in 1989 he made a dramatic signing. The arrival of Mo Johnston, a Catholic who had previously played for Celtic, caused shockwaves throughout Scottish football and struck a blow for anti-sectarianism.

A manager whose ability to motivate players produced exceptional results was John Lambie. A forthright and outspoken manager, he inspired his Hamilton Academical team to a 1–0 victory at Ibrox in the third round of the 1986/87 Scottish Cup, and then in 2001 and 2002 he led Partick Thistle from the Second Division to the Scottish Premier League in consecutive seasons.

Many Scottish managers have accepted the challenge of managing an English football club, but sometimes the grass is not always greener south of the border. In 2000, almost a hundred years after Tom Maley went south, Jim Jefferies joined struggling Bradford City in the English Premiership. Jefferies had enjoyed success in Scottish football, winning the 1993/94 First Division title with Falkirk and the 1997/98 Scottish Cup with Hearts, but he describes in *The Bradford City Story - The Pain and the Glory* how Bradford's training facilities, scouting system and youth development were not what he was accustomed to. By 2002 he was back in Scotland with Kilmarnock, and resumed his career as a manager in the SPL.

Walter Smith was head coach of the Scotland team from 2004 until early 2007. He began his managerial career by assisting Jim McLean at Dundee United and

Jock Stein.

Graeme Souness at Rangers, and then took over as manager of Rangers in 1991, leading them to seven successive championships and the 1992/93 treble. Despite this outstanding success, he too had a disappointing time in the English Premiership, where he managed Everton from 1998 to 2002. When he returned to Scotland the fortunes of the national team dramatically improved, but when the opportunity arose he left to manage Rangers for a second time.

At the start of the twenty-first century Scottish clubs were increasingly emphasising the importance of coaching, and several appointed a head coach as opposed to a manager. For example, John Hughes was appointed head coach of Falkirk in 2003 (two years before he led them into the SPL). UEFA's 'Pro Licence', a qualification that comprises sixteen modules, became recognised as a means of improving the standard of coaching, and from 2008 all managers and head coaches in the SPL must hold the UEFA Pro Licence unless they have been in their posts for five years.

Alex McLeish took over as head coach of Scotland's national team in January 2007, and both he and his predecessor Walter Smith include the Pro Licence in their CV. He was appointed after a successful playing career that saw him represent Scotland at three World Cup finals, and a managerial career that included trophies at both Hibernian and Rangers. He only stayed until November 2007, when the lure of the English Premiership proved irresistible, and he became yet another Scottish manager to move south of the border. Nevertheless, in that short time, Scotland only narrowly failed to qualify for the finals of the 2008 European championships under his leadership.

One of the biggest contrasts between the twenty-first century manager and pioneers such as William Wilton and Willie Maley is the need to communicate through the media. Television has assumed an ever-increasing importance for the men who account for their team in public, and a manager's ability to speak to a mass audience has become an important contribution to a club's profile. The manager who can master such appearances is not only able to analyse a match, but also keeps his television audience interested and entertained, as well as informed. (see also **SCOTLAND MANAGERS**)

Craig Brown managed Scotland.

MASON Jimmy (1919 – 1971)

Scotland Caps: 7

Jimmy Mason was an inside forward for the now defunct Third Lanark. He won seven Scottish caps between 1949 and 1951, including the famous 1949 victory over England at Wembley. He was a well-loved character, because of his natural ability on the field allied with his charm and modesty off it.

MASSIE Alec (1906 – 1977)

Scotland Caps: 18

Wing half for Hearts and Aston Villa in the 1930s, Alec Massie was sometimes known as 'Classy Massie' for his fine play, and with his fair hair he was an easily recognisable character on the field. He was unfortunate in that he never won any major honour for either Hearts between 1930 and 1935 or Aston Villa between 1935 and

the start of the second world war. His games for Scotland all were good examples of how well he could play, particularly the games against England in 1935 and 1937. After the war he was manager of Aston Villa until 1950, and subsequently Torquay United and Hereford United.

MATCH-FIXING

It is to be hoped that match-fixing is a rarity in Scotland, but one would be naïve to suppose that it has never happened. Whilst prior determination of the outcome of a match is uncovered in other parts of the world from time to time, notably in Italy in 2006, Scottish football is comparatively bereft of such scandals. Mutterings are heard occasionally, however, and the Hampden riot of 1909 may well have had its genesis in the widespread belief throughout Glasgow that the replayed Scottish Cup final of that year between Celtic and Rangers was 'fixed' as a draw. In this way a third game would have to be played, to yield even more money, and it was believed that this was why there was no extra time at the end of the second game. Similarly in 1963, 1966 and 1971, when the Scottish Cup finals between the Glasgow giants were drawn, and six-figure crowds appeared at the replays, cynicism was the order of the day. But such accusations were vigorously denied and remain hard to prove.

Ian St John, in his autobiography *The Saint,* tells a story concerning a game played at Fir Park, Motherwell on 11 October 1958. The Motherwell players were allegedly 'in' on a deal for £100, whereby Motherwell would lose to Third Lanark at home so that a bet placed on Third Lanark (and another unnamed team playing away from home in similar circumstances on the same day) would win at odds of 10–1. The plot fell through when Motherwell's goalkeeper Hastie Weir was approached (for the goalkeeper would really have to be part of the deal), and Hastie 'went berserk', reporting the matter immediately to manager Bobby Ancell. The Motherwell players then repented of their plan to such an extent that they beat Third Lanark 8–1 (St John actually says seven) and St John himself scored a hat-trick, admitting afterwards to a 'fever of guilt and then much relief!'.

Ian Ure, in his autobiography *Ure's Truly,* tells another story about a considerably more important game. It was April 28, the final day of the 1961/62 season, when Dundee were at Muirton Park, Perth to play St. Johnstone. A draw would have suited both teams, in that Dundee would have won the league championship and St. Johnstone would have been saved from relegation. Ure states that a message was passed to the Dundee players in the dressing room, offering them £50 per man if the game finished all square. He is understandably coy about saying much more (and one would like to think that the whole thing was a joke), but the offer was treated with contempt. Dundee then went out and defeated St. Johnstone 3-0 so that they won the league title, and St. Johnstone, thanks to all their rivals winning on the same day, were relegated.

On two occasions Aberdeen have been at the centre of allegations. One was in 1977, and appears to have been the work of an overzealous journalist with little substance to it, although the fall-out may well have hampered the Dons' challenge for the Scottish League championship that year. The 1931 scandal was rather more serious. Five players, McLaren, Hill, Yorston, Galloway and Black were all suddenly dropped from the first team and subsequently transferred. No prosecution charges were ever brought, however.

Eyebrows have been raised once or twice at certain games and with certain players. Dick Beattie, who played in goal for Celtic and St Mirren, was accused by Celtic fans for his strange performances in the 1956 Scottish Cup final and the 1957 Scottish Cup semi-final, and the allegations became more pronounced after he served nine months in prison in 1965 for taking a bribe during his time at Portsmouth. Other unofficial allegations have been made from time to time, but there have been few prosecutions in Scotland, although there was the occasion on 22 March 1924 when Johnny Browning and Archie 'Punch' Kyle were found guilty of attempting to fix the result of a match between Lochgelly United and Bo'ness.

Ian Ure is the centre of attraction for these autograph hunters in 1963 as he arrives in England. When his autobiography was published he suggested that there had been an attempt to 'fix' a game between Dundee and St Johnstone.

Before a game on 3 December 1932 between Ayr United and St Mirren, Ayr's captain Andy McCall received a letter offering him £50 if he could arrange for Ayr to lose. He passed the letter on to the police, and Ayr United duly won 1–0. After a game on 9 March 1935, Falkirk manager Willie Orr was suspended *sine die* by the SFA and the SFL, for persuading Robert Russell of Ayr United not to play. He had offered Russell £3, Russell had accepted, and Falkirk duly won 3–2. A replay was ordered, which Ayr won 3–1, and Russell never played again for Ayr United.

It would be very difficult to 'throw' a game convincingly, particularly in this age of an obtrusive press and endless television coverage. A fix would need the active cooperation of many people, and one of them might reveal the plan. It remains, however, one of the murkier areas of football.

MEIKLEJOHN Davie (1900 – 1959)

Scotland Caps: 15
Scottish League Championship medals: 12
Scottish Cup medals: 5

Davie Meiklejohn was one of Rangers' greatest ever players, and a giant of the 1920s and 1930s. He was a rugged centre half, but one who always played the game in a sporting fashion, never more so than in his attempt to still the Ibrox crowd when they were hurling abuse at the fatally injured John Thomson in 1931. He would later read the lesson at Thomson's memorial service. 'Meek', as he was called, played fifteen times for Scotland, and was the mainstay of the great Rangers side of the inter-war years. It was Meiklejohn who converted the crucial penalty kick in the Scottish Cup final of 1928, which broke Rangers' twenty-five year Scottish Cup 'hoodoo'. After the second world war he became manager of Partick Thistle, leading them to consistent respectability in the Scottish League, and to three unsuccessful Scottish League Cup finals, before his sudden death in August 1959 following a game against Airdrieonians at Broomfield.

MERCER Wallace (1946 – 2006)

Wallace Mercer was a colourful and high profile businessman who saved Heart of Midlothian from bankruptcy, and possible extinction, in the early 1980s. Chairman of the club from 1981 to 1994, Hearts became one of the best teams in Scotland during his period in office, narrowly missing out on Scottish League and Scottish Cup honours in successive weeks in May 1986. In 1990 he came up with the controversial idea of amalgamating Hearts and Hibernian. Whilst many people believed the idea was not without merit, he was fiercely opposed by Hibs supporters, and had to drop his plans.

MID-ANNANDALE FC (former Scottish League club)

Home: **Kintail Park, Lockerbie, Dumfriesshire**
Highest League Position: **46th (6th in Div. 3, 1925/26)**
Best Scottish Cup Performance: **Last 16 (3rd round, 1926/27)**

Lockerbie was the home of a Scottish League club when Mid-Annandale belonged to the short-lived Division Three that existed between 1923 and 1926. Most of its members, including the Mids, failed to complete their fixtures in the harsh economic environment of 1925/26 and when Division Three was abandoned, their time as a member of the Scottish League came to an end.

A club called Mid-Annandale was originally founded in 1877 and its exploits in the Scottish Cup included a sixth-round appearance in 1891/92, which resulted in an 11–2 defeat to Cowlairs. It went out of existence sometime in the 1890s, but around 1909 another Mid-Annandale was created from a club called Vale of Dryfe. The new club spent the 1914/15 season in the Southern District League, and after the first world war joined the Southern Counties League for the 1921/22 season. They won the title at the second attempt, and made 1922/23 an even more memorable season by reaching the final of the Scottish Qualifying Cup, although they lost 4–1 to Royal Albert.

On the back of this success, the club was invited to join the new Division Three and was one of only five members that didn't come from the Western League. They never achieved promotion and finished eighth, fifteenth and sixth between 1924 and 1926. Crowds were low and the club's finances only stayed in the black because of some shrewd transfer dealing. After 1926 they played in both the Alliance League (Southern Division) and the South of Scotland League and showed that the Mids were still a team to be reckoned with when they beat Brechin City 4–1 in the final of the 1926/27 Scottish Qualifying Cup. They went on to reach the third round of the competition proper, losing 3–0 at Falkirk. After this success, there were three more appearances in the first round of the Scottish Cup, but times were hard and the club finally folded in 1936.

MILESON Brooks (1947 –)

Brooks Mileson bought control of Gretna FC in 2003, and became one of the real characters of Scottish football. A pony-tailed multi-millionaire, he became involved with Gretna soon after they were admitted to the Scottish League, and took them to the SPL in 2007 after a record three successive promotions. Gretna also reached the Scottish Cup final of 2006, where Hearts only defeated them after a penalty shoot-out. He hails from Sunderland, supports Carlisle United, has a menagerie for sick animals on his estate, and has also distributed his largesse to various football supporters' trusts as well as Gretna. In March 2008, when he was suffering ill health, his financial support for Gretna FC was withdrawn and the club went into administration.

MILLER Kenny (1979 –)

Scotland Caps: 37
Scottish Premier League medals: 1
Scottish Cup medals: 1

Only the third man (Alfie Conn and Maurice Johnston being the others) to have played for both halves of the Old Firm in modern times, Kenny Miller is a well-known Scottish figure. A fast-running, free-scoring forward, he began his career with Hibernian in 1997 and moved to Rangers in 2000, but left for Wolverhampton Wanderers after a brief and unhappy spell (although he once scored five goals for them against St Mirren). He played for Wolves from 2001 until 2006, when he returned to Scotland to play for Celtic. Although he won

Striker Kenny Miller has played a season each for both Rangers and Celtic, and reached double figures for the national team.

a league and Scottish Cup double with them in 2006/07, he did not score as many goals as was hoped for and, not being guaranteed a first team place, was sold to Derby County in August 2007 for a reputed £3 million.

MILLER Willie (1955 –)

Scotland Caps: 65
Scottish League Championship medals: 3
Scottish Cup medals: 4
Scottish League Cup medals: 2
European Cup-Winners' Cup: 1

Willie Miller won sixty-five caps for Scotland between 1975 and 1990, and was centre half and captain for Aberdeen during their glory years. He was born in Glasgow, but the only club that he is associated with is Aberdeen. He joined the Dons in 1971, and by the end of the decade had established himself in that team, forming an excellent defensive partnership with Alex McLeish. The pair had an almost telepathic understanding of who was to attack the ball and who was to stay behind and sweep. The main fruit of his career was the European Cup-Winners' Cup win of 1983 and the Super Cup of the following year.

In 1984 he was elected Player of the Year by the Scottish Football Writers. His Scotland career encompassed World Cup finals in both 1982 and 1986, and it was his unfortunate misunderstanding with Alan Hansen that led to Scotland's defeat by the USSR in 1982. It was a very rare mistake indeed. He dominated his penalty area and it was said that he often cowed referees, sometimes leading to jokes and comments that he indeed was the referee! After his playing career was over, he became manager of Aberdeen for a spell between 1992 and 1995, and then he was a pundit for the BBC, before returning to his spiritual home of Pittodrie as Director of Football in 2004. He is not to be confused with another Willie Miller, who played as goalkeeper for Celtic and Scotland in the late 1940s.

MOCHAN Neil (1927 – 1994)

Scotland Caps: 3
Scottish League Championship: 1
Scottish Cup medals: 1
Scottish League Cup medals: 2

Neil Mochan played for Morton (1944), Middlesbrough (1951), Celtic (1953), Dundee United (1960) and Raith Rovers (1963), before in 1964 becoming trainer of Celtic's Lisbon Lions side. He is the man generally held responsible for the superb fitness of that team. It was with Celtic that he played his best football, winning a medal in each Scottish domestic competition, even though he was not always 'persona grata' with the Celtic directorate, and was often left out of the team when supporters felt he should be one of the first to be included.

He also achieved the unusual feat of winning two medals in 1953 (the Glasgow Charity Cup and the Coronation Cup) before playing a game at Parkhead! Famed for his shot, and known as the 'Cannonball Kid', his best position was left wing, but occasionally towards the end of his Celtic days he played at left back, and when the right back was Frank Meechan, the Celtic team began Beattie, Meechan and Mochan…! He won three caps for Scotland, but two of them were at the 1954 Switzerland World Cup finals, which included the 0–7 thrashing from Uruguay.

MOLDOVA

Arguably Scotland's worst-ever performance was the game against Moldova in Chisinau. Scotland were lucky to get a draw and, according to one press report, 'played like a pub league team'

2004	13 Oct	Chisinau	1–1	Thompson	Dadu
2005	4 June	Hampden Park	2–0	Dailly McFadden	

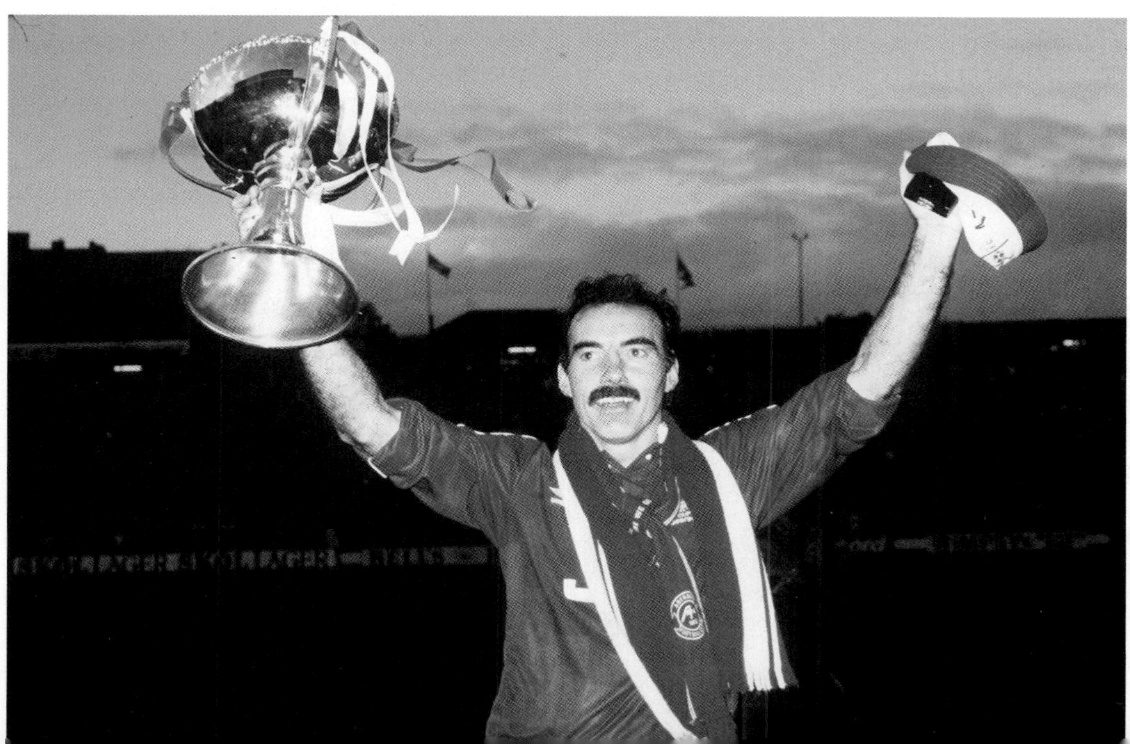

Aberdeen captain Willie Miller celebrates lifting the 1989/90 League Cup.

MONTFORD Arthur (1934 –)

Arthur Montford was the much-loved commentator and anchor man of STV's *Scotsport*, which he hosted from its beginning in the Theatre Royal on 18 September 1957 until he retired in 1989. He was born in Glasgow but raised in Greenock. He was a print journalist with the *Evening Times* and a radio broadcaster before being offered the job of hosting *Scotsport*, following a successful audition at Maryhill town hall. Such was his popularity that he was voted Lord Rector of Glasgow University from 1974 until 1977. He was famous for his checked jackets, his unashamed love of Greenock Morton, and his general enthusiasm for the game with catchphrases such as 'up go the heads!', 'things are getting a little tousy', and 'what a stramash!'. Famously in 1973, when he was commentating on the World Cup qualifier between Scotland and Czechoslovakia, he forgot his supposed neutrality, shouting advice like 'Watch your legs, Billy'; then in the final minute, when Denis Law broke through, 'C'mon, Denis'!

MONTROSE FC

Ground: **Links Park**
Nickname: **The 'Gable Endies'**
Colours: **Blue and white**
Record Attendance: **8983 v Dundee (1973)**
Record Victory: **12-0 v Vale of Leithen (1975)**
Record Defeat: **0-13 v Aberdeen (1951)**
Highest League Position: **13th (3rd in First Div., 1975/76)**
Best Scottish Cup Performance: **Last 8 (5th round 1972/73; 1975/76)**
Best League Cup Performance: **Last 4 (1975/76)**

The club was founded in 1879 and initially played on Montrose Links before moving to the first Links Park. The colours at that time were black and white. In 1887 a further move was made to the current Links Park, but financial problems were never far away and bigger clubs signed the better players on several occasions. In the 1890s this included two players, Sandy Keillor and Gordon Bowman, who had been capped for Scotland. Montrose FC was one of the founder members of the Northern League in 1891 and this was where the club played its league football for many years.

The Scottish Qualifying Cup was won in 1921/22, when Nithsdale Wanderers were beaten in a final that went to two replays, and not long afterwards Montrose joined the Scottish League, becoming a member of the short-lived Division Three from 1923 to 1926. They never finished higher than fourth, but when two places in Division Two became available in 1929, they found themselves back in the national league. Their league form was once again unremarkable and when the Scottish League resumed after the second world war they were placed in Division C. The Gable Endies were still there in 1955 when all the teams that were not second-elevens were admitted to Division B.

They remained in the lower division until league reconstruction in 1975, but now a third-place finish meant that they became part of the First Division, which was the new second tier, and in the first season they finished third. 1975/76 was also a year of memorable cup performances, with a League Cup semi-final against Rangers, after defeating Hibs over two legs, and an appearance in the quarter-finals of the Scottish Cup for the second time in four years. Montrose took Hearts to two replays before going out 2–1 at Muirton Park.

However, this good form did not continue and in 1979 the club was relegated to the Second Division. Once again good players were sold, but eventually, under manager Ian Stewart, the Second Division championship was won in 1985. Relegation back to the third tier followed in 1987. Co-managers Chic McLelland and Doug Rougvie achieved promotion as runners-up in 1991, but again it did not last and the club was relegated once more in 1992.

After further league reconstruction in 1994 Montrose found themselves in the Third Division, the new fourth tier. Promotion was achieved as runners-up in 1995, but history repeated itself when relegation followed the following season, and this signalled the beginning of many years in the bottom division.

A synthetic playing surface was installed at Links Park in the summer of 2007, which enabled the club to allow access for local teams as part of its football development programme within the local community.

A pre-season friendly between Inverurie Locos and Montrose, August 2007. Goals by Keith Gibson and Paul Stewart helped the Gable Endies to a 2-0 win.

MORGAN Willie (1944 –)

Scotland Caps: 21

A good traditional winger, who played for Burnley, Manchester United and Scotland in the early 1970s, Willie Morgan won twenty-one caps for Scotland and played his part in Scotland's qualification for, and participation in, the 1974 World Cup finals. As well as Burnley and Manchester United, he turned out for Bolton Wanderers, and was coach with Blackpool. He also played football in the USA and Canada.

MOROCCO

Scotland have played Morocco only once, but it was the game which put a disorganised and outclassed Scotland out of the 1998 World Cup.

1998	23 June	St.Etienne	0–3		Bassir (2) Hadda

MORRIS David (1899 – 1971)

Scotland Caps: 6

David Morris is often regarded as the greatest player that Raith Rovers have ever had, a centre half who will ever be remembered for season 1924/25, in which he captained Scotland to a fine international treble over Ireland, Wales and England. A great leader and captain, he earned six caps for Scotland, a record for a Raith Rovers player. On Christmas Eve 1925 he was transferred to Preston North End for £4,800 He was famed for his heading ability, for he 'could head the ball further than most men could kick it' in the view of most of his admirers.

MORRIS Henry (1919 – 1993)

Scotland Caps: 1
Scottish League Cups: 2

Henry Morris was a forward for East Fife in the late 1940s. He won two Scottish League Cup medals with them, and his career was notable for the fact that he scored a hat-trick in his international debut (Northern Ireland v. Scotland on 1 October 1949) and was never picked for Scotland again!

MORTON Alan Lauder (1893 – 1971)

Scotland Caps: 31
Scottish League Championship medals: 8
Scottish Cup medals: 2

Known as the 'Wee Blue De'il', Alan Morton was possibly Scotland's greatest-ever left winger, winning thirty-one Scottish caps, one of them being the Wembley Wizards international of 1928. He joined Queen's Park in 1913 and played for them as an amateur until he turned professional with Rangers in 1920. Unusually, he was allowed by Rangers to maintain his other career, that of a mining engineer, while playing for Rangers. He very soon became the most talked about football player of the 1920s, which was a golden era for Scottish football. Rangers' fans loved him. He was naturally a right-sided player, but developed his left side by constant practice. He was speedy, could beat a defender, and was a brilliant crosser of a ball. He was often injured, as star players were in those days, by the brutal tackles of desperate defenders, but he kept playing until he was forty in 1933.

'The Wee Blue De'il", Alan Morton of Rangers.

A mark of his greatness was that he kept outstanding left wingers like Adam McLean and Alec Troup out of the Scottish team. He had the nickname of the 'wee society man', for he was always immaculately dressed, with suit, tie, bowler hat, leather gloves and umbrella. His hair was always black with a tidy parting, and he was a stickler for discipline in behaviour and church attendance, as well as dress. On his retirement he became a director of Rangers and stayed a director until his death in 1971. Unusually for a professional footballer, Alan Morton was very much from a middle class background. He was also responsible for what is arguably the most famous supporters' song in Scottish football history, concerning the goal he scored against Charlie Shaw of Celtic in 1921. To the tune of 'The Red Flag', (a song very common in the 1920s in Glasgow, which had the nickname of 'Red Clydeside'), the song ran:

"Oh, Charlie Shaw, he never saw
Whaur Alan Morton pit the ba'
He pit the ba' straight in the net
An Charlie Shaw sat doon and gret!

MOTHERWELL FC

Ground: **Fir Park**
Nickname: **The Well; The Steelmen**
Colours: **Claret and amber**
Record Attendance: **35,632 v Rangers (1952)**
Record Victory: **12-1 v Dundee United (1954)**
Record Defeat: **0-8 v Aberdeen (1979)**
Highest League Position: **Champions (1931/32)**
Best Scottish Cup Performance: **Winners (1951/52; 1990/91)**
Best League Cup Performance: **Winners (1950/51)**

Motherwell FC was formed when two amateur works teams, Alpha and Glencairn, amalgamated in 1886. At first the new club played at Roman Road, where Alpha had played, before switching to Dalziel Park, near Airbles Street, in 1889. Six years later they finally found a permanent home on land at the edge of the fir park on Lord Hamilton's Estate. They became known as regular entrants in the Scottish Cup, and when the Scottish League decided to create a new Division Two in 1893, Motherwell were invited to be one of the founder members. At this time they played in blue shirts, and their familiar claret and amber would not be adopted until 1913 when, after frequent clashes of colour with other clubs, they adopted the colours of Bradford City, who had recently won the FA Cup.

The first few years were unremarkable and the club twice finished bottom of the league, but promotion in 1903 set the scene for a remarkable run of success. Seventy-two years later, when the league was being reconstructed, Motherwell had been in the top division for every season except two, and from 1926/27 to 1934/35 they finished in the top three for eight consecutive seasons. Their finest hour came in 1931/32 when manager John 'Sailor' Hunter led them to the league title and broke the Old Firm's twenty-seven year monopoly. Willie McFadyen scored fifty-two goals that season.

They finished as losing finalists in the Scottish Cup in 1930/31, 1932/33 and 1938/39 and it happened again in 1950/51, when Celtic defeated them 1–0. However, the Steelmen did win a major trophy that season when Hibernian were beaten 3–0 in the final of the League Cup. The following season Motherwell finally brought the Scottish Cup back to Fir Park after a 4–0 victory over Dundee in their fifth final.

Bobby Ancell was manager from 1955 to 1965, and he built a renowned team of 'Ancell Babes', including international players such as Ian St John, that achieved a top-five finish for Motherwell in three consecutive seasons from 1958/59 to 1960/61. League form deteriorated after he left, and there was a season in Division Two in 1968/69, but in 1970/71 the club raised its profile in England through victories over Tottenham Hotspur and Stoke City in the short-lived 'Texaco Cup' competition.

When the Scottish league was reconstructed in 1975, Motherwell became a founder member of the new Premier Division, but the club found it difficult to consistently compete at the top level, and four of the first ten years were spent in the First Division (second tier). It was the arrival of manager Tommy McLean in 1984 that heralded another period of sustained success. The Scottish Cup was won again in 1991, when Davie Cooper put in a star performance as Dundee United were beaten 4–3 at Hampden Park. This brought European competition in the form of the European Cup-Winners' Cup, but the Well went out to Katowice in the first round on the 'away goals' rule.

A third-place finish in 1994 brought participation in the UEFA Cup, and a second-round defeat against Borussia Dortmund. Paul Lambert, who was one of Tommy McLean's signings, made such an impression on their opponents that they subsequently signed him. Alex McLeish replaced Tommy McLean in 1994 and, although star players such as Phil O'Donnell were sold, Motherwell finished second in 1994/95. This meant another UEFA Cup campaign, but it quickly came to an end with a first-round defeat against MyPA 47 of Finland. Some difficult years ensued; Alex McLeish left to join Hibs, other managers came and went, and the club had to go through a period of financial administration.

Former England captain Terry Butcher was appointed manager in 2002 and he was forced to rely on his younger players. Relegation was only avoided in 2003 because First Division champions Falkirk didn't have a ground that satisfied the requirements of the Scottish Premier League. However, results steadily improved and Phil O'Donnell returned in 2004. There were consecutive top six finishes in 2003/04 and 2004/05, and the team also reached the final of the 2004/05 League Cup, losing 5–1 to Rangers.

Maurice Malpas took over from Terry Butcher in 2006 and, although the Well's tenth-place at the end of 2006/07 was enough for SPL survival, he left after just

one season in charge, to be replaced by Mark McGhee. He soon had to lead the club through one of the most traumatic periods of its history, when captain Phil O'Donnell collapsed during a match against Dundee United on 29 December 2007 and later died in hospital. As the season unfolded the Well became the main challengers to the Old Firm in the SPL, and they eventually finished in third place.

MOWAT Jack (1913 –)

Jack Mowat was a legendary Scottish referee of the 1950s, officiating in seven Scottish Cup finals and six Scottish League Cup finals, and generally considered to be the toughest and the fairest referee of his time, earning great respect from everyone. He was given many international honours, including the potentially difficult Sweden versus Hungary game at the 1958 World Cup finals in Sweden. His most famous match was the 1960 European Cup final at Hampden Park between Real Madrid and Eintracht, to which, legend has it, he walked from his Rutherglen home.

He was first appointed to the Scottish League list in 1933, and refereed continuously until the early 1960s, apart from during the second world war, when he was a Squadron Leader in the RAF. Such was his reputation that he was often invited to officiate at difficult games in Ireland involving Linfield, Belfast Celtic and Glentoran, where crowd trouble and civil disturbance might have been a problem. When he retired from active refereeing, he became a Referee Supervisor, and today the Jack Mowat Trophy is awarded to the referee who earns the best marks from their supervisors. He was an elder of the Church of Scotland.

MURDOCH Bobby (1944 – 2001)

Scotland Caps: 12
Scottish League Championship medals: 8
Scottish Cup medals: 4
Scottish League Cup medals: 5
European Cup medals: 1

Bobby Murdoch was possibly the best player of the Lisbon Lions Celtic team of the late 1960s. He started off with Celtic in 1962, as a moderately successful inside right, but the arrival of Jock Stein in 1965 made him a world-class wing half. He specialised in the creation of play with a long pass to the feet of Lennox or Johnstone. In 1969 the Scottish Football Writers named him Player of the Year. After struggling with a weight problem, he went to Middlesbrough in 1973 and helped them to win promotion to Division One, before a long-term injury compelled his retirement in 1976. He was a coach for a time with the Boro, and then became their manager for a brief and unhappy spell between 1981 and 1982. He played twelve times for Scotland, but tended to underperform for the national side, particularly against England in 1966 and 1969. But he did score a brilliant

goal to earn Scotland a draw against West Germany in 1969, and can consider himself unfortunate in that Scotland never made it to World Cup finals in his time.

MURRAY Sir David (1951 –)

Sir David Murray is an Edinburgh-based entrepreneur who led a takeover of Rangers FC in 1988 and became chairman. He took intense ambition to Ibrox, together with a strong determination to succeed, and under his chairmanship the club went on to win nine consecutive league titles. The period was characterised by the arrival of high-profile stars, and included the controversial signing of Mo Johnston.

His financial support enabled Rangers to make significant improvements to Ibrox Stadium, including a new tier on the stand, and Rangers' Training and Development Centre at Auchenhowie bears the name 'Murray Park' in recognition of his contribution to the club. In 1996 he set up a charitable organisation, known as 'The Murray Foundation', to provide support for amputees and their families in Scotland.

NAKAMURA Shunsuke (1978 –)

Scottish Premier League medals: 3
Scottish Cup medals: 1
Scottish League Cup medals: 1

Probably the first Japanese player to play in Scotland, Nakamura joined Celtic in 2005 from Italian club Reggina, and very soon distinguished himself by his tricky footwork and, in particular, his ability from set pieces. He has scored many goals direct from free kicks, notably against Manchester United in the Champions' League in November 2006, and against Kilmarnock in April 2007 - a strike that won the SPL for Celtic. By the end of May 2008 he had played seventy-four times for Japan.

Dunfermline's modern day fans do not know why their early counterparts nicknamed their club 'The Pars'.

NAMES and NICKNAMES

One of the problems that a non-Scottish person faces when studying Scottish football is that the names of the clubs are not necessarily geographically self-defined. Where for example do Raith Rovers play? Or the two Saints – Johnstone and Mirren? Partick Thistle? Morton? Queen's Park? This is a justified criticism but, on the other hand, a study of the nomenclature of Scottish teams can teach a great deal about Scottish cultural life. Perth, for example, is otherwise known as St John's Town, the Raith is a part of Kirkcaldy and Partick is an area in Glasgow, although ironically Partick Thistle now play in Maryhill rather than Partick. Heart of Midlothian is a well-known novel by Sir Walter Scott. Sometimes a great deal can be learned from a name, e.g. the now defunct Third Lanark were actually the Third Lanarkshire Rifle Volunteers, hence their nicknames of the 'Sodgers' and the 'Warriors' (a nickname shared with Stenhousemuir). They were also referred to as the 'Hi-Hi' and 'Thirds'.

Occasionally politics can be seen to be at work. In 1875 in Edinburgh a team was created called the Hibernians, whose very name means 'Irishmen', for this organization was intended exclusively for the Catholic Irish of that city. Twelve years later when a similar football club was formed in Glasgow, the team was at one point to be called the Glasgow Hibernians, but it was decided that a certain 'Scottishness' should be allowed as well, and thus the team became known as the Celtic, and it was some time before people could be persuaded not to call them the Keltic.

The name 'Rangers' seems to have been copied from an English rugby union team and means the same sort of thing as 'Wanderers' or 'Rovers'. The name 'United' ought to come about because of an amalgamation, but that is not always the case. Dundee United, for example, were called Dundee Hibernian until 1923 but changed their name to move away from their Irish roots and to avoid confusion with the Edinburgh team of that name. Some followers of Queen of the South claim that their team is mentioned in the Bible. So indeed do Hearts (as in 'lift up your hearts'), but there does seem to be a specific prediction of promotion for the 'Doonhamers' in the Gospel of St Matthew 12.42 or St Luke 11.31 when it says 'the queen of the south shall rise up'. The context is the day of judgement, so who knows what will happen when the Dumfries men reach the Scottish Premier League?

As for the teams who are geographically self-defined, they are to be commended for the boost that they have given to the teaching of geography in Scottish schools. Most schoolboys with an interest in football will probably be able to say where Stenhousemuir, Cowdenbeath, Forfar, Motherwell and Kilmarnock are located on a map, but what about Carluke, Biggar, Ullapool, Langholm or Oban? These latter named places have committed the fairly serious crime of not having a football team in the Scottish League! Care must be taken sometimes. There is a team loosely referred to as 'East Stirling', with the implication for the unwary that they play in the east end of Stirling. In fact their name is East Stirlingshire, and until 2008 they plied their trade at Firs Park in Falkirk.

In worldwide terms as well, football can be a help to geography. On one June day in 1990, for example, all Scotland suddenly found out that there was a country called Costa Rica.

Every team has at least one nickname. Some of them are banal, e.g. Raith Rovers are nicknamed the 'Rovers' and Brechin City the 'City'. Others have a reference to the colour or design of their strips, e.g. Airdrie United retained the same strip as Airdrieonians and are called the 'Diamonds', while Alloa's black and gold strip likens them to the 'Wasps'. Others are often shortened forms of their name e.g. 'Killie' for Kilmarnock, 'Ton' for Morton and 'Well' for Motherwell. Others reflect the name given to the town's inhabitants e.g. the 'Bairns' of Falkirk, the 'Loons' of Forfar and the 'Buddies' of Paisley, whose team St Mirren are also nicknamed the 'Saints', a nickname shared by St Johnstone. The river Don explains Aberdeen's nickname, whilst the 'Doonhamers' came about for Queen of the South because people from Dumfries would refer to their town as 'doon hame' when they were working away from home. Arbroath are the 'Red Lichties' in a reference to their lighthouse, while Dumbarton Rock explains why their team has the name the 'Sons of the Rock' or more commonly the 'Sons'. Peterhead are called the 'Blue Toon'. The 'Blue Brazil', however, became the nickname of Cowdenbeath following their promotion from the second division in 1992, while Robert Burns is directly responsible for Ayr United being called the 'Honest Men'.

In the 1960s the custom prevailed of supporters chanting the name of their team and then clapping three times. This is a great deal less effective if the team only has one syllable in its name, so Hearts fans had a problem. City rivals could call themselves the 'Hibees', but Tynecastle devotees had to resort to rhyming slang and call their team the 'Jam Tarts'. Rhyming slang also meant that Partick Thistle, already called the 'Jags' because of what a thistle can do to you, could call themselves the 'Harry Wraggs' after the famous racing jockey, and for Rangers the 'Gers' rhymed in Glasgow dialect with the 'Teddy Bears'.

Controversy rages about why Dunfermline Athletic are called the 'Pars'. They have been so called since the 1920s, and the general consensus is that it was originally a term of abuse, a shortened form of 'paralytics', which was a reference to their poor performances on the field. Similarly, it is believed that Dundee United earned the nickname the 'Arabs' because of the state of their pitch, looking more like a desert than a football field, after the hard winter of 1963. But a real mystery surrounds Montrose, who rejoice in the nickname of the 'Gable Endies'. Are there really more houses with a gable end in Montrose than elsewhere? Similarly are Stenhousemuir more warlike than anyone else to merit the nickname the 'Warriors'? And why are Clyde called the 'Bully Wee' – a nickname that they have had since their Shawfield days, and is probably the best-known nickname of them all? The generally recognised nicknames of each club are:

Aberdeen	The Dons
Airdrie United	The Diamonds
Albion Rovers	The Wee Rovers
Alloa Athletic	The Wasps
Arbroath	The Red Lichties
Ayr United	The Honest Men
Berwick Rangers	The Borderers
Brechin City	The City
Celtic	The Bhoys; The Hoops
Clyde	The Bully Wee
Cowdenbeath	The Blue Brazil
Dumbarton	The Sons of the Rock
Dundee	The Dee; The Dark Blues
Dundee United	The Arabs; The Terrors
Dunfermline Athletic	The Pars
East Fife	The Fifers
East Stirlingshire	The Shire
Elgin City	The City
Falkirk	The Bairns
Forfar Athletic	The Loons
Greenock Morton	The Ton
Hamilton Academical	The Accies
Heart of Midlothian	The Jam Tarts
Hibernian	The Hibees
Inverness Caledonian Thistle	The Caley Jags
Kilmarnock	The Killie
Livingston	The Livi Lions
Montrose	The Gable Endies
Motherwell	The Well; The Steelmen
Partick Thistle	The Jags; The Harry Wraggs
Peterhead	The Blue Toon
Queen of the South	The Doonhamers
Queen's Park	The Spiders
Raith Rovers	The Rovers
Rangers	The Gers; The Teddy Bears
Ross County	The Staggies
St Mirren	The Saints; The Buddies
St Johnstone	The Saints
Stenhousemuir	The Warriors
Stirling Albion	The Binos
Stranraer	The Blues

NAREY David (1956 –)

Scotland Caps: 35
Scottish League Championship medals: 1
Scottish League Cup medals: 3

A solid, dependable central defender, David Narey played most of his career with Dundee United. He won thirty-five caps for Scotland, and took part in the World Cup finals of 1982 and 1986. His most famous moment was the brilliant goal he scored against Brazil in the 1982 World Cup from the edge of the box. This was the goal that was infamously described by Jimmy Hill as 'a toe poke'! With Dundee United he won one Scottish Premier League championship medal and two Scottish League Cup medals, but tended to lose Scottish Cup finals. His dour defending was a potent factor in Dundee United's consistent success in Europe throughout the 1980s. He holds the Scottish record of having played seventy-six matches in Europe, and was awarded the MBE for his services to Scottish football. Towards the end of his long career he moved to Raith Rovers, and with them won a Scottish League Cup medal in 1994/95.

David Narey scores his famous goal against Brazil in the 1982 World Cup

NAYSMITH Gary (1979 –)

Scotland Caps: 40
Scottish Cup medals: 1

Gary Naysmith is a defender who has now played forty times for Scotland, in a career that began with Hearts in 1996. He showed great promise there, and in 1998 won a Scottish Cup medal with the Tynecastle side. In 2000 he was transferred to Everton for £1.7 million. He has had a few injury setbacks, and possibly suffered for playing in a team that has consistently under-performed in the English Premiership, but has continued to impress for Scotland. In summer 2007 he moved to Sheffield United.

NELSON Jimmy (1901 – 1965)

Scotland Caps: 4

Jimmy Nelson was the right back of the Wembley Wizards side of 1928, one of only four times that he played for Scotland. He was born in Greenock, but lived a great deal of his early life in Northern Ireland. He joined Cardiff City in 1921, and won the FA Cup with them in 1927 (becoming known as 'the Scotsman from Ireland who won the English Cup with a Welsh team!'). In 1930 he joined Newcastle United and captained them to an FA Cup triumph in 1932.

NEVIN Pat (1963 –)

Scotland Caps: 28

Pat Nevin was a forward who played twenty-eight times for Scotland (including participation in the 1992 European Championships), and is now a well-known journalist and television pundit, famous for his esoteric interests in music and literature as well as football. His first senior club was Clyde, whom he joined in 1981 and helped to win the Second Division championship in 1982. In 1983 he joined Chelsea for £95,000, a fee that had increased tenfold by the time he went to Everton in 1988. He then played for Tranmere Rovers, Kilmarnock and Motherwell, being director of football with the Fir Park men for a spell.

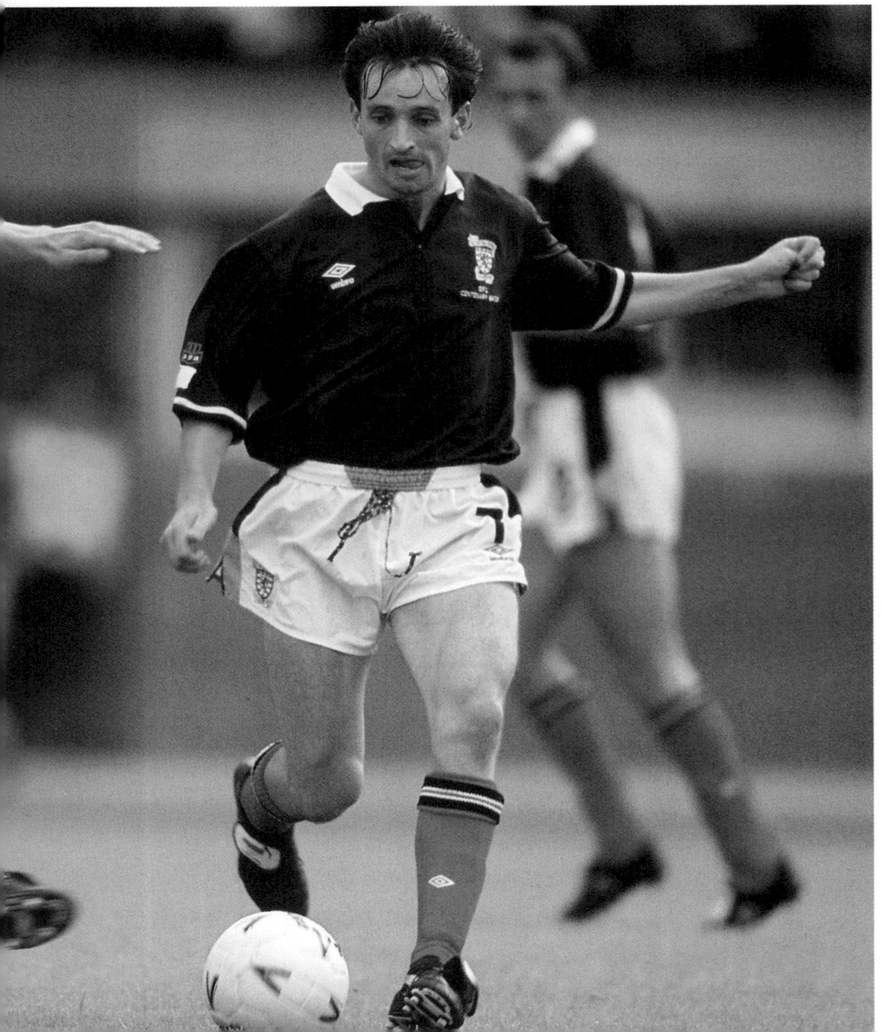

Will 'O the Wisp winger Pat Nevin in full flow.

NEW ZEALAND

Scotland have played New Zealand twice, with a win at the 1982 World Cup finals and a draw during the Bertie Vogts era.

1982	15 June	Malaga	5–2	Wark (2) Dalglish Archibald Robertson	Sumner Wooddin
2003	27 May	Tynecastle	1–1	Crawford	Nelsen

NEWSPAPERS

The circulation of newspapers drops noticeably during the summer when there is no football. Football in Scotland is what sells most newspapers, far more than pictures of almost-naked women, or gossip about celebrities, or the Royal Family, or even real news. Most men (and a great deal of women as well) will ignore the wars and the general elections on the front pages, and turn immediately to the back pages to read about knee injuries, transfer speculation (founded and unfounded), and some club's chances of playing in next season's UEFA Cup.

This has been the case since the 1880s. In the 1870s there was often a brief mention that Scotland had beaten England at football... but that would be all. It was only when Scotland began to beat England a great deal and regularly that newspapers realised their readers (even those of the bourgeois *Glasgow Herald* and *Scotsman*) wanted to hear more about this game. Accordingly, by the mid 1880s games were reported in some detail, but there was a distinct lack of speculation or opinions about the game until the early 1900s. Specific sporting newspapers like *Scottish Sport* and *The Scottish Referee* were in vogue by the 1890s, and in 1906 Queen's Park recognised their importance by providing them with the world's first ever press box at Hampden Park

The Scottish Referee in particular was a very good publication, appearing twice weekly; on a Monday with reports of Saturday's sport, and on a Friday with a preview of the next Saturday's games. It gave some indication of the massive amount of football (and other sports) played in Scotland, with a full and comprehensive coverage of all the regional and junior Leagues. It was also famous for its cartoons in the tradition of the *Punch* political cartoons, but it is usually necessary to know some of the background. For example, the Scottish League had stopped playing the Irish League for a few seasons between 1904 and 1908, on the grounds that the standard of Irish football was so low. But the Irish League was making overtures for the resumption of this fixture. A lady dressed in Irish costume appeared on the front page of *The Scottish Referee* singing the music hall song 'Come Back To Erin'.

In the same way that newspapers tended to support political parties, a certain bias could be detected in the way the football was reported. One newspaper, *The Glasgow Observer,* which catered for the Roman Catholic community, made no bones about the fact that it loved the Celtic team and was notorious for its bias towards them. *The Glasgow Herald* was a lover of Queen's Park, the Edinburgh-based *The Scotsman* supported Hearts, and the *Dundee Courier* and *Advertiser* naturally revealed a penchant for Dundee.

Newspapers come and go, but the 1950s and 1960s were the decades of the *Daily Express* and the *Daily Record,* with great journalists such as Waverley, Rex Kingsley, Gair Henderson, Cyril Horne, Jack Harkness and John McKenzie, who called himself somewhat bombastically 'The Voice of Football'. Willie Waddell also wrote for the *Daily Express* after he left his job as manager of Kilmarnock and before he became manager of Rangers in 1969. He is criticised by some Ibrox historians for the way that he used his position at the *Daily Express* to undermine his predecessor at Ibrox, Davie White. For circulation reasons, newspapers tended towards Rangers, but they were usually very careful not to upset the Celtic readership too much. It could be argued that this state of affairs continues today, but there is certainly a wealth of printers' ink spilt on all aspects of football.

Journalists can have a great deal of influence on the game. It has often been said that they can pick the Scotland team or choose the next manager. The best way to do this is not of course by a blatant campaign, for such things tend to be counter-productive, but more effectively by the insidious and assiduous mentioning, or (crucially) *not* mentioning, a man's name day after day. A clear indication that a man has fallen out with the press is when his name is not mentioned in a report of a game other than in the listing of the teams.

But if journalists can have a great influence on affairs, a good manager can also use the media for his own advantage. An example of this was Jock Stein who, when manager of Celtic, clearly knew how to manipulate journalists. He would give them a story on what he knew would be a quiet day, he would frequently invite the press to Celtic Park to see the team training, and he had the extraordinary ability, as Alan Herron of the *Sunday Mail* used to say, to knock his opponents off the back page by giving the press a story so huge that the newspapers would have to take it in place of whatever they were planning to say about Rangers.

One sad loss in recent decades has been the demise of the Saturday evening newspapers like the *Evening Citizen,* the *Evening News* and the *Evening Times* of Glasgow, the *Evening News* of Edinburgh, and the *Sporting Post* of Dundee, with reports of games written as they actually happen. Fans would often wonder at the speed with which these newspapers were produced. In such circumstances, it was of course no surprise that they were full of misprints and errors, sometimes hilarious ones – 'McGrory hit the post with a hard shit' or 'the first goal of the game is scored by Ralph Brand of the Bangers' – but they did very much capture the essence of the game. The *Sporting Post* in particular employed the vivid present tense in the same way that Latin authors use that tense to describe graphic battle scenes 'Dundee United kick off towards the Arklay Street end of the ground, but in the second minute it is Kilmarnock who make the first attempt on goal…'

Scottish Daily Mail

News Chronicle

PRINTED AND PUBLISHED IN SCOTLAND — SATURDAY, MAY 27

FANTASTIC, SAYS STEIN AS 200,000 GREET CELTIC

Champion nigh[t]

By JACK McEACHRAN, WILL JONES, GEORGE McKECHNIE, TOM STEELE, GORDON ANDERSON and RON FLOCKHART

GLASGOW belonged to Celtic last night. The newly crowned kings of European football came home to a welcome unrivalled since the end of the war.

Well over 100,000 fans gathered at Parkhead and the surrounding area to greet their heroes.

Another estimated 100,000 were on the route from Glasgow Airport.

Appeal

"Morning, Sir Francis."

SIR FRANCIS LANDS AT 11 a.m. TOMORROW

By Daily Mail Reporter

Handshake from the law for Jock Stein as he arrives at Parkhead carryi[ng]

70 FANS

Police

These evening papers have now all but disappeared, victims of radio and television programmes which inform everyone of the results, and in particular of the invention in the early 1980s of teletext. Features of such newspapers were the 'Spot The Ball' competition, based on a photograph taken at a recent game with the ball missing. There was also gossip, and an excellent 'Query Column' that settled many arguments and often (deliberately) provoked more.

For a historian, newspapers provide a wealth of information, but anyone reading his football newspaper in the present day would be well advised to take everything with a very large pinch of salt, particularly as regards transfer speculation, or the sacking or appointment of a manager. It has, indeed, been admitted by some journalists and ex-journalists that on a quiet day such a story has (lamentably) to be invented, for the editor would not like to see empty pages in his newspaper! 'Scoops' and 'exclusives' come and go with varying degrees of accuracy, but on one famous occasion in July 1989, the *Scottish Sun* broke the dominance of the *Daily Record.* This was when it published the story of Maurice Johnston signing for Rangers. The story in itself was massive, and the fact that the *Scottish Sun* was twenty-four hours ahead of everyone else was a great triumph for Iain Scott, the Sports Editor, and led to a permanent change in circulation figures.

NIBLOE Joe (1903 – 1976)

Scotland Caps: 11
Scottish Cup medals: 1

A left back with Kilmarnock in the 1920s and early 1930s, Joe Nibloe was capped eleven times for Scotland, and was on the winning side against England in 1929 and 1931. For Kilmarnock, he also won a Scottish Cup medal in 1929. He was transferred to Aston Villa in 1932, and then moved on to Sheffield Wednesday in 1935, but his best days were with Kilmarnock.

Charlie Nicholas in Celtic's colours.

NICHOLAS Charlie (1961 –)

Scotland Caps: 20
Scottish League Championship medals: 2
Scottish Cup medals: 1
Scottish League Cup medals: 2

Charlie Nicholas was an extremely talented, but in some ways disappointing, forward with Celtic, Arsenal, Aberdeen and then Celtic again, before finishing his career with Clyde. He won twenty caps for Scotland, and the goal he scored on his international debut against Switzerland at Hampden Park in March 1983 will be long remembered. But he was transferred (to the great distress of his many admirers) for £800,000 to Arsenal in 1983, where his career did not reach the high peaks that one might have expected had he stayed with Celtic. Nor has he ever been forgiven in Glasgow for his desertion of the cause. With only one English League Cup medal with Arsenal to his credit, he returned to play for Aberdeen in 1998. He then went back to Celtic in 1990 at, arguably, the worst spell in Celtic's history. He annoyed Celtic supporters by reminding them how 'Celtic-minded' he was – something that did not seem to square with the events of 1983. He finished his career with Clyde and is now a television pundit.

NICKNAMES (See NAMES AND NICKNAMES)

NICOL Steve (1961 –)

Scotland Caps: 27

A solid defender for Ayr United and Liverpool, Steve Nicol earned twenty-seven caps for Scotland and played in the 1986 World Cup finals. His strength lay in his versatility, in that he could play all over the defence and even sometimes in midfield. He made his debut for Ayr United in 1979, and joined Liverpool in 1981 for £300,000. He won a European Cup medal with Liverpool in 1984, even though he missed a penalty in the shoot-out. He won four English league medals and three FA Cup medals with Liverpool, before finishing his career with Notts County, Sheffield Wednesday and West Bromwich Albion.

NIGERIA

Scotland have played Nigeria only once, and lost.

2002	17 Apr	Pittodrie	1–2	Dailly	Aghahowa (2)

NITHSDALE WANDERERS FC
(former Scottish League club)

Home: **Crawick Holm, Sanquhar, Dumfriesshire**
Highest League Position: **32nd (12th in Div. 2, 1925/26)**
Best Scottish Cup Performances: **Last 16 (2nd round 1902/03; 1910/11; 3rd round 1920/21; 1922/23)**

Founded in the late 1890s, the Wanderers played league football in both the Scottish Combination and the Scottish Union in the years before the first world war. They regularly qualified for the early rounds of the Scottish Cup and in 1910/11 took Motherwell to a second-round replay before losing 1–0. They made their only appearance in the final of the Scottish Qualifying Cup in 1921/22, losing 2–1 to Montrose when the final went to a second replay at Ibrox.

After the war the club didn't re-enter a league until 1922/23, when they joined the Western League at the second time of asking. A year later most of its members, including the Wanderers, became part of the short-lived Division Three that existed from 1923 to 1926. Nithsdale Wanderers, however, were members of the select band that managed to escape. They were champions of Division Three in its second season, 1924/25, and, along with Queen of the South, won promotion to Division Two. Then, when Division Three folded a year later, both clubs survived and continued as members of the Scottish League. The tragedy for Nithsdale was that just one year later, in 1927, they finished bottom and failed to gain re-election. Their league membership had lasted for four seasons.

In the years that followed Nithsdale played in several different leagues and qualified for the Scottish Cup from time to time. In 1930/31 they lost 14–0 at Dundee United in the first round. There were several unsuccessful attempts to return to the Scottish League and in 1951 they decided to become a junior club. This club eventually went out of existence in 1964, but the name lives on as a new Nithsdale Wanderers has played in the South of Scotland League since 2001.

NORTHERN FC (former Scottish League club)

Home: **Hyde Park, Springburn, Glasgow**
Highest League Position: **19th (9th in Div. 2, 1893/94)**
Best Scottish Cup Performance: **Last 12 (4th round, 1876/77)**

The club only belonged to the Scottish League for one season, 1893/94. This was the season when Division Two was introduced for the first time and it had come as a surprise when Northern was named as one of its members. Although they had been founded in 1874, their only previous experience of league football had been two seasons in the Scottish Alliance between 1891 and 1893 and they had finished below clubs that were now denied membership. Northern had entered the Scottish Cup since 1875, but their form had been unremarkable.

By the end of the season the doubts had been justified. Northern finished second bottom, with just nine points from eighteen games, and failed to gain re-election. This proved to be the beginning of the end, although there was an unsuccessful attempt to rejoin the Scottish League the following year. The best players left, crowds were small, and financial problems mounted. By 1897 the club had gone out of existence.

NORTHERN IRELAND

See **IRELAND.** Northern Ireland's governing body is the Irish Football Association (IFA), which is not to be confused with the Republic's Football Association of Ireland (FAI).

The southern part of Ireland broke away from the IFA in 1921, and Scotland's fixture in February of that year was the last occasion on which Scotland played a team that represented the whole of Ireland. From 1922 onwards, games that are listed against 'Ireland' refer to games against Northern Ireland.

NORTHERN LEAGUE

The Northern League was formed in 1891 for clubs in the Tayside and Aberdeen areas, and at the end of the 1891/92 season the first championship was shared between East End and Our Boys – the two clubs that amalgamated to form Dundee FC in 1893.

The league suffered a blow in 1909 when six clubs (Arbroath, Dunfermline Athletic, East Fife, Kirkcaldy United, Lochgelly United and St Johnstone) left to become part of the new Central League, and at the end of the 1909/10 season the weakened Northern League looked as follows, with several fixtures not completed:

	P	W	D	L	Pts
Dundee 'A'	9	7	1	1	15
Brechin City	11	6	1	4	13
Dundee Hibernian	11	4	3	4	11
Montrose	9	3	3	3	9
Forfar Athletic	12	3	3	6	9
Dundee Wanderers	8	1	4	3	6
Aberdeen 'A'	6	1	1	4	3

Although Dundee Hibernian joined Division Two of the Scottish League in 1910, they also participated in the Northern League during seasons 1910/11, 1911/12, 1913/14, and 1914/15. The Northern League was suspended during the first world war, but it reformed for a final season in 1919/20, when Montrose won the championship.

NORWAY

Scotland's record against Norway is fairly impressive – played fifteen, won eight, drawn five, lost two.

Norway were Scotland's first overseas opponents in 1929.

1929	28 May	Bergen	7–3	Cheyne (3) Nisbet (2) Rankin Craig	Kongsvik (2) Berg-Johannesen
1954	5 May	Hampden Park	1–0	Hamilton	
1954	19 May	Oslo	1–1	Mackenzie	Kure
1963	4 June	Bergen	3–4	Law (3)	Nilsen Johansen Pedersen Krogh
1963	7 Nov	Hampden Park	6–1	Law (4) Mackay (2)	Kristoffersen
1974	6 June	Oslo	2–1	Jordan Dalglish	Lund
1978	25 Oct	Hampden Park	3–2	Dalglish (2) Gemmill (pen)	Aas Larsen-Okland
1979	7 June	Oslo	4–0	Jordan Dalglish Robertson McQueen	
1988	14 Sep	Oslo	2–1	McStay Johnston	Fjortoft
1989	15 Nov	Hampden Park	1–1	McCoist	Johnsen
1992	3 June	Oslo	0–0		
1998	16 June	Bordeaux	1–1	Burley	Flo
2003	20 Aug	Oslo	0–0		
2004	9 Oct	Hampden Park	0–1		Iversen (pen)
2005	7 Sep	Oslo	2–1	Miller (2)	Arst

NUMBERING

Every player must now have a number on his shirt, and in the SPL his name must appear as well. Less acceptably to the purist, the names of the shirt manufacturer and sponsor(s) are also there. Until the second world war there were no numbers on shirts, and then, as the idea which had started in England at the FA Cup final of 1923 spread northwards, the right back became number 2, left back number 3 etc., all the way to the left winger at number 11. This was not universally applied, for some teams, notably Celtic and Queen's Park, avoided the use of numbers until Celtic amazed the world in a friendly in 1960 by appearing with numbers on their shorts! With the arrival of substitutes in the mid 1960s, a

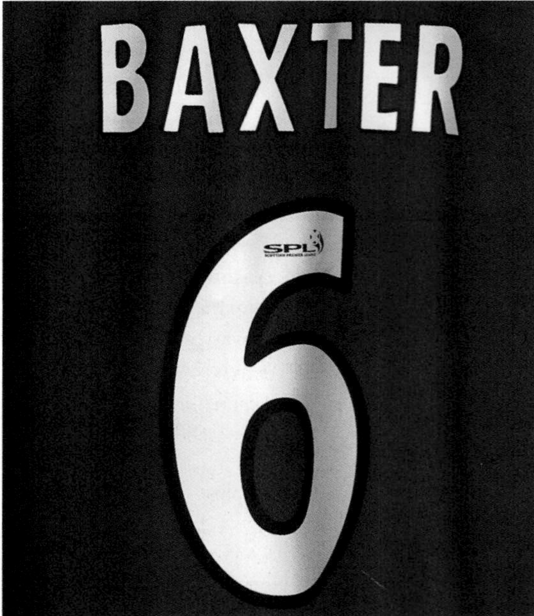

number 12 and then a number 14 was needed, although there was a certain amount of triskaidekaphobia in that number 13 was sometimes avoided. The arrival of European football meant that eventually the authorities insisted that all jerseys must be numbered so that the referees could more easily identify the players. Yet Celtic, obstinate to the end, managed to hold out against having numbers on their shirts in domestic competition until 1994. Now the bigger teams give their players a squad number that they use all season. This has an advantage in that supporters can instantly identify a player as long as they know his squad number, but it does seem incongruous to have someone running around with 44 or 27 on his back, when a game is played between two teams of eleven men each!

OFFSIDE

As this Law causes more arguments and confusion than any other, it is worth quoting Law 11 in full:

'A player is offside if he is nearer his opponents' goal line than the ball at the moment the ball is played unless;

a) He is in his own half of the field of play.
b) There are two of his opponents nearer to their own goal line than he is.
c) The ball last touched an opponent or was played by him.
d) He received the ball direct from a goal kick, a corner kick, a throw in, or when it was dropped by the referee.

Punishment – for an infringement of this Law, an indirect free kick shall be taken by a player of the opposing team, from the place where the infringement occurred.

A player in an offside position shall not be penalised unless, in the opinion of the referee, he is interfering with the play or with an opponent, or is seeking to gain an advantage by being in an offside position.'

Many directives have come from FIFA on this issue, the more recent ones being that 'any part of a player's body, head or feet being nearer to the goal line than both the ball and the second last opponent will make the attacker offside. Arms are not included in this definition'. And a closer definition of a player 'interfering with play' and being 'active' is as follows:

a) 'Interfering with the play means the involvement of a player at least touching a ball projected by his team-mate.'
b) 'Interfering means preventing an opponent playing or being able to play the ball by obstructing his vision, movements or making gestures that in the opinion of the referee deceive or distract him.'

Gaining an advantage is being initially in an offside position, not interfering with the ball, but subsequently playing it when it rebounds from posts, bar or an opponent. Although not referred to in the Laws, this is frequently termed a 'secondary offside'.

Many people are scornful of the phrase 'interfering with play', notably Bill Shankly, who once asked the pertinent question that if a player is not interfering with play, why is he on the field in the first place?

The problem remains however that everything depends on the referee and his assistant to get it right. Games played on public parks where the referee is on his own have a particular problem here, for offside decisions are virtually impossible to call with any degree of accuracy unless the official is in line. In televised games, modern technology can prove whether the referee got it right or wrong, but a decision can hardly be rescinded. Supporters of every team will no doubt be able to recall instances when they were robbed by a dodgy offside decision, never more so than in the European Cup-Winners' Cup semi final second leg of 1966 at Anfield when Celtic scored a legitimate goal through Bobby Lennox only to have it flagged offside by a linesman who could not believe the speed of Bobby Lennox. Bobby was able to move from an onside position at the time the ball was played to an apparently offside position by the time the ball reached him. A similarly unfortunate incident occurred in the 2003 Scottish League Cup final involving John Hartson. Rangers fans are able to give many examples of Ralph Brand and Ally McCoist being similarly unjustly treated.

Historically, it was the SFA who were responsible for the change of the Law in 1925. Concerned about the paucity of goals being scored, the SFA, with the backing of the English Football Association, approached FIFA (which had been formed in 1904) and successfully proposed the change. Previously there had to be three men closer to the goal line than the attacker for him to be onside, and the result was that fewer goals were being scored than was desirable. The change of the Law brought an increase in the number of goals being scored (1,337 in season 1925/6 as distinct from 1,178 in 1924/25) and it did brighten up the game. Indirectly it brought about a gradual change in the role of the centre half, because so many goals were now being scored that the centre half was pulled further back to become a central defender rather than a centre half back, as he had been originally.

From time to time, some teams have played an offside trap, notably Aberdeen in the early 1970s, but such traps often fail, for they require a well-drilled defence and a very sharp linesman or assistant referee. Such traps involve the defence charging forward en masse and leaving the forwards in an exposed and offside position.

In season 1973/74, as an experiment in the Dryburgh and Scottish League Cup, a player could only be declared offside inside his opponent's penalty area or its lateral extension. The idea was to encourage more goalscoring by allowing a forward to 'poach' in his opponents' half as far as the penalty area. There was no marked increase in the amount of goals being scored and the experiment was swiftly abandoned.

OLDEST CLUB

Documents held in the National Archives of Scotland suggest that 'The Foot-Ball Club', which existed in Edinburgh from 1824 until at least 1841, may be the earliest known football club in the world. The papers show that John Hope, who was seventeen years of age and a trainee lawyer in 1824, organised Saturday matches on the Dalry estate in southwest Edinburgh during 1824/25. One of the documents lays down a series of rules, but it is clear that the games were much rougher than modern football, and another document refers to a match that involved thirty-nine players. In 1831 the club moved to Greenhill Parks in Bruntsfield, and by 1839 was meeting in Grove Park, west of Gardeners Crescent.

In 2008 football coach Kenny Cameron resurrected the club, with a view to not only involving young people, but also raising money for charity. However, it should be noted that Sheffield FC, whilst founded thirty-three years later in 1857, is the world's oldest football club that has continuously existed.

OLD FIRM

This is the name given to the two big teams of Glasgow, Celtic and Rangers. The origin of this phrase is a cynical cartoon in the *Scottish Referee* of 16 April 1904, the day of the Scottish Cup final between Celtic and Rangers, which depicted a man with a sandwich board which advised people to 'Patronise the Old Firm – Rangers Celtic Ltd'. This was a comment on their ability to make money by drawing large crowds, particularly in cup ties, when a draw in the first game and a replay with another big gate was by no means uncommon. Indeed it was the perception that this was being done deliberately, which was one of the causes of the Hampden Riot at the Scottish Cup final of 17 April 1909.

However uncomfortable this has been to both sets of fans, there can be little doubt that the interests of both Celtic and Rangers converge oftener than they diverge. Both clubs have realised this, and very seldom in their history have they been on different sides of a political fence. This symbiotic relationship, for example, led Rangers to back Celtic in their flying of the Irish flag in the early 1950s when Celtic were under attack from

Something's caught the eye of John Greig (Rangers) and Billy McNeill (Celtic).

Bertie Peacock, Celtic and Eric Caldow, Rangers, lead their teams out in August 1960.

Harry Swan of Hibs. Celtic for their part never objected to Rangers' policy of not employing Catholics. Sectarianism and bigotry, however distasteful to Scottish society at large, has been a large goose that has laid many golden eggs at the front doors of Parkhead and Ibrox. As someone once noticed, the words of 'Sean South of Garryowen' and 'The Sash My Father Wore' fit into each other's tunes!

OLYMPIC GAMES

Football has been played in every Olympic Games since 1908 at the Crystal Palace, apart from Los Angeles in 1932. Scotland has never entered a team, but has occasionally contributed to a Great Britain entry. Great Britain has twice won the Gold Medal, in 1908 at the Crystal Palace and at Stockholm in 1912.

Ronnie Simpson, who went on to win five Scotland caps and a European Cup medal with Celtic in the late 1960s, competed for Great Britain at the Olympic Games twenty years earlier in London in 1948. Simpson was an amateur with Queen's Park at the time. The manager of the British Olympic team that year was Matt Busby, the Scottish manager of Manchester United. Great Britain beat Holland and France, but lost in the semi-final to Yugoslavia, and then in the third-place final to Denmark. Since 1960 Great Britain has failed to qualify.

Two other Queen's Park players, W. Neil and P. Buchanan, represented Great Britain in the unsuccessful qualifying rounds for the Tokyo Olympics of 1964, but Great Britain failed to qualify. Since 1972, when Great Britain lost to Bulgaria and failed to qualify for the Munich Olympics of that year, no Great Britain team has participated in the games. But with the Olympics being held in London in 2012, there will be once again a Great Britain team. In June 2007 the SFA failed to attend a meeting to discuss the situation, fearing perhaps that this might weaken their bargaining power for future World Cups, for South American countries in particular often feel that there should be one Great Britain team for the World Cup.

O'NEILL Martin (1952 –)

Born in Northern Ireland, the much-travelled Martin O'Neill's contribution to Scottish football was his managership of Celtic from 2000-2005, during which time the club won three Scottish Premier League championships, three Scottish Cups and one Scottish League Cup. He also took the club to the final of the UEFA Cup in Seville in 2003, where they lost narrowly to Jose Mourinho's Porto. He left Celtic in 2005 to look after his ill wife, but returned to football a year later to manage Aston Villa. He has also managed Wycombe Wanderers, Norwich City and Leicester City. In his playing career he won sixty-four caps for Northern Ireland and an English league championship medal, two English League Cup medals, and a European Cup medal with Nottingham Forest. He also played for Norwich City, Manchester City and Notts County.

ORDERED OFF

It is a sad fact that players do get ordered off or have 'an early bath' or 'first use of the soap' in Scottish football with regrettable regularity. Violent conduct of any kind cannot ever be justified and the red card (which has been used since the early 1980s) is clearly appropriate in these circumstances, as is the suspension that inevitably follows.

Law 12 gives seven reasons why a player may be sent off viz. serious foul play, violent conduct, spitting at opponent or other person, denying a goalscoring opportunity by deliberately handling, denying a goalscoring opportunity by an offence normally punishable by a free kick or penalty kick, using offensive, insulting or abusive language or gestures and receiving a second caution (or yellow card) in the same match.

Sometimes it can seem that Law 12 is a little tough in this regard. In particular the sending off of a goalkeeper for overstepping the penalty box with the ball in his hands does seem more than a trifle harsh in that there is often no malice or violent intent, and the goalkeeper can be merely carried over the line by his own impetus and really cannot be interpreted as deliberate handball. Famously this happened at a Scottish League Cup semi final in 1994, when Scot Thomson of Raith Rovers was sent off against Airdrie at McDiarmid Park for this 'offence'.

Similarly the last man rule as it is erroneously called or 'denying a goalscoring opportunity' can be a little draconian, as is 'deliberate hand ball' and it is often good to see wise referees not being too strict in enforcing the letter of the law. On the other hand, it is often sad to see a player sent off for a 'second bookable offence', something that really shows a lack of professionalism in that the culprit is clearly unable to take a telling.

Even then, there are times when the referee might use a little discretion as in the case in February 2007 when Jan Vennegoor of Hesselink, having been yellow carded previously, was sent off for celebrating a goal with his own fans in a game in Inverness.

'Deliberate handball' and 'denying a goalscoring opportunity' are more recent phenomena, but any kind of violent conduct was always deplored and usually rewarded with a sending off. Edwardian Scotland had two *causes célèbres* when on 25 March 1905 and 1 January 1907, Celtic's Jimmy Quinn was sent off, each time in a game against Rangers. These cases were much argued about and disputed in their time.

Willie Johnston of Rangers, West Bromwich Albion, Vancouver Whitecaps, Hearts and Scotland holds the record of being sent off twenty-one times in a lengthy and interesting career. It will be recalled that Willie was also the man sent home from Argentina for taking an illegal substance, so it is fair to say that 'Bud' has not had his troubles to seek.

On three occasions in recent years in Scottish football have four players been sent off from one side. (If five are sent off, the referee should abandon the game). The highest profile one was Rangers versus Hearts on 14 September 1996 at Ibrox when four Tynecastle men saw red. On 3 December 1994, four Stranraer players were sent off against Airdrie at Broomfield, and on 23 August 1997 four men from Albion Rovers had a premature look at the Hampden dressing room in a game against Queen's Park.

Ordered off: Colin Stein, on the ground, is sent off in the dying moments in a game against Clyde.

And Colin Stein goes again, this time with Kilmarnock's Billy Dickson joining him.

17 March 1991 saw four players sent off in a Celtic versus Rangers game in the Scottish Cup at Celtic Park. One was a Celt – Peter Grant for the comparatively minor offence of breaking from the line before a free kick – but the other three, Terry Hurlock, Mark Walters and Mark Hateley were all from Rangers and dismissed for violent conduct. This led to an apology from manager Graeme Souness, and jokes about how Rangers recovered from their defeat on time to have a dance – the eightsome reel!

On at least two other occasions – Hamilton versus Airdrie in 1993, and Ayr United versus Stranraer in 1994 have four players been sent off, the score, as it were, being 3–1 on each occasion! One of the most bizarre sendings off was at Stark's Park, Kirkcaldy in a game between Raith Rovers and Hearts in 1994. Graeme Hogg and Craig Levein of Hearts were sent off for fighting – each other! This was bad enough, but it happened in a pre-season friendly!

The suspension *sine die* (indefinitely) is a rarity in Scottish or any other kind of senior football, (less rare, sadly, in junior football) but it did happen to Willie Kelly of St. Mirren in 1954 and in the same year to Willie Woodburn of Rangers (who had been capped twenty-four times for Scotland) after he had been sent off in August 1954 for head-butting a Stirling Albion player. It was his fifth sending off, and the authorities clearly upset about the rise of violence in the game, chose to visit this draconian but not undeserved penalty on this high profile player, possibly too using this opportunity to demonstrate that they were not (as was commonly believed) 'soft' on Rangers.

Duncan Ferguson of Rangers had more reason than most to regret his violent assault on John McStay of Raith Rovers in April 1994. Curiously enough his offence was missed by the referee, but not by the TV cameras, and he was duly suspended for twelve matches. This was bad enough, but he was subsequently jailed for three months for this offence.

Dave Bowman who had had a glittering, albeit occasionally contentious, career with Dundee United, was playing for Forfar Athletic in 2001 against Stranraer when he was given five red cards for persistent foul and abusive language, even after he had been sent off! As a result he was suspended for seventeen matches – more or less to the end of the season and his career never really restarted.

Orderings off in high profile matches are comparatively rare. Only four men have ever been sent off in a Scottish Cup final – Jock Buchanan of Rangers in 1929, Roy Aitken of Celtic in 1984, Walter Kydd of Hearts in 1986 and Paul Hartley of Hearts in 2006. Significantly, on three of the four occasions, their side lost the game. Hartley's case was different in that it came at the very end of extra time, so all he really missed was the penalty shoot-out.

A sending off is slightly more common in the Scottish League Cup Final. Doug Rougvie of Aberdeen in 1978/79, Maurice Johnston of Celtic in 1986/87, Tommy Solberg of Aberdeen in 1999/2000, Chris Sutton of Celtic in 2000/01 and Neil Lennon of Celtic in 2002/03 are the guilty men, and once again (with the exception of Sutton in 2001) the men ordered off played for the losers. In the Scottish League Cup final of October 1986, there was a curious incident when Celtic's Tony Shepherd was sent off by referee Davie Syme, who thought that he had been punched by Shepherd. When Syme realised that he had in fact been hit by a missile from the crowd, Shepherd was immediately reinstated.

To be sent off in an international match is a particular disgrace. Fifteen men share that opprobrium, although some were in extenuating circumstances e.g. Jamie McFadden was for handball. But the guilty men are Billy Steel, (versus Austria 27 May 1951), Bertie Auld, (Holland 27 May 1959), Pat Crerand (Czechoslovakia 14 May 1961), Tommy Gemmell (West Germany 22 October 1969), Peter Lorimer (Denmark 15 November 1972), Andy Gray (Czechoslovakia 13 October 1976), Willie Johnston (Argentina 18 June 1977), Joe Jordan (Northern Ireland 16 May 1980), Richard Gough (Switzerland 9 September 1992), John Spencer (Japan 21 May 1995), Craig Burley (Morocco 23 June 1998) Matt Elliott (Faeroe Islands 5 June 1999), Maurice Ross (Germany 10 September 2003), Jamie McFadden (Norway 9 October 2004), and Steven Pressley (Ukraine 11 Oct 2006).

ORIGINS OF THE GAME

The origins of the game are of course lost in the mists of antiquity. The Romans apparently played a game called 'harpastum' which, from its Greek derivation, seems to mean something more akin to the Rugby Union code of the game rather than Association football as we now know it. Stories of the first game of football being played by victorious armies of soldiers using their enemies' heads as footballs are, we hope, as untrue as they are grizzly.

It is certainly true, however, that in Scotland a game called football did exist and was played throughout the realm in various forms, usually in a free-for-all in which the object was to get the ball 'one way or another' (and it did not matter too much how one did this) into the opponents' goal. There is documentary evidence of such games being played in Orkney, Shetland, Scone, Perth and the Borders. Towns like Jedburgh, for example, had a long-running fixture between the 'Uppies' and the 'Doonies'.

The six King Jameses of Scotland all seemed to be bothered by football. James I's Parliament at Perth in '*ane thousand foure hundreth tuientir foure*' (1424) decreed that '*na man shall play at the fute-ball under the paine of fiftie schillings, to be raised to the Lord of the land, als often as he be tainted or to the Schireffe of the land or his ministers, gid the Lordes will not punish sic tresspassoures*'. In 1457 the Parliament of James II in Edinburgh said that '*ye golfe and ye footieball shud be utterly cryed doon*', and in 1491 the Parliament of James IV went a step further when it said that '*in na place of the Realme there be used fute-ball, golfe or other such unprofitable sportes*'. With an attitude like that, it is perhaps not surprising that they went down so badly at Flodden! A game or two of football might well have strengthened the morale, resolve and attitude of the Scottish army. On the other hand, perhaps Flodden can be seen as merely a precursor to Argentina and not a few Wembley occasions!

Mary, Queen of Scots, may well have owned a football, for the oldest surviving football in the world – a small pig's bladder, inside a jacket of thick leather pieces, and about one and a half times the size of a cricket ball, was found in the rafters of her chamber, and has been dated to 1540. It found its way to Stirling's Smith Museum, and in April 2006 was shipped to Hamburg on loan for an exhibition to coincide with the 2006 World Cup.

Then there was the book written by the Aberdeen poet and teacher David Wedderburn, who in 1633 published a book in Latin called *Vocabula*, in which he says about the game: 'Let's pick sides. Those who are on the outside, come over here. Kick off, so that we can begin the match… Pass it here'. Phrases like 'kick off' and 'pass it' make one think that the game referred to is something like football as we know it, but to claim that the game therefore originated in Aberdeen in 1633 is hardly a convincing one.

Throughout the eighteenth and early nineteenth centuries there are a few disparaging and condemnatory references in Kirk Session records, and in newspapers, to football being played near churches, even on a Sunday – the Presbyterian Kirk not having as much power to enforce Sabbath observance as it would have liked. This is presumably the origin of the phrase 'making enough noise to awaken the dead' for, until the middle of the nineteenth century, kirkyards were the only cemeteries. But there can be little doubt that football, in its organized form, began in England rather than Scotland, particularly in the English public schools, where the ethos of teamwork was very important if an empire was to be built. After all, the Battle of Waterloo, they said, was won on the playing fields of Eton. In addition *mens sana in corpore sano* (a healthy mind in a healthy body) became an important concept.

Queen's Park, winners of the first Scottish Cup in 1874.

Queen's Park were the first Scottish team to be formed in 1867, if we ignore 'The Foot-Ball Club' (see **OLDEST CLUB**), which was founded in Edinburgh in 1824 and disappeared after 1841. This organisation, founded by a student called John Hope, played a game only vaguely similar to what we call football today. But Queen's Park used the English codification of laws of Association Football of 1863. For a long time, Queen's Park had no one to play against, so they organized games such as Married Men versus Bachelors, Young Men versus old Men, Handsome Men versus Ugly Men, and Light Weights versus Heavy Weights. They also saw that it was their duty to spread the game throughout Scotland and did so. Kilmarnock founded a football club in 1869, and by 1873 the Scottish Football Association was formed, with the first Scottish Cup being competed for in 1874. Hardly surprisingly, Queen's Park won the trophy for the first three years. (See under **SFA** and **SCOTTISH CUP**)

But before that happened there had been a very significant event on 30 November 1872, when an England team came to Hamilton Crescent in Partick to play Queen's Park, who for this game decided to call themselves Scotland, thus inaugurating the first ever Scotland versus England international. It was a 0–0 draw, attracted a huge crowd of about 4,500, and Scotland surprised England by playing a 'passing' game rather than a 'dribbling' game. The idea was that whenever a tackle was imminent, the ball would be passed from one man to another. (There had been five games between England and Scotland played prior to that date, but they are not considered official, for they were all played at the Oval in London, the Scotland team was made up only of Scotsmen who were living in England at the time, and the Scotland team was picked by the English Football Association!)

A significant quote from the world's first football international (as it came to be known) comes from a weekly newspaper called the Graphic. "Individual skill was generally on England's side... The Southrons (sic) however did not play to each other as well as their opponents, who seem to be adepts in passing the ball". This 'passing game' was clearly successful for Scotland and, crucially, Scotland beat England in 1874 at Hamilton Crescent, and again in 1876 and 1878. By this time Wales had entered the equation and Scotland beat them too. There was thus the perception that here was something that Scotland could do successfully. In these circumstances the game spread, as Queen's Park organized tours to Tayside, Aberdeen and the Highlands, but significantly not to the Borders, for on the day of their intended trip, they were heavily involved in the English FA Cup and, to this day, rugby holds the sway over football in these parts.

It is important to realise that this spreading of football throughout Scotland was not really the creation of something new. The difference now was that there would be nationally recognised rules, referees, costumes and competitions. In addition, the railways were by the 1870s in full swing, so travel was now possible. Rangers were founded in 1873, for the time of year when there was no rowing or cricket to be played, and the two Edinburgh teams were formed in 1874 and 1875; the foundation of Hibs in 1875 bringing a new and significant phenomenon into Scottish football, for their constitution clearly specified that they were for young Catholic men. (the name Hibernians does of course mean 'Irishmen'). This was laudable in that it showed that football could be a channel for an ethnic minority to take part in Scottish cultural life. Sadly, however, this aspect of the game had side effects (see **SECTARIANISM**).

The late 1870s and the early 1880s were very much the era of the Dunbartonshire villages, with teams like Vale of Leven, Renton and Dumbarton doing consistently well in the Scottish Cup and challenging the Glasgow giants, Queen's Park. It was not until 1887, when Hibs won the Scottish Cup, that we see evidence of an East of Scotland team doing well. Laudably, the SFA encouraged this trend by playing international games all over Scotland – at Easter Road and Tynecastle in Edinburgh, then Carolina Port (and later Dens Park) in Dundee, and in 1900 at Pittodrie in Aberdeen.

For a while there was confusion between the two codes of football, association and rugby. Clearly the newspapers of the time did not know the difference, and sometimes teams would agree to play two matches on the same day – one association and one rugby – or even (incredibly) to play the first half association and the second half rugby! Some of the early rules of association football now strike us as strange. At first each team produced an umpire (an idea from cricket), and there was no half way line, penalty box or goal net. Hacking (i.e. shin kicking) seems to have been tolerated, and for a long time charging into the goalkeeper and defenders was very much part of the game. It would be a long time before football would evolve into what we now know it.

The early1880s saw Scotland beat England four years in a row, something that impressed all of Scotland, even the Presbyterian Church, who gradually came to the view that playing football was a far more wholesome and healthy activity than drinking or fornication, especially if Scotland could beat England. It was the era when the term 'muscular Christianity' became current, for the epistles of St Paul (1 Corinthians 9.19) tell us that 'the body is the temple of the Holy Spirit'.

Crucially, too, the working classes began to get interested and, as Saturday was now a half-holiday in many factories and workplaces, football became the thing to do. More enlightened capitalists recognised that their young men were better off playing football than organising revolutions and other seditious activities, and encouraged the forming of works teams.

By the mid 1880s, in addition to the Scottish Cup, there was a plethora of regional tournaments, but there was as yet no Scottish league (in which each team played each other twice per season at each other's grounds) until 1890, when Abercorn, Cambuslang, Celtic, Cowlairs, Dumbarton, Hearts, Rangers, St Mirren, Third Lanark and Vale of Leven formed the Scottish League. Queen's Park made the tactical error of not joining, for they feared (correctly) that this might be the precursor of professionalism. As a result, they lost much influence, and were powerless, in any case, to stop the official legalisation of professionalism in 1893. In fact, clubs had been paying their players for some time, sometimes by 'under the counter' payments or, more commonly, by inserting a few coins into a man's shoe in the dressing room while the game was actually in progress. At least as widespread was the giving of a 'loan' to a player with a view to him setting up business, often in the licensing trade. Such was the competitive desire to do well in a sport that even in the 1880s and 1890s it was dominating Scottish culture and conversation.

ORMOND Willie (1927 – 1984)

Scotland Caps: 6

Scottish League Championship medals: 3

One of the real characters of Scottish football, Willie Ormond was born in Falkirk and his first team was Stenhousemuir, but he made his name as the outside left of the 'famous five' forward line of the great Hibs team of the early 1950s. He broke his leg three times, something that perhaps explains why he was only awarded six Scottish caps when many people felt he was worth more. He later went to Falkirk, and in 1967 became the manager of St Johnstone, leading the Perth side to undreamed-of success. He took them to the final of the Scottish League Cup in October 1969 (where they lost narrowly to Celtic 0–1), and later to Europe in season 1971/72, where they famously beat SV Hamburg and Vasas Budapest, with excellent players like John Connolly and goal scorer Henry Hall.

In January 1973 Willie became the manager of Scotland. After a disastrous 0–5 defeat from England in his first match, the unpretentious little man led them to the World Cup finals in Germany in 1974, from where they emerged undefeated. He is therefore arguably

Scotland's most successful-ever manager, and deserving of the OBE that he was awarded in 1975. He was often accused of being too soft on his players, and certainly, during his tenure, a few well-documented occasions of players' indiscipline took place. In 1977 he became manager of Hearts, but this coincided with a low point in Hearts' history, and he became manager of Hibs for a brief spell in 1980, but was unable to save them from relegation before ill health compelled his resignation. He died in 1984. In his latter years he was a publican in Musselburgh.

OTHER SPORTS PLAYED AT FOOTBALL GROUNDS

As a general rule this does not happen as much as one would expect. The problem often is the fear that the turf would be churned up. Most activities other than football that take place on grounds tend to take place round rather than on the field. But Hampden Park has in its time played host to rugby, famously hosting Scottish internationals in 1896 and 1906. On 14 March 1896, at Second Hampden, Scotland beat England 11–0 before a large but unspecified attendance, and ten years later on 17 November 1906, at the brand new Hampden Park, 32,000 saw Scotland beat the touring South Africans 6–0 with tries from MacLeod and Purves. McDiarmid Park, Perth has also had a fair amount of rugby played on it, as has Firhill in Glasgow, but the 'down side' of this was seen in 2008 at the Falkirk Stadium where the amount of rugby being played led to Falkirk FC complaining of the damage done to the surface.

American football and boxing, as well as pop concerts, have all taken place at Hampden Park (disgracefully, in September 2006, a Scotland international had to be re-routed from Hampden to Celtic Park because of a pop concert). Celtic Park used to have cycling (for many years, a cycling track was a feature of the ground) and athletics. On 28 April 1928 it became the first ground in Great Britain to host motorcycle speedway racing, and in recent years has hosted a Billy Graham evangelical rally. Ibrox used to boast about being a 'stadium', which hosted many sports rather than a 'ground' or a 'park', and a floodlit cricket match has been played at Stark's Park, Kirkcaldy.

Athletic internationals have been staged at Hampden, Ibrox and Celtic Park. A triangular international between Scotland, Ireland and England was held at Hampden in 1914, 1922 and 1930; Ibrox hosted the Scotland versus Ireland international athletics match in 1907 and 1910, while Celtic Park did the same in 1895. The Scottish Amateur Athletic Championships were held at Hampden every year between 1919 and 1939, apart from 1920, 1922, 1925, 1926 and 1928, and then every year after the second world war until 1951. Celtic Park and Ibrox also hosted this event before the first world war. On one occasion, on 1 April 1922, the Scottish Amateur Athletic Association's cross country event began at Hampden at half time in the game between Queen's Park and Celtic, and then the athletes ran round the south side of Glasgow, returning after the game was over. A problem arose however when the athletes met the crowd coming out, and this idea was not repeated. In 1927 Hampden also staged a tennis match involving Suzanne Lenglen, the French star who shocked 1920s society by revealing far too much arm and shoulder, and who had been on six occasions Wimbledon Ladies Singles champion. In 1947 the new machine called a helicopter gave a demonstration; and between 1969 and 1972 some speedway was staged there as well.

On at least four occasions football stadia in Glasgow have hosted world title boxing bouts. One was at Shawfield on 16 September 1936, when Benny Lynch successfully defended his word flyweight title by knocking out Pat Palmer, and at the same weight, Jackie Paterson won the world title at Hampden on 19 June 1943, knocking out Peter Kane in 61 seconds. Then on 10 July 1946, again at Hampden, he successfully defended the title with a points win over Joe Curran. He was less lucky at the same venue against Theo Medina on 30 October of that year.

Until the mid 1960s, a feature on most football grounds towards the end of July used to be the 'Sports' or the 'Games', which involved cycling, athletics, tossing the caber, highland dancing and other things, and then, in a clear indication that the football season was just round the corner, a five-a-side football tournament. These events attracted huge crowds and brought in a great deal of income. Meadowbank Thistle played in Edinburgh on the ground that had been used for the 1970 Commonwealth Games.

Of the sports still played *round* the field, Shawfield, at one point the home of Clyde, was, and remains, the mecca for greyhound racing in Glasgow. Armadale were so financially hard pressed in the 1930s that they had reluctantly to allow such activities as well, in a vain effort to remain solvent, and Central Park, Cowdenbeath has stock car racing.

OWN GOALS

Scoring an own goal is a distressing experience for a defender. Two of the most famous in Scottish football were the own goal scored by Tom Boyd for Brazil in Paris in the opening game of the World Cup on 10 June 1998, and the own goal scored by Alan Craig of Motherwell in the last minute of the 1931 Scottish Cup Final on 11 April, which allowed Celtic a replay. In a Scottish Cup tie between Clyde and Raith Rovers on 11 February 1950, Clyde scored all three goals for Raith Rovers in their 3–2 win, Jimmy Campbell, Frank Mennie and Bob Milligan being the unlucky men. It is not unknown for players to score for both sides in a game, i.e. for their own team and also an own goal, but Alan Mackin of East Stirlingshire actually managed to score for both teams within forty-five seconds of each other! This was in a game at Hampden Park against Queen's Park on 3 December 1977.

PARAGUAY

Scotland have played Paraguay once, in the World Cup finals of 1958 in Sweden.

1958	11 June	Norrkoping	2–3	Mudie Collins	Aguero Re Parodi

PARKER Alex (1935 –)

Scotland Caps: 15
Scottish Cup medals: 1

A right back for Falkirk and Everton, who won fifteen caps for Scotland, Alex Parker was named Player of the Year in 1957. He also won the Scottish Cup with Falkirk in 1957 and the English League Cup with Everton in 1963, by which time his position had changed to right half. He featured in the World Cup finals of 1958, a matter of weeks after he had been transferred to Everton

for £18,000. In season 1970/71 he was coach and manager of Southport after having tasted football in Ireland with Ballymena and Drumcondra.

PARTICK THISTLE FC

Ground: **Firhill Stadium, Glasgow**
Nickname: **The Jags**
Colours: **Red and yellow**
Record Attendance: **49,838 v Rangers (1922)**
Record Victory: **16-0 v Royal Albert (1931)**
Record Defeat: **0-10 v Queen's Park (1881)**
Highest League Position: **3rd (1947/48; 1953/54; 1962/63)**
Best Scottish Cup Performance: **Winners (1920/21)**
Best League Cup Performance: **Winners (1971/72)**

The club's date of formation is usually recorded as 1876, although it may just have been December 1875. It wasn't long before Partick Thistle won a trophy, winning the West of Scotland Cup in 1879 with a 1–0 victory over Marchton in the final. The fixture list of cup-ties and friendlies soon included challenge matches in the north of England and in 1885 they became one of the small group of Scottish clubs to enter the English FA Cup. In 1886/87 they got all the way to the fifth round before losing 1–0 to Old Westminsters at the Oval.

There were several different homes in those early years, and by the time the Jags moved to Firhill in 1909 they had already played at Overnewton Park (a public area), Jordanvale Park in Whiteinch, Muir Park in Dumbarton Road, Inchview and Meadowside. At Jordanvale Park two Scottish cup-ties had to be replayed in 1881 after protests that spectators had encroached on to the pitch. Willie Paul became a famous player for Partick Thistle towards the end of the nineteenth century. A prolific goal scorer, he became their first international player when he was capped for Scotland against Wales in 1888.

There was disappointment when the club was not invited to be part of the new Scottish League that was formed in 1890 and the Jags decided to join the Scottish Alliance league. They played in it from 1891 to 1893, when the Scottish League decided to create a second division and elected them into the inaugural Division Two for the 1893/94 season. At first they moved between the two divisions on several occasions, but when they were promoted to the top flight in 1902 they remained there until 1970. Even then they only spent only two more seasons, 1970/71 and 1975/76, out of the top tier before 1982.

The Jags' history in the twentieth century is dominated by their two cup victories. In 1920/21 the Scottish Cup was won after Rangers were beaten 1–0 in a final held at Celtic Park and in 1971/72 the League Cup was added to the trophy cabinet when Jock Stein's Celtic were beaten 4–1 in the final. Jimmy Bone and Alan Rough were two of the stars who shocked the football world that day.

Partick Thistle is also one of Scotland's clubs with a European pedigree. The Jags earned a place in the

Partick Thistle FC 1960/61.

1963/64 Inter-Cities Fairs Cup by virtue of a third-place finish in the league and went out to Spartak Brno of Czechoslovakia in the second round after beating them 3–2 at home. Then their League Cup victory earned them a place in the 1972/73 UEFA Cup, but this time they went out to Honved of Hungary in the first round.

Since 1982 Thistle have spent many years in the second tier of the Scottish League, but there have also been forays into both the first and third tiers. After ten seasons in the First Division (second tier) they achieved promotion in 1992 when manager John Lambie led them back to the top. He left in 1995 and they stayed in the Premier Division until 1996. When he returned in March 1999 he took over a club in the Second Division (third tier) and by 2002 had led them all the way up to the SPL. He left again in 2003 and, despite a brief return as caretaker-manager, they were back in the Second Division by 2005.

The introduction of play-offs for the 2005/06 season enabled the Jags to bounce back to the First Division at the first attempt, and then manager Dick Campbell was sacked in March 2007. Two months later he was replaced by Ian McCall, but Thistle went on to settle in the middle of the First Division.

The club suffered severe financial difficulties in the late 1990s and the supporters launched a 'Save the Jags' campaign that helped the club to survive. The money raised was converted into shares and in 1998 a Jags' Trust was inaugurated that enables each member to be a part owner of the shares. The chairperson of the Trust has a seat on the board and this provides a means for supporters to have a say in the future direction of the club.

PART-TIME PLAYERS

It may surprise many people, given the sheer amount of interest in the game of football in Scotland, that most senior clubs are part-time organisations and most professional players are part-time. The larger organizations in the SPL are not, but most teams in the SFL are, although some have a few full-time professionals. A young man with a career outside football might be reluctant to turn full-time, for life as a footballer is short and unpredictable, and playing part-time football for East Fife, Arbroath or Dumbarton can be a healthy and enjoyable way of supplementing a livelihood without running the risk of financial ruin in the wake of relegation. Part-time clubs are the backbone of Scottish football, and much hard work and energy goes into the running of a senior football club, often without any great financial reward.

Historians may be even more surprised that two of the greatest footballers of the 1920s, Alan Morton of Rangers and Patsy Gallacher of Celtic, were part-time. Alan Morton was a mining engineer and frequently arrived at Ibrox carrying a briefcase, whereas Patsy Gallacher would disappear from Parkhead in the afternoon to run his wine and spirits business. Both managers, Willie Struth and Willie Maley disapproved, but great players are able to dictate terms. Normally, players for the larger clubs are full-time, but the practice varies and full-timers often line up with part-timers in the same team.

PEEBLES ROVERS FC (former Scottish League club)

Home: **Whitestone Park, Peebles**
Highest League Position: **48th (8th in Div. 3 1924/25)**
Best Scottish Cup Performance: **Last 16 (2nd round 1912/13; 1913/14)**

The club is a former member of the Scottish League because of its three years in the Division Three that existed from 1923 to 1926. At the end of the 1925/26 season Rovers, like many other clubs, were heavily in

Peebles Rovers FC with Scottish Qualifying Cup (South) 1953/54.

debt and unable to complete their fixtures, but their long history contains much more than involvement with this ill-fated experiment.

Founded in 1893, Peebles won the championships of the Border League in 1903/04 and the Scottish Union in 1910/11, and their name became familiar to all Scottish football fans when the draw for the Scottish Cup twice took them to Parkhead in the space of six years. Celtic beat them 4–0 in a first round tie in 1907/08 and then won 3–0 in the third round of the 1912/13 competition.

By 1922/23 Rovers were playing in the Western League and once again the Scottish Cup enabled them to raise their profile. A 0–0 draw against Hibernian at Easter Road was a shock result in the second round, although Hibs won the replay 3–0. It was soon after the elation of this result that the club began its time in Division Three but three years later the picture looked very different.

After 1926 the club briefly adopted junior status, and then found a new home in the East of Scotland League. In 1953/54 they won the Scottish Qualifying Cup (South), and there were occasional forays into the later rounds of the Scottish Cup, including a 15–1 second round defeat away to Hibs in 1960/61. (Their 1955/56 tie against Brechin City is referred to in **LONGEST GAMES**). In 1966 Rovers began another spell of junior football, but they rejoined the East of Scotland League in 1980 and remained there until 2006 when they combined with other clubs from the town to form Peebles FC.

PENALTIES

The penalty kick from twelve yards, with only the goalkeeper to beat, was introduced into football as early as 2 June 1891, and remains a great and dramatic event in the game. A referee's decision to award, or not to award, a penalty kick is frequently the talking point of a game, and some clubs are often accused of getting more penalties than others from sympathetic referees who may, or may not, be swayed by the home crowd. A penalty should be scored, and the statistics show that a goal results from a penalty about four times out of five. Scotland claims to have staged the world's first-ever penalty kick. Four days after its introduction, on 6 June 1891, in the Airdrie Charity Cup final at Mavisbank, Airdrie, a man called McLuggage of Royal Albert scored a penalty after Andrew Mitchell of Airdrieonians had handled 'in the vicinity of the goal'. In the Scottish League, the first penalty ever converted was by Alex McColl of Renton against Leith Athletic at Bank Place, Leith on 22 August 1891.

Johnny Hubbard of Rangers in the 1950s is often claimed to be the 'penalty king'. Certainly his success rate of fifty-four out of fifty-seven would be hard to beat, and he deserved his nickname of 'Johnny-on-the-spot'. Hat-tricks of penalties are rare, but not unheard of, and have happened at least eight times in Scottish football history. The first occasion was on 9 January 1904 at Love Street, Paisley, when David Lindsay of St Mirren scored three in a game against Rangers, and men such as Bobby Collins and Eddie Turnbull subsequently emulated this.

There have been several pivotal penalties in Scottish football history. The most famous, certainly among Rangers fans, was during the 1928 Scottish Cup final. Rangers had not won the Scottish Cup since 1903, and there was much was talk of a 'hoodoo', and even of a curse laid by the ghosts of the dead of the Ibrox disaster of 1902. The final against Celtic on 14 April 1928 was deadlocked at 0–0 when Rangers were awarded a penalty. Captain Davie Meiklejohn, with the weight of Ibrox history on his shoulders, took it and scored to open the floodgates for a 4–0 Rangers victory. It was only the second-ever penalty kick that had been awarded in a Scottish Cup final, the first having been in 1907, converted by Willie Orr of Celtic in their 3-0 victory over Hearts.

A similar occasion, except in reverse, occurred on 23 October 1965 in the Scottish League Cup final, when

Celtic, just coming out of their trophy famine, were awarded two penalties against Rangers. This time it was John Hughes who took the penalties and scored both, leading to a 2–1 win.

The coolest penalty taker must be Tommy Walker of Hearts. In the international against England at Wembley on 4 April 1936, Scotland were 1–0 down with only thirteen minutes to go, when they were awarded a penalty. It was a windy day, and three times the ball was blown from the spot. Three times the ice-cool Walker (only twenty years of age) replaced the ball before scoring the goal that gave Scotland their deserved draw.

There was also an occasion in 1962 when Scotland, not having beaten England at Hampden Park for twenty-five years, were only one up, and under severe pressure with England pressing hard. Then they were awarded a penalty, which Eric Caldow of Rangers calmly slotted home. The following year Jim Baxter scored with a penalty at Wembley, and he claimed afterwards that it was his first-ever penalty kick!

Qualification for the 1978 and 1986 World Cups depended on penalty kicks, and the nation was grateful to Don Masson of Derby County and Davie Cooper of Rangers respectively. On the other hand, Scotland's Argentine adventure of 1978 might have been different if the same Don Masson had sunk his penalty in the first game against Peru, and the same can be said of Scotland's meeting with England in the finals of Euro 96. England were leading 1–0 when Scotland were awarded a penalty, and Gary McAllister's miss was followed almost immediately by England's second goal.

Perhaps the most infamous Scotland penalty howler was that of the otherwise excellent Billy Liddell of Liverpool, in a great victory over Austria in a friendly in Vienna in 1955. Liddell missed the penalty and in the words of the radio commentator 'narrowly missed the corner flag as well'!

PENALTY SHOOT-OUTS

These are an effective, although sometimes cruel, way of deciding drawn cup games without any need for a replay. Each team takes five penalties, and if the teams are still level, the contest moves on to sudden death with a player from each team taking alternate penalties until someone misses and the other team scores. This means of deciding a football match first affected a Scottish club when Airdrieonians and Nottingham Forest settled their Texaco Cup tie on 28 September 1970 by this method. Airdrie won 5–2 on penalties at Broomfield after two 2–2 draws. Two days later on 30 September Aberdeen were less fortunate when they went out of the European Cup-Winners' Cup, losing 5–4 to Honved in Hungary. Jim Forrest was the unlucky Aberdeen player to miss and the Aberdeen players were astounded to see the Hungarian goalkeeper take the decisive penalty.

Scottish League Cup games are settled like this if the teams are level after extra time, and the Scottish Cup final and semi-finals also. Earlier rounds of the Scottish Cup, however, are granted a replay. The shoot-outs are

March 1969: Rangers John Greig misses from the penalty spot against Athletic Bilbao in the Inter-Cities Fairs Cup at Ibrox.

great attractions on television (even to those who don't like football) and are infinitely preferable to other ways of settling a game, which have in the past included dubious methods like counting corners or even tossing a coin.

The cruelty lies in the fact that one player may well be the only one to miss. For example the excellent playing record of Dixie Deans is stained by the memory of a missed penalty in a high-profile shoot-out. It was during Celtic's first contact with a penalty shoot-out, on live TV throughout Europe, in a European Cup semi-final at Parkhead on 19 April 1972. Penalties were used after playing for 210 minutes with neither Inter Milan nor Celtic scoring a goal, and Deans was the luckless player who sent the ball over the bar. Seventeen days later he scored a hat trick in the Scottish Cup final.

Scottish teams in Europe have frequently gone out in this cruel fashion. The excellent Aberdeen team of 1984 lost on penalties to Dynamo Berlin, Celtic went out to Valencia in 2001/02 and Rangers to Borussia Dortmund in 1999/2000. On the other hand, there have been successes too, for Rangers beat Paris St Germain in 2001/02 and Maritimo of Portugal in 2004/05 in such circumstances, whilst Celtic qualified for the group stages of the 2007/08 Champions League after a thrilling shoot-out against Spartak Moscow.

On the domestic front, Rangers beat Aberdeen on penalties in the Scottish League Cup final of 1987/88, and a similar method was employed in 1994/95 to give Raith Rovers the Scottish League Cup over Celtic. Interestingly, Raith Rovers had also won their semi-final against Airdrie in a similar way that year. Only twice has the Scottish Cup final been decided in this manner and those occasions were in 1990, when Aberdeen beat Celtic 9–8 on penalties, and in 2006 when Hearts beat Gretna 4–2.

PERU

In a game considered to be pivotal in Scottish football history, Scotland lost to Peru in the first game of the

Argentina World Cup of 1978. There has also been one victory and one draw.

1972	26 Apr	Hampden Park	2–0	O'Hare Law	
1978	3 June	Cordoba	1–3	Jordan	Cubillas (2) Cueto
1979	12 Sep	Hampden Park	1–1	Hartford	Leguia

PETERHEAD FC

Ground: **Balmoor Stadium**
Nickname: **The Blue Toon**
Colours: **Blue and white**
Record Attendance: **8,643 at Recreation Park v Raith Rovers (1987)**
3,700 at Balmoor Stadium v Partick Thistle (2006)
Record Victory: **17-0 v Fort William (1998)**
Record Defeat: **0-13 v Aberdeen (1923)**
Highest League Position: **25th (3rd in Second Division 2005/06)**
Best Scottish Cup Performance: **Last 8 (5th round, 2000/01)**
Best League Cup Performance: **Last 28 (2nd round, 2003/04; 2004/05; 2005/06; 2006/07; 2007/08)**

Peterhead can trace their roots back to 1890, when the first committee was formed, and the club played its first match in 1891 at the newly opened Recreation Park. In 1900 they joined the Aberdeenshire League and continued to play in it until the early 1930s, when they transferred to the Highland Football League. There were occasional forays into the early stages of the Scottish Cup, and in 1923 they reached a third-round tie against Aberdeen, when a weakened team went out 13–0.

In the late 1940s, under manager Percy Dickie, Peterhead became a dominant force in Highland football. The Highland League championship was won in 1946/47, 1948/49 and 1949/50, and in the 1948/49 season the team scored one hundred and twenty goals. The Scottish Qualifying Cup (North) was also won in 1946/47. This successful period was not to last, however, and the Qualifying Cup did not return to Peterhead until the 1970s, when it was won in 1975/76, 1977/78 and 1978/79.

The club survived severe financial problems in the early 1980s and then in 1986/87 embarked on a run in the Scottish Cup that saw Raith Rovers require two fourth-round replays before beating them 3–0 at Gayfield Park, Arbroath. The Highland League title was won on two further occasions, in 1988/89 and 1998/99, and there was further success in the Scottish Qualifying Cup (North) in 1985/86 and 1997/98.

In 1997 the Blue Toon left 'The Rec' and moved to a modern new home at Balmoor Stadium. A new era of success soon followed, and when the Scottish League was expanded in 2000 the club was elected to the Third Division. In 2000/01 they reached the fifth round of the Scottish Cup, losing 3–1 at Livingston, but their progress had been helped by a walkover in the fourth round against Airdrieonians, who were refused permission to postpone the tie at a time of financial difficulty. Then, after five seasons in the Third Division, Peterhead finished the 2004/05 season in second place behind Gretna, and were promoted to the third tier.

In their first season in the Second Division manager Iain Stewart led them to the final of the play-offs, where they only lost on penalties to Partick Thistle, and their two home matches each broke the attendance record at Balmoor Stadium. Steve Paterson took over as manager in October 2006, and when former Ross County manager Neale Cooper replaced him in January 2008, his first match produced a 9–2 demolition of Berwick Rangers.

PETERSHILL FC (see JUNIOR FOOTBALL)

PITCHES

Not all pitches are the same size, and not all of them are made from natural grass. The properties of artificial turf have improved considerably since it was first introduced, but its use as a playing surface has been the subject of much controversy. It is sometimes derisively referred to as a 'plastic pitch', and many people argue that a game on plastic will never provide the same spectacle as one on real grass. Some, however, argue that its benefits cannot be ignored, particularly for a club with limited training facilities. The resilient nature of a synthetic surface can permit several teams to regularly train and play on it despite the rigours of a Scottish winter, and the advocates of 'all-weather pitches' claim that in poor weather the surface performs better than a grass pitch does.

Stirling Albion installed an artificial surface at Annfield, their original home, and the league match against Ayr United in September 1987 was the first to be played on such a pitch in Scotland. When Dunfermline Athletic laid one as part of a UEFA programme it proved so controversial that the SPL decided its clubs must only play on a natural surface, and it was replaced in 2005. This ruling did not apply in the SFL though, and Hamilton Academical, Stenhousemuir, Montrose and Alloa have all gone on to enjoy the benefits of modern synthetic turf after installing pitches that meet FIFA's two-star standard. However, when Hamilton won promotion to the SPL in 2008, they immediately announced that they would be laying real turf for their matches in the top flight. The Falkirk Stadium attempts to combine the benefits of new technology with a traditional grass surface, with the Bairns' pitch having a special fibre membrane under the surface that helps to prevent the formation of divots.

Celtic were required to play on Spartak Moscow's synthetic pitch in the third qualifying round of the Champions League tournament in August 2007, amid allegations of inconsistency from UEFA. Three years previously Dunfermline Athletic had to switch their UEFA Cup tie against FH Hafnarfjordur to McDiarmid Park, when UEFA ruled that their synthetic pitch was unsuitable for European football, but now the Luzhniki Stadium was deemed to be suitable. In the end Celtic were able to adjust to the difference and came away with a 1–1 draw. Spectators at the match reported that the ball did not behave erratically, but it did bounce in a different way to a ball on grass.

The vast majority of playing surfaces in the SPL and SFL are between 110 and 115 yards long, with a width that is between 70 and 75 yards. The laws of the game impose maximum and minimum requirements, and for domestic games these are a length between 100 and 130 yards with a width between 50 and 100 yards. If a club seeks to enter one of UEFA's club competitions, it must gain their approval for its pitch, amongst many other matters, before it can be admitted.

PLAYER OF THE YEAR

There are two such awards. The older one, awarded by the Scottish Football Writers Association, began in 1965, but since 1978 there has also been a set of awards (one for each division, plus the 'young player of the year') awarded by the Scottish Professional Footballers' Association. It is possible to win both, and indeed to win one or other several times. Both these awards are much coveted by players.

Scottish Football Writers Association

1965	Billy McNeill	Celtic
1966	John Greig	Rangers
1967	Ronnie Simpson	Celtic
1968	Gordon Wallace	Raith Rovers
1969	Bobby Murdoch	Celtic
1970	Pat Stanton	Hibernian
1971	Martin Buchan	Aberdeen
1972	Dave Smith	Rangers
1973	George Connelly	Celtic
1974	Scotland World Cup Squad	
1975	Sandy Jardine	Rangers
1976	John Greig	Rangers
1977	Danny McGrain	Celtic
1978	Derek Johnstone	Rangers
1979	Andy Ritchie	Morton
1980	Gordon Strachan	Aberdeen
1981	Alan Rough	Partick Thistle
1982	Paul Sturrock	Dundee United
1983	Charlie Nicholas	Celtic
1984	Willie Miller	Aberdeen
1985	Hamish McAlpine	Dundee United
1986	Sandy Jardine	Hearts
1987	Brian McClair	Celtic
1988	Paul McStay	Celtic
1989	Richard Gough	Rangers
1990	Alex McLeish	Aberdeen
1991	Maurice Malpas	Dundee United
1992	Ally McCoist	Rangers
1993	Andy Goram	Rangers
1994	Mark Hateley	Rangers
1995	Brian Laudrup	Rangers
1996	Paul Gascoigne	Rangers
1997	Brian Laudrup	Rangers
1998	Craig Burley	Celtic
1999	Henrik Larsson	Celtic
2000	Barry Ferguson	Rangers
2001	Henrik Larsson	Celtic
2002	Paul Lambert	Celtic
2003	Barry Ferguson	Rangers
2004	Jackie McNamara	Celtic
2005	John Hartson	Celtic
2006	Craig Gordon	Hearts
2007	Shunsuke Nakamura	Celtic
2008	Carlos Cuellar	Rangers

Scottish Professional Footballers' Association

1978	Premier Division	Derek Johnstone	Rangers
	First Division	Billy Pirie	Dundee
	Second Division	Dave Smith	Berwick Rangers
	Young Player	Graeme Payne	Dundee United
1979	Premier Division	Paul Hegarty	Dundee United
	First Division	Brian McLaughlin	Ayr United
	Second Division	Michael Leonard	Dunfermline Ath
	Young Player	Raymond Stewart	Dundee United
1980	Premier Division	Davie Provan	Celtic
	First Division	Sandy Clark	Airdrieonians
	Second Division	Paul Leetion	Falkirk
	Young Player	John MacDonald	Rangers
1981	Premier Division	Mark McGhee	Aberdeen
	First Division	Eric Sinclair	Dundee
	Second Division	Jimmy Robertson	Queen of the South
	Young Player	Charlie Nicholas	Celtic
1982	Premier Division	Sandy Clark	Airdrieonians
	First Division	Brian McLaughlin	Motherwell
	Second Division	Pat Nevin	Clyde
	Young Player	Frank McAvennie	St Mirren
1983	Premier Division	Charlie Nicholas	Celtic
	First Division	Gerry McCabe	Clydebank
	Second Division	John Colquhoun	Stirling Albion
	Young Player	Paul McStay	Celtic
1984	Premier Division	Willie Miller	Aberdeen
	First Division	Gerry McCabe	Clydebank
	Second Division	Jim Liddle	Forfar Athletic
	Young Player	John Robertson	Hearts
1985	Premier Division	Jim Duffy	Morton
	First Division	Gerry McCabe	Clydebank
	Second Division	Bernie Slaven	Albion Rovers
	Young Player	Craig Levein	Hearts
1986	Premier Division	Richard Gough	Dundee United
	First Division	John Brogan	Hamilton Acad
	Second Division	Mark Smith	Queen's Park
	Young Player	Craig Levein	Hearts
1987	Premier Division	Brian McClair	Celtic
	First Division	Jim Holmes	Morton
	Second Division	John Sludden	Ayr United
	Young Player	Robert Fleck	Rangers
1988	Premier Division	Paul McStay	Celtic
	First Division	Alex Taylor	Hamilton Acad
	Second Division	Henry Templeton	Ayr United
	Young Player	John Collins	Hibernian
1989	Premier Division	Theo Snelders	Aberdeen
	First Division	Ross Jack	Dunfermline Ath
	Second Division	Paul Hunter	East Fife
	Young Player	Billy McKinlay	Dundee United
1990	Premier Division	Jim Bett	Aberdeen
	First Division	Ken Eadie	Clydebank
	Second Division	Willie Watters	Kilmarnock
	Young Player	Scott Crabbe	Hearts
1991	Premier Division	Paul Elliott	Celtic
	First Division	Simon Stainrod	Falkirk
	Second Division	Kevin Todd	Berwick Rangers
	Young Player	Eoin Jess	Aberdeen
1992	Premier Division	Ally McCoist	Rangers
	First Division	Gordon Dalziel	Raith Rovers
	Second Division	Andy Thomson	Queen of the South
	Young Player	Phil O'Donnell	Motherwell
1993	Premier Division	Andy Goram	Rangers
	First Division	Gordon Dalziel	Raith Rovers
	Second Division	Sandy Ross	Brechin City
	Young Player	Eoin Jess	Aberdeen
1994	Premier Division	Mark Hateley	Rangers
	First Division	Richard Cadette	Falkirk
	Second Division	Andy Thomson	Queen of the South
	Young Player	Phil O'Donnell	Motherwell
1995	Premier Division	Brian Laudrup	Rangers
	First Division	Stephen Crawford	Raith Rovers
	Second Division	Derek McInnes	Morton
	Third Division	David Bingham	Forfar Athletic
	Young Player	Charlie Miller	Rangers

Jackie McNamara.

Paolo di Canio.

FOOTBALL

AND SPORT SURVEY

No. 10 Official Organ of the Scottish Football Players Union March, April, May, 1948

Chief of the German Intelligence Service is kicking himself now. Says if he had signed Johnny Divers, Germany would have won the War in a canter.

* * *

Jim Davies, however, is hugging himself. Says he'll be satisfied with the Scottish Cup.

* * *

Saw Jimmy M'Grory the other day. If he gets any more wrinkles on his forehead, he'll have to screw his hat on. Jock Weir didn't arrive too soon.

* * *

Speaking of Jock Weir. Isn't it funny about all those Hibs men floating around? We were tempted to make a crack here, but that alert Bell of *Reynolds' News* sounded first.

* * *

And what's Jimmy Carabine up to? That guy gets moseying around to some tune. But Jimmy ain't talking. He believes in action. Meantime we're keeping him in our binoculars.

* * *

Getting a ticket for the big How-d'ye-do at Hampden on 10th April is as easy as trying to crack Dumbarton Rock with that tie your auntie sent you at Christmas.

* * *

Even the Players' Union got bawled out. When they made a mild request at Carlton Place, the S.F.A. threatened to send for Dick Barton.

* * *

And, anyway, why *should* the players get any better treatment than the goal-posts?

* * *

If that *Opera Bouffe* at Carlton Place could only foresee the tornado that's about to break around their ears, they'd feel like changing their minds. Snag is, no one would ever swop with them.

Walter Galbraith (Clyde)

Trouble with those Bashi-Bazouks of the S.F.A. is, they love themselves so much they get chapped lips kissing mirrors. But, *Mene, mene, mene, Tekel upharsin.*

* * *

Maybe we shall write to Stafford Cripps about it. The Scottish Football Association is a non-essential luxury, and we know that Cripps is keen on the export drive.

* * *

Dundee people will remember Bert Robertson, who played for Stobswell and Dundee United. Bert went to Australia last year and has now been appointed coach to the Western Australia State Junior Football Association. By coaching and training the youngsters, Bert hopes to raise the standard of play to the high level that exists in New South Wales.

* * *

Bill Sweeney is fitting in admirably with Carlisle United and is quite happy. He is still resident in Glasgow and training at Shawfield with his old Clyde colleagues.

* * *

Charlie Briggs, now with Chesterfield, spent an hour or so with Bill recently comparing notes on English and Scottish League football.

* * *

Jimmy Dykes, ex-Hearts pivot and Scottish International, has been appointed Manager of Portadown.

* * *

Jimmy M'Kerley broke an arm recently while playing for Newtonards. The ex-Kilmarnock man was at the top of his form, too, when he met with this unfortunate accident. Speedy recovery, Jimmy.

The Paper Rationing severely limits the number of copies that may be printed of "FOOTBALL" per month. If you want to be sure of getting your Regular Copy, you are requested to register with us without delay. Subscription Rates are 7/- per year, or 3/- per half-year. Write, enclosing Postal Order for the amount in question to MANAGER, "FOOTBALL," 81 St. Vincent Street, Glasgow, C.2

The journal of the Players Union in 1948.

1996	Premier Division	Paul Gascoigne	Rangers
	First Division	George O'Boyle	St Johnstone
	Second Division	Steven McCormick	Stirling Albion
	Third Division	Jason Young	Livingston
	Young Player	Jackie McNamara	Celtic
1997	Premier Division	Paolo di Canio	Celtic
	First Division	Roddy Grant	St Johnstone
	Second Division	Paul Ritchie	Hamilton Acad
	Third Division	Ian Stewart	Inverness CT
	Young Player	Robbie Winters	Dundee United
1998	Premier Division	Jackie McNamara	Celtic
	First Division	James Grady	Dundee
	Second Division	Paul Lovering	Clydebank
	Third Division	Willie Irvine	Alloa Athletic
	Young Player	Barry Ferguson	Rangers
1999	Scottish Premier	Henrik Larsson	Celtic
	First Division	Russell Latapy	Hibernian
	Second Division	David Bingham	Livingstone
	Third Division	Neil Tarrant	Ross County
	Young Player	Barry Ferguson	Rangers
2000	Scottish Premier	Mark Viduka	Celtic
	First Division	Stephen Crawford	Dunfermline Ath
	Second Division	Brian Carrigan	Clyde
	Third Division	Steve Milne	Forfar Athletic
	Young Player	Kenny Miller	Hibernian
2001	Scottish PremieR	Henrik Larsson	Celtic
	First Division	David Bingham	Livingston
	Second Division	Scott McLean	Partick Thistle
	Third Division	Steve Hislop	East Stirlingshire
	Young Player	Stilian Petrov	Celtic
2002	Scottish Premier	Lorenzo Amoruso	Rangers
	First Division	Owen Coyle	Airdrieonians
	Second Division	John O'Neill	Queen of the South
	Third Division	Paul McManus	East Fife
	Young Player	Kevin McNaughton	Aberdeen
2003	Scottish Premier	Barry Ferguson	Rangers
	First Division	Derek Wyness	Inverness CT
	Second Division	Chris Templeman	Brechin City
	Third Division	Alex Williams	Morton
	Young Player	James McFadden	Motherwell
2004	Scottish Premier	Chris Sutton	Celtic
	First Division	Ian Harty	Clyde
	Second Division	Paul Tosh	Forfar Athletic
	Third Division	Michael Moore	Stranraer
	Young Player	Stephen Pearson	Celtic
2005	Scottish Premier	John Hartson	Celtic
		Fernando Ricksen	Rangers
	First Division	Russell Latapy	Falkirk
	Second Division	Steven Hampshire	Brechin City
	Third Division	David Bingham	Gretna
	Young Player	Derek Riordan	Hibernian
2006	Scottish Premier	Shaun Maloney	Celtic
	First Division	John Rankin	Ross County
	Second Division	James Grady	Gretna
	Third Division	Markus Paatelainen	Cowdenbeath
	Young Player	Shaun Maloney	Celtic
2007	Scottish Premier	Shunsuke Nakamura	Celtic
	First Division	Colin McMenamin	Gretna
	Second Division	Iain Russell	Brechin City
	Third Division	Scott Chaplain	Albion Rovers
	Young Player	Steven Naismith	Kilmarnock
2008	Scottish Premier	Aiden McGeady	Celtic
	First Division	Graham Dorrans	Livingston
	Second Division	Allan Russell	Airdrie United
	Third Division	Jonathan Smart	East Fife
	Young Player	Aiden McGeady	Celtic

PLAYERS UNION

The football industry is not generally associated with labour problems such as strikes. To an outsider, footballers appear to have a great lifestyle, earning very large sums of money, and there seems to be no need for militancy, nor indeed any need for player representation at negotiating tables. But that is a simplistic way of looking at things, and the Players Union (or to give it its full name, the Scottish Professional Footballers Association, which is a branch of the General Municipal and Boilermakers Union, having amalgamated with them in 1974), with negotiators like Tony Higgins and Fraser Wishart, plays an important part in the representation of players. This may be in circumstances such as injury compensation, a club going into administration (as happened, for example, with Dundee, Livingston and Motherwell) and the protection of players against a club that is none too scrupulous in its dealings with staff. There is also an education department that gives advice on what to do when a footballing career comes to an end, as it inevitably does in a player's mid-30s.

The first mention of a Players Union was in 1898 when Jimmy Millar of Rangers and Dan Doyle of Celtic formed this organization, with Doyle its first Chairman. It came to prominence in the 1960s under the leadership of its energetic secretary Johnny Hughes (not to be confused with John Hughes who played for Celtic) when, with the maximum wage having been abolished, there was a need for contract negotiations, a function now often handled by agents. There had been a union before then, but it was often not recognised and treated with disdain by clubs who felt there was no need for players to do anything other than carry out their orders.

The only time when there was the slightest hint of any militancy came in the winter of the 1945/46 season when the players detected a reluctance on the part of clubs to return to peace time wages, even though the war had been over for several months. A strike was threatened for New Year's Day 1946, but a meeting a few days before Christmas saw the players accept the pay and conditions of the clubs, albeit under protest. Industrial action would almost certainly not have enjoyed a huge amount of popular support.

PLAY-OFFS

These events have not been a regular feature of the Scottish scene. Before the arrival of goal average and goal difference they were used from time to time to decide between teams that had finished on equal points. There was even a play-off for the league title in 1890/91, which was the very first season of the Scottish League. When Celtic and Rangers finished on equal points at the end of the 1904/05 season, they agreed that a previously arranged fixture in the Glasgow League would also be used as a play-off to decide the championship of the Scottish League.

In season 1994/95 onwards, after the Scottish League was re-arranged into four divisions, the second-bottom club in the Premier Division played the second-top club in the First Division to decide who would play in the next season's Premier Division. In 1998 the team second from the top of the First Division was Falkirk and their Brockville stadium was deemed unsuitable for the Premier Division. They were therefore not granted a play-off. The Scottish Premier League was established for the 1998/99 season and these play-offs were discontinued.

In 2005 it was decided that end-of-season play-offs between clubs in the lower divisions would generate extra interest in the Scottish League and from 2005/06 the second-bottom club in the First Division and the second, third and fourth clubs in the Second Division have played two semi-finals and a final. A similar thing has happened between the Second Division and the Third Division.

Play-Offs In The Scottish League

1890/91-Between two teams with equal points at the top of Division One

Dumbarton	2	Rangers	2
Dumbarton and Rangers declared joint champions of Scottish League			

1895/96-Between two teams with equal points that finished third-top of Division Two.

Renton	2	Kilmarnock	1
Renton put forward for election to Division One (not elected - Abercorn promoted)			

1897/98-Between two teams with equal points that finished third-bottom of Division One

Dundee	2	Partick Thistle	0
Partick Thistle had to apply for re-election to Division One (re-elected)			

1899/1900-Between two teams with equal points that finished second-bottom of Division One

St. Mirren	2	St. Bernard's	1
St. Bernard's had to apply for re-election to Division One (relegated)			

1904/05-Between two teams with equal points at the top of Division One

Rangers	1	Celtic	2
Celtic declared champions of Scottish League			

Aberdeen celebrate retaining their SPL status by defeating Dunfermline 6-2 in the 1995 play-off.

A member of the tartan army celebrates the 1-0 away win over England in the 1999 play-off against England, but Scotland lost 2-1 on aggregate.

1905/06-Between two teams with equal points that finished second-bottom of Division One

Port Glasgow Athletic	6	Kilmarnock	0
Kilmarnock had to apply for re-election to Division One (re-elected)			

1906/07-Between two teams with equal points that finished second-bottom of Division Two

Raith Rovers	3	East Stirlingshire	2
East Stirlingshire had to apply for re-election to the league (re-elected)			

1914/15-Between three teams with equal points at the top of Division Two

Cowdenbeath	1	Leith Athletic	0
Cowdenbeath	3	St. Bernard's	1
Leith Athletic	2	St. Bernard's	1
Cowdenbeath declared champions of Division Two			

1994/95-Between second-bottom club in Premier Division (first tier) and runners-up in First Division (second tier)

Aberdeen	3	Dunfermline Athletic	1
Dunfermline Athletic	1	Aberdeen	3
Aberdeen won 6–2 on aggregate (stayed in Premier Div)			

1995/96 -Between second-bottom club in Premier Division (first tier) and runners-up in First Division (second tier)

Partick Thistle	1	Dundee United	1
Dundee United	2	Partick Thistle	1
United won 3–2 on aggregate aet in 2nd leg (promoted to Premier Div)			

1996/97-Between second-bottom club in Premier Division (first tier) and runners-up in First Division (second tier)

Hibernian	1	Airdrieonians	0
Airdrieonians	2	Hibernian	4
Hibernian won 5–2 on aggregate (stayed in Premier Div)			

Hibernian fans rejoice as they defeat Airdrieonians to keep their SPL place in 1997.

2005/06-Between second-bottom club in First Division (second tier) and second, third and fourth clubs in Second Division (third tier)

Semi-final 1	Stranraer	1	Partick Thistle	3
	Partick Thistle	1	Stranraer	2
	Partick Thistle won 4–3 on aggregate			
Semi-final 2	Morton	0	Peterhead	0
	Peterhead	1	Morton	0
	Peterhead won 1–0 on aggregate			
Final	Partick Thistle	1	Peterhead	2
	Peterhead	1	Partick Thistle	2
	Partick Thistle won 4–2 on penalties (promoted to 1st Div)			

2005/06-Between second-bottom club in Second Division (third tier) and second, third and fourth clubs in Third Division (fourth tier)

Semi-final 1	Arbroath	1	Alloa Athletic	1
	Alloa Athletic	1	Arbroath	0
	Alloa Athletic won 2–1 on aggregate			
Semi-final 2	Stenhousemuir	0	Berwick Rangers	1
	Berwick Rangers	0	Stenhousemuir	0
	Berwick Rangers won 1–0 on aggregate			
Final	Alloa Athletic	4	Berwick Rangers	0
	Berwick Rangers	2	Alloa Athletic	1
	Alloa Athletic won 5–2 on aggregate (stayed in 2nd Div)			

2006/07-Between second-bottom club in First Division (second tier) and second, third and fourth clubs in Second Division (third tier)

Semi-final 1	Brechin City	1	Airdrie United	3
	Airdrie United	3	Brechin City	0
	Airdrie United won 6–1 on aggregate			
Semi-final 2	Raith Rovers	0	Stirling Albion	0
	Stirling Albion	3	Raith Rovers	1
	Stirling Albion won 3–1 on aggregate			
Final	Stirling Albion	2	Airdrie United	2
	Airdrie United	2	Stirling Albion	3
	Stirling Alb'n won 5–4 on aggregate (promoted to 1st Div)			

2006/07-Between second-bottom club in Second Division (third tier) and second, third and fourth clubs in Third Division (fourth tier)

Semi-final 1	Queen's Park	2	Arbroath	0
	Arbroath	1	Queen's Park	2
	Queen's Park won 4–1 on aggregate			
Semi-final 2	East Fife	4	Stranraer	1
	Stranraer	1	East Fife	0
	East Fife won 4–2 on aggregate			
Final	Queen's Park	4	East Fife	2
	East Fife	0	Queen's Park	3
	Queen's Park won 7–2 on aggregate (promoted to 2nd Div)			

2007/08-Between second-bottom club in First Division (second tier) and second, third and fourth clubs in Second Division (third tier)

Semi-final 1	Alloa Athletic	2	Clyde	1
	Clyde	5	Alloa Athletic	3
	Clyde won 6–5 on aggregate			
Semi-final 2	Raith Rovers	0	Airdrie United	2
	Airdrie United	2	Raith Rovers	2
	Airdrie United won 4–2 on aggregate			
Final	Airdrie United	0	Clyde	1
	Clyde	2	Airdrie United	0
Clyde won 3–0 on aggregate (Clyde stayed in 1st Div; Airdrie promoted to 1st Div)				

2007/08-Between second-bottom club in Second Division (third tier) and second, third and fourth clubs in Third Division (fourth tier)

Semi-final 1	Arbroath	1	Cowdenbeath	1
	Cowdenbeath	1	Arbroath	2
	Arbroath won 3–2 on aggregate			
Semi-final 2	Montrose	1	Stranraer	1
	Stranraer	3	Montrose	0
	Stranraer won 4–1 on aggregate			
Final	Arbroath	2	Stranraer	0
	Stranraer	1	Arbroath	0
Arbroath won 2–1 on aggregate (Arbroath and Stranraer both promoted to 2nd Div)				

International Play-Offs

29th November 1961

Between two countries that finished on equal points at the top of their qualifying group for the 1962 World Cup

Brussels	Scotland	2	Czechoslovakia	4
a.e.t. - Czechoslovakia qualified for the finals in Chile				

20th November 1985 and 4th December 1985

Between the country that finished top of the Oceania qualifying group for the 1986 World Cup and the runners-up in a European qualifying group

Hampden Park	Scotland	2	Australia	0
Melbourne	Australia	0	Scotland	0
Scotland won 2–0 on aggregate and qualified for the finals in Mexico				

13 November 1999 and 17 November 1999

Between two countries that finished as runners-up in their qualifying groups for the 2000 European Championship.

Hampden Park	Scotland	0	England	2
Wembley	England	0	Scotland	1
England won 2–1 on aggregate and qualified for the finals in Holland / Belgium				

15th November 2003 and 19th November 2003

Between two countries that finished as runners-up in their qualifying groups for the 2004 European Championship.

Hampden Park	Scotland	1	Holland	0
Amsterdam	Holland	6	Scotland	0
Holland won 6–1 on aggregate and qualified for the finals in Portugal				

POINTS

Traditionally, two points were awarded for a win and one for a draw, but this was changed in season 1994/95 to three points for a win and one for a draw. The idea was that teams would be less likely to settle for a draw, given the greater differential between a win and a draw. It does not necessarily seem to have had any positive effect.

The deduction of points has been used as a punishment since the very first season of the Scottish Football League in 1890/91, when Celtic, Third Lanark and Cowlairs all had points deducted for fielding ineligible players.

In the case of Celtic, for example, they had fielded their newly signed goalkeeper James Bell against Hearts when less than a fortnight had elapsed since his last game for Dumbarton. There have been several further instances of Scottish League clubs being punished for fielding unregistered or ineligible players over the following years, and in 2000 Hamilton Academical had fifteen points deducted for failing to fulfil a fixture at Stenhousemuir.

In 2004 the SPL introduced a penalty for clubs that go into financial administration, and brought in a rule that requires the deduction of ten points when an administrator is appointed. In March 2008 Gretna, who

Don Hutchison reflects on what might have followed his goal at Wembley in November 1999.

were already sitting at the bottom of the SPL, went into administration and felt the effect of this ruling.

Season	Club(s)	Points Deducted
1890/91	Celtic; Third Lanark; Cowlairs	4
1893/94	Port Glasgow Athletic	7
1896/97	Linthouse	4
1903/04	Albion Rovers	2
1906/07	Cowdenbeath	2
1907/08	Dumbarton	2
1922/23	St. Johnstone; Cowdenbeath; St. Bernard's	2
1947/48	Alloa Athletic	2
1988/89	Queen of the South; Cowdenbeath	2
1989/90	Forfar Athletic	2
1994/95	Meadowbank Thistle	3
1999/00	Hamilton Academical	15
2007/08	Gretna	10

POLAND

Scotland does not enjoy a good record against Poland with only one victory and three draws in seven games.

1958	1 June	Warsaw	2–1	Collins 2	Cieslik
1960	4 June	Hampden Park	2–3	Law St John	Baszkiewicz Brychczy Pol
1965	23 May	Chorzow	1–1	Law	Lentner
1965	13 Oct	Hampden Park	1–2	McNeill	Liberda Sadek
1980	28 May	Poznan	0–1		Boniek
1990	19 May	Hampden Park	1–1	Johnston	Gillespie o.g.
2001	25 April	Bydgoszcz	1–1	Booth (pen)	Kaluzny

POLLOK FC (see JUNIOR FOOTBALL)

PORTERFIELD Ian (1946 – 2007)

Ian Porterfield managed Aberdeen from 1986 to 1988 after playing for Raith, Sunderland, Reading and Sheffield Wednesday.

Born in Dunfermline, Ian Porterfield was a successful manager who took his coaching skills around the world, but he will always be remembered for scoring the only goal in the 1973 FA Cup final at Wembley. His Sunderland side beat the high-flying Leeds United 1–0, and became the first second division team to win the English Cup for forty-two years.

He began his playing career with Raith Rovers, and was part of the team that won promotion to Division One in 1967. In December 1967 he was sold to Sunderland for £45,000, and by the time he left them ten years later he had become one of their legendary players. After also playing for Reading (on loan) and Sheffield Wednesday, he began a managerial career that took him to Rotherham, Sheffield United, Aberdeen, Reading and Chelsea. His Aberdeen side lost the 1987/88 League Cup final to Rangers on penalties after a 3–3 draw.

After leaving Chelsea in 1993, he managed the national teams of Zambia, Saudi Arabia, Zimbabwe, Oman and Trinidad & Tobago, followed by a spell as manager of South Korean club side Busan I'Park. At the time of his death from colon cancer he was managing the Armenian national side, and had achieved some creditable results during the qualifying campaign for the 2008 European championships.

PORT GLASGOW ATHLETIC FC
(former Scottish League club)

Home: **Clune Park, Port Glasgow, Renfrewshire**
Highest League Position: **9th (1903/04)**
Best Scottish Cup Performances: **Last 4 (Semi-finals 1898/99; 1905/06)**

Founded as Broadfield FC in 1880 and renamed Port Glasgow Athletic in 1881, the 'Port' was an amateur club that became a founder member of the original Division Two in 1893. After playing in it for nine seasons, they eventually won the title in 1902 and were promoted to the top division. The club then played in Division One until 1910, despite finishing bottom in both 1907 and 1908. However, when they finished bottom yet again, their fellow members no longer re-elected them to the top division and they were finally relegated back to Division Two. The club was not well supported, financial difficulties were mounting, and after just one more season Port Glasgow resigned from the league in 1911. They were accepted into the Scottish Union for 1911/12, but failed to complete their fixtures and soon went out of existence.

The club first entered the Scottish Cup in 1881/82 and enjoyed considerable success in its relatively short lifetime, reaching the semi-finals twice and the last eight on a further three occasions. The cup run of 1905/06 was the most dramatic. It took three replays before Kilmarnock were knocked out 1–0 at Celtic Park and in the quarter-final Port Glasgow beat Rangers for the first time in their history, in front of a record crowd of 11,000 at their Clune Park ground. In the semi-final they lost 2–0 to the eventual winners Hearts.

PORTUGAL

Scotland's record against Portugal is played fourteen, won four, drawn three, and lost seven:

1950	21 May	Lisbon	2–2	Bauld Brown	Travacos Albano
1955	4 May	Hampden Park	3–0	Gemmell Liddell Reilly	
1959	3 June	Lisbon	0–1		Matateu
1966	18 June	Hampden Park	0–1		Torres
1971	21 April	Lisbon	0–2		Stanton o.g. Eusebio
1971	13 Oct	Hampden Park	2–1	O'Hare Gemmill	Rodrigues
1975	13 May	Hampden Park	1–0	Artur o.g.	
1978	29 Nov	Lisbon	0–1		Alberto
1980	26 Mar	Hampden Park	4–1	Dalglish Gray Archibald Gemmill	Gomes
1980	15 Oct	Hampden Park	0–0		
1981	18 Nov	Lisbon	1–2	Sturrock	Fernandes (2)
1992	14 Oct	Ibrox	0–0		
1993	28 April	Lisbon	0–5		Barros (2) Cadete (2) Futre
2002	20 Nov	Braga	0–2		Pauleta (2)

PRE-SEASON MATCHES

Many people believe these games are given more significance than they deserve, for they are really nothing more than practice matches. At one time every club would have a public trial match the week before the football season started and it was normally held on the first weekend in August, with the crowd being admitted free or perhaps a collection taken for charity. It tended to be along the lines of First Team versus Reserves, Probables versus Possibles, Blues versus Reds etc and frequently the teams would be changed around at half time. In the mid 1960s there began to be organized a few games against English clubs, for example, and such games were well attended, for the weather was normally good and a favourite cliché was that they were 'pipe openers' to the season. Jock Stein's Celtic laid down a marker by thrashing Sunderland 5–0 at Roker Park at the start of the 1965/66 season, then on August 6 1966 (the Saturday after England won the World Cup), beat Manchester United 4–1 at Parkhead on the same day that Rangers beat Arsenal 2–0, each game being played before a crowd in excess of 50,000. The Manchester United side contained World Cup winners like Bobby Charlton and Nobby Stiles and it was a perfect 'put down' for some of the hype.

Then there were even pre-season tournaments, sometimes in the USA or Canada, and there was a danger that the 'pre-season' was becoming almost as important as the season itself. A **DRYBURGH CUP** (q.v.) was introduced for the big teams in the early 1970s, but it did not last long, being as it was a rather too blatant attempt at money making rather than a serious pre-season event in which players could be tried out. There has been a calming down of such activity in recent years, but there will still be a need for a few pre-season matches. They should not be taken too seriously because for most football fans it is a relief when the real, competitive football begins in earnest.

PRENTICE John (1927 – 2006)

Scottish League Championship medals: 1
Scottish Cup medals: 2

John Prentice was manager of Scotland for a brief spell in 1966, the highlight being a 1–1 draw with Brazil, as

Barcelona's Thierry Henry (right) runs with the ball while Hearts' Marius Zaliukas (left) and Robbie Neilson challenge him during their pre-season friendly at Murrayfield in July 2007.

Brazil warmed up for the 1966 World Cup finals. His playing career started with Hearts, but in 1951 he moved to Rangers, with whom he won a Scottish League championship medal in 1952/53 in the left half position. In 1956 he was transferred to Falkirk, whom he captained to Scottish Cup success in 1957, before finishing his playing career at Dumbarton. He managed Arbroath, and was then sufficiently impressive as manager with Clyde to be offered the Scotland job. His departure from the post in October 1966 was abrupt, but he then moved to Falkirk, Dundee, and Falkirk again, before emigrating to Australia in 1975.

PRESSLEY Steven (1973 –)

Scotland Caps: 32
Scottish Premier League medals: 1
Scottish Cup medals: 3

Steven Pressley, a tall and commanding defender, is one of the few players to have played for Rangers, Celtic and Hearts. Inevitably nicknamed 'Elvis', Pressley was a stalwart of Hearts from 1998 until 2007, and won thirty-two caps for Scotland. He became the most capped Heart of Midlothian player, beating the record of Bobby Walker, which had stood for almost a century. He started off with Rangers in 1990, but never really claimed a permanent spot there, and moved to Coventry in 1994. He then played for Dundee United before eventually joining Hearts in 1998. With Rangers he won a Scottish Cup medal (as a substitute) in 1993, and did the same, this time playing the full ninety minutes, with Hearts in 2006. Having said that there was 'significant unrest in the dressing room' in a statement to the media in November 2006, Pressley was disciplined by the club and eventually left by mutual consent to join Celtic in January 2007. There he played an important part in securing Celtic's double of the Scottish League and Scottish Cup in 2007 and, by playing in the winning side at the Scottish Cup final, he completed the unique feat of having won three Scottish Cup winners' medals with three separate teams.

PROFESSIONALISM

There was a tremendous struggle to get professionalism legalised in Scotland. England officially sanctioned professionalism in 1885, but it was not until 1893 that it was officially recognised north of the border. On 4 October 1884 Hearts won a second-round Scottish Cup-tie 11–1 away to Dunfermline FC, and the Fife club protested that payments had been made to certain Hearts players, in breach of the rules. It emerged that Hearts' James Maxwell (a defender) and Chris McNee (a forward) were being paid twenty-six shillings per week. The SFA expelled the club from the Scottish Cup, disqualified Maxwell and McNee for two years, and Hearts became the first club to be suspended from the SFA. However, the Edinburgh club had foreseen the possibility of suspension and, after they admitted the offence and showed the SFA that all the club's office-bearers had been replaced, the suspension was immediately lifted. (An interesting footnote was that by December 1884 Chris McNee was playing for Burnley FC, and presumably receiving unofficial payments for his services.).

The eventual legalisation of professionalism brought to an end a period of hypocrisy in which, for example, players were 'enticed' from Renton and Vale of Leven to the big city clubs, and society was expected to believe that there were no financial inducements involved (also see **ST BERNARD'S FC**). There was even the case where the Celtic centre forward Sandy McMahon in 1892 was (legally) persuaded to join Nottingham Forest for a sum of money. Then a Celtic rescue party, under committee member John Glass, had to be sent from Glasgow to woo him back, and did so without apparently offering

Defender Steven Pressley scores for Celtic against Hearts in April 2007.

him any illegal payment – a statement not universally believed either then or now.

There were those who objected to professionalism, notably Queen's Park who have bucked all trends and whose motto remains 'ludere causa ludendi' – 'to play for the sake of playing'. After the legalisation of professionalism in 1893 they refused to join the Scottish League until season 1900/01 as they associated it with the concept of professionalism.

Professionalism changed the whole face of Scottish football. Queen's Park, who in 1893 won the Scottish Cup for the tenth time (a record then), have not won it since, and the power shifted irrevocably from the village teams of Dumbartonshire such as Vale of Leven and Renton, and Dumbarton itself, to big city teams such as Celtic, Rangers and Hearts, who had a larger following and who could therefore afford to pay more for star players.

Some argue that professionalism has got out of hand, and people point to what appear to be absurd salaries earned by some players, who sometimes seem to do little to justify them. It must be pointed out, though, that not all players earn huge salaries, and those who do earn such amounts do so because people are prepared to pay money at the turnstiles (one in forty-three of the Scottish population regularly attends a football match – the highest per capita rate in Europe), watch games on television, or buy the goods that are advertised.

Professionalism also implies certain standards of commitment, dedication and proper conduct. Sometimes these are not met, notably by players who, for example, manage to get themselves sent off for a double yellow card. The failure to accept the first one as a warning appears as a lack of professionalism to many spectators.

PROGRAMMES

Sometimes known as 'matchday magazines', programmes are very much part of the Scottish football scene, and the cry of 'offeeshul programme' can be heard from sellers at Scotland's grounds. Collecting programmes is a popular hobby and credit is due to John Litster for his work in promoting the collection and collation of football programmes through the magazine *Programme Monthly and Football Collectable*, and books called *The Football Programme–A History and Guide* and *Famous Football Programmes.*

Programmes tell us a great deal about an actual game. For example, the earliest Scottish programme is for a game between Queen's Park and The Wanderers, played at the first Hampden Park on 9 October 1875. The programme is little more than a team sheet, but from it we learn that the Queen's Park team, containing famous players like Charlie Campbell and Moses McNeil, played in a 1–2–2–3–3 formation, whereas the formation of The Wanderers was 1–2–2–6. The Wanderers played in white, with Queen's Park in black and white, but players wore different colours of stockings. It states that Moses McNeil (the left back-up) 'will play in blue and white

stockings', while Charlie Campbell (the right half back) 'will play in red, white and blue stockings'. It also mentions that 'there will be a referee and two umpires' (one of them provided by Queen's Park, but the other from Clydesdale rather than The Wanderers), and 'play will begin at 3.30 and finish at 5.00' (it is not clear whether there was an allowance for half-time, and if so for how long). Spectators were told not to 'strain the ropes'.

Although there were a few programmes before the first world war, they only really proliferated in the 1920s – and even then there was no uniformity, for programme production was a haphazard business, often depending on advertising revenue. A fan might buy a programme so that he could understand the ground's half time scoreboard, which would contain information such as A 1–0, B 2–1, and the programme would tell him which matches 'A' and B' referred to. However, knowledge of the alphabet and the day's fixtures would mean that 'A' was likely to be Aberdeen v. Hibs, and 'B' would be Celtic v. St Mirren etc. The teams were listed in the programme, but were often guesswork on the part of the editor (as indeed they still are in some cases). The manager would make non-contentious statements such as 'Welcome to our visitors from Dundee today. A keen contest is anticipated, but I feel confident that we can come out on top . . . ' and there would be advertisements, including one from British Railways about a football special for the next week's away game.

Programmes have since developed, usually with glossy paper and a consequent rise in price. The content can sometimes be less important than the souvenir aspect, yet some programmes have excellent sections on a club's history and good reports on the previous week's game. *Programme Monthly and Football Collectable* organises awards for the best programmes, and in 2006 Clyde won 'Scottish programme of the year' for the eleventh consecutive season.

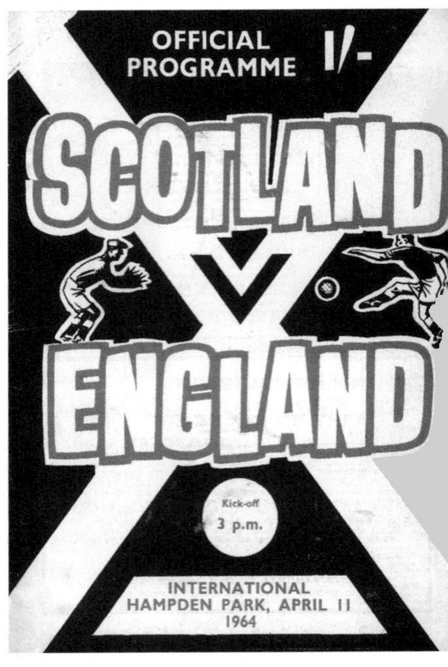

ARBROATH FOOTBALL CLUB
Ground — GAYFIELD PARK, ARBROATH

President: .... Mr. Hugh S. Nelson
Vice-President: .... Mr. D. F. McKechnie
Hon. Treasurer: .... Mr. J. D. McCulloch

Members of Committee:
Messrs J. C. Blair, W. Ford, Geo. Hardie, Geo. Pelling, G. Potter

Secretary: Mr. Wilfred E. Forrester, Gayfield Park.
Telephones: Ground 2157; Office 2087/2088; Home 2520

Arbroath v. Celtic 3rd October 1959
LEAGUE CHAMPIONSHIP

THE BRITISH LINEN BANK
Incorporated by Royal Charter 1746
All classes of banking business transacted.
Enquiries will be welcomed at any of the Bank's Branches throughout Scotland.
ARBROATH BRANCH
BROTHOCK BRIDGE R. A. Henderson, Manager.

ISH FOOTBALL ASSOCIATION • OFFICIAL PROGRAMME
Scotland
VERSUS
ENGLAND
AMPDEN PARK
GLASGOW
PRICE 1/-
. 3rd APRIL, 1954 Kick-off 3 p.m.

THE CIS INSURANCE CUP
Final 2001
OFFICIAL MATCHDAY MAGAZINE £4.00
Kilmarnock v Celtic
Sunday 18th March 2001
The National Stadium, Hampden Park, Glasgow

TENNENT'S
SCOTTISH CUP
SEMI-FINAL
GRETNA VS
DUNDEE
THE NATIONAL STADIUM, HAMPDEN PARK
SATURDAY 1 APRIL 2006 KICK-OFF 12.15PM
GRETNA
F.C.

OFFICIAL PROGRAMME
COTTISH LEAGUE CUP FINAL
CELTIC
v.
ST. JOHNSTONE
HAMPDEN PARK
Saturday, 25th October, 1969
KICK-OFF 3 p.m.

OFFICIAL PROGRAMME
SCOTTISH FOOTBALL LEAGUE CUP
1946
6D
SCOTTISH
LEAGUE CUP
CELTIC
versus
PARTICK THISTLE
KICK-OFF — 2.15 p.m.
FINAL
HAMPDEN PARK
SATURDAY
OCTOBER 27th, 1956

OFFICIAL PROGRAMME
DUNDEE FOOTBALL CLUB
LIMITED
FAIRS CUP — Semi-Final (1st leg)
DUNDEE v. LEEDS UNITED
WEDNESDAY, 1st MAY, 1968
You'll save well by using
MELDRUMS
FOOTBALL GEAR
SUPPLIERS TO THE DUNDEE FOOTBALL CLUB
Club Secretaries should write for illustrated list sent post free and Special Terms Offered
7-9 REFORM STREET, DUNDEE
Phone 24751

UVENIR PROGRAMME £2.00
the LOONS
ENNENT'S SCOTTISH CUP QUARTER FINAL
FORFAR ATHLETIC
v RANGERS
TATION PARK · SUNDAY 24th FEBRUARY 2002

FORFAR ATHLETIC
FOOTBALL CLUB
BELL'S
BELL'S SCOTTISH DIVISION TWO
FORFAR ATHLETIC v
BERWICK RANGERS
STATION PARK – SATURDAY, SEPTEMBER 18, 2004
MATCH SPONSORED BY FINDLAY & CO
Match ball sponsor - NORTH STREET DAIRY
OFFICIAL PROGRAMME – £1.00

Bairns
View
Official Programme 15p
Scottish League Division One
Falkirk
v.
Hearts
September 12, 1981 Issue No. 4

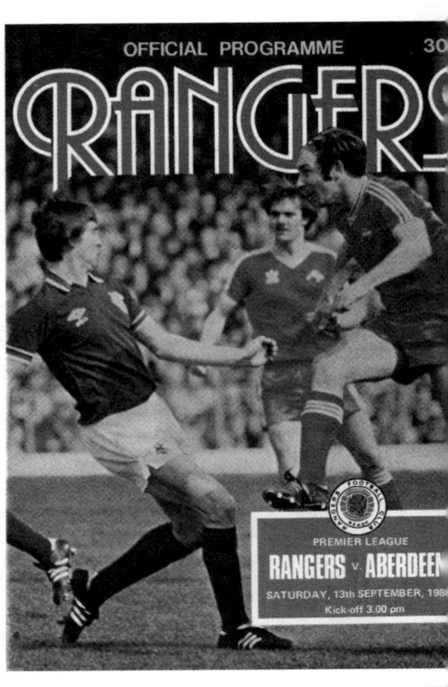

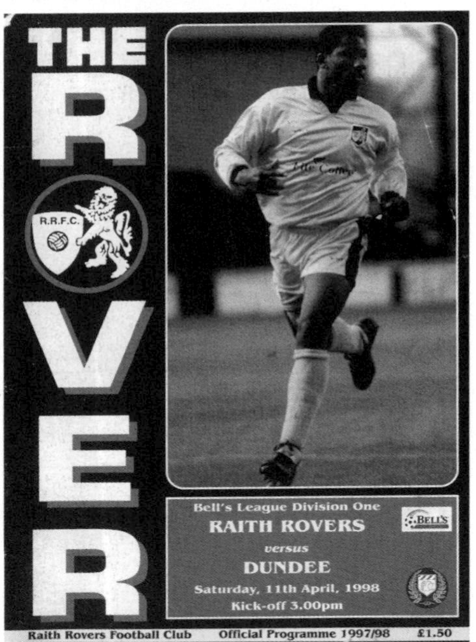

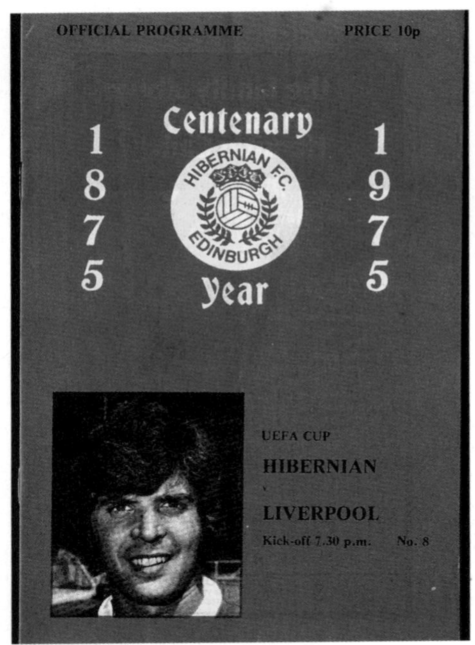

SATURDAY, JANUARY 11, 1969

ARBROATH

versus

DUNDEE UNITED

№ 240

FIRST DIVISION PRICE — 6d. KICK-OFF 3 p.m.

THE MANAGER SAYS . . .

We were all happy to see the team record their first League win last week against Morton, and no one would deny that it was a well-deserved victory, although it was the final minutes of the game before a Jimmy Jack header, his second of the game, made this certain.

The most pleasing factor was the grand support and encouragement given to the players throughout the game by the Gayfield fans, and I feel that this contributed greatly to the success of the side. There's nothing better than supporters encouraging their team, even when things aren't going too well with the team at times, and I can assure our supporters that the support given by them, particularly on Saturday, is appreciated by us all at Gayfield Park, officials and players alike.

We welcome to-day's opponents, Dundee United, who are having their best season for some time, and are at present in second place in the League. Although coming a cropper last week against Aberdeen to the tune of 4 goals to 1, the Tannadice side do not occupy their present position in the League without good reason. They will certainly be all out to make amends for last week's reverse as soon as possible.

Last week our lads showed plenty of ability and fighting spirit, and the same determined effort to-day should see us emerge as worthy winners.

A. W. HENDERSON, Manager.

SCOTTISH LEAGUE DIVISION 1
ISSUE No. 17
Today's match is sponsored by Strathleven Bonded Warehouses Ltd.
BOGHEAD
DUMBARTON FOOTBALL CLUB
D F C
OFFICIAL PROGRAMME 1983 - 84
BANTER
LUCKY NUMBER
Nº 000138
30p
DUMBARTON v CLYDE
BOGHEAD PARK, DUMBARTON
Saturday, 28th April, 1984 — Kick-off 3.00 pm

CENTRAL PARK
OFFICIAL PROGRAMME
COWDENBEATH F.C.
ESTABLISHED 1881
COWDENBEATH
v
PARTICK THISTLE

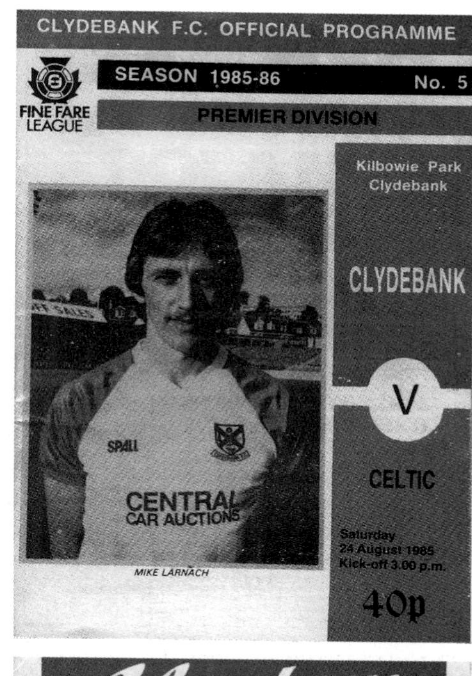
CLYDEBANK F.C. OFFICIAL PROGRAMME
SEASON 1985-86
No. 5
FINE FARE LEAGUE
PREMIER DIVISION
Kilbowie Park Clydebank
CLYDEBANK
V
CELTIC
Saturday 24 August 1985 Kick-off 3.00 p.m.
40p
CENTRAL CAR AUCTIONS
MIKE LARNACH

MONTROSE FOOTBALL CLUB
Season 1987/88
40p
Vol. 5, No. 1
TUESDAY, JULY 28, 1987
FORFARSHIRE CUP
MONTROSE
v.
Dundee United
KICK-OFF 7.30 p.m.
MAIN SPONSORS
PLASBOARD PLASTICS LTD.

THISTLE REVIEW
Award Winning Programme
Official Match Programme of Buckie Thistle F.C.
SEASON 2006/2007
BUCKIE THISTLE F.C.
versus
ROTHES F.C.
Saturday, NOVEMBER 28th, 2006 (kick-off 3.00pm)
SCOT ADS HIGHLAND LEAGUE
Programme No 11 ~ Price £1.00

Aberdeen
FOOTBALL CLUB Ltd.
SEASON 1964-65
AFC
ADENHEADS
Andy Kerr beats Niven for Aberdeen's fifth goal against Partick Thistle.
PITTODRIE PARK
SCOTTISH LEAGUE — FIRST DIVISION
Saturday, 10th October, 1964
Kick-off 3 p.m.
ABERDEEN v. CELTIC
OFFICIAL PROGRAMME 3d

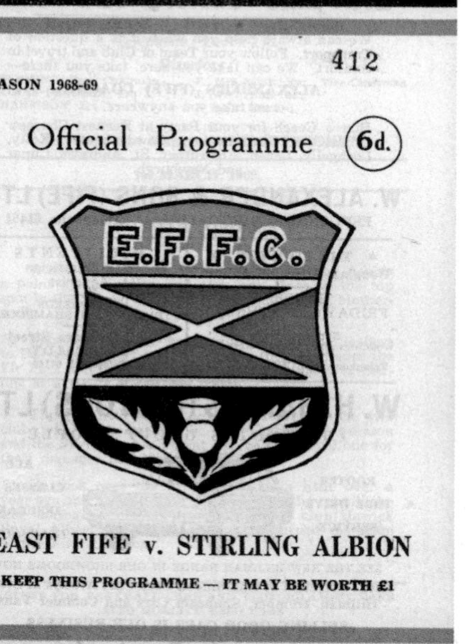
412
SEASON 1968-69
Official Programme
6d.
E.F.F.C.
EAST FIFE v. STIRLING ALBION
KEEP THIS PROGRAMME — IT MAY BE WORTH £1

STRANRAER FOOTBALL CLUB
S F C
FINE FARE LEAGUE SECOND DIVISION
STRANRAER
v
Raith Rovers
Stair Park,
Saturday, 9th May, 1987
SHIRT SPONSOR - BURGESS MOTORS
GO FOR TENNENT'S LAGER
STRANRAER F.C. SOCIAL CLUB
9/15 NORTH STRAND STREET
WEEKEND ENTERTAINMENT
TUESDAY NIGHT BINGO
QUALITY COMES FIRST
OFFICIAL PROGRAMME - 20p

CELTIC
Official Programme
JOHN HUGHES
SCOTTISH LEAGUE — FIRST DIVISION
CELTIC v. ST. MIRREN
Saturday, 9th March, 1963
Kick-off 3.00 p.m.
No. 15.
PRICE THREEPENCE

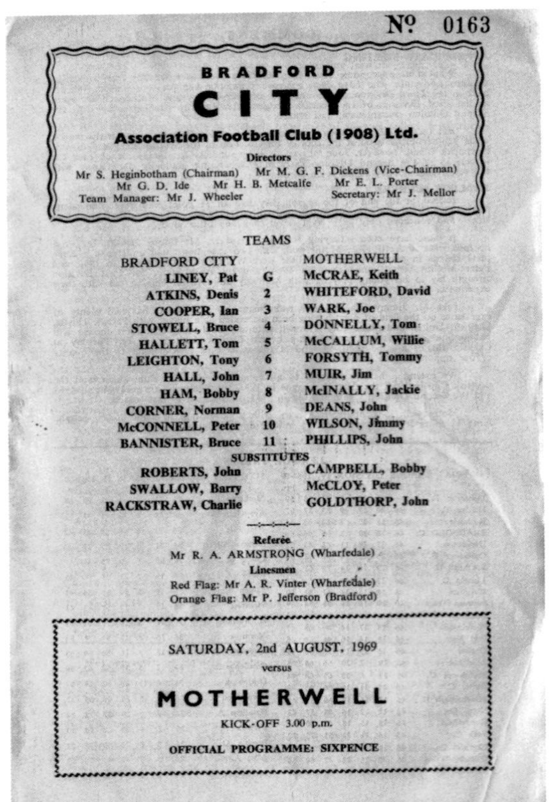

№ 0163

BRADFORD
CITY
Association Football Club (1908) Ltd.

Directors
Mr S. Heginbotham (Chairman) Mr M. G. F. Dickens (Vice-Chairman)
Mr G. D. Ide Mr H. B. Metcalfe Mr E. L. Porter
Team Manager: Mr J. Wheeler Secretary: Mr J. Mellor

TEAMS

BRADFORD CITY		MOTHERWELL
LINEY, Pat	G	McCRAE, Keith
ATKINS, Denis	2	WHITEFORD, David
COOPER, Ian	3	WARK, Joe
STOWELL, Bruce	4	DONNELLY, Tom
HALLETT, Tom	5	McCALLUM, Willie
LEIGHTON, Tony	6	FORSYTH, Tommy
HALL, John	7	MUIR, Jim
HAM, Bobby	8	McINALLY, Jackie
CORNER, Norman	9	DEANS, John
McCONNELL, Peter	10	WILSON, Jimmy
BANNISTER, Bruce	11	PHILLIPS, John
	SUBSTITUTES	
ROBERTS, John		CAMPBELL, Bobby
SWALLOW, Barry		McCLOY, Peter
RACKSTRAW, Charlie		GOLDTHORP, John

Referee
Mr R. A. ARMSTRONG (Wharfedale)
Linesmen
Red Flag: Mr A. R. Vinter (Wharfedale)
Orange Flag: Mr P. Jefferson (Bradford)

SATURDAY, 2nd AUGUST, 1969
versus
MOTHERWELL
KICK-OFF 3.00 p.m.
OFFICIAL PROGRAMME: SIXPENCE

Occasionally a player may regret what he has said to his programme editor, eg a goalkeeper once talked about which way he dived at a penalty kick. The penalty taker of the opposite side read it… and remembered! Every programme is indeed an 'official' publication, so editors must be careful what they say about the opposition, or indeed about their own team's performances. In the last part of the twentieth century this was a factor in the rise of the fanzine. These are unofficial publications and, providing the laws of libel are respected, can be as virulent and scurrilous as the editor wants them to be. (see **FANZINES**). Old programmes are very expensive. A good copy of a Scottish Cup final programme from the 1950s, for example, can fetch a three-figure sum at one of the programme fairs that are held from time to time, or indeed at stalls outside some of the big grounds. Particularly sought-after collectors' items are programmes for games that were not played for some reason, or perhaps abandoned at half time, as well as games that are significant in Scottish football history, eg cup giant killings, or games that saw league championships won.

PROMOTION

Promotion to a higher division was not automatic until the 1921/22 season. Before then the clubs in Division One held a vote at the end of the season to elect their members for the following year, and this sometimes produced results that now seem unfair. For example in 1905 the champions of Division Two, Clyde, were not elected to Division One, but Falkirk, who finished second, and Aberdeen, who finished seventh, were promoted.

By the 1920/21 season Division Two had still not been re-introduced, following its suspension in 1915. The Central League, which included clubs that had previously been in Division Two, had become popular and an arrangement was agreed whereby the Central League would form the backbone of a new Division Two for 1921/22. A crucial part of the deal was that there would be automatic promotion and relegation between the divisions.

Although Division Two clubs had proposed play-offs to decide promotion and relegation as long ago as 1895, they were not adopted in Scotland until 1994, as part of a restructuring of the Scottish Football League.

First club to be promoted (decided by means of a vote)	Clyde (from Division Two to Division One)	1894
First club to be automatically promoted	Alloa Athletic (from Division Two to Division One)	1922
First club to be promoted as a result of a play-off	Dundee United (from First Division to Premier Division)	1996

PROVAN Davie (1941 –)

Scotland Caps: 5
Scottish League Championship medals: 1
Scottish Cup medals: 3
Scottish League Cup medals: 2

A left back for Rangers during their glory years of the1960s, Davie Provan picked up five Scottish caps as well. He was tall and rugged, never disdaining the 'big boot up the park' to clear his lines. With Rangers he grasped the opportunity provided by the absence of Eric Caldow, due to injury, and won many honours in the fine Rangers side of the mid 1960s. He was unlucky enough to be in the side that lost the 1967 European Cup-Winners' Cup final. Later in his career he played for Crystal Palace, Plymouth Argyle and St. Mirren before becoming manager of Albion Rovers.

Davie Provan (left) and Frank McGarvey celebrate with the 1985 Scottish FA Cup.

PROVAN Davie (1956 –)

Scotland Caps: 10
Scottish League Championship medals: 4
Scottish Cup medals: 2
Scottish League Cup medals: 1

This Davie Provan played for Celtic, whom he joined from Kilmarnock in 1978, and is not to be confused with the previous entry. He was fast, direct, and a brilliant crosser of the ball. In 1980 he won the Scottish Professional Footballers' Player Of The Year award. He earned ten Scottish caps, his best match being the 1981 victory over England at Wembley. His most famous game for Celtic was the 1985 Scottish Cup final, when his free kick turned the game around, but trouble followed in the shape of an injury and the illness ME, which effectively curtailed his career. He is now a pundit and commentator on television.

PUNDITS AND PHONE-INS

A pundit is defined in the Chambers Dictionary as 'any learned man', although originally it was an expert in the customs of India. A football pundit therefore portrays himself as an expert of football, and invites people to listen to his views or talk to him on a phone-in.

There is a plethora of pundits in Scottish football, and people have said that Scottish football lacks the 'senior statesman' sort of figure that Richie Benaud is in cricket, or Dan Maskell was in tennis – venerable, sharp, unbiased, fair, helpful and supportive. Bob Crampsey, now retired, was considered to come close to this, and creditable mentions have been given to Archie McPherson and Arthur Montford. Many of the modern day pundits are said to play to the gallery, saying what the fans want to hear in the short-term, in a contentious and provocative way, so that people will buy their newspaper or keep listening to their radio programme. Pundits have been ridiculed in TV satirical programmes for their clichés such as 'indubitably so', 'only one thing on his mind', 'I can exclusively reveal', and 'to tell you the truth', and it is probably true to say that any pundit is guaranteed to upset someone. A slight indication of praise for Rangers will, for example, upset the other half, whereas people who live outside Glasgow are convinced that all pundits back up both members of the Old Firm against everyone else.

Radio Clyde claims to have the highest audience penetration for any radio market in the UK, but their radio phone-ins, like those of Radio Scotland, have been said to become tedious when too many people telephone to challenge Jim Traynor or Hugh Keevins for a perceived Rangers or Celtic bias. They do provide, though, an opportunity for members of the public to get their point of view across on national radio. It is not unknown for a caller to be cut off if he becomes abusive or foul-mouthed, although there are time-delay devices to prevent this from happening. There is too the occasional spoof caller, the most famous example being one 25 January when the presenter's voice intoned 'the next caller is Robert Burns from Ayrshire. What have you got to say, Robert?' 'Robert then took a deep breath and burst into 'Scots Wha Hae Wi' Wallace Bled…'!

Respected Scottish pundits include Graham Spiers, of various newspapers, and Richard Gordon, an anchorman on Radio Scotland with an astonishingly wide knowledge of the game. Gordon Smith, now the SFA Chief Executive, was similarly considered very knowledgeable when he worked for the BBC. Others who are less good have called to mind Robbie Burns when he says 'mair o horrible and awful, which even to name wad be unlawful'.

QUEEN OF THE SOUTH FC

Ground: **Palmerston Park, Dumfries**
Nickname: **The Doonhamers**
Colours: **Royal blue**
Record Attendance: **26,552 v Hearts (1952)**
Record Victory: **11-1 v Stranraer (1932)**
Record Defeat: **2-10 v Dundee (1962)**
Highest League Position: **4th (1933/34)**
Best Scottish Cup Performance: **Runners-up (2007/08)**
Best League Cup Performances: **Last 4 (1950/51; 1960/61)**

Queen of the South was founded in 1919, when three teams from Dumfries and Maxwelltown united to form a new club after the end of the first world war. At first they played in the Western League and went on to win the title in 1922/23. This was the year when the Scottish League introduced the short-lived Division Three and, like most of the other clubs in the Western League, they left to join it. For some of these clubs the three seasons of Division Three were to be their only taste of Scottish League football, but for Queen of the South it was a springboard to greater things.

By finishing as runners-up in the 1924/25 season, albeit only because their goal average was better than Solway Star's, the club got into Division Two and eight years later in 1933 they were promoted to Division One.

Queen of the South in the early 1960s.

These were good times for the Dumfries club and, with the exception of one season, they stayed in the top division until 1959. There were some impressive runs in cup competitions too and in 1949/50 they beat Aberdeen in a Scottish Cup fourth-round replay before Rangers needed two matches to dispose of them in the semi-finals. The following season the Doonhamers reached the semi-finals of the League Cup before losing 3–1 to Hibernian. It was around this time that centre forward Billy Houliston was capped three times for Scotland. A member of the team that beat England 3–1 at Wembley in 1949, he remains the only man to have gained full international caps whilst playing for Queen of the South.

After relegation to Division Two in 1959 success was hard to come by, although they once again reached the semi-finals of the League Cup in 1960/61. They stayed in the lower division, with the exception of two seasons, until league reconstruction in 1975, when they then found themselves in the First Division (second of three tiers). Goalkeeper Allan Ball had by now become an established member of the team and his appearances would eventually add up to a new club record, with a total of 819 senior games between 1963 and 1982.

By the time of the next major reconstruction of the Scottish League in 1994 they had only spent eight seasons in the First Division and were more often found in the bottom tier. Now they were placed in the Second Division (third of four tiers), but the years without a trophy were about to come to an end. It started with the appointment of John Connolly as manager in 2000. He led the club to the Second Division title in 2002 and the following season Queen of the South won the Scottish League Challenge Cup when they beat Brechin City 2–0 at Broadwood Stadium.

By the middle of 2005/06 it looked as though the Doonhamers might be about to slip back into the Second Division, but Ian McCall returned to manage his hometown club in November 2005 and kept them in the second tier. He resigned at the end of the 2006/07 season, to be replaced by his assistant Gordon Chisholm, and twelve months later the Doonhamers surprised the world of Scottish football by qualifying for Europe. A 2–0 quarter-final victory over Dundee in the Scottish Cup featured an astonishing seventy yard goal from Ryan McCann, and then Aberdeen were beaten 4–3 in a thrilling semi-final at Hampden Park. The final against Rangers was lost 3–2, but the Doonhamers had still earned participation in the 2008/09 UEFA Cup.

QUEEN'S PARK FC

Ground: **Hampden Park, Glasgow (also see HAMPDEN PARK)**
Nickname: **The Spiders**
Colours: **White and black**
Record Attendance: **95,772 v Rangers (1930)**
Record Victory: **16-0 v St Peter's (1885)**
Record Defeat: **0-9 v Motherwell (1930)**
Highest League Position: **5th (1928/29)**
Best Scottish Cup Performance: **Winners (1873/74; 1874/75; 1875/76; 1879/80; 1880/81; 1881/82; 1883/84; 1885/86; 1889/90; 1892/93)**
Best League Cup Performance: **Last 8 (Quarter-Finals 1967/68)**

Queen's Park FC is the Scottish League's only amateur club and it enjoys the privilege of having Scotland's national stadium as its home, but the most remarkable thing about the club is its unique history. Queen's Park once dominated Scottish football and also made a major contribution to the development of the game.

Founded in 1867, the club is believed to have taken its name from the Queen's Park Recreation Grounds, where early football was played in Glasgow, and its members led the way in developing rules and tactics for the new sport. When Scotland played England in 1872, in what is believed to be the first ever international fixture, the club supplied all eleven players for the Scottish team and the dark blue of their club shirts still remains the colour of the national team.

Alan Morton in action for Queen's Park at Hampden.

Queen's Park was a founder member of the Scottish FA and won the first Scottish Cup competition, when they beat Clydesdale 2–0 in the 1873/74 final. They then went on to win the trophy on nine further occasions before the end of the nineteenth century, and even at the start of the twenty-first century no other club outside the old firm had won the trophy as many times. Their strength and reputation can also be gauged from the fact that they were invited to take part in the first English FA Cup competition and later reached the final on two occasions, losing to Blackburn Rovers in both 1884 and 1885.

When the Scottish League was formed in 1890, the amateurs declined to join and tried to stay at arm's length from the professionalism that was starting to take root. However, by 1900 the benefits of regular competition against the best teams had become irresistible and the club was elected to Division One for the 1900/01 season. By 1915 they had finished bottom on four occasions, but on each occasion they were spared relegation by the re-election system. When they finished second bottom in 1922 it was the same year that automatic relegation was introduced and this time they went down.

Their experience of lower division football only lasted for one year though, because they won the Division Two title in 1923 and then went on to stay in the top flight until relegation in 1939. This time life in the bottom division only lasted for four games, because the advent of the second world war caused the 1939/40 season to be abandoned, and after the war they were placed back in the top division for the 1945/46 season.

They finished bottom of Division A in 1948 and since then success has been hard to find. There were two seasons in Division One from 1956 to 1958, but from then on there have been very few seasons when the Spiders were not playing their football in the lowest division of the Scottish League. The years from 1981 to 1983 were spent in the second of Scottish football's three tiers and in 1999/2000 their first full-time head coach, John McCormack, led them to the Third Division championship and a single season in the Second Division (third tier).

There was a memorable result in the second round of the 2006/07 League Cup when Queen's Park defeated Aberdeen 5–3 on penalties after a goalless draw, although they lost 3–0 to Motherwell in the third round. At the end of that season the Spiders finished third in the league and, after convincing wins in their play-off matches, were promoted back to the Second Division. In January 2008 Billy Stark, who had been Head Coach since 2004, left to become national coach for Scotland's youth teams and Gardner Spiers took over.

QUICKEST GOALS

There are two claims for the quickest goal scored in Scottish football. In the Scottish League Willie Sharp of Partick Thistle scored in seven seconds against Queen of the South at Firhill on 30 December 1947 and in the Scottish Cup John Hewitt of Aberdeen scored in nine and a half seconds against Motherwell at Fir Park on 30 January 1982. It was the only goal of the game.

In the Scottish Cup final of 1976, Rangers actually scored before the start of the game! The game started a few minutes before the scheduled time of 3.00 pm and Derek Johnstone put Rangers one up before 3.00 pm was reached. They went on to beat Hearts 3–1.

QUINN Jimmy (1878 – 1945)

Scotland Caps: 11
Scottish League Championship medals: 6
Scottish Cup medals: 5

Jimmy Quinn was a centre forward, and one of Celtic and Scotland's greatest-ever players. Born in Croy and joining Celtic in 1900, Quinn scored a hat trick in the

1904 Scottish Cup final, and then became an integral part of the Celtic team that won almost everything between 1905 and 1910. His goal scoring was legendary, although he was no angel, and was twice suspended, some say incorrectly, for serious foul play. He won eleven Scottish caps, his most famous internationals being the victory over England in 1910, and the time he scored four goals against Ireland in Dublin in 1908. He kept playing for Celtic, in spite of many injuries, until 1915, whereupon he retired to private life, working in the pits in his native Croy.

RADIO (see BROADCASTING, RADIO AND TV)

RAITH ROVERS FC

Ground: **Stark's Park, Kirkcaldy**
Nickname: **The Rovers**
Colours: **Navy blue and white**
Record Attendance: **31,306 v Hearts (1953)**
Record Victory: **10-1 v Coldstream (1954)**
Record Defeat: **2-11 v Morton (1936)**
Highest League Position: **3rd (1921/22)**
Best Scottish Cup Performance: **Runners-up (1912/13)**
Best League Cup Performance: **Winners (1994/95)**

Founded in 1883, the club takes its name from the man who owned its first ground, the Laird of Raith and Novar. At first the team played junior football, but then stepped up to senior level in 1889. The early years were spent playing friendly matches and cup-ties and they played in the first round of the 1889/90 Scottish Cup, losing 2–1 at home to Dunfermline Athletic.

In 1891 they moved to their present home at Stark's Park and by the end of the century the club was enjoying considerable success in local cup competitions. After winning the Northern League in 1902, they were elected to Division Two of the Scottish League. Rovers beat St. Bernard's 3–1 in the replayed final of the 1906/07 Scottish Qualifying Cup and the victory was consolidated with a run to the last eight of the competition proper. A 2–2 draw with Hearts was followed by a 1–0 defeat in the replay. Six years later, Rovers went all the way to the 1912/13 final and finished as runners-up after a 2–0 defeat to Falkirk.

Jimmy Delaney on the wing for Aberdeen in a game against Raith Rovers at Stark's Park. Willie McNaught and Harry Colville are the Raith players.

During the first world war, Scotland was experiencing severe transport problems and Rovers, along with Dundee and Aberdeen, were considered a 'remote' club. The Scottish League asked them to resign in 1917, but they were re-admitted two years later. By the early 1920s, under manager James Logan, Rovers had one of their best ever teams, and finished the 1921/22 season in third place. Then they were joined by the legendary Alex James, who played for them between 1922 and 1925, before going on to Preston and Arsenal.

In the 1930s they spent most of their time in Division Two, but then in 1937/38, under manager Sandy Archibald, Raith Rovers entered the record books. Not only did they win the Division Two championship, they scored 142 goals in the process, a British record. Sadly, this remarkable achievement only brought one season in Division One, and Rovers were relegated twelve months later.

When league football started again after the second world war, Bert Herdman was appointed manager and he went on to lead the club to many successes during his seventeen years with the club. The 1948/49 championship of Division B was accompanied by an appearance in that season's League Cup final, although it was lost 2–0 to Rangers, and then there were five top-ten finishes in nine years. He was also the man who brought Jim Baxter to Stark's Park, before 'Slim Jim' went on to become one of Scotland's all-time greats.

Relegation came in 1963 and the club entered a period of many years in the lower divisions. There were, however, two notable exceptions. First of all, when George Farm led the club to promotion in 1967, and a team that included the high-scoring Gordon Wallace spent three seasons in the top flight. The second came in the 1990s, and another three years in the top division. It was in 1994/95, though, that Rovers scaled the heights, under Jimmy Nicholl. Not only did they win the First Division (second tier) title that season, they also won the League Cup, beating Celtic 6–5 on penalties after a 2–2 draw. This brought qualification for the 1995/96 UEFA Cup and a second-round tie against Bayern Munich. The Germans won 4–1 on aggregate, but it is the halftime scoreboard in the Olympic Stadium that is remembered by Raith fans, when Rovers were winning 1–0. Unfortunately those heady times were followed by disappointments, and the club once again reverted to seasons in the second and third tiers of Scottish football.

In 2004 they hit the headlines when Claude Anelka, brother of Nicolas, invested in the club and took over as coach. Although he only stayed for about three months, Rovers never recovered from a string of disastrous results and were relegated from the First Division at the end of 2004/05. A few months later they were in the news again when it was announced that the club might have to close unless a buyer could be found. Gordon Brown, then the Chancellor of the Exchequer, and a life-long fan, helped to organise a community buyout and a consortium that included authors such as Ian Rankin, Val McDermid and Nick Hornby came to the rescue.

Craig Levein replaced manager Gordon Dalziel in September 2006, but he only stayed for a few weeks before Hearts' coach John McGlynn took over. Rovers reached the play-offs in both 2007 and 2008, but lost in the semi-finals on both occasions.

RANGERS FC

Ground: **Ibrox Stadium, Glasgow**
Nickname: **The Gers**
Colours: **Blue, red and white**
Record Attendance: **118,567 v Celtic (1939)**
Record Victory: **14-2 v Blairgowrie (1934)**
Record Defeat: **2-10 v Airdrie (1886)**
Highest League Position: **1st (1890/91 (shared); 1898/99; 1899/1900; 1900/01; 1901/02; 1910/11; 1911/12; 1912/13; 1917/18; 1919/20; 1920/21; 1922/23; 1923/24; 1924/25; 1926/27; 1927/28; 1928/29; 1929/30; 1930/31; 1932/33; 1933/34; 1934/35; 1936/37; 1938/39; 1946/47; 1948/49; 1949/50; 1952/53; 1955/56; 1956/57; 1958/59; 1960/61; 1962/63; 1963/64; 1974/75; 1975/76; 1977/78; 1986/87; 1988/89; 1989/90; 1990/91; 1991/92; 1992/93; 1993/94; 1994/95; 1995/96; 1996/97; 1998/99; 1999/2000; 2002/03; 2004/05)**
Best Scottish Cup Performance: **Winners (1893/94; 1896/97; 1897/98; 1902/03; 1927/28; 1929/30; 1931/32; 1933/34; 1934/35; 1935/36; 1947/48; 1948/49; 1949/50; 1952/53; 1959/60; 1961/62; 1962/63; 1963/64; 1965/66; 1972/73; 1975/76; 1977/78; 1978/79; 1980/81; 1991/92; 1992/93; 1995/96; 1998/99; 1999/2000; 2001/02; 2002/03); 2007/08)**
Best League Cup Performance: **Winners (1946/47; 1948/49; 1960/61; 1961/62; 1963/64; 1964/65; 1970/71; 1975/76; 1977/78; 1978/79; 1981/82; 1983/84; 1984/85; 1986/87; 1987/88; 1988/89; 1990/91; 1992/93; 1993/94; 1996/97; 1998/99; 2001/02; 2002/03; 2004/05; 2007/08)**

It was in February 1872 that Peter and Moses McNeil, together with Peter Campbell and William McBeath, decided to form a football team called Rangers, and a few weeks later in May the newly formed side played its first match. It took place at Fleshers' Haugh on Glasgow Green, and a 0–0 draw against Callander FC, played in a public space, became the first entry in the Rangers record book. The club was officially formed the following year, and by 1875 it had its own ground at Burnbank, near Kelvin Bridge. In August 1876 Rangers were able to move to a ground at Kinning Park that had previously been used by Clydesdale, and this became their home until 1887, when they moved to Ibrox.

They soon challenged the dominance of Queen's Park and Vale of Leven, and reached the final of the Scottish Cup in 1876/77. A 1–1 draw against Vale of Leven was followed by a replay that had to be abandoned because of a pitch invasion during extra time, and then a third match was lost 3–2. Rangers even reached the semi-finals of the 1886/87 English FA Cup before the SFA put a stop to cross-border participation. They became founder members of the Scottish League in 1890/91 and won the first of their many honours in that very first season when they shared the championship with Dumbarton.

In 1899 they moved the short distance to 'New Ibrox' and, after the new ground had been expanded into 'Greater Ibrox', it was selected to host the 1902 Scotland v England fixture. The decision was to lead to tragedy when the match took place on 5 April 1902. Part of the terracing collapsed, leaving twenty-six people killed, plus 587 injured, and William Wilton, the club's first manager (and secretary), led a programme of intense fundraising for the injured and the dependants of those killed. A major reconstruction of the stadium followed and players were sold to meet the cost.

Rangers began the twentieth century with four league titles in a row, and by April 1920 they were on the point of winning the league for the ninth time when William Wilton drowned in a boating accident at Gourock. Despite the many titles, he had not held the Scottish Cup since 1903, and even his successor, William Struth, did not do so until 1928. Bill Struth was in charge for thirty-four years, and had a reputation for ensuring smartness and discipline among the players. One of his first signings was Alan Morton from Queen's Park, who went on to play at Ibrox for thirteen seasons, and become a Rangers legend. Another signing was Sam English from Coleraine in 1931 and he went on to score a record forty-four goals in the 1931/32 season.

The Rangers team of 1896/97. Standing: (left to right): McCade (assistant trainer), Oswald, N.Smith, Hyslop, Dickie, Turnbull, Muir (linesman). Seated: McPherson, Miller, McCreadie, Drummond, Mitchell, Gibson, Neil. On ground: Low, A.Smith. This season Rangers won the Scottish Cup, the Glasgow Cup and the Glasgow Merchants' Charity Cup.

In 1945 Rangers played a match against a touring Moscow Dynamo side that is still remembered as a classic encounter; trailing by 2–0, Rangers came back to earn a 2–2 draw. As the 1940s progressed, the Rangers defence became known as the 'Iron Curtain', and in 1948/49 the team won the first ever treble of league championship, Scottish Cup and League Cup. In 1954 Scot Symon, the manager of East Fife and a former Rangers player, returned to Ibrox, where he would be manager until 1967. He introduced young players such as Eric Caldow and Bobby Shearer alongside experienced ones such as George Young and in 1960 signed Jim Baxter, whom many people consider to be one of Rangers greatest ever players, from Raith Rovers.

This was the time when Rangers first made their mark in European competition and in 1959/60 Scot Symon led Rangers to the semi-finals of the European Cup, where they lost to Eintracht Frankfurt. The following season they went one better and became the first British team to reach a major European final, when they reached the final of the 1960/61 European Cup-

Winners' Cup, although they lost 4–1 on aggregate to Fiorentina. There was a second treble in 1963/64 and three seasons later Rangers again reached the final of the European Cup-Winners' Cup, this time a one-off match against Bayern Munich in Nuremburg. There were no goals after ninety minutes, but then the Germans scored a single goal in extra time, and Franz Beckenbauer's men took the trophy. This was just four months after a 1–0 defeat by Berwick Rangers in the first round of the Scottish Cup and before the end of 1967 Scot Symon had been replaced as manager by his assistant Davie White.

There continued to be good runs in European competition and a Rangers side that was captained by John Greig reached the semi-finals of the 1968/69 Inter-Cities Fairs Cup, before losing 2–0 on aggregate to eventual winners Newcastle United. There were, however, no domestic trophies to console the Rangers fans and in March 1969 Davie White was dismissed. Former Rangers player Willie Waddell replaced him and he quickly established a reputation for fitness and discipline. Jock Wallace, goalkeeper and manager of the Berwick Rangers side that embarrassed Rangers in 1967, was appointed chief trainer and coach and his intensive training regimes became legendary.

The League Cup was won when Celtic were defeated 1–0 in the 1970/71 final, and a sixteen year old Derek Johnstone scored the winner. Then, on 2 January 1971 disaster struck again. In the New Year game against Celtic at Ibrox, Jimmy Johnstone headed Celtic into a 1–0 lead with just over a minute left, and then Colin Stein equalised with just seconds remaining. The goals resulted in large numbers of fans both leaving and returning and the pressure of the crowds on stairway thirteen resulted in a crush that left sixty-six people dead and more than 140 injured. These were dark days for the club and Willie Waddell was a source of inspiration that helped everyone get through them.

A European trophy finally arrived at Ibrox with the 1971/72 European Cup-Winners' Cup. The semi-finals brought revenge against Bayern Munich, who were beaten 3–1 on aggregate, and then thousands of Rangers supporters went to Barcelona to see their team defeat Dynamo Moscow in the final. The celebrations were marred by the behaviour of over-exuberant fans and Rangers were banned from European games for two years, but this was later reduced to one year. Two weeks after the win in Barcelona Jock Wallace became team manager, whilst Willie Waddell assumed the role of general manager. He devoted his energies to the reconstruction of the ground and, when a modern new stadium was eventually opened in 1981, it was a testament to his efforts.

Rangers stars McPhail, English, Meiklejohn and Fleming pictured the day after the club beat Kilmarnock 3-0 in the replayed final at Hampden.

In 1972 a Dutch journalist proposed the idea of a European Super Cup to be competed for by the winners of the European Cup and the winners of the European Cup-Winners' Cup. The idea was not immediately endorsed by UEFA because of the ban imposed on Rangers, but the De Telegraaf newspaper provided financial support and the competition took place without official backing in its first year. Rangers played Ajax, the holders of the European Cup, over two legs with Alex McDonald scoring in both a 3–1 defeat at Ibrox and a 3–2 defeat in Amsterdam. Thus a strong Ajax side, for whom Johan Cruyff also scored in both legs, deprived Rangers of another trophy in their centenary year.

Jock Wallace led Rangers to the 1974/75 league championship that ended Celtic's run of nine

Rangers, League winners in 1910/11.

consecutive titles, and this was followed up with the treble of three domestic trophies in both 1975/76 and 1977/78. Shortly after the 1977/78 Scottish Cup final Jock Wallace left for Leicester City and long-serving captain John Greig took on the job. His signings included Ian Redford from Dundee, Craig Paterson from Hibernian and Ally McCoist from Sunderland, and his teams won two Scottish Cups and two League Cups. The all important league title was not, however, brought back to Ibrox and John Greig resigned in October 1984. The club turned once more to Jock Wallace, who was by now at Motherwell, and he oversaw a period that included two League Cup victories, but not the success that Rangers desired.

In 1986 Rangers appointed Graeme Souness as their first player-manager, together with Walter Smith as assistant manager, and they assembled a squad of big-name players that included Terry Butcher the England captain. The most controversial acquisition was Maurice Johnstone, the former Celtic star, but the signing of a Catholic player was seen by many as a sign of the club's determination to reach the top. In November 1988 David Murray took over control of the club from Lawrence Marlborough and a new era of investment and expansion commenced, which complemented the continuing acquisition of trophies.

Graeme Souness shocked the world of football when he resigned, to return to Liverpool, in April 1991, but the 'Souness revolution' during his time in Glasgow inspired the club to new heights. Championship wins in 1989, 1990, and 1991 turned out to be the first three of nine consecutive titles that equalled Celtic's record, with Walter Smith now in charge for the last six. In 1992/93 he not only led Rangers to their fifth treble, he also took them to second place in the group stage of the European Champions League, missing qualification for the semi-finals by just one point.

His successor was Dutchman Dick Advocaat, the first non-Scot to be manager of Rangers, and his side adopted a European style of play that won another treble in his first season of 1998/99. The double of league title and Scottish Cup followed in 1999/2000 and the side was further strengthened by the arrival of Ronald de Boer from Barcelona. Dick Advocaat was a major influence in the development of a youth academy and training centre, and although he made way for Alex McLeish in 2001, Murray Park continues as a reminder of the standards that he set.

Alex McLeish led Rangers to their seventh treble in 2002/03, and in 2005/06 he took them to the last sixteen in the European Champions League, where a goal from Peter Lovenkrands in each leg was not enough to overcome Villareal. However, the search for improvement did not let up and at the end of that season Frenchman Paul Le Guen arrived from Lyon to take over as manager. After a series of disappointing results he left by mutual consent in January 2007 and soon afterwards Walter Smith left his job as Scotland coach to return to Ibrox for a second period in charge.

His first full season of 2007/08 saw Rangers win both the Scottish Cup and the League Cup, and they almost won two other trophies despite a backlog of fixtures. The UEFA Cup final in Manchester was lost 2–0 to Zenit St Petersburg, and the fight for the SPL title went to the last game of the season before the Gers had to settle for the runners-up position.

RED CARD (see ORDERED OFF)

REFEREE

The man or woman who presides over a game of Association Football has many powers and duties, and they are all laid down in the laws of the game. The referee controls the match in co-operation with two assistant referees, and is responsible for disciplining players who do not comply with the laws. He or she also acts as the official timekeeper and recordkeeper.

Originally, the team captains would attempt to resolve disputes on the pitch, but then this job was given to two umpires. Each side brought their own official. Eventually, a third, neutral, person was appointed, who would be referred to if the umpires could not agree. In 1891 this referee took his place on the pitch, and the two umpires became linesmen or assistant referees, as they are known today.

A referee must not only have a thorough knowledge of the laws, he or she must be very fit in order to keep up with the play. Also, if a person is to take control of a football match, they must have excellent communication skills in order to enforce the laws when two teams are both determined to win.

Jack Mowat, one-time referee and then a referee supervisor, is compelled to make a come-back in the snow at Cappielow when the linesman was injured.

Scotland has had many famous referees throughout the ages. There was Tom Robertson of Queen's Park in the 1890s and 1900s (in Victorian and Edwardian times a referee was often a member of a club, although he could not officiate in games played by that club), Tom Dougray of Bellshill in the 1910s and 1920s, Peter Craigmyle of Aberdeen in the 1930s, Jack Mowat of Rutherglen in the 1950s, Tom (Tiny) Wharton of Clarkston in the 1950s and 1960s, Hugh Phillips of Wishaw of the same era and Hugh Dallas of Bonkle, near Motherwell, in the 1990s and 2000s. It is now the custom not to mention where a referee comes from, to avoid problems such as intimidation and threats.

Scottish referees who have controlled European finals are as follows:

1960	Jack Mowat	European Cup
	Hampden Park	Real Madrid versus Eintracht Frankfurt
1962	Tom Wharton	European Cup-Winners' Cup
	Hampden Park	Atletico Madrid versus Fiorentina
1975	Bobby Davidson	European Cup-Winners' Cup
	Basle	Dinamo Kiev versus Ferencvaros
1999	Hugh Dallas	UEFA Cup
	Moscow	Parma versus Marseille

In the 1960 European Cup Final at Hampden Jack Mowat, who lived in Rutherglen, saved the authorities expenses by walking from his house to the game! He was

Scottish Cup final 1958. Famous referee Jack Mowat supervises an injury.

fifty-two at the time, and a couple of years earlier had become FIFA's oldest referee when he controlled the Hungary versus Mexico game at the 1958 World Cup in Sweden.

The Scottish Football Association has over 2000 registered referees, including almost 150 on a list of Category 1 Referees, who are qualified to officiate in Scotland's principal league and cup competitions. Every year some of these are appointed to the FIFA international list, and will officiate in European competitions. The grading system goes all the way down to Category 6 Referees, who will referee in youth and amateur football, as well as probationary and trainee referees.

The compulsory retirement age for referees has been a subject of much debate. A Category 1 referee is currently obliged to retire from domestic football at the age of fifty, and from the FIFA international list at the age of forty-five. Referees are constantly monitored on their performance by a supervisor, and may have to stop even earlier if they do not maintain the required standard.

The duties of the assistant referees, which are laid down in the laws of the game, are subject to the decision of the referee. They include indicating when the ball has left the field of play, and which side is entitled to return it. He or she will also indicate to the referee when a player may have committed an offside offence, as well as providing an opinion on other matters when the referee requires clarification. Along with the referee, they operate in a diagonal system of control in order to be as effective as possible, and will stay level with the last defender to judge on the always-contentious issue of offside. In the many games that take place every week without the benefit of neutral assistant referees, no decision is more difficult for a referee than offside.

In 1991 the International Football Association Board created the position of fourth official, whose job is to assist the referee at all times. As well as serving as a replacement official when a referee or assistant referee cannot continue, there are many other ways in which assistance is provided. These include the assessment of players' equipment, ensuring that substitutions are properly carried out, and making sure that the referee doesn't make a serious error, such as cautioning the wrong player.

The fourth official can sometimes be seen helping to keep things calm in the teams' technical areas when people become agitated, and also serves as a point of contact between the other officials and non-participants such as television crews.

REGISTRATION OF PLAYERS

Clubs are occasionally fined, or have points deducted, for not having registered a player, and Cowdenbeath in 1989, Forfar Athletic in 1990 and Meadowbank Thistle in 1995 all lost points for this reason.

In January 2008, Brechin City were expelled from the Scottish Cup after evidence came to light that they had fielded two ineligible players in their fourth-round replay against Hamilton Academical on 28 January. Michael Paton and Willie Dyer had not been properly registered, for although they were signed before the replay, it was after the original game on 12 January. Rule 15 (b) of the competition rules states that only those players who were eligible at the date fixed for originally playing the round may play in a replay.

There can be a particular problem with the Scottish Cup and the Scottish League Cup, for once a player plays for a team in one of these tournaments he may not play for any other team in that season's competition, even though he is transferred to them. It is what is known as being 'cup-tied', and is a relic from the Victorian amateur days when a player could play for any club he wished. Its idea was to stop the winners of a particular cup game persuading the best player of the defeated team to play for them in the next round, but it is still rigorously applied in the professional era. In the 2006 Scottish League Cup final, for example, Mark Wilson was ineligible to play for Celtic as he had already played in the competition that season for Dundee United.

Regulations are less tight for amateur players, but tighter now than they were in 1909, in the remarkable case of John Atkinson. Celtic had to play eight games in twelve days to finish their league programme and one of their games was against Hamilton Accies at home. They won, but outside left Davie Hamilton was injured. Celtic manager Willie Maley had, however, been impressed by opposition left winger John Atkinson. Finding out that he was an amateur and playing on a freelance basis, Maley engaged him for the following day's fixture against Morton, having sent a telegram to SFA Headquarters to ask if he could be registered for this one game. Permission was granted, and not only did John Atkinson play, he scored two goals. He thus has the unique distinction of having played against Celtic one day and for them the next.

REILLY Lawrie (1928 –)

Scotland Caps: 38
Scottish League Championship medals: 3

Commonly known as 'Last minute Reilly', because of his ability to score vital goals late in the game, Lawrie Reilly was capped thirty-eight times for Scotland. He was the centre forward of Hibs' 'famous five' forward line, and is considered by many to be the most famous Hibernian player of all time. His most famous last-minute goal was at Wembley in 1953, to earn Scotland a 2–2 draw against England. He scored twenty-two goals in his thirty-eight Scotland games, which means that his strike-rate is better than that of Kenny Dalglish or Denis Law. He played for Hibs between 1945 and 1958. He never won the Scottish Cup, or the Scottish League Cup, but he did score 185 goals for Hibernian.

Wembley 1953: The famous goal scored by Lawrie Reilly in the last minute to earn Scotland a draw against England

REILLY Rose (1955 –)

Born in Ayrshire, Rose Reilly won the highest honours in women's football. In a career that started with a boys' team in Stewarton, she first played for Scotland at the age of thirteen, and had won ten Scottish caps by the time she moved to French club Reims four years later. After just six months in France she was signed by AC Milan, and began a career in Italian football that eventually saw her play for eight different clubs. There were two Serie A titles during her four years at the San Siro, and by the time she retired at the age of forty she had amassed a total of eight Italian championships, four Italian cups and one French title. At one stage she was playing for both Lecce in Italy and Reims in France, and won the league championship in both countries in the same season.

Rose became an Italian citizen during her time in Italy, and went on to play thirteen times for her adopted country. The highlight of her career came in 1983 when she captained Italy to a 3–1 victory over the USA in the Women's World Cup final in China. As well as scoring a goal, she was voted the best player in the Italian squad. In March 2007 she was acknowledged as one of Scotland's sporting greats when she was inducted into the Scottish Sports Hall of Fame, and in November that year she became the first woman to be inducted into the Scottish Football Hall of Fame at Hampden Park.

Rose Reilly receives the 1975 player of the year award at AC Milan.

RELEGATION

Relegation to a lower division was not automatic until the 1921/22 season. Before then the clubs in Division One held a vote at the end of the season to elect their members for the following year. This sometimes produced results that now seem unfair. For example in 1907/08 Port Glasgow Athletic finished bottom of Division One after finishing joint bottom in 1906/07 and second bottom in 1905/06. They maintained their Division One status for the following season and Raith Rovers, who had topped Division Two, were denied promotion.

By the 1920/21 season Division Two had still not been re-introduced, following its suspension in 1915. The Central League, which included clubs that had previously been in Division Two, had become popular and an arrangement was agreed whereby the Central League would form the backbone of a new Division Two for 1921/22. A crucial part of the deal was that there would be automatic promotion and relegation between the divisions.

The reality of relegation from the SPL sinks in to Dundee fans in May 2005.

Although the Division Two clubs had proposed play-offs to decide promotion and relegation as long ago as 1895, they were not adopted in Scotland until 1994, as part of a restructuring of the Scottish Football League.

First clubs to be relegated (decided by means of a vote)	Abercorn and Clyde (from Division One to Division Two)	1893
First clubs to be automatically relegated	Dumbarton, Queen's Park and Clydebank (from Division One to Division Two)	1922
First club to be relegated as a result of a play-off	Partick Thistle (from Premier Division to First Division)	1996

In May 2008 Gretna FC fell all the way from the SPL to the Third Division. The club was already in administration and relegated from the SPL, and the administrator said he could not guarantee that they would be able to fulfil their fixtures. The SFL therefore decided that, if Gretna were going to continue to exist at all, their next season would be spent in the Third Division. They resigned from the Scottish League soon afterwards.

RENFREW FC (see JUNIOR FOOTBALL)

RENFREWSHIRE CUP

This is one of the many regional cups played for throughout Scotland that have now fallen out of fashion. This particular trophy suffered from lack of competition in later years in that it was usually an annual pre-season game between Morton and St Mirren. For a while in the early years of the twenty-first century, Morton withdrew from the Renfrewshire FA, leaving St Mirren to play the winners of the Renfrewshire Junior Cup, but Morton then rejoined. Past winners are:

1879	Thornliebank	1880	Thornliebank	1881	Arthurlie
1882	Arthurlie	1883	St Mirren	1884	St Mirren
1885	Port Glasgow Ath.	1886	Abercorn	1887	Abercorn
1888	St Mirren	1889	Abercorn	1890	Abercorn
1891	St Mirren	1892	Abercorn	1893	Morton
1894	St Mirren	1895	Port Glasgow Ath.	1896	Port Glasgow Ath.
1897	St Mirren	1898	St Mirren	1899	Morton
1900	Port Glasgow Ath.	1901	Morton	1902	Morton
1903	Morton	1904	St Mirren	1905	Morton
1906	Morton	1907	Morton	1908	Morton
1909	Port Glasgow Ath.	1910	St Mirren	1911	St Mirren
1912	Morton	1913	Morton	1914	Morton
1915	Morton	1916	No Competition	1917	No Competition
1918	Morton	1919	No Competition	1920	Morton
1921	No Competition	1922	Morton	1923	Morton
1924	St Mirren	1925	St Mirren	1926	St Mirren
1927	St Mirren	1928	No Competition	1929	St Mirren
1930	St Mirren	1931	Morton	1932	St Mirren
1933	St Mirren	1934	St Mirren	1935	Morton
1936	St Mirren	1937	Morton	1938	St Mirren
1939	Morton	1940	No Competition	1941	St Mirren
1942	Morton	1943	Morton	1944	St Mirren
1945	Morton	1946	St Mirren	1947	St Mirren
1948	St Mirren	1949	Morton	1950	St Mirren
1951	Morton	1952	Morton	1953	Morton
1954	Babcock & Wilcox	1955	No Competition	1956	Morton
1957	Morton	1958	Morton	1959	St Mirren
1960	St Mirren	1961	St Mirren	1962	Morton
1963	St Mirren	1964	Morton	1965	Morton
1966	Morton	1967	St Mirren	1968	Morton
1969	No Competition	1970	No Competition	1971	No Competition
1972	Morton	1973	Morton	1974	St Mirren
1975	No Competition	1976	No Competition	1977	St Mirren
1978	Morton	1979	St Mirren	1980	St Mirren
1981	Morton	1982	No Competition	1983	St Mirren
1984	St Mirren	1985	St Mirren	1986	St Mirren
1987	Morton	1988	St Mirren	1989	Morton
1990	St Mirren	1991	Morton	1992	No Competition
1993	No Competition	1994	No Competition	1995	No Competition
1996	Morton	1997	Morton	1998	St Mirren
1999	St Mirren	2000	St Mirren	2001	St Mirren
2002	St Mirren	2003	Morton	2004	Morton
2005	St Mirren	2006	St Mirren	2007	St Mirren

RENNIE Harry (1873 – 1954)

Scotland Caps: 13
Scottish League Championship medals: 1
Scottish Cup medals: 1

Harry Rennie was undeniably one of the best-ever goalkeepers in Scottish football history, as his thirteen international matches for Scotland between 1900 and 1908 indicate. He had tremendous agility and versatility, being sometimes prepared to join in attacks, as befitted a man who had been a half back before he became a goalkeeper. With Hibernian he won a Scottish Cup winners' medal in 1902, and a Scottish League championship winners' medal the following year. He also played for Morton, Hearts, Rangers and Kilmarnock.

RENNY-TAILYOUR Henry (1849 – 1920)

Scotland Caps: 1

Renny-Tailyour is the only man to have represented Scotland at both football and rugby. He was born in

India of Scottish descent, and became a colonel in the British Army. He scored the first goal for Scotland in international football, as the team went down 4–2 to England in 1873 at the Oval. He played football for the Royal Engineers and won the FA Cup with them in 1875. His rugby appearance for Scotland was against England at the Oval in 1872. He also played cricket for Aberdeenshire, Kent, and the Gentlemen (amateurs) versus the Players (professionals). He is an excellent example of an all-round Victorian sportsman, for he was a noted runner as well.

RENTON FC (former Scottish League club)

Home: **Tontine Park, Renton, Dunbartonshire**
Highest League Position: **7th (1891/92)**
Best Scottish Cup Performances: **Winners (1884/85; 1887/88)**

Founded in 1872, the club from the village of Renton has a remarkable number of achievements to its name. Renton played, and won, the very first Scottish cup-tie when they beat Kilmarnock 2–0 on 18 October 1873. Not only did they go on to twice win the Scottish Cup, they were losing finalists on a further three occasions and in 1886/87 they even took part in the English FA Cup. After their Scottish Cup success in 1888, when Cambuslang were beaten 6–1 in the final, Renton played West Bromwich Albion, the holders of the English FA Cup. The match was advertised as being for the 'championship of the world' and Renton won 4–1.

Another 'first' associated with the club is that Henry (Harry) Campbell (q.v.), one of their players against Cambuslang, went on to become the first player to win both Scottish and English cup-winners medals when he played for Blackburn Rovers in the 1890 FA Cup final.

Renton was one of the founder members of the Scottish League when it was formed on 30 April 1890, but in the first season the club was expelled after only five league matches, for contravening the amateur code. They played a match against 'Edinburgh Saints', even though they had been refused permission by the Scottish FA. 'Saints' was really just another name for St Bernard's, a club that had been suspended for professionalism. Renton pursued the matter in the courts and the club was re-instated the following season.

The club's league form never matched its successes in the Scottish Cup and in 1894 they were relegated to Division Two. Poor crowds and financial difficulties followed, and by 1897 they had lost their best players and were having difficulty in raising a team. After just four matches of the 1897/98 season they resigned, to be replaced by Hamilton Academical.

Nevertheless, the tradition of cup success carried on and they reached the final of the Scottish Qualifying Cup in 1904/05. In 1907/08 they reached the last eight of the Scottish Cup and even reached the second round as late as 1920/21, when they lost 2–0 to Motherwell. However, by 1922 their financial problems had become too great and they went out of existence.

The trophy awarded to Renton FC in 1888 for 'The Championship of the United Kingdom and the World'

RESERVE-TEAM FOOTBALL

It is desirable for a club to have a reserve side from the point of view of developing youngsters, but some teams find them an expensive luxury. It is still encouraging, however, to see youngsters fighting their way through the reserve teams to reach the top grade.

The Scottish Reserve League was established in 1909, but was disbanded in 1915 after one year of the first world war. After the war it was reformed into the Scottish Football Alliance, and for one season divided into north and south sections. It later included a few other clubs that had been left homeless when Division Three of the Scottish League imploded after season 1925/26, but thereafter the non-reserve teams began to be excluded, although this process did not become formalised until the AGM of 1938, when the Scottish Football Alliance became the Scottish Reserve League once again.

For a few years after the second world war, the Reserve League amalgamated with 'C' Division (the teams that were in the Scottish League, but not good enough for 'A' and 'B' divisions). This was an unusual, but successful, concept, although it suffered from the fact that only a non-reserve team could win promotion to the 'B' Division. Stirling Albion and Leith Athletic in 1947, East Stirlingshire in 1948, Forfar Athletic in 1949 and Brechin City in 1954 earned promotion in this way, but on other occasions the 'C' Division was won by a reserve side, which could not be promoted.

From season 1955/56 onwards, the Scottish Reserve League contained only the second XI teams of those clubs whose first XIs were in the first division. From season 1975/76 onwards, there was a Premier Reserve League, mirroring developments with the first teams, and in 1978/79 came the welcome development of a Reserve League (East) and a Reserve League (West) for clubs that were not in the Premier Division. From the inception of the Scottish Premier League in 1998/99 until 2003/04 there was no Reserve League as such, just Under 21 and Under 19 leagues, but from 2004/05 onwards a Reserve League (with no age restriction) replaced the Under 21 League. Celtic won the Scottish Premier Reserve League in 2004/05, 2005/06, 2006/07 and 2007/08, and as they won the Under 21 League three years before that, can claim to have won the title seven years in a row. It is Rangers, however, who can claim to have been the reserve champions (i.e. winners of the reserve league, under its various names) on twenty-nine occasions since 1909/10, followed by Celtic with twenty-five, then by Hearts and Aberdeen with eight each.

There was a Scottish Second XI Cup from 1882 until 1988. It was competed for exactly one hundred times, with Rangers winning it on twenty-five occasions, followed by Hearts who were victorious twelve times. Dundee United were the last winners in 1988, although the tournament had been struggling for some time - for example not being competed for in 1986 or 1987. In addition, in 1960, the competition was abandoned when the two finalists Rangers and Hibernian could not agree a date. A Reserve League Cup came into existence after the second world war, running in tandem with the Scottish League Cup. In fifty-six years of competition, Celtic won it thirteen times, Rangers ten and Aberdeen nine.

A Combined Reserve League was also in existence between 1959 and 1971, for clubs that had a reserve team but were not themselves in the top flight of first XI football. Both Celtic and Rangers entered what amounted to their third XI in this competition, which suffered from a lack of teams and was sometimes played for twice per season in the autumn and the spring. On five occasions the spring section was either not contested or was left unfinished.

Although reserve matches were, and are, competed for fiercely, consistent team selection is very difficult to achieve, for a good player is likely to be invited to step up a grade. The practice used to be that if Aberdeen, say, were playing against Hibs at Pittodrie, then the reserves would be playing at Easter Road. This is no longer the case, because so many of the 'reserves' are needed to be on the bench for the first team game, and it is not viable to have a reserve game at the same time. Thus reserve games can be played at any time, often on junior grounds, or other grounds hired by a rich club, lest they damage their pitch.

Reserve sides were often called the 'Swifts', and in the case of Queen's Park, the 'Strollers'. Less officially, they are called the 'second string', the 'seconds', the 'stiffs', the 'cannabees', the 'wannabees' and other less complimentary names, but none is so vivid as the 'ham and eggers'. This is because in the old days, reserves were not paid, but were engaged on a match-to-match basis, and instead of payment they were given high tea after the game – usually ham and egg, hence their nickname.

REST OF EUROPE

On two occasions, a Great Britain side has played against the Rest of Europe, and on each occasion, the Scottish input has been significant. The first game was on 10 May 1947 at Hampden when Great Britain, playing in all blue Scotland jerseys beat the Rest of Europe 6–1 before 135,000 in what was dubbed 'The Match of the Century'. The British team contained three Scotsmen in Archie Macaulay, Billy Steel and Billy Liddell. The team was Swift, Hardwick, Hughes, Macaulay, Vernon, Burgess, Matthews, Mannion, Lawton, Steel and Liddell.

On 13 August 1955, to commemorate seventy-five years of the Irish Football Association, another match was held against the Rest of Europe. This time, Great Britain, wearing the green jerseys of Northern Ireland, did less well, losing to the Rest of Europe 1–4. This team also had three Scotsmen – Joe McDonald, Bobby Johnstone and Billy Liddell, and an Irishman with Scottish connections, namely Bertie Peacock of Celtic. The team was Kelsey, Sillett, McDonald, Blanchflower, Charles, Peacock, Matthews, Johnstone, Bentley, McIlroy and Liddell.

REST OF THE WORLD

Two Scotsmen, Jim Baxter and Denis Law, played in the Rest of the World team which played England at Wembley on 23 October 1963 to mark the centenary of the English Football Association, which was founded on 26 October 1863. The Rest of the World had a squad of seventeen players, including Yashin, Di Stefano, Puskas and Pele, and they rotated their formation. It was Denis Law who scored their only goal in the 1–2 defeat.

RIOCH Bruce (1947 –)

Scotland Caps: 24

Bruce Rioch was a midfield player in the 1970s, mainly with Derby County and Everton, although he also had spells with Luton Town, Aston Villa, Birmingham City and Sheffield United. He won an English league championship medal with Derby County in 1975. He gained twenty-four caps for Scotland, but had the misfortune to be Scotland's captain in the disastrous World Cup in Argentina, and his career and credibility

A Scottish fan embraces midfielder Bruce Rioch after Scotland's famous 2-1 victory over England at Wembley in 1977.

never really recovered from that. He was born in Aldershot, and was the first man born in England to be captain of Scotland. In later years he was manager of Torquay United and Middlesbrough.

ROBERTSON John (1964 –)

Scotland Caps: 16

John Robertson was a centre forward for Hearts in the 1980s and early 1990s, with sixteen Scottish caps to his credit. With Hearts, he became an instant success in the mid 1980s and, following a brief and unsuccessful spell with Newcastle in 1988, returned to play the rest of his career at Tynecastle. He was a cult hero at Tynecastle for the number of goals that he scored (214 in league games). On leaving Hearts, he played for Dundee and Livingston. His playing career over, John became manager of Inverness Caledonian Thistle (whom he guided to the SPL), Hearts, Ross County and Livingston. He was sacked from his job at Livingston in April 2007, and there then followed a brief and unhappy time in Ireland with Derry City.

ROBERTSON John Neilson (1953 –)

Scotland Caps: 28

Not to be confused with the John Robertson who played for Hearts in the 1980s (supra), this John Robertson was a left-winger who played for Derby County and Nottingham Forest, and earned twenty-eight caps for Scotland between 1978 and 1984, playing in the World Cup finals of 1982. He will also be remembered for the penalty that he took at Wembley in 1981 to win the game for Scotland against England. With Notts Forest he won the English league championship in 1978, and then the European Cup in the following two years, and he was looked upon as one of the star men in Brian Clough's side. He also won the English League Cup in both 1978 and 1979. From 2000 until 2005 he was assistant manager to Martin O'Neill (with whom he had played at Nottingham Forest) at Celtic, and deserves credit for the part he played in the success that Celtic had in those years. He moved with Martin O'Neill to Aston Villa in 2006.

ROMANIA

All square with Romania – played six, won two, drawn two, lost two with home advantage being significant:

1975	1 June	Bucharest	1–1	McQueen	Georgescu
1975	17 Dec	Hampden Park	1–1	Rioch	Crisan
1986	26 Mar	Hampden Park	3–0	Strachan Gough Aitken	
1990	12 Sep	Hampden Park	2–1	Robertson McCoist	Camataru
1991	16 Oct	Bucharest	0–1		Hagi (pen)
2004	31 Mar	Hampden Park	1–2	McFadden	Chivu Pancu

ROMANOV Vladimir (1948 –)

Vladimir Romanov is the controlling shareholder of Hearts, a position he has been in since 2005. He is a Russian, but has been based in Lithuania for many years. He gained control of Hearts after various attempts to gain control of other Scottish clubs, but won the affections of the Hearts supporters by guaranteeing that he would keep them at Tynecastle. He appointed George Burley (see **BURLEY George**) as manager in summer 2005 and, for a while, things went well. Then Burley was sacked in October 2005, in a move which puzzled Hearts supporters. Graham Rix, whose reign was equally short-lived, replaced Burley and Hearts were plunged into a period of instability, characterised by player and supporter unrest. Yet, to Romanov's credit, Hearts won the Scottish Cup in 2006, were second in the SPL in that year, and finished fourth in 2007.

ROSEBERY Lord (1847 – 1929)

Lord Rosebery was a sponsor of the Scotland international team around the turn of the nineteenth / twentieth centuries. He was born in London, but as one of his houses was at Dalmeny near the Forth Bridge, he considered himself to be Scottish, and following his brief spell as Liberal Prime Minister between 1894 and 1895, retired to the House of Lords and began supporting the Scotland team. He had already given them a set of strips as early as 1881 and 1882, but now equipped the team in his racing colours of yellow and purple on numerous occasions. The international between Scotland and England in 1900 at Celtic Park became known as the 'Rosebery International' because he himself was there and had paid for the decking out of the Celtic Park pavilion in his colours. He addressed the crowd at the end, paying tribute to the Scottish team who had won 4–1, but expressing hope that between Scotland and England 'there would be no greater civil war than football' in the future!

ROSS COUNTY FC

Ground: **Victoria Park, Dingwall**
Nickname: **The County; The Staggies**
Colours: **Navy blue, white and red**
Record Attendance: **8,500 (disputed by some) v Rangers (1966)**
Record Victory: **11-0 v St. Cuthbert Wanderers (1993)**
Record Defeat: **1-10 v Inverness Thistle**
Highest League Position: **16th (4th in First Div., 2001/02; 2005/06)**
Best Scottish Cup Performance: **Last 14 (1933/34)**
Best League Cup Performance: **Last 8 (1998/99; 2001/02)**

Although the current Ross County FC was founded in 1929, a previous club with that name was a founder member of the Highland League in 1893. They resigned in November of that year after failing to fulfil a fixture against Caledonian at Dingwall, and then being ordered to play the match at Inverness without a share of the gate receipts. Thirty-six years later members of a local amateur club, Dingwall Victors, successfully applied for membership of the Highland League and the name of Ross County returned to senior football. County reached the final of the Scottish Qualifying Cup (North) in 1933/34, losing 4–1 to Rosyth Dockyard at Pittodrie. They went on to play in the Scottish Cup for the first time, and reached the last fourteen, losing 6–1 away to Albion Rovers. Over the following years they earned a reputation as giant-killers, and reached the last sixteen in both 1961/62 and 1965/66. On the latter occasion victories over Forfar Athletic and Alloa Athletic brought Rangers to Dingwall for a second-round tie and a 2–0 defeat to the eventual winners of the trophy was a respectable result. There was a 6–2 away win against Queen of the South in a replayed second-round tie in 1990/91, and a 4–0 second-round win at Forfar came just days before they were voted into the Scottish League in 1994.

In 1966/67 player/manager Ian McNeill led them to the first of their three Highland League titles, and the Staggies topped the table again in 1990/91 and 1991/92. They also won the Qualifying Cup (North) in 1993/94, beating Huntly 2–1 in the final. Then the Scottish League was expanded in 1994 and the club was awarded one of two new places in the Third Division (fourth tier).

Manager Neale Cooper led them to successive promotions in 1998/99 and 1999/2000 before he left in 2002, and after his departure Alex Smith, John Robertson, Gardner Spiers and Scott Leitch all occupied the manager's post whilst the Staggies stayed in the First Division for seven seasons. However, this consistency finally came to an end in 2006/07, when they finished bottom and were relegated. In November 2007, Derek Adams, a former player who had become assistant coach, accepted the challenge of managing his old club and went on to take County straight back to the second tier after they won the 2007/08 Second Division title. .

Once they had become members of the Scottish League, the League Cup provided further opportunities for cup success against the bigger clubs. In 1998/99 County beat Dundee United 2–0 to earn a place in the last eight, and Hearts had to win a penalty shoot-out in order to prevent them from reaching the semi-finals. This result was avenged in 2001/02 when Hearts were beaten on penalties in the first round and then Dundee were beaten 2–1, before a 2–1 quarter-final defeat to Rangers.

ROUGH Alan (1951 –   )

Scotland Caps: 53
Scottish League Cup medals: 1

Alan Rough earned fifty-three Scottish caps as Scotland's goalkeeper between 1976 and 1986, and took part in the World Cup finals of 1978 and 1982. He was capable of occasional 'howlers', but is generally recognised as one of Scotland's best-ever goalkeepers. He played for Partick Thistle between 1966 and 1982, winning a Scottish League Cup medal in the famous 4–1 victory over Celtic in 1971 and a Scottish League First Division medal in 1976. Voted 'Player of the Year' by the Scottish Football Writers in 1981, he joined Hibernian in 1982 after playing 410 times for Thistle. In 1988 he left

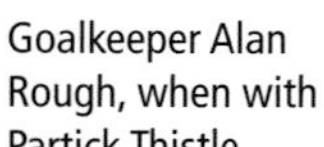
Goalkeeper Alan Rough, when with Partick Thistle.

Hibs for Orlando Lions, and then played briefly for Celtic, Hamilton Academical and Ayr United towards the end of his career. He became player-manager of junior side Glenafton Athletic in 1990, and was their manager when they won the Scottish Junior Cup in 1992/93. In later years he became a radio presenter and pundit.

ROYAL ALBERT FC (former Scottish League club)

Home: **Raploch Park, Larkhall, Lanarkshire**
Highest League Position: **45th (5th in Div 3, 1925/26)**
Best Scottish Cup Performance: **Last 12 (5th round, 1890/91)**

Royal Albert was only part of the Scottish Football League because it was a member of the Division Three that existed between 1923 and 1926. Many of the teams in this bottom division were in financial trouble in 1926, and the Scottish League decided to revert to just two divisions. There was no longer a place for the club from Larkhall.

The club had been around for over forty years before becoming part of the Scottish League. It had first entered the Scottish Cup in 1881/82, losing 5–0 to Cambuslang in the first round, and is believed to have come into existence not long before then. In those days, the only games were cup-ties and friendly matches and Royal Albert didn't join a league until 1891, when they became a founder member of the Scottish Federation.

There was modest cup success in the early years. The Lanarkshire Cup was won on four occasions and in 1890/91 they reached the fifth round of the Scottish Cup before going out 2–0 to Celtic. The match had to be replayed at Ibrox after a crowd invasion caused the first match at Larkhall to be abandoned. However, the club found it hard to repeat these successes and by the start of the first world war little more had been achieved. By this time they had also played their football in three more leagues, the Scottish Alliance, the Football Combination and the Scottish Union.

By 1919 they were playing in the Western League and the club's fortunes started to improve. The Qualifying Cup was won in 1922/23 and then in 1923, like many other teams in the Western League, the Larkhall club became part of Division Three. The Qualifying Cup was won for a second time in 1924/25, but a year or two later things started to look very different. Division Three had folded, and with dwindling support for their matches in the Scottish Alliance (South), and later in the Provincial League, Royal Albert decided to reform as a junior club in 1928.

There was, however, a footnote. Despite the existence of the junior club, a team calling itself 'Royal Albert' continued to compete in the Qualifying Cup and in 1930/31 a team under this name made a final appearance in the Scottish Cup, with a 16–0 first round defeat away to Partick Thistle.

ROYALTY

Perhaps it was necessary to fight and defeat Edward II at Bannockburn in June 1314 because of what he had done in April of that year, when he issued a proclamation banning the playing of football. Perhaps there is also little wonder that England got her revenge at Flodden in 1513, for in 1457 James II of Scotland had said that *'footballe and golfe be utterly cryed doon and not be used'*, and in 1491 James IV of Scotland decreed that *'nowhere in the realm ther be used futeball, golfe or other sik unprofitable sports'*.

In recent times a more enlightened attitude towards the sport has been evident. Members of the royal family have been present at Scottish football games, although no evidence can be found of a reigning British monarch attending a Scottish domestic match. In 1893, Princess Mary of Teck (who would become Queen Mary, the wife of King George V) was presented to the captains (in Scotland's case, James Kelly of Celtic) of the Scotland and England teams before the international game at Richmond. The reason why only the captains were called over to be introduced was that they were still nominally amateurs in 1893, whereas some of the English and Scottish teams may well have been professional, albeit unofficially so in the case of the Scotsmen. This was the first royal occasion, and was considered a significant milestone in the development of the game.

On 27 January 1923, the Duke of York (who would in 1936 become King George VI) attended the Scottish Cup tie between Queen's Park and Bathgate at Hampden Park, and in 1928 the same Duke of York (who was a genuine football fan) was present with his guest King Amanullah of Afghanistan at the 'Wembley Wizards' game on 31 March. In 1973 Princess Alexandra, the cousin of the Queen, was present at the centenary Scottish Cup final between Rangers and Celtic, and in 1995 the Duchess of Kent, normally a devotee of the tennis at Wimbledon, attended the Scottish Cup final between Celtic and Airdrie and was kissed by all the Airdrie team! Celtic players were more restrained and were rewarded for their forbearance with a 1–0 victory. The 2002 Champions League final at Hampden Park between Real Madrid and Bayer Leverkusen had a royal presence in King Juan Carlos of Spain, an unashamed lover of Real Madrid, and he would appear to be the only reigning monarch ever to have attended a football match in Scotland.

Prince Rainier and Princess Grace (the former Hollywood actress Grace Kelly) came from the principality of Monaco to attend the Dundee United v AS Monaco game on 30 September 1981. Monaco won 2–1, but Dundee United had beaten them 5–2 in the first leg. They watched the game from manager Jim McLean's glass-fronted office, which faced the Tannadice pitch.

When Prince William attended St Andrews University in the early years of the twenty- first century, efforts were made to persuade him to declare an allegiance for a local team, but he wisely kept silent counsel. Those close to him said that he had a fondness for Aberdeen because it is close to Balmoral. His great-grandmother, the Queen Mother, who lived for a long time at Glamis Castle, is believed to have been a supporter of Forfar Athletic. Indeed, her father, the Earl of Strathmore, and her brother were frequent attenders at Station Park in the 1930s.

RUSSIA

Not to be confused with the USSR, which broke up at the end of 1991, or the CIS (Commonwealth of Independent States) that briefly followed it, the Russians have since played two draws with Scotland:

1994	16 Nov	Hampden Park	1–1	Booth	Radchenko
1995	29 Mar	Moscow	0–0		

The Queen meets 1998 World Cup stars (L-R) England's Graeme Le Saux and captain Alan Shearer, Jamaica captain Warren Barrett and Scotland captain Colin Hendry at a Buckingham Palace reception.

ST ANDREWS UNITED FC (see JUNIOR FOOTBALL)

ST BERNARD'S FC (former Scottish League club)

Home: **Edinburgh (list of grounds below)**
Highest League Position: **3rd (1893/94)**
Best Scottish Cup Performance: **Winners (1894/95)**

Founded in 1878, the club played at various locations in the northern suburbs of Edinburgh, including the Royal Gymnasium Ground in Stockbridge ('the gymmie'), and these are listed below. Its name was taken from the well near Dean Village that still bears the name of the saint and which featured on the club badge. At first the local connection was emphasised by a residential qualification that required all members to live in the area.

Saints first entered the Scottish Cup in 1881/82 and beat Hearts 1–0 in the first round, although they went on to lose 2–1 to Hibs in the second. It wasn't long before they started to lose their best players to bigger clubs and the residential rule was soon scrapped. It was in the Scottish Cup of 1890/91 that St Bernard's achieved notoriety. After a 7–0 victory over Adventurers in the first round, the opposition lodged a protest on the grounds that Saints were a professional club. The complaint was upheld and, in those days of amateur football, this resulted in disqualification and a six-week ban. During this period the club claimed to have re-formed as 'Edinburgh Saints' and played a match against Renton. This attempted disguise did not impress the authorities and both clubs were banned for a year.

Renton went on to challenge the decision in the courts, but Saints took their punishment and then soon tasted success. When the ban was over, they joined the Scottish Alliance, where they were one of the stronger teams, and also reached the semi-finals of the 1892/93 Scottish Cup, where they lost 5–0 to Celtic. Saints were then voted into Division One of the Scottish League for the 1893/94 season, which was the fourth season of its existence, and achieved a third-place finish at the first attempt. The next year they did even better in the Scottish Cup, beating Renton 2–1 in the 1894/95 final at Ibrox, and the following year reached the semi-finals once again, losing 1–0 to Hearts.

When this eventful decade came to an end, so did St Bernard's time as one of Scotland's most successful clubs and in 1900 they were voted into Division Two, along with Clyde, after losing a play-off against St Mirren at Dens Park. They did finish top of Division Two in 1901 and 1907, and they also won the Scottish Qualifying Cup in both 1907/08 and 1914/15, but were never elected back into the top flight. The club was suffering financial difficulties and these were never far away for the rest of its days.

From now on, Saints were usually to be found in the middle reaches of Division Two at the end of the season and, apart from a brief spell in the Central League at the end of the first world war, they were still there in the 1930s. There was, however, to be one final fling before the end. Their league form was improving, with third-place finishes in Division Two in both 1934/35 and 1936/37, and then in 1937/38 Saints took East Fife to two replays in the semi-finals of the Scottish Cup before losing 2–1 at Tynecastle.

It wasn't long before the second world war brought about the suspension of league football and in September 1939 Saints played their last Scottish League match, a 0–0 draw with Queen's Park at their Royal Gymnasium ground. Their very last match was in the wartime North-Eastern League, when they lost 3–2 at home to East Fife in May 1942. A director who had loaned money to the club died in 1943 and, when the executors of his will sought its return, St Bernard's FC was wound up, although there was an unsuccessful revival attempt after the war.

The following table lists the various grounds in the Edinburgh area where St Bernard's played in the Scottish League:

(Royal Gymnasium Ground, New Powderhall, New Logie Green)	
Scottish League	
New Logie Green	1893 - 1899
New Powderhall	1900 - 1900
Royal Gymnasium Ground	1900 - 1915
Old Logie Green	1921 - 1924
Tynecastle	1924 - 1924
Royal Gymnasium Ground	1924 - 1939

ST JOHN Ian (1938 –)

Scotland Caps: 21

A great centre forward for Motherwell and Liverpool, with a tremendous capacity for scoring goals, Ian St John played twenty-one times for Scotland. But Scotland never qualified for the World Cup finals in his heyday, so the world was deprived of the chance to see what he could do on the really big stage. Many people, including St John himself, felt that his international career suffered because he was an Anglo. He joined Motherwell in 1956,

May 1959: Three Motherwell players appeared for Scotland against West Germany at Hampden Park. Bert McCann, Andy Weir and Ian St John.

St. Johnstone in season 1933/34.

scoring what is believed to be one of the fastest hat-tricks ever in a game against Hibernian on 15 August 1959, and earning international recognition. Financial necessity compelled Motherwell to sell him to Liverpool in 1961 for £37,500. Under Bill Shankly, St John played a great part in the successes achieved at Anfield, winning the English league in 1964 and 1966, and the FA Cup in 1965, when he scored the winning goal against Leeds United in the final. He also played for Coventry and became their assistant manager; then he managed or coached at Motherwell, Portsmouth and Sheffield Wednesday. Later he became a TV pundit, and his 'Saint and Greavsie' programme with Jimmy Greaves became very popular in the 1980s. He was a journalist with *The Sunday Post* for a spell.

ST JOHNSTONE FC

Ground: **McDiarmid Park, Perth**
Nickname: **The Saints**
Colours: **Blue and white**
Record Attendance: **29,972 at Muirton Park v Dundee (1951)**
10,545 at McDiarmid Park v Dundee (1999)
Record Victory: **9-0 v Albion Rovers (1946)**
Record Defeat: **1-10 v Third Lanark (1903)**
Highest League Position: **3rd (1970/71; 1998/99)**
Best Scottish Cup Performance: **Last 4 (Semi-finals 1933/34; 1967/68; 1988/89; 1990/91; 1998/99; 2006/07; 2007/08)**
Best League Cup Performance: **Runners-up (1969/70; 1998/99)**

The origins of the club can be traced back to 1884, when a group of cricketers turned their attention to football in the winter months. The cricket team took its name from the old name for the city of Perth, Saint John's Toun, which referred to Perth's patron saint. The football club was formed the following year and moved to Craigie Haugh, near the present South Inch, on land which would be named the 'Recreation Grounds'. In 1911 Port Glasgow Athletic dropped out of the Scottish League, and St Johnstone left the Central League in order to replace them.

The club then continued as a member of Division Two until 1915, when the Scottish League was cut back to just Division One during the first world war. When the war was over, St Johnstone played in the Eastern League in 1919/20 and the Central League in 1920/21, before becoming part of the reformed Division Two in 1921. In 1923/24 they won the title and were promoted to the top flight. Newspaper reports of the time describe the pitch at the Recreation Grounds as 'in a deplorable condition', and at the end of 1924 the Saints moved to Muirton Park on the north side of Perth, which would be their home until 1989. The opening fixture was a 2–1 win over Queen's Park on Christmas Day 1924. By 1939, when the Scottish League was suspended at the start of the second world war, there had only been two seasons without first division football at Muirton Park and they finished the 1938/39 season in eighth place.

It was therefore something of a shock when the club was placed in the new Division B in 1945, and fifteen seasons elapsed before they were back in the top division, after winning the Division Two title in 1959/60. There was a single further season in the lower division, but the Division Two championship was won again in 1962/63, and then St Johnstone moved on to a period of greater success. In 1970, manager Willie Ormond

took them to the League Cup final, where they lost 1–0 to Celtic, and then the following season a third-place finish in the league brought qualification for the UEFA Cup. The ensuing European campaign saw both SV Hamburg and Vasas Budapest eliminated before a third-round defeat to Zeljeznicar of Yugoslavia.

Between the two major reconstructions of the league in 1975 and 1994, St Johnstone played in all three divisions and there were both highs and lows. Although they were founder members of the Premier Division in 1975, just ten years later in 1985 they began three seasons in the Second Division (third tier). However, the club's fortunes were improving by the time Muirton Park was sold in 1989 and the Saints moved to a newly built, all-seated stadium on land donated by local farmer Bruce McDiarmid on the western side of Perth.

Manager Alex Totten led the club back into the Premier Division in 1990, but the 1994 league reconstruction saw them placed in the First Division (second tier). Three years later it was Paul Sturrock who led them back to the top division and this paved the way for a repeat of their success in the 1970s. In 1999, after Sandy Clark had become manager, Saints again reached the League Cup final, where they lost 2–1 to Rangers, and they again finished third in the league, which brought qualification for Europe. This time VPS Vaasa of Finland were beaten in the qualifying round of the UEFA Cup before AS Monaco put them out in the first round, but Saints can claim to be unbeaten at home in Europe after two campaigns.

After five seasons in the Scottish Premier League, a bottom-place finish in 2002 resulted in the Saints returning to the First Division (second tier). Owen Coyle was appointed manager in April 2005 and they soon became regular challengers for promotion. In 2006/07 there were semi-final appearances in both the Scottish Cup and the League Cup, as well as a second consecutive runners-up place in the First Division. Owen Coyle left for Burnley in November 2007, and his assistant Sandy Stewart, who later joined him at Turf Moor, guided the club to a 3–2 victory over Dunfermline in the final of the Scottish League Challenge Cup.

Derek McInnes, who had joined Saints as a player at the start of 2007, became the new manager, and in April 2008 his side was unlucky not to become the first St Johnstone team to reach a Scottish Cup final when they lost on penalties to Rangers, after a 1–1 draw in the semi-final.

ST MIRREN FC

Ground: **St Mirren Park, Love Street, Paisley**
Nickname: **The Buddies**
Colours: **Black and white**
Record Attendance: **47,438 v Celtic (1949)**
Record Victory: **15-0 v Glasgow University (1960)**
Record Defeat: **0-9 v Rangers (1897)**
Highest League Position: **3rd (1892/93; 1979/80)**
Best Scottish Cup Performance: **Winners (1925/26; 1958/59; 1986/87)**
Best League Cup Performance: **Runners-up (1955/56)**

St Mirren can trace their roots as a football club back to 1877, although they began life as a cricket club around two years earlier. The club has competed in the Scottish Cup since 1880 and became one of the founder members of the Scottish League in 1890. They moved home several times in those early years, playing first at Shortroods, followed by Thistle Park and then Westmarch, before moving to Love Street in 1894, which would be their home for over a hundred years.

In 1908 the Buddies reached the Scottish Cup final for the first time, losing 5–1 to Celtic. They finished bottom of Division One in both 1911/12 and 1913/14, but survived in the top flight because there was no automatic relegation and they were re-elected. They again finished bottom in 1920/21 and once again survived, as the league was expanded at the end of the

St. Mirren with the (rather small) Victory Cup of 1919.

season. In 1919 St Mirren won the Victory Cup, which marked the end of the first world war, and in 1926 the Scottish Cup was added to the trophy cabinet when Celtic were defeated 2–0 at Hampden Park. Division One status was finally lost in 1935 when they were relegated, but only one season was spent in Division Two before they were back in the top flight. In 1956 the club reached its first League Cup final, losing 2–1 to Aberdeen, but gained revenge by defeating Aberdeen 3–1 in the Scottish Cup final three years later.

In 1966 Paisley-born Archie Gemmill, who would later score one of Scotland's most famous goals at the 1978 World Cup finals in Argentina, entered the record books with the Buddies. The use of substitutes had only just been officially permitted in Scottish football, and when he replaced Jim Clunie in a League Cup-tie at Shawfield on 13 August 1966 he became the country's first.

St Mirren were once again relegated to Division Two in 1971 and achieved their worst-ever league position in 1973/74 (twenty-ninth, which was ninth bottom of Division Two). New manager Alex Ferguson led them to a sixth-place finish in 1975, and this brought membership of the newly created First Division (second tier). Two years later the Buddies finished top, and commenced a run of fifteen consecutive seasons in the Premier Division, although Alex Ferguson was sacked in 1978 and joined Aberdeen not long afterwards.

In 1980 St Mirren became the only Scottish club to win the Anglo-Scottish Cup when Bristol City were defeated 5–1 over two legs in the final. Also in 1980, a team containing Scotland internationals Iain Munro and Billy Thomson finished third in the Premier Division and the Buddies qualified for European competition for the first time. They went on to defeat Elfsborg of Sweden in the first round of the UEFA Cup, but went out to St Etienne in the second round. There was more UEFA Cup football in 1983/84 and then again in 1985/86, when they almost reached the third round. A Brian Gallagher hat-trick had earned them a 3–3 draw away to Hammarby of Sweden, and then Frank McGarvey put them 1–0 ahead at Love Street, but two late goals by the Swedes put an end to their hopes.

The Scottish Cup was won for a third time in 1987, when Dundee United were beaten 1–0 after extra time, and qualification for European competition was again achieved. Tromso were defeated in the first round of the 1987/88 European Cup-Winners' Cup, but once more the campaign finished in the second round, this time to eventual winners Mechelen.

In 1990/91 St Mirren finished bottom of the Premier League, despite having the services of former Scotland international Steve Archibald and Victor Munoz, the former captain of Spain, but once again they were saved from relegation by league re-construction. The reprieve only lasted for one year and in 1992 they were relegated to the second tier. After winning the First Division title and promotion to the SPL in 1999/2000, they were relegated back down after just one season.

Five years later they returned to the top flight, when manager Gus MacPherson's team won the 2005/06 First Division championship by ten points, and their season was completed with a 2–1 victory over Hamilton Academical in the final of the Scottish League Challenge Cup. Goals from John Sutton helped them survive in the SPL, and the Buddies now prepared to leave their Love Street home. In January 2008 construction commenced on a new stadium in Greenhill Road, and St Mirren Park was sold to become the site of a supermarket.

April 1960: Willie Bauld scores for Hearts against St Mirren at Love Street. It is late in the game and wins the League for Hearts.

ST MUNGO CUP

This was a one-off trophy played for in 1951 as part of the Festival of Britain celebrations. It was Glasgow's contribution, and they put up a trophy to be called the St Mungo Cup named after the patron saint of Glasgow. The sixteen teams in the then first division of the Scottish Football League were invited to take part in a pre-season tournament. The trophy was won by Celtic who beat Aberdeen 3–2 in the final at Hampden before a crowd of over 81,000 on 1 August 1952, having defeated Hearts, Clyde and Raith Rovers on the way.

There was however a funny and embarrassing sequel. The trophy itself was beautiful and ornate in Victorian style, but had dolphins, mermaids and other nautical phenomena on it rather than anything to do with football. In addition, it tended to disintegrate whenever anyone touched it! Investigations as to the provenance of the trophy led to the scandalous conclusion that Glasgow Corporation (council) had bought this trophy second-hand, on the cheap, for it had originally been a trophy awarded at a yachting regatta in 1894 – hence the dolphins and the mermaids. It had re-emerged some eighteen years later, this time as a football trophy won by Provan Gas Works in a game against the Glasgow Constabulary. The trophy remains at Celtic Park, to be seen by visitors, but not to be touched!

SAN MARINO

Scotland have now played the tiny San Marino six times and have won them all, with San Marino yet to score a goal. Scotland will be hoping that they draw them in every competition!

1991	1 May	Serravalle	2–0	Strachan (pen) Durie	
1991	13 Nov	Hampden Park	4–0	McStay Gough Durie McCoist	
1995	26 Apr	Serravalle	2–0	Collins Calderwood	
1995	15 Nov	Hampden Park	5–0	Jess Booth McCoist Nevin Francini o.g.	
2000	7 Oct	Serravalle	2–0	Elliott Hutchison	
2001	28 Mar	Hampden Park	4–0	Hendry (2) Dodds Cameron	

SAUDI ARABIA

1988	17 Feb	Riyadh	2–2	Johnston Collins	Jazaa Majed

SCHOOLS FOOTBALL

Football in schools is a very important part of the game in Scotland. Unfortunately, schools football took a knock in the industrial action in Scottish schools in the mid-1980s and has not yet totally recovered, in that teachers are now less willing than previously to give up Saturday mornings to coach and to referee when there are so many other demands on their time. However, the Scottish Schools Football Association, which was founded in 1904, oversees primary and secondary school football at regional, national, and international level. Among the many competitions are the national trophies for regional select primary sides and U-14s, as well as the Scottish Shield at U-12s, U-13s, U-14s, U-15s and senior levels for individual schools. There are also five-a-side and seven-a-side competitions, and a great effort has been made in recent years to encourage girls' football. The Senior Shield has been played for every year since 1904, when it was won by Paisley Grammar School. Knightswood Secondary School won in both 2006 and 2007, and Our Lady's High School took the Shield to Cumbernauld in 2008.

The SSFA is responsible for the international schoolboy sides at U-14, U-15, U-16, U-17 and U-18 levels, with girls now playing U-15 internationals against the other British countries. For boys, the oldest international fixture is the U-16 game against England, which was first played in 1911. The SSFA currently operates twenty centres of excellence throughout the length and breadth of the country. The centres are staffed by coaching experts, and young players who shine progress to the Scotland trials system. Many of today's international stars began their careers by impressing at schoolboy level for Scotland.

SCOTLAND MANAGERS

This high profile post has been occupied by seventeen men, many of them on a part-time or short-term basis, and two of them have held the office twice – Andy Beattie (1954), Matt Busby (1958), Andy Beattie (again) (1959–60), Ian McColl (1960–65), Jock Stein (1965), John Prentice (1966), Malky MacDonald (1966), Bobby Brown (1967–71), Tommy Docherty (1971–72), Willie Ormond (1973–1977), Ally MacLeod (1977–78), Jock Stein (again) (1978–1985), Alex Ferguson (1985–1986), Andy Roxburgh (1986–1993), Craig Brown (1993–2001), Berti Vogts (2001–2004), Walter Smith (2005–2007), Alex McLeish (January 2007–November 2007) and George Burley (from January 2008).

Walter Smith.

Prior to 1954, Scotland had seen no need to have a manager in that selectors picked the team, and the argument was that the players chosen should be good enough not to need any tactical talks or discussion. To be fair, this ramshackle way of working was by no means a failure, for Scotland's record prior to 1954 is vastly superior to what it has been since!

Berti Vogts.

Andy Beattie had been a good player for Scotland and Preston North End before the second world war, and he was manager of Huddersfield Town when he was appointed to the Scotland job for the World Cup of 1954, and a few pre-tournament games. He managed to lose 2–4 to England at Hampden, then in the World Cup itself, after a narrow and unlucky defeat by Austria, he astonished the world by resigning *before* the game against Uruguay, which Scotland lost 0–7! No reason was forthcoming for this amazing move, but it is possible that interference from selectors had something to do with it. Even more astonishing is the fact that in 1959 he was invited back to be Scotland manager, a role he fulfilled for a year and a half before resigning with dignity this time.

Matt Busby was the manager of Manchester United. In January 1958 he was half-heartedly asked if he would like to lead Scotland in the 1958 World Cup. Equally half-heartedly he agreed, but then came the Munich Air Crash of 1958, which prevented him taking Scotland to Sweden. Amazingly, Scotland did not appoint anyone else, leaving trainer Dawson Walker in charge with a few experienced players like Tommy Younger and Bobby Evans to help. Busby took up the reins after the World Cup, but soon found that managing Manchester United and Scotland was too much for one man.

Ian McColl was still playing for Rangers when he was appointed the manager of Scotland. It was never clear how much control McColl had over the selection of the team, but he certainly deserves a great deal of credit for recovering from the 9–3 thrashing by England and then beating them three times in a row, a feat not achieved since the 1880s. Sadly, Scotland did not make it to the Chile World Cup of 1962, going down to the eventual runners-up, Czechoslovakia in a play-off in Rotterdam. McColl left in 1965 to become manager of Sunderland.

Jock Stein's first tenure of the job was when he was also manager of Celtic, and with a bit of luck, he might have taken the excellent Scottish talent of 1965 to the World Cup in England in 1966. He then became manager of Scotland after the Argentina fiasco and brought back a little self-respect for the nation when he took them to the World Cup in Spain in 1982. He was on the very brink of qualifying for a second World Cup final when he collapsed and died in tragic fashion on the bench at Ninian Park, Cardiff on 10 September 1985.

John Prentice was manager of the team for four games in 1966, the highlight of which was a 1–1 draw with Brazil before he resigned abruptly in October 1966 to return to club football. No satisfactory reason was given for the sudden departure, other than a feeling that he preferred the daily contact with players.

Malky MacDonald, a player with Celtic before the second world war, was called upon in late 1966 to do the Scotland job on a short-term basis, before Bobby Brown was appointed in February 1967. Brown got off to a great start by beating England in 1967 at Wembley but failed to qualify for either the European Nations Cup in 1968 or the World Cup in 1970. He had lost the confidence of the nation long before his inevitable resignation in 1971.

Tommy Docherty restored some Scottish pride between 1971 and 1972, but did not endear himself to his country by suddenly leaving to take over at Manchester United and leaving the reins to Willie Ormond. It was Willie who brought Scotland her best World Cup moments in 1974 after an epic game in 1973 when Scotland beat Czechoslovakia. But his reign was char-

George Burley took over from Alex McLeish as Scotland manager in January 2008.

acterised by a few indiscipline scandals, and he left in 1977. Ally MacLeod will always be associated with the Argentina disaster but he deserves credit for getting Scotland there and for firing the nation up, even though the expectations were unrealistic.

Following Jock Stein's untimely death, Alex Ferguson, then manager of Aberdeen, took the team to the 1986 Mexico World Cup on a temporary basis, but then Andy Roxburgh took over. Andy did well to take the team to Italy in 1990, but his credibility was seriously impaired by the shocking defeat by Costa Rica, the defeat that perhaps killed the last vestige of credibility for Scotland, and led to a dramatic downfall in international attendances in a nation that had been disappointed too often. Craig Brown did something to arrest the decline by reaching the European Championships in 1996 and the World Cup of 1998, but his failure to reach the World Cup of 2002 led to his downfall and the appointment of Berti Vogts, a man who had been a success as a player and a coach in his native Germany, but whose time of office was characterised by repeated failures against even the most moderate of opposition. To be fair to Vogts, it was also a time when Scottish talent seemed to have temporarily dried up, but his departure was not a matter for national distress. More people were upset when Walter Smith departed to return to Rangers in January 2007. He had taken over in January 2005, and had made a creditable beginning. In October 2006, for example, he produced one excellent result as Scotland beat France, the beaten finalists in that year's World Cup.

Alex McLeish then took over and Scotland's revival continued. For a while it looked as if Scotland might qualify for the European Championships of 2008, especially after Scotland had one of their best results for years when they beat France in Paris in September, but disappointing results in their last two fixtures against Georgia in Tbilisi, and in a high-profile match against Italy at Hampden Park, meant that Scotland were narrowly squeezed out. McLeish then left for Birmingham City soon afterwards, and in January 2008 George Burley, then manager of Southampton, replaced him.

SCOTT Alex (1937 – 2001)

Scotland Caps: 16
Scottish League Championship medals: 4
Scottish Cup medals: 1
Scottish League Cup medals: 2

Alex Scott was a fine right winger for Rangers, Everton, Hibernian and Falkirk from the 1950s until the early 1970s. Fast, direct, and fit, Alex is primarily associated with Rangers, and was one of their best players under Scott Symon, scoring their only goal in their first-ever European Cup-Winners' Cup final against Fiorentina in 1961. But Alex lost his place to Willie Henderson and moved to Everton in 1963, winning both English league and FA Cup medals with them. Towards then end of his career, he returned to Hibs and his hometown team, Falkirk, for whom he played along with his brother Jim, who had played for Hibs and Newcastle United.

SCOTTISH ALLIANCE

After the Scottish League was formed in 1890, the clubs that were not part of the new set-up found it harder to arrange matches against the top clubs. There were occasional friendly games, and of course cup-ties, but it soon became apparent that another league was required in order to maintain interest. On 26 February 1891 the decision was taken to form the Scottish Alliance league, and twelve clubs participated in its first season of 1891/92. They were Airdrieonians, Ayr FC, East Stirlingshire, Greenock Morton, Kilmarnock, King's Park, Linthouse, Northern, Partick Thistle, Port Glasgow Athletic, St Bernard's and Thistle. Some clubs found the cost of travelling to away fixtures to be too much, and five dropped out after one year. Cambuslang, Cowlairs and Vale of Leven replaced them for the league's second season, and the numbers dropped to ten.

All but one of these clubs found that the Scottish Alliance provided a route into the Scottish League, with five being elected at the end of the 1892/93 season, when the Scottish Alliance league table looked like: -

	P	W	D	L	F	A	Pts.
Cowlairs	18	14	2	2	68	31	30
St Bernard's	18	11	1	6	60	40	23
Linthouse	18	11	1	6	52	46	23
Airdrieonians	18	10	2	6	62	48	22
Thistle	18	9	1	8	49	44	19
Partick Thistle	18	7	1	10	44	61	15
Northern	18	6	2	10	46	57	14
Vale of Leven	18	5	2	11	33	53	12
Kilmarnock	18	3	5	10	41	51	11
Cambuslang	18	3	5	10	30	52	11

St Bernard's were elected into Division One of the Scottish League, whilst Cowlairs, Thistle, Partick Thistle and Northern were elected into the inaugural Division Two. Airdrieonians (1894), Kilmarnock and Linthouse (1895), and Vale of Leven (1905) eventually followed them into Division Two, although the Scottish Alliance came to an end in 1897. There was a brief attempt to resurrect a Scottish Alliance in 1905/06, but the next important league with that name was formed in 1919, principally to provide competitive football for reserve teams, although some first teams did take part. Arbroath and Forfar Athletic competed in 1920/21, before joining the new Division Two of the Scottish League, and when Celtic 'A' left in 1922, they were replaced by Dundee Hibernian, who had just dropped out of the Scottish League. The table at the end of the 1922/23 season looked like:

	P	W	D	L	Pts
Airdrieonians A	26	16	6	4	38
St Mirren A	26	14	6	6	34
Hearts A	26	13	6	7	32
Aberdeen A	26	11	9	6	31
Queen's Park Strollers	26	12	6	8	30
Rangers A	26	12	6	8	30
Dundee A	26	11	5	10	27
Partick Thistle A	26	10	5	11	25
Raith Rovers A	26	8	9	9	25
Kilmarnock A	26	7	10	9	24
Albion Rovers A	26	7	6	13	20
Dundee Hibernian	26	5	7	14	17
Ayr United A	26	7	2	17	16
Third Lanark A	26	4	7	15	15

Dundee Hibs were elected back into the Scottish League for 1923/24, under their new name of Dundee United. In 1926/27 the Scottish Alliance was split into northern and southern sections for a single season, and then it continued until 1938, although there were short-lived attempts to revive it in the years that followed.

SCOTTISH CUP

First competed for in 1873/74, the actual cup is the oldest trophy competed for in football history for, although the English FA Cup is two years older, there have been three actual trophies, whereas the Scottish Cup has remained the same since 1874. The first games were on 18 October 1873 and the results were:

Alexandra Athletic	3	Callander	0
Renton	2	Kilmarnock	0
Western	0	Blythswood	1
Third Lanark walkover versus Southern			

Queen's Park, who received a bye, went on to win the first trophy, beating Clydesdale 2–0 in the final.

The success of the tournament lies in the fact that it retains the same format, and has a straight draw. Celtic have won the trophy thirty-four times, Rangers come next with thirty-two, and then third are Queen's Park with ten, while Aberdeen and Hearts are joint fourth with seven each. Three teams, Queen's Park, Dumbarton and Kilmarnock have entered every single competition.

The record winners' medal holder is Charlie Campbell of Queen's Park with eight, although in one cup final, that of 1884, no game took place, as Vale of Leven didn't turn up! Bobby Lennox of Celtic also has eight winners' medals, but he started in only five finals, came on once as a substitute and on another two occasions was an unused substitute. Three men have seven winners' medals – Jimmy McMenemy (six with Celtic and one with Partick Thistle) Bob McPhail (six with Rangers and one with Airdrie) and Billy McNeill (all seven with Celtic). In 2007 Steven Pressley completed a remarkable treble of Scottish Cup medals with three separate clubs – Rangers in 1993, Hearts in 2006 and Celtic in 2007.

The full-time whistle has gone in the replay of the 1909 Scottish Cup final. The players wait to see if there will be extra-time. There won't be and a riot will ensue.

The Scottish Cup final is regarded as one of the showpieces of the season. It was televised live in 1955 and 1957 (in both cases the first game, but not the replay) and from 1977 onwards. The final has had a variety of venues, but only once has it been played outwith Glasgow, and that was in 1896 when Logie Green in Edinburgh, the home of St Bernard's, housed the all-Edinburgh final between Hibernian and Hearts. (also see **REGISTRATION OF PLAYERS**)

The cup final results since 1874 are as follows:

1874	21 Mar	Queen's Park	2	0	Clydesdale	1st Hampden Park
		W. McKinnon Leckie				
Queen's Park: Dickson, Taylor, Neill, Thomson, Campbell, Weir, Leckie, W. McKinnon, Lawrie, McNeil, A. McKinnon						
Clydesdale: Gardner, Wotherspoon, McArley, Henry, Raeburn, Anderson, Gibb, Wilson, Lang, McPherson, Kennedy						
Referee: J. McIntyre						2500

1875	10 April	Queen's Park	3	0	Renton	1st Hampden Park
		A. McKinnon Highet W. McKinnon				
Queen's Park: Neil, Taylor, Philips, Campbell, Dickson, McNeil, Highet, W. McKinnon, A. McKinnon, Lawrie, Weir						
Renton: Turnbull, A. Kennedy, McKay, Scallion, McGregor, Melville, McRae, M. Kennedy, J. Brown, Glen, L. Brown						
Referee: A. Campbell, Glasgow						7,000

1876	11 Mar	Queen's Park	1	1	Third Lanark	Hamilton Crescent
		Highet			Drinnan	
Queen's Park: Dickson, Taylor, Neil, Campbell, Phillips, Lawrie, McGill, Highet, W. McKinnon, A. McKinnon, McNeil						
Third Lanark: Wallace, Hunter, Watson, White, Davidson, Crichton, Drinnan, Scoular, Walker, Millar, McDonald						
Referee: A. McBride, Vale of Leven						10,000

1876	18 Mar	Queen's Park	2	0	Third Lanark	Hamilton Crescent
		Highet (2)				
Queen's Park: Hillcote and Smith replaced Lawrie and A. McKinnon						
Third Lanark: As per first game						
Referee: A. McBride, Vale of Leven						6,000

1877	17 Mar	Vale of Leven	1	1	Rangers	Hamilton Crescent
		Paton			McDougall o.g.	
Vale of Leven: Wood, McIntyre, Michie, Jamieson, McLintock, Ferguson, Paton, McGregor, McDougall, Baird, Lindsay						
Rangers: Watt, Vallance, Gillespie, Ricketts, W. McNeill, M. McNeill, Watson, Dunlop, Campbell, Marshall, Hill						
Referee: J. Kerr, Hamilton						12,000

1877	7 April	Vale of Leven:	1	1	Rangers	Hamilton Crescent
		McDougall			Dunlop	a.e.t.
Vale of Leven: As per first game						
Rangers: As per first game						
Referee: J. Kerr, Hamilton						15,000

1877	13 April	Vale of Leven	3	2	Rangers	1st Hampden Park
		Watson o.g. Baird Paton			Campbell W. McNeill	
Vale of Leven: As per first and second games						
Rangers: As per first and second games						
Referee: J. Kerr, Hamilton						8,000

1878	30 Mar	Vale of Leven	1	0	Third Lanark	1st Hampden Park
		McDougall				
Vale of Leven: Parlane, McLintock, McIntyre, McPherson, Jamieson, Ferguson, McFarlane, McGregor, James Baird, McDougall, John Baird						
Third Lanark: Wallace, Somers, J. Hunter, Kennedy, McKenzie, Miller, A. Hunter, Lang, Peden, McCririck, Kay						
Referee: R. Gardner, Clydesdale						5,000

1879	19 April	Vale of Leven	1	1	Rangers	1st Hampden Park
		Ferguson			Struthers	
Vale of Leven: Parlane, McLintock, A. McIntyre, J. McIntyre, McPherson, McFarlane, Ferguson, James Baird, McGregor, J. Baird, McGougall						
Rangers: Gillespie, A. Vallance, T. Vallance, Drinnan, McIntyre, Hill, Dunlop, Steel, Struthers, Campbell, McNeil						
Referee: J. Wallace, Beith						6,000
Vale of Leven awarded the cup after Rangers failed to appear for the replay on 26 April.						

1880	21 Feb	Queen's Park	3	0	Thornliebank	1st Cathkin Park
		Highet (2) Ker				
Queen's Park: Graham, Somers, Neil, Campbell, Davidson, Richmond, Weir, Highet, Ker, Kay, McNeil						
Thornliebank: Cadden, Jamieson, Marshall, Henderson, McFetridge, A. Brannan, Clark, Wham, Anderson, Hutton, T. Brannan						
Referee: D. Hamilton, Ayr						7,000

1881	9 April	Queen's Park	3	1	Dumbarton:	Kinning Park
		Smith (2) Ker			Meikleham	
Queen's Park: McCallum, Watson, Holm, Campbell, Davidson, Anderson, Fraser, Ker, Smith, Allan, Kay						
Dumbarton: Kennedy, Hutcheson, Paton, Miller, Anderson, Meikleham, Brown, Lindsay, McAulay, McKinnon, Kennedy						
Referee: D. Hamilton, Ayr						10,000
This game followed a protested 2–1 win for Queen's Park on 26 March at Kinning Park. Dumbarton claimed that crowd encroachment prevented the referee or the umpire seeing if the ball had crossed the line before Queen's Park scored. The SFA upheld the appeal.						

1882	18 Mar	Queen's Park	2	2	Dumbarton	1st Cathkin Park
		Harrower (2)			Brown Meikleham	
Queen's Park: McCallum, Watson, A. Holm, Davidson, J. Holm, Fraser, Anderson, Ker, Harrower, Richmond, Kay						
Dumbarton: Kennedy, Hutcheson, Paton, P. Miller, Watt, Brown, Meikleham, McAulay, Lindsay, Kennedy, J. Miller						
Referee: J. Wallace, Beith						12,000

1882	1 April	Queen's Park:	4	1	Dumbarton	1st Cathkin Park
		Richmond Ker Harrower Kay			J. Miller	
Queen's Park: Campbell for J. Holm						
Dumbarton: Watt for McKinnon						
Referee: J. Wallace, Beith						15,000

1883	31 Mar	Dumbarton	2	2	Vale of Leven	1st Hampden Park
		Paton McArthur			Johnstone McCrae	
Dumbarton: McAuley, Hutcheson, Paton, P. Miller, Lang, Keir, R. Brown I, R. Brown II, J. Miller, Lindsay, McArthur						
Vale of Leven: McLintock, McIntyre, Forbes, McLeish, McPherson, Gillies, McCrae, Johnston, Friel, Kennedy, McFarlane						
Referee: T. Lawrie, Queen's Park						15,000

1883	7 April	Dumbarton	2	1	Vale of Leven	1st Hampden Park
		Anderson Brown 1			Friel	
Dumbarton: Anderson for Lang						
Vale of Leven: as per first game						
Referee: T. Lawrie, Queen's Park						8,000

1884	23 Feb					1st Cathkin Park
Queen's Park beat Vale of Leven after Vale of Leven failed to turn up, following a dispute about the date. Queen's Park's team would have been: McCallum, Arnott, Holm, Campbell, Gow, Christie, Allan, Smith, Harrower, Anderson, Watt.						

1885	21Feb	Renton	0	0	Vale of Leven	2nd Hampden Park
Renton: Lindsay, Hannah, A. McCall, Kelso, McKechnie, Barbour, Kelly, McIntyre, J. McCall, Thomson, Grant						
Vale of Leven: James Wilson, A. McIntyre, Forbes, Abraham, John Wilson, Galloway, D. McIntyre, Ferguson, Johnstone, Gillies, Kennedy						
Referee: J. E. McKillop, Cartvale						2,500

1885	28 Feb	Renton	3	1	Vale of Leven	2nd Hampden Park
		J. McCall McIntyre Unknown			Gillies	
Renton: As per first game						
Vale of Leven: McPherson for John Wilson						
Referee: J. E. McKillop, Cartvale						3,500

The Scottish FA Cup is the oldest football trophy still to be actively played for in the world.

1886	13 Feb	Queen's Park	3	1	Renton	1st Cathkin Park
		Hamilton Christie Somerville			Kelso	
Queen's Park: Gillespie, Arnot, Watson, Campbell, Gow, Christie, Somerville, Hamilton, Allan, Harrower, Lambie						
Renton: Lindsay, Hannah, A. McCall, Kelso, McKechnie, Thomson, Grant, Barbour, J. McCall, McIntyre, Kelly						
Referee: J. E. McKillop, Cartvale						7,000

1887	12 Feb	Hibernian	2	1	Dumbarton	2nd Hampden Park
		Smith Groves			Aitken	
Hibernian: Tobin, Lundy, Fagan, McGhee, McGinn, McLaren, Lafferty, Groves, Montgomery, Clark, Smith						
Dumbarton: McAulay, Hutcheson, Fergus, Miller, McMillan, Kerr, Brown, Robertson, Madden, Aitken, Jamieson						
Referee: R. Brown, Queen's Park						10,000

1888	4 Feb	Renton	6	1	Cambuslang	2nd Hampden Park
		McCall (2) D. Campbell J. Campbell McCallum McNee			H. Gourlay	
Renton: Lindsay, Hannah, A. McCall, Kelso, Kelly, McKechnie, McCallum, J. Campbell, D. Campbell, J. McCall, McNee						
Cambuslang: Dunn, Smith, Semple, McKay, J. Gourlay, Jackson, James Buchanan, John Buchanan, Plenderleith, H. Gourlay, J. Gourlay						
Referee: A. McA. Kennedy, Dumbarton						10,000

1889	9 Feb	Third Lanark	2	1	Celtic	2nd Hampden Park
		Oswald (minor) Marshall			McCallum	
Third Lanark: Downie, Thomson, Rae, Lochead, Auld, McFarlane, Marshall, Oswald (minor), Oswald (major), Hannah, Johnstone						
Celtic: John Kelly, Gallacher, McKeown, W. Maley, James Kelly, McLaren, McCallum, Dunbar, Groves, Coleman, T. Maley						
Referee: C.Campbell, Queen's Park						16,000
Followed a game played on 2nd February at 2nd Hampden Park that was declared a friendly, because of shocking ground conditions. Third Lanark won 3–0.						

1890	15 Feb	Queen's Park	1	1	Vale of Leven	1st Ibrox
		Hamilton			McLachlan	
Queen's Park: Gillespie, Arnot, Smellie, McAra, Stewart, Robertson, Berry, Gulliland, Hamilton, Sellar, Allan						
Vale of Leven: Wilson, Murray, Whitelaw, Sharp, McNicol, Osborne, McLachlan, Rankin, Paton, Bruce, McMillan						
Referee: C. Campbell, Queen's Park						10,000

1890	22 Feb	Queen's Park	2	1	Vale of Leven	1st Ibrox
		Hamilton Stewart			Bruce	
Queen's Park: As per first game						
Vale of Leven: As per first game						
Referee: C. Campbell, Queen's Park						14,000

1891	7 Feb	Hearts	1	0	Dumbarton	2nd Hampden Park
		Russell				
Hearts: Fairbairn, Adams, Goodfellow, Begbie, McPherson, Hill, Taylor, Mason, Russell, Scott, Baird						
Dumbarton: McLeod, Watson, Miller, McMillan, Boyle, Keir, Taylor, Galbraith, Mair, McNaught, Bell						
Referee: T. R. Park, Cambuslang						14,000

1892	9 April	Celtic	5	1	Queen's Park	1st Ibrox
		Campbell (2) McMahon (2) Sillars o.g.			Waddell	
Celtic: Cullen, Reynolds, Doyle, Gallacher, Kelly, Maley, Campbell, Dowds, McCallum, McMahon, Brady						
Queen's Park: Baird, Sillars, Sellar, Gillespie, Robertson, Stewart, Waddell, Lambie, Gulliland, Hamilton, Scott						
Referee: G. Sneddon						20,000
Following a game on 12 March that was won 1–0 by Celtic, but declared a friendly following repeated encroachment of the 40,000 crowd at 1st Ibrox						

1893	11 Mar	Queen's Park	2	1	Celtic	1st Ibrox
		Sellar (2)			Blessington	
Queen's Park: Baird, Sillars, Smellie, Gillespie, McFarlane, Stewart, Gulliland, Waddell, Hamilton, Lambie, Sellar						
Celtic: Cullen, Reynolds, Doyle, Maley, Kelly, Dunbar, Towie, Blessington, Madden, McMahon, Campbell						
Referee: R. Harrison, Kilmarnock						15,000
Following a game on 25 February that was won 1–0 by Celtic, but declared a friendly because of a frozen pitch at 1st Ibrox. The game was not postponed for fear of upsetting the 20,000 crowd.						

1894	17 Feb	Rangers	3	1	Celtic	2nd Hampden Park
		H. McCreadie Barker McPherson			Maley	
Rangers: Haddow, Smith, Drummond, Marshall, A. McCreadie, Mitchell, Steel, H. McCreadie, Gray, McPherson, Barker						
Celtic: Cullen, Reynolds, Doyle, Curran, Kelly, Maley, Blessington, Madden, Cassidy, Campbell, McMahon						
Referee: J. Marshall, Third Lanark						15,000

1895	20 April	St Bernard's	2	1	Renton	1st Ibrox
		Clelland (2)			Duncan	
St Bernard's: Sneddon, Hall, Foyers, McManus, Robertson, Murdoch, Laing, Paton, Oswald, Crossan, Clelland						
Renton: Dickie, Ritchie, McCall, Glen, McColl, Tait, McLean, Murray, Price, Gilfillan, Duncan						
Referee: J. Robertson						13,500

1896	14 Mar	Hearts	3	1	Hibernian	Logie Green
		Baird King Michael			O'Neill	
Hearts: Fairbairn, McCartney, Mirk, Begbie, Russell, Hogg, McLaren, Baird, Michael, King, Walker						
Hibernian: McColl, Robertson, McFarlane, Breslin, Neill, Murphy, Murray, Kennedy, Groves, Smith, O'Neill						
Referee: Mr. McLeod, Cowlairs						16,034

R.S.McColl of Queen's Park has an attempt saved by Celtic's McArthur in the 1900 final.

1897	20 Mar	Rangers	5	1	Dumbarton	2nd Hampden Park
		Miller (2) Hyslop McPherson A. Smith			W. Thomson	
Rangers: Dickie, N. Smith, Drummond, Gibson, McCreadie, Mitchell, Low, McPherson, Miller, Hyslop, A. Smith						
Dumbarton: Docherty, D. Thomson, Mauchlan, Miller, Gillan, Sanderson, Mackie, Speedie, Hendry, W. Thomson, Fraser						
Referee: Mr. Simpson, Aberdeen						15,000

1898	26 Mar	Rangers	2	0	Kilmarnock	2nd Hampden Park
		A. Smith Hamilton				
Rangers: Dickie, N. Smith, Drummond, Gibson, Neil, Mitchell, Miller, McPherson, Hamilton, Hyslop, A. Smith						
Kilmarnock: McAllan, Busby, Brown, McPherson, Anderson, Johnstone, Muir, Maitland, Campbell, Reid, Finlay						
Referee: Mr. Colville, Inverness						14,000

1899	22 April	Celtic	2	0	Rangers	2nd Hampden Park
		McMahon Hodge				
Celtic: McArthur, Welford, Storrier, Battles, Marshall, King, Hodge, Campbell, Divers, McMahon, Bell						
Rangers: Dickie, N. Smith, Crawford, Gibson, Neill, Mitchell, Campbell, McPherson, Hamilton, Miller, A. Smith						
Referee: T. Robertson, Queen's Park						25,000

1900	14April	Celtic	4	3	Queen's Park	2nd Ibrox
		McMahon Divers (2) Bell			Christie W. Stewart Battles o.g.	
Celtic: McArthur, Storrier, Battles, Russell, Marshall, Orr, Hodge, Campbell, Divers, McMahon, Bell						
Queen's Park: Gourlay, D. Stewart, Swan, Irons, Christie, Templeton, W. Stewart, Wilson, McColl, Kennedy, Hay						
Referee: J. Walker, Kilmarnock						17,000

1901	6 April	Hearts	4	3	Celtic	Ibrox
		Bell (2) Walker Thomson			McOustra (2) McMahon	
Hearts: Philip, Allan, Baird, Key, Buick, Hogg, Porteous, Walker, Thomson, Houston, Bell						
Celtic: McArthur, Davidson, Battles, Russell, Loney, Orr, McOustra, Divers, Campbell, McMahon, Quinn						
Referee: A. Jackson						15,000

1902	26 April	Hibernian	1	0	Celtic	Celtic Park
		McGeachen				
Hibernian: Rennie, Gray, Glen, Breslin, Harrower, Robertson, McCall, McGeachen, Divers, Callaghan, Atherton						
Celtic: McFarlane, Watson, Battles, Loney, Marshall, Orr, McCafferty, McDermott, McMahon, Livingstone, Quinn						
Referee: R.T. Murray, Stenhousemuir						16,000

1903	11 April	Rangers	1	1	Hearts	Celtic Park
		Stark			Walker	
Rangers: Dickie, Fraser, Drummond, Gibson, Stark, Robertson, McDonald, Speedie, Hamilton, Walker, Smith						
Hearts: McWattie, Thomson, Orr, Key, Buick, Hogg, Dalrymple, Walker, Porteous, Hunter, Baird						
Referee: T. Robertson, Queen's Park						28,000

1903	18 April	Rangers	0	0	Hearts	Celtic Park
Rangers: As per first game						
Hearts: As per first game						
Referee: T. Robertson, Queen's Park						16,000

1903	25 April	Rangers	2	0	Hearts	Celtic Park
		Mackie Hamilton				
Rangers: Henderson and Mackie for Gibson and Walker						
Hearts: Anderson for Buick						
Referee: T. Robertson, Queen's Park						32,000

1904	16 April	Celtic	3	2	Rangers	3rd Hampden Park
		Quinn (3)			Speedie (2)	
Celtic: Adams, McLeod, Orr, Young, Loney, Hay, Muir, McMenemy, Quinn, Somers, Hamilton						
Rangers: Watson, N. Smith, Drummond, Henderson, Stark, Robertson, Walker, Speedie, Mackie, Donnachie, A. Smith						
Referee: T. Robertson, Queen's Park						64,323

1905	8 April	Third Lanark	0	0	Rangers	Hampden Park
Third Lanark: Raeside, Barr, McIntosh, Comrie, Sloan, Neilson, Johnstone, Kidd, McKenzie, Wilson, Munro						
Rangers: Rangers: Sinclair, Fraser, Craig, Henderson, Stark, Robertson, Hamilton, Speedie, McColl, Kyle, Smith						
Referee: J. Deans, Dalkeith						55,000

1905	15 April	Third Lanark	3	1	Rangers	Hampden Park
		Wilson (2) Johnstone			Smith	
Third Lanark: As per first game						
Rangers: Low for Hamilton						
Referee: J. Deans, Dalkeith						40,000

1906	28 April	Hearts	1	0	Third Lanark	Ibrox
		G. Wilson				
Hearts: G. Philip, McNaught, D. Philip, McLaren, Thomson, Dickson, Cooper, Walker, Menzies, D. Wilson, G. Wilson						
Third Lanark: Raeside, Barr, Hill, Cross, Neilson, Comrie, Johnstone, Graham, Reid, Wilson, Munro						
Referee: R. T. Murray, Stenhousemuir						30,000

1907	20 April	Celtic	3	0	Hearts	Hampden Park
		Somers (2) Orr pen				
Celtic: Adams, McLeod, Orr, Young, McNair, Hay, Bennett, McMenemy, Quinn, Somers, Templeton						
Hearts: Allan, Reid, Collins, Philip, McLaren, Henderson, Bauchope, Walker, Axford, Yates, Wombwell						
Referee: D. Philp, Dunfermline						50,000

1908	18 April	Celtic	5	1	St Mirren	Hampden Park
		Bennett (2) Hamilton Somers Quinn			Cunningham	
Celtic: Adams, McNair, Weir, Young, Loney, Hay, Bennett, McMenemy, Quinn, Somers, Hamilton						
St Mirren: Grant, Gordon, White, Key, Robertson, McAvoy, Clements, Cunningham, Wylie, Paton, Anderson						
Referee: J. R. W. Ferguson, Falkirk						55,000

1909	10 April	Celtic	2	2	Rangers	Hampden Park
		Quinn Munro			Gilchrist Bennett	
Celtic: Adams, McNair, Weir, Young, Dodds, Hay, Munro, McMenemy, Quinn, Somers, Hamilton						
Rangers: Rennie, Law, Craig, May, Stark, Galt, Bennett, Gilchrist, Campbell, McPherson, Smith						
Referee: J. B. Stark, Airdrie						70,000

1909	17 April	Celtic	1	1	Rangers	Hampden Park
		Quinn			Gordon	
Celtic: Kivlichan for Munro						
Rangers: Gordon, McDonald and Reid for May, Gilchrist and Campbell						
Referee: J. B. Stark, Airdrie						60,000
Cup withheld after a riot when spectators expected extra time after second game.						

1910	9 April	Dundee	2	2	Clyde	Ibrox
		Own goal Langlands			Chalmers Booth	
Dundee: Crumley, Lawson, Chaplin, Lee, Dainty, Comrie, Bellamy, Langlands, Hunter, McFarlane, Fraser						
Clyde: McTurk, Watson, Blair, Walker, McAteer, Robertson, Stirling, McCartney, Chalmers, Jackson, Booth						
Referee: T. Dougray, Bellshill						60,000

1910	16 April	Dundee	0	0	Clyde	Ibrox
Dundee: Neal for Lawson						
Clyde: As per first game						
Referee: T. Dougray, Bellshill						20,000

1910	20 April	Dundee	2	1	Clyde	Ibrox
		Bellamy Hunter			Chalmers	
Dundee: McEwan for Chaplin						
Clyde: Wyllie and Wyse for Stirling and Jackson						
Referee: T. Dougray, Bellshill						24,000

1911	8 April	Celtic	0	0	Hamilton Ac.	Ibrox
Celtic: Adams, McNair, Dodds, Young, McAteer, Hay, Kivlichan, McMenemy, Quinn, Hastie, Hamilton						
Hamilton Academical: J. Watson, Davie, Miller, P. Watson, W. McLaughlin, Eglinton, J. McLaughlin, Waugh, Hunter, Hastie, McNeil						
Referee: T. Dougray, Bellshill						45,000

1911	15 April	Celtic	2	0	Hamilton Ac.	Ibrox
		Quinn McAteer				
Celtic: McAteer for Hastie						
Hamilton Academical: As per first game						
Referee: T. Dougray, Bellshill						25,000

1912	6 April	Celtic	2	0	Clyde	Ibrox
		McMenemy Gallacher				
Celtic: Mulrooney, McNair, Dodds, Young, Loney, Johnstone, McAtee, Gallacher, Quinn, McMenemy, Brown						
Clyde: Grant, Gilligan, Blair, Walker, McAndrew, Collins, Hamilton, Jackson, Morrison, Carmichael, Stevens						
Referee: T. Dougray, Bellshill						45,000

1913	12 April	Falkirk	2	0	Raith Rovers	Celtic Park
		Robertson Logan				
Falkirk: Stewart, Orrock, Donaldson, McDonald, Logan, McMillan, McNaught, Gibbons, Robertson, Croal, Terris						
Raith Rovers: McLeod, Morrison, Cumming, J. Gibson, Logan, Anderson, Cranston, Graham, Martin, Gourlay, F. Gibson						
Referee: T. Robertson, Glasgow						45,000

1914	11 April	Celtic	0	0	Hibernian	Ibrox
Celtic: Shaw, McNair, Dodds, Young, Johnstone, McMaster, McAtee, Gallacher, Owers, McMenemy, Browning						
Hibernian: Allan, Girdwood, Templeton, Kerr, Paterson, Grossert, Wilson, Fleming, Hendren, Wood, Smith						
Referee: T. Dougray, Bellshill						55,000

Celtic show off the 1914 Scottish Cup.

1914	16 April	Celtic	4	1	Hibernian	Ibrox
		McColl (2) Browning (2)			Smith	
Celtic: McColl for Owers						
Hibernian: As per first game						
Referee: T. Dougray, Bellshill						45,000
Competition suspended between 1915 and 1919 because of first world war.						

1920	17 April	Kilmarnock	3	2	Albion Rovers	Hampden Park
		Culley Shortt J. Smith			Watson Hillhouse	
Kilmarnock: Blair, Hamilton. Gibson, Bagan, Shortt, Neave, McNaught, M. Smith, J. Smith, Culley, McPhail						
Albion Rovers: Short, Penman, Bell, Wilson, Black, Ford, Ribchester, James White, John White, Watson, Hillhouse						
Referee: W. Bell, Hamilton						95,000

1921	16 April	Partick Thistle	1	0	Rangers	Celtic Park
		Blair				
Partick Thistle: Campbell, Crichton, Bulloch, Harris, Wilson, Borthwick, Blair, Kinloch, Johnston, McMenemy, Salisbury						
Rangers: Robb, Manderson, McCandless, Meiklejohn, Dixon, Bowie, Archibald, Cunningham, Henderson, Cairns, Morton						
Referee: H. Humphreys, Greenock						28,294

1922	15 April	Morton	1	0	Rangers	Hampden Park
		Gourlay				
Morton: Edwards, McIntyre, R. Brown, Gourlay, Wright, McGregor, McNab, McKay, Buchanan, A. Brown, McMinn						
Rangers: Robb, Manderson, McCandless, Meiklejohn, Dixon, Muirhead, Archibald, Cunningham, Henderson, Cairns, Morton						
Referee: T. Dougray, Bellshill						75,000

1923	31 Mar	Celtic	1	0	Hibernian	Hampden Park
		Cassidy				
Celtic: Shaw, McNair, W. McStay, J. McStay, Cringan, McFarlane, McAtee, Gallacher, Cassidy, McLean, Connolly						
Hibernian: Harper, McGinnigle, Dornan, Kerr, Miller, Shaw, Ritchie, Dunn, McColl, Halligan, Walker						
Referee: T. Dougray, Bellshill						80,100

1924	19 April	Airdrieonians	2	0	Hibernian	Ibrox
		Russell (2)				
Airdrieonians: Ewart, Dick, McQueen, Preston, McDougall, Bennie, Reid, Russell, Gallacher, McPhail, Sommerville						
Hibernian: Harper, McGinnigle, Dornan, Kerr, Miller, Shaw, Ritchie, Dunn, McColl, Halligan, Walker						
Referee: T. Dougray, Bellshill						59,214

1925	11 April	Celtic	2	1	Dundee	Hampden Park
		Gallacher McGrory			McLean	
Celtic: Shevlin, W. McStay, Hilley, Wilson, J. McStay, McFarlane, Connolly, Gallacher, McGrory, Thomson, McLean						
Dundee: Britton, Brown, Thomson, Ross, W. Rankine, Irving, Duncan, McLean, Halliday, J. Rankine, Gilmour						
Referee: T. Dougray, Bellshill						75,137

1926	10 April	St Mirren	2	0	Celtic	Hampden Park
		McCrae Howieson				
St Mirren: Bradford, Findlay, Newbiggin, Morrison, Summers, McDonald, Morgan, Gebbie, McCrae, Howieson, Thomson						
Celtic: Shevlin, W. McStay, Hilley, Wilson, J. McStay, McFarlane, Connolly, Thomson, McGrory, McInally, Leitch						
Referee: P. Craigmyle, Aberdeen						98,620

1927	16 April	Celtic	3	1	East Fife	Hampden Park
		Robertson o.g. McLean Connolly			Wood	
Celtic: J. Thomson, W. McStay, Hilley, Wilson, J. McStay, McFarlane, Connolly, A. Thomson, McInally, McMenemy, McLean						
East Fife: Gilfillan, Robertson, Gillespie, Hope, Brown, Russell, Weir, Paterson, Wood, Barrett, Edgar						
Referee: T. Dougray, Bellshill						80,070

1928	14 April	Rangers	4	0	Celtic	Hampden Park
		Meiklejohn McPhail Archibald (2)				
Rangers: T. Hamilton, Gray, R. Hamilton, Buchanan, Meiklejohn, Craig, Archibald, Cunningham, Fleming, McPhail, Morton						
Celtic: J. Thomson, W. McStay, Donoghue, Wilson, J. McStay, McFarlane, Connolly, A. Thomson, McGrory, McInally, McLean						
Referee: W. Bell, Motherwell						118,115

1929	6 April	Kilmarnock	2	0	Rangers	Hampden Park
		Aitken Williamson				
Kilmarnock: Clemie, Robertson, Nibloe, Morton, McLaren, McEwan, Connell, Smith, Cunningham, Williamson, Aitken						
Rangers: T. Hamilton, Gray, R. Hamilton, Buchanan, Meiklejohn, Craig, Archibald, Muirhead, Fleming, McPhail, Morton						
Referee: T. Dougray, Bellshill						114,708

1930	12 April	Rangers	0	0	Partick Thistle	Hampden Park
Rangers: T. Hamilton, Gray, R. Hamilton, Buchanan, Meiklejohn, Craig, Archibald, Marshall, Fleming, McPhail, Nicholson						
Partick Thistle: Jackson, Calderwood, Rae, Elliot, Lambie, McLeod, Ness, Grove, Boardman, Ballantyne, Torbet						
Referee: W. Bell, Motherwell						107,475

1930	16 April	Rangers	2	1	Partick Thistle	Hampden Park
		Marshall Craig			Torbet	
Rangers: McDonald and Morton for Buchanan and Nicholson						
Partick Thistle: As per first game						
Referee: W. Bell, Motherwell						103,686

1931	11 April	Celtic	2	2	Motherwell	Hampden Park
		McGrory Craig o.g.			Stevenson McMenemy	
Celtic: J. Thomson, Cook, McGonagle, Wilson, McStay, Geatons, R. Thomson, A. Thomson, McGrory, Scarff, Napier						
Motherwell: McClory, Johnman, Hunter, Wales, Craig, Telfer, Murdoch, McMenemy, McFadyen, Stevenson, Ferrier						
Referee: P. Craigmyle, Aberdeen						105,000

1931	15 April	Celtic	4	2	Motherwell	Hampden Park
		R. Thomson (2) McGrory (2)			Murdoch Stevenson	
Celtic: As per first game						
Motherwell: As per first game						
Referee: P. Craigmyle, Aberdeen						98,579

1932	16 April	Rangers	1	1	Kilmarnock	Hampden Park
		McPhail			Maxwell	
Rangers: Hamilton, Gray, McAuley, Meiklejohn, Simpson, Brown, Archibald, Marshall, English, McPhail, Morton						
Kilmarnock: Bell, Leslie, Nibloe, Morton, Smith, McEwan, Connell, Muir, Maxwell, Duncan, Aitken						
Referee: P. Craigmyle, Aberdeen						111,982

1932	20 April	Rangers	3	0	Kilmarnock	Hampden Park
		Fleming McPhail English				
Rangers: Fleming for Morton						
Kilmarnock: As per first game						
Referee: P. Craigmyle, Aberdeen						104,695

1933	15 April	Celtic	1	0	Motherwell	Hampden Park
		McGrory				
Celtic: Kennaway, Hogg, McGonagle, Wilson, McStay, Geatons, R. Thomson, A. Thomson, McGrory, Napier, O'Donnell						
Motherwell: McClory, Crapnell, Ellis, Wales, Blair, McKenzie, Murdoch, McMenemy, McFadyen, Stevenson, Ferrier						
Referee: T. Dougray, Bellshill						102,339

1934	21 April	Rangers	5	0	St Mirren	Hampden Park
		Nicholson (2) McPhail Main Smith				
Rangers: Hamilton, Gray, McDonald, Meiklejohn, Simpson, Brown, Main, Marshall, Smith, McPhail, Nicholson						
St. Mirren: McCloy, Hay, Ancell, Gebbie, Wilson, Miller, Knox, Latimer, McGregor, McCabe, Phillips						
Referee: M. Hutton, Glasgow						113,403

1935	20 April	Rangers	2	1	Hamilton Acad.	Hampden Park
		Smith (2)			Harrison	
Rangers: Dawson, Gray, McDonald, Kennedy, Simpson, Brown, Main, Venters, Smith, McPhail, Gillick						
Hamilton Academical: Morgan, Wallace, Bulloch, Cox, McStay, Murray, King, McLaren, Wilson, Harrison, Reid						
Referee: H. Watson, Glasgow						87,286

1936	18 April	Rangers	1	0	Third Lanark	Hampden Park
		McPhail				
Rangers: Dawson, Gray, Cheyne, Meiklejohn, Simpson, Brown, Fiddes, Venters, Smith, McPhail, Turnbull						
Third Lanark: Muir, Carabine, Hamilton, Blair, Denmark, McInnes, Howe, Gallacher, Hay, Kennedy, Kinnaird						
Referee: J. Martin, Ladybank						88,859

Ian Ferguson of St Mirren with the spoils after the 1987 final.

1937	24 April	Celtic	2	1	Aberdeen	Hampden Park
		Crum Buchan			Armstrong	
Celtic: Kennaway, Hogg, Morrison, Geatons, Lyon, Paterson, Delaney, Buchan, McGrory, Crum, Murphy						
Aberdeen: Johnstone, Cooper, Temple, Dunlop, Falloon, Thomson, Benyon, McKenzie, Armstrong, Mills, Laing						
Referee: M. Hutton, Glasgow						147,365

1938	23 April	East Fife	1	1	Kilmarnock	Hampden Park
		McLeod			McAvoy	
East Fife: Milton, Laird, Tait, Russell, Sneddon, Herd, Adams, McLeod, McCartney, Miller, McKerrell						
Kilmarnock: Hunter, Fyfe, Milloy, Robertson, Stewart, Ross, Thomson, Reid, Collins, McAvoy, McGrogan						
Referee: H. Watson, Glasgow						80,091

1938	27 April	East Fife	4	2	Kilmarnock	Hampden Park
		McKerrell (2) McLeod Miller			Thomson McGrogan	
East Fife: Harvey for Herd						
Kilmarnock: as per first game						
Referee: H. Watson, Glasgow						92,716

1939	22 April	Clyde	4	0	Motherwell	Hampden Park
		Martin (2) Wallace Noble				
Clyde: Brown, Kirk, Hickie, Beaton, Falloon, Weir, Robertson, Noble, Martin, Wallace, Gillies						
Motherwell: Murray, Wales, Ellis, McKenzie, Blair, Telfer, Ogilvie, Bremner, Mathie, Stevenson, McCulloch						
Referee: W. Webb, Glasgow						94,799

1947	19 April	Aberdeen	2	1	Hibernian	Hampden Park
		Hamilton Williams			Cuthbertson	
Aberdeen: Johnstone, McKenna, Taylor, McLaughlin, Dunlop, Waddell, Harris, Hamilton, Williams, Baird, McCall						
Hibernian: Kerr, Govan, Shaw, Howie, Aird, Kean, Smith, Finnigan, Cuthbertson, Turnbull, Ormond						
Referee: R. Calder, Glasgow						82,140

1948	17 April	Rangers	1	1	Morton	Hampden Park
		Gillick			Whyte	a.e.t.
Rangers: Brown Young, Shaw, McColl, Woodburn, Cox, Rutherford, Gillick, Thornton, Findlay, Duncanson						
Morton: Cowan, Mitchell, Whigham, Campbell, Miller, Whyte, Hepburn, Murphy, Cupples, Orr, Liddell						
Referee: J. Martin, Blairgowrie						129,176

1948	21 April	Rangers	1	0	Morton	Hampden Park
		Williamson				a.e.t.
Rangers: Williamson for Findlay						
Morton: As per first game						
Referee: J. Martin, Blairgowrie						131,975

1949	23 April	Rangers	4	1	Clyde	Hampden Park
		Young (2) Williamson Duncanson			Galletly	
Rangers: Brown, Young, Shaw, McColl, Woodburn, Cox, Waddell, Duncanson, Thornton, Williamson, Rutherford						
Clyde: Cullan, Gibson, Mennie, Campbell, Milligan, Long, Davies, Wright, Linwood, Galletly, Bootland						
Referee: R. Benzie, Irvine						108,435

1950	22 April	Rangers	3	0	East Fife	Hampden Park
		Findlay Thornton (2)				
Rangers: Brown, Young, Shaw, McColl, Woodburn, Cox, Rutherford, Findlay, Thornton, Duncanson, Rae						
East Fife: Easson, Laird, Stewart, Philp, Finlay, Aitken, Black, Fleming, Morris, Brown, Duncan						
Referee: J. Mowat, Glasgow						118,262

1951	21 April	Celtic	1	0	Motherwell	Hampden Park
		McPhail				
Celtic: Hunter, Fallon, Rollo, Evans, Boden, Baillie, Weir, Collins, McPhail, Peacock, Tully						
Motherwell: Johnstone, Kilmarnock, Shaw, McLeod, Paton, Redpath, Humphries, Forrest, Kelly, Watson, Aitkenhead						
Referee: J. Mowat, Glasgow						131,943

1952	19 April	Motherwell	4	0	Dundee	Hampden Park
		Watson Redpath Humphries Kelly				
Motherwell: Johnstone, Kilmarnock, Shaw, Cox, Paton, Redpath, Sloan, Humphries, Kelly, Watson, Aitkenhead						
Dundee: Henderson, Fallon, Cowan, Gallacher, Cowie, Boyd, Hill, Patillo, Flavell, Steel, Christie						
Referee: J. Mowat, Glasgow						136,304

1953	25 April	Rangers	1	1	Aberdeen	Hampden Park
		Prentice			Yorston	
Rangers: Niven, Young, Little, McColl, Stanners, Pryde, Waddell, Greirson, Paton, Prentice, Hubbard						
Aberdeen: Martin, Mitchell, Shaw, Harris, Young, Allister, Rodger, Yorston, Buckley, Hamilton, Hather						
Referee: J. Mowat, Glasgow						129,861

1953	29 April	Rangers	1	0	Aberdeen	Hampden Park
		Simpson				
Rangers: Woodburn and Simpson for Stanners and Prentice						
Aberdeen: As per first game						
Referee: J. Mowat, Glasgow						112,619

1954	24 April	Celtic	2	1	Aberdeen	Hampden Park
		Young o.g. Fallon			Buckley	
Celtic: Bonnar, Haughney, Meechan, Evans, Stein, Peacock, Higgins, Fernie, Fallon, Tully, Mochan						
Aberdeen: Martin, Mitchell, Caldwell, Allister, Young, Glen, Leggat, Hamilton, Buckley, Clunie, Hather						
Referee: C. Faultless, Giffnock						129,926

1955	23 April	Clyde	1	1	Celtic	Hampden Park
		Robertson			Walsh	
Clyde: Hewkins, Murphy, Haddock, Granville, Anderson, Laing, Divers, Robertson, Hill, Brown, Ring						
Celtic: Bonnar, Haughney, Meechan, Evans, Stein, Peacock, Collins, Fernie, McPhail, Walsh, Tully						
Referee: C. Faultless, Giffnock						106,111

1955	27 April	Clyde	1	0	Celtic	Hampden Park
		Ring				
Clyde: As per first game						
Celtic: Fallon for Collins						
Referee: C. Faultless, Giffnock						68,735

1956	21 April	Hearts	3	1	Celtic	Hampden Park
		Crawford (2) Conn			Haughney	
Hearts: Duff, Kirk, McKenzie, Mackay, Glidden, Cumming, Young, Conn, Bauld, Wardhaugh, Crawford						
Celtic: Beattie, Meechan, Fallon, Smith, Evans, Peacock, Craig, Haughney, Mochan, Fernie, Tully						
Referee: R. Davidson, Airdrie						133,399

1957	20 April	Falkirk	1	1	Kilmarnock	Hampden Park
		Prentice			Curlett	
Falkirk: Slater, Parker, Rae, Wright, Irvine, Prentice, Murray, Greirson, Merchant, Moran, O'Hara						
Kilmarnock: Brown, Collins, J. Stewart, R. Stewart, Toner, Mackay, Mays, Harvey, Curlett, Black, Burns						
Referee: J. Mowat, Glasgow						81,057

Hearts with the Scottish Cup of 1956. The trophy is held by Freddie Glidden.

1957	24 April	Falkirk	2	1	Kilmarnock	Hampden Park
		Merchant Moran			Curlett	a.e.t.
Falkirk: As per first game						
Kilmarnock: As per first game						
Referee: J. Mowat, Glasgow						79,785

1958	26 April	Clyde	1	0	Hibernian	Hampden Park
		Coyle				
Clyde: McCulloch, Murphy, Haddock, Walters, Finlay, Clinton, Herd, Currie, Coyle, Robertson, Ring						
Hibernian: Leslie, Grant, McClelland, Turnbull, Plenderleith, Baxter, Fraser, Aitken, Baker, Preston, Ormond						
Referee: J. Mowat, Glasgow						95, 123

1959	25 April	St Mirren	3	1	Aberdeen	Hampden Park
		Bryceland Miller Baker			Baird	
St Mirren: Walker, Lapsley, Wilson, Neilson, McGugan, Leishman, Rodger, Bryceland, Baker, Gemmell, Miller						
Aberdeen: Martin, Caldwell, Hogg, Brownlie, Clunie, Glen, Ewan, Davidson, Baird, Wishart, Hather						
Referee: J. Mowat, Glasgow						108,591

1960	23 April	Rangers	2	0	Kilmarnock	Hampden Park
		Millar (2)				
Rangers: Niven, Caldow, Little, McColl, Paterson, Stevenson, Scott, McMillan, Millar, Brand, Wilson						
Kilmarnock: Brown, Richmond, Watson, Beattie, Toner, Kennedy, Stewart, McInally, Kerr, Black, Muir						
Referee: R. Davidson, Airdrie						108,017

1961	22 April	Dunfermline	0	0	Celtic	Hampden Park
Dunfermline: Connachan, Fraser, Cunningham, Mailer, Williamson, Miller, Peebles, Smith, Dickson, McAlindon, Melrose						
Celtic: Haffey, McKay, Kennedy, Crerand, McNeill, Clark, Gallagher, Fernie, Hughes, Chalmers, Byrne						
Referee: H. Phillips, Wishaw						113,618

1961	26 April	Dunfermline	2	0	Celtic	Hampden Park
		Thomson Dickson				
Dunfermline: Sweeney and Thomson for Williamson and McAlindon						
Celtic: O'Neill for Kennedy						
Referee: H. Phillips, Wishaw						87,866

1962	21 April	Rangers	2	0	St Mirren	Hampden Park
		Brand Wilson				
Rangers: Ritchie, Shearer, Caldow, Davis, McKinnon, Baxter, Henderson, McMillan, Millar, Brand, Wilson						
St Mirren: Williamson, Campbell, Wilson, Stewart, Clunie, McLean, Henderson, Bryceland, Kerrigan, Fernie, Beck						
Referee: T. Wharton, Clarkston						126,930

1963	4 May	Rangers	1	1	Celtic	Hampden Park
		Brand			Murdoch	
Rangers: Ritchie, Shearer, Caldow, Greig, McKinnon, Baxter, Henderson, McLean, Miller, Brand, Wilson						
Celtic: Haffey, McKay, Kennedy, McNamee, McNeill, Price, Johnstone, Murdoch, Hughes, Divers, Brogan						
Referee: T. Wharton, Clarkston						129,527

1963	15 May	Rangers	3	0	Celtic	Hampden Park
		Brand (2) Wilson				
Rangers: McMillan for McLean						
Celtic: Craig and Chalmers for Johnstone and Brogan						
Referee: T. Wharton, Clarkston						120,263

1964	25 April	Rangers	3	1	Dundee	Hampden Park
		Millar (2) Brand			Cameron	
Rangers: Ritchie, Shearer, Caldow, Greig, McKinnon, Baxter, Henderson, McLean, Millar, Brand, Wilson						
Dundee: Slater, Hamilton, Cox, Seith, Ryden, Stuart, Penman, Cousin, Cameron, Gilzean, Robertson						
Referee: H. Phillips, Wishaw						120,982

1965	24 April	Celtic	3	2	Dunfermline	Hampden Park
		Auld (2) McNeill			Melrose McLaughlin	
Celtic: Fallon, Young, Gemmell, Murdoch, McNeill, Clark, Chalmers, Gallagher, Hughes, Lennox, Auld						
Dunfermline: Herriot, W. Callaghan, Lunn, Thomson, McLean, T. Callaghan, Edwards, Smith, McLaughlin, Melrose, Sinclair						
Referee: H. Phillips, Wishaw						108,800

1966	23 April	Rangers	0	0	Celtic	Hampden Park
Rangers: Ritchie, Johansen, Provan, Greig, McKinnon, Millar, Henderson, Watson, Forrest, Johnston, Wilson						
Celtic: Simpson, Young, Gemmell, Murdoch, McNeill, Clark, Johnstone, McBride, Chalmers, Gallagher, Hughes						
Referee: T. Wharton, Clarkston						126,552

1966	27 April	Rangers	1	0	Celtic	Hampden Park
		Johansen				
Rangers: McLean for Forrest						
Celtic: Craig and Auld for Young and Gallagher						
Referee: T. Wharton, Clarkston						98,202

1967	29 April	Celtic	2	0	Aberdeen	Hampden Park
		Wallace (2)				
Celtic: Simpson, Craig, Gemmell, Murdoch, McNeill, Clark, Johnstone, Wallace, Chalmers, Auld, Lennox						
Aberdeen: Clark, Whyte, Shewan, Munro, McMillan, Petersen, Wilson, Smith, Storrie, Melrose, Johnston						
Referee: W. Syme, Glasgow						127,117

1968	27 April	Dunfermline	3	1	Hearts	Hampden Park
		Gardner (2) Lister			Lunn o.g.	
Dunfermline: Martin, W. Callaghan, Lunn, McGarty, Barry, T. Callaghan, Lister, Paton, Gardner, Robertson, Edwards						
Hearts: Cruikshank, Sneddon, Mann, Anderson, Thomson, Miller, Jensen (Moller), Townsend, Ford, Irvine, Traynor						
Referee: W. Anderson, East Kilbride						56,366

1969	26 April	Celtic	4	0	Rangers	Hampden Park
		McNeill Lennox Connelly Chalmers				
Celtic: Fallon, Craig, Gemmell, Murdoch, McNeill, Brogan (Clark), Connelly, Chalmers, Wallace, Lennox, Auld						
Rangers: Martin, Johansen, Mathieson, Greig, McKinnon, Smith, Henderson, Penman, Ferguson, Johnston, Persson						
Referee: J. Callaghan, Glasgow						132,870

1970	11 April	Aberdeen	3	1	Celtic	Hampden Park
		Harper McKay (2)			Lennox	
Aberdeen: Clark, Boel, Murray, Hermiston, McMillan, Buchan, McKay, Robb, Forrest, Harper, Graham						
Celtic: Williams, Hay, Gemmell, Murdoch, McNeill, Brogan, Johnstone, Wallace, Connelly, Lennox, Hughes (Auld)						
Referee: R. Davidson, Airdrie						108,244

1971	8 May	Celtic	1	1	Rangers	Hampden Park
		Lennox			D. Johnstone	
Celtic: Williams, Craig, Brogan, Connelly, McNeill, Hay, Johnstone, Lennox, Wallace, Callaghan, Hood						
Rangers: McCloy, Miller, Mathieson, Greig, McKinnon, Jackson, Henderson, Penman (D. Johnstone), Stein, MacDonald, W. Johnston						
Referee: T. Wharton, Clarkston						120,027

1971	12 May	Celtic	2	1	Rangers	Hampden Park
		Macari Hood pen			Craig o.g.	
Celtic: Macari for Wallace, who substituted for Hood						
Rangers: Denny for Miller. D. Johnstone again substituted for Penman.						
Referee: T. Wharton, Clarkston						103,297

1972	6 May	Celtic	6	1	Hibernian	Hampden Park
		Deans (3) Macari (2) McNeill			Gordon	
Celtic: Williams, Craig, Brogan, Murdoch, McNeill, Connelly, Johnstone, Deans, Macari, Dalglish, Callaghan						
Hibernian: Herriot, Brownlie, Schaedler, Stanton, Black, Blackley, Edwards, Hazel, Gordon, O'Rourke, Duncan (Auld)						
Referee: A. MacKenzie, Larbert						105,909

1973	5 May	Rangers	3	2	Celtic	Hampden Park
		Parlane Conn Forsyth			Dalglish Connelly	
Rangers: McCloy, Jardine, Mathieson, Greig, Johnstone, MacDonald, McLean, Forsyth, Parlane, Conn, Young						
Celtic: Hunter, McGrain, Brogan (Lennox), Murdoch, McNeill, Connelly, Johnstone, Deans, Dalglish, Hay, Callaghan						
Referee: J.R.P. Gordon						122,714

1974	4 May	Celtic	3	0	Dundee United	Hampden Park
		Hood Murray Deans				
Celtic: Connaghan, McGrain (Callaghan), Brogan, Murray, McNeill, McCluskey, Johnstone, Hood, Deans, Hay, Dalglish						
Dundee United: Davie, Gardner, Kopel, Copland, D. Smith (Traynor), W. Smith, Payne (Rolland), Knox, Gray, Fleming, Houston						
Referee: W. Black, Glasgow						75,959

1975	3 May	Celtic	3	1	Airdrieonians	Hampden Park
		Wilson (2) McCluskey			McCann	
Celtic: Latchford, McGrain, Lynch, Murray, McNeill, McCluskey, Hood, Glavin, Dalglish, Lennox, Wilson						
Airdrieonians: McWilliams, Jonquin, Cowan, Menzies, Black, Whiteford, McCann, Walker, McCulloch (March), Lapsley (Reynolds), Wilson						
Referee: I. Foote, Glasgow						75,457

1976	1 May	Rangers	3	1	Hearts	Hampden Park
		Johnstone (2) MacDonald			Shaw	
Rangers: McCloy, Miller, Greig, Forsyth, Jackson, MacDonald, McKean, Hamilton (Jardine), Henderson, McLean, Johnstone						
Hearts: Cruickshank, Brown, Burrell (Aird), Jefferies, Gallagher, Kay, Gibson (Park), Busby, Shaw, Callachan, Prentice						
Referee: R. Davidson, Airdrie						85,250

1977	7 May	Celtic	1	0	Rangers	Hampden Park
		Lynch				
Celtic: Latchford, McGrain, Lynch, Stanton, McDonald, Aitken, Dalglish, Edvaldsson, Craig, Conn, Wilson						
Rangers: Kennedy, Jardine, Greig, Forsyth, Jackson, Watson (Robertson), McLean, Hamilton, Parlane, MacDonald, Johnstone						
Referee: R. Valentine, Dundee						54,252

1978	6 May	Rangers	2	1	Aberdeen	Hampden Park
		MacDonald Johnstone			Ritchie	
Rangers: McCloy, Jardine, Greig, Forsyth, Jackson, MacDonald, McLean, Russell, Johnstone, Smith, Cooper (Watson)						
Aberdeen: Clark, Kennedy, Ritchie, McMaster, Garner, Miller, Sullivan, Fleming (Scanlon), Harper, Jarvie, Davidson						
Referee: B. McGinlay, Balfron						61,563

1979	12 May	Rangers	0	0	Hibernian	Hampden Park
Rangers: McCloy, Jardine, Dawson, Johnstone, Jackson, MacDonald (Miller), McLean, Russell, Parlane, Smith, Cooper						
Hibernian: McArthur, Brazil, Duncan, Bremner, Stewart, McNamara, Hutchison (Rae), McLeod, Campbell, Callachan, Higgins						
Referee: B. McGinlay, Balfron						50,260

1979	16 May	Rangers	0	0	Hibernian	Hampden Park
						a.e.t.
Rangers: As per first game. Miller substituted for McLean						
Hibernian: Rae for Hutchison. Brown substituted for Higgins						
Referee: B. McGinlay, Balfron						33,508

1979	28 May	Rangers	3	2	Hibernian	Hampden Park
		Johnstone (2) Duncan o.g.			Higgins McLeod	a.e.t.
Rangers: Watson for Smith. Miller and Smith substituted for Watson and McLean						
Hibernian: Rae for Hutchison. Brown and Hutchison substituted for Callachan and Higgins						
Referee: I. Foote, Glasgow						30,602

1980	10 May	Celtic	1	0	Rangers	Hampden Park
		McCluskey				a.e.t.
Celtic: Latchford, Sneddon, McGrain, Aitken, Conroy, MacLeod, Provan, Doyle (Lennox), McCluskey, Burns, McGarvey						
Rangers: McCloy, Jardine, Dawson, Forsyth (Miller), Jackson, Stevens, Cooper, Russell, Johnstone, Smith, MacDonald (McLean)						
Referee: G. Smith, Edinburgh						70,303

Davie Wilson scores in the 1962 Scottish Cup final.

Scottish Cup final 1969: Billy McNeill scores the opening goal in a 4-0 win over Rangers from a corner kick.

1981	9 May	Rangers	0	0	Dundee United	Hampden Park
						a.e.t.
Rangers: Stewart, Jardine, Dawson, Stevens, Forsyth, Bett, McLean, Russell, McAdam (Cooper), Redford, W. Johnston						
Dundee United: McAlpine, Holt, Kopel, Phillip (Stark), Hegarty, Narey, Bannon, Milne (Pettigrew), Kirkwood, Sturrock, Dodds						
Referee: I. Foote, Glasgow						53,000

1981	12 May	Rangers	4	1	Dundee United	Hampden Park
		Cooper Russell MacDonald (2)			Dodds	
Rangers: Cooper, D. Johnstone and MacDonald for McLean, McAdam and W. Johnston						
Dundee United: As per first game, with Stark again substituting for Phillip						
Referee: I. Foote, Glasgow						43,099

1982	22 May	Aberdeen	4	1	Rangers	Hampden Park
		McLeish McGhee Strachan Cooper			MacDonald	a.e.t.
Aberdeen: Leighton, Kennedy, Rougvie, McMaster (Bell), McLeish, Miller, Strachan, Cooper, McGhee, Simpson, Hewitt (Black)						
Rangers: Stewart, Jardine (McAdam), Dawson, McClelland, Jackson, Bett, Cooper, Russell, Dalziel (McLean), Miller, MacDonald						
Referee: B. McGinlay, Balfron						53,788

1983	21 May	Aberdeen	1	0	Rangers	Hampden Park
		Black				a.e.t.
Aberdeen: Leighton, Rougvie (Watson), McMaster, Cooper, McLeish, Miller, Strachan, Simpson, McGhee, Black, Weir						
Rangers: McCloy, Dawson, McClelland, McPherson, Paterson, Bett, Cooper (Davis), McKinnon, Clark, Russell, MacDonald (Dalziel)						
Referee: D. Syme, Rutherglen						62,979

1984	19 May	Aberdeen	2	1	Celtic	Hampden Park
		Black McGhee			P. McStay	a.e.t.
Aberdeen: Leighton, McKimmie, Rougvie (Stark), Cooper, McLeish, Miller, Strachan, Simpson, McGhee, Black, Weir (Bell)						
Celtic: Bonner, McGrain, Reid (Melrose), Aitken, W. McStay, MacLeod, Provan, P. McStay, McGarvey, Burns, McClair (Sinclair)						
Referee: R. Valentine, Dundee						58,900

1985	18 May	Celtic	2	1	Dundee United	Hampden Park
		Provan McGarvey			Beedie	
Celtic: Bonner, W. McStay, McGrain, Aitken, McAdam, MacLeod, Provan, P. McStay (O'Leary), Johnston, Burns (McClair), McGarvey						
Dundee United: McAlpine, Malpas, Beedie (Holt), Gough, Hegarty, Narey, Bannon, Milne, Kirkwood, Sturrock, Dodds						
Referee: B. McGinlay, Balfron						60,346

1986	10 May	Aberdeen	3	0	Hearts	Hampden Park
		Hewitt (2) Stark				
Aberdeen: Leighton, McKimmie, McQueen, McMaster (Stark), McLeish, W. Miller, Hewitt (J. Miller), Cooper, McDougall, Bett, Weir						
Hearts: Smith, Kidd, Whittaker, Jardine, Berry, Levein, Colquhoun, Black, Clark, Mackay, Robertson						
Referee: H. Alexander, Irvine						62,841

1987	16 May	St Mirren	1	0	Dundee United	Hampden Park
		Ferguson				a.e.t.
St Mirren: Money, Wilson, D. Hamilton, Abercromby, Winnie, Cooper, McGarvey, Ferguson, McDowall (Cameron), B. Hamilton, Lambert (Fitzpatrick)						
Dundee United: Thomson, Holt, Malpas, McInally, Clark, Narey, Ferguson, Bowman, Bannon, Sturrock (Gallacher), Redford (Hegarty)						
Referee: K. Hope (Clarkston)						51,782

1988	14 May	Celtic	2	1	Dundee United	Hampden Park
		McAvennie (2)			Gallacher	
Celtic: McKnight, Morris, Rogan, Aitken, McCarthy, Whyte (Stark), Miller, McStay, McAvennie, Walker (McGhee), Burns						
Dundee United: Thomson, Bowman, Malpas, McInally, Hegarty, Narey, Bannon, Gallacher, Paatelainen (Clark), Ferguson, McKinlay						
Referee: G. Smith, Edinburgh						74,000

1989	20 May	Celtic	1	0	Rangers	Hampden Park
		Miller				
Celtic: Bonner, Morris, Rogan, Aitken, McCarthy, Whyte, Grant, McStay, Miller, McGhee, Burns						
Rangers: Woods, Stevens, Munro (Souness), Gough, Sterland (Cooper), Butcher, Drinkell, Ferguson, McCoist, Brown, Walters						
Referee: R. Valentine, Dundee						72,069

1990	12 May	Aberdeen	0	0	Celtic	Hampden Park
						a.e.t.
Aberdeen won 9–8 on penalties						
Aberdeen: Snelders, McKimmie, Robertson, Grant, McLeish, Irvine, Nicholas, Bett, Mason (Watson), Connor, Gilhaus						
Celtic: Bonner, Wdowczyk, Rogan, Grant, Elliott, Whyte, Stark (Galloway), McStay, Dziekanowski, Walker (Coyne), Miller						
Referee: G. Smith, Edinburgh						60,493

1991	18 May	Motherwell	4	3	Dundee United	Hampden Park
		Ferguson O'Donnell Angus Kirk			Bowman O'Neil Jackson	a.e.t.
Motherwell: Maxwell, Nijholt, Boyd, Griffin, Paterson, McCart, Arnott, Angus, Ferguson (Kirk), O'Donnell, Cooper (O'Neill)						
Dundee United: Main, Clark, Malpas, McInally, Krivokapic, Bowman, Van der Hoorn, McKinnon (McKinlay), French, Ferguson (O'Neil), Jackson						
Referee: D. Syme, Rutherglen						57,319

1992	9 May	Rangers	2	1	Airdrieonians	Hampden Park
		Hateley McCoist			Smith	
Rangers: Goram, Stevens, Robertson, Gough, Spackman, Brown, Durrant (Gordon), McCall, McCoist, Hateley, Mikhailichenko						
Airdrieonians: Martin, Kidd, Stewart, Honor, Caesar, Jack, Boyle, Balfour, Lawrence (Smith), Coyle, Kirkwood (Reid)						
Referee: D. Hope, Linburn						44,045

1993	29 May	Rangers	2	1	Aberdeen	Celtic Park
		Murray Hateley			Richardson	
Rangers: Goram, McCall, Robertson, Gough, McPherson, Brown, Murray, Ferguson, Durrant, Hateley, Huistra (Pressley)						
Aberdeen: Snelders, McKimmie, Wright (Smith), Grant, Irvine, McLeish, Richardson, Mason, Booth, Shearer (Jess), Paatelainen						
Referee: J. McCluskey, Stewarton						50,715

1994	21 May	Dundee United	1	0	Rangers	Hampden Park
		Brewster				
Dundee United: Van de Kamp, Cleland, Malpas, McInally, Petric, Welsh, Bowman, Hannah, McLaren (Nixon), Brewster, Dailly						
Rangers: Maxwell, Stevens (Mikhailichenko), Robertson, McPherson, Gough, McCall, Murray, I. Ferguson, McCoist (D. Ferguson), Hateley, Durie						
Referee: D. Hope, Erskine						37,450

1995	27 May	Celtic	1	0	Airdrieonians	Hampden Park
		Van Hooijdonk				
Celtic: Bonner, Boyd, McKinlay, Vata, McNally, Grant, McLaughlin, McStay, van Hooijdonk (Falconer), Donnelly (O'Donnell), Collins						
Airdrieonians: Martin, Stewart, Jack, Sandison, Hay (McIntyre), Black, Boyle, A. Smith, Cooper, Harvey (T. Smith), Lawrence						
Referee: L. Mottram, Wilsontown						36,915

1996	18 May	Rangers	5	1	Hearts	Hampden Park
		Laudrup (2) Durie (3)			Colquhoun	
Rangers: Goram, Cleland, Robertson, Gough, McLaren, Brown, Durie, Gascoigne, Ferguson (Durrant), McCall, Laudrup						
Hearts: Rousset, Locke (Lawrence), Ritchie, McManus, McPherson, Bruno (Robertson), Johnston, Mackay, Colquhoun, Fulton, Pointon						
Referee: H. Dallas, Motherwell						37,730

1997	24 May	Kilmarnock	1	0	Falkirk	Ibrox
		Wright				
Kilmarnock: Lekovic, MacPherson, Kerr, Montgomerie, McGowne, Reilly, Bagen (Mitchell), Burke, Wright (Henry), McIntyre (Brown), Holt						
Falkirk: Nelson, McGowan, Seaton, Oliver, James, Gray, McAllister, McKenzie, Crabbe (Craig), Hagen, McGrillen (Fellner)						
Referee: H. Dallas, Motherwell						48,953

1998	16 May	Hearts	2	1	Rangers	Celtic Park
		Cameron Adam			McCoist	
Hearts: Rousset, McPherson, Naysmith, Weir, Salvatori, Ritchie, McCann, Fulton, Adam (Hamilton), Cameron, Flogel						
Rangers: Goram, Porrini, Stensaas (McCoist), Gough, Amoruso, Bjorklund, Gattuso, Ferguson, Durie, McCall (Durrant), Laudrup						
Referee: W. Young, Clarkston						48,946

1999	29 May	Rangers	1	0	Celtic	Hampden Park
		Wallace				
Rangers: Klos, Porrini (Kanchelskis), Amoruso, Hendry, Vidmar, McCann (Ferguson), McInnes, van Bronckhorst, Wallace, Amato (Wilson), Albertz						
Celtic: Gould, Boyd, Mahe (O'Donnell), Mjallby, Stubbs, Annoni (Johnson), Lambert, Wieghorst, Larsson, Moravcik, Blinker						
Referee: H. Dallas, Motherwell						51,746

2000	27 May	Rangers	4	0	Aberdeen	Hampden Park
		van Bronckhorst Vidmar Dodds Albertz				
Rangers: Klos, Reyna, Moore (Porrini), Vidmar, Numan, Kanchelskis, Ferguson, Albertz, van Bronckhorst (Kerimoglu), Wallace (McCann), Dodds						
Aberdeen: Leighton (Winters), Solberg, McAllister, Whyte, Anderson (Belabed), Dow, Bernard, Jess, Rowson, Guntweit, Stavrum (Zerouali)						
Referee: J. McCluskey, Stewarton						50,685

2001	26 May	Celtic	3	0	Hibernian	Hampden Park
		McNamara Larsson (2)				
Celtic: Douglas, Mjallby, Valgaeren, Vega, Thompson (Johnson), Agathe, Lennon, Lambert (Boyd), Moravcik (McNamara), Larsson, Sutton						
Hibernian: Colgan, Fenwick, Smith, Sauzee, Jack, Laursen, Murray, Brebner (Arpinon) (Lovell), O'Neill, Paatelainen (Zitelli), Libbra						
Referee: K. Clark, Paisley						51,284

Jock Wallace and Alex McDonald after Rangers' 3–2 win over Celtic in the 1973 Scottish Cup final.

2002	4 May	Rangers	3	2	Celtic	Hampden Park
		Lovenkrands (2) Ferguson			Hartson Balde	
Rangers: Klos, Ricksen, Amoruso, Moore, Numan, Ross, Ferguson, Lovenkrands, de Boer, Caniggia (Arveladze), McCann						
Celtic: Douglas, Mjallby, Sutton, Balde, Thompson, Petrov, Lennon, Lambert (McNamara), Agathe, Larsson, Hartson						
Referee: H. Dallas, Motherwell						51,138

2003	31 May	Rangers	1	0	Dundee	Hampden Park
		Amoruso				
Rangers: Klos, Ricksen, Moore, Amoruso, Numan (Muscat), Malcolm, Ferguson, McCann, de Boer, Mols (Ross), Arveladze (Thompson)						
Dundee: Speroni, Mackay (Milne), Hernandez, Khizivanishvili, Muir, Smith, Nemsadze, Rae (Brady), Lovell, Caballero, Burchill (Novo)						
Referee: K. Clark, Paisley						47,136

2004	22 May	Celtic	3	1	Dunfermline	Hampden Park
		Larsson (2) Petrov			Skerla	
Celtic: Marshall, Varga, Balde, McNamara, Agathe, Lennon, Petrov, Pearson (Wallace), Thompson, Larsson, Sutton						
Dunfermline: Stillie, Labonte, Mason (Grondin), Skerla, Byrne (Tod), Darren Young, Nicholson, Dempsey (Bullen), Derek Young, Crawford, Brewster						
Referee: S. Dougall, Burnside						50,846

2005	28 May	Celtic	1	0	Dundee United	Hampden Park
		Thompson				
Celtic: Douglas, Agathe, Varga, Balde, McNamara, Petrov, Lennon, Thompson (McGeady), Sutton, Hartson (Valgaeren), Bellamy						
Dundee United: Bullock, Ritchie, Archibald, Wilson, Kenneth, McInnes (Samuel), Brebner (Duff), Kerr, Robson, Crawford (Grady), Scotland						
Referee: J. Rowbotham, Kirkcaldy						50,635

2006	13 May	Hearts	1	1	Gretna	Hampden Park
		Skacel			McGuffie pen	a.e.t.
Hearts won 4–2 on penalties						
Hearts: Gordon, Neilson, Pressley, Tall, Fyssas, Cesnauskas (Mikoliunas), Aguiar (Brellier), Hartley, Skacel, Bednar (Pospisil), Jankauskas						
Gretna: Main, Birch, Townsley, Innes, Nicholls (Graham), McGuffie, Tosh, O'Neil, Skelton, Grady, Deuchar (McQuilken)						
Referee: D. McDonald, Edinburgh						51,232

2007	26 May	Celtic	1	0	Dunfermline	Hampden Park
		Perrier-Doumbe				
Celtic: Boruc, Perrier-Doumbe, McManus, Pressley, Naylor, Nakamura, Lennon (Caldwell), Hartley, McGeady, Vennegoor of Hesselink, Miller (Beattie)						
Dunfermline: de Vries, Shields, Wilson, Bamba, Morrison (Crawford), Hammill, Young, McCunnie, Muirhead, McIntyre (Hamilton), Burchill						
Referee: K. Clark, Paisley						49,600

Mark Hateley after scoring against Airdrieonians in the 1992 Scottish Cup final.

2008	24 May	Rangers	3	2	Queen of the S'th	Hampden Park
		Boyd (2) Beasley			Tosh Thomson	
Rangers: Alexander, Whittaker, Cuellar, Weir, Papac, McCulloch, Ferguson, Thomson, Beasley (Davis), Boyd, Darcheville (Fleck)						
Queen of the South: MacDonald, McCann (Robertson), Thomson, Aitken, Harris, McQuilken (Stewart), MacFarlane, Tosh, Burns, Dobbie (O'Neill), O'Connor						
Referee: S. Dougall, Burnside						48,821

The trophy has been competed for 123 times, and the winners are as follows:

Celtic	34
Rangers	32
Queen's Park	10
Aberdeen	7
Hearts	7
Clyde	3
Kilmarnock	3
Vale of Leven	3
St Mirren	3
Dunfermline	2
Falkirk	2
Hibernian	2
Motherwell	2
Renton	2
Third Lanark	2
Airdrieonians	1
Dumbarton	1
Dundee	1
Dundee United	1
East Fife	1
Greenock Morton	1
Partick Thistle	1
St Bernard's	1
In 1909 the Scottish Cup was withheld, following the Hampden riot.	

In 2007/08 junior clubs were admitted for the first time, the Scottish Qualifying Cup was discontinued, and clubs entered the competition according to the following new format:

First Round (36 clubs)	Fourteen clubs that would have participated in Scottish Qualifying Cup (North) (does not include top two clubs in Highland League); eighteen clubs that would have participated in Scottish Qualifying Cup (South) (does not include champions of East of Scotland League and South of Scotland League); winners of Scottish Junior Cup; winners of East, North and West junior Super Leagues
Second Round (32clubs)	Eighteen first-round winners; top two clubs in Highland League; East of Scotland League champions; South of Scotland League champions; ten Third Division clubs
Third Round (32 clubs)	Sixteen second-round winners; ten Second Division clubs; bottom six clubs in First Division;
Fourth Round (32 clubs)	Sixteen third-round winners; top four clubs in First Division; twelve SPL clubs
Fifth Round (16 clubs)	Sixteen fourth-round winners
Quarter-Finals (8 clubs)	Eight fifth-round winners
Semi-Finals (4 clubs)	Four quarter-final winners (No replays; extra-time and penalties if necessary)
Final (2 clubs)	Two semi-final winners

SCOTTISH FOOTBALL ASSOCIATION

The Scottish Football Association was formed on 13 March 1873, a few days after Scotland's 4–2 defeat by England at the Kennington Oval in the second-ever international. The association was formed (after a few advertisements in newspapers such as the North British Daily Mail) at a small temperance hotel called Dewar's Hotel at 11 Bridge Street, Glasgow. Queen's Park, who

Scottish FA Chief Executive Gordon Smith (left) and Scottish FA President George Peat (right) announce the appointment of new Scotland manager George Burley (centre) in January 2008.

would continue to be dominant in Scottish football for many years, were the driving force behind the SFA's formation, but the other clubs who attended on that fateful day were Clydesdale, Vale of Leven, Dumbreck, Third Lanarkshire Rifle Volunteers, Eastern and Granville. In addition, Kilmarnock could not attend but sent a letter indicating their willingness to join. The eight teams resolved that '*the clubs here represented form themselves into an Association for the promotion of football according to the rules of The Football Association (of England) and that the clubs connected with this Association subscribe for a challenge cup to be played for annually, the Committee to propose the laws of the competition.*' That first important decision was the establishment of the Scottish Cup, which was first competed for in 1874.

Along with the English Football Association, the Football Association of Wales and the Irish Football Association, the SFA set up the International Football Association Board to control the laws of the game. The IFAB still acts as guardian of the laws of the game, although FIFA, which was founded in 1904 and became a member of the IFAB, has significant, and possibly paramount input. The SFA joined FIFA in 1910 and was a founder member of UEFA in 1954

The SFA retains control of at least three very important aspects of the game. One is discipline, with the powers to fine, suspend and ban; another is the administration of the Scottish Cup (the second oldest tournament in the world); and yet another is the Scotland international team. The SFA states that its principal objects are to 'promote, foster and develop in all its branches the game of association football in Scotland, and to take all steps as may be deemed necessary or advisable to prevent infringements of the rules of the game, thus protecting the game from abuses'. To this end, it provides assistance on football matters to its member clubs, organizes domestic and international competitive events at all levels, trains, selects and appoints referees, develops coaching and liaises with national and international organisations.

The SFA directly organises the Scottish Cup and the Scottish Youth Cup, and organised the Scottish Qualifying Cup before it came to an end in 2007. It takes part in fifteen FIFA or UEFA organised competitions from the World Cup down to the UEFA Regions' Cup for amateur regional representative clubs, including several women's competitions.

There is a board of eleven directors who control everything, and there are eight Standing Committees with specific remits – namely the General Purposes Committee, the Professional Football Committee, the Recreational Football Committee, the Disciplinary Committee, the Referee Committee, the Appeals Committee, the Medical Committee and the Emergency Committee.

The SFA Council is an advisory body which meets periodically under the chairmanship of the president (currently George Peat) and two vice-presidents (currently Campbell Ogilvie and Alan McRae), and consists of three representatives of the SPL, three of the SFL, a representative from each of the fifteen affiliated associations and a representative from each of the Highland League, the East of Scotland League and the South of Scotland League.

In summer 2008 there were seventy-six full member clubs and two associate members. The affiliated associations are the Aberdeenshire and District FA, the East of Scotland FA, the Fife FA, the Forfarshire FA, the Glasgow FA, the North of Scotland FA, the Southern Counties FA, the Stirlingshire FA, the West of Scotland FA, the Scottish Amateur FA, the Scottish Junior FA, the Scottish Schools FA, the Scottish Youth FA, the Scottish Welfare FA and the Scottish Women's FA.

Most of the SFA's work is unseen and unobtrusive, and it often fails to receive credit for the large amount of work that is done, for example, at youth level and with the training and supervision of referees. It often gets the blame for things that go wrong in the game, but not the credit for the many things that go right. The SFA is now the umbrella body under which every other body works – the SPL, the SFL and other organizations – and they all now have their headquarters at Hampden Park. In June 2007 Gordon Smith replaced David Taylor as chief executive.

SCOTTISH FOOTBALL LEAGUE

The Scottish Football League (sometimes simply called the Scottish League) was formed in 1890 with ten members – Abercorn, Cambuslang, Celtic, Cowlairs, Dumbarton, Hearts, Rangers, St Mirren, Third Lanark and Vale of Leven. Only five of these teams remain in senior football, Cambuslang disappearing in 1892, Cowlairs in 1895, Abercorn in 1915, Vale of Leven in 1926 and Third Lanark in 1967.

The league was split into Divisions One and Two in 1893. Division One was contested during the first world war, but the lower division was not. Division Two was not re-formed until 1921, and this was when promotion became automatic for the first time. There was also a Division Three between 1923 and 1926. After the second world war there was a season of unofficial competition in 1945/46, and then there were Divisions A, B, and C from 1946 until 1955, when Division C was scrapped. A year later Divisions A and B became Divisions One and Two again.

In 1975 the league was re-formed into Premier, First and Second Divisions, and these lasted until 1994, when clubs were placed into Premier, First, Second and Third Divisions. In 1998, after decades of wrangling about the distribution of income, ten teams broke away to form their own organization, which they called the Scottish Premier League (see **SCOTTISH PREMIER LEAGUE**). This left the SFL to run three divisions, from which the top team in the First Division may earn promotion to the SPL. The word 'may' has been used because such are the strict regulations of the SPL about ground accommodation that promotion cannot be guaranteed. In 2003 the Scottish Premier League blocked promotion for Falkirk because their ground (Brockville) was deemed to be unsuitable.

The SFL also organizes the competition known as the Scottish League Cup (see **SCOTTISH LEAGUE CUP**), although it is normally disguised by a sponsor's name. It has been in existence since season 1946/47. There is also the **SCOTTISH LEAGUE CHALLENGE CUP** for those clubs who are not in the SPL. The Scottish League used to also be responsible for 'League' Internationals (see **INTER-LEAGUE INTERNATIONALS**) in which players playing for

The winners of the Scottish League Cup (right) were also presented with the Skol Cup between 1984 and 1993.

a Scottish League club were eligible to play against teams representing the English (or Football) League, the Irish League, and others.

The champions of the various divisions of the league over the years are listed below:

Willie Waddell congratulates his Kilmarnock players after their dramatic last-day Chanpionship win at Tynecastle in April 1965.

	Division One	Division Two
1890/91	Dumbarton & Rangers (Shared)	
1891/92	Dumbarton	
1892/93	Celtic	
1893/94	Celtic	Hibernian
1894/95	Hearts	Hibernian
1895/96	Celtic	Abercorn
1896/97	Hearts	Partick Thistle
1897/98	Celtic	Kilmarnock
1898/99	Rangers	Kilmarnock
1899/00	Rangers	Partick Thistle
1900/01	Rangers	St Bernard's
1901/02	Rangers	Port Glasgow
1902/03	Hibernian	Airdrieonians
1903/04	Third Lanark	Hamilton Academical
1904/05	Celtic	Clyde
1905/06	Celtic	Leith Athletic
1906/07	Celtic	St Bernard's
1907/08	Celtic	Raith Rovers
1908/09	Celtic	Abercorn
1909/10	Celtic	Leith Athletic
1910/11	Rangers	Dumbarton
1911/12	Rangers	Ayr United
1912/13	Rangers	Ayr United
1913/14	Celtic	Cowdenbeath
1914/15	Celtic	Cowdenbeath
1915/16	Celtic	No competition
1916/17	Celtic	No competition
1917/18	Rangers	No competition
1918/19	Celtic	No competition
1919/20	Rangers	No competition
1920/21	Rangers	No competition
1921/22	Celtic	Alloa Athletic
1922/23	Rangers	Queen's Park
1923/24	Rangers	St Johnstone
1924/25	Rangers	Dundee United
1925/26	Celtic	Dunfermline Athletic
1926/27	Rangers	Bo'ness
1927/28	Rangers	Ayr United
1928/29	Rangers	Dundee United
1929/30	Rangers	Leith Athletic
1930/31	Rangers	Third Lanark
1931/32	Motherwell	East Stirlingshire
1932/33	Rangers	Hibernian
1933/34	Rangers	Albion Rovers
1934/35	Rangers	Third Lanark
1935/36	Celtic	Falkirk
1936/37	Rangers	Ayr United
1937/38	Celtic	Raith Rovers
1938/39	Rangers	Cowdenbeath
Suspended because of the second world war		
1946/47	Rangers	Dundee
1947/48	Hibernian	East Fife
1948/49	Rangers	Raith Rovers
1949/50	Rangers	Morton
1950/51	Hibernian	Queen of the South
1951/52	Hibernian	Clyde
1952/53	Rangers	Stirling Albion
1953/54	Celtic	Motherwell
1954/55	Aberdeen	Airdrieonians
1955/56	Rangers	Queen's Park
1956/57	Rangers	Clyde
1957/58	Hearts	Stirling Albion
1958/59	Rangers	Ayr United
1959/60	Hearts	St Johnstone
1960/61	Rangers	Stirling Albion
1961/62	Dundee	Clyde
1962/63	Rangers	St Johnstone
1963/64	Rangers	Morton
1964/65	Kilmarnock	Stirling Albion
1965/66	Celtic	Ayr United
1966/67	Celtic	Morton
1967/68	Celtic	St Mirren
1968/69	Celtic	Motherwell
1969/70	Celtic	Falkirk
1970/71	Celtic	Partick Thistle
1971/72	Celtic	Dumbarton
1972/73	Celtic	Clyde
1973/74	Celtic	Airdrieonians
1974/75	Rangers	Falkirk

Third Lanark Championship winners 1903/04. Back row, left to right: Graham, Raeside, Sloan, Campbell, Neilson, Cross. Front row: Barr, McIntosh, McKenzie, Wardrope (chairman) Livingstone, Wilson, Johnstone.

	Premier Division	First Division	Second Division
1975/76	Rangers	Partick Thistle	Clydebank
1976/77	Celtic	St Mirren	Stirling Albion
1977/78	Rangers	Morton	Clyde
1978/79	Celtic	Dundee	Berwick Rangers
1979/80	Aberdeen	Hearts	Falkirk
1980/81	Celtic	Hibernian	Queen's Park
1981/82	Celtic	Motherwell	Clyde
1982/83	Dundee United	St Johnstone	Brechin City
1983/84	Aberdeen	Morton	Forfar Athletic
1984/85	Aberdeen	Motherwell	Montrose
1985/86	Celtic	Hamilton Ac.	Dunfermline Ath.
1986/87	Rangers	Morton	Meadowbank This.
1987/88	Celtic	Hamilton Ac.	Ayr United
1988/89	Rangers	Dunfermline Ath.	Albion Rovers
1989/90	Rangers	St Johnstone	Brechin City
1990/91	Rangers	Falkirk	Stirling Albion
1991/92	Rangers	Dundee	Dumbarton
1992/93	Rangers	Raith Rovers	Clyde
1993/94	Rangers	Falkirk	Stranraer

	Premier Div.	First Div.	Second Div.	Third Div.
1994/95	Rangers	Raith Rovers	Morton	Forfar Athletic
1995/96	Rangers	Dunfermline Ath.	Stirling Alb.	Livingston
1996/97	Rangers	St Johnstone	Ayr United	Inverness CT
1997/98	Celtic	Dundee	Stranraer	Alloa Athletic

	SPL	First Div.	Second Div.	Third Div.
1998/99	Rangers	Hibernian	Livingston	Ross County
1999/00	Rangers	St Mirren	Clyde	Queen's Park
2000/01	Celtic	Livingston	Partick Thistle	Hamilton Ac.
2001/02	Celtic	Partick Thistle	Queen of S.	Brechin City
2002/03	Rangers	Falkirk	Raith Rovers	Morton
2003/04	Celtic	Inverness CT	Airdrie Utd.	Stranraer
2004/05	Rangers	Falkirk	Brechin City	Gretna
2005/06	Celtic	St Mirren	Gretna	Cowdenbeath
2006/07	Celtic	Gretna	Morton	Berwick Rangers
2007/08	Celtic	Hamilton Ac.	Ross County	East Fife

This chart shows how the structure of the Scottish Football League has changed over the years, and the figure in brackets gives the number of clubs in each division at a given time:

1890-1891	Div One (10)			
1891-1892	Div One (12)			
1892-1893	Div One (10)			
1893-1900	Div One (10)	Div Two (10)		
1900-1901	Div One (11)	Div Two (10)		
1901-1902	Div One (10)	Div Two (12)		
1902-1903	Div One (12)	Div Two (12)		
1903-1905	Div One (14)	Div Two (12)		
1905-1906	Div One (16)	Div Two (12)		
1906-1912	Div One (18)	Div Two (12)		
1912-1913	Div One (18)	Div Two (14)		
1913-1914	Div One (20)	Div Two (12)		
1914-1915	Div One (20)	Div Two (14)		
1915-1917	Div One (20)			
1917-1919	Div One (18)			
1919-1921	Div One (22)			
1921-1922	Div One (22)	Div Two (20)		
1922-1923	Div One (20)	Div Two (20)		
1923-1926	Div One (20)	Div Two (20)	Div Three (16)	
1926-1932	Div One (20)	Div Two (20)		
1932-1939	Div One (20)	Div Two (18)		
1939-1940	Div A (20)	Div B (18)		
1945-1946*	Div A (16)	Div B (14)		
1946-1947	Div A (16)	Div B (14)	Div C (10)	
1947-1949	Div A (16)	Div B (16)	Div C (12)	
1949-1950	Div A (16)	Div B (16)	Div C SouthEast-16	Div C SouthWest-18
1950-1952	Div A (16)	Div B (16)	Div C NorthEast-16	Div C SouthWest-16
1952-1953	Div A (16)	Div B (16)	Div C NorthEast-15	Div C SouthWest-14
1953-1954	Div A (16)	Div B (16)	Div C NorthEast-13	Div C SouthWest-14
1954-1955	Div A (16)	Div B (16)	Div C NorthEast-13	Div C SouthWest-13
1955-1956	Div A (18)	Div B (19)		
1956-1974	Div One (18)	Div Two (19)		
1974-1975	Div One (18)	Div Two (20)		
1975-1986	Premier Div (10)	First Div (14)	Second Div (14)	
1986-1988	Premier Div (12)	First Div (12)	Second Div (14)	
1988-1991	Premier Div (10)	First Div (14)	Second Div (14)	
1991-1994	Premier Div (12)	First Div (12)	Second Div (14)	
1994-1998	Premier Div (10)	First Div (10)	Second Div (10)	Third Div (10)
1998-2000	SPL (10)	First Div (10)	Second Div (10)	Third Div (10)
2000-Present	SPL (12)	First Div (10)	Second Div (10)	Third Div (10)

*(unofficial)

Celtic celebrate clinching the title on the last day of the 2007/08 season.

SCOTTISH LEAGUE CHALLENGE CUP

This tournament is competed for each year by all the teams in the Scottish Football League, but not those in the Scottish Premier League (and before that the Premier Division). It began in season 1990/91, but sadly does not usually receive as much attention from the press, public and media as other national competitions. This table shows the result of each final, together with the venue:

1990/91	Dundee	3	Ayr United	2	Fir Park	aet
1991/92	Hamilton Ac.	1	Ayr United	0	Fir Park	
1992/93	Hamilton Ac.	3	Morton	2	Love Street	
1993/94	Falkirk	3	St Mirren	0	Fir Park	
1994/95	Airdrieonians	3	Dundee	2	McDiarmid Park	aet
1995/96	Stenhousemuir	0	Dundee United	0	McDiarmid Park	aet
	Stenhousemuir won 5–4 on penalties					
1996/97	Stranraer	1	St Johnstone	0	Broadwood Stadium	
1997/98	Falkirk	1	Queen of the South	0	Fir Park	
1998/99	no competition					
1999/00	Alloa Athletic	4	Inverness CT	4	Excelsior Stadium	aet
	Alloa Athletic won 5–4 on penalties					
2000/01	Airdrieonians	2	Livingston	2	Broadwood Stadium	aet
	Airdrieonians won 4–3 on penalties					
2001/02	Airdrieonians	2	Alloa Athletic	1	Broadwood Stadium	
2002/03	Queen of the South	2	Brechin City	0	Broadwood Stadium	
2003/04	Inverness CT	2	Airdrie United	0	McDiarmid Park	
2004/05	Falkirk	2	Ross County	1	McDiarmid Park	
2005/06	St Mirren	2	Hamilton Ac.	1	Excelsior Stadium	
2006/07	Ross County	1	Clyde	1	McDiarmid Park	aet
	Ross County won 5–4 on penalties					
2007/08	St Johnstone	3	Dunfermline	2	Dens Park	

SCOTTISH LEAGUE CUP

This competition started life as the Southern League Cup during the years of the second world war, but since 1946/47 has been played as the Scottish League Cup, although its name has changed many times because of sponsorship. It is organised by the Scottish Football League and the format has varied over the years. Between 1946/47 and 1976/77 it was played on a sectional basis followed by a knock-out competition, but since then it has been on a knock-out basis with many variations – e.g. home and away ties; replays allowed; straight knock-out games; and in 1983/84 there was a knock-out phase followed by sections and then more knock-out!

Such tinkering is considered by many people to have worked to its detriment, and in recent seasons teams in the SPL are given an exemption from the early rounds, and teams competing in Europe are allowed a further exemption to the quarter-final stage. Some record books include the 1945/46 'League Cup', (won by Aberdeen) but 1945/46 is an unofficial wartime season. Rangers lead the way with twenty-five wins, followed by Celtic on thirteen and Aberdeen on five. Sometimes the final was played in the autumn, but more recently it has been in the spring. Thus it is necessary to give the years of the season concerned (eg 1955/56 rather than just 1956)

1946/47	5 Apr	Rangers	4	0	Aberdeen	Hampden Park
		Duncanson (2) Williamson Gillick				
Rangers: Brown, Young, Shaw, McColl, Woodburn, Rae, Rutherford, Gillick, Williamson, Thornton, Duncanson						
Aberdeen: Johnstone, Cooper, McKenna, McLaughlin, Dunlop, Taylor, Harris, Hamilton, Williams, Baird, McCall						
Referee: R. Calder, Rutherglen						82,584

1947/48	25 Oct	East Fife	0	0	Falkirk	Hampden Park
East Fife: Niven, Laird, Stewart, Philip, Finlay, Aitken, Adams, D. Davidson, Norris, J. Davidson, Duncan						
Falkirk: J. Dawson, Whyte, McPhie, Bolt, R. Henderson, Whitelaw, Fiddes, Fleck, Aikman, J. Henderson, K. Dawson						
Referee: P. Craigmyle, Aberdeen						52,781

1947/48	1 Nov	East Fife	4	1	Falkirk	Hampden Park
		Duncan (3) Adams			Aikman	
East Fife: As per first game						
Falkirk: Gallagher and Alison for Whitelaw and Fleck						
Referee: P. Craigmyle, Aberdeen						30,664

1948/49	12 Mar	Rangers	2	0	Raith Rovers	Hampden Park
		Gillick Paton				
Rangers: Brown, Young, Shaw, McColl, Woodburn, Cox, Gillick, Paton, Thornton, Duncanson, Rutherford						
Raith Rovers: Westland, McClure, McNaught, Young, Colville, Leigh, Hall, Collins, Penman, Brady, Joiner						
Referee: W. G. Livingstone, Glasgow						53,359

1949/50	29 Oct	East Fife	3	0	Dunfermline Ath.	Hampden Park
		Fleming Duncan Morris				
East Fife: McGarrity, Laird, Stewart, Philip, Finlay, Aitken, Black, Fleming, Morris, Brown, Duncan						
Dunfermline Athletic: Johnstone, Kirk, McLean, McCall, Clarkson, Whyte, Mayes, Cannon, Henderson, McGairy, Smith						
Referee: W. Webb, Glasgow						38,897

1950/51	28 Oct	Motherwell	3	0	Hibernian	Hampden Park
		Kelly Forrest Waters				
Motherwell: Johnstone, Kilmarnock, Shaw, McLeod, Paton, Redpath, Watters, Forrest, Kelly, Watson, Aitkenhead						
Hibernian: Younger, Govan, Ogilvie, Buchanan, Paterson, Coombe, Smith, Johnstone, Reilly, Ormond, Bradley						
Referee: J. Mowat, Glasgow						63,074

1951/52	27 Oct	Dundee	3	2	Rangers	Hampden Park
		Flavell Pattillo Boyd			Findlay Thornton	
Dundee: Brown, Fallon, Cowan, Gallacher, Cowie, Boyd, Toner, Pattillo, Flavell, Steel, Christie						
Rangers: Brown, Young, Little, McColl, Woodburn, Cox, Waddell, Findlay, Thornton, Johnson, Rutherford						
Referee: J. Mowat, Glasgow						91,075

Scottish League Cup final of 1959/60. Alex Young of Hearts heads for goal.

1952/53	25 Oct	Dundee	2	0	Kilmarnock	Hampden Park
		Flavell (2)				
Dundee: R. Henderson, Fallon, Frew, Ziesing, Boyd, Cowie, Toner, A. Henderson, Flavell, Steel, Christie						
Kilmarnock: Niven, Collins, Hood, Russell, Thyne, Middlemass, Henaughan, Harvey, Mayes, Jack, Murray						
Referee: J. Mowat, Glasgow						51,830

1953/54	24 Oct	East Fife	3	2	Partick Thistle	Hampden Park
		Gardiner Fleming Christie			Walker McKenzie	
East Fife: Curran, Emery, S. Stewart, Christie, Finlay, McLennan, J. Stewart, Fleming, Bonthrone, Gardiner, Matthew						
Partick Thistle: Ledgerwood, McGowan, Gibb, Crawford, Davidson, Kerr, McKenzie, Howitt, Sharp, Wright, Walker						
Referee: J. Cox, Rutherglen						88,529

1954/55	23 Oct	Hearts	4	2	Motherwell	Hampden Park
		Bauld (3) Wardhaugh			Redpath Bain	
Hearts: Duff, Parker, McKenzie, Mackay, Glidden, Cumming, Souness, Conn, Bauld, Wardhaugh, Urquhart						
Motherwell: Weir, Kilmarnock, McSeveney, Cox, Paton, Redpath, Hunter, Aitken, Bain, Humphries, Williams						
Referee: J. Mowat, Glasgow						55,640

1955/56	22 Oct	Aberdeen	2	1	St Mirren	Hampden Park
		Mallan o.g. Leggat			Holmes	
Aberdeen: Martin, Mitchell, Caldwell, Wilson, Clunie, Glen, Leggat, Yorston, Buckley, Wishart, Hather						
St Mirren: Lornie, Lapsley, Mallon, Neilson, Telfer, Holmes, Rodger, Laird, Brown, Gemmell, Callan						
Referee: H. Phillips, Wishaw						44,103

1956/57	27 Oct	Celtic	0	0	Partick Thistle	Hampden Park
Celtic: Beattie, Haughney, Fallon, Evans, Jack, Peacock, Walsh, Collins, McPhail, Tully, Fernie						
Partick Thistle: Ledgerwood, Kerr, Gibb, Collins, Davidson, Mathers, McKenzie, Smith, Hogan, Wright, Ewing						
Referee: J. Mowat, Glasgow						58,794

1956/57	31 Oct	Celtic	3	0	Partick Thistle	Hampden Park
		McPhail (2) Collins				
Celtic: Mochan for Walsh						
Partick Thistle: Crawford and McParland for Davidson and Smith						
Referee: J. Mowat, Glasgow						31,126

1957/58	19 Oct	Celtic	7	1	Rangers	Hampden Park
		McPhail (3) Mochan (2) Wilson Fernie			Simpson	
Celtic: Beattie, Donnelly, Fallon, Fernie, Evans, Peacock, Tully, Collins, McPhail, Wilson, Mochan						
Rangers: Niven, Shearer, Caldow, McColl, Valentine, Davis, Scott, Simpson, Murray, Baird, Hubbard						
Referee: J. Mowat, Glasgow						82,293

1958/59	25 Oct	Hearts	5	1	Partick Thistle	Hampden Park
		Bauld (2) Murray (2) Hamilton			Smith	
Hearts: Marshall, Kirk, Thomson, Mackay, Glidden, Cumming, Hamilton, Murray, Bauld, Wardhaugh, Crawford						
Partick Thistle: Ledgerwood, Hogan, Donlevy, Mathers, Davidson, Wright, McKenzie, Thomson, Smith, McParland, Ewing						
Referee: R. H. Davidson, Airdrie						59,960

1959/60	24 Oct	Hearts	2	1	Third Lanark	Hampden Park
		Hamilton Young			Gray	
Hearts: Marshall, Kirk, Thomson, Bowman, Cumming, Higgins, Smith, Crawford, Young, Blackwood, Hamilton						
Third Lanark: Robertson, Lewis, Brown, Reilly, McCallum, Cunningham, McInnes, Craig, D. Hilley, Gray, L. Hilley						
Referee: R. H. Davidson, Airdrie						57,974

1960/61	29 Oct	Rangers	2	0	Kilmarnock	Hampden Park
		Brand Scott				
Rangers: Niven, Shearer, Caldow, Davis, Paterson, Baxter, Scott, McMillan, Millar, Brand, Wilson						
Kilmarnock: J. Brown, Richmond, Watson, Beattie, Toner, Kennedy, H. Brown, McInally, Kerr, Black, Muir						
Referee: T. Wharton, Clarkston						82,063

1961/62	28 Oct	Rangers	1	1	Hearts	Hampden Park
		Millar			Cumming	a.e.t.
Rangers: Ritchie, Shearer, Caldow, Davis, Paterson, Baxter, Scott, McMillan, Millar, Brand, Wilson						
Hearts: Marshall, Kirk, Holt, Cumming, Polland, Higgins, Ferguson, Elliott, Wallace, Gordon, Hamilton						
Referee: R. H. Davidson, Airdrie						88, 635

1961/62	18 Dec	Rangers	3	1	Hearts	Hampden Park
		Millar Brand McMillan			Davidson	
Rangers: Baillie for Paterson						
Hearts: Cruickshank, Davidson, Bauld and Blackwood for Marshall, Elliott, Wallace and Gordon						
Referee: R. H. Davidson, Airdrie						47,552

1962/63	27 Oct	Hearts	1	0	Kilmarnock	Hampden Park
		Davidson				
Hearts: Marshall, Polland, Holt, Cumming, Barry, Higgins, Wallace, Paton, Davidson, W. Hamilton, J. Hamilton						
Kilmarnock: McLaughlin, Richmond, Watson, O'Connor, McGrory, Beattie, Brown, Black, Kerr, McInally, McIlroy						
Referee: T. Wharton, Clarkston						51,280

1963/64	26 Oct	Rangers	5	0	Morton	Hampden Park
		Forrest (4) Willoughby				
Rangers: Ritchie, Shearer, Provan, Greig, McKinnon, Baxter, Henderson, Willoughby, Forrest, Brand, Watson						
Morton: Brown, Boyd, Mallan, Reilly, Keirman, Strachan, Adamson, Campbell, Stevenson, McGraw, Wilson						
Referee: H. Phillips, Wishaw						105,907

1964/65	24 Oct	Rangers	2	1	Celtic	Hampden Park
		Forrest (2)			Divers	
Rangers: Ritchie, Provan, Caldow, Greig, McKinnon, Wood, Brand, Millar, Forrest, Baxter, Johnston						
Celtic: Fallon, Young, Gemmell, Clark, Cushley, Kennedy, Johnstone, Murdoch, Chalmers, Divers, Hughes						
Referee: H. Phillips, Wishaw						91,423

1965/66	23 Oct	Celtic	2	1	Rangers	Hampden Park
		Hughes (2 pens)			Young o.g.	
Celtic: Simpson, Young, Gemmell, Murdoch, McNeill, Clark, Johnstone, Gallagher, McBride, Lennox, Hughes						
Rangers: Ritchie, Johansen, Provan, Wood, McKinnon, Greig, Henderson, Willoughby, Forrest, Wilson, Johnston						
Referee: H. Phillips, Wishaw						107,600

1966/67	29 Oct	Celtic	1	0	Rangers	Hampden Park
		Lennox				
Celtic: Simpson, Gemmell, O'Neill, Murdoch, McNeill, Clark, Johnstone, Lennox, McBride, Auld, Hughes (Chalmers)						
Rangers: Martin, Johansen, Provan, Greig, McKinnon, D. Smith, Henderson, Watson, McLean, A. Smith, Johnston						
Referee: T. Wharton, Clarkston						94,532

1967/68	28 Oct	Celtic	5	3	Dundee	Hampden Park
		Chalmers (2) Hughes Lennox Wallace			G. McLean (2) J. McLean	
Celtic: Simpson, Craig, Gemmell, Murdoch, McNeill, Clark, Chalmers, Lennox, Wallace, Auld (O'Neill), Hughes						
Dundee: Arrol, Wilson, Houston, Murray, Stewart, Stuart, Campbell, J. McLean, Wilson, G. McLean, Bryce						
Referee: R. H. Davidson, Airdrie						66,600

1968/69	5 Apr	Celtic	6	2	Hibernian	Hampden Park
		Lennox (3) Wallace Auld Craig			O'Rourke Stevenson	
Celtic: Fallon, Craig, Gemmell (Clark), Murdoch, McNeill, Brogan, Johnstone, Wallace, Chalmers, Auld, Lennox						
Hibernian: Allan, Shevlane, Davis, Stanton, Madsen, Blackley, Marinello, Quinn, Cormack, O'Rourke, Stevenson						
Referee: W. Syme, Airdrie						74,000

1969/70	25 Oct	Celtic	1	0	St Johnstone	Hampden Park
		Auld				
Celtic: Fallon, Craig, Hay, Murdoch, McNeill, Brogan, Callaghan, Hood, Hughes, Chalmers (Johnstone), Auld						
St Johnstone: Donaldson, Lambie, Coburn, Gordon, Rooney, McPhee, Aird, Hall, McCarry (Whitelaw), Connolly, Aitken						
Referee: J. Paterson, Bothwell						73,067

1970/71	24 Oct	Rangers	1	0	Celtic	Hampden Park
		D. Johnstone				
Rangers: McCloy, Jardine, Miller, Conn, McKinnon, Jackson, Henderson, MacDonald, D. Johnstone, Stein, W. Johnston						
Celtic: Williams, Craig, Quinn, Murdoch, McNeill, Hay, Johnstone, Connelly, Wallace, Hood (Lennox), Macari						
Referee: T. Wharton, Clarkston						106,263

1971/72	23 Oct	Partick Thistle	4	1	Celtic	Hampden Park
		Rae Lawrie McQuade Bone			Dalglish	
Partick Thistle: Rough, Hansen, Forsyth, Glavin (Gibson), Campbell, Strachan, McQuade, Coulston, Bone, Rae, Lawrie						
Celtic: Williams, Hay, Gemmell, Murdoch, Connelly, Brogan, Johnstone (Craig), Dalglish, Hood, Callaghan, Macari						
Referee: W. Mullan, Dalkeith						62, 740

Partick Thistle's finest hour as they beat Celtic 4-1 in the Scottish League Cup final of 1971/72.

Aberdeen's Peter Nicholas misses from the penalty spot against Rangers in the 1987/88 League Cup final at Hampden. After drawing 3–3 Rangers won the trophy 5–3 on penalties.

1972/73	9 Dec	Hibernian	2	1	Celtic	Hampden Park
		Stanton O'Rourke			Dalglish	
Hibernian: Herriot, Brownlie, Schaedler, Stanton, Black, Blackley, Edwards, O'Rourke, Gordon, Cropley, Duncan						
Celtic: Williams, McGrain, Brogan, McCluskey, McNeill, Hay, Johnstone (Callaghan), Connelly, Dalglish, Hood, Macari						
Referee: A. MacKenzie, Larbert						71,696

1973/74	15 Dec	Dundee	1	0	Celtic	Hampden Park
		Wallace				
Dundee: Allan, Wilson, Gemmell, Ford, Stewart, Phillip, Duncan, Robinson, Wallace, Scott, Lambie						
Celtic: Hunter, McGrain, Brogan, McCluskey, McNeill, Murray, Hood (Johnstone), Hay (Connelly), Wilson, Callaghan, Dalglish						
Referee: R. H. Davidson, Airdrie						27,974

1974/75	26 Oct	Celtic	6	3	Hibernian	Hampden Park
		Deans (3) Johnstone Wilson Murray			Harper (3)	
Celtic: Hunter, McGrain, Brogan, Murray, McNeill, McCluskey, Johnstone, Dalglish, Deans, Hood, Wilson						
Hibernian: McArthur, Brownlie (Smith), Bremner, Stanton, Spalding, Blackley, Edwards, Cropley, Harper, Munro, Duncan (Murray)						
Referee: J. R. P. Gordon, Newport on Tay						53,848

1975/76	25 Oct	Rangers	1	0	Celtic	Hampden Park
		MacDonald				
Rangers: Kennedy, Jardine, Greig, Forsyth, Jackson, MacDonald, McLean, Stein, Parlane, Johnstone, Young						
Celtic: Latchford, McGrain, Lynch, McCluskey, MacDonald, Edvaldsson, Hood (McNamara), Dalglish, Wilson (Glavin), Callaghan, Lennox						
Referee: W. Anderson, East Kilbride						50,806

1976/77	6 Nov	Aberdeen	2	1	Celtic	Hampden Park
		Jarvie Robb			Dalglish	a.e.t.
Aberdeen: Clark, Kennedy, Williamson, Smith, Garner, Miller, Sullivan, Scott, Harper, Jarvie (Robb), Graham						
Celtic: Latchford, McGrain, Lynch, Edvaldsson, MacDonald, Aitken, Doyle, Glavin, Dalglish, Burns (Lennox), Wilson						
Referee: J. Paterson, Bothwell						69,707

1977/78	18 Mar	Rangers	2	1	Celtic	Hampden Park
		Cooper Smith			Edvaldsson	a.e.t.
Rangers: Kennedy, Jardine, Jackson, Forsyth, Greig, Hamilton (Miller), MacDonald, Smith, McLean, Johnstone, Cooper (Parlane)						
Celtic: Latchford, Sneddon, Lynch (Wilson), Munro, MacDonald, Dowie, Glavin (Doyle), Edvaldsson, McCluskey, Aitken, Burns						
Referee: D. Syme, Rutherglen						60,168

1978/79	31 Mar	Rangers	2	1	Aberdeen	Hampden Park
		McMaster o.g. Jackson			Davidson	
Rangers: McCloy, Jardine, Dawson, Johnstone, Jackson, MacDonald, McLean, Russell, Urquhart (Miller), Smith (Parlane), Cooper						
Aberdeen: Clark, Kennedy, McLelland, McMaster, Rougvie, Miller, Strachan, Archibald, Harper, Jarvie (McLeish), Davidson						
Referee: I. Foote, Glasgow						54,000

1979/80	8 Dec	Dundee United	0	0	Aberdeen	Hampden Park
						a.e.t.
Dundee United: McAlpine, Stark, Kopel, Phillip (Fleming), Hegarty, Narey, Bannon, Sturrock, Pettigrew, Holt, Payne (Murray)						
Aberdeen: Clark, Kennedy, Rougvie, McLeish, Garner, Miller, Strachan, Archibald, McGhee (Jarvie), McMaster (Hamilton), Scanlon						
Referee: B. McGinlay, Balfron						27, 173

1979/80	12 Dec	Dundee United	3	0	Aberdeen	Dens Park
		Pettigrew (2) Sturrock				
Dundee United: Fleming and Kirkwood for Phillip and Payne						
Aberdeen: As per first game. Jarvie substituted for McGhee, and Hamilton for Scanlon						
Referee: B. McGinlay, Balfron						28,933

1980/81	6 Dec	Dundee United	3	0	Dundee	Dens Park
		Sturrock (2) Dodds				
Dundee United: McAlpine, Holt, Kopel, Phillip, Hegarty, Narey, Bannon, Payne, Pettigrew, Sturrock, Dodds						
Dundee: R. Geddes, Barr, Schaedler, Fraser, Glennie, McGeachie, Mackie, Stephen, Sinclair, Williamson, A. Geddes						
Referee: R. Valentine, Dundee						24,466

1981/82	28 Nov	Rangers	2	1	Dundee United	Hampden Park
		Cooper Redford			Milne	
Rangers: Stewart, Jardine, Miller, Stevens, Jackson, Bett, Cooper, Johnstone, Russell, MacDonald, Dalziel (Redford)						
Dundee United: McAlpine, Holt, Stark, Narey, Hegarty, Phillip, Bannon, Milne, Kirkwood, Sturrock, Dodds						
Referee: E. Pringle, Edinburgh					53,777	

1982/83	4 Dec	Celtic	2	1	Rangers	Hampden Park
		Nicholas MacLeod			Bett	
Celtic: Bonner, McGrain, Sinclair, Aitken, McAdam, MacLeod, Provan, McStay (Reid), McGarvey, Burns, Nicholas						
Rangers: Stewart, McKinnon, Redford, McClelland, Paterson, Bett, Cooper, Prytz (Dawson), Johnstone, Russell (MacDonald), Smith						
Referee: K. Hope, Clarkston					55,372	

1983/84	25 Mar	Rangers	3	2	Celtic	Hampden Park
		McCoist (3)			McClair Reid	a.e.t.
Rangers: McCloy, Nicholl, Dawson, McClelland, Paterson, McPherson, Russell, McCoist, Clark (McAdam), MacDonald (Burns), Cooper						
Celtic: Bonner, McGrain, Reid, Aitken, McAdam, MacLeod, Provan (Sinclair), McStay, McGarvey (Melrose), Burns, McClair						
Referee: R. Valentine, Dundee					66,369	

1984/85	28 Oct	Rangers	1	0	Dundee United	Hampden Park
		Ferguson				
Rangers: McCloy, Dawson, McClelland, Fraser, Paterson, McPherson, Russell (Prytz), McCoist, Ferguson (Mitchell), Redford, Cooper						
Dundee United: McAlpine, Holt (Clark), Malpas, Gough, Hegarty, Narey, Bannon, Milne (Beedie), Kirkwood, Sturrock, Dodds						
Referee: B. McGinlay, Balfron						44,698

1985/86	27 Oct	Aberdeen	3	0	Hibernian	Hampden Park
		Black (2) Stark				
Aberdeen: Leighton, McKimmie, Mitchell, Stark, McLeish, Miller, Black (Gray), Simpson, McDougall, Cooper, Hewitt						
Hibernian: Rough, Sneddon, Munro, Brazil (Harris), Fulton, Hunter, Kane, Chisholm, Cowan, Durie, McBride (Collins)						
Referee: R. Valentine, Dundee						40,065

1986/87	26 Oct	Rangers	2	1	Celtic	Hampden Park
		Durrant Cooper			McClair	
Rangers: Woods, Nicholl, Munro, Fraser (MacFarlane), Dawson, Butcher, Ferguson, McMinn, McCoist (Fleck), Durrant, Cooper						
Celtic: Bonner, Grant, MacLeod, Aitken, Whyte, McGhee (Archdeacon), McClair, McStay, Johnston, Shepherd, McInally						
Referee: D. Syme, Rutherglen					74,219	

1987/88	25 Oct	Rangers	3	3	Aberdeen	Hampden Park
		Cooper Durrant Fleck			Bett Falconer Hewitt	a.e.t.
Rangers won 5–3 on penalties						
Rangers: Walker, Nicholl, Munro, Roberts, Ferguson (Francis), Gough, McGregor (Cohen), Fleck, McCoist, Durrant, Cooper						
Aberdeen: Leighton, McKimmie, Connor, Simpson (Weir), McLeish, W. Miller, Hewitt, Bett, J. Miller, Nicholas, Falconer						
Referee: R. Valentine, Dundee						71,961

1988/89	23 Oct	Rangers	3	2	Aberdeen	Hampden Park
		McCoist (2) Ferguson			Dodds (2)	
Rangers: Woods, Stevens, Brown, Gough, Wilkins, Butcher, Drinkell, Ferguson, McCoist, Cooper, Walters						
Aberdeen: Snelders, McKimmie, Robertson, Simpson (Irvine), McLeish, Miller, Nicholas, Bett, Dodds, Connor, Hewitt						
Referee: G. Smith, Edinburgh						72,122

1989/90	22 Oct	Aberdeen	2	1	Rangers	Hampden Park
		Mason (2)			Walters	a.e.t.
Aberdeen: Snelders, McKimmie, Robertson, Grant (Van der Ark), McLeish, Miller, Nicholas, Bett, Mason, Connor, Jess (Irvine)						
Rangers: Woods, Stevens, Munro, Gough, Wilkins, Butcher, Steven, Ferguson, McCoist, Johnston, Walters (McCall)						
Referee: G. Smith, Edinburgh						61,190

1990/91	28 Oct	Rangers	2	1	Celtic	Hampden Park
		Walters Gough			Elliott	a.e.t.
Rangers: Woods, Stevens, Munro, Gough, Spackman, Brown, Steven, Hurlock (Huistra), McCoist (Ferguson), Hateley, Walters						
Celtic: Bonner, Grant, Wdowczyk, Fulton (Hewitt), Elliott, Rogan, Miller (Morris), McStay, Dziekanowski, Creaney, Collins						
Referee: J. McCluskey, Stewarton						62,817

1991/92	27 Oct	Hibernian	2	0	Dunfermline	Hampden Park
		McIntyre Wright				
Hibernian: Burridge, Miller, Mitchell, Hunter, McIntyre, MacLeod, Weir, Hamilton, Wright, Evans, McGinlay						
Dunfermline: Rhodes, Wilson, Sharp (Cunnington), McCathie, Moyes, Robertson, McWilliams, Kozma, Leitch, Davies, Sinclair (McCall)						
Referee: B. McGinlay, Balfron						40,377

1992/93	25 Oct	Rangers	2	1	Aberdeen	Hampden Park
		McCall Smith o.g.			Shearer	a.e.t.
Rangers: Goram, McCall, Robertson, Gough (Mikhailichenko), McPherson, Brown, Steven (Gordon), Ferguson, McCoist, Hateley, Durrant						
Aberdeen: Snelders, Wright, Winnie, Grant, McLeish, Smith, Aitken (Richardson), Bett (Booth), Jess, Shearer, Paatelainen						
Referee: D.D. Hope, Erskine						45,298

1993/94	24 Oct	Rangers	2	1	Hibernian	Celtic Park
		Durrant McCoist			McPherson o.g.	
Rangers: Maxwell, Stevens, Robertson, Gough, McPherson, McCall, Steven, Ferguson, Durrant, Hateley, Huistra (McCoist)						
Hibernian: Leighton, Miller, Mitchell, Farrell, Tweed, Hunter, McAllister, Hamilton, Wright, Jackson (Evans), O'Neill						
Referee: J. McCluskey, Stewarton						47,632

1994/95	27 Nov	Raith Rovers	2	2	Celtic	Ibrox
		Crawford Dalziel			Walker Nicholas	a.e.t.
Raith Rovers won 6–5 on penalties						
Raith Rovers: Thomson, McAnespie, Broddle (Rowbotham), Narey, Dennis, Sinclair, Crawford, Dalziel (Redford), Graham, Cameron, Dair						
Celtic: Marshall, Galloway, Boyd, McNally, Mowbray, O'Neil, Donnelly (Falconer), McStay, Nicholas (Byrne), Walker, Collins						
Referee: J. McCluskey, Stewarton						45,384

1995/96	26 Nov	Aberdeen	2	0	Dundee	Hampden Park
		Dodds Shearer				
Aberdeen: Watt, McKimmie, Glass, Grant, Inglis, Smith, Miller (Robertson), Shearer, Bernard, Dodds, Jess (Hetherston)						
Dundee: Pageaud, J. Duffy, McQueen, Manley, Wieghorst, C. Duffy, Shaw, Vrto (Farningham), Tosh (Britton), Hamilton, McCann (Anderson)						
Referee: L. Mottram, Forth						33,096

1996/97	24 Nov	Rangers	4	3	Hearts	Celtic Park
		McCoist (2) Gascoigne (2)			Fulton Robertson Weir	
Rangers: Goram, Cleland (Robertson), Moore, Gough, Petric, Bjorklund, Miller, Gascoigne, McCoist, Albertz, Laudrup						
Hearts: Rousset, Weir, Pointon, Mackay, Ritchie, Bruno, Paille (Beckford), Fulton, Robertson, Cameron, McCann						
Referee: H. Dallas, Motherwell						48,599

Rangers with the League Cup after defeating Dundee United in October 1984.

1997/98	30 Nov	Celtic	3	0	Dundee United	Ibrox
		Rieper Larsson Burley				
Celtic: Gould, Boyd, Mahe, McNamara (Annoni), Rieper, Stubbs, Larsson, Burley, Thom (Donnelly), Wieghorst, Blinker (Lambert)						
Dundee United: Dijkstra, Skoldmark (McSwegan), Malpas, Pressley, Perry, Pedersen, Olofsson, Zetterlund, Winters, Easton, Bowman						
Referee: J. McCluskey, Stewarton						49,305

1998/99	29 Nov	Rangers	2	1	St Johnstone	Celtic Park
		Guivarc'h Albertz			Dasovic	
Rangers: Niemi, Porrini, Numan, Amoruso, Hendry, Albertz (I. Ferguson), B. Ferguson, van Bronckhorst, Kanchelskis, Wallace, Guivarc'h (Durie)						
St Johnstone: Main, McQuillan, Dods, Kernaghan, Bollan, Scott, O'Neil (Preston), Kane, O'Boyle (Lowndes), Dasovic, Simao (Grant)						
Referee: H. Dallas, Motherwell						45,533

1999/00	19 Mar	Celtic	2	0	Aberdeen	Hampden Park
		Riseth Johnson				
Celtic: Gould, Boyd, Riseth, Mjallby, Mahe, McNamara, Wieghorst, Petrov, Moravcik (Stubbs), Johnson (Berkovic), Viduka						
Aberdeen: Leighton, Perry, McAllister, Solberg, Anderson, Dow, Bernard, Jess (Mayer), Guntweit (Belabed), Zerouali (Winters), Stavrum						
Referee: K. Clark, Paisley						50,073

2000/01	18 Mar	Celtic	3	0	Kilmarnock	Hampden Park
		Larsson (3)				
Celtic: Gould, Mjallby, Valgaeren, Vega, Petta (Crainey) (Boyd), Healy, Lennon, Lambert, Moravcik (Smith), Larsson, Sutton						
Kilmarnock: Marshall, MacPherson, McGowne, Dindeleux (Canero), Innes, Hay, Holt, Durrant (Reilly), Mahood, Cocard (McLaren), Dargo						
Referee: H. Dallas, Motherwell						48,830

2001/02	17 Mar	Rangers	4	0	Ayr United	Hampden Park
		Flo Ferguson Caniggia (2)				
Rangers: Klos, Ricksen, Vidmar (Hughes), Amoruso, Numan, Konterman, Ferguson, Latapy (Dodds), Caniggia, Flo, Lovenkrands (McCann)						
Ayr United: Nelson, Robertson, Lovering, Duffy, Hughes, Craig, Wilson (Chaplain), McGinlay, McLaughlin (Kean), Grady, Sheerin						
Referee: H. Dallas, Motherwell:						50,049

2002/03	16 Mar	Rangers	2	1	Celtic	Hampden Park
		Caniggia Lovenkrands			Larsson	
Rangers: Klos, Ricksen, Moore, Amoruso, Bonnisel (Ross), Arteta (Konterman), Ferguson, Caniggia, de Boer (Arveladze), Mols, Lovenkrands						
Celtic: Douglas, Mjallby (Petrov), Valgaeren, Balde, Thompson, Lennon, Smith (Sylla), Lambert, Sutton (Maloney), Larsson, Hartson						
Referee: K. Clark, Paisley						52,000

Rangers' Andrei Kanchelskis shoots as Airdrie's Paul Jack slides in during the 1998 League Cup semi-final.

2003/04	14 Mar	Livingston	2	0	Hibernian	Hampden Park
		Lilley McAllister				
Livingston: McKenzie, McNamee (McLaughlin), McAllister, Rubio, Andrews, Dorado, Makel, O'Brien (McGovern), Lovell, Fernandez (Pasquinelli), Lilley						
Hibernian: Anderson, Murdock, Smith (McManus), Edge, Doumbe, Caldwell, Thomson, Reid (Dobbie), Riordan, O'Connor, Brown						
Referee: W. Young, Clarkston						45,443

2004/05	20 Mar	Rangers	5	1	Motherwell	Hampden Park
		Kyrgiakos (2) Ross Ricksen Novo			Partridge	
Rangers: Waterreus, Ross, Malcolm, Kyrgiakos, Ball, Ricksen, Ferguson, Vignal (Rae), Buffel, Novo (Thompson), Prso						
Motherwell: Marshall, Corrigan, Partridge, Hammell, Craigan, McBride (Quinn), O'Donnell, Leitch, Paterson (Fitzpatrick), Foran (Clarkson), McDonald						
Referee: M. McCurry						50,182

2005/06	19 Mar	Celtic	3	0	Dunfermline	Hampden Park
		Zurawski Maloney Dublin				
Celtic: Boruc, Telfer, Balde, McManus, Wallace, Nakamura, Keane (Dublin), Lennon, Maloney, Zurawski, Petrov						
Dunfermline: McGregor, Shields, Wilson, Ross (Donnelly), Campbell (Derek Young), Mason, Thomson, Daquin (Tarachulski), Labonte, Makel, Burchill						
Referee: S. Dougal, Burnside						50,090

2006/07	18 Mar	Hibernian	5	1	Kilmarnock	Hampden Park
		Jones Benjelloun (2) Fletcher (2)			Greer	
Hibernian: McNeil, Whittaker (Martis), Hogg (McCann), Jones, Murphy, Sproule (Zemmama), Brown, Beuzelin, Stevenson, Benjelloun, Fletcher						
Kilmarnock: Combe, Wright, Greer, Ford, Hay, Di Giacomo (Locke), Johnston, Fowler, Leven (Wales), Nish, Naismith						
Referee: D. McDonald, Edinburgh						50,162

2007/08	16 Mar	Rangers	2	2	Dundee Utd	Hampden Park
		Boyd (2)			Hunt De Vries	a.e.t.
Rangers won 3–2 on penalties						
Rangers: McGregor, Broadfoot, Cuellar, Weir, Papac (Boyd), Hemdani (Darcheville), Dailly, Burke (Whittaker), Ferguson, Davis, McCulloch						
Dundee United: Zaluska, Kovacevic, Kenneth, Wilkie, Kalvenes, Buaben (Robertson), Flood, Kerr, Gomis, Hunt (Conway), DeVries						
Referee: K. Clark, Paisley						50, 019

The trophy has been competed for sixty-two times and the winners are as follows:

Rangers	25
Celtic	13
Aberdeen	5
Hearts	4
Dundee	3
East Fife	3
Hibernian	3
Dundee United	2
Livingston	1
Motherwell	1
Partick Thistle	1
Raith Rovers	1

SCOTTISH PLAYERS PLAYING ABROAD

There has been no lack of Scottish footballers who have tried their luck abroad, although England has tended to be the most popular port of call for talented Scots. It was a Scotsman who was the driving force behind the formation of the English League, or the Football League, as it became known. Ironically, some Scots accuse the English of arrogance by talking about the Football League as if football was played nowhere other than England, but the Football League was so called by its Scottish founder so that Scottish clubs would not be deterred from joining it at some future stage.

This was Perthshire man William McGregor who, in his capacity as director of Aston Villa, sent out letters to Accrington Stanley, Bolton Wanderers, Burnley, Blackburn Rovers, Derby County, Everton, Nottingham County, Preston North End, Stoke, West Bromwich Albion, and Wolverhampton Wanderers, inviting them to meet Aston Villa at the Royal Hotel, Manchester on 17 April 1888 with a view to founding a Football League. The clubs all agreed with McGregor, and by September of that year, the world's first-ever competition in which all teams played each other home and away was underway.

From then on, Scottish influence on English football was very noticeable, with many young Scotsmen crossing the border to grace the English game. Most English teams, in particular the northern ones like Newcastle and Sunderland, would have more than their fair share of Scotsmen playing for them, and in April 1955, Scottish manager Walter Galbraith of Accrington Stanley chose a team of eleven Scotsmen to play a League fixture against York City.

The most famous travelling Scot of the early years was Johnnie Madden who actually played in Celtic's

John Collins left Celtic to play in Monaco.

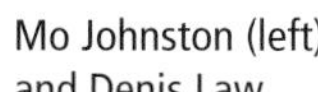

Mo Johnston (left) and Denis Law.

first-ever game in 1888, then after playing for Dumbarton, Dundee and Tottenham Hotspur, emigrated in 1905 to Czechoslovakia where he coached and even played for a newly founded team called Slavia Prague. He is deservedly much honoured and feted in Prague.

The name Archie McLean (q.v.) is well known in Brazil in relation to the development of football there, for it is he who is credited with taking the 'passing game' to Brazil. He had played for Ayr United and Johnstone before his firm, Coats of Paisley, sent him to Brazil in 1912. There he started a team called the Scottish Wanderers, and also played for a few other teams. Although to call him the 'father of Brazilian football' is something of an exaggeration, his influence was significant. Similarly in Uruguay, Scotsmen William Poole and John Harley made a tremendous contribution, while Alexander Hutton (q.v.) is considered by many to be the father of Argentine football. Other Scotsmen who deserve a mention for their role in the development of world football are Thomas Boyd in Trinidad, David Forsyth in Canada and John Prentice in China.

A fascinating character was Bruce Lockhart, from Anstruther in Fife, who in 1912 won a Moscow League medal with a team called Morozovski, who after the revolution would be called Moscow Dynamo. Lockhart was a British diplomat, but in the first world war, there was a fine line between diplomacy and spying. British policy was aimed at preventing a Bolshevik Revolution and keeping Russia in the war, but Lockhart was deemed to have crossed that particular line, and in 1918, following an assassination attempt on Lenin, Lockhart spent a few days in the Lubyanka prison and in the Kremlin. He was released, however, and eventually died in 1970.

Edward McIlvenny (1924-1989) played a significant part in the 1950 World Cup. He was born in Greenock but emigrated to the USA in 1949, was chosen for their team, and was actually captain on the famous day of 29 June 1950 at Belo Horizonte in the World Cup when they shocked the world by beating England 1–0.

A high-profile Scotsman playing abroad was Denis Law, who played for Torino in season 1961/62 after signing from Manchester City. He suffered a great deal of misfortune with a car crash and injury, and eventually fell out with them because they were not too willing to release him to play for Scotland. He joined Manchester United at the end of the season.

In the 1980s and 1990s there was no lack of Scottish players playing for big teams on the continent of Europe, although a move to Canada or the USA has tended to be the epilogue of a fine career. The most famous Scotsmen who have tried it abroad are Joe Jordan, who joined AC Milan in 1981 and subsequently played for Verona; Jim Bett played for Lokeren in Belgium; Steve Archibald helped Barcelona win the Spanish championship in 1985 and was beaten in the European Cup final of 1986 after underachievement for Scotland and disappointment with Tottenham Hotspur; Maurice Johnston, between his spells for Celtic and Rangers, played with Nantes in France in the mid 1980s at about the same time that Graeme Souness was playing for Sampdoria in Italy.

Paul Lambert actually won a European Cup medal with Borussia Dortmund in 1997 before homesickness encouraged him to return to Celtic, and another ex-Celt who played for Dortmund was Murdo MacLeod. John Collins, who had played for Hibs and Celtic, had a spell with Monaco, as did Alan McInally with Bayern Munich. John Inglis was freed by Aberdeen in 1999 and became the first known Scotsman to play in Bulgaria when he signed for Levski Sofia.

SCOTTISH PREMIER LEAGUE

This was formed in 1998 after the top ten teams broke away from the Scottish Football League, and decided to go it alone while remaining under the auspices of the Scottish Football Association. There were ten teams for the first two years, but from 2000 onwards the SPL was enlarged to twelve teams. This necessitates the controversial 'split' after every team has played all the others three times each. After thirty-three games, the top six play each other another once and the bottom six do likewise. It is thus possible (and has happened) for the team placed seventh in the SPL to have more points than the team placed sixth!

The SPL has rigid requirements for ground standards. In 2003, for example, Falkirk won the SFL first division, but were refused admission because Brockville did not come up to their standards, and in 2004 Inverness Caledonian Thistle were only allowed in on sufferance, having to play their home games at Pittodrie (over 100 miles away) until such time as their ground met the requirements. Gretna were similarly obliged to play their home games at Motherwell in 2007/08, a move that did no favours to the turf at Fir Park, and led to a few postponements and the eventual relaying of the turf.

The reason for the breakaway was to allow the top teams to negotiate their own terms about TV deals (with SKY from 1998 until 2002, with the BBC from 2002 until 2004, and then with Setanta), but if the object was to make the top tier more competitive, no one can claim that this has been a success. Up to 2008, no team other than a member of the Old Firm has won the SPL (see **HONOURS**). Nor can any convincing claim be made that the general standard of Scottish football has been enhanced by the existence of the SPL.

Celtic hold the record for the biggest victory when they defeated Dunfermline Athletic 8–1 on 19 February 2006, and Henrik Larsson holds the record for the number of SPL goals scored in one season, namely thirty-five in 2000/01. The oldest player to play in the SPL is Andy Millen, who was forty-two years nine months and five days when he played for St Mirren against Hearts on 15 March 2008. The youngest is Scott Robinson, who was sixteen years one month and fourteen days when he played for Hearts against Inverness Caledonian Thistle on 26 April 2008.

SCOTTISH QUALIFYING CUP

Until 2007 only clubs that were members of the Scottish Football League or Scottish Premier League were allowed direct entry into the Scottish Cup. Others had to take part in a qualifying competition, which was open to them if they were members of the SFA, and had a ground and facilities that met the SFA's criteria. The Scottish Qualifying Cup began in 1895 and operated as a national tournament at first. The number of clubs that qualified for the main competition varied over the years, but after the creation of qualifying cup competitions for both the north and south of Scotland in 1931 the four semi-finalists from each tournament were given a place in the first round of the Scottish Cup.

There were two interruptions to this system, as well as suspension of the tournaments during the war years. Between 1946 and 1948 there was also a Midlands Cup, and this increased the number of qualifying clubs. There were also three seasons between 1954 and 1957 when there was no qualifying competition. During these years the Scottish Cup was organised so that the early stages were exclusively for clubs outwith the Scottish League and the league sides did not become involved until the later rounds.

On 1 June 2007 the SFA took the decision to once again abolish the Qualifying Cups and replace them with an expanded format for the Scottish Cup. From 2007/08 onwards clubs that would have been eligible for the Scottish Qualifying Cup were given automatic entry to the Scottish Cup, along with the winners of the four main competitions in junior football.

Dundee United's Brian Welsh takes on Rangers' Trevor Steven in 1994 SPL action.

The following table lists each of the finals:

Single Competition

1895/96	Annbank	3	East Stirlingshire	1
1896/97	Kilmarnock	4	Motherwell	1
1897/98	Port Glasgow	4	East Stirlingshire	2
1898/99	East Stirlingshire	4	Arthurlie	1
1899/1900	Galston	5	Arbroath	2
1900/01	Stenhousemuir	3	East Stirlingshire	0
1901/02	Stenhousemuir	2	Motherwell	1
1902/03	Motherwell	2	Stenhousemuir	1
1903/04	Arbroath	4	Albion Rovers	2
1904/05	Aberdeen	2	Renton	0
1905/06	Leith Athletic	2	Beith	0
1906/07	Raith Rovers	2	St. Bernard's	2
Replay	Raith Rovers	3	St. Bernard's	1
1907/08	St. Bernard's	3	Raith Rovers	1
1908/09	Vale of Leven	5	Brechin City	2
1909/10	Leith Athletic	4	Bathgate	0
1910/11	East Stirlingshire	0	Johnstone	0
Replay	East Stirlingshire	1	Johnstone	0
1911/12	Dunfermline Athletic	1	Dumbarton	0
1912/13	Abercorn	1	Arbroath	1
Replay	Abercorn	2	Arbroath	2
2nd Replay	Abercorn	4	Arbroath	1
1913/14	Albion Rovers	1	Dundee Hibernian	1
Replay	Albion Rovers	1	Dundee Hibernian	1
2nd Replay	Albion Rovers	3	Dundee Hibernian	0
1914/15	St. Bernard's	2	Dykehead	2
Replay	St. Bernard's	1	Dykehead	1
2nd Replay	St. Bernard's	3	Dykehead	0
1915/16	no competition			
1916/17	no competition			
1917/18	no competition			
1918/19	no competition			
1919/20	Bathgate	2	Cowdenbeath	0
1920/21	East Fife	3	Bo'ness	1
1921/22	Montrose	3	Nithsdale Wanderers	3
Replay	Montrose	0	Nithsdale Wanderers	0
2nd Replay	Montrose	2	Nithsdale Wanderers	1
1922/23	Royal Albert	4	Mid Annandale	1
1923/24	Queen of the South	0	Dykehead	0
Replay	Queen of the South	3	Dykehead	0
1924/25	Royal Albert	3	Clachnacuddin	1
1925/26	Leith Athletic	3	Solway Star	1
1926/27	Mid Annandale	4	Brechin City	1
1927/28	Beith	3	Forres Mechanics	1
1928/29	Murrayfield Amateurs	8	Thornhill	1
1929/30	Bathgate	1	St Cuthbert Wanderers	0
1930/31	Bathgate	1	Dalbeattie Star	1
Replay	Bathgate	1	Dalbeattie Star	0

Midlands Competition

1946/47	Forfar Athletic	2	East Stirlingshire	1
1947/48	Montrose	4	East Stirlingshire	4
Replay	Montrose	3	East Stirlingshire	0

South and North Competitions

	South				North			
1931/32	Beith	6	Dalbeattie Star	1	Citadel	3	Murrayfield A	3
Replay					Citadel	2	Murrayfield A	2
2nd Replay					Citadel	4	Murrayfield A	1
1932/33	Beith	4	Falkirk Amateurs	2	Inverness Thistle	4	Penicuik Athletic	3
1933/34	Penicuik Athletic	3	Galston	1	Rosyth D Recn	4	Ross County	1
1934/35	Beith	1	Bo'ness	1	Clachnacuddin	2	Rosyth D Recn	0
Replay	Beith	2	Bo'ness	1				
1935/36	Galston	4	Bo'ness	0	Elgin City	4	Blairgowrie	2
1936/37	Duns	2	Galston	1	Vale Ocoba	2	Keith	2
Replay					Vale Ocoba	0	Keith	0
2nd Replay					Vale Ocoba	4	Keith	2
1937/38	Stranraer	5	Bo'ness	3	Elgin City	6	Blairgowrie	2
1938/39	Penicuik Athletic	5	St Cuthbert W.	3	Clachnacuddin	5	Babcock & W.	3
1939/40	No Competn				No Competn.			
1940/41	No Competn.				No Competn.			
1941/42	No Competn.				No Competn.			
1942/43	No Competn.				No Competn.			
1943/44	No Competn.				No Competn.			
1944/45	No Competn.				No Competn.			
1945/46	No Competn.				No Competn.			
1946/47	Edinburgh City	1	Stranraer	0	Peterhead	3	Clachnacuddin	2
1947/48	Berwick Rngrs	3	Stranraer	2	Clachnacuddin	3	Caledonian	1
1948/49	Leith Athletic	3	Montrose	2	Caledonian	2	Elgin City	2
Replay					Caledonian	4	Elgin City	3
1949/50	Leith Athletic	5	Brechin City	2	Caledonian	3	Clachnacuddin	0
1950/51	Brechin City	3	Duns	1	Caledonian	5	Peterhead	0
	Brechin City	9	Duns	1	Caledonian	3	Peterhead	1
Aggregate	Brechin City	12	Duns	2	Caledonian	8	Peterhead	1
1951/52	Wigtown & B.	2	Duns	0	Deveronvale	4	Clachnacuddin	1
	Wigtown & B.	2	Duns	0	Deveronvale	1	Clachnacuddin	3
Aggregate	Wigtown & B.	4	Duns	0	Deveronvale	5	Clachnacuddin	4
1952/53	Eyemouth Utd.	2	Newton Stewart	0	Buckie Thistle	3	Clachnacuddin	2
	Eyemouth Utd.	1	Newton Stewart	3	Buckie Thistle	1	Clachnacuddin	1
Aggregate	Eyemouth Utd.	3	Newton Stewart	3	Buckie Thistle	4	Clachnacuddin	3
Play-off	Eyemouth Utd.	3	Newton Stewart	2				
1953/54	Peebles Rovers	3	Tarff Rovers	4	Buckie Thistle	2	Inverness Thistle	2
	Peebles Rovers	3	Tarff Rovers	1	Buckie Thistle	2	Inverness Thistle	0
Aggregate	Peebles Rovers	6	Tarff Rovers	5	Buckie Thistle	4	Inverness Thistle	2
1954/55	No Competn.				No Competn.			
1955/56	No Competn.				No Competn.			
1956/57	No Competn.				No Competn.			
1957/58	Vale of Leithen	1	Peebles Rovers	3	Fraserburgh	3	Caledonian	0
	Vale of Leithen	6	Peebles Rovers	0	Fraserburgh	3	Caledonian	1
Aggregate	Vale of Leithen	7	Peebles Rovers	3	Fraserburgh	6	Caledonian	1
1958/59	Eyemouth Utd.	3	Babcock & W.	2	Buckie Thistle	2	Fraserburgh	2
	Eyemouth Utd.	7	Babcock & W.	1	Buckie Thistle	2	Fraserburgh	1
Aggregate	Eyemouth Utd.	10	Babcock & W.	3	Buckie Thistle	4	Fraserburgh	3
1959/60	Eyemouth Utd	2	Peebles Rovrs.	0	Elgin City	3	Rothes	2
	Eyemouth Utd	4	Peebles Rovrs.	1	Elgin City	3	Rothes	2
Aggregate	Eyemouth Utd	6	Peebles Rovrs.	1	Elgin City	6	Rothes	4
1960/61	Duns	6	Peebles Rovrs.	1	Keith	4	Buckie Thistle	2
	Duns	3	Peebles Rovrs.	6	Keith	3	Buckie Thistle	3
Aggregate	Duns	9	Peebles Rovrs.	7	Keith	7	Buckie Thistle	5
1961/62	Gala Fairydean	3	Vale of Leithen	3	Caledonian	1	Peterhead	0
	Gala Fairydean	1	Vale of Leithen	0	Caledonian	2	Peterhead	2
Aggregate	Gala Fairydean	4	Vale of Leithen	3	Caledonian	3	Peterhead	2
1962/63	Duns	5	Eyemouth Utd	2	Keith	3	Caledonian	1
	Duns	2	Eyemouth Utd	2	Keith	1	Caledonian	2
Aggregate	Duns	7	Eyemouth Utd	4	Keith	4	Caledonian	3
1963/64	Duns	3	St Cuthbert W.	0	Forres Mech'cs	3	Buckie Thistle	1
	Duns	4	St Cuthbert W.	1	Forres Mech'cs	5	Buckie Thistle	3
Aggregate	Duns	7	St Cuthbert W.	1	Forres Mech'cs	8	Buckie Thistle	4
1964/65	Edinburgh Uni.	2	Peebles Rovers	2	Elgin City	4	Clachnacuddin	3
	Edinburgh Uni.	2	Peebles Rovers	1	Elgin City	4	Clachnacuddin	2

Aggregate	Edinburgh Uni.	4	Peebles Rovers	3	Elgin City	8	Clachnacuddin	5
1965/66	Gala Fairydean	5	Glasgow Uni.	3	Caledonian	1	Ross County	2
	Gala Fairydean	4	Glasgow Uni.	2	Caledonian	3	Ross County	0
Aggregate	Gala Fairydean	9	Glasgow Uni.	5	Caledonian	4	Ross County	2
1966/67	Gala Fairydean	5	Vale of Leithen	3	Caledonian	3	Elgin City	0
	Gala Fairydean	3	Vale of Leithen	2	Caledonian	2	Elgin City	1
Aggregate	Gala Fairydean	8	Vale of Leithen	5	Caledonian	5	Elgin City	1
1967/68	Hawick R. Albert.	2	Tarff Rovers	2	Elgin City	1	Nairn County	1
	Hawick R. Albert.	6	Tarff Rovers	0	Elgin City	4	Nairn County	3
Aggregate	Hawick R. Albert	8	Tarff Rovers	2	Elgin City	5	Nairn County	4
1968/69	Glasgow Uni.	2	St Cuthbert W.	0	Nairn County	3	Fraserburgh	1
	Glasgow Uni.	2	St Cuthbert W.	1	Nairn County	1	Fraserburgh	1
Aggregate	Glasgow Uni.	4	St Cuthbert W.	1	Nairn County	4	Fraserburgh	2
1969/70	Tarff Rovers	4	St Cuthbert W.	0	Caledonian	1	Ross County	1
	Tarff Rovers	0	St Cuthbert W.	3	Caledonian	4	Ross County	1
Aggregate	Tarff Rovers	4	St Cuthbert W.	3	Caledonian	5	Ross County	2
1970/71	Glasgow Uni.	4	St Cuthbert W.	1	Elgin City	0	Nairn County	1
	Glasgow Uni.	1	St Cuthbert W.	3	Elgin City	1	Nairn County	0
Aggregate	Glasgow Uni.	5	St Cuthbert W.	4	Elgin City	1	Nairn County	1
Play-off					Elgin City	6	Nairn County	1
1971/72	St Cuthbert W.	4	Burntisland S.	1	Caledonian	0	Elgin City	0
	St Cuthbert W.	1	Burntisland S.	2	Caledonian	2	Elgin City	2
Aggregate	St Cuthbert W.	5	Burntisland S.	3	Caledonian	2	Elgin City	2
Play-off					Caledonian	4	Elgin City	2
1972/73	Vale of Leithen	3	Duns	0	Inverness Thistle	2	Ross County	0
	Vale of Leithen	1	Duns	0	Inverness Thistle	3	Ross County	4
Aggregate	Vale of Leithen	4	Duns	0	Inverness Thistle	5	Ross County	4
1973/74	Ferranti Thistle	4	Civil Service S	0	Clachnacuddin	1	Ross County	1
	Ferranti Thistle	2	Civil Service S	0	Clachnacuddin	2	Ross County	0
Aggregate	Ferranti Thistle	6	Civil Service S	0	Clachnacuddin	3	Ross County	1
1974/75	Selkirk	2	St. Cuthbert W.	1	Clachnacuddin	1	Inverness Thistle	0
	Selkirk	2	St. Cuthbert W.	1	Clachnacuddin	1	Inverness Thistle	1
Aggregate	Selkirk	4	St. Cuthbert W.	2	Clachnacuddin	2	Inverness Thistle	1
1975/76	Selkirk	2	Civil Service S.	0	Peterhead	2	Elgin City	0
	Selkirk	6	Civil Service S.	2	Peterhead	1	Elgin City	1
Aggregate	Selkirk	8	Civil Service S.	2	Peterhead	3	Elgin City	1
1976/77	Vale of Leithen	1	Girvan	2	Elgin City	1	Inverness Thistle	1
	Vale of Leithen	4	Girvan	0	Elgin City	2	Inverness Thistle	0
Aggregate	Vale of Leithen	5	Girvan	2	Elgin City	3	Inverness Thistle	1
1977/78	Selkirk	2	Civil Service S.	1	Peterhead	2	Caledonian	1
	Selkirk	0	Civil Service S.	1				
Aggregate	Selkirk	2	Civil Service S.	2				
Play-off	Selkirk	2	Civil Service S.	1				
1978/79	Gala Fairydean	2	Vale of Leithen	1	Peterhead	2	Inverness Thistle	0
	Gala Fairydean	1	Vale of Leithen	1				
Aggregate	Gala Fairydean	3	Vale of Leithen	2				
1979/80	Spartans	2	Coldstream	0	Brora Rangers	1	Peterhead	1
	Spartans	0	Coldstream	0				
Aggregate	Spartans	2	Coldstream	0				
Replay					Brora Rangers	5	Peterhead	0
1980/81	Whitehill Welfare	2	Hawick R. Albert	0	Inverness Thistle	5	Buckie Thistle	0
	Whitehill Welfare	6	Hawick R. Albert	1				
Aggregate	Whitehill Welfare	8	Hawick R. Albert	1				
1981/82	Hawick R. Albert	2	Gala Fairydean	1	Caledonian	1	Elgin City	1
	Hawick R. Albert	1	Gala Fairydean	0				
Aggregate	Hawick R. Albert	3	Gala Fairydean	1				
Replay					Caledonian	2	Elgin City	1
1982/83	Gala Fairydean	1	Vale of Leithen	0	Caledonian	3	Peterhead	2
	Gala Fairydean	4	Vale of Leithen	3				
Aggregate	Gala Fairydean	5	Vale of Leithen	3				
1983/84	Gala Fairydean	3	Vale of Leithen	2	Caledonian	2	Elgin City	1
1984/85	Gala Fairydean	3	Whitehill Welf.	2	Keith	1	Caledonian	1
Replay					Keith	2	Caledonian	2
2nd Replay					Keith	2	Caledonian	0
1985/86	Gala Fairydean	2	Whitehill Welfare	1	Peterhead	5	Buckie Thistle	1
1986/87	Whitehill Welfare	1	Vale of Leithen	0	Caledonian	2	Rothes	1
1987/88	Gala Fairydean	3	Vale of Leithen	0	Caledonian	2	Fraserburgh	0

(top) Spartans FC; (middle) Nairn County FC; (bottom) Inverurie Loco Works FC.

1988/89	Spartans	5	Gala Fairydean	0	Inverness Thistle	1	Caledonian	1
Replay					Inverness Thistle	3	Caledonian	0
1989/90	Gala Fairydean	2	Whitehill Welfare	0	Elgin City	1	Cove Rangers	0
1990/91	Vale of Leithen	3	Spartans	2	Cove Rangers	1	Fraserburgh	0
1991/92	Gala Fairydean	3	Civil Service S	1	Caledonian	3	Peterhead	2
1992/93	Vale of Leithen	4	Gala Fairydean	0	Huntly	2	Cove Rangers	2
Penalties					Huntly	5	Cove Rangers	3
1993/94	Whitehill Welfare	5	St Cuthbert W.	0	Ross County	2	Huntly	1
1994/95	Whitehill Welfare	4	Burntisland S.	1	Huntly	1	Keith	1
Penalties					Huntly	5	Keith	3
1995/96	Whitehill Welfare	4	Annan Athletic	2	Fraserburgh	4	Keith	3
1996/97	Spartans	2	Gala Fairydean	1	Huntly	2	Elgin City	1
1997/98	Whitehill Welfare	3	Annan Athletic	2	Peterhead	8	Fraserburgh	0
1998/99	Whitehill Welfare	2	Civil Service S.	0	Clachnacuddin	3	Keith	1
1999/2000	Whitehill Welfare	4	Threave Rovers	0	Huntly	2	Fraserburgh	0
2000/01	Whitehill Welfare	3	Spartans	2	Cove Rangers	4	Keith	2
2001/02	Spartans	2	Tarff Rovers	1	Deveronvale	5	Buckie Thistle	1
2002/03	Whitehill Welfare	3	Threave Rovers	0	Keith	2	Cove Rangers	2
Penalties					Keith	3	Cove Rangers	1
2003/04	Spartans	1	Edinburgh City	1	Clachnacuddin	1	Buckie Thistle	1
Penalties	Spartans	4	Edinburgh City	2	Clachnacuddin	6	Buckie Thistle	5
2004/05	Whitehill Welfare	0	Edinburgh City	0	Inverurie LW	4	Cove Rangers	0
Penalties	Whitehill Welfare	4	Edinburgh City	3				
2005/06	Spartans	2	Threave Rvrs	0	Inverurie LW	2	Forres Mech'cs	1
2006/07	Annan Athletic	3	Preston Athletic	1	Fraserburgh	2	Keith	1

SCOUTS

Most teams have a scouting system for young talent, often in an unofficial way where 'a friend of the manager' passes on a tip that, for example, number eight for some juvenile side might be worth another look. The larger clubs are better organized than that, but the whole business is sometimes very clandestine. A man will pretend to be strolling through a public park, will stop and watch a game, strike up a friendly conversation with one of the other spectators, find out the name of the good central defender and take it from there. Sometimes a club will write to the amateur team and say that they are coming to watch someone. One way or other in Scottish football, 'Big Brother' is watching.

The most famous scout in the old days was Bobby Calder of Aberdeen, a former referee, who had a lot of contacts and introduced many players to the game. Celtic and Rangers will naturally have a network of spies, and Willie Maley, Celtic's legendary manager, told the amusing story about the time when he met William Wilton, the manager of Rangers on a train. Not wishing to tell Wilton that he was going to check up on good reports he had heard about a young player called James Quinn, Maley had to go to the game that Wilton was going to, talked sociably with him (they were good friends), then feigned boredom at half time and said he was going home early, whereas he was really slipping away to watch the game in which Quinn was playing!

SEASON

Football has always been a 'winter' sport in Scotland, and there seems little likelihood that this will change in

Stark's Park is under water as Raith Rovers attempt to take on Alloa.

the foreseeable future. Contrary to common perception, Scottish weather in the winter is not outrageously bad in comparison with many other European countries, and it is rare for there to be huge backlog of fixtures, although 1947, 1963 and 1979 were examples of bad winters. In any case, undersoil heating of pitches (a prerequisite of the Scottish Premier League) does usually prevent postponements.

Traditionally, from the 1880s onwards, the season began at the beginning of August and finished at the end of April. The first Saturday in August was usually a public trial match of Team versus Others, Blues versus Reds, Probables versus Possibles etc., and then the season began in earnest the following week. Players were not usually paid in the month of May (although they were given a retainer for the duration of the close season), so there was usually a scramble to get all fixtures played by the end of April. The Scotland versus England international was played in early or mid April, the Scottish Cup final a week after that, and then the curtain came down on the season the following week.

The arrival of European football in the 1950s and the expanding fixture list changed all that, and since the 1970s the season has encroached into the month of May. Curiously enough, there has been no marked increase in attendances in better weather. Often the competitions are 'dead', and fixtures meaningless, but in any case a Scottish football fan is a creature of habit, and summer is the time for other activities. A Summer Cup was attempted at the end of seasons 1964/65 and 1965/66, but it suffered from the lack of Old Firm participation and was quickly abandoned.

Several times the Scottish Cup final has been scheduled for late May, (the very last day of May in 2003) and in 1979, for example, the Scottish League was not decided until 21 May when Celtic beat Rangers 4–2. This was the forerunner of things to come, for on several occasions in the early twenty-first century, it has been late May before the SPL season has finished. An effect, however, of the World Cup and the European Championships (scheduled normally for the month of June) has been to compel the domestic seasons to finish earlier, even if it means clubs playing two (or occasionally three) times per week.

International matches, whether World Cup qualifiers or friendlies, are often played in the month of May at the end of the domestic season. This is to their detriment, for it can give the impression that they are an afterthought. Player motivation is sometimes lacking, and there is an element of 'turnstile fatigue' in the low attendances for what would otherwise be attractive and indeed sometimes vital fixtures.

The arrival of the Scottish Premier League brought with it the concept of a mid-winter break, whereby football stops for about three weeks in January to allow for bad weather. This idea works in other European countries but, significantly, it has never been tried in England. In Scotland it happened in seasons 1998/99, 1999/2000, 2000/01 and 2002/03. It was hardly a success

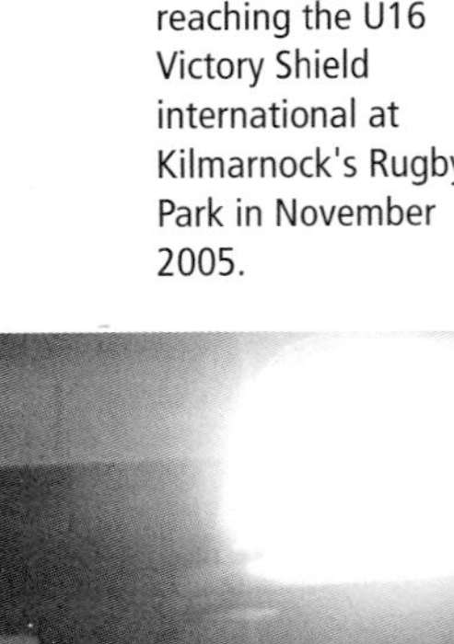

Snow prevents fans reaching the U16 Victory Shield international at Kilmarnock's Rugby Park in November 2005.

in Scotland, where Scottish weather is so unpredictable. (February, for example, is the worst month statistically for postponements). In any case, clubs that maintain players need a rest, and injuries need time to heal, sometimes cut the ground from under their own feet by disappearing to Florida to play a few games! One thing in its favour is that it does give the media a chance to focus in on the Scottish Football League for a few weeks. The mid-winter break cannot easily be operated in a season where there is a World Cup or European Championship, for there is simply not enough time to play the fixtures. In any case, it is not popular with the fans, who enjoy their weekly 'fix' of football. Indeed, in the dark depressing days of January it is needed all the more!

Occasionally the argument of 'summer football' is adduced, and people argue that March to November would be a better time for the Scottish season, pointing to the Republic of Ireland, where this has been the case for several years. The idea has superficial attractions, but there are arguments against it as well. It may be, for example, that the counter-attractions of holidays and other summer activities (not least other sports) might have a bad effect on attendances, and clubs would certainly miss the traditional money-spinning New Year fixtures. There has so far been no strong pressure for such a change in Scotland.

SECTARIANISM

This is one of the least acceptable aspects of Scottish football, and one that is currently being addressed by the authorities. It has been called a 'blight', a 'disease' and a 'cancer' and it has been acknowledged that it should have been tackled many decades ago. People hoped that it would all go away or, in some cases, tacitly supported it by doing nothing. It has also, although no one likes to admit it, contributed to the generation of income.

It is a particularly Scottish problem. The Irish potato famine of 1846 caused an influx of Irish Catholics in huge numbers as these luckless people sought a job in Scotland's industrial revolution. Scotland was a staunchly Protestant country and resented their intrusion to an extent that the north of England, London, or new countries like Australia, USA and Canada, for example, did not. When football became a huge game for the working classes in the late nineteenth century, the Irish communities formed their own football teams. Edinburgh Hibernian, for example, founded in 1875, specifically stated that their club was for Irish Catholics. Naturally there was a reaction, and Protestants would tend to gravitate to the opponents of the Irish team.

In the late nineteenth century, the problem was more acute in Edinburgh than in Glasgow, for Hibs' 'Catholics Only' policy did cause resentment amongst the rest of the Edinburgh population. Not only that, it led Hibs into trouble when they refused to sign players of the other denomination. Thomas Jenkinson, for example, was all set to join Hibs in 1884 until it was discovered

Jimmy Quinn from Croy was one of Celtic's early Scots-Irish heroes with whom working class Irish immigrants wholly identified.

that he was a non-Catholic. Jenkinson then went to Hearts, became a star for them and was eventually capped for Scotland. Hibs' short-sighted policy was proved to be even more foolish when a rival Irish team in Glasgow called the Celtic appeared in 1888 and denuded Hibs of most of their players, forcing them out of business for a few years.

In Glasgow, as late as the first world war of 1914-1918, there was no huge discriminatory policy on the part of either team. Protestants were employed by Celtic, and Catholics by Rangers, and in the case of Celtic, such was the success of Willie Maley's side, which won six League championships in a row between 1905 and 1910 with several Protestant players on board, that a substantial number of Protestants throughout Scotland supported them as well, attracted by the excellence of their play rather than any ethnic consideration.

But the end of the first world war brought complications. These lay in the Irish struggle for independence, an influx of Orange shipbuilding workers to the Clyde and, crucially, extreme poverty as Lloyd George failed to deliver on his 'land fit for heroes to live in' promise. Poverty and deprivation were breeding grounds for bigotry at a time when Rangers moved to their unstated, but nevertheless very real, 'No Catholics' policy. For a spell they were tacitly encouraged by the Church of Scotland, which in the 1920s made several utterances about the 'purity of the Scottish nation' and 'the Catholic menace'.

Catholic schools, which were enshrined in the Education Act of 1918, were a laudable attempt to ensure that Roman Catholic teaching was not eschewed and ignored by secular or Protestant teaching, but they made it very obvious that a person was a Catholic and therefore made discrimination against him or her all the easier.

The problem in football was that the Old Firm teams (so-called because of their ability to make money) both prospered as a result of this. Rangers, under Bill Struth, built up a great side, which between the wars won every League championship except 1919, 1922, 1926, 1932, 1936 and 1938. It must be emphasised that not all of this success was built on the rock of religious bigotry. There were also many football supporters who were attracted by the play of Sandy Archibald, Andy Cunningham, Alan Morton and Bob McPhail. Celtic on the other hand, although less consistently successful and holding on to the moral high ground by fielding non-Catholic players like John Thomson and Willie Lyon, now enjoyed the undivided love of the Catholic community in Scotland. Although they employed Protestants as players, their manager Willie Maley was Catholic, as indeed were all the directors. Maley, although himself a devout Catholic, would be often quoted as saying 'It is not the man's creed or his nationality that counts – it is the man himself'.

The end of the second world war, and the arrival of a Labour Government pledged to create a Welfare State and National Health Service, made at first no great difference to this state of affairs. Rangers' policy continued unchallenged until the 1960s and 1970s, even when the Church of Scotland had visibly eased from its hard line into, for example, holding ecumenical services with a neighbouring Catholic church. Visitors to Ibrox, however, could not help hearing offensive remarks about the Pope and Fenians from people who clearly did not know what they were talking about. On the other side, there were songs about Irish rebels and the Irish Republican Army. The emphasis from the Celtic side was political rather than religious, with demands for a united Ireland rather than hatred of anyone because of his religion.

Once again, it must be emphasised that this attitude was far from universal, and tended to be concentrated in the minds of those who were not successful in the world of education, and particularly so in the minds of supporters who lived in either Glasgow itself, or the strongholds of either side namely, Larkhall, Wishaw or Govan on one side as distinct from Carfin, Cleland or Croy on the other. Supporters of Celtic and Rangers from the east or the north of Scotland were often incredulous about what they heard from fellow supporters.

Even more distressing for supporters of Scotland was the abuse hurled at Celtic players. Jimmy Johnstone, Davie Hay, Tommy Gemmell and Billy McNeill often suffered in this regard. Gradually, however, such behaviour became a matter for jest and scorn, particularly when Celtic, under Protestant manager Jock Stein, (appointed, perhaps reluctantly, by the Celtic establishment in 1965) showed what could be done in Europe with a team composed of men of both religious traditions.

At various points throughout the 1970s, notably after their fans rioted at a 'friendly' in Birmingham in October 1976, Rangers made statements about signing players of all persuasions, but 1980 saw a riot at the Scottish Cup final between Celtic and Rangers, and still no Catholic player donned a Rangers jersey. Then Graeme Souness, in one fell swoop, killed seventy years of bigotry and outwitted the Celtic board of directors. This was in July 1989 when he signed Maurice Johnston, a Catholic player who had played for Celtic and who had made a vague promise to Celtic that he was about to

Maurice Johnston became the first Catholic player to sign for Rangers in 1989, causing as much controversy for snubbing former club Celtic as he did for joining the other half of Glasgow's Old Firm.

return. He appeared with a Celtic jersey and said that Celtic were 'the only team he ever wanted to play for'. Souness's coup could hardly have been more spectacular, and the floodgates were opened. A few diehard Rangers fans did not go back, but most did, and there were occasions in the 1990s when Rangers took the field for an Old Firm game with more Catholics than Celtic did.

The problem is not confined to Glasgow. It has been seen in Edinburgh as well, and even Dundee. In Edinburgh, the Irish immigrants tended to settle in Leith and Hibs grew up out of them, but Hibs very soon became the Leith team, attracting Protestants and Catholic supporters alike. Indeed, the divide in Edinburgh today is more geographical than religious. Dundee United were formed in 1909 under the name of Dundee Hibernian, and to this day Catholics in the City of Discovery will probably support Dundee United, if they don't follow Celtic. Most people believe, however, that this does not justify, for example, a flag with 'Dundee Derry' on it among the supporters of Dundee FC.

In the early years of the twenty-first century, the problem still exists – but only in the minds of the supporters. Rangers fans have been in trouble more than once with UEFA for their songs about 'being up to the knees in Fenian blood' (the club was fined for this in 2006) and the offensive three words at the end of the song 'The Sash My Father Wore', but perhaps those who talk about 'a ninety minute bigot' are correct in that in Glasgow and the surrounding areas most Catholics and Protestants live together in peace, harmony and mutual tolerance. The trouble is that a ninety minute bigot is a bigot for ninety minutes too long, and there is surely no place for such behaviour today. Perhaps the best way to deal with prejudice is to hold it up to ridicule. Indeed, great efforts have been made by politicians and the clubs themselves (Rangers banned some supporters from East Kilbride in December 2006 after offensive chants at a game at Tynecastle the previous month) to rid Scottish society of the menace of bigotry. Organizations like 'Bhoys Against Bigotry' and 'Nil By Mouth', as well as several initiatives from the former First Minister Jack McConnell, are playing their part, and it is to be hoped that one day the issue of someone's religion will be a thing of the past.

SELECT TEAM FROM THE SCOTTISH FOOTBALL LEAGUE

A select team from the Scottish Football League played Scotland, in a special match to mark the SFL's centenary, on 18 August 1990 at Hampden Park. Managed by Jim McLean of Dundee United and Alex Smith of Aberdeen, the select team won 1–0, in front of just 15,085 people, with a twelfth-minute penalty from Hans Gillhaus of Aberdeen. The team included four players who had competed in the world cup finals in Italy two months previously – Pat Bonner (Ireland), Hans Gillhaus (Holland), Chris Morris (Ireland), and Gary Stevens (England). Gary Stevens was the captain. The teams were:

SFL Select: Theo Snelders (Aberdeen) (Pat Bonner, Celtic, 45); Gary Stevens (Rangers); Miodrag Krivokapic (Dundee United) (Chris Morris, Celtic, 71); Freddy van der Hoorn (Dundee United); David Robertson (Aberdeen); Istvan Kozma (Dunfermline Athletic) (Tom Boyd, Motherwell, 60); Paul Lambert (St Mirren); Jim McInally (Dundee United); Robert Connor (Aberdeen) (Billy McKinlay, Dundee United, 83); Hans Gillhaus (Aberdeen); Charlie Nicholas (Celtic) (Keith Wright, Dundee, 45).

Policemen were ordered to draw batons on the warring factions during this Celtic-Rangers Scottish Cup final in 1980.

Tom Boyd (top) and Billy McKinlay (bottom) both were both part of the SFL select team.

Scotland: Andy Goram (Hibernian) (Campbell Money, St Mirren, 66); Stewart McKimmie (Aberdeen); Dave McPherson (Hearts); Maurice Malpas (Dundee United – captain); Gary McAllister (Leeds United); Paul McStay (Celtic) (Chris McCart, Motherwell, 71); John Collins (Celtic) (Gary Mackay, Hearts, 60); Stuart Munro (Rangers) (Roy Aitken, Newcastle United, 27); Pat Nevin (Everton); Ally McCoist (Rangers); Robert Fleck (Norwich City) (John Robertson (Hearts, 66). Manager: Andy Roxburgh.
Referee: J. McCluskey (Stewarton)

SHANKLY Bill (1913 – 1981)

Scotland Caps: 5
Bill Shankly was the legendary manager of Liverpool in the 1960s and 1970s. He was born in Glenbuck in East Ayrshire, but never appeared in Scottish domestic football either as a player or a manager, other than as a player for Partick Thistle during the second world war. He played for Carlisle United and Preston North End, appearing in two FA Cup finals, winning one and losing the other. He was a cultured right half, and is one of the many players of whom it is true that he would have won more Scottish caps if it had not been for the war. He managed Carlisle United, Grimsby Town, Workington

and Huddersfield Town (during which time he played a part in the discovery and development of Denis Law), before moving to Liverpool in December 1959. He transformed the under-performing second division side into a major European power, winning the English league on three occasions, the FA Cup twice, and the UEFA Cup once, before he retired in 1974. He is famous for making remarks like 'football is more important than life or death' (a slight misquotation of something probably said with tongue in cheek) and, with reference to the phrase 'interfering with play' to determine whether or not a player is offside, 'a player should be interfering with play, otherwise he shouldn't be on the park!'

SHANKLY Bob (1910 – 1982)

Bill Shankly's elder brother Bob is less well known, but he was the manager of Falkirk, Dundee and Hibs, being best known for the great Dundee team that won the Scottish League in 1962, and which reached the semi-final of the European Cup the following year.

SHEARER Bobby (1931 – 2006)

Scotland Caps: 4
Scottish League Championship medals: 6
Scottish Cup medals: 3
Scottish League Cup medals: 3
Bobby Shearer was a right back and captain for Rangers. He joined Rangers from Hamilton Academical in 1955, and played for the Ibrox side for a decade with 407

appearances, before moving on to Queen of the South, Third Lanark, and Hamilton Accies in a coaching/managerial capacity. His robust and determined style of play for the successful Rangers side of that period earned him the nickname 'Captain Cutlass'. He

Skipper Bobby Shearer with the League Cup in 1963.

played four times for Scotland, but it was his misfortune to be the right back on the occasion of the 3–9 debacle at Wembley in 1961. Outside football, he ran a bus company in Hamilton, and his coaches would frequently be seen ferrying Rangers (and even Celtic) fans to games.

SHINGUARDS

The invention of shinguards is credited to Sam Widdowson of Nottingham Forest in 1874, who cut down some cricket pads and strapped them to the outside of his stockings. This was an era when hacking at a player's shins was not uncommon, even though the rules forbade it, and shin protection soon became routine for many players in the Scottish game as well. However, the wearing of shin-guards was not made compulsory until 1990 and this brought an end to the sight of a tired player with his socks rolled down towards the end of a match.

Law 4 of the rules of the game requires that they must provide a reasonable degree of protection, be made of a suitable material, and be covered entirely by the stockings. Modern shin-guards are designed with energy-absorbing characteristics and frequently have a hard outer casing and a softer inner layer. They are made in different styles so that, for example, a striker can be given extra ankle protection.

SHOTTS BON ACCORD FC (see JUNIOR FOOTBALL)

SIMPSON Ronnie (1930 – 2004)

Scotland Caps: 5
Scottish League Championship medals: 4
Scottish Cup medals: 1
Scottish League Cup medals: 3
European Cup medals: 1

Ronnie Simpson had a remarkable career as goalkeeper for Queen's Park, the British Olympic team, Third Lanark, Newcastle United, Hibernian, Celtic and Scotland. His father was Jimmy Simpson of Rangers, and when Ronnie made his debut for Queen's Park in 1945, he was reputed to be the youngest player ever in Scottish football. After playing for Great Britain in the 1948 Olympics, he turned professional and played for Third Lanark before joining Newcastle United in 1951. With the 'Geordies', Ronnie won the FA Cup in 1952 and 1955, before returning to Scotland to play for Hibs in 1960. When Jock Stein took over at Hibs, Ronnie was transferred to Celtic to the bewilderment of Celtic fans, who could not see him, the son of a Rangers player, as anything other than a stop-gap at the age of thirty-four. It seemed that Jock Stein did not like him, and when Stein returned to Celtic Park, Ronnie contemplated retirement, but a combination of circumstances saw Ronnie in goal for Celtic, earning the grudging respect, then the total admiration, of Jock Stein and the Celtic fans.

He then went on to win a European Cup medal, and a total of eight domestic medals before injury compelled retirement in 1970. He played five times for Scotland, his international debut at the age of 36 years 196 days being the famous 3–2 win for Scotland over England at Wembley in April 1967. Against Northern Ireland in October of that year, he saved a penalty. As if 1967 had not given him enough, he was also Player of the Year in the eyes of the Scottish Football Writers. After giving up the playing of the game, he was manager of Hamilton Accies and goalkeeping coach for Celtic, St Johnstone,

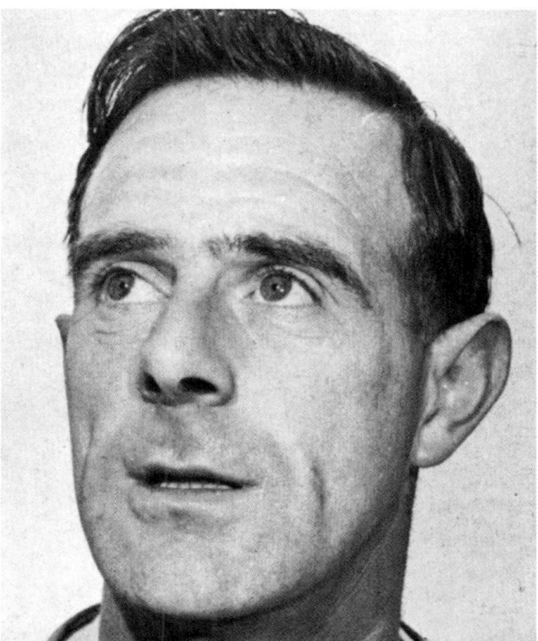

Ronnie Simpson was once a member of Britiain's 1948 Olympic team

Partick Thistle and Dunfermline Athletic, as well as sitting on the Pools Panel and being a Conservative councillor in Edinburgh.

SLOVENIA

Slovenia were the side responsible for getting Scotland's World Cup bid off to a disappointing start in 2004, but Scotland (typically, perhaps) finished off in style once the damage was done, and there was no longer any possibility of qualification for the 2006 finals.

2004	8 Sep	Hampden Park	0–0		
2005	12 Oct	Celje	3–0	Fletcher McFadden Hartley	

SMITH Alex (1876 – 1954)

Scotland Caps: 20
Scottish League Championship medals: 7
Scottish Cup medals: 3

One of the great players of the early years of the twentieth century, Alex Smith played for Rangers from 1894 until 1915, winning seven Scottish League championship medals and three Scottish Cup medals during that time. He was a left-winger, and is fit to be included in the same breath as Alan Morton. He played twenty times for Scotland, and possibly his greatest game was in the Rosebery International against England in 1900, but he also featured in the victories over England in 1903 and 1906.

SMITH Gordon (1924 – 2004)

Scotland Caps: 18
Scottish League Championship medals: 5
Scottish League Cup medals: 1

This Gordon Smith is not to be confused with the SFA Chief Executive and former BBC pundit of that name. This one is forever identified with Hibernian, and indeed is one of their 'Famous Five' forward line of Smith, Johnstone, Reilly, Turnbull and Ormond, but there is a great deal more to him than that. He is generally regarded as one of the best outside rights that Scotland has ever seen, combining artistry and wizardry, and earning nicknames in the 1950s like 'the Gay Gordon' for his devastating speed, ball control and crossing ability. He could score goals himself, once notching five in a game for Hibs against Third Lanark in 1947.

It is with Hibs that he is most associated, but he played elsewhere as well. He played eighteen times for Scotland between 1947 and 1957, and was Scotland's Player of the Year in 1951.

He achieved the remarkable feat of winning Scottish League championship medals with three separate teams (and none of them were either Celtic or Rangers!). He did this with Hibs in 1948, 1951, and 1952, then with Hearts in 1960, and then with Dundee in 1962 at the age of thirty-eight.

He also won the Scottish League Cup with Hearts in October 1959. Occasionally it was felt that he disappointed in his Scotland appearances, but it is hard not to feel that Scotland might have benefited from his presence in the disastrous World Cup of 1954 in Switzerland.

Alex Smith of Rangers

Gordon Smith (far right), with Dundee towards the end of his career

Gordon Smith progressed from elegant Rangers striker to Chief Executive of the Scottish FA.

SMITH Gordon (1954 –)

Scottish League Championship medals: 1
Scottish Cup medals: 2
Scottish League Cup medals: 2

An articulate, intelligent man with a degree in accountancy and the ability to speak fluent German, Gordon Smith became a respected pundit on the Scottish game in the course of his career as a journalist and BBC broadcaster. He was brought up in Stevenson, Ayrshire and his grandfather was Matt (or Matta) Smith of Kilmarnock in the 1920s. It was with Kilmarnock that Gordon Smith began his career in 1972. He moved to Rangers in 1977, won a domestic treble with them the following season, and then moved on to Brighton, with whom he famously missed a great chance to win the FA Cup final of 1983. He subsequently played for Manchester City, as well as in Austria and Switzerland, and was assistant manager with St Mirren for a spell.

He worked as an agent for a time, and in June 2007 was appointed Chief Executive of the SFA (the first former professional football player to hold the post) – immediately laying stress on overhauling the youth development side of the game. His appointment was controversial in the eyes of some, but Smith does not shirk from admitting his Rangers background or from dealing with questions on sectarianism, always stressing the 'Scottishness' of his character. He is a guitar player, and his other sporting interests include golf and boxing, in which on one occasion he beat the politician Tommy Sheridan on points.

SMITH Nick (1873 – 1905)

Scotland Caps: 12
Scottish League Championship medals: 4
Scottish Cup medals: 3

A fair-haired full back for Rangers and Scotland, Nick Smith joined Rangers in 1893, and was a mainstay in their team that won four Scottish League championships in a row at the turn of the century, and three Scottish Cups in the 1890s. He was a hard tackler, and infamously in the Glasgow Charity Cup final of 1904 exacted a brutal revenge on Celtic's Jimmy Quinn for the hat-trick that Quinn scored in the Scottish Cup final a month earlier. He played twelve times for Scotland, including the famous Rosebery International against England in 1900, when he and his Rangers full back partner Jock Drummond played brilliantly in Scotland's 4–1 win. He died tragically in January 1905 of enteric fever, only a few weeks after the death of his wife who had died of the same illness.

SMITH Walter (1948 –)

Walter Smith joined Dundee United in 1966 and played for them until 1980, with a short break at Dumbarton. He learned coaching at Tannadice as assistant manager to Jim McLean and then became coach of the Scotland under-18 team, whom he helped to the European Championship in 1982. Having been assistant manager to Alex Ferguson in the Mexico World Cup of 1986, he became assistant manager to Graeme Souness at Ibrox

and, on the departure of Souness in April 1991, inherited the managerial chair. With Rangers he won six League championships, three Scottish Cups and three Scottish League Cups. 1997/98 saw his departure to Everton, where he was less successful and was sacked in March 2002. He was briefly assistant manager to Alex Ferguson at Manchester United before being appointed to the Scotland job in December 2004. Under Smith, Scotland's performances improved, notably with the victory over France in October 2006, and Scotland were top of their 2008 European Championship qualifying group before he returned to Ibrox as manager in January 2007.

SOLWAY STAR FC (former Scottish League club)

Home: **Kimmeter Park Green, Annan, Dumfriesshire**
Highest League Position: **43rd (3rd in Div. 3 1924/25)**
Best Scottish Cup Performance: **Last 16 (3rd round 1924/25)**

The club from Annan was a member of the Division Three that existed between 1923 and 1926. They nearly escaped in 1925, only missing promotion on goal average, but then Division Three was abandoned in 1926 and there was no longer a place for Solway Star in the Scottish League.

Founded in 1911, Solway's early years were often confined to friendly matches and cup football, although they occasionally spent a season in a local league. In 1921/22 they belonged to the Southern Counties League and then in 1922/23 joined the Western League, which gave them a springboard to the newly formed Division Three a year later.

Star, who played in black and gold, competed in the Scottish Cup before, during and after their period of Scottish League membership, but their most successful season was 1924/25. After two second-round replays against Vale of Leven, they reached the third round and an away tie with Celtic, which they lost 2–0. The following season, in 1925/26, they reached the final of the Scottish Qualifying Cup, but were defeated 3–1 by Leith Athletic at Love Street, Paisley.

After 1926 Solway spent a single season in each of several different leagues and in 1929/30 confined themselves to friendlies and cup-ties once again. By 1930 financial difficulties were mounting and they adopted amateur status. There was a short time in the Southern Counties League, but as the 1930s progressed their football became more and more sporadic, until the second world war brought it to an end altogether.

At the end of the hostilities they spent the 1946/47 season in the South of Scotland League, but then resigned when it emerged that the league would no longer be in a regional format for the 1947/48 season. Not long afterwards they went out of existence.

SOUNESS Graeme (1953 –)

Scotland Caps: 54

A somewhat controversial character, Graeme Souness is generally agreed to be one of the best players that Scotland produced during the second half of the twentieth century. He was born in Edinburgh and, after an unhappy spell at Tottenham Hotspur, moved to Middlesbrough in 1973. In January 1978 he was transferred to Liverpool for a record £352,000. By then he was an accomplished midfielder and with Liverpool he won three European Cups, five English league championships and four English League Cups – all in the space of six years before he moved on to Sampdoria in Italy.

In 1986 he was brought back to Scotland to be player-manager of Rangers, and although he was sent off in his first game and had a poor disciplinary record, he pulled

Graeme Souness in typically commanding form for Scotland against West Germany at the 1986 World Cup in Mexico.

Rangers up to success in Scotland, although not in Europe. During his time at Ibrox Rangers won the league championship in 1986/87, 1988/89 and 1989/90, as well as the League Cup on four occasions. It is to his credit that he signed Maurice Johnston in 1989, thereby striking a blow against sectarianism, and wrong-footing Celtic. After he left Glasgow in 1991 he survived major heart surgery, and was manager at Liverpool, Galatasaray, Southampton, Torino (for six games), Benfica, Blackburn Rovers and Newcastle United. He won the 1991/92 FA Cup with Liverpool, the 1995/96 Turkish Cup with Galatasaray, and the 2001/02 English League Cup with Blackburn Rovers.

For Scotland he won fifty-four caps and took part in the World Cup finals of 1978, 1982 and 1986. In 1978 he was only given a game against Holland when the damage had been done, and he helped Scotland to a great but belated success. In 1986 he was controversially dropped for the last game against Uruguay. He later became a TV pundit with SKY Television.

SOUTH AFRICA

2002	20 May	Hong Kong	0–2		Mokoena Koumantarakis
2007	22 Aug	Pittodrie	1–0	Boyd	

SOUTH KOREA

2002	16 May	Busan	1–4	Dobie	Ahn (2) Lee Yoon

SOUTH OF SCOTLAND LEAGUE

Its members are situated throughout Dumfries & Galloway, and it is usually referred to as 'non-league' football because its status is below that of the Scottish Football League, but it is nevertheless a 'senior league' in that it is not part of Scottish junior football (the Highland League and the East of Scotland League also fall into this category). The league was founded in 1946 and Ayr United 'A' won the first championship at the end of the 1946/47 season.

Two clubs, Annan Athletic and Dalbeattie Star, field their 'A' teams in this league whilst their first teams play in the East of Scotland League, and in 2007 the 'A' team of Stranraer FC re-joined the SOSL. Threave Rovers, searching for a higher standard of football, left for the East of Scotland League in 1998, but moved back in 2004 when travelling costs and bonus payments proved expensive. In 2000/01 the league programme was not completed because of the outbreak of foot and mouth disease.

Not all the clubs are eligible to enter the Scottish Cup, but Threave Rovers have been regular participants, playing in the second round on four occasions between 2001/02 and 2005/06. They had to qualify by virtue of reaching the last four of the Scottish Qualifying Cup (South), but on 1 June 2007 the SFA decided that in future SOSL clubs that met their criteria would automatically be entered into a revamped Scottish Cup. Rovers responded by beating Stenhousemuir 1–0 in the new-look second round, and earned a home tie with Raith Rovers, which they lost 5–0.

Nithsdale Wanderers and Mid-Annandale bear the names of clubs that once belonged to the Scottish Football League, although the original clubs have gone out of existence. Tarff Rovers were once one of the league's most successful teams, winning the championship on eight occasions between 1950 and 2002, but they folded in 2005.

Member Club	League Champions	Best Post-War Scottish Cup Performance
Abbey Vale Maryfield Park, New Abbey		Non-participant
Annan Athletic 'A' Galabank, Annan		
Creetown Castle Carie Park, Creetown		Non-participant
Crichton Crichton Hospital Park, Dumfries	2007/08	Non-participant
Dalbeattie Star 'A' Islecroft Stadium, Dalbeattie		
Dumfries Norfolk Park, Glencaple		Non-participant
Fleet Star Garries Park, Gatehouse of Fleet		Non-participant
Mid Annandale King Edward Park, Lockerbie		Non-participant
Newton Stewart Blairmount Park, Newton Stewart	1950/51; 1955/56; 1987/88;	Last 40 (first round 1949/50)
Nithsdale Wanderers Lorimer Park, Sanquhar		Non-participant
St Cuthbert Wanderers St Mary's Park, Kirkcudbright	1954/55; 1956/57; 1958/59; 1970/71; 1973/74; 1980/81; 1995/96;	Last 40 (second preliminary round 1967/68; 1968/69; 1969/70)
Stranraer Athletic Stranraer Academy, Stranraer	2002/03; 2003/04; 2004/05	Non-participant
Stranraer FC 'A' Stair Park, Stranraer	1956/57; 1957/58; 1961/62; 1963/64; 1968/69; 1973/74; 1976/77	
Threave Rovers Meadow Park, Castle Douglas	1964/65; 1968/69; 1971/72; 1978/79; 1992/93; 1993/94; 1994/95; 2005/06; 2006/07	Last 40 (second round 1979/80; 1985/86)
Wigtown & Bladnoch Trammondford Park, Wigtown	1951/52 1953/54 1991/92	Last 32 (second round 1951/52; 1952/53; 1961/62)

SPAIN

Under-performers on the world stage, they just have the better over Scotland. Scotland have played them eleven

Gordon McQueen in action for Scotland against Spain at Hampden.

times, won three, drawn three, and lost four, with one abandoned (a rare fate for an international match).

1957	8 May	Hampden Park	4–2	Mudie (3) Hewie (pen)	Kubala Suarez
1957	26 May	Madrid	1–4	Smith	Basora (2) Mateos Kubala
1963	13 June	Madrid	6–2	Law Gibson McLintock Wilson Henderson St. John	Adelardo Veloso
1965	8 May	Hampden Park	0–0		
1974	20 Nov	Hampden Park	1–2	Bremner	Castro (2)
1975	5 Feb	Valencia	1–1	Jordan	Mejido
1982	24 Feb	Valencia	0–3		Munoz Castro Gallego
1984	14 Nov	Hampden Park	3–1	Johnston (2) Dalglish	Goicoechea
1985	27 Feb	Seville	0–1		Clos
1988	27 Apr	Madrid	0–0		
2004	3 Sept	Valencia	1-1	Baraja o.g.	Raul (pen)
Match abandoned after 60 minutes due to power failure					

SPECTACLES

It is not practical for players to wear spectacles on the field of play, although a few have tried. For those whose vision is not what it might be, this can cause problems. Willie Henderson of Rangers, for example, in an Old Firm game wandered over to the dugout to ask how long was left to play. The answer '5 minutes' was a little gruffer and less welcoming than Willie would have expected. He had in fact asked the question of Jock Stein in the Celtic dugout! In the game that became famous for all the wrong and tragic reasons, namely the game at Cardiff in which Jock Stein died, Scotland's goalkeeper Jim Leighton had to be replaced at half time because he had lost his contact lens! Often a referee's eyesight is called into question. It is not absolutely unheard of for a referee to wear glasses, and of course in recent years, referees have been sponsored by a well-known ophthalmic business!

STANTON Pat (1944 –)

Scotland Caps: 16
Scottish League Championship medals: 1
Scottish Cup medals: 1
Scottish League Cup medals: 1

Pat Stanton is indelibly associated with the great Hibernian team of the early 1970s. He joined the Edinburgh club in 1963, and soon became recognised as one of the best defenders in the game, winning sixteen caps for Scotland, and captaining Hibs to their Scottish League Cup triumph of 1972/73. To the surprise of many observers, he joined Celtic in 1976, when his

career seemed over, but won a double with the Parkhead team in season 1976/77. Turning to management, he became Alex Ferguson's assistant at Aberdeen, and then became manager at Cowdenbeath, Dunfermline and Hibs, but without great success at any of them. He remains a great Hibs supporter.

STEEL Billy (1923 – 1982)

Scotland Caps: 30
Scottish League Cup medals: 2

Those who saw him claim that he was the best player of them all, and certainly most accounts agree that he was a very tricky inside forward with a fine tactical brain. The 'steel' in his name was matched by the 'steel' in his character. He played for Morton during the war, was given his international debut in 1947 against England,

Billy Steel with Third Lanark's Jimmy Mason.

and then was chosen for Great Britain against the Rest of Europe in May of that year. He scored a goal in the 6–1 victory. Later in 1947 he was transferred to Derby County for a record fee of £11,500. Dundee paid £17,500 for him in September 1950 (some say £23,000), and this was a record fee paid by a Scottish club. He was well worth his fee and helped Dundee win the Scottish League Cup twice. Dens Park habitués of the early 1950s averred that he was the greatest of them all.

The unfortunate side of Steel, however, was that he did not always get on with his team-mates, and the Dens Park crowd was frequently treated to shouting matches between Steel and his colleagues! He played thirty times for Scotland, was on the winning side at Wembley in 1949 and 1951, and in November 1950 at Hampden Park scored four times against Northern Ireland. He also has the unwelcome distinction of being the first Scottish player ever to be sent off in an international match, in an incident in Austria in 1951. He played in the USA later in his career.

STEIN Colin (1947 –)

Scotland Caps: 21
Scottish League Cup medals: 1
European Cup Winners Cup medals: 1

Colin Stein was a centre forward for Hibernian and Rangers in the late 1960s. He was an accomplished player and his blonde hair and good looks ensured his popularity at Ibrox when he joined them from Hibs in 1968, for the first six-figure transfer between two Scottish clubs. Surviving the apparent handicap of sharing the same surname as the Celtic manager, Colin could take goals, but sometimes his discipline let him down – e.g. a violent indiscretion against Clyde, late in a game that Rangers won 6–0, cost him a place in the 1969 Scottish Cup final. With Rangers he won the European Cup-Winners' Cup in 1972, but for all his talent his only domestic honour was the Scottish League Cup of 1970/71. He played for Coventry City from 1972 onwards, before returning unsuccessfully to Rangers in 1975. For Scotland, he played twenty-one times, the highlight of his international career being the time he scored four goals against Cyprus in the World Cup qualifier of 1969.

No game for softies! Colin Stein of Rangers has slid right into the net.

STEIN Jock (1922 – 1985)

Scottish League Championship medals: 1
Scottish Cup medals: 1

A truly colossal figure in Scottish football history, Jock Stein was best known for being the manager of the Lisbon Lions who won the European Cup for Celtic in 1967. He was never a great player, starting off in wartime for Albion Rovers, before moving to the Welsh side Llanelli. In 1951 he was surprisingly brought back to Scotland as emergency centre half cover for Celtic. Very soon he began to show great qualities as a leader, if not as a player (he would describe himself with deliberate ambiguity as a passable centre half), and Celtic won the Coronation Cup in 1953, and a league and cup double in 1954. A bad ankle injury in 1955 curtailed his career, but he was given a job as Youth Coach at Parkhead, where he brought on young boys like Billy McNeill, Pat Crerand and John Clark.

He might have become the Celtic manager at that point, but perhaps (as he himself stated) his non-Catholic background counted against him, and he moved to Dunfermline, where he won the Scottish Cup in 1961 and had some European success. He moved to Hibs in 1964, before the irresistible call came from Parkhead on 31 January 1965. Celtic's Chairman Bob Kelly may have wondered whether the Celtic supporters would take kindly to a Protestant manager, but he needn't have. History changed at that point, for apart from the European Cup in 1967, Celtic won nine Scottish titles in a row and Scottish Cups and Scottish League Cups galore.

He had a few health problems, notably in midwinter 1972/73, and in 1975 he had a bad road accident, from which he took some time to recover, but he never recovered (in the footballing sense) from the transfer of Kenny Dalglish to Liverpool in 1977. He left Celtic in 1978 to become manager of Leeds United, but then the Scotland job (a job he had always coveted) became available a couple of months later, and Stein jumped at the chance. For Scotland, he earned respectability after the Argentina fiasco by taking them to the 1982 World Cup finals in Spain. It was at the end of the final qualifying group game between Scotland and Wales at Ninian Park, Cardiff on September 10th 1985 that Jock collapsed and died, having suffered a fatal heart attack. The game had earned Scotland a play-off for the 1986 World Cup. It was somehow a fitting way for him to die.

STENHOUSEMUIR FC

Ground: **Ochilview Park**
Nickname: **The Warriors**
Colours: **Maroon and white**
Record Attendance: **12,500 v East Fife (1950)**
Record Victory: **9-2 v Dundee United (1937)**
Record Defeat: **2-11 v Dunfermline (1930)**
Highest League Position: **20th (4th in Div. B, 1953/54)**
Best Scottish Cup Performance: **Last 4 (Semi-finals 1902/03)**
Best League Cup Performance: **Last 8 (Quarter-finals 1947/48; 1960/61; 1975/76)**

The club was formed in 1884, when members of a team called Heather Rangers broke away to form Stenhousemuir FC. In the early years they played in the Midland Central League, the Central Combination League and then the Central League, but the highlights

Jock Stein has just told Celtic fans to cut out offensive songs before a game against Stirling Albion at Annfield in the Scottish League Cup in August 1972.

Ochilview Park, home of Stenhousemuir FC.

of this period were the Warriors' cup exploits. They won the Scottish Qualifying Cup in consecutive seasons, beating East Stirlingshire 3–0 in the 1900/01 final, and then winning 2–0 against Motherwell in 1901/02. They reached the final again in 1902/03, and although Motherwell beat them 2–1 on this occasion, the Warriors went all the way to the semi-finals of the Scottish Cup, when a 4–1 defeat by Rangers prevented an appearance in the final.

In 1921 the Central League was taken under the umbrella of the Scottish League's new Division Two and Stenhousemuir remained in the lower of the two divisions all the way through to league reconstruction in 1975. Alex Smith was appointed as the club's first manager in 1969, and in October 1972 he oversaw a 2–1 victory over Rangers at Ibrox in the second leg of a second-round League Cup tie, although Rangers had already won the first leg 5–0. In 1975 their eleventh-place finish saw them become members of a division that was called the Second Division, but was actually the third of three tiers, and they remained there until 1994, when the league was reconstructed once again. Terry Christie was now their manager and he led them to a third-place finish in 1993/94, which earned membership of the new Second Division, which had become the third of four tiers.

Not long after their elevation out of the bottom tier Stenhousemuir won a trophy, when the 1995/96 Scottish League Challenge Cup was brought to Ochilview. In a close match at McDiarmid Park they beat Dundee United on penalties after the match had finished 0–0 despite extra time. The Warriors' season was further enhanced by a 2–0 victory over Premier Division Falkirk at Brockville in the third round of the Scottish Cup, although they lost 1–0 at home to Caledonian in the next round.

In 1998 the club was relegated for the first time, when a second-bottom finish took them to the Third Division (fourth tier), but the following year the club was then promoted for the first time, when the runners-up position was enough to take Stenhousemuir back into the Second Division. This time the Warriors remained there for five seasons, until they finished bottom in 2003/04 and were relegated again. They would have been relegated in 2001/02, but were reprieved when Airdrieonians went out of existence.

No account of Stenhousemuir is complete without mentioning their place in the history of floodlit football in Scotland. On 7 November 1951 they hosted Scotland's first floodlit match when visitors Hibs won a friendly encounter 5–3. Then on Wednesday 8 February 1956 they became the first winners of a first-class competitive match played under floodlights in Scotland. Their fifth-round Scottish cup-tie away to East Fife had been postponed the previous Saturday, and the SFA gave permission for the re-arranged match to be played under the lights. The Warriors won 3–1 at Bayview, but were defeated by Clyde in the next round.

The Warriors continued to be innovative in the twenty-first century. In 2006 they installed a multi-layered synthetic pitch with a rubber infill that is designed to make the ball interact with the playing surface in the same way that it would with natural grass.

STIRLING ALBION FC

Ground: **Forthbank Stadium**
Nickname: **The Binos**
Colours: **Red and white**
Record Attendance: **28,600 (disputed by some) at Annfield Park v Celtic (1959)**
3,808 at Forthbank Stadium v Aberdeen (1996)
Record Victory: **20-0 v Selkirk (1984)**
Record Defeat: **0-9 v Dundee United 1967**
Highest League Position: **12th (1958/59)**
Best Scottish Cup Performance: **Last 8 (4th round 1949/50; 1958/59; 1961/62) (3rd round 1964/65) (5th round 1989/90)**
Best League Cup Performance: **Last 4 (Semi-finals 1961/62)**

Stirling lost its football club during the second world war, when a German bomb fell on the ground of the King's Park club, and so in 1945 a group of local businessmen founded Stirling Albion FC. The Annfield Estate was purchased, close to the town centre, and Annfield Stadium was created as a home for the new club. Admitted to the newly formed Division C for the 1946/47 season, Albion proceeded to become its first ever champions and in the years since then their name has been entered into the record books on several further occasions.

By 1949 they had climbed into Division A, but Stirling quickly became known as the 'Yo-Yo' club. In the period from 1948 to 1968 they were promoted into the higher division and relegated back down again on no fewer than six occasions. In season 1954/55 they suffered the ignominy of setting a record for the fewest points in a season, when they amassed just six from thirty games. Even today this is a record low for both Scotland and England. There was almost an appearance in a cup final when they reached the semi-finals of the League Cup in 1961/62, and Hearts needed extra time before beating them 2–1.

On 8 December 1984 the club made headlines around the world when Selkirk were beaten 20–0 in the first round of the Scottish Cup, the biggest victory in the competition since the nineteenth century. The euphoria was short lived, however, as the second round brought a 2–1 defeat at Cowdenbeath. There was another record on 5 September 1987 when Stirling hosted the Scottish

Scotland's Under 17s take on the Faeroe Islands at Stirling Albion's Forthbank Stadium.

League's first ever match on artificial turf, with the Second Division game against Ayr United finishing as a 1–1 draw.

In 1993 the club, which was by now being referred to as the Binos, moved to a new Stadium on the outskirts of the town. It has the same name, Forthbank Stadium, as the ground that was once the home of King's Park, and a view of the Ochil hills provides a superb backdrop behind one of the goals. In 1995/96 the new ground was the scene of yet another record when the Second Division title was won with eighty-one points, the division's most in a season under the 'three points for a win' system. This marked the eighth occasion on which Stirling Albion had won a divisional title, but this success was to be followed by several years of disappointment.

Relegated back to the Second Division in 1997/98, they finished bottom in 2000/01 and were relegated down to the fourth tier. Even then things got worse, for by the end of the 2001/02 season the Binos were the second-bottom club in the Scottish League. At this point Allan Moore was appointed as head coach, and under his leadership the journey back up the league began. Promotion to the Second Division in 2003/04 was followed by another promotion in 2006/07 when Airdrie United were beaten in the play-off final, but then Albion's reputation as a 'Yo-Yo' club returned, and twelve months later they were back in the third tier.

STRACHAN Gordon (1957 –)

Scotland Caps: 50
Scottish League Championship medals: 2
Scottish Cup medals: 3
European Cup-Winners' Cup medals: 1

Gordon Strachan is one of the characters of Scottish football. Born in Edinburgh in 1957, he began his playing career for Dundee, but it was for Aberdeen, to whom he was transferred in 1977, that he really began to shine. He was part of Alex Ferguson's great Aberdeen team of the early 1980s, winning many domestic honours and famously the European Cup-Winners' Cup in 1983. He was not always popular with opposing supporters and, ironically in view of later events, a fan at Celtic Park once attacked him. He won the first of his fifty Scottish caps in 1980 and the last in 1992, and took part in the World Cup finals of 1982 and 1986, scoring a goal for Scotland against West Germany in Mexico.

His tenacious style of midfield play and his never-say-die attitude endeared him to the Tartan Army. He moved to Manchester United in 1984, won an FA Cup medal in 1985, and was re-united with Alex Ferguson in 1986, but did not shine for Manchester United the way that he did for Aberdeen. He then moved to Leeds United in 1989, winning a Second Division championship medal in 1990, and a First Division championship medal in 1992, before becoming manager of Coventry and Southampton. In summer 2005 he took over at Celtic from Martin O'Neill, and in his first season won the Scottish Premier League, the Scottish League Cup, and was also named Manager of the Year. In 2007 he won a league and cup double, and followed this up in 2008 with his third SPL trophy for the club.

Gordon Strachan scored 5 goals in 50 appearances for Scotland before going on to a successful managerial career.

STRANRAER FC

Ground: **Stair Park**
Nickname: **The Blues**
Colours: **Blue and white**
Record Attendance: **6,500 v Rangers (1948)**
Record Victory: **7-0 v Brechin (1965)**
Record Defeat: **1-11 v Queen Of The South (1932)**
Highest League Position: **20th (10th in First Div., 1994/95 &1998/99)**
Best Scottish Cup Performance: **Last 8 (5th round 2002/03)**
Best League Cup Performance: **Last 8 (Quarter-finals 1968/69)**

Stranraer FC was founded in 1870, following an amalgamation of clubs in the town. They played at various grounds, and even briefly disbanded during 1907, when players left to form Dalrymple Harriers. Before the end of that year they were back in business at their new home of Stair Park under the name of Stranraer United, and it was not long before the word 'United' was dropped. Despite their early beginning, the Blues did not gain admission to the Scottish League until 1949, and over the years played in different leagues from time to time, including the Wigtownshire League, the Southern Counties League, the Scottish Combination, the Scottish Alliance and the South of Scotland League. They won the championship of the South of Scotland League in 1948/49, and shortly afterwards were admitted to Division C (South West) of the national league. Division C was discontinued in 1955, and Stranraer became part of an expanded Division B, which later became Division Two.

The Qualifying Cup (South) was won in 1937/38, with a 5–3 victory over Bo'ness, but it was cup performances in the late 1940s that did much to raise the profile of the club prior to its admission to the Scottish League. There were appearances in two consecutive finals of the Scottish Qualifying Cup (South) in 1946/47 and 1947/48, although both matches were lost, and then Stranraer became the focus of national attention when Rangers visited in the first round of the 1947/48 Scottish Cup and only won 1–0.

There were more headlines in 1968/69 when an appearance in the last eight of the Scottish League Cup resulted in a 10–0 aggregate defeat by Dundee, but performances in the league were unremarkable. The Blues stayed in the lower division from 1955 until league reconstruction in 1975, when they became a member of the new Second Division (third of three tiers). On 19August 1981 Stair Park became the last of the Scottish League grounds at that time to stage a match under floodlights, when Albion Rovers were defeated 2–0 in the League Cup.

Stranraer finished bottom of the new-look Scottish League on four occasions, but in 1993/1994, under manager Alex McAnespie, the team won the Second Division championship. This was the final season before the league was again reconstructed, and they were now placed in the second of four tiers. Life in the First Division only lasted for one season and relegation

Stranraer defenders Allan Jenkins (left) and Billy MacDonald (right) close down Celtic striker Chris Sutton at Stair Park in January 2001.

followed in 1995. However, after Campbell Money became manager, the team won the Scottish League Challenge Cup in 1996/97, beating St Johnstone 1–0 in the final, and then in 1997/1998 became champions of the Second Division (now the third of four tiers). Once again life at the higher level only lasted for a single season.

In 2002/2003, despite a Scottish Cup run that took them to a 4–0 quarter-final defeat against Motherwell, the club was relegated to the Third Division. This time however, under the management of former captain Neil Watt, relegation was followed by two consecutive promotions. In 2004/05 a second-place finish in the Second Division followed the 2003/04 Third Division title, and this took Stranraer back to the First Division (second tier). The new status again lasted for only a single season, and they slid back down the league after losing a play-off semi-final in two consecutive seasons. Defeats to Partick Thistle in 2006 and East Fife in 2007 meant that they were back in the bottom tier of Scottish football, and in February 2008 former Rangers player Derek Ferguson took on the challenge of returning Stranraer to a higher division. His team lost the 2007/08 play-off final to Arbroath, but the Blues were still promoted when the fall of Gretna FC created an extra place in the Second Division.

STRUTH Bill (1875 – 1956)

Bill Struth was the legendary manager of Rangers between the years of 1920 and 1954, during which time the team won eighteen Scottish League championships, ten Scottish Cups and two Scottish League Cups. He was born in Milnathort and became a stonemason, playing football with no great success. After being trainer at Hearts and Clyde for a spell, during which time he was also appointed trainer of the Scotland national team, he became assistant manager of Rangers in 1914. He then took over as manager in 1920 when William Wilton drowned in a boating accident on the river Clyde.

A physical fitness fanatic, he built up a succession of great teams and placed an emphasis on discipline and dress among his players, who included luminaries such as Tommy Cairns, Alan Morton, Bob McPhail, Willie Thornton, and George Young. Church attendance on a Sunday morning was a *sine qua non* of playing for Rangers. His toughness was legendary, and for a while he earned the nicknames of 'ruthless Struth' or 'God's truth'. He devoted himself to Rangers, living in a flat around the corner from Ibrox, and walking to work every day. As a result of this, Rangers were clearly the most successful team in Scotland during the inter-war years, and exerted an almost total domination of Scottish football during the second world war. Indeed, some Rangers historians claim that Struth's side was the first to win nine league championships in a row, from 1938/39 until season 1946/47 if unofficial wartime seasons are allowed for. Less happily, Struth is associated with what many people believe was a religious discrimination policy at Rangers during the years when he was their manager. The main stand at Ibrox has now been named after him.

STURROCK Paul (1956 –)

Scotland Caps: 20
Scottish League Championship medals: 1
Scottish League Cup medals: 2

Commonly known as 'Luggy', Paul Sturrock played for Dundee United from 1974 onwards, winning two Scottish League Cups and one Scottish Premier League championship, as well as playing consistently well for them in their many successful European forays. When he retired from playing in 1989, he became a coach, and then managed St Johnstone, Dundee United, Plymouth Argyle, Southampton (for a brief and unhappy spell) Sheffield Wednesday, Swindon Town (who gained promotion from Division Two to Division One under his managership), and then Plymouth Argyle again. He won twenty caps for Scotland and participated in the World Cup finals of 1986 in Mexico.

SUBSTITUTES

Now an essential part of the game, substitutes were frowned upon until 1966. This often meant that a match could be ruined if a player was injured and his team was thus reduced to ten men. This sometimes led to situations where players hobbled about the field when they were palpably unfit, or injured players were put in goal, or on the left wing, where it was felt they would do themselves less harm. It also made life difficult for the left winger, who would then have to swap places with the injured man. It was not unknown for teams to finish with nine or even eight men.

In friendly international matches, teams could often make a substitution by prior agreement. Thus, on 29 May 1960 in Vienna, Alex Young of Hearts replaced the injured Denis Law of Manchester City after twelve minutes. Alex must have wished that he had remained on the bench, for Scotland went on to lose 4–1 to Austria. A curious case arose with the unassuming Billy Ritchie of Rangers. Billy was a good goalkeeper and unfortunate not to be capped by Scotland until 2 May 1962 at Hampden, when he was called upon to replace Dunfermline's Eddie Connachan at half time in a game against Uruguay. Billy conceded a goal almost immediately, (Uruguay were already 2–0 up) and, although Scotland fought back to make the final score 3–2, Billy never again played for Scotland. He can therefore claim to have half a Scottish cap!

The most remarkable substitution at international level must be that of Joe Craig of Celtic on 27 April 1977 at Hampden Park in a friendly against Sweden. He was brought on in the seventy-ninth minute and almost immediately headed a goal before he had kicked the ball. Legend has it that he never kicked the ball for the remainder of the game, and he certainly never won another Scottish cap. So, if he never did kick the ball, he can claim to have scored a goal without kicking a ball in his entire international career!

England allowed one substitute for an injury in season 1965/66, but it was not until the following season that this was allowed in Scotland. Archie Gemmill of St Mirren became Scotland's first-ever substitute on the first day of the season, 13 August 1966, against Clyde at Shawfield in the Scottish League Cup, when he replaced the injured Jim Clunie. Ten days later on 23 August at Cliftonhill, the home of Albion Rovers, Peter Conn of Queen's Park became the first substitute in a Scottish League game. The following season, 1967/68, a substitute was allowed for any reason, because it had been obvious the previous year that 'injured' players were sometimes not really injured at all, merely having a poor game. It was far better to allow substitution for any reason than have the spectacle of players unconvincingly pretending to be injured.

The first substitute in a Scottish Cup final was Rene Moller of Hearts for Raold Jensen on 27 April 1968, and in a Scottish League Cup final it was Steve Chalmers of Celtic for John Hughes on 29 October 1966. Gradually, as people saw that substitutes were a good idea, two substitutes were allowed, then three, and now

Kris Boyd prepares to enter the fray for Scotland against the Ukraine in October 2006.

substitutions are looked upon as part of a manager's skill. In the SPL seven substitutes may be nominated, although only three can be used. The manager must know when to substitute and when not to do so. In particular, he must judge the precise moment in the game when fresh blood is necessary.

SULLIVAN Neil (1970 –)

Scotland Caps: 28

A sound goalkeeper, Neil Sullivan earned twenty-eight caps for Scotland between 1997 and 2003. He was not born in Scotland, but was eligible by virtue of the 'ancestry rule'. His first club was Wimbledon, whom he joined in 1988, but he took some time to break into their first team. In 2000 he moved to Tottenham Hotspur and, after a brief spell with Chelsea, moved to Leeds United in 2004 and then Doncaster Rovers in 2007.

SUMMER CUP

In theory a good idea, in practice a Summer Cup has never really worked, for the simple reason that football needs a rest. There have been two incarnations of the Summer Cup – one in wartime, won by Hibs in 1941, Rangers in 1942, St.Mirren in 1943, Motherwell in 1944 and Partick Thistle in 1945, and the other in the mid-sixties when Hibs won the trophy in 1964 and Motherwell in 1965. The competition never really got off the ground in the 1960s as the non-entrance of Rangers and Celtic lessened its appeal, but the Summer Cup of 1964 (the final was actually played before the start of the 1964/65 season) was the only trophy won by Jock Stein in his brief spell as manager of Hibernian.

SUNDAY FOOTBALL

For many years Scotland was a too-strictly Sabbatarian and Presbyterian country ever to countenance the idea of Sunday football, even when some people in the Church of Scotland dared to suggest that perhaps Saturday, if the Book of Genesis is looked at closely, is the day intended for God's 'day of rest'. Football, even when played by boys in the street, was frowned upon, but so too were women doing their washing, the running of trains, and the opening of shops. As early as 1628, the minute book of the kirk session in Carstairs records sadly and angrily, 'the minister has occasion to complain of the insolent behaviour of his parishioners, both men and women, in footballing (sic) instead of observing Sunday as a solemn day devoted to God.'

In Dundee in March 1898, thirteen youths were fined by the Sheriff for playing football on the Sabbath, the ringleaders being fined seven shillings and sixpence, and the others five shillings, for playing football in the Dens Road area of the town. Their parents pleaded that they were returning from the 'school', and when the Sheriff asked sarcastically if this was the 'football school', they said it was the 'Sabbath school' ie what became known as Sunday school at the Church. *The Courier* of 21 March 1898 states disapprovingly, 'at four o'clock on Sunday, when respectable citizens were on their way home from church, the match was in full swing', and 'a lady had to stop to avoid being hit by the ball'.

During the first world war, when it might have made sense to play some games on a Sunday, and when even the Church of Scotland was moved to allow 'war work' on a Sunday, the authorities would instead insist on teams playing two games on the same Saturday. Celtic, for example, on 15 April 1916 beat Raith Rovers at Parkhead on a Saturday afternoon and then went to Motherwell that same evening to record another victory.

Even when Scotland played a few games abroad on a Sunday, heads were shaken and fingers pointed. On Sunday 19 May 1957, for example, Scotland played a World Cup tie in Switzerland and the BBC televised the game. This provoked letters of outrage in newspapers, and prayers were said for those who watched this 'sinful' game. Even more heat was generated on Sunday 23 May 1965 when Scotland played in Poland in another World Cup tie. This time the game was only broadcast on the radio, but with only two minutes left and the game poised at 1–1, the game was taken off the air and replaced by the normal Sunday evening religious programme. This decision pleased no one because football fans were incensed, and religious people felt that football should not have been on the radio anyway!

But more and more sports and other entertainments were beginning to take place on a Sunday, and it was clear that it would make a lot of sense for football to use this day as well. In fact the catalyst was the 1973/74 'miners versus Conservative government' conflict. Prime Minister Edward Heath reacted to the miners' overtime ban by placing the country on a three-day week to save energy. Half the country would work Monday, Tuesday and Wednesday and the other half would work Thursday, Friday and Saturday. This deprived football of half its potential customers, so Sunday football was reluctantly allowed – beginning in England on 6 January and in Scotland with the Scottish Cup matches of Sunday 27 January 1974. To Dixie Deans of Celtic belongs the honour of scoring Scotland's first-ever Sunday goal as Celtic beat Clydebank 6–1. The following week, 3 February 1974, saw the first-ever Scottish League game on a Sunday as Dundee beat Partick Thistle 4–1 at Dens Park.

The miners' dispute was eventually resolved, but it would take some time before Sunday football became commonplace. It was probably live television that made the difference. The Scottish League Cup final of March 1984 was played on a Sunday for the benefit of live television and has been played on that day ever since, although the Scottish Cup final has retained a sacrosanct Saturday. But now, no matter which television company has the contract, there is always plenty of football available on live television on a Sunday, whether from Scotland, England or elsewhere in Europe.

Rangers have just won the League Cup after beating Celtic 3-2 after extra-time in the first-ever League Cup final played on a Sunday (in March 1984.)

There are those who deplore all this, but the gainers are definitely the fans, who are given more opportunity to watch their favourites. It also means that it is possible to see more than one game per weekend. One disadvantage is that it can sometimes favour a team playing on a Sunday to know how well or how badly their rivals have done on the Saturday, but one way round that is to play all games towards the climax of the season on a Sunday and televise them. Those who recall the thrilling finishes to the SPL in 2003 and 2005 will vouch for that.

SUNNYBANK FC (see JUNIOR FOOTBALL)

SUSPENSIONS AND FINES

It lies within the authority of the SFA to impose fines and suspensions for infringements of discipline such as a red card, or a collection of yellow cards. Suspensions are normally for a given number of games rather than a set period of days and, while serving a suspension in the SPL for example, a player is normally allowed to play a UEFA fixture, for it has its own disciplinary code. Normally a red card in a game carries the automatic penalty of missing the next game as well as whatever else the disciplinary committee may decide to impose.

Since the second world war, there have been very few *sine die* suspensions. *Sine die* is Latin for 'without a day', and means an indefinite suspension, ie without a day being given for its lifting. One very high-profile one was in September 1954 when *sine die* was imposed on Willie Woodburn of Rangers, who was sent off in a game against Stirling Albion. It was his fifth sending-off in six years. In September 2001 Dave Bowman (ex-Dundee United and Scotland) of Forfar Athletic was suspended for seventeen games after being shown five red cards for 'persistent foul and abusive language' in a game against Stranraer. His first red card resulted in him being sent off, but as he persisted in his offences after he left the park, the red cards continued to be shown. In a case that had legal and judicial implications as well, Duncan Ferguson of Rangers was suspended for twelve games for violent conduct in a game against Raith Rovers in April 1994. He was sent to jail for three months for the assault on Raith Rovers' Jock McStay. Billy McLafferty of Stenhousemuir was banned from the game for eight months in April 1993 (the rest of the calendar year of 1993) for failing to appear at a disciplinary hearing after he had been sent off against Arbroath in February. He was also fined £250 (also see **PROFESSIONALISM, RENTON FC** and **ST BERNARD'S FC**)

SUTER Fergus (dates unknown)

There has been speculation that Fergus Suter was the first professional footballer, but this is simply a possibility that remains unproven. Nevertheless, he should be remembered for his role in the introduction of the Scottish passing game to the football clubs of Lancashire, at a time when English sides were still adopting a more individual approach.

A stonemason from Glasgow, Suter was a full back in the Partick Thistle side that toured Lancashire over the New Year period of 1878. Having come to the attention of some of the county's leading clubs, he joined Darwen in 1879 and moved on to Blackburn Rovers a year later. By the time he left them in 1889 he had appeared in four FA Cup finals and collected three winners' medals, winning them in consecutive seasons.

Some historians believe that Suter did not work for a living outside football, or at least was given a job that amounted to a sinecure, in an era before professionalism had become officially accepted. The evidence is less strong in the case of goalkeeper James Love, who had accompanied Suter from Scotland, and hence it has been suggested that Fergus Suter was the first professional, but could not admit it.

SWEDEN

Scotland's record against Sweden is all-square, for they have played eleven, won five, drawn one, and lost five.

1952	30 May	Stockholm	1–3	Liddell	Sandberg Lofgren Bengtsson
1953	6 May	Hampden Park	1–2	Johnstone	Lofgren Eriksson
1975	16 Apr	Gothenburg	1–1	MacDougall	Sjoberg
1977	27 Apr	Hampden Park	3–1	Hellstrom o.g. Dalglish Craig	Wendt
1980	10 Sep	Stockholm	1–0	Strachan	
1981	9 Sep	Hampden Park	2–0	Jordan Robertson (pen)	
1990	16 June	Genoa	2–1	McCall Johnston (pen)	Stromberg
1995	11 Oct	Stockholm	0–2		Pettersson Schwarz
1996	10 Nov	Ibrox	1-0	McGinlay	
1997	30 Apr	Gothenburg	1–2	Gallacher	K. Andersson (2)
2004	17 Nov	Easter Road	1–4	McFadden (pen)	Allback (2) Elmander Berglund

SWITZERLAND

Scotland's record against the Swiss is a good one – played fifteen, won seven, drawn three, and lost five.

1931	24 May	Geneva	3–2	Easson Boyd Love	Buche Faugel
1948	17 May	Berne	1–2	Johnston	Maillard Fatton
1950	26 Apr	Hampden Park	3–1	Bauld Campbell Brown	Antenen
1957	19 May	Basle	2–1	Mudie Collins	Vonlanthen
1957	6 Nov	Hampden Park	3–2	Robertson Mudie Scott	Riva Vonlanthen
1973	22 June	Berne	0–1		Mundschin
1976	7 Apr	Hampden Park	1–0	Pettigrew	
1982	17 Nov	Berne	0–2		Sulser Egli
1983	30 Mar	Hampden Park	2–2	Wark Nicholas	Egli Hermann
1990	17 Oct	Hampden Park	2–1	Robertson (pen) McAllister	Knup (pen)
1991	11 Sep	Berne	2–2	Durie McCoist	Chapuisat Hermann
1992	9 Sep	Berne	1–3	McCoist	Knup (2) Bregy
1993	8 Sep	Pittodrie	1–1	Collins	Bregy (pen)
1996	18 June	Villa Park	1–0	McCoist	
2006	1 Mar	Hampden Park	1–3	Miller	Barnetta Gygax Cabanas

SYMON Scot (1911 – 1985)

Scotland Caps: 1
Scottish League Championship medals: 1

Scot Symon played for Dundee, Portsmouth and Rangers in the 1930s. He earned only one cap, and would have earned more but for the second world war. He was also capped for Scotland at cricket when he played for Perthshire, and is one of the few men to have played for Scotland at both disciplines. He won a Scottish League championship medal with Rangers in 1939, but it is as a manager that he is best known. In the

Joe Jordan nets a header against Sweden in a World Cup qualifier in September 1981.

years immediately after the second world war, he took East Fife to two Scottish League Cup successes, and discovered men like Charlie 'Legs' Fleming, Henry Morris, and 'Dod' Aitken before going to Preston North End, whom he took to the final of the FA Cup in his first year.

He was then appointed manager of Rangers in 1954, and his tenure at Ibrox over the next thirteen years brought him a total of fifteen domestic trophies. In addition he spotted and brought on talent like Jim Baxter and John Greig, and made Rangers a respected name in Europe, twice reaching the final of the European Cup-Winners' Cup. In 1967, several months after the infamous loss at Berwick, and to the incredulity of the footballing world, Symon was dismissed while his team were at the top of the league. He subsequently became manager of Partick Thistle. He was well respected in the game for his gentlemanly, if somewhat austere, demeanour.

TACTICS AND TEAM EVOLUTION

Very little is known for certain about team formations in the early years of the game, and the word 'tactics' is perhaps a misnomer until at least the professional era of the 1890s and onwards.

In the first international match between Scotland and England in 1872, there was a clear differentiation in the way that both sides played the game, for England specialised in dribbling, whereas Scotland (all of them players for Queen's Park) had evolved a passing game and only used dribbling occasionally to draw an opponent out of position and then pass to a colleague who was now unmarked. This method of play was clearly the more successful way, for Scotland consistently beat England in the 1870s and 1880s, until such time as England too adopted a passing game.

As regards team formation, there was always a goalkeeper, who would have a hard job avoiding the (legal) shoulder charges of his opponents and who would have to get used to the idea of changing ends every time a goal was scored lest one team had too much of an advantage with the wind, sun or the slope of the pitch. The rest of the team would all be called 'forwards' and their team talks would be little more than 'go out and chase the ball' and 'when you've got it either pass it to your team mate or score a goal'.

By the time that official domestic football began to be played in the 1870s, wiser elements began to realise that if some players stayed in certain areas of the field, they would do a lot better. Big, burly fellows would make good defenders or centre forwards (for they had to charge the goalkeeper), whereas the slighter-built fellows might do better on the edges of the field and, as they were lighter, they were called the wingers.

By 1875, a team sheet for a game between Queen's Park and London Wanderers had Queen's Park with a goalkeeper, two full backs, two half backs, three back-ups, and three forwards. This is getting very close to the traditional one, two, three and five formula of the first fifty years of the twentieth century, for all that is required is that two of the back-ups go forward and became inside men, and the other one goes back to became a centre half. Wanderers, on the other hand, had a different formation with a goalkeeper, a full back, two half backs, two men on each wing (one a full winger, the other a half winger or what would be called a wing half) and three inside forwards. This would develop into the template that lasted fairly rigidly until the early 1960s.

A key person was often the centre half. He was not simply a defender, but was expected to attack as well, almost like a double centre forward. In the mid 1920s however, the authorities were concerned that not enough goals were being scored and from season 1925/26 onwards the offside rule was changed so that only two defenders needed to be between the attacker and the goal for a man to be onside, rather than three. To counteract this advantage to the attacking side, and to prevent the scoring of the goals so desired by the legislators, the centre half evolved into a pure defender, except for the occasional foray up the field for a corner kick, for example.

Scottish football has always been rich in wingers. Examples are Alan Morton, Jimmy Delaney, Willie Waddell, Billy Liddell, Jimmy Johnstone, Willie Henderson, Tommy McLean, Davie Cooper and many others whose skill was to get the ball at the edge of the field, beat a defender or two, reach the dead-ball line and cross. This was a standard move in Scottish football and some say that the decline in wingers over the past fifty years has impoverished the game. Significantly, two Englishmen who were always much loved in Scotland (although they frequently did much damage to Scotland) were Stanley Matthews and Tom Finney, two great wingers.

The wing halves and the inside men (who would wear 4, 6, 8 and 10) were the key to a good team. They were the foragers, the 'fetch and carry' men and the creators of the attack. They had to be able to win a ball, bring it forward, pass with accuracy and spread it to the wingers or their centre forward. The centre forward was the goal

The Celtic squad that won the 1967 European Cup. Back row, left to right: Willie O'Neil, Billy McNeill, Jim Craig, Tommy Gemmill, Ronnie Simpson, John Hughes, Bobby Murdoch, John Clark. Front row: Jimmy Johnstone, Bobby Lennox, Willie Wallace, Steve Chalmers, Charlie Gallacher, Joe McBride and Bertie Auld.

scorer, but his role was also to lead the line, meaning he had to receive the ball and distribute it to other forwards. A feature of successful teams was the way that the forward line could interchange positions

This 'goalkeeper, two full backs, three half backs and five forwards' formula lasted so long, and was so embedded in Scottish thinking, that it was as though there was no other way of playing the game. It came as shock therefore in the early 1960s when some teams began to play in a 4–2–4 formation, with four defenders, two midfielders and four forwards (without any recognised winger, or perhaps only one). They were immediately branded defensive, and thought almost heretical in their attack on Scotland's tradition, but it was a successful system.

The first team to play like this was Hearts, but very soon other teams followed suit. In November 1963 two of Scotland's younger managers, Jock Stein and Willie Waddell, managers at the time of Dunfermline Athletic and Kilmarnock respectively, visited Italy to consult the great Helenio Herrera about tactics, and the days of the 1–2–3–5 formation were numbered after that. By the mid 1960s, every Scottish team was playing some variation or other of the 4–2–4 formation, however much the media and conservative fans kept talking about wing halves and outside rights.

To take as an example, Celtic's side in 1967, the team that won the European Cup in Lisbon was recited (and still is) by its fans as:

Simpson
Craig Gemmell
Murdoch McNeill Clark
Wallace Auld
Johnstone Chalmers Lennox

This is the traditional Scottish set-up. Both defence and attack would play in a W or M formation. In fact the way the team played in Lisbon was as follows:

Simpson
Craig McNeill Clark Gemmell
Murdoch Auld
Johnstone Wallace Chalmers Lennox

The system was very fluid with Tommy Gemmell being an attacking full back and Jimmy Johnstone having a 'roving commission', but the team formation was far more akin to 4–2–4 than anything else. Many Celtic fans persisted in their denial that this was the way that their team played, but the edge was taken off the objection when it was observed how well the team played.

Since the 1960s there have been many changes of formation with 4–3–3, and 3–4–3 and even 3–3–4 being practised successfully. There have even been changes in nomenclature. A centre forward has become a striker, one of the two centre halves has become a sweeper and inside men and wing halves have given way to right-sided midfield players etc. A 'flat back four' means four defenders, and the 'arc formation' means five defenders, but not playing in a straight line. In this day of super-fit professionals, it is probably fluidity and ability to interchange that is the key thing.

Team formation and tactics probably matter less than how players perform in a given formation. The route to success has much more to with ability and (possibly even more importantly) attitude than any coaching methods.

TAYLOR David (1954 –)

David Taylor is an able administrator who became the General Secretary of UEFA, a post he moved to in 2007 after he had been the Chief Executive of the SFA since 1999. He had established his credentials by the fine work he did from his Hampden base, although he was unfairly blamed by some fans for the poor performances of the national team during his period of office.

TAYPORT FC (see JUNIOR FOOTBALL)

TELEVISION (see BROADCASTING, RADIO AND TV)

TEMPLETON Bobby (1879 – 1919)

Scotland Caps: 11
Scottish League Championship medals: 1
Scottish Cup medals: 1

Bobby Templeton was a remarkable and much-travelled footballing personality of the Edwardian and pre-first world war era, who won eleven Scotland caps. His international debut was the Ibrox disaster of 1902, when twenty-five people were killed as a wooden stand behind the goal collapsed – largely because, it was said, people all swayed to one side to see Bobby Templeton receive a cross-field pass. He had happier international appearances as well, notably the great victory over England at Hampden Park in 1910. He came from Kilmarnock and played for the Rugby Park side before moving to Hibs, Aston Villa, Newcastle United, Arsenal, Celtic, Kilmarnock (again), Fulham and Kilmarnock (the third time).

He had already won two English league medals with Aston Villa and Newcastle United, but it was his year with Celtic (1906/07) that was his most successful, in that he won the league and cup double with the club. Bobby Templeton, however, could never cope with Maley's strict discipline and his career did not last long there. He was a crowd pleaser and a personality, and his street credibility grew when, after playing for Kilmarnock against Celtic, he entered a lion's cage at a circus, patted its head and tweaked its tail. When his career was over, he went into partnership with his old friend Sunny Jim Young, to run a pub in Kilmarnock, but he died at the tragically young age of forty in 1919 from a heart attack, following a bout of Spanish flu.

TERRACE CHANTS (see ATMOSPHERE)

TERRIBLE TRIO

This was the name given to the inside right, centre forward and inside left of the successful Hearts team of the mid 1950s – Alfie Conn, Willie Bauld and Jimmy Wardhaugh. Playing at the same time as Hibs' 'Famous Five' (see **FAMOUS FIVE**), they came together for the first time in the 1948/49 season, and began to break up in season 1957/58, but not before they had played a large part in Hearts' winning of the championship that year. Previously they had been influential in ending Hearts' trophy famine of almost fifty years when the Tynecastle side won the Scottish League Cup in October 1954 (Willie Bauld scored a hat-trick in the 4-2 won over Motherwell and Jimmy Wardhaugh the other goal), and then the Scottish Cup of 1956 when Hearts beat Celtic 3-1.

Curiously, they were under-represented at international level, with only six caps between them. Wardhaugh's selection for his two games was controversial, for he was technically an Englishman, born at Marshall Meadows, a mile into England! Bauld, playing for Scotland on a famous occasion in 1950, hit the bar with a shot late in the game at Hampden Park against England. Had that gone in, Scotland would have gone to the 1950 World Cup finals in Brazil. Alfie Conn had a son, also called Alfie (see **CONN Alfie jr.**), who famously played for both Rangers and Celtic in the 1970s.

TESTIMONIAL MATCHES

Perhaps surprisingly, in this age of highly paid professional footballers, testimonials have not yet become an anachronism. In less affluent times, they would be awarded to players who had come to the end of their career and at the age of almost forty, and having done nothing but play football all their lives, faced an uncertain future. It would be a friendly match against a big team, and the man himself would be allowed to keep the gate money. In the early twenty-first century, however, men like Henrik Larsson and Roy Keane (hardly paupers) have had testimonial games, and they have been surprisingly well attended. They do give fans a chance to record their thanks and say farewell to their heroes.

As famous as Hibernian's Famous Five, Hearts Terrible Trio are: Willie Bauld, Jimmy Wardhaugh and Alfie Conn.

Third Lanark, Cup winners of 1889. Back row, left to right: A. Thompson, R. Downie, J. Rae. Second row: J. Marshall, J. Thomson (umpire), R. MacFarlane, A. Lochhead, W. French (secretary), J. Hannah. Centre row: John Oswald, W. Brown (President), W. Johnstone,. Front row: James Oswald, J. Auld.

TEXACO CUP

This was a knockout cup competition for leading clubs from Scotland, England, Northern Ireland and the Republic of Ireland that had failed to qualify for Europe. There were five tournaments, from 1970/71 to 1974/75, although Irish clubs ceased to take part after the first two. When Airdrieonians beat Nottingham Forest in the first round of the 1970/71 competition they took part in the UK's first penalty shoot-out.

The final was contested on a home and away basis in every year except one, when Newcastle United and Burnley played a single match in 1973/74. After the sponsor withdrew in 1975, Scottish and English clubs took part in the Anglo-Scottish Cup for a further six years. The results of the Texaco finals are as follows:

1970/1971	Heart of Midlothian	1	Wolverhampton Wndrs.	3
	Wolverhampton Wndrs.	0	Heart of Midlothian	1
	Wolverhampton Wanderers won 3–2 on aggregate			
1971/1972	Airdrieonians	0	Derby County	0
	Derby County	2	Airdrieonians	1
	Derby County won 2–1 on aggregate			
1972/1973	Ipswich Town	2	Norwich City	1
	Norwich City	1	Ipswich Town	2
	Ipswich Town won 4–2 on aggregate			
1973/1974	Newcastle United	2	Burnley	1
	After extra time			
1974/1975	Southampton	1	Newcastle United	0
	Newcastle United	3	Southampton	0
	Newcastle United won 3-1 on aggregate (aet in second leg)			

THIRD LANARK FC (former Scottish League club)

Home: **Cathkin Park / New Cathkin Park, Glasgow**
Highest League Position: **1st (1903/04)**
Best Scottish Cup Performance: **Winners (1888/89; 1904/05)**
Best League Cup Performance: **Runners-up (1959/60)**

Formed by members of the 3rd Lanarkshire Rifle Volunteers in 1872, the club's first home, Cathkin Park, was situated at one end of the field where the soldiers used to drill.

Thirds were founder members of the Scottish FA and took part in the first ever Scottish Cup competition in 1873/74, when Clydesdale needed a second replay before beating them 2–0. Their form in the Scottish Cup soon established them as one of Scotland's leading clubs and by 1890 they had been winners once (recording a 2–1 victory over Celtic in the final), runners-up twice, and losing semi-finalists on a further two occasions.

When the Scottish League was formed for the 1890/91 season, Thirds were once again founder members of a new organisation and for many years they finished the season as one of Scotland's top clubs. In 1903 they moved to the second Hampden Park when it was vacated by Queen's Park and, after extensive rebuilding, renamed it New Cathkin Park. Thirds had to play several 'home' matches away from their new ground whilst the rebuilding was going on, but despite this handicap they completed a momentous season by winning the 1903/04 league title under the management of a man with the unlikely name of Frank Heaven. By the start of the first world war in 1914 they had only failed to finish in the top ten on three occasions, and there had been a second Scottish Cup victory too, when Rangers were beaten 3–1 in the final of the 1904/05 competition.

The Hi-Hi, as they were also known, experienced relegation for the first time in 1924/25 and the period between the two world wars was a relatively unsuccessful one. By 1939 they had been relegated on a further two occasions, although there had also been two Division Two championships. In the Scottish Cup the highlight was an appearance in the 1935/36 final, although Rangers won 1–0.

In the 1950s there were four more seasons in the lower division but, after promotion in 1957, Thirds enjoyed eight consecutive seasons in Division One. There was an appearance in the 1959/60 League Cup final, which resulted in a 2–1 defeat to Hearts, and then they finished the 1960/61 season in third place, which was their highest finish since 1905. Alex Harley scored forty-two goals in the league, which was a club record, but the supporters' optimism for the future was soon to be cruelly dashed.

In 1964/65 Thirds finished bottom of Division One with just seven points from thirty-four games. There were two years in Division Two and then in 1967 the club's financial difficulties became so severe that they resigned from the Scottish League. There were allegations of asset stripping, coupled with speculation about plans to redevelop the ground, and even a Board of Trade enquiry, but Third Lanark FC had gone out of existence.

Since then the local authority has landscaped Cathkin Park and a commemorative design at the entrance provides a tribute to a once great club. The visitor can stand in silence and try to imagine the record crowd of 45,455 that watched the Hi-Hi play a Scottish Cup-tie against Rangers in 1954.

Third Lanark FC 1960/61.

THISTLE FC (former Scottish League club)

Home: **Braehead Park, near Richmond Park, Glasgow**
Best League Position: **20th (10th in Div. 2 1893/94)**
Best Scottish Cup Performance: **Last 10 (5th round 1880/81)**

Founded in 1875, Thistle's first experience of league football was in the Scottish Alliance, from 1891 to 1893. That league became Division Two of the Scottish League in 1893/94 and this resulted in the club becoming members of the Scottish League for just a single season. They went on to finish bottom, with just seven points from 18 games, and their results included a 13–1 defeat away to Partick Thistle. Crowds were low and their financial problems became so bad that they did not apply for re-election in 1894. Not long afterwards they went out of existence.

The club has nevertheless left its mark in the records of the Scottish Cup. Thistle regularly entered the competition from 1878 onwards and in 1886/87 they won their first and second-round matches 13–0 and 12–0, against Blairvaddick and St. Andrew's respectively. In 1890 a record crowd of 3000 saw them lose 5–3 in a first-round tie against neighbours Queen's Park.

THOMPSON Eddie (1940 –)

Eddie Thompson became chairman of Dundee United in 2002. Originally an accountant in Glasgow, his company was taken over by a Dundee firm in 1964 and he re-located to Tayside, where he soon became a United fan. After leaving his company to start a chain of convenience stores, he embarked on a lengthy campaign to acquire a controlling interest in the club in the late 1990s.

His efforts to purchase shares from Jim McLean (q.v.) attracted considerable interest from the media, but his determination eventually won through, and he gained a majority shareholding.

THOMSON Charlie (1878 – 1936)

Scotland Caps: 21
Scottish Cup medals: 2

Charlie Thomson was a centre half for Hearts and Sunderland in the years before the first world war. As was the custom in those days, he often played as a double centre forward, before settling down as a centre half. He won twenty-one caps for Scotland, and was considered one of Scotland's best-ever captains. With Hearts he won two Scottish Cup medals, and after his transfer to Sunderland in 1908 he won an English league championship medal.

His international career included Scotland's victories over England in 1910 and 1914.

5 September 1931: This is the moment of John Thomson's fatal collision with Sam English's knee.

THOMSON John (1909 – 1931)

Scotland Caps: 4
Scottish Cup medals: 2

John Thomson remains one of the most tragic figures in Scottish football history, and one of the very few who has ever died as a result of an accident on the field of play. He was born in Kirkcaldy, Fife, in January 1909, although his family lived in Cardenden at the time that he played professional football. He joined Celtic in late 1925 from Wellesley Juniors, and made his debut in February 1927 at Dens Park. He was very soon seen to be a brilliant goalkeeper, lithe, agile and courageous. He won two Scottish Cup medals with Celtic in 1927 and 1931, and was capped for Scotland four times. His death came after the Rangers versus Celtic game at Ibrox on 5 September 1931, as a result of a fracture of the skull, following an accidental collision with Sam English of Rangers. He died in Victoria Hospital, Glasgow that evening.

A young lad named John Thomson
From the Wellesley Fife he came
To play for Glasgow Celtic
And to give himself a name.
On the fifth day of September
Against the Rangers club he played
From defeat he saved the Celtic
Ah! But what a price he paid!

THORNTON Willie (1920 – 1991)

Scotland Caps: 7
Scottish League Championship medals: 4
Scottish Cup medals: 3
Scottish League Cup medals: 2

Willie Thornton was an outstanding centre forward for Rangers in the late 1940s and early 1950s. He had joined Rangers in 1936, but his career was interrupted by service in the second world war. During the war he won the Military Medal, for which he was cheered on his first post-war appearance – at Parkhead! He scored prolifically for Rangers but, sadly, Thornton often tended to disappoint while playing for Scotland. He scored only one goal for the national side and his only appearance against England was a 2–0 defeat at Hampden Park on 10 April 1948.

When he left Rangers in 1954 he went on to be manager of Dundee, Partick Thistle, and assistant manager of Rangers.

THROW-INS

A throw-in is used to restart play when it has been judged that the whole of the ball has passed over the touchline, either on the ground or in the air. Awarded to the opponents of the player who was the last to touch the ball, a throw-in must be taken from the point where the ball crossed the line and opponents must stand at least two metres away. A goal cannot be scored direct from a throw-in.

Some players have developed the 'long throw' into a means of exerting pressure on the opposing goalkeeper and creating a goal-scoring opportunity. David Hopkin did this twice for Scotland during the qualifying campaign for the 2000 European championship. Against the Czech Republic at Celtic Park his long throw resulted in a headed goal from Eoin Jess, and against Bosnia in Sarajevo he pressurised the goalkeeper into conceding a corner-kick from which Don Hutchison scored the opening goal.

Law fifteen of the rules of the game describes the procedure that must be followed and the sanctions that will be applied when it is not.

Failure to comply results in a 'foul throw' and will result in the throw-in being awarded to the opposition.

TICKETS

The first game in Scotland with tickets was the 1884 Scotland versus England international at the Second Hampden Park (Cathkin Park), where 10,000 tickets were sold, although there were also facilities to pay at the gate. For many years after that Scotland did not need all-ticket games, for the stadia were always considered big enough for the crowds. After the third Hampden Park was built in 1903, it was always vast enough to cope with whatever crowds decided to appear, even the six-figure crowds that regularly turned up for the Scotland versus England international, or Scottish Cup finals involving one or other of the Old Firm. Once or twice, notably at the 1906 and 1908 Scotland versus England internationals, the gates had to be closed before the start for fear of overcrowding, but all-ticket games were not considered necessary. Wembley was a different matter, for it had to have an all-ticket policy after the overcrowding at the 1923 FA Cup final, the first game at the new stadium.

At Hampden Park serious overcrowding at the 1935 international match (involving the gates having to be closed before the start and thousands being locked outside) compelled the SFA to issue tickets for the Scotland versus England game on 17 April 1937. Possibly the novelty of tickets, or simply an overwhelming desire to see the game at a time when football was clearly booming in Great Britain once the economic depression was over, meant that although 147,000 legitimate tickets were sold, 149,547 actually managed to get in through the turnstiles because of forged tickets and hundreds, possibly thousands, more climbed over the wall. The 149,547 crowd was a world record until 1950 and remains a record for any game in Europe, although the Scottish Cup final of the following week ran it close.

After the second world war clubs were reluctant, for financial reasons, to declare a game 'all ticket', thereby imperilling the safety of those who turned up, but the Scotland versus England international at Hampden Park was always all-ticket, as were the 1963, 1966 and 1969 Scottish Cup finals between Celtic and Rangers. Usually if Celtic or Rangers were drawn against a provincial team away from home in the Scottish Cup, these games were made all-ticket, and such tickets are now collectors' items for souvenir hunters. The arrival of European football also necessitated the use of tickets for those who wished to see Rangers versus Real Madrid in 1963 or Celtic versus AC Milan in 1969. All-ticket games were necessary too for Dundee's run in the European Cup in 1962/63, particularly the games in the quarter-final against Anderlecht and the semi-final against AC Milan, for Dens Park is a small ground for such big occasions. Newspapers would frequently carry photographs of queues snaking away into the distance for such tickets.

In the wake of the Ibrox disaster of 1971, the regulations about all-ticket games were toughened, and the creation of all-seater stadia in the 1980s was a step towards making every big game in these large stadia all-ticket, in that a ticket is bought for a specific seat, perhaps by virtue of a season ticket.

Every two years, when Scotland played at Wembley, there was an annual scramble for tickets to go to the game. Many were the complaints about such tickets going to people who would not normally go to watch Stenhousemuir versus Forfar on a wet November day, but who were quite prepared to don the kilt for a Wembley outing in April. Demand always exceeded supply. Clubs were given an allocation and they could dispose of them in any way that they thought fit. Even less defensibly, many tickets found their way to business companies whose contact with the game was negligible, but who could give out tickets to impress clients.

There thus grew a black market for tickets, with 'touts' asking, and getting, many times their face value. Amazingly, this activity was tolerated, even though several newspapers would run campaigns against it. A way of beating them often was to wait until 2.55 pm and watch the price drop until the tickets were virtually given away. This did not always work, however, for the public were often prepared to pay exorbitant sums of money to the vendors of tickets.

To a large extent, the arrival of television coverage of most, if not all, big games has meant that everyone who wishes to see a game will probably be able to do so, but this does not seem to lessen demand. Nor does it seem to lessen complaints of unfair treatment in favour of smaller teams, who may have an average home crowd of 6,000 but are nevertheless given 20,000 tickets for a cup final, whereas a team that attracts close to 60,000 for home games is perhaps given 25,000 for such occasions.

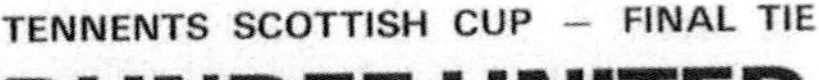

TENNENTS SCOTTISH CUP – FINAL TIE

DUNDEE UNITED

v.

MOTHERWELL

HAMPDEN PARK, GLASGOW

SATURDAY 18th MAY, 1991

Kick-off 3.00 p.m.

In the event of a draw after 90 minutes, extra time of 30 minutes will be played.
In the event of a draw after extra time, kicks from the Penalty Mark will decide the tie.

be in their position on the terracing not later than 30 minutes prior

FAMILY SECTION

ADULT Price £7·00

Turnstile M

NORTH ENCLOSURE UNCOVERED

ALID UNLESS PRESENTED IN FULL – SEE BACK FOR PLAN

TOURS

Tours are almost a thing of the past. The sheer length of the season, which now normally extends well into May, together with European and international commitments, means that there is little time for leisurely end-of-season visits abroad and the introduction of the game to others. Now, if there is any tour at all, it is often in the 'pre-season' in July with a few games played in the United States or Canada or Europe.

Queen's Park was the first Scottish club to tour. This was to Denmark in 1898, where they played two games against the Danish Boldspiel Union and won them both. The games were held in Copenhagen and formed part of a 'Carnival of Sports and Gymnastics'. Queen's Park took very seriously what they saw as their 'missionary commitment' to further the game abroad, having done so in Scotland itself. It is often said that the reason why rugby holds sway over football in the Borders (the only area in Scotland in which it does so) is because Queen's Park never toured there in the 1870s, whereas they toured every other part of Scotland. Thus, having evangelised most of Scotland, Queen's Park felt that it was their duty to travel elsewhere as well.

Celtic too were active in European tours in the years before and after the first world war, even visiting Germany in the early 1920s to the disapproval of certain elements of British society who were still wanting to 'Hang the Kaiser'. The 1920s were a great era for Scottish teams to tour abroad, feeling that they had to spread the gospel of Scottish football. Third Lanark even toured South America in 1923.

Raith Rovers went to Denmark in 1922 and then, en voyage for their trip to the Canary Islands in 1923, found themselves shipwrecked on June 30 as their ship the *Highland Loch* ran aground off the Spanish coast at a place called Villa Garcia. Mighty men like Alex James, Davie Morris and manager James Logan took to the lifeboats, perhaps thinking of recent maritime tragedies like the *Titanic* and the *Lusitania*, but everyone was safe, and the party continued on another vessel to the Canaries where the Kirkcaldy men won all their four scheduled matches.

Scotland's first overseas tour was in May/June 1929 to Norway, Germany and Holland, beating Norway 7–3, Holland 2–0 and drawing 1–1 with Germany. Even as late as 1929 there was a certain amount of eyebrow raising about the German leg of the tour and letters appeared in newspapers disapproving of 'fraternising with the Hun'. In 1930 there was a one-game tour to France, and subsequent tours to Europe in 1931, 1932, 1937 and 1938. After the second world war Scotland arranged several tours of the USA and Canada, playing friendlies and unofficial international matches.

In 1931 Celtic, taking the Scottish Cup with them, went to the USA and Canada, and have been there several times. The great Hibs team of the late 1940s and early 1950s always went on a summer tour. Rangers toured North America on several occasions. Interestingly, they took their players there in 1954, and their players were denied a chance to participate in Scotland's first World Cup finals, in Switzerland. Rangers were involved in one of the most famous tour matches by a visiting team when, the second world war having been won by the combined strengths of the eastern and western allies, Moscow Dynamo visited Ibrox in November 1945 as part of their three-match tour of Great Britain, having already played Arsenal and Chelsea. The game ended as a draw, but any effort to cement Soviet–Scottish relationships must have hit a serious obstacle, when Moscow Dynamo at one point tried to play with twelve men!

Seventeen years later, Rangers broke new ground by touring the Soviet Union. This tour did not necessarily meet with wholehearted approval from the British Foreign Office, for 1962 was the height of the cold war, with tension in Cuba, but the tour was an outstanding success as they played Lokomotiv Moscow, Dinamo

Dynamo Moscow goalkeeper Khomich punches clear from a Rangers attack at Ibrox in November 1945.

Tblisi and Dynamo Kiev, ending up with two victories and one draw. They were very popular wherever they went, and the tour was the time that John Greig emerged as a great player.

In late Victorian times 'the tour' meant the trip undertaken by the national side on the railway, the marvel of the era, to play England (normally in London) and then, on the Monday on the way back, calling in at Wrexham to play Wales as well. In 1875, 1881, 1883 and 1887 the Scotland team returned to a triumphal reception at Glasgow Central Station on the Tuesday, having defeated both nations and therefore able to claim with justice that they were the champions of Great Britain. Given that football was not really played elsewhere in the world in those days, it would be the closest that Scotland would come to winning the World Cup!

Scotland often had tours at the end of a season, playing about three games in Europe, and often getting a shock at how much the European nations had developed and indeed how tough were their tactics. In 1972 and 1977 Scotland broke new ground by making a successful tour of South America. In 2002 they visited the Far East on a tour that was good for finance but disastrous in playing terms.

Such is the ease of air travel now that the idea of 'tour' is probably an anachronism. They are expensive and very often the manager must exercise a great deal of control over his players. Players are not always the greatest ambassadors for their club or their country, for incidents can happen, eg in 1975 when Billy Bremner and others found themselves banned from playing for Scotland after an incident in a Copenhagen nightclub, and sometimes players abroad have formed cliques and conspiracies against the manager, or worse still, each other.

Celtic's Jan Vennegoor of Hesselink receives treatment to a nasty cut after clashing heads with Kilmarnock's Simon Ford in January 2008.

TRAINERS

The image of a trainer running on to the field to attend to an injured player with little more than a water bag and a bottle of smelling salts is a dated one. The man (or woman) who treats injured players is more likely to be called a 'physio' and will have at his/her disposal a whole panoply of sprays, bandages, splints, ointments, tablets etc in a fairly large suitcase or holdall. The actual 'training' of the team will be in the hands of a coach with an assistant or two, and there probably no longer is any such person as a trainer.

Yet in days gone by, the trainer, usually an ex-player, often had more direct control of the game than the manager, who was often an aloof figure sitting among the other Olympian figures in the stand, while the actual tactical decisions, if instructions like 'keep an eye on that big no 8' can be so called, were the province of the trainer. From the 1920s onwards, the trainer might have the luxury of a 'dug out'. The name comes from the first world war, for soldiers would dig a hole in the walls of their trenches so that they could sit or even sleep in lulls during the fighting. When Donald Colman, the trainer of Aberdeen, felt that he needed some shelter on the touchline in inclement weather, a hut was built and likened to the first world war 'dug out'. Often the trainer was a great character in the game like Matta Gemmell of Clyde who was offered a job as manager of another club and accepted it – if only he could have Saturday afternoon off to go and watch his beloved Clyde! Bill Struth, the legendary manager of Rangers, served his time by being trainer of Clyde before being appointed to the Ibrox managerial job in 1920. Celtic and Rangers had great trainers such as Celtic's Neil Mochan in the Jock Stein era, while Rangers were well served by Davie Kinnear for many years.

The trainer had to be a master of psychology, knowing when to encourage a player and when to take him down a peg or two. He had to be able to spot a serious injury, and tell a shirker a mile away. He had to keep spirits up, remain optimistic, have a ready supply of jokes, and be the life and soul of the party on the bus for away trips when some players were becoming nervous.

TRANSFERS

The less pleasant side of football is seen often in transfer deals, where the desire to make money on the part of players, clubs and agents can be more apparent than any love of the game. Behind the 'A dream come true' and 'The only team I ever wanted to play for' cant sometimes lies a great deal of dirty dealing, with the interest of true fans shamefully betrayed, and gold digging and pocket lining paramount.

Transfers do generate a great deal of interest from fans, and can often be life-savers for smaller clubs, but the often-repeated statement that a small team needs to sell to survive is only at best half true. In any case, the English market for Scottish players has dried up to a large extent in recent decades, and the selling of players to wealthy English clubs is, at best, a short-term way of making money. Dundee has suffered repeated and serious financial troubles, and to a large extent this was due to financial mismanagement by successive boards of directors, but many people believe that the root cause lay in the way their support was alienated in the 1960s. Dundee won the Scottish league championship in 1962 and reached the semi-final of the European Cup the following year. A fine performance from a fine side, but then Ian Ure, Alan Gilzean and Charlie Cooke were sold at a time when the emphasis should surely have been the retention of that winning team, if fans were to believe the statements about 'mounting and maintaining a challenge to the old firm'.

Dundee is far from being the only provincial club to asset-strip, although they are perhaps a particularly spectacular example. But the Old Firm have been guilty of the same thing. Celtic, for example, sold Kenny Dalglish to Liverpool in 1977 for £440,000 (a British record) at a time when they might have mounted another attempt on Europe. The blunder was compounded by the failure to replace Dalglish, and Celtic were never again a force in Europe for the rest of the twentieth century, and frequently struggled in Scotland.

Things have changed in two respects in the twenty-first century. In the first place the 'Bosman' ruling means that a player can negotiate his own terms after his contract comes to an end, so that a club really has to sell a player before that date to make any money off him, and the other is that Celtic, Rangers and Hearts have all had major investments of money, so that they are 'buying' rather than 'selling' clubs.

Rangers in November 2000 paid out £12 million for Tore Andre Flo (and not all Ibrox fans would agree that they got their money's worth), and Celtic have on at least two occasions paid over £6 million, on John Hartson and Chris Sutton, for example. Another feature of early twentieth-first century transfer dealings has been the prohibition of transfer activity from the end of August until the end of the season, other than the 'January window'. It is still possible to sign players on pre-contract agreements for the following season while they play out the rest of the season with their current club.

Inflation has meant that any attempt to talk about record transfers is fairly meaningless. It is a far cry from the days when Morton raked in £15,000 from the sale of Billy Steel to Derby County in 1947, and when Dundee amazed the world by finding £17,500 to bring him back to Scotland in 1950. It was a Scotsman, Denis Law who became the world's first-ever six-figure transfer when £100,000 changed hands for him as he went from Manchester City to Torino in June 1961. He did not last long there, for Torino sold him a year later to Manchester United, for £115,000.

A particular problem involves agents. Their remit is to ensure that the player gets the best possible deal in any transfer. The problem is that the agent himself will get a cut of what is agreed. Some agents are honest, but others are to be viewed with the gravest of suspicion, for they will 'only' get a cut if a transfer is agreed, and therefore may well persuade a gullible player that a transfer is necessary for the furtherance of his career.

Rangers spent £12m on Tore Andre Flo.

TRAVELLING

In a comparatively small country like Scotland, travelling to fixtures need not always be a huge problem, and only in extreme circumstances does it seriously affect anyone. In 1917, during the first world war, Dundee, Raith Rovers and Aberdeen were compelled to withdraw from the Scottish League because of the problems of travelling in war-time transport, but generally, Aberdeen and Inverness on the one hand, and Berwick and Stranraer on the other, are not, by the standards of most European countries, all that far away or inaccessible. (Occasionally, however, there are absurdities such as a fixture between Stranraer and Peterhead on a Wednesday night!) Normally teams hire their own bus and travel there and back on the day of a game. Sometimes an overnight stay before or after the game is called for, but normally in Scotland (a small country when compared to the likes of Russia) a day trip is all that is required.

Travelling for a European fixture is a different matter altogether, for UEFA insists that the away team is in the foreign country twenty-four hours in advance of the kick off. In any case, that is when they are allowed to practice on the pitch where the game will be played. Air travel is therefore necessary, and some players do not fly well. The late Jimmy Johnstone, for example, was so afraid of air travel after one unpleasant experience that he once persuaded Jock Stein to excuse him a trip to Red Star Belgrade if Celtic were far enough ahead after the first leg. Johnstone inspired Celtic to a 5–1 triumph at Parkhead and Johnstone ran off the field saying 'I'll no need tae go! I'll no need tae go!'

Yet it is often hard to explain, in this age of professionalism, how it is that teams play so much better at home than they do away from home. In addition, the experience of being abroad often leads to a bad result in Scotland the following Saturday or Sunday in the SPL, and it is clear that travelling, as far as Scottish football is concerned, is far from the glamorous thing that many people think it is. A trip to eastern Europe or Turkey, for example, can be a severe culture shock for Scottish-based players.

Celtic fans from the island of Barra in the Western Isles of Scotland prepare to board the bus to Seville for the UEFA Cup final in May 2003.

TREBLES

Trebles, meaning the capture of the Scottish League championship, the Scottish Cup and the Scottish League Cup in the same season, are fairly rare in Scottish football, and have only been possible since 1946/47 with the introduction of the Scottish League Cup. Only Rangers and Celtic have achieved this feat – Rangers on six occasions in 1949, 1964, 1976, 1978, 1993 and 2003, and Celtic on three occasions in 1967, 1969 and 2001. As Celtic's triumphs in 1967 also included the European Cup and the Glasgow Cup, thus meaning that they won every competition they entered, 1966/67 has a good claim to be the best season of any Scottish team, although Parkhead historians will point to 1908 and say that that side accomplished the same in that they won the Scottish League, the Scottish Cup, the Glasgow Cup and the Glasgow Charity Cup, the four competitions that they entered. Rangers can claim that they did the same in 1930 and 1934. Other than Celtic or Rangers, the closest that any team has come to a treble was Aberdeen in 1984, when they won the Scottish League and the Scottish Cup, but not the Scottish League Cup.

TRINIDAD and TOBAGO

Not famous for being footballing islands, Trinidad and Tobago have nevertheless played Scotland once.

2004	30 May	Easter Road	4–1	Fletcher Holt G. Caldwell Quashie	John

TROPHIES

Every team's supporters love to see trophies, bedecked in the team colours, being lifted by the victorious captain to the adoring cheers of the support. It can be guaranteed that a club's boardroom will have a picture of its best ever team with a piece of silverware. Scotland possesses the oldest trophy in continuous existence in the world. This is the Scottish Cup, first competed for in 1874. The English FA Cup tournament is a couple of years older, but there have been three actual trophies. The Scottish Cup is presented to the winning captain every year, but then kept in the Hampden Museum, while the winning team is given an exact replica to retain for the next year. The SPL trophy, the various SFL trophies, and the Scottish League Cup are all lovely pieces of silver as well, but the Glasgow Cup and the Glasgow Charity Cup (sadly no longer played for) are possibly better examples of Victorian craftsmanship. On the other hand, the Champions League trophy, for all the passion and money that is generates, is not generally considered to be a particularly handsome piece.

Alec Troup, when with Everton.

TROUP Alec (1895 – 1952)

Scotland Caps: 5

A diminutive, but tricky, left winger for Forfar Athletic, Dundee, Everton and Dundee again in the years from 1914 to 1933, Alec Troup earned five caps for Scotland, being on the winning side in 1926 against England. He also won an English league championship medal with Everton in 1928, and famously took the corner kick for legendary centre forward Dixie Dean to reach the record of scoring the most goals per season in the very last minute of the season's last game.

TULLY Charlie (1924 – 1971)

Scottish League Championship medals: 1
Scottish Cup medals: 2
Scottish League Cup medals: 2

Charlie Tully was an Irishman who played for Celtic between the years of 1948 and 1958. Famous as a wit, crowd pleaser and personality player, he was one of the real characters of Scottish football of his time, yet he was never a great 'team' man, and was frequently accused of selfishness. His most famous moment was when he took a corner kick at Falkirk, scored direct, had the goal disallowed because the ball was not in the arc, took the corner again, and scored direct again!

TURKEY

Scotland visited Turkey once, and lost.

1960	8 June	Ankara	2–4	Caldow pen Young	Lefter (2) Metin Senol

TURNBULL Eddie (1923 –   )

Scotland Caps: 9
Scottish League Championship medals: 3

The inside left of Hibernian's 'famous five' forward line, Eddie Turnbull served in the Royal Navy on the Murmansk convoys in the second world war. With Hibs, Eddie won the Scottish League championship three times, and has the honour of being the first British player to score a goal in European competition when, on 14 September 1955, he scored against Rot Weiss Essen.

He is also one of the few players to have scored a hat trick of penalties, a feat he achieved against Celtic at Easter Road on 4 February 1950. He played nine times for Scotland, earning a surprise recall for the 1958 World Cup finals in Sweden, years after it had seemed that his Scotland days were over.

He retired from playing in 1959, and became the trainer with Hibs, then coach with Queen's Park in 1963, before being appointed manager of Aberdeen in 1965. He had an impressive six years with the Dons, guiding them to the Scottish Cup in 1970, but not managing to break down entirely the stranglehold of Jock Stein's Celtic.

Hibs appointed him as their manager in 1971, a post he occupied until 1980, bringing on a fine team of players but with no sustained trophy success other than the Scottish League Cup of December 1972 and some success in the pre-season Dryburgh Cup. Eddie Turnbull was one of the players who had played for Scotland but was never 'capped', on the grounds that his international games were not against any of the home countries. For a long time people protested against this injustice, and the SFA remedied the situation on 1 March 2006 when Eddie was chosen as the token player to be presented with a cap at half time in the Scotland versus Switzerland international.

UEFA CUP

This name given to the tournament that was previously known as the Inter-Cities Fairs Cup when it was re-branded in 1971 and the link to trade fairs was dropped. Four years later the 'one club per city' rule was also dropped. Qualification is based on a club's league position at the end of the previous season, with some countries being allocated more places than others according to their ranking. It is often regarded as the 'consolation' trophy for clubs that have not managed to reach the Champions League.

Following the demise of the European Cup-Winners' Cup in 1999, a place was also provided for the winners of the Scottish Cup. Since 1996/97 there has been a 'parachute' for clubs that have been eliminated from the Champions League after finishing the group stages in third place. Places can also be earned via the Intertoto Cup and the UEFA fair play rankings.

The final was changed to a single game at a neutral venue in 1998 and in 2004/05 the format was changed so that clubs progress to a group stage after the first round. Scotland has had its moments in this tournament, although no Scottish team has ever won it. The closest have been Dundee United, Celtic and Rangers, who reached the final in 1987, 2003 and 2008 respectively.

The results of Scottish clubs are as follows:

Season	Scottish Club	Opposition	Agg.	Round
1971/72	Aberdeen	Celta Vigo	3–0	First
		Juventus	1–3	Second
	Dundee	Akademisk	5–2	First
		Cologne	5–4	Second
		AC Milan	2–3	Third
	St Johnstone	SV Hamburg	4–2	First
		Vasas Budapest	2–1	Second
		Zeljeznicar	2–5	Third
1972/73	Aberdeen	Borussia M'gladbach	5–9	First
	Partick Thistle	Honved	0–4	First
1973/74	Aberdeen	Finn Harps	7–2	First
		Tottenham Hotspur	2–5	Second
	Dundee	Twente Enschede	3–7	First
	Hibernian	Keflavik	3–1	First
		Leeds United	0–0	Second
		Leeds United won 5–4 on penalties		
1974/75	Dundee	RWD Molenbeek	2–5	First
	Hibernian	Rosenborg	12–3	First
		Juventus	2–8	Second
1975/76	Dundee United	Keflavik	6–0	First
		Porto	2–3	Second
	Hibernian	Liverpool	2–3	First
1976/77	Celtic	Wisla Krakow	2–4	First
	Hibernian	Sochaux	1–0	First
		Osters Vaxjo	3–4	Second
1977/78	Aberdeen	RWD Molenbeek	1–2	First
	Dundee United	KB Copenhagen	1–3	First
1978/79	Dundee United	Standard Liege	0–1	First
	Hibernian	Norrkoping	3–2	First
		Strasbourg	1–2	Second
1979/80	Aberdeen	Eintracht Frankfurt	1–2	First
	Dundee United	Anderlecht	1–1	First
		Dundee United won on away goals		
		Diosgyor	1–4	Second
1980/81	Dundee United	Slask Wroclaw	7–2	First
		Lokeren	1–1	Second
		Lokeren won on away goals		
	St Mirren	Elfsborg	2–1	First
		St Etienne	0–2	Second
1981/82	Aberdeen	Ipswich Town	4–2	First
		Arges Pitesti	5–2	Second
		SV Hamburg	4–5	Third
	Dundee United	Monaco	6–4	First
		Borussia M'gladbach	5–2	Second
		Winterslag	5–0	Third
		Radnicki Nis	2–3	Quart-final
1982/83	Dundee United	PSV Eindhoven	3–1	First
		Viking Stavanger	3–1	Second
		Werder Bremen	3–2	Third
		Bohemians	0–1	Quart-final
	Rangers	Borussia Dortmund	2–0	First
		FC Cologne	2–6	Second
1983/84	Celtic	Aarhus	5–1	First
		Sporting Lisbon	5–2	Second
		Nottingham Forest	1–2	Third
	St Mirren	Feyenoord	0–3	First
1984/85	Dundee United	AIK Stockholm	3–1	First
		ASK Linz	7–2	Second
		Manchester United	4–5	Third
	Hearts	Paris St Germain	2–6	First
	Rangers	Bohemians	4–3	First
		Inter Milan	3–4	Second
1985/86	Dundee United	Bohemians	7–4	First
		Vardar Skopje	3–1	Second
		Neuchatel Xamax	3–4	Third
	Rangers	Osasuna	1–2	First
	St Mirren	Slavia Prague	3–1	First
		Hammarby	4–5	Second
1986/87	Dundee United	Lens	2–1	First
		Universitaria Craiova	3–1	Second
		Hadjuk Split	2–0	Third
		Barcelona	3–1	Quart-final
		Borussia M'gladbach	2–0	Semi-final
		IFK Gothenburg	1–2	Final
	Hearts	Dukla Prague	3–3	First
		Dukla Prague won on away goals		
	Rangers	Ilves	4–2	First
		Boavista	3–1	Second
		Borussia M'gladbach	1–1	Third
		Borussia Monchengladbach won on away goals		
1987/88	Aberdeen	Bohemians	1–0	First
		Feyenoord	2–2	Second
		Feyenoord won on away goals		
	Celtic	Borussia Dortmund	2–3	First
	Dundee United	Coleraine	4–1	First
		Vitkovice	2–3	Second
1988/89	Aberdeen	Dinamo Dresden	0–2	First
	Hearts	St Patrick's Athletic	4–0	First
		FK Austria	1–0	Second
		Velez Mostar	4–2	Third
		Bayern Munich	1–2	Quart-final
	Rangers	Katowice	5–2	First
		FC Cologne	1–3	Second
1989/90	Aberdeen	Rapid Vienna	2–2	First
		Rapid Vienna won on away goals		

The Dundee United team at the first leg of the UEFA Cup final at IFK Gothenburg's Ullevi stadium on 6 May 1987.

Rangers' Nacho Novo celebrates the winning penalty against Fiorentina in the UEFA Cup semi-final to send his team through to the 2008 final.

	Dundee United	Glentoran	5–1	First
		Antwerp	3–6	Second
	Hibernian	Videoton	4–0	First
		FC Liege	0–1	Second
1990/91	Dundee United	FH Hafnafjordur	5–3	First
		Arnhem	1–4	Second
	Hearts	Dnepr	4–2	First
		Bologna	3–4	Second
1991/92	Aberdeen	BK Copenhagen	0–3	First
	Celtic	Germinal Ekeren	3–1	First
		Neuchatel Xamax	2–5	Second
1992/93	Celtic	FC Cologne	3–2	First
		Borussia Dortmund	1–3	Second
	Hearts	Slavia Prague	4–3	First
		Standard Liege	0–2	Second
	Hibernian	Anderlecht	3–3	First
		Anderlecht won on away goals		
1993/94	Celtic	Young Boys	1–0	First
		Sporting Lisbon	1–2	Second
	Dundee United	Brondby	3–3	First
		Brondby won on away goals		
	Hearts	Atletico Madrid	2–4	First
1994/95	Aberdeen	Skonto Riga	1–1	Prelim.
		Skonto Riga won on away goals		
	Motherwell	Hanvar	7–1	Prelim.
		Borussia Dortmund	0–3	First
1995/96	Motherwell	My-Pa 47	3–3	Prelim.
		My-Pa 47 won on away goals		
	Raith Rovers	Gotu	6–4	Prelim.
		Akranes	3–2	First
		Bayern Munich	1–4	Second
1996/97	Aberdeen	FK Zalgiris	5–4	Qualifying
		Barry Town	6–4	First
		Brondby	0–2	Second
	Celtic	Kosice	1–0	Qualifying
		Hamburg	0–4	First
1997/98	Celtic	Inter Cable Tel	8–0	1st Qual.
		FC Tirol Innsbruck	7–5	2nd Qual.
		Liverpool	2–2	First
		Liverpool won on away goals		
	Dundee United	CE Principat	17–0	1st Qual.
		Trabzonspor	1–2	2nd Qual.
	Rangers	Strasbourg	2–4	First
1998/99	Celtic	Vitoria Guimares	4–2	First
		FC Zurich	3–5	Second
	Kilmarnock	Zeljeznicar	2–1	1st Qual.
		Sigma Olomouc	0–4	2nd Qual.
	Rangers	Shelbourne	7–3	1st Qual.
		PAOK Salonika	2–0	2nd Qual.
		Beitar	5–3	First
		Bayer Leverkusen	3–2	Second
		Parma	2–4	Third
1999/00	Celtic	Cwmbran Town	10–0	Qualifying
		Hapoel Tel Aviv	3–0	First
		Lyon	0–2	Second
	Kilmarnock	KR Reykjavik	2–1	Qualifying
		Kaiserslautern	0–5	First
	Rangers	Borussia Dortmund	2–2	Third
		Borussia Dortmund won 3–1 on penalties		
	St Johnstone	VPS Vaasa	3–1	Qualifying
		Monaco	3–6	First
2000/01	Aberdeen	Bohemians	2–2	Qualifying
		Bohemians won on away goals		
	Celtic	Jeunesse Esch	11–0	Qualifying
		HJK Helsinki	3–2	First
		Bordeaux	2–3aet	Second
	Hearts	IBV	5–0	Qualifying
		VFB Stuttgart	3–3	First
		Stuttgart won on away goals		
	Rangers	Kaiserslautern	1–3	Third
2001/02	Celtic	Valencia	1–1aet	Third
		Valencia won 5–4 on penalties		
	Hibernian	AEK Athens	3–4aet	First
	Kilmarnock	Glenavon	2–0	Qualifying
		Viking Stavanger	1–3	First
	Rangers	Anzhi	1–0	First
		Moscow Dynamo	7–2	Second
		Paris St Germain	0–0aet	Third
		Rangers won 4–3 on penalties		
		Feyenoord	3–4	Fourth
2002/03	Aberdeen	Nistru Otaci	1–0	Qualifying
		Hertha Berlin	0–1	First
	Celtic	FK Suduva	10–1	First
		Blackburn Rovers	3–0	Second
		Celta Vigo	3–1	Third
		VFB Stuttgart	5–4	Fourth
		Liverpool	3–1	Quart-final
		Boavista	2–1	Semi-final
		Porto	2–3aet	Final
	Livingston	Vaduz	1–1	Qualifying
		Livingston won on away goals		
		Sturm Graz	6–8	First
	Rangers	Viktoria Zizkov	3–3aet	First
		Viktoria Zizkov won on away goals		
2003/04	Celtic	Teplice	3–1	Third
		Barcelona	1–0	Fourth
		Villarreal	1–3	Quart-final
	Dundee	Vllaznia Shkoder	6–0	Qualifying
		Perugia	1–3	First
	Hearts	Zeljeznicar	2–0	First
		Bordeaux	1–2	Second
2004/05	Dunfermline	FH Hafnarfjordur	3–4	2nd Qual.
	Hearts	Sporting Braga	5–3	First
		Feyenoord (A)	0–3	Grp. Stage
		Schalke 04 (H)	0–1	
		FC Basel (A)	2–1	
		Ferencvaros (H)	0–1	
	Rangers	Maritimo	1–1aet	First
		Rangers won 4–2 on penalties		
		Amica Wronki (A)	5–0	Grp.Stage
		Graf AZ (H)	3–0	
		AZ Alkmaar (A)	0–1	
		Auxerre (H)	0–2	
2005/06	Dundee United	My-Pa 47	2–2	2nd Qual.
		My-Pa 47 won on away goals		
	Hibernian	Dnipro	1–5	First
2006/07	Gretna	Derry City	3–7	2nd Qual.
	Rangers	Molde	2–0	First
		Livorno (A)	3–2	Grp. Stage
		Maccabi Haifa (H)	2–0	
		Auxerre (A)	2–2	
		Partizan Belgrade (H)	1–0	

		Hapoel Tel Aviv	5–2	Rd of 32
		Osasuna	1–2	Rd of 16
2007/08	Aberdeen	Dnipro	1–1	First
		Aberdeen won on away goals		
		Panathinaikos (A)	0–3	Grp. Stage
		Loko'tiv Moscow (H)	1–1	
		Atletico Madrid (A)	0–2	
		FC Copenhagen (H)	4–0	
		Bayern Munich	3–7	Rd of 32
	Dunfermline	BK Hacken	1–2	2nd Qual.
	Rangers	Panathinaikos	1–1	Rd of 32
		Rangers won on away goals		
		Werder Brenan	2–1	Rd of 16
		Sporting Lisbon	2–0	Quart-final
		Fiorentina	0–0aet	Semi-final
		Rangers won 4-2 on penalties		
		Zenit St. Petersburg	0–2	Final

The following table summarises the progress of Scottish clubs by showing which round/stage they reached each year:

1971/72	Aberdeen	2nd	Dundee	3rd	St. Johnstone	3rd		
1972/73	Aberdeen	1st	Partick Thstl.	1st				
1973/74	Dundee	1st	Aberdeen	2nd	Hibernian	2nd		
1974/75	Dundee	1st	Hibernian	2nd				
1975/76	Hibernian	1st	Dundee Utd.	2nd				
1976/77	Celtic	1st	Hibernian	2nd				
1977/78	Aberdeen	1st	Dundee Utd.	1st				
1978/79	Dundee Utd.	1st	Hibernian	2nd				
1979/80	Aberdeen	1st	Dundee Utd.	2nd				
1980/81	Dundee Utd.	2nd	St. Mirren	2nd				
1981/82	Aberdeen	3rd	Dundee Utd	QF				
1982/83	Rangers	2nd	Dundee Utd.	QF				
1983/84	St. Mirren	1st	Celtic	3rd				
1984/85	Hearts	1st	Rangers	2nd	Dundee Utd.	3rd		
1985/86	Rangers	1st	St. Mirren	2nd	Dundee Utd.	3rd		
1986/87	Hearts	1st	Rangers	3rd	Dundee Utd.	RU		
1987/88	Celtic	1st	Aberdeen	2nd	Dundee Utd.	2nd		
1988/89	Aberdeen	1st	Rangers	1st	Hearts	QF		
1989/90	Aberdeen	1st	Hibernian	2nd				
1990/91	Dundee Utd.	2nd	Hearts	2nd				
1991/92	Aberdeen	1st	Celtic	2nd				
1992/93	Hibernian	1st	Celtic	2nd	Hearts	2nd		
1993/94	Dundee Utd.	1st	Hearts	1st	Celtic	2nd		
1994/95	Aberdeen	1st	Motherwell	1st				
1995/96	Motherwell	PR	Raith Rovers	2nd				
1996/97	Celtic	1st	Aberdeen	2nd				
1997/98	Dundee Utd.	2QR	Celtic	1st	*Rangers	1st		
1998/99	Kilmarnock	2QR	*Celtic	2nd	Rangers	3rd		
1999/00	Kilmarnock	1st	St. Johnstone	1st	Celtic	2nd	*Rangers	3rd
2000/01	Aberdeen	QR	Hearts	1st	Celtic	2nd	*Rangers	3rd
2001/02	Hibernian	1st	Kilmarnock	1st	*Celtic	3rd	Rangers	4th
2002/03	Aberdeen	1st	Livingston	1st	Rangers	1st	*Celtic	RU
2003/04	Dundee	1st	Hearts	2nd	*Celtic	QF		
2004/05	Dunf'mline	2QR	Hearts	GS	*Rangers	GS		
2005/06	Dundee Utd.	2QR	Hibernian	1st				
2006/07	Gretna	2QR	*Hearts	1st	Rangers	16		
2007/08	Dunf'mline	2QR	Aberdeen	32	*Rangers	RU		

*Denotes qualified via European Champions League

PR-Preliminary round; QR-Qualifying round; GS-Group stage; 32-Round of 32; 16-Round of 16; QF-Quarter-final; RU-Runners-up. The terms 'Round of 32' and 'Round of 16' were introduced for season 2004/05.

UKRAINE

Scotland have played twice against this country in the qualification section for Euro 2008, with home advantage telling on both occasions.

2006	11 Oct	Kiev	0–2		Kucher Shevchenko (pen)
2007	13 Oct	Hampden Park	3–1	Miller McCulloch McFadden	Shevchenko

UNDEFEATED

Celtic hold the record, for going sixty-two games undefeated. This was in the somewhat unreal circumstances of the first world war. They lost 0–2 to Hearts at Tynecastle on 13 November 1915, and not again until 21 April 1917 when they lost 0–2 to Kilmarnock at Parkhead. The Scottish Cup was not competed for in wartime, but in that sequence they won the Scottish League of 1915/16, the Scottish League of 1916/17, the Glasgow Charity Cup of 1915/16, and the Glasgow Cup of 1916/17. Two teams have completed a league season undefeated – Celtic in 1897/98, and Rangers the following year 1898/99, but only eighteen league games were played in the 1890s. Rangers in fact had a 100% league record in 1898/99, but lost to Celtic in the Scottish Cup final that year.

Celtic in season 2003/04 almost went through a season in the Scottish Premier League undefeated. They drew at Dunfermline on the first day of the season, then went twenty-five games without dropping a point, before losing twice in the latter part of the season, after the league had been won, to Aberdeen and Dunfermline. Morton went through the 1963/64 season in Division Two of the Scottish League with only one defeat – to East Fife at Bayview on 1 February.

UNDER-17

In 2008 Scotland qualified for the finals of the UEFA Under 17 championships for the first time, under the leadership of coach Ross Mathie. They were the only country to win all their games in the second qualifying stage, known as the 'Elite Round', but the team lost their games against Serbia, Turkey and the Netherlands at the final tournament in Turkey.

UNDER-19

Scotland has enjoyed success in the UEFA Under-19 championship and its predecessor the Under 18 championship. In 1982 a team managed by Andy Roxburgh and Walter Smith won the Under-18 tournament with a 3–1 victory over Czechoslovakia in the final, and Scotland reached the semi-finals in both 1978 and 1986.

In 2006 a team coached by Archie Gemmill and Tommy Wilson finished as runners-up to Spain, losing 2–1. Earlier they had beaten Turkey, drawn with Portugal, and lost to Spain in the group stage, before defeating the Czech Republic in the semi-final. This earned a place at the 2007 FIFA Under-20 World Cup, formerly known as the World Youth Championships, held in June/July 2007 in Canada, but Scotland failed to qualify after losing their matches against Japan, Nigeria and Costa Rica.

A team coached by Archie Knox and captained by Greg Cameron of Dundee United topped their qualifying group and went on to be group hosts in the Elite Round of the 2007 tournament, but were eliminated in a group that also included Turkey, Georgia and Portugal.

UNDER-21

Since 1976 there has been an Under-21 World Cup and European Championship, but Scotland have seldom done well. The poor performances of the Under-21 team were not always taken seriously enough by the authorities or by the public, and the result has been poor performances by the seniors as well. Normally such games are played against the same opposition as the full international team and normally a day earlier to facilitate travelling. Only once have Scotland qualified from the group stage of the European Championships. This was in 1992, when they won a strong group of Bulgaria, Romania and Switzerland (losing only once, in Bulgaria), then they beat Germany 5–4 on aggregate in the quarter final before going down to Sweden 0–1 on aggregate in the semi final. In January 2008 Billy Stark was appointed manager of the Scotland Under-21 side.

UNDER-23

Between 1955 and 1976, when Under-21 became the key age group, Under-23 internationals were played against England (on virtually an annual basis), Wales (less often), and sporadically against the British Army, Belgium, Denmark, France, Holland, Sweden and Rumania. They were considered to be a good stepping-stone to the other international sides – Scottish League, Scotland 'B' and Scotland itself.

	P	W	D	L	Aban'dn
Belgium	1	0	1	0	0
British Army	1	1	0	0	0
Denmark	1	1	0	0	0
England	17	2	5	9	1
France	2	1	1	0	0
Holland	4	3	0	1	0
Romania	2	2	0	0	0
Sweden	1	1	0	0	0
Wales	11	6	2	3	0

Attendances and interest declined over the twenty-one years, but the last Under-23 international, which Scotland won 2–0 over Holland at Easter Road on 24 March 1976, attracted a crowd of 32,593. This game was the quarter-final of the European Championship and sadly Scotland's 2–0 win only equalled the 0–2 scoreline in Holland, and Scotland subsequently lost on penalties.

URE Ian (1939 –)

Scotland Caps: 11
Scottish League Championship medals: 1

The centre half and mainstay of the Dundee side that won the Scottish League in 1962, Ian Ure was a tall, blonde, commanding centre half who won eleven caps for Scotland, and might have won more if Scotland had not been so rich in centre halves at that time (with Billy McNeill of Celtic and Ron McKinnon of Rangers also being around). He was born in Ayr and attended Ayr Academy at the same time as Mike Denness the cricketer and Moira Anderson the singer. Ian did not play football until the age of eighteen, for Ayr Academy played rugby.

He joined Dundee in 1958 and very soon became a favourite with their fans, earning the nickname 'Yogi' after the cartoon character Yogi Bear, a nickname he shared with John Hughes of Celtic. Following Dundee's successful run to the semi-final of the European Cup in 1963, he was transferred to Arsenal for £62,500 in August of that year – a decision that was disastrous for Dundee in the context of their long-term decline. With Arsenal he reached the final of the English League Cup twice, but never won any medals. He moved to Manchester United in 1969, and then returned to Scotland to play for St Mirren in 1972. In later years he was manager of East Stirlingshire.

URUGUAY

Uruguay delivered one of the biggest shocks of all time to the Scottish system with their 7–0 victory in the 1954 World Cup in Switzerland. In a subsequent World Cup (1986) they produced a shock of a different kind with their cynical approach to the game. Played four, won one, drawn one and lost two.

1954	19 June	Basle	0–7		Borges (3) Miguez (2) Abbadie (2)
1962	2 May	Hampden Park	2–3	Baxter Brand	Cubilla (2) Sacia
1983	21 Sep	Hampden Park	2–0	Robertson (pen) Dodds	
1986	13 June	Nezahualcoyotl	0–0		

USA

Comparative newcomers to the football scene (although they famously beat England in the World Cup of 1950), the USA are now respected opponents. Played five, won two, drawn two, and lost one.

1952	30 Apr	Hampden Park	6–0	Reilly (3) McMillan (2) O' Connell o.g.	
1992	17 May	Denver	1–0	Nevin	
1996	26 May	New Britain	1–2	Durie	Wynalda (pen) Jones
1998	30 May	Washington	0–0		
2005	11 Nov	Hampden Park	1–1	Webster	Wolff (pen)

USSR

Scotland never beat the USSR in the four times that they met, and now they will never have an opportunity to do so, as the USSR is no more. The best result was a draw in Malaga, which effectively put Scotland out of the 1982 World Cup in Spain. Scotland did beat a team called the Commonwealth of Independent States in the European Championships in Sweden in 1992. This team was effectively the USSR, but for political reasons could no longer be so called. Played four, drawn one, and lost three.

1967	10 May	Hampden Park	0–2		Gemmell o.g. Medved
1971	14 June	Moscow	0–1		Yevryuzhikhin
1982	22 June	Malaga	2–2	Jordan Souness	Chivadze Shengalia
1991	6 Feb	Ibrox	0–1		Kuznetsov

VALE OF LEVEN FC (former Scottish League club)

Home: **Millburn Park, Alexandria, Dunbartonshire**
Highest League Position: **9th (1890/91)**
Best Scottish Cup Performance: **Winners (1876/77; 1877/78; 1878/79)**

The Vale of Leven club was formed in 1872, at a time when Association football was in its infancy, and exhibition matches against Queens Park helped to popularise the game in Alexandria and the surrounding area. A founder member of the Scottish FA, the club played its first Scottish Cup tie in 1875/76 and embarked on a cup run that ended in a semi-final defeat against Queens Park.

This early success was soon surpassed and by 1879 the trophy had been won in three consecutive years, although the 1879 final produced a 1–1 draw against Rangers. When the Glasgow team didn't appear for the replay, as a protest against a disallowed goal, the cup was awarded to Vale of Leven. By 1890 the club had followed up these wins by becoming runners-up on four occasions and in 1884 it was Vale's turn to fail to appear. Several players were unavailable, the SFA would not agree to a postponement, and the cup was awarded to Queens Park.

The newly built Millburn Park was opened in 1888, and the previous ground at North Street was vacated to make way for a foundry. When Vale became founder members of the Scottish League in 1890 they had been losing their best players to top clubs in both Scotland and England for years and the standard of their football had declined. In their first season they finished second bottom and in 1892 they were the bottom club with no wins from twenty-two games. After just two seasons they decided to resign. The crowds soon dwindled, financial problems mounted, and it wasn't long before Vale of Leven FC was virtually defunct.

However, a small group of men was determined that this famous club shouldn't die and in 1896 they set about the long process of returning it to the Scottish League. It took them nine years and when the Scottish League was expanded in 1905 the club was elected into Division Two. Over the subsequent years they were never promoted and they finished at the bottom of the league in both 1910/11 and 1914/15. When Division Two was suspended in 1915, Vale joined a re-formed Western League and won the title in 1915/16.

Division Two was eventually brought back in 1921 and there was a place for Vale of Leven. However, after just three seasons, Vale were voted into Division Three, even though they had only finished fifth bottom. Then, when Division Three was abandoned in 1926, their time in the Scottish League also came to an end. There were seasons in each of the Scottish Alliance and the Scottish Provincial League, but by 1928 the club was no longer playing in recognised football. Eleven years later there was a brief attempt to resurrect senior football, but soon afterwards the club switched to the junior code and it has remained there until the present day. (see **JUNIOR FOOTBALL**)

VENTERS Alex (1913 – 1959)

Scotland Caps: 3
Scottish League Championship medals: 4
Scottish Cup medals: 2

One of Rangers' best-ever players, Alex Venters was an inside right, and many people believe he deserved more than just three caps for Scotland. He started off his senior career playing for Cowdenbeath, but was transferred to Rangers in November 1933. With the Ibrox men he impressed everyone with his skills, stamina and hard work. The second world war badly disrupted his career, but after the war he played for Third Lanark, Blackburn Rovers and Raith Rovers.

VICTORY CUP

A Victory Cup has been contested on two occasions. In 1919 and 1946, although the respective wars were over, the seasons were still considered unofficial and there was no Scottish Cup. A Victory Cup was contested to take the place of the Scottish Cup in both years. St Mirren won the 1919 Victory Cup, beating Hearts 3–0 after extra time on 26 April 1919 at Hampden Park, but because of war shortages no cup was available for presentation. An old shield had to be presented to the Buddies until such time as a proper cup could be commissioned! Less embarrassing for the authorities was the trophy presented to Rangers after they had beaten Hibs 3–1 in the Victory Cup final at Hampden on 15 June 1946. They used the Southern League Cup, which Aberdeen had won a couple of months previously. Rangers were allowed to keep this trophy, but the Southern League Cup tournament was re-launched in the first official season of 1946/47 as the Scottish League Cup.

VICTORY INTERNATIONALS

These games are not officially recognised. This seems strange to many people, because the 1919 Victory Internationals were played over several months after the armistice of November 1918, and the 1946 Victory Internationals continued until almost a year after the end of hostilities. On 26 April 1919 the game at Goodison Park was a thrilling 2–2 draw between England and Scotland, and on 3 May 1919 over 80,000 people were at Hampden Park (in spite of transport problems) to see one of the best games between Scotland and England. Scotland were 3–0 down at half-time, pulled two goals back through Andy Wilson and Alan Morton and then, after England scored a fourth, Andy Wilson scored a third to set up a great finale.

A six-figure crowd was at Hampden Park (and millions more listened on the radio throughout the world) to see the 1946 Victory International against England, in which Jimmy Delaney scored a late winner to bring some cheer to a football-starved nation. As the games were contested between the best available players for both England and Scotland, there seems no reason for their continued exclusion from the official list.

22 Mar 1919	Scotland	2	1	Ireland	Ibrox
5 Apr 1919	Scottish League	3	2	English League	Ibrox
19 Apr 1919	Ireland	0	0	Scotland	Belfast
26 Apr 1919	England	2	2	Scotland	Goodison Park
3 May 1919	Scotland	3	4	England	Hampden Park
10 Nov 1945	Scotland	2	0	Wales	Hampden Park
23 Jan 1946	Scotland	2	2	Belgium	Hampden Park
2 Feb 1946	Ireland	2	3	Scotland	Belfast
13 Apr 1946	Scotland	1	0	England	Hampden Park
15 May 1946	Scotland	2	1	Switzerland	Hampden Park

VIOLENCE

Violence amongst Scottish football fans has historically been part of the scene, and has been so from the start. It is true to say, however, that crowd behaviour ebbs and flows and, for several years now, there have been comparatively few serious incidents. The troughs were in the aftermath of both wars, when aggressive young men had perhaps learned a little too well in the brutalising atmosphere of army barracks, and in the period from the 1950s until the 1970s, when some young men could not cope with the comparative freedom and prosperity that the affluent society had bestowed on them. From the 1980s onwards, however, all-seater stadia and the banning of alcohol from football grounds made a considerable difference to football matches in Scotland. It is not necessarily true elsewhere in the world.

An unfortunate setback to Scotland's image occurred, however, in May 2008 at the UEFA Cup final between Rangers and Zenit St. Petersburg in Manchester. The game itself passed peacefully enough, but at one of the centres where the game was to be shown on large-screen television, a combination of alcohol, the technical failure of the television system, and an unfavourable result led to some shocking scenes as Rangers fans went berserk. TV viewers were treated, for example, to scenes of a policeman being set upon and kicked by a gang of about a dozen youths. Most Rangers fans were, of course, embarrassed and upset by this minority, but the damage done to their and Scotland's credibility was considerable.

Psychologists and sociologists wax eloquent about 'housing schemes', 'alienation from mainstream life', the 'culture of under-achievement', 'group frustration of a delinquescent sub-culture', and whatever happen to be the buzz-words of the moment. The failure of the Scottish educational system to solve its problems of violence and indiscipline must be borne in mind as well, and many people are tired of politicians who promise to be tough on crime and disorder, but lack the political will to do so when they are in office. But Scottish football does in itself throw up a few components. The Celtic versus Rangers sectarian issue cannot really be ignored, especially when it spreads to Edinburgh and Dundee. Most teams, however, do attract an unpleasant element. For example, there was a time in the 1980s when Aberdeen attracted the 'Aberdeen Casuals', whose interest in football was limited, and some say their intelligence was too.

The Scotland national team can claim to have a civilized support. The 'Tartan Army', as they call themselves, are not exactly teetotallers in their trips abroad, but seldom is there any scandal or disgrace attached to them. They did dent their haloes a little in

Tension on the terraces at Wembley in the 1980s as England and Scotland fans clash.

1977 when they managed to rip up the turf and demolish the Wembley goalposts after a 2–1 victory, but while nobody would ever try to minimise that offence, it is important to stress that no one was hurt. It is in contrast to some of the supporters of other countries, including England, whose imminent arrival frequently sends a shiver down the spine wherever they visit.

On several occasions there has been serious violence in Scottish football. There was the 1909 Scottish Cup final replay between Celtic and Rangers. This was not a sectarian riot, but rather a protest at the denial of extra-time by a large crowd who suspected that a game had been deliberately drawn in order to get another big 'gate'. The previous autumn's Glasgow Cup semi-final between the two teams had gone to a replay, and the first Scottish Cup final on 10 April had also been drawn. Suggestions had been made in the press that there might be extra time if this replay on 17 April was drawn, but nothing official had been said. The game finished 1–1, and some players lingered on the field, not sure whether there would be extra time or not. But the referee Mr. Stark picked up the ball and went off. A few youths came on to the field, possibly for no other purpose than to see their heroes, but then a stone or two was thrown at the pavilion, and one thing led to another. Goalposts, pay boxes and the stand were all put to the sword in an orgy of violence. A bonfire was lit by the none-too-intelligent, and even firemen who were trying to put the fire out were attacked. Fortunately the players (not that they were really in any great danger) escaped, as did the Scottish Cup trophy itself, saved by Alec Maley, the brother of Celtic's manager Willie, but the violence went on for several hours. Hampden Park was seriously damaged and the Scottish Cup was withheld that season, as Edwardian Scotland received a severe shock to its system.

The League Cup final of 23 October 1965 finished peacefully, but after Celtic were presented with the League Cup, a few Rangers fans took exception to them parading the trophy and invaded the field. Fortunately, although they reached the Celtic players, no damage was done, but 'laps of honour' were subsequently banned for many years.

Far more serious was the Scottish Cup final between the Old Firm on May 10 1980. Celtic had been presented with the trophy, and some of their own fans came on the field to celebrate, before there was a less friendly counter-invasion from the other end. Violence did ensue then and a few split heads occurred, although fortunately nothing more serious than that. Although this was perhaps a rather pathetic playing out of some grudge, and proved little other than the failure of the Scottish educational system, it was the catalyst for some radical thinking about the game. One thing that came out of it was the banning of alcohol from grounds, and a gradual, albeit reluctant, move to all-seater stadia.

Abroad in Europe, Scottish fans have generally behaved well, but there was an outbreak of bottle throwing at Liverpool in 1966, when Celtic appeared to be cheated out of an equalizing goal, and serious fighting at Waterford versus Celtic in 1970. In 1972 in Barcelona, when Rangers won the European Cup-Winners' Cup, the occasion was spoiled by a whole night of fighting between Rangers' fans and Franco's *guardia civil*, some of whom were upset by an anti-Catholic atmosphere amongst the Rangers support, and who, in any case, were totally different creatures from the traditional Scottish 'bobby'.

In recent years, the large Celtic support have been a credit to the country, notably at Seville in 2003, but it was not always so. As recently as four years previously, in 1999, the club had been fined after referee Hugh Dallas

Referee Mike Ritchie breaks up a fight between Livingston's Greg Strong and Caley Thistle's Liam Fox in an SPL fixture in October 2005.

was hit by a missile at Parkhead in the game against Rangers in which Rangers won the SPL championship. Fighting and bottle throwing in 1941(when there were surely far more important things going on in the world) at Ibrox saw Celtic Park closed for a few games (for it was Celtic fans who were perceived to be the trouble makers). Similar occurrences in the early 1950s encouraged the SFA, (under the leadership of George Graham, considered by many to be a bigoted Secretary), to begin a fruitless campaign to persuade Celtic fans not to fly the Irish flag at home games.

Falkirk repeatedly beat Celtic in the late 1950s and early 1960s – and its good citizens suffered as a result. Perth was savagely ransacked after a League Cup defeat by St Johnstone on 30 August 1961, as was Dundee on 4 November of that year, but the worst occasion for Celtic FC was in the semi-final of the Scottish Cup on 31 March 1962. Celtic were 3–0 down to St Mirren with ten minutes remaining when their fans invaded the field in a misguided attempt to abandon the game. The game was eventually re-started, but by that time the Celtic directors had conceded the tie.

It must, however, be stressed that these incidents, bad though they were, were not necessarily typical. They were abhorred and deplored by the decent elements of their support, and most games, even Old Firm games, pass without any serious violence. There are some clubs indeed who have never been in any way associated with violent supporters, notably Dunfermline Athletic, Dundee United, St. Johnstone, Ayr United, Partick Thistle and many others. Many years have now passed since the last serious outbreak of violence at a Scottish football match, and it is to be hoped that the corner has been turned. The 'casual culture' already referred to has fortunately not been as serious as it might have been. Yet books continue to appear on bookshelves written by people claiming to have been 'casuals'.

VOGTS Berti (1946 –)

The Scotland manager from 2002 till 2004, Berti Vogts' reign coincided with a major drought of Scottish talent, and his spell in charge was nothing short of disastrous. During his reign of thirty-one games, Scotland won nine, lost six and drew fifteen, with one game abandoned because of floodlight failure. It is fair to say that the largest nails in his coffin were the repeated failures to beat teams like Slovenia, Moldova and the Faeroe Islands. Incredibly, he handed out forty new caps, in many cases to men who were totally unknown in Scotland. Yet he had been a successful manager for Germany and a great player for them as well. It was a case of a man who simply did not appear to understand the complex and peculiar problems of Scotland, and who had the misfortune to be the manager at a bad time. In January 2007 he took over as manager of Nigeria, but a poor performance at the African Nations Cup in 2008 led to his resignation. A short while later he became manager of Azerbaijan.

WADDELL Willie (1921 – 1992)

Scotland Caps: 17
Scottish League Championship medals: 4
Scottish Cup medals: 2

A talented right winger for Rangers and Scotland in the years immediately after the second world war, Willie Waddell played seventeen times for Scotland. His career lasted from 1938 to 1956 and included 558 games, with 143 goals. He was well built and powerful, had tremendous ball control, and was nicknamed 'Deedle'. In 1957 he became manager of Kilmarnock, where he built up a strong side, but Killie tended to be the bridesmaids rather than the bride, until that epic day in 1965 when they clinched the league championship by beating Hearts 2–0 at Tynecastle. He resigned soon after, in favour of a career in journalism with the Scottish Daily Express that lasted until December 1969, when he was invited to become manager of Rangers. It was sometimes said, perhaps unfairly, that he used his column in the Scottish Daily Express to undermine Rangers' manager Davie White, and thus gain the position for himself.

His managerial career at Rangers coincided with the Ibrox Disaster of 1971, but although domestic success was difficult to achieve, he won the European Cup-Winners' Cup in 1972 in Barcelona, although the triumph was marred by hooliganism and a resultant ban on European competition. He became general manager later, then a director, but lost a little credibility by claiming in 1976 that Rangers would sign Roman Catholics, and then failing to do so. On the other hand, he does deserve a great deal of praise for leading the club through the stormy waters of the aftermath of the Ibrox Disaster of 1971 and the Barcelona hooliganism, and for making Ibrox into one of the best stadia in Europe.

WAGES

Wages are, of course, confidential to each player. His earnings depend on how much he, perhaps together with an agent, has been able to negotiate from the club at the start of the contract. Some players are reputed to earn colossal sums per week, but it is important to realise that one must not generalise. Those who play for the Old Firm will not be poor (although Pierre van Hooijdonk, with considerable insensitivity, once compared his earnings for Celtic with the income of the homeless!), but there is the other side of the coin as well, for without doubt the livelihoods of those who play for some Scottish teams that have been in and out of administration will not be high. Yet a part-time player will often find his football earnings to be a welcome supplement.

Until 1961, there was a maximum wage in force throughout Great Britain. This did not stop talented Scottish players moving south for financial betterment, and it was often suspected in any case that the restrictions of the maximum wage were honoured more in their breach than in their observance. In any case there were ways around the maximum wage by virtue of bonuses, appearance money etc, but in 1961 the Professional Footballers Association in England, with the tacit support of some of the wealthier clubs, managed to remove the clause that contained the maximum wage. Once it was lifted, the 1960s saw a depressing trek of talented Scottish players to high-paying English clubs. Some players, like MacKay, Crerand, Ure, Gilzean and St John were very successful; others less so.

In the 1960s, a really good player could command a wage of £100 per week, something that was about three times better than the average wage. Naturally only the richest clubs could afford to pay that. Today the wages can be very high, but only at the very top, and as the Bible might say, 'although many are called, few are chosen'. In addition, young players would be well advised to bear in mind that the life of a professional footballer is a short one.

WALES

Scotland played Wales annually in the Home International Championship from 1876 until 1985. Sometimes Scotland fielded teams which they would not necessarily have fielded against England, but this practice stopped once Wales began to improve as a team in the Edwardian era. The defeat by Wales at Tynecastle in 1906 in particular was a major shock to the Scottish national psyche, and marked the end of Scotland fielding a 'reserve team' against Wales. Some of the fixtures were World Cup or European Championship Qualifying games, including the famous game in 1977 when Scotland qualified for Argentina at Anfield, and the time in 1985 when they earned a play-off for Mexico. Tragically this was the night that Jock Stein collapsed and died. Of the 103 games played, Scotland has won sixty, Wales twenty, and twenty-three have been drawn.

1876	25 Mar	Hamilton Crescent	4–0	Ferguson Lang MacKinnon H. McNeil	
1877	5 Mar	Wrexham	2–0	Campbell Evans o.g	
1878	23 Mar	1st Hampden Park	9–0	Campbell (2) Weir (2) Ferguson (2) Baird Watson Lang	
1879	7 April	Wrexham	3–0	Smith (2) Campbell	
1880	27 Mar	1st Hampden Park	5–1	Davidson Beveridge Lindsay McAdam Campbell	W. Roberts
1881	14 Mar	Wrexham	5-1	Ker (2) McNeil Bell o.g. Morgan o.g	Crosse
1882	25 Mar	1st Hampden Park	5-0	Fraser (2) Kay Ker McAulay	
1883	12 Mar	Wrexham	3–0	Smith Fraser Anderson	
1884	29 Mar	Cathkin Park	4–1	Lindsay Shaw Kay Ker	R. Roberts
1885	23 Mar	Wrexham	8–1	Lindsay (3) Calderwood (2) Anderson (2) Allan	R. Jones
1886	10 April	2nd Hampden Park	4–1	McCormack McCall Allan Harrower	Vaughan
1887	21 Mar	Wrexham	2–0	Robertson Allan	
1888	10 Mar	Easter Road	5–1	Latta (2) Paul Munro Groves	J. Doughty
1889	15 April	Wrexham	0–0		
1890	22 Mar	Underwood, Paisley	5–0	Paul (4) Wilson	
1891	21 Mar	Wrexham	4–3	Boyd (2) Logan Buchanan	Bowdler (2) Owen
1892	26 Mar	Tynecastle	6–1	Hamilton (2) McPherson (2) Thomson Baird	B. Lewis
1893	18 Mar	Wrexham	8–0	Madden (4) Barker (3) Lambie	
1894	24 Mar	Rugby Park	5–2	Berry Barker Chambers Alexander Johnstone	Morris (2)
1895	23 Mar	Wrexham	2–2	Madden Divers	W. Lewis Chapman
1896	21 Mar	Carolina Port, Dundee	4–0	Neil (2) Keillor Paton	
1897	20 Mar	Wrexham	2–2	Ritchie (pen) Walker	Morgan-Owen Pugh

1898	19 Mar	Fir Park	5–2	Gillespie (3) McKie (2)	Thomas Morgan-Owen
1899	18 Mar	Wrexham	6–0	McColl (3) Campbell (2) Marshall	
1900	3 Feb	Pittodrie	5–2	Wilson (2) Bell Hamilton A. Smith	Parry Butler
1901	2 Mar	Wrexham	1–1	Robertson	T. Parry
1902	15 Mar	Cappielow	5–1	Smith (3) Buick Drummond	Morgan-Owen
1903	9 Mar	Cardiff	1–0	Speedie	
1904	12 Mar	Dens Park	1–1	R. Walker	Atherton
1905	6 Mar	Wrexham	1–3	Robertson	Watkins A. Morris Meredith
1906	3 Mar	Tynecastle	0–2		W. Jones J. Jones
1907	4 Mar	Wrexham	0–1		A. Morris
1908	7 Mar	Dens Park	2–1	Bennett Lennie	Jones
1909	1 Mar	Wrexham	2–3	Walker Paul	Davies (2) Jones
1910	5 Mar	Rugby Park	1–0	Devine	
1911	6 Mar	Cardiff	2–2	Hamilton (2)	A. Morris (2)
1912	2 Mar	Tynecastle	1–0	Quinn	
1913	3 Mar	Wrexham	0–0		
1914	28 Feb	Celtic Park	0–0		
1920	26 Feb	Cardiff	1–1	Cairns	Evans
1921	12 Feb	Pittodrie	2–1	Wilson (2)	Collier
1922	4 Feb	Wrexham	1–2	Archibald	L. Davies S. Davies
1923	17 Mar	Love Street	2–0	Wilson (2)	
1924	16 Feb	Cardiff	0–2		W. Davies L. Davies
1925	14 Feb	Tynecastle	3–1	Gallacher (2) Meiklejohn	Williams
1925	31 Oct	Cardiff	3–0	Duncan McLean Clunas	
1926	30 Oct	Ibrox	3–0	Jackson (2) Gallacher	
1927	29 Oct	Wrexham	2–2	Gallacher Hutton	Curtis Gibson o.g.
1928	27 Oct	Ibrox	4–2	Gallacher (3) Dunn	W. Davies (2)
1929	26 Oct	Cardiff	4–2	Gallacher (2) James Gibson	O'Callaghan L. Davies
1930	25 Oct	Ibrox	1–1	Battles	Bamford
1931	31 Oct	Wrexham	3–2	Stevenson Thomson McGrory	Curtis O'Callaghan
1932	26 Oct	Tynecastle	2–5	Dewar Duncan	O'Callaghan (2) Griffiths Astley J. Thomson o.g.
1933	4 Oct	Cardiff	2–3	McFadyen Duncan	Evans Robbins Astley
1934	21 Nov	Pittodrie	3–2	Napier (2) Duncan	Phillips Astley
1935	5 Oct	Cardiff	1–1	Duncan	Phillips
1936	2 Dec	Dens Park	1–2	Walker	Glover (2)
1937	30 Oct	Cardiff	1–2	Massie	B. Jones Morris
1938	9 Nov	Tynecastle	3–2	Walker (2) Gillick	Astley L. Jones
1946	19 Oct	Wrexham	1–3	Waddell (pen)	B. Jones Ford Stephen o.g.
1947	12 Nov	Hampden Park	1–2	McLaren	Ford Lowrie
1948	23 Oct	Cardiff	3–1	Waddell (2) Howie	B. Jones
1949	9 Nov	Hampden Park	2–0	McPhail Linwood	
1950	21 Oct	Cardiff	3–1	Reilly (2) Waddell	A. Powell
1951	14 Nov	Hampden Park	0–1		Allchurch
1952	18 Oct	Cardiff	2–1	Brown Liddell	Ford
1953	4 Nov	Hampden Park	3–3	Brown Johnstone Reilly	Charles (2) Allchurch
1954	16 Oct	Cardiff	1–0	Buckley	
1955	9 Nov	Hampden Park	2–0	Johnstone (2)	
1956	20 Oct	Cardiff	2–2	Fernie Reilly	Ford Medwin
1957	13 Nov	Hampden Park	1–1	Collins	Medwin
1958	18 Oct	Cardiff	3–0	Leggat Law Collins	

1959: Action from Scotland v Wales at Hampden with Graham Leggat in the centre of the photograph. The game ended in a 1-1 draw.

1959	4 Nov	Hampden Park	1–1	Leggat	Charles
1960	22 Oct	Cardiff	0–2		Jones Vernon
1961	8 Nov	Hampden Park	2–0	St. John (2)	
1962	20 Oct	Cardiff	3–2	Caldow Law Henderson	Allchurch Charles
1963	20 Nov	Hampden Park	2–1	White Law	B. Jones
1964	3 Oct	Cardiff	2–3	Chalmers Gibson	Leek (2) Davies
1965	24 Nov	Hampden Park	4–1	Murdoch (2) Henderson Greig	Allchurch
1966	22 Oct	Cardiff	1–1	Law	R. Davies
1967	22 Nov	Hampden Park	3–2	Gilzean (2) McKinnon	R. Davies Durban
1969	3 May	Wrexham	5–3	McNeill Stein Gilzean Bremner McLean	R. Davies (2) Toshack
1970	22 April	Hampden Park	0–0		
1971	15 May	Cardiff	0–0		
1972	24 May	Hampden Park	1–0	Lorimer	
1973	12 May	Wrexham	2–0	Graham (2)	
1974	14 May	Hampden Park	2–0	Dalglish Jardine (pen)	
1975	17 May	Cardiff	2–2	Jackson Rioch	Toshack Flynn
1976	6 May	Hampden Park	3–1	Pettigrew Rioch Gray	Griffiths (pen)
1976	17 Nov	Hampden Park	1–0	Evans o.g.	
1977	28 May	Wrexham	0–0		
1977	12 Oct	Anfield, Liverpool	2–0	Masson (pen) Dalglish	
1978	17 May	Hampden Park	1–1	Johnstone	Donachie o.g.
1979	19 May	Cardiff	0–3		Toshack (3)
1980	21 May	Hampden Park	1–0	Miller	
1981	16 May	Swansea	0–2		Walsh (2)
1982	24 May	Hampden Park	1–0	Hartford	
1983	28 May	Cardiff	2–0	A. Gray Brazil	
1984	28 Feb	Hampden Park	2–1	Cooper (pen) Johnston	James
1985	27 Mar	Hampden Park	0–1		Rush
1985	10 Sept	Cardiff	1–1	Cooper (pen)	Hughes
1997	27 May	Rugby Park	0–1		Hartson
2004	18 Feb	Cardiff	0–4		Earnshaw (3) Taylor

WALKER Bobby (1879 – 1930)

Scotland Caps: 29
Scottish Cup medals: 2

Bobby Walker was one of Hearts and Scotland's greatest-ever players, but is not to be confused with Tommy Walker, who played for Hearts in the 1930s and managed them in the 1950s and 1960s. Bobby was a star player of the Edwardian era, and won twenty-nine caps for Scotland between 1900 and 1913, his best game being the 2–1 win over England at Bramall Lane in 1903. Hearts' side of that era revolved around his brilliant inside right play, and it was his inspirational performances that won the 1901 and 1906 Scottish Cups for Hearts. He was also on the losing side in Scottish Cup finals in 1903 and 1907. He was essentially a very shy man, but for all that he was freely compared to Houdini for his ability to avoid tackles, and his mesmerising dribbles were often referred to as 'Walkerism'.

WALKER Tommy (1915 – 1993)

Scotland Caps: 20

A legendary figure in Hearts' history both as player and manager, Tommy Walker joined the club in 1932, and soon sufficiently impressed as an inside right to be chosen for Scotland in 1935. He had the distinction of scoring twice for Scotland at Wembley, earning Scotland a draw from the penalty spot in 1936 (famously having to replace the ball several times because of the wind before he took the kick), and scoring in 1938 to give Scotland a 1–0 victory. He played twenty times for Scotland and would have played more often if it had not been for the second world war. After the war he played for Chelsea, and then returned to Tynecastle in 1948 as assistant manager, taking over as manager in 1951. He then built a phenomenally successful Hearts side that challenged the Old Firm all though the 1950s and into the early 1960s, winning the Scottish League championship twice, the Scottish Cup once, and the Scottish League Cup four times.

His great players included Dave Mackay, Alec Young and the 'Terrible Trio' of Alfie Conn, Willie Bauld and Jimmy Wardhaugh. He was awarded the OBE in 1960 (one of the first-ever footballers to be so honoured), but a key moment in Hearts' subsequent decline was the last day of the 1964/65 season at home to Kilmarnock, when a 2–0 defeat was enough to hand the league championship to the Ayrshire men. Tommy was surprisingly sacked in September 1966 – a blow from which Hearts took a long time to recover. He then went on to work with Dunfermline for a spell before becoming manager of Raith Rovers from 1967-1969. In 1974 he made his peace with Hearts and became a director. Throughout his career he was renowned for his gentlemanly and dignified approach to the game.

Willie Wallace (left), soon after arriving from Hearts to sign for Celtic.

(Right) Rangers in the European Cup-Winners' Cup 1972. Rangers v Moscow Dynamo. Rangers dugout right to left: Jock Wallace,Willie Waddell, Andy Penman, Jim Denny, Derek Parlane, Gerry Neff, Stan Anderson, Tom Craig and Tom Paterson .

WALLACE Jock (1935 – 1996)

Jock Wallace was one of Rangers greatest managers, winning for them a domestic treble of honours in seasons 1975/76 and 1977/78. He first came to prominence in 1967 when, as goalkeeper and player/manager of Berwick Rangers, his side put Glasgow Rangers out of the Scottish Cup. In 1970, having been a coach at Hearts for a spell, he joined Rangers as coach and, working with Willie Waddell, won the European Cup-Winners' Cup in 1972. It was not until 1975, however, that he won the Scottish League with them. Immediately after the second domestic treble success in 1978, Wallace amazed Rangers fans by departing for Leicester City, for reasons that have never been adequately explained. He returned to Scotland, however, to manage Motherwell in 1982, and then went back to Ibrox in 1983 for a less successful spell, even though he won the Scottish League Cup twice for them. He lost his job in the 'Souness Revolution' of 1986, and then moved on to manage Seville and Colchester United. He was well liked by the Rangers fans for his tough, militaristic approach to training (he had served in the jungles of Malaysia). He died of Motor Neurone Disease in 1996.

WALLACE Willie (1940 –)

Scotland Caps: 7
Scottish League Championship medals: 5
Scottish Cup medals: 3
Scottish League Cup medals: 3
European Cup medals: 1

A man with the same name as the famous Scottish patriot, Willie is a Lisbon Lion and earned one of his seven Scottish caps by playing in the 1967 game at Wembley, in which Scotland beat England 3–2. He was nicknamed 'wispy', not so much because of his speed as because his full name is William Semple Brown Wallace and 'wispy' Wallace is a fast way of saying WSB Wallace. He was a fast centre forward with an eye for goal, although his aggressive approach to the game often got him into trouble with referees. His first senior team was Stenhousemuir, then Raith Rovers, before he joined Hearts in 1961 and won a Scottish League Cup medal with them. Then Jock Stein signed him for Celtic in December 1966, and by the end of that season he had won a European Cup medal, scoring a couple of vital goals in the semi-final against Dukla Prague. With Celtic he tasted a great deal of success, but was transferred to Crystal Palace in 1971, returning to Dumbarton in 1972, before coaching for a variety of teams. He later emigrated to Australia, where he opened a sports shop.

WAR HEROES

Scottish footballers served their country well during both world wars of the twentieth century, and possibly every club in the Scotland had someone who went to war and did not come back. Pride of place must go to the Heart of Midlothian team who enlisted virtually en masse in the first year of the first world war, and who are commemorated on the impressive memorial near Haymarket Station in Edinburgh. (See below under **WARTIME FOOTBALL**) Some footballers were decorated for gallantry, notably Willie Lyon of Celtic and Willie Thornton of Rangers in the second world war – the latter receiving perhaps Scottish football's ultimate accolade of a cheer every time he touched the ball in his first appearance after the war at Celtic Park!

WARK John (1957 –)

Scotland Caps: 29

A versatile and successful player for Ipswich Town and Liverpool in the 1970s and 1980s, John Wark won twenty-nine caps for Scotland and took part in the 1982 World Cup finals in Spain. Like many a Scottish player, his best form came for his clubs, where he shone. He

joined Ipswich in the mid-1970s, winning the FA Cup with them in 1978 and the UEFA Cup in 1981, scoring a record fourteen goals in that competition, and being chosen as Player of The Year. Whilst at Portman Road he also appeared in football film Escape To Victory, alongside Pele and Sylvester Stallone. He joined Liverpool in March 1984 and won English league championship medals in 1983/84 and 1985/86, although a broken leg in 1986 kept him on the sidelines for a long time. In 1988 he moved back to Ipswich for £100,000 and, after a brief and unsuccessful spell with Middlesbrough, joined Ipswich for a third time, helping the club win promotion to the first ever Premier League in 1992. Throughout his career his position gradually moved back from goal scorer to attacking midfielder, to defensive midfielder, to out and out defender, and this may have prolonged his time in the game, which lasted until his late thirties. He remains a legendary figure at Ipswich.

WARTIME FOOTBALL

It is sometimes assumed that interest in football dipped during wartime. This is not so. In fact, if anything, people were more interested in the game, in the same way that the cinema and theatre all boomed during wartime. War conditions, however, had a tremendous effect on the game. Not only were many players and spectators called up to the forces, but hours of work and transport problems also had an effect. On the other hand, there were always many army, navy and air force teams, and it was generally held that football was good for morale. Yet in the first world war in particular, there were always those who complained that twenty-two fit young men should have been wearing khaki in France, rather than entertaining those who were labelled 'war dodgers' or 'conscientious objectors'.

In the first world war, league football continued as normal, at least for the big teams in the central belt, although by the end of the war Dundee, Raith Rovers and Aberdeen found it impossible, through transport difficulties, to fulfil fixtures, and were compelled to withdraw from the League. 1914/15 saw the first and second divisions of the Scottish League in existence, but by 1915 the second division was not a viable entity. The Scottish Cup and international matches were no longer played, but regional competitions like the Glasgow Cup flourished, as did the Scottish Junior Cup and all the regional leagues. In the 1918/19 season, a Scottish Victory Cup was played for instead of the 'real' Scottish Cup, and it was won by St. Mirren.

Full-time professional football was not allowed, and every player had to have a job in munitions or war-related industries before he could play football on a part-time basis. Saturday (or the occasional Monday Holiday) was the only day allowed for football, and

April 1944. Field Marshall Montgomery is introduced to Scotland's team by captain Matt Busby before the international at Hampden versus England.

occasionally, as on 15 April 1916 for example, Celtic had to play two games on the one day. They beat Raith Rovers 6–0 in the afternoon at Parkhead, and then headed off to Motherwell where they won 3–1in the evening. Motherwell had also been active that afternoon, losing 3–0 to Ayr United.

The end of season 1916/17 also saw games having to be played on the same day. On 14 April Clyde beat St. Mirren 2–1 at Shawfield, then lost 1–0 to Third Lanark at Cathkin Park in the evening. On 21 April Queen's Park beat Partick Thistle 2–0 at Firhill in the afternoon, while Rangers lost 3–1 to Hamilton Accies at Douglas Park. In the evening at Ibrox Rangers then beat Queen's Park 1–0.

Celtic were indeed the team of the first world war, winning the championship in 1915, 1916, 1917 and 1919 (although losing to Rangers in 1918), and it was often said that the most talked-about person in the trenches was Patsy Gallacher. The same Patsy, however, was fined for bad timekeeping at his job in the shipyards. The football authorities took such a dim view of this that he was also suspended from playing football as well!

At the start of the first world war, there had been a certain amount of pressure on the Government to stop football altogether, such was the hysteria of the day. This was resisted, although many footballers joined the colours, including the Hearts players who enlisted virtually en masse, and are commemorated on a war memorial at Haymarket. Tribute must be paid to Private James Speedie, Corporal Tom Gracie, Private Henry Wattie, Private Ernest Ellis, Lance Corporal James Boyd, Sergeant Duncan Currie and Sergeant John Allan, who made the ultimate sacrifice, but they were not the only ones, for most teams suffered several casualties in the war.

In 1939 the circumstances were different, for immediately on the declaration of war, all football was suspended and it was feared that there might be no football at all 'for the duration'. But the authorities relented and allowed unofficial football. Initially, no internationals were allowed for fear of such a large crowd being bombed, but the restrictions were gradually relaxed before being eventually dispensed with as the threat of aerial bombing receded. The Scottish Cup and league were suspended, but regional competitions continued. There was a southern division of the Scottish League and a long-term benefit was the introduction of a Southern League Cup to replace the Scottish Cup. This trophy became the Scottish League Cup after the end of the war. Rangers won the southern division of the Scottish League every year, and Ibrox historians can claim that Rangers actually won nine championships in a row from 1938/39 until 1946/47 (before Celtic from 1965/66 to 1973/74 and Rangers from 1988/89 to 1996/97) if we include the unofficial war years.

Goalkeeper Crozier punches clear of Lawton in the wartime international against England at Hampden in April 1944.

Rangers in 1941, 1942 and 1943, Hibs in 1944, Rangers again in 1945, and Aberdeen in 1946 won the Southern League Cup. Aberdeen historians claim with some justification that this victory in 1946 should be looked upon as an official Scottish League Cup win, for Aberdeen are hardly a 'southern' team!

Hibs in 1941, Rangers in 1942, St. Mirren in 1943, Motherwell in 1944 and Partick Thistle in 1945 won the Summer Cup. Rangers won the Scottish Emergency Cup of 1940 and the Scottish Victory Cup of 1946, whereas Celtic won the Victory in Europe Cup of 1945.

Players were paid a maximum of £2 per week and had to have another job as well, usually in the shipyards or the mines. 'Guesting' was allowed, and thus enterprising clubs were able to recruit for a game or two famous internationalists who just happened to be based nearby. Morton in particular were able to cash in on this opportunity. As the threat of invasion and bombing receded towards the end of the war, more and more internationals were allowed and the Scotland versus England games were much enjoyed by the troops overseas as they listened to BBC World Service, although Scotland generally did badly. They were also a great opportunity to boost morale, and Winston Churchill, King George VI and Field Marshall Montgomery were frequently seen at big matches. The war finished in 1945, and the next season was still considered unofficial. It is unfortunate that the famous Victory International of April 1946, in which Jimmy Delaney scored his famous goal, is not a 'real' international.

A problem often arose with equipment. Footballs were hardly a war priority and football strips were, like all other clothing, affected by rationing. Bobby Hogg of Celtic had picked up so many unused Scotland strips before the second world war in his capacity as travelling reserve that he was able to supply a whole set for Scotland to use in their wartime internationals. Otherwise, faded and moth-eaten strips would have had to be deployed, as they were at club level.

Patched-up balls were very often the order of the day. Loudspeaker appeals for someone to make up the numbers, or even to act as referee or linesman, were not unknown. But none of these emergency conditions should ever allow anyone to think that football was not taken seriously in wartime. Indeed, quite a few teams made a consistent financial profit, for wages were perforce minimal and soldiers home on leave had enough money to go to football matches, as did those who worked in the munitions industries. What is also true is that wartime army games were of a high standard, and soldiers who happened to be good footballers, or who had played at professional level before the war, often found that army life was not quite as unpleasant as might have been the case.

WARTIME INTERNATIONALS

There were no wartime internationals played during the first world war. In the second they were discouraged for a spell, and attendance severely limited for fear of air raids, but as the war progressed the benefit to morale far outweighed any possible danger. The authorities, however, insisted in the early years of the war that such games should not be played at Wembley, which was well within range of the Luftwaffe. These internationals are not considered official, for neither country had its best players available, but that is not to say that they were not taken seriously or that they were not eagerly anticipated and looked forward to. The 1944 game at Hampden Park, for example, attracted a six-figure crowd, who were delighted with the surprise appearance of Field Marshall Montgomery before the start. In particular, the BBC World Service did a great job in broadcasting these internationals to troops all over the world. Scotland did not do particularly well in these games, so it is perhaps better that they remain 'unofficial'. There were also many unofficial internationals between Scotland and The Army, or Scotland versus The RAF etc, but no attempt seems to have been made to arrange fixtures against Wales or Ireland.

2 Dec 1939	Newcastle	England	2	1	Scotland
11 May 1940	Hampden Park	Scotland	1	1	England
8 Feb 1941	Newcastle	England	2	3	Scotland
3 May 1941	Hampden Park	Scotland	1	3	England
4 Oct 1941	Wembley	England	2	0	Scotland
11 Oct 1941	Blackpool	English League	3	2	Scottish League
17 Jan 1942	Wembley	England	3	0	Scotland
18 Apr 1942	Hampden Park	Scotland	5	4	England
10 Oct 1942	Wembley	England	0	0	Scotland
17 Apr 1943	Hampden Park	Scotland	0	4	England
16 Oct 1943	Maine Road	England	8	0	Scotland
19 Feb 1944	Wembley	England	6	2	Scotland
22 Apr 1944	Hampden Park	Scotland	2	3	England
14 Oct 1944	Wembley	England	6	2	Scotland
3 Feb 1944	Villa Park	England	3	2	Scotland
14 Apr 1945	Hampden Park	Scotland	1	6	England

WATSON Andrew (1857 – Unknown)

Scotland Caps: 3
Scottish Cup medals: 3

Scotland's first-ever black player, Andrew Watson earned three caps for Scotland, and won three Scottish Cup medals with Queen's Park. He was born in Demarara in British Guyana, the son of a Scottish sugar planter and his black paramour. Unlike some sugar planters, Watson's father took his responsibilities towards his son seriously and paid for him to attend Glasgow University. Queen's Park observed his skill as a full back and picked him up. His three games for Scotland included a 6–1 win over England in 1881 and a 5–1 win the following year. No one ever seems to have made the colour of his skin an issue. He later emigrated to India and is believed to have died in Australia in the 1920s.

WEATHER

Any outdoor game is subject to the whims of the weather, although for Scottish football, this is less so than it once was. The insertion of undersoil heating (a requirement for the SPL, and many other clubs have it as well) means that frost will seldom now result in a major game being put off. Heavy snow, water logging, fog and even high winds can of course still cause a postponement.

The Scottish weather is nothing if not quixotic and unpredictable with, statistically, February being the worst month, although in some years (notably 2006) March was a bigger problem. 1947 saw a great deal of snow, but the worst year for postponements was 1963 when between early January and early March only a very few games were played in what became known as the 'big freeze'. 1979, 1981 and 1982 were difficult years as well, but since then perhaps 'global warming' and 'the greenhouse effect' have begun to have an effect and many seasons have passed without any serious problems.

Cries for 'summer football' are heard from time to time, but this might also cause problems, with summer holidays, other sports, and the sheer fact that it is often more difficult to play football (certainly the Scottish style of football, with emphasis on running and speed) in the heat than in the cold. The midwinter shut down happened in the SPL in 1999, 2000, 2001 and 2003, but it was to give players a rest rather than for climatic reasons, and in any case it did not enjoy widespread support among supporters.

All this does not necessarily make it any more comfortable for spectators to watch football, although more and more grounds now have adequate shelter, and the SPL grounds are all-seated. But in any case, Scottish football has never been a game for 'softies'!

This is what Scottish football is all about! Morton fans try to shelter from the wintry blast at Stranraer.

Andy Webster's move from Hearts to Wigan triggered a debate about players walking away from a club when still under contract.

WEBSTER RULING

The 'Webster Ruling' is the name popularly given to a decision by the Court of Arbitration for Sport in relation to Andy Webster's move from Hearts to Wigan Athletic. The case centred on article 17 of FIFA's 'Regulations for the Status and Transfer of Players', which lays down the rules for the payment of compensation when a player aged under twenty-eight years, such as Webster, leaves his club after completing three years of a four or five-year contract, and has given adequate notice. FIFA decided that Hearts should be paid compensation of £625,000.

The player and Wigan Athletic proceeded to appeal to the CAS because they believed the amount was too high, and Hearts appealed because they believed the amount was too low. In January 2008 the court announced that Hearts' compensation would be £150,000, and the decision sparked a debate about the rights and wrongs of players walking away from a club when still under contract. The debate was fuelled by other aspects of FIFA's regulations, which open up the possibility of a player aged twenty-eight or over deciding it is worth leaving a club when he has served just two years of his contract.

WEIGHT

This is often a problem for footballers, never more obvious than in the years immediately after they retire, when they suddenly stop training and put on a lot of weight. Some players, notably two giants of the 1960s, Jim Baxter of Rangers and Bobby Murdoch of Celtic, had tremendous problems with weight – in Murdoch's case, he twice went to a 'fitness farm' in England in order to reduce weight.

It is sometimes desirable for a defender to possess a certain amount of weight so that he can bundle forwards off the ball. Indeed, the stereotype of a defender is just that, and the normal words to be applied would be burly or rotund. There was, for example, Jock Hutton of Aberdeen and Blackburn Rovers in the 1920s who weighed in at thirteen stone six pounds, and who wasn't easily shoved around. He played ten times for Scotland in an era when Scotland were the best in Great Britain. On the other hand, in those pre-welfare state days, there were the slight figures of men like Patsy Gallacher of Celtic, who was little more than eight stone when he started to play in 1911.

Today's football demands that a player be super-fit. This does involve certain restrictions in lifestyle, and particularly in diet. Certainly an overweight footballer will immediately become obvious, and in this respect some foreign players are far better organised than Scottish ones. For example, a well-known foreign player, playing for a Scottish club, was invited to the annual function of a supporters' club and amazed them all by giving detailed instructions to the chef about how he wanted his food cooked and served, and in what quantity etc , including the temperature of his drinking water. And this was on a Saturday night *after* a game!

WEIR David (1970 –   )

Scotland Caps: 61
Scottish Cup medals: 2
Scottish League Cup medals: 1

A solid defender who played for Falkirk, Hearts and Everton, and won fifty-eight caps for Scotland (at a time when Scotland were not always doing well), David Weir played two games in the 1998 World Cup finals in France. He was transferred to Everton in 1998/99, after having won a Scottish Cup medal with Hearts the previous season. In 2007 Walter Smith signed him for Rangers.

WEMBLEY

Wembley is a stadium that will always have a mystique about it as far as Scottish football fans are concerned. Not only was there the famous 'Wembley Wizards' international in 1928 (see below and under GREAT DAYS), it was the scene of the biennial pilgrimage from the 1930s until the 1980s, as Scottish fans descended on London to see the game that meant so much to the whole nation. Before the second world war, the international at Wembley was played in even years, after the war it was played in odd years.

The stadium was opened in 1923 and Scotland was the first international team to play there in 1924, in a game that was a 1–1 draw. For some reason the international was played at Old Trafford in 1926, but from the 'wizards' international onwards, there was no doubt where the game would be played. For a while Scotland did badly (often because of incomprehensible team selections), but they earned a draw in 1936 and won in 1938.

It was in the immediate aftermath of the second world war, and the gradual dawning of the affluent society, that the travelling Scottish hordes (they were not yet named the tartan army) saw the best Scottish performances. 1949 was Cowan's Wembley, when Morton goalkeeper Jimmy Cowan defied English forwards like Jackie Milburn and Stan Pearson to inspire Scotland to victory. There was another win in 1951, and then Lawrie Reilly scored in the last minute in 1953 to earn a draw. After that the dark ages descended, with heavy defeats in 1955 and 1961, and two less crushing, but still clear, defeats in 1957 and 1959. 1963 was a narrow win, 1965 a draw that most people believe should have been a win, and 1967 will be remembered as the day that Scotland beat England after they had won the World Cup. This victory was an isolated phenomenon, unfortunately, with defeats in 1969, 1971, and 1973, and a thrashing in 1975, until Scotland again won in 1977. This occasion was largely spoiled, it must be said, by Scotland supporters breaking the cross bar. Sadly this image tended to detract from what was a fine Scottish performance.

The collapse of the home international championship, and the moving of the fixture to midweek, did not help this fixture, but it continued in a desultory sort of way throughout the 1980s, often with players' priorities elsewhere. The last games between the two nations at Wembley were in the European Championship of June 1996, when Paul Gascoigne of Rangers broke Scottish hearts after Gary McAllister infamously missed a penalty. Then, in November 1999, Scotland actually beat England 1–0 in the play–off for the European Championships, but this was not enough to reverse England's 2–0 win at Hampden Park a few days previously.

It is to be hoped that the Scotland versus England fixture is restored to the calendar in the new Wembley Stadium… but only if the game is to be given its due importance.

WEMBLEY WIZARDS

'Wembley Wizards' was the name that was popularly given to the Scotland team of Harkness, Nelson and Law; Gibson, Bradshaw and McMullen; Jackson, Dunn, Gallagher, James and Morton, who on 31 March 1928 defeated England 5–1 at Wembley before the Duke of York (later to become King George VI) and King Amanullah of Afghanistan. (See **GREAT DAYS**).

In 1928 Scotland defeated England 5-1 at Wembley Stadium and thereafter became known as the 'Wembley Wizards'.

WESTERN LEAGUE

This was a regional league that was formed in 1915 when Division Two was discontinued because of the first world war (also see **EASTERN LEAGUE**). A mix of former league clubs and non-league clubs, it eventually served as a springboard to the Scottish League for most of its members. The first club to make the transition was Clydebank in 1917. They replaced Aberdeen, Dundee and Raith Rovers, who all had to leave the Scottish League because they were deemed 'remote' clubs in wartime.

The next club to do so was Albion Rovers, who joined Aberdeen, Dundee and Raith Rovers when they were re-admitted to the Scottish League in 1919, and which now consisted of a single division of twenty-two clubs. Two years later two more Western League clubs, Johnstone and Vale of Leven, left when Division Two was finally re-introduced for the 1921/22 season. They joined sixteen clubs from the Central League, plus Forfar Athletic and Arbroath, in the new second tier.

However, it was in 1923 that the Western League acquired its main historical significance. The Scottish League created a Division Three for the 1923/24 season and ten of its sixteen members came from the Western League. The only clubs in the Western League that didn't participate were Hurlford and Queen's Park Victoria XI. The final Western League table, with some matches left unfulfilled, looked like this on 1 May 1923 –

	P	W	D	L	F	A	Pts.
Queen of the South	20	17	3	0	69	12	37
Arthurlie	21	11	3	7	46	29	25
Beith	20	10	3	7	45	29	23
Nithsdale Wanderers	18	8	6	4	27	17	22
Galston	19	8	6	5	35	22	22
Peebles Rovers	19	9	4	6	35	38	22
Royal Albert	20	7	6	7	35	39	20
Dykehead	21	6	7	8	30	32	19
Helensburgh	22	6	4	12	29	58	16
Solway Star	20	3	7	10	13	35	13
Queen's Park Victoria XI	18	3	3	12	25	44	9
Hurlford	18	3	2	13	14	45	8

All the clubs except Hurlford and Queen's Park Victoria XI joined Brechin City, Clackmannan, Dumbarton Harp, East Stirlingshire, Mid-Annandale and Montrose in a new Division Three of sixteen clubs. Division Three only lasted for three seasons, and by 1925/26 the clubs were experiencing such financial problems that only one, Helensburgh, managed to complete its fixtures.

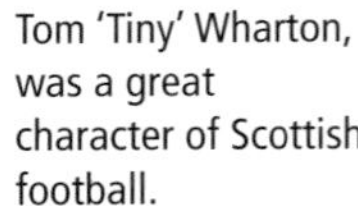

Tom 'Tiny' Wharton, was a great character of Scottish football.

WHARTON Tom ('Tiny') (1928 – 2005)

Tom Wharton was one of the most famous referees of the 1960s. He was called 'Tiny' because he was anything but tiny. He had a huge bulk and a tremendous presence on the field. He refereed the game with a smile on his face and clearly enjoyed the game, often preferring the 'quiet word' approach to the heavy-handed one of bookings and sendings-off. After he retired from active refereeing, he was a referee supervisor for a long time before retiring in 2003. He was one of the great characters of Scottish football.

WHITBURN JUNIOR FC (see JUNIOR FOOTBALL)

WHITE John (1937 – 1964)

Scotland Caps: 22

John White was a skilful inside forward for Alloa, Falkirk and, from 1959 onwards, Tottenham Hotspur. He played a big part in their double-winning season of 1961 and the lifting of the FA Cup in 1962. He also won the European Cup-Winners' Cup with them in 1963. His twenty-two Scottish Caps included the three wins in a

John White shoots at goal for Spurs in the 1961 FA Cup final at Wembley.

row against England in 1962, 1963 and 1964. He was a frail figure and nicknamed 'the ghost'. He died young as the result of a tragic accident when he was struck by lightning on a golf course at Enfield, near London, in July 1964.

WILSON Andrew Nesbit (1896 – 1973)

Scotland Caps: 12

Scotland's centre forward in the years immediately after the first world war, he is not to be confused with another Andrew Wilson who played *before* the 1914–18 war. He played for Dunfermline Athletic immediately after the war, Middlesbrough from 1921, Chelsea (for a record £6,000) from 1923, then Queen's Park Rangers and a French team called Sporting Club Nimois, until he retired in 1934. He then became manager of Walsall. He was actually registered with Middlesbrough in 1914, but after the war went to play for Dunfermline Athletic, who

Wembley, 1961: Davie Wilson scores a second goal as Ian St John and Denis Law jump for joy.

were then playing in the unofficial Central League. When Dunfermline re-joined the official Scottish League, he became ineligible to play for them and was compelled to return to Middlesbrough, who still held his registration documents.

He played in twelve games for Scotland (and twice in the unofficial victory internationals of 1919) and scored thirteen goals, scoring at least once in every game except two. He scored against England four years in a row between 1920 and 1923, and was twice on the winning side against them.

WILSON Davie (1939 –)

Scotland Caps: 22
Scottish League Championship medals: 3
Scottish Cup medals: 5
Scottish League Cup medals: 2

A fair-haired left winger for Rangers in their glory days of the early 1960s, Davie Wilson was a frequent goal scorer for both Rangers and Scotland. It was Wilson who scored the first goal in the 1962 defeat of England. He took part in each of the defeats of England between 1962 and 1964, winning twenty-two caps in all between 1961 and 1965. For Rangers the left wing pairing of Brand and Wilson was regarded as one of the best in the history of the club. If it had not been for Alan Morton, Wilson may well be regarded as the best left winger that Rangers ever had. His best single performance for the club was on 17 March 1962, when he scored six goals as a centre forward in a 7–1 victory over Falkirk. He then had the misfortune to suffer a broken leg in autumn 1963, but came back brilliantly. In 1967 he moved on to Dundee United and then Dumbarton (as player and subsequently manager), before becoming assistant-manager with Kilmarnock. Another spell as manager of Dumbarton followed before he gave up the game.

WINS

The game is all about winning, and therefore the number of games won at the end of a season is usually what determines the winners of the various divisions of the league. This is especially true since season 1994/95, when three points were awarded for a win, rather than two, in an attempt to encourage attacking football and to discourage teams from settling for a draw.

Celtic, who managed thirty-three wins from thirty-eight matches in season 2001/02, hold the record for the most wins in a season in the Scottish Premier League. In the Scottish League Premier Division, Rangers recorded thirty-three wins on two occasions, but that was out of a possible forty-four games.

In the old Division One of the Scottish League, Rangers recorded thirty-five wins out of forty-four in season 1920/21, yet that is not as good as 1898/99 when they 'only' won eighteen games, but that is because they only played eighteen! In the old Division Two Morton managed thirty-three out of thirty-eight in season 1966/67. In the new ten-team divisions of the Scottish League, where thirty-six games are played, credit must be given to Hibs, who managed twenty-eight wins in the First Division in 1998/99, Gretna in the Second Division in 2005/06 with twenty-eight, and to Gretna (again) who registered thirty-two in the Third Division of 2004/05.

WINNING RUNS

Celtic set a new British record of twenty-five consecutive league wins in season 2003/04. This was when they went from 15 August 2003 to 14 March 2004 without even drawing. In their memorable season of 1966/67 they won twenty-three games in all competitions from the start of the season on 13 August until 5 November.

Scotland's women: Back, from Left: Ifeoma Dieke, Suzanne Robertson, Stacey Cook, Michelle Kerr, Gemma Fay, Julie Fleeting, Claire Johnstone, Denise Brolly, Joanne Love, Rhonda Jones, Suzanne Malone Middle Row: Stephen Boyle (team doctor), Wayne Henderson (GK coach), Elaine Stewart (administrator), Pauline Hamill, Leanne Ross, Amanda Burns, Amy McDonald, Suzanne Lappin, Jayne Sommerville, Johanne Wilson (physio), Sheila Begbie (coach), Tim Berridge (video technician) Front Row: Ann-Helen Grahm, Kirsty McBride, Julie Ferguson, Megan Sneddon, Suzanne Grant, Kim Little, Nichola Grant, Anna Signeul (team manager)

WITHOUT A WIN

This unwanted distinction belongs to the now defunct Vale of Leven, who managed to go through a league season in 1891/92 without a single win in twenty-two matches. They did achieve five draws though!

Six teams have gone through a season with only one win in the old Division One – Renton in 1893/94, Abercorn in 1896/97, Clyde in 1897/98, Dundee in 1898/99, Morton in 1901/02 and Ayr United in 1966/67.

Two teams have gone through a league season with only one victory in the old Division Two – East Stirlingshire in 1905/06 and Forfar Athletic, who registered only one victory out of thirty-eight in season 1974/75. On two other occasions East Stirlingshire managed only two – and it was in consecutive seasons 2002/03 and 2003/04.

Queen of the South holds the record for the new First Division with two in season 1988/89, and for the Premier Division it is Dunfermline with four in 1998/99. Forfar Athletic went from 25 September 1974 until 4 October 1975 without a league win, although they did win two League Cup games. This was a total of thirty-six league games. In the middle of this, they went from 1 February 1975 until the end of the season on 26 April scoring only one goal. But they maintained their sense of humour and dignity throughout it all. On one occasion, during a dire defeat by East Stirlingshire, their goalkeeper waved to a solitary spectator on the terracing!

WOMEN'S FOOTBALL

The women's game is regulated by FIFA, with rules that are the same as for the men. It has enjoyed a continuous growth in popularity around the world since the 1970s, but Scottish women were leading the way as long ago as the 1930s.

Nancy Thomson played for the Edinburgh City Girls' team in the 1930s, and then joined the famous 'Dick, Kerr's Preston Ladies Team', becoming captain in 1939. The team had originated at the Dick, Kerr's munitions factory in Preston, where women worked during the first world war, and was virtually unbeatable in the 1920s and 1930s. One of her games was against the Belgian Ladies international team. At that time many people disapproved of women playing football, and the team found it increasingly hard to find a ground where they would be allowed to play.

International football officially began for Scotland's women with a fixture against England on 18 November 1972 at Ravenscraig Stadium, Greenock. After taking a two goal lead, Scotland eventually lost 3–2. Rab Stewart, who played for Kilmarnock and St. Mirren, was in charge of a team that had been selected after three months of trials and Margaret McAuley Reid was the captain.

1972 was also the year when the Scottish Women's FA was formed, although it did not receive recognition

from the SFA until 1974, which was the year that the introduction of a Sex Discrimination Act was announced. Elsie Cook became the first manager of the Scotland women's side, and Home International Championships for women were first held in May 1976 at Bedford, Enfield and Watford in England.

Several Scottish women went to play in Italy during the 1970s and some of them were very successful. Edna Neillis played semi-professional football for AC Milan and in a match against Roma she scored a hat-trick in front of a crowd of 50,000. Rose Reilly (q.v.) also played for AC Milan, and in 1975 was part of the team that won both the Italian Cup and the League Cup.

After two unofficial Women's World Cups in 1970 and 1971, steps were taken to structure the development of women's football, and there is now a European Women's championship every four years in the year following the men's competition. The 2005 finals were held in England, but Scotland did not qualify from a difficult group that included Germany, the eventual winners of the tournament. The finals were contested by the host country and four group winners, plus three countries that qualified from play-offs between the four runners-up and the two best countries in third place.

2005 UEFA European Women's Championship

27 Mar 2003	Germany	5	0	Scotland	
18 May 2003	Scotland	5	1	Ukraine	Ralph; Brown; Fleeting (3)
7 Jun 2003	Portugal	1	8	Scotland	Brown (3); Fleeting (5)
19 Oct 2003	Czech Rep	2	0	Scotland	
10 Apr 2004	Ukraine	1	0	Scotland	
2 May 2004	Scotland	1	3	Germany	Fleeting
23 May 2004	Scotland	2	1	Portugal	Grant; Hamill
5 Sep 2004	Scotland	3	2	Czech Republic	Malone; Fleeting; Jones

2009 UEFA European Women's Championship

6 May 2007	Scotland	0	0	Portugal	
30 May 2007	Ukraine	2	1	Scotland	Fleeting
27 Oct 2007	Slovakia	0	3	Scotland	Kerr; Hamill; Fleeting
31 Oct 2007	Scotland	0	1	Denmark	
27 Apr 2008	Denmark	2	1	Scotland	Sneddon
3 May 2008	Portugal	1	4	Scotland	Beattie; Fleeting (3)
28 May 2008	Scotland	0	1	Ukraine	
28 Sep 2008	Scotland			Slovakia	

Vera Pauw, from the Netherlands, was appointed national coach in 1994 and under her leadership

Scotland became one of Europe's better sides. In 1998 Sheila Begbie, a former captain of the national side, joined her at the SFA and later became Head of Girls and Women's football. Anna Signeul, an experienced player in the Swedish Women's Premier League, took over from Vera Pauw in January 2005.

It was an indication of how much Scotland had improved when they participated as a 'first category' team in the qualifying campaign for the 2007 World Cup finals in China. They finished third in a group that again included Germany, who went on to finish top and qualify for the finals.

2007 FIFA Women's World Cup

28 Aug 2005	Russia	6	0	Scotland	
25 Sep 2005	Scotland	0	0	Ireland	
13 Oct 2005	Germany	4	0	Scotland	
26 Apr 2006	Scotland	1	0	Switzerland	Grant
6 May 2006	Ireland	0	2	Scotland	Love; Fleeting
24 May 2006	Scotland	0	4	Russia	
26 Aug 2006	Switzerland	1	1	Scotland	Fleeting
23 Sep 2006	Scotland	0	5	Germany	

The under-19 team, coached by Tony Gervaise, provided evidence of a successful youth policy when they won their first round qualifying group for the 2006/07 UEFA Women's Under-19 championship with victories over Russia, Slovenia and Israel. They came third in their second round qualifying group, but then in 2007/08 they did even better, coming through both qualifying groups to reach the finals along with England, Germany, Italy, Norway, Spain, Sweden and hosts France.

By the beginning of the twenty-first century more than four thousand girls were registered with the SFA and over eighty schools were taking part in an annual regional festival. Nationwide development centres were created for girls at under-13, under-16 and under-18 levels. One of Scotland's most famous players is Julie Fleeting (q.v.), who won her first Scotland cap at the age of fifteen against Wales and went on to become captain of the national side. A prolific goal scorer, she scored her 100th international goal during her 99th appearance for Scotland, against Slovakia in October 2007. Julie spent two seasons with San Diego Spirit in the USA and joined Arsenal in 2004.

Another player with USA connections is Ifeoma Dieke, a defender who played for Cumbernauld before switching to women's soccer in the United States. However, it was Pauline Hamill (q.v.) who became the first woman to gain one hundred caps for her country, when she played in the 3–2 victory over Belgium in August 2007.

Women's club football

The top women's football league in Scotland is the Scottish Women's Premier League, which comprises twelve teams. The Scottish Women's Football League is organised at a level below this and comprises a First Division, a Second Division, a Third Division (East) and a Third Division (West). There is also an annual Scottish Women's FA Cup tournament, and a League Cup for both the SWPL and the SWFL.

	SW Premier League Champions	SWFA Cup Winners
2003/04	Hibernian	Glasgow City
2004/05	Glasgow City	Hibernian
2005/06	Hibernian	Glasgow City
2006/07	Hibernian	Hibernian
2007/08	Glasgow City	Hibernian

In 2006/07 Hibernian set a new SWPL record by winning every one of their twenty-two league games: Scottish Women's Premier League 2006/07

	P	W	D	L	F	A	GD	Pts.
Hibernian	22	22	0	0	115	17	+98	66
Glasgow City	22	19	1	2	92	19	+73	58
Edinburgh Ladies	22	16	0	6	73	31	+42	48
Newburgh	22	13	5	4	67	41	+26	44
Kilmarnock	22	10	4	8	51	38	+13	34
Aberdeen	22	8	4	10	55	55	0	28
Hamilton	22	8	4	10	42	55	-13	28
Raith Rovers	22	9	1	12	33	54	-21	28
Forfar Farmington	22	7	2	13	37	62	-25	23
Arsenal North	22	3	3	16	45	79	-34	12
Lochee United	22	4	0	18	22	79	-57	12
Hutchison Vale	22	1	0	21	10	112	-102	3

The winners of the Premier League go on to participate in the UEFA Women's Cup, which was introduced in season 2001/02. Clubs play in a qualifying group that takes the form of a mini-tournament, and one member of each group hosts the tournament in their country. The table below shows where Scotland's representatives have participated at European level:

	Venue for Qualifying Tournament	Participating Club
2001/02	Scotland	Ayr United LFC
2002/03	Austria	FC Kilmarnock
2003/04	Denmark	FC Kilmarnock
2004/05	Belgium	Hibernian LFC
2005/06	Holland	Glasgow City
2006/07	Scotland	Hibernian LFC
2007/08	Austria	Hibernian LFC

Julie Fleeting in action against Denmark as she gains her 100th cap.

Premier League winners Hibernian hosted their qualifying group in 2006/07, with five matches taking place at Livingston and one at the home of Linlithgow Rose junior club. The final table was:

Espanyol (Spain)	3	3	0	0	12	1	9
Juvisy (France)	3	2	0	1	12	1	6
Hibernian	3	1	0	2	3	11	3
KI Klaksvik (Faroe Islands)	3	0	0	3	1	15	0

In 2007/08 Hibernian travelled to Austria, where they finished second in their group behind the host club:

	P	W	D	L	GF	GA	Pts
Neulengbach (Austria)	3	3	0	0	15	4	9
Hibernian	3	2	0	1	15	5	6
Sportowy GOL (Poland)	3	1	0	2	6	13	3
Mayo FC (Ireland)	3	0	0	3	1	15	0

WOODBURN Willie (1919 – 2001)

Scotland Caps: 24
Scottish League Championship medals: 4
Scottish Cup medals: 4
Scottish League Cup medals: 2

Willie Woodburn was a tall, commanding, centre half for Rangers, who enjoyed the nickname 'Big Ben', and epitomised the Iron Curtain defence that Rangers had in the late 1940s and early 1950s. He played twenty-four times for Scotland, the highlights being the Wembley triumphs of 1949 and 1951. For Rangers he played between the years of 1937 and 1954, winning four Scottish League championship medals, four Scottish Cup medals and two Scottish League Cup medals, and was recognised as the mainstay of that successful team. But he had a bad disciplinary record, and his career

came to a sudden halt in August 1954 when he was ordered off against Stirling Albion for a violent indiscretion and was subsequently suspended sine die. Some have argued that his sine die suspension should have debarred him from a place in Hampden's Hall of Fame.

WORLD CLUB CHAMPIONSHIP

Only once has a Scottish team been involved in this competition, and it was a far from happy experience. This was Celtic in the autumn of 1967. On the strength of their capture of the European Cup the previous May, Celtic took on Racing Club of Argentina, the winners of the South American Cup. The first game was played at Hampden Park on 18 October 1967, and a Billy McNeill goal gave Celtic a 1–0 victory to take to South America. But the behaviour of the Argentineans should have given a clue as to what was about to happen.

Celtic, having won the Scottish League Cup that afternoon, flew out to Argentina on the night of Saturday 28 October and faced Racing Club in Buenos Aires on 1 November. Before the game started goal-keeper Ronnie Simpson was felled by a missile (which might even have been thrown from the playing area) and John Fallon had to go into goal. Celtic did well, but in such an atmosphere of intimidation it was no surprise that they went down 2–1. Had the 'away goals' rule counted, Celtic would have won, but as it was, a play-off was scheduled for Montevideo, Uruguay on Saturday 4 November.

Some in the party, including Chairman Bob Kelly, felt that Celtic should go home and allow Racing Club to win the game by default, but he was persuaded to play the third game. Kelly's original judgement was correct, for not only did Celtic lose, Jimmy Johnstone and John Hughes were sent off, as was Bobby Lennox, (it was a case of mistaken identity and he had to be threatened by a policeman's sword before he eventually went). Bertie Auld was sent off but didn't go, and Tommy Gemmell should have been for his violent indiscretion (highlighted endlessly on TV) on an Argentinian. Every member of the Celtic squad was fined £250 for his behaviour. This was grossly unfair to many members of the squad, for the violence, spitting and intimidation were hard for anyone to accept phlegmatically. It took Celtic a long time to recover from this fiasco.

As for the title 'world champions', there are times when it has seemed as if a Scottish team should be world champions – the Celtic team of 1908 would have had a strong case, for example, but not as strong as that of Renton. In 1888, the Dumbartonshire team, having beaten Cambuslang 6–1 in the Scottish Cup final (there was as yet no Scottish League) promptly challenged both West Bromwich Albion (winners of the 1888 FA Cup) and Preston North End (the runners-up) and beat them both. As no other country as yet played football to the standard of England or Scotland, a reasonable case could therefore be made out for Renton being world champions of 1888. Less substantial are Hearts claims in 1902. Being the Scottish Cup winners of 1901, they challenged Tottenham Hotspur, the FA Cup winners of that year, although not yet members of the English League. After a 0–0 draw in London, Hearts beat Spurs 3–1 at Tynecastle on 4 January 1902. But as Rangers won the Scottish League in 1901 and would do so again in 1902, it is hard to sustain the claim of Hearts. There is even less justification for Hibs' claim to the same title in 1887. In a match billed as the championship of the world, they beat Preston North End 2–1, but although Hibs did indeed win the Scottish Cup that year, Preston did not win the English Cup.

WORLD CUP

Scotland have entered every World Cup tournament since 1950, and have qualified for the final stages in 1954, 1958, 1974, 1978, 1982, 1986, 1990 and 1998. In common with other British nations, they showed no interest in the first three World Cup competitions of 1930, 1934 and 1938, and even in 1950, when they were invited to enter, they refused to do so unless they were British Champions! England beat them in the crucial game, and thus Scotland was deprived of a trip to Brazil. Since then qualification for the World Cup has become an important part of the Scottish psyche. The first player to score for Scotland in the World Cup finals was Jimmy Murray of Hearts in 1958, but the first Scotsman to score was Jimmy Brown, an Ayrshire man who scored for the USA versus Argentina in the semi-final of the 1930 World Cup.

1950 Qualifying Stages

1 Oct 1949	Northern Ireland	Belfast	8–2
9 Nov 1949	Wales	Hampden Park	2–0
15 Apr 1950	England	Hampden Park	0–1
Scotland refused to go to Brazil			

1954 Qualifying Stages

3 Oct 1953	Northern Ireland	Belfast	3–1
4 Nov 1953	Wales	Hampden Park	3–3
3 Apr 1954	England	Hampden Park	2–4

Finals in Switzerland

16 June 1954	Austria	Zurich	0–1
19 June 1954	Uruguay	Basle	0–7

Scotland's half-hearted and amateurish approach to this tournament got what it deserved in terms of results. Only thirteen men were in the squad (although twenty-two would have been allowed) and no training kit was supplied. Only one goalkeeper, Fred Martin of Aberdeen, was chosen.

The strips supplied were the thick ones that one would have expected for a cold day in February, not for the sweltering heat of Switzerland in midsummer. Scotland played only two games, for they were to play the other team in the group, Czechoslovakia, only if there was a tie.

In spite of this, Scotland played respectably in their first game against Austria and were unlucky to see a late Neil Mochan shot saved by the goalkeeper. Then before the next game against Uruguay, Andy Beattie the manager announced his resignation, although he would stay with the squad for the duration of the World Cup.

For inept timing, this was breathtaking, and Scotland, suffering from a lack of leadership, the heat and a total lack of preparation for their South American opponents went down 0–7 before a 43,000 crowd and a live TV audience.

1958 Qualifying Stages

8 May 1957	Spain	Hampden Park	4–2
19 May 1957	Switzerland	Basle	2–1
26 May 1957	Spain	Madrid	1–4
6 Nov 1957	Switzerland	Hampden Park	3–2

Cheers from Scotland as they return undefeated from the 1974 World Cup in West Germany.

Finals in Sweden

8 June 1958	Yugoslavia	Vasteras	1–1
11 June 1958	Paraguay	Norrkoping	2–3
15 June 1958	France	Orebro	1–2

Incredibly, Scotland approached a World Cup finals tournament without a manager, Matt Busby having not yet fully recovered from the injuries sustained in the Munich air crash in February. The job was not offered to any other accredited manager and the organization of the team was in the hands of the selectors. Team talks were given by trainer Dawson Walker and a few more experienced players. In each of the three games played, Scotland lost an early goal. The first game against Yugoslavia was a respectable draw, and indeed Scotland might have won if the referee had not disallowed a late goal. It was against Paraguay that Scotland came a real cropper, losing 2–3 in a game that was characterised by heavy tackling and a weak referee, as well as Scottish naivety. The final game against France saw Scotland 0–2 down, then fight back and they were unlucky not to get an equalizer after Jimmy Murray had pulled one back. It is hard to resist the feeling that a little organization and leadership would not have gone amiss.

1962 Qualifying Stages

3 May 1961	Eire	Hampden Park	4–1
7 May 1961	Eire	Dublin	3–0
14 May 1961	Czechoslovakia	Bratislava	0–4
26 Sep 1961	Czechoslovakia	Hampden Park	3–2
29 Nov 1961	Czechoslovakia	Brussels	2–4
	(After extra time in a play-off on a neutral ground)		
Scotland failed to qualify for Chile			

1966 Qualifying Stages

21 Oct 1964	Finland	Hampden Park	3–1
23 May 1965	Poland	Chorzow	1–1
27 May 1965	Finland	Helsinki	2–1
13 Oct 1965	Poland	Hampden Park	1–2
9 Nov 1965	Italy	Hampden Park	1–0
7 Dec 1965	Italy	Naples	0–3
Scotland failed to qualify for England			

1970 Qualifying Stages

6 Nov 1968	Austria	Hampden Park	2–1
11 Dec 1968	Cyprus	Nicosia	5–0
16 Apr 1969	West Germany	Hampden Park	1–1
17 May 1969	Cyprus	Hampden Park	8–0
22 Oct 1969	West Germany	Hamburg	2–3
5 Nov 1969	Austria	Vienna	0–2
Scotland failed to qualify for Mexico			

1974 Qualifying Stages

18 Oct 1972	Denmark	Copenhagen	4–1
15 Nov 1972	Denmark	Hampden Park	2–0
26 Sep 1973	Czechoslovakia	Hampden Park	2–1
17 Oct 1973	Czechoslovakia	Bratislava	0–1

Finals in West Germany

14 June 1974	Zaire	Dortmund	2–0
18 June 1974	Brazil	Frankfurt	0–0
22 June 1974	Yugoslavia	Frankfurt	1–1

This was arguably Scotland's best-ever performance in the World Cup finals, but Willie Ormond's side, although undefeated, did not get past the group stage, largely as a result of not having scored enough goals in the first game against Zaire. The goals by Lorimer and

Kenny Dalglish against Yugoslavia in the 1974 World Cup finals.

Jordan were satisfactory but both Yugoslavia and Brazil beat Zaire by more goals. In the second game against Brazil, Scotland were distinctly unlucky. Billy Bremner missed one good chance and several others might have been put away as well, and a 0–0 draw was all that Scotland could claim. It was, however, a good result against Brazil, although it meant that Scotland now had to beat Yugoslavia to qualify. Once again a draw was all that could be achieved, both goals coming late. Yugoslavia scored with eight minutes to go, then Jordan equalized at the death. Some thought that Scotland had qualified because Zaire were holding Brazil to two goals in the other game, but a comical goalkeeping error by the Zaire goalkeeper allowed Brazil to score again and qualify.

In spite of the disappointment, Scotland deserved the acclaim that they received when they came back to Scotland.

1978 Qualifying Stages

13 Oct 1976	Czechoslovakia	Prague	0–2
17 Nov 1976	Wales	Hampden Park	1–0
21 Sep 1977	Czechoslovakia	Hampden Park	3–1
12 Oct 1977	Wales	Anfield	2–0

Finals in Argentina

3 June 1978	Peru	Cordoba	1–3
7 June 1978	Iran	Cordoba	1–1
11 June 1978	Holland	Mendoza	3–2

A major disaster for Scotland that affected the credibility of Scottish football for a time, and rocked the whole nation in a way that is hard to parallel elsewhere. Following the winter of 1977/78, in which unrestrained optimism and euphoria was the order of the day, manager Ally MacLeod failed to read the danger signals highlighted by some dreadful performances in the British International Championship, particularly a poor performance against England. The draw was looked upon as comparatively easy, but no research had been done on Peru or Iran, whom the management took far too lightly. Scotland went ahead in the first game against Peru through Jordan, then at a crucial stage missed a penalty and subsequently collapsed.

Following the sending home of Willie Johnston for using an illegal substance, Scotland then proceeded to draw with Iran, needing an own goal to do so. Then, ironically, once the damage had been done, Scotland beat Holland on the night of Archie Gemmill's famous goal (Dalglish scored the first goal, then Gemmill scored a penalty for the second) but the 3–2 scoreline was not enough.

1982 Qualifying Stages

10 Sep 1980	Sweden	Stockholm	1–0
15 Oct 1980	Portugal	Hampden Park	0–0
25 Feb 1981	Israel	Tel Aviv	1–0
25 Mar 1981	Northern Ireland	Hampden Park	1–1
28 Apr 1981	Israel	Hampden Park	3–0
9 Sep 1981	Sweden	Hampden Park	2–0
14 Oct 1981	Northern Ireland	Belfast	0–0
18 Nov 1981	Portugal	Lisbon	1–2

World Cup finals 1982: Eder's goal for Brazil in their 4-1 victory,

Finals in Spain

15 June 1982	New Zealand	Malaga	5–2
18 June 1982	Brazil	Seville	1–4
22 June 1982	USSR	Malaga	2–2

Jock Stein's men did creditably in Spain, but once again disappointment was the order of the day. The game against New Zealand brought five good goals (Dalglish, Wark 2, Robertson and Archibald), but two were conceded through defensive errors, and at one point New Zealand brought it back to 3–2. The game against Brazil was the game of Dave Narey's famous goal as Scotland went ahead. Unfortunately it was too good to last, and Scotland then conceded four. Thus Scotland had to beat the USSR in the final game. For a while it looked possible as Jordan opened the scoring, but then after the USSR had equalized, with time running out, Miller and Hansen made the classic mistake of going for the same ball and collided into one another, allowing the USSR the chance to go ahead. Although Graeme Souness scored near the end, the 2–2 draw was not enough, and for the third successive time, Scotland went out of the tournament on goal difference.

1986 Qualifying Stages

17 Oct 1984	Iceland	Hampden Park	3–0
14 Nov 1984	Spain	Hampden Park	3–1
27 Feb 1985	Spain	Seville	0–1
27 Mar 1985	Wales	Hampden Park	0–1
28 May 1985	Iceland	Reykjavik	1–0
10 Sep 1985	Wales	Cardiff	1–1

Play–offs

20 Nov 1985	Australia	Hampden Park	2–0
4 Dec 1985	Australia	Melbourne	0–0

Finals in Mexico

4 June 1986	Denmark	Nezahualcoyotl	0–1
8 June 1986	West Germany	Queretaro	1–2
13 June 1986	Uruguay	Nezahualcoyotl	0–0

Costa Rica's Juan Cayasso scores a shock goal, which effectively ended Scotland's hopes at Italia '90.

Scotland, under the temporary charge of Alex Ferguson, was placed into what was called the 'group of death' by the draw, and it was generally acknowledged to be the most difficult of all. The first game against Denmark saw a good performance from Scotland, but it was Denmark who got the only goal of the game. The game against the Germans produced a great goal by Gordon Strachan to put Scotland ahead, but then Germany scored twice in a game played in searing heat. Scotland might yet have qualified as one of the best-placed third countries if they beat Uruguay, but in spite of the Uruguayans losing a man, Batista sent off in the first minute for a bad tackle on Strachan, Scotland could not score against a defensive-minded Uruguayan side.

1990 Qualifying Stages

14 Sep 1988	Norway	Oslo	2–1
19 Oct 1988	Yugoslavia	Hampden Park	1–1
8 Feb 1989	Cyprus	Limassol	3–2
8 Mar 1989	France	Hampden Park	2–0
26 Apr 1989	Cyprus	Hampden Park	2–1
6 Sep 1989	Yugoslavia	Zagreb	1–3
11 Oct 1989	France	Paris	0–3
15 Nov 1989	Norway	Hampden Park	1–1

Finals in Italy

11 June 1990	Costa Rica	Genoa	0–1
16 June 1990	Sweden	Genoa	2–1
20 June 1990	Brazil	Turin	0–1

Scotland shot themselves in the foot in this tournament with a disgraceful first game against Costa Rica which the third-world unknowns won 1–0. This result was greeted with incredulity throughout the world, but then Scotland bounced back with a fine win over Sweden five days later. Stuart McCall and Mo Johnston (with a penalty) scored for Scotland, and although Sweden pulled a goal back in the last few minutes, Scotland held out for a deserved victory. It now all depended on the game against Brazil, who had already qualified, and it looked as if a draw might be sufficient. Everything went well until a ball bounced off Jim Leighton's chest and Muller tapped the ball in to win the game for Brazil and to put Andy Roxburgh's side out.

1994 Qualifying Stages

19 Sep 1992	Switzerland	Berne	1–3
14 Oct 1992	Portugal	Ibrox	0–0
18 Nov 1992	Italy	Ibrox	0–0
17 Feb 1993	Malta	Ibrox	3–0
28 Apr 1993	Portugal	Lisbon	0–5
19 May 1993	Estonia	Tallinn	3–0
2 June 1993	Estonia	Pittodrie	3–1
8 Sep 1993	Switzerland	Pittodrie	1–1
13 Oct 1993	Italy	Rome	1–3
17 Nov 1993	Malta	Valletta	2–0
Scotland failed to qualify for the USA			

1998 Qualifying Stages

31 Aug 1996	Austria	Vienna	0–0
5 Oct 1996	Latvia	Riga	2–0
10 Nov 1996	Sweden	Ibrox	1–0
11 Feb 1997	Estonia	Monaco	0–0
29 Mar 1997	Estonia	Rugby Park	2–0
2 Apr 1997	Austria	Celtic Park	2–0
30 Apr 1997	Sweden	Gothenburg	1–2
8 June 1997	Belarus	Minsk	1–0
7 Sep 1997	Belarus	Pittodrie	4–1
11 Oct 1997	Latvia	Celtic Park	2–0

Finals in France

10 June 1998	Brazil	Paris	1–2
16 June 1998	Norway	Bordeaux	1–1
23 June 1998	Morocco	St Etienne	0–3

Craig Brown's team found themselves opening the tournament by playing against Brazil (yet again) and once again not getting the breaks from Lady Luck. Brazil scored early, but then Scotland equalized through a penalty from John Collins, and looked for a long time as if they might get a draw, until a freakish own goal, when the ball bounced off Tom Boyd to give the Brazilians the lead. A creditable draw against Norway followed, with Craig Burley equalizing for Scotland and a little luck might well have brought a winner. Scotland had to beat Morocco in their final game, but collapsed and went down 0–3 before a large and disappointed Scottish support.

2002 Qualifying Stages

2 Sep 2000	Latvia	Riga	1–0
7 Oct 2000	San Marino	Serravalle	2–0
11 Oct 2000	Croatia	Zagreb	1–1
24 Mar 2001	Belgium	Hampden Park	2–2
28 Mar 2001	San Marino	Hampden Park	4–0
1 Sep 2001	Croatia	Hampden Park	0–0
5 Sep 2001	Belgium	Brussels	0–2
6 Oct 2001	Latvia	Hampden Park	2–1
Scotland failed to qualify for Korea / Japan			

2006 Qualifying Stages

8 Sep 2004	Slovenia	Hampden Park	0–0
9 Oct 2004	Norway	Hampden Park	0–1
13 Oct 2004	Moldova	Chisinau	1–1
26 Mar 2005	Italy	Milan	0–2
4 June 2005	Moldova	Hampden Park	2–0
8 June 2005	Belarus	Minsk	0–0
3 Sep 2005	Italy	Hampden Park	1–1
7 Sep 2005	Norway	Oslo	2–1
8 Oct 2005	Belarus	Hampden Park	0–1
12 Oct 2005	Slovenia	Celje	3–0
Scotland failed to qualify for Germany			

WORLD CUP WINNERS

World Cup winners and Scotland do not necessarily go hand in hand, but several men who have won a World Cup medal have played for a Scottish team, eg Rino Gattuso and Stephane Guivarc'h have played for Rangers, and Juninho for Celtic.

YELLOW CARD (See DISCIPLINE and SUSPENSION AND FINES)

YOUNG Alec (1937 –)

Scotland Caps: 8
Scottish League Championship medals: 2
Scottish Cup medals: 1
Scottish League Cup medals: 1

Alec Young is not to be confused with an earlier Alec (Sandy) Young, who played for Everton some fifty years

Kenny Miller (left) celebrates with Darren Fletcher after scoring against Italy during the World Cup 2006 qualifying match at Hampden Park in September 2005.

previously. This one played for Hearts as well as Everton, and was capped eight times for Scotland. He was fair-haired and a very versatile forward, with an ability to play almost anywhere in the forward line. After his transfer to Everton for £55,000 in 1960, he won an English league medal and an FA Cup medal, and is considered to be one of the Merseyside club's best-ever players. He also played for Glentoran and Stockport County.

YOUNG George (1922 – 1997)

Scotland Caps: 53
Scottish League Championship medals: 6
Scottish Cup medals: 4
Scottish League Cup medals: 2

George Young was an outstanding centre half and captain of Rangers and Scotland, playing 428 times for Rangers and fifty-three times for Scotland, before his retirement in 1957. He was commonly known as 'Corky', either for his ability to bottle-up attacks or because he always carried the cork of a champagne bottle that was opened when Rangers won the Scottish Cup of 1948. Young was the mainstay of the Rangers 'iron curtain' defence of the late 1940s and early 1950s, although he was often at right back to accommodate Willie Woodburn. On one famous occasion, in the Scottish Cup final of 1953 against Aberdeen, he was compelled through an injury to goalkeeper George Niven to don the yellow jersey and play in goal. The problem was that Young's physique was somewhat larger than that of Niven and he is described in contemporary accounts as looking 'like a skinned rabbit'. He was big and tough, but his play did not lack sophistication. He was always a great ambassador for both the club and the game. His retirement from the playing side of the game in 1957 was abrupt, and he was manager of Third Lanark in the 1960s.

YOUNG James (1882 – 1922)

Scotland Caps: 1
Scottish League Championship medals: 9
Scottish Cup medals: 6

A fair-haired right back commonly known as 'Sunny Jim', James Young was the epitome of the successful Celtic sides of the pre-first world war era. He played for Kilmarnock, Barrow and Bristol Rovers before joining Celtic in 1903. As part of the half-back line of Young, Loney and Hay he dominated Scottish football from 1904 until his retirement through injury in 1917. He was captain of Celtic from 1911 onwards, but only won one Scottish cap. He met his death in a motorcycle accident in his native Ayrshire in 1922. In the opinion of Eugene MacBride, who wrote the massive work '*An Alphabet of the Celts*', Sunny Jim is the greatest Celt of all time.

YOUNGER Tommy (1930 – 1984)

Scotland Caps: 24
Scottish League Championship medals: 2

Generally regarded as one of the safest goalkeepers of the mid 1950s, Tommy Younger won twenty-four caps for Scotland and (unusually for a goalkeeper) captained the side for two games in the 1958 World Cup finals. He played for Hibernian between 1948 and 1956, and won two Scottish League medals with the Edinburgh side in the early 1950s. He was transferred to Liverpool in 1956 for £9,000, and later in his career played briefly with Falkirk, Stoke City and Leeds United. His heart lay with Hibs, however, and he became a director with the Easter Road side, and was also President of the Scottish League.

YOUTH FOOTBALL

This aspect of football is indispensable to the future of the game in Scotland. There exists a Scottish Youth Football Association, affiliated to the Scottish Football Association, which coordinates all youth football played throughout the country.

Its aims are "legislate for, foster, develop and improve the game of association football among all classes of youth football clubs, leagues or associations of such clubs in Scotland and to conduct annually the cup competitions of the Scottish Youth Football Association." In particular there is a Scottish Youth Cup for seven levels of youth football, namely Age 13s, Age 14s, Age 15s, Age 16s, Age 17s, Age 19s (which replaced Age 18s from 2003 onwards) and Age 21s. The practice is to have a whole weekend dedicated to the playing of these cup finals (four on Saturday, three on Sunday) at a senior ground (in 2006 and 2007 the Excelsior Stadium, Airdrie). Previous winners have been:

Scottish Youth FA Challenge Cup Winners

Age 12s

1999/2000	Renfrew Victoria BC
2000/01	Leith Athletic FC
2001/02	Leith Athletic FC
2002/03	Leith Athletic FC

Age 13s

1999/2000	Dalkeith BC
2000/01	Rangers SABC
2001/02	Greig Park Rangers
2002/03	Tynecastle Hearts
2003/04	Hutchison Vale FC
2004/05	Hutchison Vale FC
2005/06	Hutchison Vale FC
2006/07	Hutchison Vale FC
2007/08	Edinburgh City FC

Age 14s

1999/2000	Tranmere Rovers BC
2000/01	Albion BC
2001/02	Musselburgh Windsor
2002/03	Gairdoch United
2003/04	Hutchison Vale FC
2004/05	Hutchison Vale FC
2005/06	Blue Brazil BC
2006/07	Albion BC
2007/08	Clyde Soccer, Cumbernauld

Age 15s

1999/2000	Star 'A' BC
2000/01	Gairdoch United
2001/02	Middlefield Wasps SC
2002/03	Hutchison Vale BC
2003/04	Fairmuir BC
2004/05	Musselburgh Windsor
2005/06	Hamilton Palace BC
2006/07	Tynecastle FC
2007/08	Albion BC

Age 16s

1999/2000	Queen's Park FC BC
2000/01	Rossvale BC
2001/02	Gairdoch United
2002/03	Middlefield Wasps SC
2003/04	Albion BC
2004/05	Crosshouse BC
2005/06	Albion BC
2006/07	Syngenta Juveniles
2007/08	Hutchison Vale FC

Age 17s

2003/04	Calderwood Blue Star
2004/05	Dyce BC
2005/06	Crosshouse BC
2006/07	Townhead Amateurs
2007/08	Leith Athletic FC

Age 18s

1999/2000	Banks O'Dee BC 'A'
2000/01	Goldenhill BC
2001/02	Paisley United
2002/03	Bonnyton Thistle FC

Age 19s

2003/04	Edina Hibs Colts
2004/05	Bonnyton Thistle FC
2005/06	Goldenhill BC
2006/07	Lenzie Youth Club
2007/08	Drumchapel United

Age 21s

1999/2000	Easthouses BC 'A'
2000/01	Knightswood Juveniles
2001/02	Hillwood BC
2002/03	Hutchison Vale BC
2003/04	Hutchison Vale BC
2004/05	Harmony Row
2005/06	Glasgow Amateurs
2006/07	Harmony Row
2007/08	Harmony Row

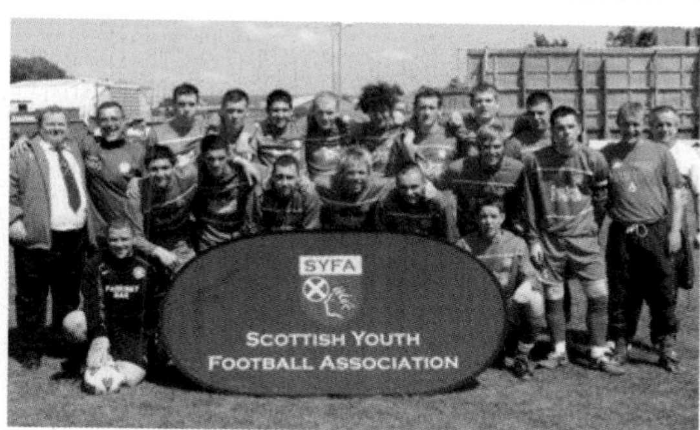

The Lady Darling Supplementary Challenge Cup final, 2008 between Barrhead Arthurlie Junior BC 21's and Hillwood Boys Club 21's .

Lady Darling Supplementary Cup

1999/2000	Knightswood Juveniles
2000/01	Viewfield Rovers
2001/02	Knightswood Juveniles
2002/03	Knightswood Juveniles
2003/04	Campsie Black Watch
2004/05	Colville Park
2005/06	Kilwinning Rangers
2006/07	St Peters Juveniles
2007/08	Barrhead Arthurlie

In addition there are regional leagues organized by the six regions – Eastern, Western, Northern, Midland, Tayside/Fife and Ayrshire/Southwest. Each of these regions has leagues at the levels indicated above. An exciting development in recent years has been the Tesco Cup for Under-13s. This is a British tournament in which the winners of the Scottish Under-13 Cup represent Scotland against the winners of the equivalent tournaments in England, Wales and Northern Ireland. On 20 May 2006 at the City of Manchester Stadium, Hutchison Vale did Scotland proud by winning the trophy. They defeated Percival Youth, the representatives of England, 2–1 after extra time in the final, having defeated Linfield of Northern Ireland in the semi-final.

YUGOSLAVIA

This country no longer exists, but when it did Scotland played them eight times, winning two, drawing five and losing only once.

1955	15 May	Belgrade	2–2	Reilly Smith	Veselinovic Vukas
1956	21 Nov	Hampden Park	2–0	Mudie Baird	
1958	8 June	Vasteras	1–1	Murray	Petakovic
1972	29 June	Bello Horizonte	2–2	Macari (2)	Bajevic Jerkovic
1974	22 June	Frankfurt	1–1	Jordan	Karasi
1984	12 Sep	Hampden Park	6–1	Cooper Souness Dalglish Sturrock Johnston Nicholas	Vokri
1988	19 Oct	Hampden Park	1–1	Johnston	Katanec
1989	6 Sep	Zagreb	1–3	Durie	Katanec Nicol o.g. Gillespie o.g.

ZAIRE

When Scotland played Zaire at the World Cup finals of 1974, beating them 2–0, it was Scotland's first-ever win at a World Cup finals tournament. The country is now known as the Democratic Republic of the Congo.

1974	14 June	Dortmund	2–0	Lorimer Jordan	

APPENDIX

A – International appearances for Scotland
B – Goals scored for Scotland

			A	B	
ADAM	Charlie	Rangers	2	0	2007
ADAMS	James	Hearts	3	0	1889-1893
AGNEW	William	Kilmarnock	3	0	1907-1908
AIRD	John	Burnley	4	0	1954
AITKEN	Andrew	Newcastle Utd. Middlesbrough Leicester Fosse	14	0	1901 -1911
AITKEN	George	East Fife Sunderland	8	0	1949-1954
AITKEN	Ralph	Dumbarton	2	1	1886-1888
AITKEN	Roy	Celtic Newcastle Utd. St Mirren	57	1	1980-1992
AITKENHEAD	Walter	Blackburn Rovers	1	2	1912
ALBISTON	Arthur	Man. Utd.	14	0	1982-1986
ALEXANDER	David	East Stirlingshire	2	0	1894
ALEXANDER	Graham	Preston N E Burnley	33	0	2002-2008
ALEXANDER	Neil	Cardiff City	3	0	2006
ALLAN	David	Queen's Park	3	1	1885-1886
ALLAN	George	Liverpool	1	0	1897
ALLAN	Henry	Hearts	1	0	1902
ALLAN	John	Queen's Park	2	1	1887
ALLAN	Thomson	Dundee	2	0	1974
ANCELL	Bobby	Newcastle Utd.	2	0	1937
ANDERSON	Andrew	Hearts	23	0	1933-1939
ANDERSON	Fred	Clydesdale	1	1	1874
ANDERSON	George	Kilmarnock	1	0	1901
ANDERSON	Harry	Raith Rovers	1	0	1914
ANDERSON	John	Leicester City	1	0	1954
ANDERSON	Kenny	Queen's Park	3	0	1896-1898
ANDERSON	Russell	Aberdeen Plymouth Argyle	11	0	2003-2008
ANDERSON	William	Queen's Park	6	2	1882-1885
ANDREWS	Peter	Eastern	1	1	1875
ARCHIBALD	Sandy	Rangers	8	1	1921-1932
ARCHIBALD	Steve	Aberdeen Tottenham H. Barcelona	27	4	1980-1986
ARMSTRONG	Matt	Aberdeen	3	0	1936-1937
ARNOT	Wattie	Queen's Park	14	0	1883-1893
AULD	Bertie	Celtic	3	0	1959-1960
AULD	John	Third Lanark	3	0	1887-1889
BAIRD	Andrew	Queen's Park	2	0	1892-1894
BAIRD	David	Hearts	3	1	1890-1892
BAIRD	Hugh	Airdrie	1	0	1956
BAIRD	John	Vale of Leven	3	2	1876-1880
BAIRD	Sammy	Rangers	7	2	1957-1958
BAIRD	William	St.Bernard's	1	0	1897
BANNON	Eamonn	Dundee Utd.	11	1	1980-1986
BARBOUR	Alexander	Renton	1	1	1885
BARKER	John	Rangers	2	4	1893-1894
BARRETT	Francis	Dundee	2	0	1894-1895
BATTLES	Barney sr.	Celtic	3	0	1901
BATTLES	Barney jr.	Hearts	1	1	1931
BAULD	Willie	Hearts	3	2	1950
BAXTER	Jim	Rangers Sunderland	34	3	1961-1968
BAXTER	Robert	Middlesbrough	3	0	1939
BEATTIE	Andy	Preston N E	7	0	1937-1939
BEATTIE	Craig	Celtic W B A	7	1	2005-2007
BEATTIE	Robert	Preston N E	1	0	1939
BEGBIE	Isaac	Hearts	4	0	1890-1894
BELL	Alec	Man. Utd.	1	0	1912
BELL	Jack	Dumbarton Everton Celtic	10	5	1890-1900
BELL	Mark	Hearts	1	0	1901
BELL	William	Leeds United	2	0	1966
BENNETT	Alec	Celtic Rangers	11	2	1904-1913
BENNIE	Bob	Airdrieonians	3	0	1925-1926
BERNARD	Paul	Oldham Ath.	2	0	1995
BERRA	Christophe	Hearts	1	0	2008
BERRY	Davidson	Queen's Park	3	1	1894-1899
BERRY	William	Queen's Park	4	0	1888-1891
BETT	Jim	Rangers Lokeren Aberdeen	25	1	1982-1990
BEVERIDGE	William	Glasgow Univ.	3	1	1879-1880
BLACK	Andrew	Hearts	3	3	1938-1939
BLACK	David	Hurlford	1	0	1889
BLACK	Eric	Metz	2	0	1988
BLACK	Ian	Southampton	1	0	1948
BLACKBURN	John	Royal Engineers	1	0	1873
BLACKLAW	Adam	Burnley	3	0	1963-1965
BLACKLEY	John	Hibernian	7	0	1974-1977
BLAIR	Danny	Clyde Aston Villa	8	0	1929-1933
BLAIR	Jimmy	Sheffield Wed. Cardiff City	8	0	1920-1924
BLAIR	Jimmy	Blackpool	1	0	1947
BLAIR	John	Motherwell	1	0	1934
BLAIR	William	Third Lanark	1	0	1896
BLESSINGTON	Jimmy	Celtic	4	0	1894-1896
BLYTH	Jim	Coventry City	2	0	1978
BONE	Jimmy	Norwich City	2	1	1972
BOOTH	Scott	Aberdeen B. Dortmund Twente	21	6	1993-2001
BOWIE	James	Rangers	2	0	1920
BOWIE	William	Linthouse	1	0	1891
BOWMAN	Dave	Dundee United	6	0	1992-1994
BOWMAN	George	Montrose	1	0	1892
BOYD	James	Newcastle Utd.	1	0	1934
BOYD	Kris	Rangers	14	7	2006-2008
BOYD	Robert	Mossend Swifts	2	2	1889-91
BOYD	Tom	Motherwell Chelsea Celtic	72	1	1991-2001
BOYD	William	Clyde	2	1	1931
BRADSHAW	Tom	Bury	1	0	1928
BRAND	Ralph	Rangers	8	8	1961-1962
BRANDON	Thomas	Blackburn Rovers	1	0	1896
BRAZIL	Alan	Ipswich Town Tottenham H.	13	1	1980-1983
BRECKENRIDGE	Thomas	Hearts	1	1	1888
BREMNER	Billy	Leeds United	54	3	1965-1975
BREMNER	Des	Hibernian	1	0	1976
BRENNAN	Frank	Newcastle Utd.	7	0	1947-1954
BRESLIN	Bernard	Hibernian	1	0	1897
BREWSTER	George	Everton	1	0	1921
BROGAN	Jim	Celtic	4	0	1971
BROWN	Alex	Middlesbrough	1	0	1904
BROWN	Allan	East Fife Blackpool	14	6	1950-1954
BROWN	Andrew	St Mirren	2	0	1890-1891
BROWN	Bill	Dundee Tottenham H.	28	0	1958-1965
BROWN	Bobby	Rangers	3	0	1947-1952
BROWN	George	Rangers	19	0	1931-1938
BROWN	Hugh	Partick Thistle	3	0	1946-1947
BROWN	James	Cambuslang	1	0	1890
BROWN	James	Sheffield United	1	0	1975
BROWN	John	Clyde	1	0	1938
BROWN	Robert	Dumbarton	2	0	1884
BROWN	Robert	Dumbarton	1	0	1885
BROWN	Scott	Hibernian Celtic	9	0	2005-2008
BROWNING	Johnny	Celtic	1	0	1914
BROWNLIE	Jimmy	Third Lanark	16	0	1909-1914
BROWNLIE	John	Hibernian	7	0	1971-1975
BRUCE	Daniel	Vale of Leven	1	0	1890
BRUCE	Robert	Middlesbrough	1	0	1934
BUCHAN	Martin	Aberdeen Man. Utd.	34	0	1971-1978
BUCHANAN	Jock	Rangers	2	0	1929-1930
BUCHANAN	John	Cambuslang	1	0	1889
BUCHANAN	Peter	Chelsea	1	1	1937

			A	B	
BUCHANAN	Robert	Abercorn	1	1	1891
BUCKLEY	Paddy	Aberdeen	3	1	1954
BUICK	Albert	Hearts	2	2	1902
BURCHILL	Mark	Celtic	6	0	1999-2000
BURKE	Chris	Rangers	2	2	2006
BURLEY	Craig	Chelsea Celtic Derby County	46	3	1995-2002
BURLEY	George	Ipswich Town	11	0	1979-1982
BURNS	Frank	Man.Utd	1	0	1969
BURNS	Kenny	Birmingham C. Nottingham F.	20	1	1974-1981
BURNS	Tommy	Celtic	8	0	1981-1988
BUSBY	Matt	Manchester C.	1	0	1933
CAIRNS	Tommy	Rangers	8	1	1920-1925
CALDERHEAD	David	Q. Of South Wanderers	1	0	1889
CALDERWOOD	Colin	Tottenham H. Aston Villa	36	1	1995-1999
CALDERWOOD	Robert	Cartvale	3	3	1885
CALDOW	Eric	Rangers	40	4	1957-1963
CALDWELL	Gary	Newcastle Utd. Hibernian Celtic	27	2	2002-2008
CALDWELL	Steve	Newcastle Utd. Sunderland	9	0	2001-2006
CALLAGHAN	Pat	Hibernian	1	0	1900
CALLAGHAN	Willie	Dunfermline Ath.	2	0	1969-70
CAMERON	Colin	Hearts Wolves	28	2	1999-2004
CAMERON	John	Rangers	1	0	1886
CAMERON	John	Queen's Park	1	0	1896
CAMERON	John	St Mirren Chelsea	2	0	1904-1909
CAMPBELL	Charles	Queen's Park	13	1	1874-1886
CAMPBELL	Henry	Renton	1	0	1889
CAMPBELL	James	Kilmarnock	2	0	1891-1892
CAMPBELL	James	Sheffield Wed.	1	0	1913
CAMPBELL	John	South Western	1	1	1880
CAMPBELL	John	Celtic	12	5	1893-1903
CAMPBELL	John	Rangers	4	4	1899-1901
CAMPBELL	Kenneth	Liverpool Partick Thistle	8	0	1920-1922
CAMPBELL	Peter	Rangers	2	3	1878-1879
CAMPBELL	Peter	Morton	1	0	1898
CAMPBELL	Robert	Falkirk Chelsea	5	1	1947-1950
CAMPBELL	William	Morton	5	0	1946-1948
CANERO	Peter	Leicester City	1	0	2004
CARABINE	Jimmy	Third Lanark	3	0	1938-1939
CARR	Willie	Coventry	6	0	1970-1972
CASSIDY	Joe	Celtic	4	1	1921-1924
CHALMERS	Steve	Celtic	5	3	1964-1966
CHALMERS	William	Rangers	1	0	1885
CHALMERS	William	Queen's Park	1	0	1929
CHAMBERS	Thomas	Hearts	1	1	1894
CHAPLIN	George	Dundee	1	0	1908
CHEYNE	Alec	Aberdeen	5	4	1929-1930
CHRISTIE	Alec	Queen's Park	3	1	1898-1899
CHRISTIE	Robert	Queen's Park	1	0	1884
CLARK	Bobby	Aberdeen	17	0	1967-1973
CLARK	John	Celtic	4	0	1966-1967
CLARKE	Steve	Chelsea	6	0	1987-1994
CLARKSON	David	Motherwell	1	1	2008
CLELAND	James	Royal Albert	1	0	1891
CLEMENTS	Robert	Leith Athletic	1	0	1891
CLUNAS	William	Sunderland	2	1	1924-1926
COLLIER	Will	Raith Rovers	1	0	1922
COLLINS	Bobby	Celtic Everton Leeds United	31	10	1950-1965
COLLINS	John	Hibernian Celtic Monaco Everton	58	12	1988-1999
COLLINS	Thomas	Hearts	1	0	1909
COLMAN	Donald	Aberdeen	4	0	1911-1913
COLQUHOUN	Eddie	Sheffield Utd.	9	0	1971-1973
COLQUHOUN	John	Hearts	2	0	1988
COMBE	James	Hibernian	3	1	1948
CONN	Alfie jr.	Tottenham H.	2	0	1975
CONN	Alfie sr.	Hearts	1	1	1956

			A	B	
CONNACHAN	Eddie	Dunfermline Ath.	2	0	1961-1962
CONNELLY	George	Celtic	2	0	1973
CONNOLLY	John	Everton	1	0	1973
CONNOR	James	Airdrieonians	1	0	1886
CONNOR	James	Sunderland	4	0	1930-34
CONNOR	Robert	Dundee Aberdeen	4	0	1986-1990
COOK	Willie	Everton	3	0	1934
COOKE	Charlie	Dundee Chelsea	16	0	1965-1975
COOPER	Davie	Rangers Motherwell	22	6	1979-1990
CORMACK	Peter	Hibernian Nottingham F.	9	0	1966-1971
COWAN	James	Aston Villa	3	0	1896-1898
COWAN	James	Morton	25	0	1948-1952
COWAN	William	Newcastle Utd.	1	1	1924
COWIE	Doug	Dundee	20	0	1953-58
COX	Sammy	Rangers	24	0	1948-1954
CRAIG	Allan	Motherwell	3	0	1929-32
CRAIG	Jim	Celtic	1	0	1967
CRAIG	Joe	Celtic	1	1	1977
CRAIG	Tom	Rangers	8	1	1927-1930
CRAIG	Tommy	Newcastle Utd.	1	0	1976
CRAINEY	Stephen	Celtic Southampton	6	0	2002-2004
CRAPNELL	James	Airdrieonians	9	0	1929-1932
CRAWFORD	David	St Mirren Rangers	3	0	1894-1900
CRAWFORD	James	Queen's Park	5	0	1931-1933
CRAWFORD	Steve	Raith Rovers Dunfermline Plymouth Arg.	25	4	1995-2004
CRERAND	Pat	Celtic Man. Utd.	16	0	1961-1965
CRINGAN	Willie	Celtic	5	0	1920-1923
CROAL	James	Falkirk	3	0	1913-1914
CROPLEY	Alex	Hibernian	2	0	1971
CROSBIE	James	Ayr United Birmingham	2	0	1920-1922
CROSS	John	Third Lanark	1	0	1903
CRUICKSHANK	Jim	Hearts	6	0	1964-1975
CRUM	Johnny	Celtic	2	0	1936-1938
CULLEN	Michael	Luton Town	1	0	1956
CUMMING	David	Middlesbrough	1	0	1938
CUMMING	John	Hearts	9	0	1954-1960
CUMMINGS	George	Partick Thistle Aston Villa	9	0	1935-1939
CUMMINGS	Warren	Chelsea	1	0	2002
CUNNINGHAM	Andy	Rangers	12	5	1920-1927
CUNNINGHAM	Willie	Preston N E	8	0	1954-1955
CURRAN	Hugh	Wolves	5	1	1969-1971
DAILLY	Christian	Derby County Blackburn R. West Ham Utd. Rangers	67	6	1997-2008
DALGLISH	Kenny	Celtic Liverpool	102	30	1971-1986
DAVIDSON	Callum	Blackburn R. Leicester City	17	0	1998-2002
DAVIDSON	David	Queen's Park	5	1	1878-1881
DAVIDSON	Jimmy	Partick Thistle	8	1	1954-1955
DAVIDSON	Stewart	Middlesbrough	1	0	1921
DAWSON	Ally	Rangers	5	0	1980-1983
DAWSON	Jerry	Rangers	14	0	1934-1939
DEANS	Dixie	Celtic	2	0	1974
DELANEY	Jimmy	Celtic Man. Utd.	13	7	1935-1948
DEVINE	Andrew	Falkirk	1	1	1910
DEVLIN	Paul	Birmingham C.	10	0	2002-2003
DEWAR	George	Dumbarton	2	1	1888-1889
DEWAR	Neil	Third Lanark	3	4	1932
DICK	John	West Ham U.	1	0	1959
DICKIE	Matthew	Rangers	3	0	1897-1900
DICKOV	Paul	Manchester C. Leicester City Blackburn R.	10	1	2000-2004
DICKSON	William	Dundee Strathmore	1	4	1888
DICKSON	Willie	Kilmarnock	5	0	1970-1971
DIVERS	John	Celtic	1	1	1895
DIVERS	John	Celtic	1	0	1938
DOBIE	Scott	W B A	6	1	2002

			A	B	
DOCHERTY	Tommy	Preston N E Arsenal	25	1	1951-1959
DODDS	Billy	Aberdeen Dundee Utd. Rangers	26	7	1996-2001
DODDS	Davie	Dundee Utd.	2	1	1983
DODDS	Joe	Celtic	3	0	1914
DOIG	Ned	Arbroath Sunderland	5	0	1887-1903
DONACHIE	Willie	Manchester C.	35	0	1972-1978
DONALDSON	Alex	Bolton Wandrs.	6	1	1914-1922
DONNACHIE	Joe	Oldham Ath.	3	1	1913-1914
DONNELLY	Simon	Celtic	10	0	1997-1998
DOUGALL	Cornelius	Birmingham C.	1	0	1946
DOUGALL	Jimmy	Preston N E	1	1	1939
DOUGAN	Bobby	Hearts	1	0	1950
DOUGLAS	Angus	Chelsea	1	0	1911
DOUGLAS	James	Renfrew	1	0	1880
DOUGLAS	Rab	Celtic	19	0	2002-2005
DOWDS	Peter	Celtic	1	0	1892
DOWNIE	Robert	Third Lanark	1	0	1892
DOYLE	Dan	Celtic	8	0	1892-1898
DOYLE	Johnny	Ayr United	1	0	1975
DRUMMOND	John	Falkirk Rangers	14	1	1892-1903
DUNBAR	Mick	Cartvale	1	1	1886
DUNCAN	Arthur	Hibernian	6	0	1975
DUNCAN	David	East Fife	3	1	1948
DUNCAN	Dally	Derby County	14	7	1932-1937
DUNCAN	James	Alexandra A.	2	0	1878-1882
DUNCAN	John	Leicester City	1	1	1925
DUNCANSON	Jimmy	Rangers	1	0	1946
DUNLOP	Jimmy	St Mirren	1	0	1890
DUNLOP	Willie	Liverpool	1	0	1906
DUNN	Jimmy	Hibernian Everton	6	2	1925-1928
DURIE	Gordon	Chelsea Tottenham H. Rangers	43	7	1987-1998
DURRANT	Iain	Rangers Kilmarnock	20	0	1987-2000
DYKES	James	Hearts	2	0	1938
EASSON	James	Portsmouth	3	1	1931-1933
ELLIOTT	Matt	Leicester City	18	1	1997-2001
ELLIS	James	Mossend Swifts	1	1	1892
EVANS	Allan	Aston Villa	4	0	1982
EVANS	Bobby	Celtic Chelsea	48	0	1948-1960
EWART	Jock	Bradford City	1	0	1921
EWING	Tommy	Partick Thistle	2	0	1957-1958
FARM	George	Blackpool	10	0	1952-1959
FERGUSON	Barry	Rangers Blackburn R.	43	3	1998-2007
FERGUSON	Bobby	Kilmarnock	7	0	1965-1966
FERGUSON	Derek	Rangers	2	0	1988
FERGUSON	Duncan	Dundee Utd. Everton	7	0	1992-1997
FERGUSON	Ian	Rangers	9	0	1988-1997
FERGUSON	John	Vale of Leven	6	5	1874-1878
FERNIE	Willie	Celtic	12	1	1954-1958
FINDLAY	Robert	Kilmarnock	1	0	1898
FITCHIE	Tommy	Arsenal Queen's Park	4	1	1905-1907
FLAVELL	Robert	Airdrieonians	2	2	1947
FLECK	Robert	Norwich City	4	0	1990-1991
FLEMING	Charlie	East Fife	1	2	1953
FLEMING	James	Rangers	3	3	1929-1930
FLEMING	Robert	Morton	1	0	1886
FLETCHER	Darren	Man.Utd.	36	4	2003-2008
FLETCHER	Steven	Hibernian	1	0	2008
FORBES	Alex	Sheffield Utd Arsenal	14	1	1947-1952
FORBES	John	Vale of Leven	5	0	1884-1887
FORD	Donald	Hearts	3	0	1973-1974
FORREST	James	Motherwell	1	0	1958
FORREST	Jim	Rangers Aberdeen	5	0	1965-1971
FORSYTH	Alex	Partick Thistle Man. Utd.	10	0	1972-1975
FORSYTH	Campbell	Kilmarnock	4	0	1964

			A	B	
FORSYTH	Tom	Motherwell Rangers	22	0	1971-1978
FOYERS	Robert	St. Bernard's	2	0	1893-1894
FRASER	Douglas	W B A	2	0	1968
FRASER	J ?	Moffat	1	0	1891
FRASER	John	Dundee	1	0	1907
FRASER	Malcolm	Queen's Park	5	0	1880-1883
FRASER	William	Sunderland	2	0	1954
FREEDMAN	Douggie	Crystal Palace	2	1	2001-2002
FULTON	William	Abercorn	1	0	1884
FYFE	John	Third Lanark	1	0	1895
GABRIEL	Jimmy	Everton	2	0	1960-1963
GALLACHER	Hughie	Airdrieonians Newcastle Utd. Chelsea Derby County	20	24	1924-1935
GALLACHER	Kevin	Dundee Utd. Coventry City Blackburn R. Newcastle Utd.	53	9	1988-2001
GALLACHER	Patrick	Sunderland	1	1	1934
GALLACHER	Paul	Dundee Utd.	8	0	2002-2004
GALLAGHER	Paul	Blackburn R.	1	0	2004
GALLOWAY	Mike	Celtic	1	0	1991
GALT	Jimmy	Rangers	2	1	1908
GARDINER	James	Motherwell	1	0	1957
GARDNER	David	Third Lanark	1	0	1897
GARDNER	Robert	Queen's Park	5	0	1872-1878
GEMMELL	Tommy	St.Mirren	2	1	1955
GEMMELL	Tommy	Celtic	18	1	1966-1971
GEMMILL	Archie	Derby County Nottingham F. Birmingham C.	43	8	1971-1981
GEMMILL	Scott	Nottingham F. Everton	26	1	1995-2003
GIBB	William	Clydesdale	1	1	1873
GIBSON	David	Leicester City	7	3	1963-1964
GIBSON	James	Partick Thistle Aston Villa	8	1	1926-1930
GIBSON	Neil	Rangers Partick Thistle	14	1	1895-1905
GILCHRIST	Johnny	Celtic	1	0	1922
GILHOOLEY	Michael	Hull City	1	0	1922
GILLESPIE	Gary	Liverpool	13	0	1987-1990
GILLESPIE	George	Rangers Queen's Park	7	0	1880-1891
GILLESPIE	James	Third Lanark	1	3	1898
GILLESPIE	John	Queen's Park	1	0	1896
GILLESPIE	Robert	Queen's Park	4	0	1926-1933
GILLICK	Torry	Everton	5	3	1937-1938
GILMOUR	John	Dundee	1	0	1930
GILZEAN	Alan	Dundee Tottenham H.	22	12	1963-1971
GLASS	Stephen	Newcastle U.	1	0	1998
GLAVIN	Ronnie	Celtic	1	0	1977
GLEN	Archie	Aberdeen	2	0	1955-1956
GLEN	Robert	Renton Hibernian	3	0	1895-1900
GORAM	Andy	Oldham Ath. Hibernian Rangers	43	0	1985-1998
GORDON	Craig	Hearts Sunderland	31	0	2004-2008
GORDON	Jimmy	Rangers	10	0	1912-1920
GOSSLAND	James	Rangers	1	2	1884
GOUDIE	John	Abercorn	1	1	1884
GOUGH	Richard	Dundee Utd. Tottenham H. Rangers	61	6	1983-1993
GOULD	Jonathan	Celtic	2	0	1999-2000
GOURLAY	Jimmy	Cambuslang	2	1	1886-1888
GOVAN	John	Hibernian	6	0	1947-1948
GOW	Donald	Rangers	1	0	1888
GOW	John J	Queen's Park	1	0	1885
GOW	John R	Rangers	1	0	1888
GRAHAM	Arthur	Leeds United	11	2	1977-1981
GRAHAM	George	Arsenal Man. Utd.	12	3	1971-1973
GRAHAM	John	Annbank	1	0	1884
GRAHAM	John	Arsenal	1	0	1921
GRANT	John	Hibernian	2	0	1958
GRANT	Peter	Celtic	2	0	1989

Simon Donnelly

			A	B	
GRAY	Andy	Aston Villa Wolves Everton	20	7	1975-1985
GRAY	Andy	Bradford City	2	0	2003
GRAY	Archie	Hibernian	1	0	1903
GRAY	Duggie	Rangers	10	0	1928-1932
GRAY	Eddie	Leeds United	12	3	1969-1976
GRAY	Frank	Leeds United Nottingham F.	32	1	1976-1983
GRAY	Woodville	Pollokshields	1	0	1886
GREEN	Tony	Blackpool Newcastle U.	6	0	1971-1972
GREIG	John	Rangers	44	3	1964-1975
GROVES	Willie	Hibernian Celtic	3	4	1888-1890
GULLILAND	William	Queen's Park	4	0	1891-1895
GUNN	Bryan	Norwich City	6	0	1990-1994
HADDOCK	Harry	Clyde	6	0	1954-1958
HADDOW	David	Rangers	1	0	1894
HAFFEY	Frank	Celtic	2	0	1960-1961
HAMILTON	Alex	Queen's Park	4	0	1885-1888
HAMILTON	Alex	Dundee	24	0	1961-1965
HAMILTON	Bob	Dundee Rangers	11	15	1899-1911
HAMILTON	George	Aberdeen	5	4	1946-1954
HAMILTON	Gladstone	Port Glasgow A.	1	0	1906
HAMILTON	James	Queen's Park	3	3	1892-1893
HAMILTON	James	St Mirren	1	0	1924
HAMILTON	T ?	Hurlford	1	0	1891
HAMILTON	Tom	Rangers	1	0	1932
HAMILTON	Willie	Hibernian	1	0	1965
HAMMELL	Steve	Motherwell	1	0	2004
HANNAH	Andrew	Renton	1	0	1888
HANNAH	James	Third Lanark	1	0	1889
HANSEN	Alan	Liverpool	26	0	1979-1987
HANSEN	John	Partick Thistle	2	0	1971-1972
HARKNESS	Jack	Queen's Park Hearts	12	0	1927-1933
HARPER	Joe	Aberdeen Hibernian	4	2	1972-1978
HARPER	Willie	Hibernian Arsenal	11	0	1923-1926
HARRIS	Joe	Partick Thistle	2	0	1921
HARRIS	Neil	Newcastle Utd.	1	0	1924
HARROWER	Willie	Queen's Park	3	4	1882-1886
HARTFORD	Asa	W B A Manchester City Everton	50	4	1972-1982
HARTLEY	Paul	Hearts Celtic	19	1	2005-2008
HARVEY	David	Leeds United	16	0	1972-1976
HASTINGS	Alex	Sunderland	2	0	1935-1937
HAUGHNEY	Mike	Celtic	1	0	1954
HAY	Davie	Celtic	27	0	1970-1974
HAY	James	Celtic Newcastle Utd.	11	0	1905-1914
HEGARTY	Paul	Dundee Utd.	8	0	1979-1983
HEGGIE	Charles	Rangers	1	4	1886
HENDERSON	George	Rangers	1	0	1904
HENDERSON	Jack	Portsmouth	7	1	1953-1958
HENDERSON	Willie	Rangers	29	5	1962-1971
HENDRY	Colin	Blackburn R. Rangers Coventry City Bolton Wandrs.	51	3	1993-2001
HEPBURN	James	Alloa	1	0	1891
HEPBURN	Bob	Ayr United	1	0	1931
HERD	Andrew	Hearts	1	0	1934
HERD	David	Arsenal	5	3	1958-1961
HERD	George	Clyde	5	1	1958-1960
HERRIOT	Jim	Birmingham C.	8	0	1968-1969
HEWIE	John	Charlton Athletic	19	2	1956-1960
HIGGINS	Alex	Kilmarnock	1	3	1885
HIGGINS	Sandy	Newcastle Utd.	4	1	1910-1911
HIGHET	Thomas	Queen's Park	4	1	1875-1878
HILL	David	Rangers	3	1	1881-1882
HILL	David	Third Lanark	1	0	1906
HILL	Frank	Aberdeen	3	0	1930-1931
HILL	John	Hearts	2	0	1891-1892
HOGG	Bobby	Celtic	1	0	1937
HOGG	George	Hearts	2	0	1896
HOGG	James	Ayr United	1	0	1922

			A	B	
HOLM	Andrew	Queen's Park	3	0	1882-1883
HOLT	Davie	Hearts	5	0	1963-1964
HOLT	Gary	Kilmarnock Norwich City	10	1	2000-2004
HOLTON	Jim	Man. Utd.	15	2	1973-1974
HOPE	Bobby	W B A	2	0	1968
HOPKIN	David	Crystal Palace Leeds United	7	2	1997-1999
HOULISTON	Billy	Queen of the S.	3	2	1948-1949
HOUSTON	Stewart	Man. Utd.	1	0	1975
HOWDEN	William	Partick Thistle	1	0	1905
HOWE	Robert	Hamilton Ac.	2	0	1929
HOWIE	Hugh	Hibernian	1	1	1948
HOWIE	James	Newcastle Utd.	3	2	1905-1908
HOWIESON	Jimmy	St Mirren	1	0	1927
HUGHES	Billy	Sunderland	1	0	1975
HUGHES	John	Celtic	8	1	1965-1969
HUGHES	Richard	Portsmouth	5	0	2004-2005
HUMPHRIES	Wilson	Motherwell	1	0	1952
HUNTER	Ally	Kilmarnock Celtic	4	0	1972-1973
HUNTER	John	Eastern Third Lanark	4	0	1874-1877
HUNTER	John	Dundee	1	0	1909
HUNTER	R?	St Mirren	1	0	1890
HUNTER	Willie	Motherwell	3	1	1960
HUSBAND	Jackie	Partick Thistle	1	0	1946
HUTCHISON	Don	Everton Sunderland West Ham Utd.	26	6	1999-2003
HUTCHISON	Tom	Coventry City	17	1	1973-1975
HUTTON	Alan	Rangers Tottenham H.	7	0	2007-2008
HUTTON	J?	St. Bernard's	1	0	1887
HUTTON	Jock	Aberdeen Blackburn R.	10	1	1923-1928
HYSLOP	Tommy	Stoke City Rangers	2	1	1896-1897
IMLACH	Stewart	Nottingham F.	4	0	1958
IMRIE	Willie	St Johnstone	2	1	1929
INGLIS	John	Rangers	2	0	1883
INGLIS	John	Kilmarnock Ath.	1	0	1884
IRONS	James	Queen's Park	1	0	1900
IRVINE	Brian	Aberdeen	9	0	1990-1994
JACKSON	Alex	Aberdeen Huddersfield T.	17	8	1925-1930
JACKSON	Andrew	Cambuslang	2	0	1886-1888
JACKSON	Colin	Rangers	8	1	1975-1976
JACKSON	Darren	Hibernian Celtic	28	4	1995-1998
JACKSON	John	Partick Thistle Chelsea	8	0	1931-1935
JACKSON	Thomas	St Mirren	6	0	1904-1907
JAMES	Alex	Preston N E Arsenal	8	3	1925-1932
JARDINE	Sandy	Rangers	38	1	1970-1979
JARVIE	Drew	Airdrieonians	3	0	1971
JENKINSON	Tommy	Hearts	1	1	1887
JESS	Eoin	Aberdeen Coventry City	18	2	1992-1999
JOHNSTON	Allan	Sunderland Rangers Middlesbrough	18	2	1998-2002
JOHNSTON	Leslie	Clyde	2	1	1948
JOHNSTON	Mo	Watford Celtic Nantes Rangers	38	14	1984-1991
JOHNSTON	Robert	Sunderland	1	0	1937
JOHNSTON	Willie	Rangers W B A	22	2	1965-1978
JOHNSTONE	Bobby	Hibernian Manchester C.	17	10	1951-1956
JOHNSTONE	Derek	Rangers	14	2	1973-1979
JOHNSTONE	James	Abercorn	1	0	1888
JOHNSTONE	Jimmy	Celtic	23	2	1964-74
JOHNSTONE	John	Hearts	3	0	1929-1932
JOHNSTONE	John	Kilmarnock	1	1	1894
JOHNSTONE	William	Third Lanark	3	1	1887-1890
JORDAN	Joe	Leeds United Man. Utd. AC Milan	52	11	1973-1982

			A	B	
KAY	John	Queen's Park	6	5	1880-1884
KEILLOR	Alex	Montrose Dundee	6	2	1891-1897
KEIR	Leitch	Dumbarton	5	1	1885-1888
KELLY	Hugh	Blackpool	1	0	1952
KELLY	James	Renton Celtic	8	1	1888-1896
KELLY	John	Barnsley	2	0	1948
KELSO	Robert	Renton Dundee	7	0	1885-1898
KELSO	Thomas	Dundee	1	0	1914
KENNAWAY	Joe	Celtic	1	0	1934
KENNEDY	Alex	Eastern Third Lanark	6	0	1875-1884
KENNEDY	John	Hibernian	1	0	1897
KENNEDY	John	Celtic	1	0	2004
KENNEDY	Jim	Celtic	6	0	1963-1964
KENNEDY	Sam	Partick Thistle	1	0	1905
KENNEDY	Stewart	Rangers	5	0	1975
KENNEDY	Stuart	Aberdeen	8	0	1978-1981
KER	Geordie	Queen's Park	5	10	1880-1882
KER	William	Queen's Park	2	0	1872-1873
KERR	Andy	Partick Thistle	2	0	1955
KERR	Brian	Newcastle Utd.	3	0	2003-2004
KERR	Peter	Hibernian	1	0	1924
KEY	George	Hearts	1	0	1902
KEY	William	Queen's Park	1	0	1907
KING	Alex	Hearts Celtic	6	1	1896-1899
KING	James	Hamilton Ac.	2	1	1932-1933
KING	William	Queen's Park	1	0	1929
KINLOCH	James	Partick Thistle	1	0	1922
KINNAIRD	Arthur	Wanderers	1	0	1873
KINNEAR	Davie	Rangers	1	1	1937
KYLE	Kevin	Sunderland	9	1	2002-2004
LAMBERT	Paul	Motherwell Borussia Dort. Celtic	40	1	1995-2003
LAMBIE	John	Queen's Park	3	1	1886-1888
LAMBIE	William	Queen's Park	9	5	1892-1897
LAMONT	W?	Pilgrims	1	1	1885
LANG	Archie	Dumbarton	1	0	1880
LANG	James	Clydesdale Third Lanark	2	2	1876-1878
LATTA	Alex	Dumbarton Ath.	2	2	1888-1889
LAW	Denis	Huddersfield T. Manchester C. Torino Man.Utd	55	30	1958-1974
LAW	George	Rangers	3	0	1910
LAW	Tommy	Chelsea	2	0	1928-1930
LAWRENCE	James	Newcastle Utd.	1	0	1911
LAWRENCE	Tommy	Liverpool	3	0	1963-1969
LAWSON	Denis	St Mirren	1	0	1923
LECKIE	Robert	Queen's Park	1	0	1872
LEGGAT	Graham	Aberdeen Fulham	18	8	1956-1960
LEIGHTON	Jim	Aberdeen Man.Utd Hibernian	91	0	1982-1998
LENNIE	Willie	Aberdeen	2	1	1908
LENNOX	Bobby	Celtic	10	3	1966-1970
LESLIE	Lawrie	Airdrieonians	5	0	1960-1961
LEVEIN	Craig	Hearts	16	0	1990-1994
LIDDELL	Billy	Liverpool	28	6	1946-1955
LIDDLE	Danny	East Fife	3	0	1931
LINDSAY	David	St Mirren	1	0	1903
LINDSAY	John	Renton	3	0	1888-1893
LINDSAY	Joseph	Dumbarton	8	6	1880-1886
LINWOOD	Alex	Clyde	1	1	1949
LITTLE	John	Rangers	1	0	1953
LIVINGSTONE	George	Manchester C. Rangers	2	0	1906-07
LOCHHEAD	Alex	Third Lanark	1	0	1889
LOGAN	James	Ayr United	1	1	1891
LOGAN	Thomas	Falkirk	1	0	1913
LOGIE	Jimmy	Arsenal	1	0	1952
LONEY	Willie	Celtic	2	0	1910
LONG	Hugh	Clyde	1	0	1946
LONGAIR	William	Dundee	1	0	1894
LORIMER	Peter	Leeds United	21	4	1969-1975
LOVE	Andrew	Aberdeen	3	1	1931

			A	B	
LOW	Alex	Falkirk	1	0	1933
LOW	James	Cambuslang	1	1	1891
LOW	Thomas	Rangers	1	0	1897
LOW	Wilfred	Newcastle Utd.	5	0	1911-1920
LOWE	James	St. Bernard's	1	1	1887
LUNDIE	James	Hibernian	1	0	1886
LYALL	John	Sheffield Wed.	1	0	1905
McADAM	J?	Third Lanark	1	1	1880
McALLISTER	Brian	Wimbledon	3	0	1997
McALLISTER	Gary	Leicester City Leeds United Coventry City	57	5	1990-1999
McALLISTER	Jamie	Livingston	1	0	2004
MACARI	Lou	Celtic Man. Utd.	24	5	1972-1978
McARTHUR	Dan	Celtic	3	0	1895-1899
McATEE	Andy	Celtic	1	0	1913
MACAULEY	Archie	Brentford Arsenal	7	0	1947-1948
McAULAY	J?	Arthurlie	1	0	1884
McAULAY	James	Dumbarton	9	1	1882-1887
McAULAY	Robert	Rangers	2	0	1931
McAVENNIE	Frank	West Ham Utd. Celtic	5	1	1985-1988
McBAIN	Edward	St Mirren	1	0	1894
McBAIN	Neil	Man. Utd Everton	3	0	1922-1924
McBRIDE	Joe	Celtic	2	0	1966
McBRIDE	Peter	Preston N E	6	0	1904-1909
McCALL	Archie	Renton	1	0	1888
McCALL	James	Renton	5	2	1886-1890
McCALL	Stuart	Everton Rangers	40	1	1990-1998
McCALLIOG	Jim	Sheffield Wed. Wolves	5	1	1967-1971
McCALLUM	Neil	Renton	1	1	1888
McCANN	Bert	Motherwell	5	0	1959-1961
McCANN	Neil	Hearts Rangers Southampton	26	1	1998-2005
McCARTNEY	Willie	Hibernian	1	0	1902
McCLAIR	Brian	Celtic Man. Utd	30	2	1986-1993
McCLORY	Allan	Motherwell	3	0	1926-1934
McCLOY	Peter	Rangers	4	0	1973
McCLOY	Philip	Ayr United	4	0	1924-1925
McCOIST	Ally	Rangers Kilmarnock	61	19	1986-1998
McCOLL	Ian	Rangers	14	0	1950-1958
McCOLL	Robert	Queen's Park Newcastle Utd.	13	13	1896-1908
McCOLL	William	Renton	1	0	1895
McCOMBIE	Andrew	Sunderland Newcastle Utd.	4	0	1903-1905
McCORKINDALE	J?	Partick Thistle	1	0	1891
McCORMACK	Ross	Motherwell	1	0	2008
McCORMICK	Robert	Abercorn	1	1	1886
McCRAE	David	St Mirren	2	0	1929
McCREADIE	Andrew	Rangers	2	0	1893-1894
McCREADIE	Eddie	Chelsea	23	0	1965-1969
McCULLOCH	David	Hearts Brentford Derby County	7	3	1934-1938
McCULLOCH	Lee	Wigan Rangers	15	1	2004-2007
MacDONALD	Alec	Rangers	1	0	1976
McDONALD	Joe	Sunderland	2	0	1955
McDONALD	John	Edinburgh Univ.	1	0	1886
MacDOUGALL	Eddie	Norwich City	7	3	1975
McDOUGALL	James	Liverpool	2	0	1931
McDOUGALL	John	Airdrie	1	0	1926
McDOUGALL	John	Vale of Leven	5	4	1877-1879
McEVELEY	James	Derby County	3	0	2007-2008
McFADDEN	Jamie	Motherwell Everton	37	13	2002-2007
McFADYEN	Willie	Motherwell	2	2	1933
MacFARLANE	Sandy	Dundee	5	1	1904-1911
MacFARLANE	Willie	Hearts	1	0	1947
McFARLANE	Robert	Morton	1	0	1896
McGARR	Ernie	Aberdeen	2	0	1969

Tosh McKinlay.

			A	B	
McGARVEY	Frank	Liverpool Celtic	7	0	1979-1984
McGEOCH	Alex	Dumbreck	4	0	1876-1877
McGHEE	Jimmy	Hibs	1	0	1886
McGHEE	Mark	Aberdeen	4	2	1983-1984
McGINLAY	John	Bolton Wandrs.	13	4	1994-1997
McGONAGLE	Peter	Celtic	6	0	1933-1934
McGRAIN	Danny	Celtic	62	0	1973-1982
McGREGOR	Allan	Rangers	1	0	2007
McGREGOR	John	Vale of Leven	4	1	1877-1880
McGRORY	John	Kilmarnock	3	0	1964-1965
McGRORY	Jimmy	Celtic	7	6	1928-1933
McGUIRE	William	Beith	2	0	1881
McGURK	Frank	Birmingham	1	0	1933
McHARDY	Hugh	Rangers	1	0	1885
McINALLY	Alan	Aston Villa Bayern Munich	8	3	1989-1990
McINALLY	Jim	Dundee United	10	0	1987-1993
McINALLY	Tommy	Celtic	2	0	1926
McINNES	Derek	W B A	2	0	2002
McINNES	Thomas	Cowlairs	1	1	1889
McINTOSH	William	Third Lanark	1	0	1905
McINTYRE	Andrew	Vale of Leven	2	0	1878-1882
McINTYRE	Hugh	Rangers	1	0	1880
McINTYRE	James	Rangers	1	0	1884
MacKAY	Dave	Hearts Tottenham H.	22	4	1957-1965
MacKAY	Dunky	Celtic	14	0	1959-1962
MacKAY	Gary	Hearts	4	1	1987-1988
MacKAY	Malky	Norwich City	5	0	2004
McKAY	Bob	Newcastle Utd	1	0	1927
McKAY	John	Blackburn R.	1	0	1924
McKEAN	Bobby	Rangers	1	0	1976
MacKENZIE	John	Partick Thistle	9	1	1953-1956
McKENZIE	Duncan	Brentford	1	0	1937
McKEOWN	Michael	Celtic	2	0	1889-1890
McKIE	James	E. Stirlingshire	1	2	1898
McKILLOP	Tommy	Rangers	1	0	1938
McKIMMIE	Stewart	Aberdeen	40	1	1989-1996
McKINLAY	Billy	Dundee United Blackburn R.	29	4	1993-1998
McKINLAY	Donald	Liverpool	2	0	1922
McKINLAY	Tosh	Celtic	22	0	1995-1998
MacKINNON	William	Dumbarton	4	0	1883-1884
MacKINNON	William	Queen's Park	9	5	1872-1879
McKINNON	Angus	Queen's Park	1	1	1874
McKINNON	Rob	Motherwell	3	0	1993-1995
McKINNON	Ron	Rangers	28	1	1965-1971
McLAREN	Alan	Hearts Rangers	24	0	1992-1995
McLAREN	Alex	St Johnstone	5	0	1929-1932
McLAREN	Andy	Preston N E	4	3	1947
McLAREN	Andy	Kilmarnock	1	0	2001
McLAREN	James	Hibernian Celtic	3	1	1888-1890
McLEAN	Adam	Celtic	4	1	1925-1927
McLEAN	Davie	Sheffield Wed.	1	0	1912
McLEAN	Duncan	St Bernard's	2	0	1896-1897
McLEAN	George	Dundee	1	0	1968
McLEAN	Tommy	Kilmarnock	6	1	1968-1971
McLEISH	Alex	Aberdeen	77	0	1980-1993
MacLEOD	John	Hibernian	4	0	1961
MacLEOD	Murdo	Celtic Borussia Dort. Hibernian	20	1	1985-1991
McLEOD	Donny	Celtic	4	0	1905-1906
McLEOD	John	Dumbarton	5	0	1888-1893
McLEOD	William	Cowlairs	1	0	1886
McLINTOCK	Alexander	Vale of Leven	3	0	1875-1880
McLINTOCK	Frank	Leicester City Arsenal	9	1	1963-1971
McLUCKIE	James	Manchester C.	1	0	1933
McMAHON	Sandy	Celtic	6	6	1892-1902
McMANUS	Stephen	Celtic	13	1	2006-2008
McMENEMY	Jimmy	Celtic	12	5	1905-1920
McMENEMY	John	Motherwell	1	0	1933
McMILLAN	Ian	Airdrieonians Rangers	6	2	1952-1961
McMILLAN	J?	St Bernard's	1	0	1897
McMILLAN	Thomas	Dumbarton	1	0	1887
McMULLAN	Jimmy	Partick Thistle Manchester C.	16	0	1920-1929

			A	B	
McNAB	Alex	Morton	2	0	1921
McNAB	Alex	Sunderland W B A	2	0	1937-1939
McNAB	Colin	Dundee	6	0	1930-1932
McNAB	John	Liverpool	1	0	1923
McNAIR	Alec	Celtic	15	0	1906-1920
McNAMARA	Jackie	Celtic Wolves	33	0	1996-2005
McNAMEE	David	Livingston	4	0	2004-2006
McNAUGHT	Willie	Raith Rovers	5	0	1950-1954
McNAUGHTON	Kevin	Aberdeen Cardiff City	3	0	2002-2008
McNEILL	Billy	Celtic	29	3	1961-1972
McNIEL	Henry	Queen's Park	10	6	1874-1881
McNIEL	Moses	Rangers	2	0	1876-1880
McPHAIL	Bob	Airdrieonians Rangers	17	7	1927-1937
McPHAIL	John	Celtic	5	3	1949-1953
McPHERSON	Dave	Hearts Rangers	27	0	1989-1993
McPHERSON	David	Kilmarnock	1	0	1892
McPHERSON	John	Clydesdale	1	0	1875
McPHERSON	John	Hearts	1	0	1891
McPHERSON	John	Kilmarnock Cowlairs Rangers	9	7	1888-1897
McPHERSON	John	Vale of Leven	8	0	1879-1885
McPHERSON	Robert	Arthurlie	1	1	1882
McQUEEN	Gordon	Leeds United Man. Utd	30	5	1974-1981
McQUEEN	Matthew	Leith Athletic	2	0	1890-1891
McRORIE	Danny	Morton	1	0	1930
McSPADYEN	Alex	Partick Thistle	2	0	1938-1939
McSTAY	Paul	Celtic	76	9	1983-1997
McSTAY	Willie	Celtic	13	0	1921-1928
McSWEGAN	Gary	Hearts	2	1	1999
McTAVISH	John	Falkirk	1	0	1910
McWATTIE	George	Queen's Park	2	0	1901
McWILLIAM	Peter	Newcastle Utd.	8	0	1905-1911
MADDEN	Johnnie	Celtic	2	5	1893-1895
MAIN	James	Hibernian	1	0	1909
MAIN	Robert	Rangers	1	0	1937
MALEY	Willie	Celtic	2	0	1893
MALONEY	Shaun	Celtic Aston Villa	11	1	2005-2008
MALPAS	Maurice	Dundee United	55	0	1984-1992
MARSHALL	David	Celtic	2	0	2004
MARSHALL	Gordon	Celtic	1	0	1992
MARSHALL	Harry	Celtic	2	1	1899-1900
MARSHALL	James	Rangers	3	0	1932-1934
MARSHALL	John	Middlesbrough Llanelli	7	0	1921-1924
MARSHALL	John	Third Lanark	4	1	1885-1887
MARSHALL	Robert	Rangers	2	0	1892-1894
MARTIN	Brian	Motherwell	2	0	1995
MARTIN	Fred	Aberdeen	6	0	1954-1955
MARTIN	Neil	Hibernian Sunderland	3	0	1965
MARTIS	John	Motherwell	1	0	1960
MASON	Jimmy	Third Lanark	7	4	1948-1951
MASSIE	Alec	Hearts Aston Villa	18	1	1931-1937
MASSON	Don	Q P R Derby County	17	5	1976-1978
MATHERS	David	Partick Thistle	1	0	1954
MATTEO	Dominic	Leeds United	6	0	2000-2002
MAXWELL	William	Stoke City	1	0	1898
MAY	John	Rangers	5	0	1906-1909
MEECHAN	Peter	Celtic	1	0	1896
MEIKLEJOHN	Davie	Rangers	15	3	1922-1933
MENZIES	Alec	Hearts	1	0	1906
MERCER	Bob	Hearts	2	0	1912-1913
MIDDLETON	Bob	Cowdenbeath	1	0	1930
MILLAR	James	Rangers	3	2	1897-1898
MILLAR	Jimmy	Rangers	2	0	1963
MILLER	Archie	Hearts	1	0	1938
MILLER	Charlie	Dundee United	1	0	2001
MILLER	John	St Mirren	5	0	1931-1934
MILLER	Kenny	Rangers Wolves Celtic Derby County	37	11	2001-2008

			A	B	
MILLER	Lee	Dundee United	1	0	2006
MILLER	Peter	Dumbarton	3	0	1882-1883
MILLER	Tommy	Liverpool Man.Utd	3	2	1920-1921
MILLER	William	Third Lanark	1	0	1876
MILLER	Willie	Aberdeen	65	1	1975-1989
MILLER	Willie	Celtic	6	0	1946-1947
MILLS	Willie	Aberdeen	3	0	1935-1936
MILNE	Jackie	Middlesbrough	2	0	1938-1939
MITCHELL	Bobby	Newcastle Utd.	2	1	1951
MITCHELL	David	Rangers	5	0	1890-1894
MITCHELL	James	Kilmarnock	3	0	1908-1910
MOCHAN	Neil	Celtic	3	0	1954
MOIR	Willie	Bolton Wandrs.	1	0	1950
MONCUR	Bobby	Newcastle Utd.	16	0	1968-1972
MORGAN	Hugh	St Mirren			
		Liverpool	2	0	1898-1899
MORGAN	Willie	Burnley			
		Man. Utd	21	1	1967-1974
MORRIS	David	Raith Rovers	6	1	1923-1925
MORRIS	Henry	East Fife	1	3	1949
MORRISON	Tommy	St Mirren	1	0	1927
MORRISON	James	W B A	1	0	2008
MORTON	Alan	Queen's Park Rangers	31	5	1920-1932
MORTON	Hugh	Kilmarnock	2	0	1929
MUDIE	Jackie	Blackpool	17	9	1956-1958
MUIR	William	Dundee	1	0	1907
MUIRHEAD	Tommy	Rangers	8	0	1922-1929
MULHALL	George	Aberdeen			
		Sunderland	3	1	1959-1963
MUNRO	Alex	Hearts			
		Blackpool	3	1	1936-1938
MUNRO	Frank	Wolves	9	0	1971-1975
MUNRO	Iain	St Mirren	7	0	1979-1980
MUNRO	Neil	Abercorn	2	2	1888-1889
MURDOCH	Bobby	Celtic	12	5	1965-1969
MURDOCH	John	Motherwell	1	0	1931
MURPHY	Frank	Celtic	1	1	1938
MURRAY	Ian	Hibernian Rangers	6	0	2002-2006
MURRAY	Jimmy	Hearts	5	1	1958
MURRAY	John	Vale of Leven	1	0	1890
MURRAY	John	Renton	1	0	1895
MURRAY	Patrick	Hibernian	2	1	1896-1897
MURRAY	Stevie	Aberdeen	1	0	1971
MURTY	Graeme	Reading	4	0	2004-2007
MUTCH	George	Preston N E	1	0	1938
NAISMITH	Stephen	Kilmarnock	1	0	2007
NAPIER	Charlie	Celtic Derby County	5	3	1932-37
NAREY	Dave	Dundee United	35	1	1977-1989
NAYSMITH	Gary	Hearts Everton Sheffield United	40	1	2000-2008
NEIL	Robert	Hibernian Rangers	2	2	1896-1900
NEILL	Robert	Queen's Park	5	0	1876-1880
NEILSON	Robbie	Hearts	1	0	2006
NELLIES	Peter	Hearts	2	0	1913-1914
NELSON	James	Cardiff City	4	0	1925-1930
NEVIN	Pat	Chelsea Everton Tranmere Rov.	28	5	1986-1996
NIBLO	Thomas	Aston Villa	1	0	1904
NIBLOE	Joe	Kilmarnock	11	0	1929-1932
NICHOLAS	Charlie	Celtic Arsenal Aberdeen	20	5	1983-1989
NICHOLSON	Barry	Dunfermline A.	3	0	2001-2004
NICOL	Steve	Liverpool	27	0	1984-1991
NISBET	James	Ayr United	3	2	1929
NIVEN	James	Moffat	1	0	1885
O'CONNOR	Garry	Hibernian Lok. Moscow Birmingham C.	15	4	2002-2007
O'DONNELL	Frank	Preston N E Blackpool	6	2	1937-1938
O'DONNELL	Phil	Motherwell	1	0	1993
OGILVIE	Duncan	Motherwell	1	0	1933
O'HARE	John	Derby County	13	5	1970-1972

			A	B	
O'NEIL	Brian	Celtic Wolfsburg Derby County Preston N E	7	0	1996-2005
O'NEIL	John	Hibernian	1	0	2001
ORMOND	Willie	Hibernian	6	2	1954-1959
O'ROURKE	Frank	Airdrieonians	1	1	1907
ORR	James	Kilmarnock	1	0	1892
ORR	Ronald	Newcastle Utd.	2	1	1902-1904
ORR	Tommy	Morton	2	1	1951
ORR	Willie	Celtic	3	0	1900-1904
ORROCK	Robert	Falkirk	1	0	1913
OSWALD	James	Third Lanark St Bernard's Rangers	3	1	1889-1897
PARKER	Alex	Falkirk Everton	15	0	1955-1958
PARLANE	Derek	Rangers	12	1	1973-1977
PARLANE	Robert	Vale of Leven	3	0	1878-1879
PATERSON	George	Celtic	1	0	1938
PATERSON	James	Cowdenbeath	3	0	1931
PATERSON	John	Leicester City	1	0	1920
PATON	Andy	Motherwell	2	0	1952
PATON	Daniel	St Bernard's	1	1	1896
PATON	Michael	Dumbarton	5	0	1883-1886
PATON	Robert	Vale of Leven	2	0	1879
PATRICK	John	St Mirren	2	0	1897
PAUL	Harold	Queen's Park	3	2	1909
PAUL	William	Dykebar	1	0	1891
PAUL	William	Partick Thistle	3	5	1888-1890
PEARSON	Stephen	Celtic Derby County	10	0	2003-2007
PEARSON	Tommy	Newcastle Utd.	2	0	1947
PENMAN	Andy	Dundee	1	0	1966
PETTIGREW	Willie	Motherwell	5	2	1976-1977
PHILLIPS	James	Queen's Park	3	0	1877-1878
PLENDERLEITH	John	Manchester C.	1	0	1961
PORTEOUS	William	Hearts	1	0	1903
PRESSLEY	Steven	Hearts	32	0	2000-2006
PRINGLE	Charles	St Mirren	1	0	1921
PROVAN	Davie	Rangers	5	0	1963-1966
PROVAN	Davie	Celtic	10	1	1979-1982
PURSELL	Peter	Queen's Park	1	0	1914
QUASHIE	Nigel	Portsmouth Southampton W B A	14	1	2004-2006
QUINN	Jimmy	Celtic	11	7	1905-1912
QUINN	Pat	Motherwell	4	1	1961-1962
RAE	Gavin	Dundee Rangers Cardiff City	13	0	2001-2008
RAE	James	Third Lanark	2	0	1889-1890
RAESIDE	James	Third Lanark	1	0	1906
RAISBECK	Alex	Liverpool	8	0	1900-1907
RANKIN	Gilbert	Vale of Leven	2	2	1890-1891
RANKIN	Robert	St Mirren	3	2	1929
REDPATH	Willie	Motherwell	9	0	1948-1952
REID	James	Airdrie	3	0	1914-1924
REID	Robert	Brentford	2	0	1937-1938
REID	Willie	Rangers	9	4	1911-1914
REILLY	Lawrie	Hibernian	38	22	1948-1957
RENNIE	Harry	Hearts Hibernian	13	0	1900-1908
RENNY-TAILYOUR	Henry	R. Engineers	1	1	1873
RHIND	Alex	Queen's Park	1	0	1872
RICHMOND	Andrew	Queen's Park	1	0	1906
RICHMOND	James	Clydesdale Queen's Park	3	1	1877-1882
RING	Tommy	Clyde	12	2	1953-1957
RIOCH	Bruce	Derby County Everton	24	6	1975-1978
RIORDAN	Derek	Hibs	1	0	2005
RITCHIE	Archibald	E. Stirlingshire	1	0	1891
RITCHIE	Billy	Rangers	1	0	1962
RITCHIE	Henry	Hibernian	2	0	1923-1928
RITCHIE	John	Queen's Park	1	1	1897
RITCHIE	Paul	Hearts Bolton W. Walsall	7	1	1999-2004
ROBB	Davie	Aberdeen	5	0	1971
ROBB	Willie	Hibernian Rangers	2	0	1925-1927

			A	B	
ROBERTSON	Archie	Clyde	5	2	1955-1958
ROBERTSON	David	Rangers	3	0	1992-1994
ROBERTSON	George	Motherwell Sheffield Wed.	4	0	1910-1913
ROBERTSON	George	Kilmarnock	1	0	1937
ROBERTSON	Hugh	Dundee	1	0	1961
ROBERTSON	James	Dundee	2	0	1931
ROBERTSON	James	Tottenham H.	1	0	1964
ROBERTSON	John	Hearts	16	3	1990-1995
ROBERTSON	John	Nottingham F. Derby County	28	8	1978-1983
ROBERTSON	John	Everton Southampton Rangers	16	2	1898-1905
ROBERTSON	Peter	Dundee	1	0	1903
ROBERTSON	Tom	Queen's Park	4	0	1889-1892
ROBERTSON	Tom	Hearts	1	1	1898
ROBERTSON	William	Dumbarton	2	1	1887
ROBINSON	Robert	Dundee	4	0	1974-1975
ROBSON	Barry	Dundee Utd. Celtic	2	0	2007-2008
ROSS	Maurice	Rangers	13	0	2002-2003
ROUGH	Alan	Partick Thistle	53	0	1976-1986
ROUGVIE	Doug	Aberdeen	1	0	1983
ROWAN	Archibald	Caledonian Queen's Park	2	0	1880-1882
RUSSELL	David	Hearts Celtic	6	1	1895-1901
RUSSELL	J?	Cambuslang	1	0	1890
RUSSELL	Willie	Airdrieonians	2	0	1924-1925
RUTHERFORD	Eddie	Rangers	1	0	1948
ST. JOHN	Ian	Motherwell Liverpool	21	9	1959-1965
SAWERS	William	Dundee	1	0	1895
SCARFF	Peter	Celtic	1	0	1931
SCHAEDLER	Erich	Hibernian	1	0	1974
SCOTT	Alec	Rangers Everton	16	5	1956-1966
SCOTT	Jim	Hibernian	1	0	1966
SCOTT	Jocky	Dundee	2	0	1971
SCOTT	Matthew	Airdrieonians	1	0	1898
SCOTT	Robert	Airdrieonians	1	0	1894
SCOULAR	Jimmy	Portsmouth	9	0	1951-1952
SELLAR	William	Battlefield Queen's Park	9	4	1885-1893
SEMPLE	William	Cambuslang	1	0	1886
SEVERIN	Scott	Hearts Aberdeen	15	0	2001-2006
SHANKLY	Bill	Preston N E	5	0	1938-1939
SHARP	Graeme	Everton	12	1	1985-1988
SHARP	James	Dundee Arsenal Fulham	5	0	1904-1909
SHAW	Davie	Hibernian	8	0	1946-1948
SHAW	Frank	Pollokshields A.	2	1	1884
SHAW	Jock	Rangers	4	0	1947
SHEARER	Bobby	Rangers	4	0	1961
SHEARER	Duncan	Aberdeen	7	2	1994-1995
SILLARS	Donald	Queen's Park	5	0	1891-1895
SIMPSON	James	Third Lanark	3	0	1895
SIMPSON	Jimmy	Rangers	14	1	1934-1937
SIMPSON	Neil	Aberdeen	5	0	1983-1988
SIMPSON	Ronnie	Celtic	5	0	1967-1968
SINCLAIR	George	Hearts	3	0	1910-1912
SINCLAIR	John	Leicester City	1	0	1966
SKENE	Leslie	Queen's Park	1	0	1904
SLOAN	Thomas	Third Lanark	1	0	1904
SMELLIE	Robert	Queen's Park	6	0	1887-1893
SMITH	Alex	Rangers	20	5	1898-1911
SMITH	Dave	Aberdeen Rangers	2	0	1966-1968
SMITH	Eric	Celtic	2	0	1959
SMITH	Gordon	Hibernian	18	4	1946-1957
SMITH	Henry	Hearts	3	0	1988-1992
SMITH	James	Queen's Park	1	0	1872
SMITH	Jamie	Celtic	2	0	2003
SMITH	John	Ayr United	1	0	1924
SMITH	John	Mauchline Edinburgh Univ. Queen's Park	10	10	1877-1884
SMITH	Jimmy	Rangers	2	1	1934-1937
SMITH	Jimmy	Aberdeen Newcastle Utd.	4	0	1968-1974
SMITH	Nick	Rangers	12	0	1897-1902
SMITH	Robert	Queen's Park	2	0	1872-1873
SMITH	Tommy	Kilmarnock Preston N E	2	0	1934-1938
SOMERS	Peter	Celtic	4	0	1905-1909
SOMERS	William	Third Lanark Queen's Park	3	0	1879-1880
SOMERVILLE	George	Queen's Park	1	0	1886
SOUNESS	Graeme	Middlesbrough Liverpool Sampdoria	54	4	1974-1986
SPEEDIE	David	Chelsea Coventry City	10	0	1985-1989
SPEEDIE	Finlay	Rangers	3	2	1903
SPEIRS	James	Rangers	1	0	1908
SPENCER	John	Chelsea QPR.	14	0	1994-1997
STANTON	Pat	Hibernian	16	0	1966-1974
STARK	James	Rangers	2	0	1909
STEEL	Billy	Morton Derby County Dundee	30	12	1947-1953
STEELE	David	Huddersfield T.	3	0	1923
STEIN	Colin	Rangers Coventry City	21	10	1968-1973
STEPHEN	James	Bradford PA	2	0	1946-1947
STEVENSON	George	Motherwell	12	4	1927-1934
STEWART	Allan	Queen's Park	2	1	1888-1889
STEWART	Andrew	Third Lanark	1	0	1894
STEWART	David	Queen's Park	3	0	1893-1897
STEWART	David	Leeds United	1	0	1977
STEWART	Duncan	Dumbarton	1	0	1888
STEWART	George	Hibernian Manchester C.	4	0	1906-1907
STEWART	James	Kilmarnock Middlesbrough	2	0	1977-78
STEWART	Michael	Man. Utd.	3	0	2002
STEWART	Ray	West Ham Utd.	10	1	1981-1987
STEWART	William	Queen's Park	2	1	1898-1900
STOCKDALE	Robbie	Middlesbrough	5	0	2002
STORRIER	Davie	Celtic	3	0	1899
STRACHAN	Gordon	Aberdeen Man. Utd. Leeds United	50	5	1980-1992
STURROCK	Paul	Dundee United	20	3	1981-1987
SULLIVAN	Neil	Wimbledon Tottenham H.	28	0	1997-2003
SUMMERS	William	St Mirren	1	0	1926
SYMON	Scott	Rangers	1	0	1938
TAIT	Thomas	Sunderland	1	0	1911
TAYLOR	John	Dumbarton St Mirren	4	1	1892-1895
TAYLOR	Joseph	Queen's Park	6	0	1872-1876
TAYLOR	William	Hearts	1	0	1892
TEALE	Gary	Wigan Athletic Derby County	11	0	2006-2008
TELFER	Paul	Coventry City	1	0	2000
TELFER	Willie	Motherwell	2	0	1932
TELFER	Willie	St Mirren	1	0	1953
TEMPLETON	Bobby	Aston Villa Newcastle Utd. Arsenal Celtic Kilmarnock	11	1	1902-1913
THOMPSON	Steve	Dundee United Rangers	16	3	2002-2004
THOMSON	Alec	Airdrieonians	1	1	1909
THOMSON	Alec	Celtic	3	0	1926-1932
THOMSON	Andrew	Arthurlie	1	0	1886
THOMSON	Andrew	Third Lanark	1	0	1889
THOMSON	Bertie	Celtic	1	1	1931
THOMSON	Billy	St Mirren	7	0	1980-1983
THOMSON	Charlie	Hearts Sunderland	21	4	1904-1914
THOMSON	Charlie	Sunderland	1	0	1937
THOMSON	David	Dundee	1	0	1920
THOMSON	James	Queen's Park	3	0	1872-1874
THOMSON	John	Celtic	5	0	1930-1931

			A	B	
THOMSON	John	Everton	1	0	1932
THOMSON	Robert	Falkirk	1	0	1927
THOMSON	Samuel	Lugar Boswell	2	0	1884
THOMSON	William	Dumbarton	4	1	1892-1898
THOMSON	William	Dundee	1	0	1896
THORNTON	Willie	Rangers	7	1	1946-1952
TONER	Willie	Kilmarnock	2	0	1958
TOWNSLEY	Tom	Falkirk	1	0	1925
TROUP	Alec	Dundee Everton	5	0	1920-1926
TURNBULL	Eddie	Hibernian	9	0	1948-1958
TURNER	Thomas	Arthurlie	1	0	1884
TURNER	William	Pollokshields A.	2	1	1885-1886
URE	Ian	Dundee Arsenal	11	0	1961-1967
URQUHART	Duncan	Hibernian	1	0	1933
VALLANCE	Thomas	Rangers	7	0	1877-1881
VENTERS	Alex	Cowdenbeath Rangers	3	0	1933-1939
WADDELL	Thomas	Queen's Park	6	1	1891-1895
WADDELL	Willie	Rangers	17	6	1946-1954
WALES	Hugh	Motherwell	1	0	1932
WALKER	Andy	Celtic	3	0	1988-1994
WALKER	Bobby	Hearts	29	7	1900-1913
WALKER	Frank	Third Lanark	1	0	1922
WALKER	George	St Mirren	4	0	1930-1931
WALKER	John	Hearts Rangers	5	3	1895-1904
WALKER	John	Swindon Town	9	0	1911-1913
WALKER	Nicky	Hearts Partick Thistle	2	0	1993-1996
WALKER	Tommy	Hearts	20	9	1934-1939
WALKER	William	Clyde	2	0	1909-1910
WALLACE	Ian	Coventry City	3	1	1978-1979
WALLACE	Willie	Hearts Celtic	7	0	1964-1969
WARDHAUGH	Jimmy	Hearts	2	0	1954-1956
WARK	John	Ipswich Town Liverpool	29	7	1979-1984
WATSON	Andrew	Queen's Park	3	0	1881
WATSON	Bobby	Motherwell	1	0	1971
WATSON	James	Motherwell Huddersfield T.	2	0	1947-1953
WATSON	James	Sunderland Middlesbrough	6	0	1903-1909
WATSON	James	Rangers	1	1	1878
WATSON	Philip	Blackpool	1	0	1933
WATSON	W?	Falkirk	1	0	1898
WATT	Frank	Balbirnie	4	3	1889-1891
WATT	William	Queen's Park	1	1	1887
WAUGH	William	Hearts	1	0	1937
WEBSTER	Andy	Hearts	22	1	2003-2006
WEIR	Andy	Motherwell	6	1	1959-1960
WEIR	Davie	Hearts Everton Rangers	61	1	1997-2007
WEIR	James	Queen's Park	4	2	1872-1878
WEIR	John	Third Lanark	1	0	1887
WEIR	Peter	St Mirren Aberdeen	6	0	1980-1983
WHITE	John	Albion Rovers Hearts	2	0	1922-1923
WHITE	John	Falkirk Tottenham H.	22	3	1959-1964
WHITE	Walter	Bolton W.	2	0	1907-1908
WHITELAW	Andrew	Vale of Leven	2	0	1887-1890
WHYTE	Derek	Celtic Middlesbrough Aberdeen	12	0	1987-1999
WILKIE	Lee	Dundee	11	1	2002-2004
WILLIAMS	Gareth	Nottingham F.	5	0	2002
WILSON	Andrew	Sheffield Wed.	6	2	1907-1914
WILSON	Andrew Nesbit	Dunfermline A. Middlesbrough	12	13	1920-1923
WILSON	Alex	Portsmouth	1	0	1954
WILSON	Bob	Arsenal	2	0	1971
WILSON	David	Queen's Park	1	2	1900
WILSON	David	Oldham Ath.	1	0	1913
WILSON	Davie	Rangers	22	9	1960-1965
WILSON	George	Hearts Everton Newcastle Utd.	6	0	1904-1909

			A	B	
WILSON	Hugh	Newmilns Sunderland Third Lanark	4	1	1890-1904
WILSON	Ian	Leicester City Everton	5	0	1987
WILSON	James	Vale of Leven	4	0	1888-1891
WILSON	Paul	Celtic	1	0	1975
WILSON	Peter	Celtic	4	0	1926-1933
WINTERS	Robbie	Aberdeen	1	0	1999
WISEMAN	William	Queen's Park	2	0	1926-1930
WOOD	George	Everton Arsenal	4	0	1979-1982
WOODBURN	Willie	Rangers	24	0	1947-1952
WOTHERSPOON	David	Queen's Park	2	0	1872-1873
WRIGHT	Keith	Hibernian	1	0	1992
WRIGHT	Stephen	Aberdeen	2	0	1993
WRIGHT	Tommy	Sunderland	3	0	1952-1953
WYLIE	Tom	Rangers	1	1	1890
YEATS	Ron	Liverpool	2	0	1964-1965
YORSTON	Benny	Aberdeen	1	0	1931
YORSTON	Harry	Aberdeen	1	0	1954
YOUNG	Alec	Everton	2	0	1905-1907
YOUNG	Alec	Hearts Everton	8	5	1960-1966
YOUNG	George	Rangers	53	0	1946-1957
YOUNG	Jim	Celtic	1	0	1906
YOUNGER	Tommy	Hibernian Liverpool	24	0	1955-1958

Darren Jackson of Celtic.

Dave Wilson of Rangers.